JUSTICE

AND

JURISPRUDENCE:

AN

Inquiry concerning the Constitutional
Limitations of the Thirteenth,
Fourteenth, and Fifteenth
Amendments.

Brotherhood of Liberty.

NEGRO UNIVERSITIES PRESS
NEW YORK

75-77191

9— 21553

Originally published in 1889
by the J. B. Lippincott Company

Reprinted 1969 by
Negro Universities Press
A DIVISION OF GREENWOOD PUBLISHING CORP.
NEW YORK

SBN 8371-1301-6

PRINTED IN UNITED STATES OF AMERICA

PREFACE.

AN inquiry concerning the constitutional provisions of the Thirteenth, Fourteenth, and Fifteenth Amendments seemed to the Brotherhood of Liberty the primal step to be taken by an Order instituted for the advancement of the African race in America.

Their Dedicatory Address and Epistles make a full revealment of the objective points of this Christian, constitutional, sociological, and political treatise. The author has contributed a fitting introductory accompaniment to his work, in a cold and critical, but lucid, vigorous, and trenchant dissertation upon the peril of juristic innovation upon the Constitution.

As a generalization, this work may be said to consist of two parts. The first concerns the Positive Law of the Fourteenth Amendment, by which the whole power of the American state is pledged to maintain the equality of civil rights of every American citizen by Due Process of Law. The second discloses the transparent veils of legal fiction under cover of which the civil rights of all races are being slowly undermined. It shows how judicial construction has so impaired the *lex scripta* that, although the letter may remain, yet the heart has been eaten out.

Mature reflection and a close observation of the course of events have led the Brotherhood to the conclusion that, if the complex constitutional questions, and the perplexing social problems involved in the much-mooted race-question could be examined, and their deep, broad, ethical and political significance demonstrated by an interesting discussion, free as possible from dry abstraction, sectionalism, and partisanship, public opinion might become disentangled from the many knotty disputes by which it is now obscured, chiefly through the chicanery of a narrow system of vicious politics.

They believe that no more important service can be per-

i

formed than the publication of an accessible treatise which points out the unconstitutional drift of the courts and public sentiment away from the Fourteenth Amendment. They entertain no suspicion that, in the opinion of considerate, thoughtful men, the value of such a work could be diminished by the consideration that the evidence of this unconstitutional trend was discovered in the course of a patient investigation of civil rights.

JUSTICE AND JURISPRUDENCE opens with a colloquy of absorbing interest between the Chief Justice of the Supreme Court and a foreign jurist "void of the intellectual and social bias generated by slavery." The character of the foreign student's subsequent interview with an eminent representative of the American Press is an original conceit, executed with consummate skill, and the striking narrative which ensues is constructed with no *apparent* labor or art : it is interwoven with law and history—with philosophy and politics. There are no digressions, unnecessary descriptions, or long speeches; grace, incisive wit, sometimes bitter but never malignant sarcasm, distinguish the fanciful allegories of the journalist, as well as the more sober reflections of the Chief Justice. The characters in this dialogue are shrewd, observant, dispassionate men of the world, philosophers with large faculties harmoniously balanced. They seem fully to comprehend the elements of human nature and the laws of their combination, and display extensive knowledge of American politics.

The intercourse of the Chief Justice with the student is characterized by manly grace and dignity. In his presentation of the jurist to Mr. Blaine the Chief Justice is natural, graceful, and polite. His eulogy of Mr. Blaine, inwrapped in the encomium upon his work, is fraught with delicacy and elegance. There is a marvellous picturing power displayed in the imagery of the student's dream, a noble extravagance in the sudden conjuring up and representation of the spirits of Fame, Ambition, and Destiny, so weird and yet so majestic do they appear as they approach Mr. Blaine with thoughts intent upon his doom. The augury of his future, by the ministers of the fates, is a masterpiece.

The work abounds with important definitions, lofty aspirations, political, religious, and philosophic truths. Copiousness of quotation from the great storehouses of literature is a novel feature of the book. These citations point with warmth and quickness to the subjects of discourse; like heralds, they proclaim the advent; as couriers, they precede the main body of themes. The preliminary Address and Letters are inlaid with an infinite variety of precious literary gems. Every chapter is crowned with a fitting diadem of thought, often reflecting the wisdom of by-gone ages; and their glittering light is no more dimmed by time than is that of the starry heavens. But this collection, gathered through unwearied industry, is not merely for the purpose of artificial ornamentation: all this multiform treasure of intellect, derived from separate ages, different hemispheres, and every class of genius, demonstrates that among patriots of the noblest and most extended views, and statesmen of the most vigorous understanding, there is a wondrous harmony in regard to the truths with which the animated discussion abounds. The satiric reprehension, the tart irony of some of these selections may appear too bold and uncharitable, and others may exhibit human infirmities in a somewhat humorous light, but these weapons have been used only on the side of truth. The husbandman has scattered broadcast these seeds of knowledge, and it is humbly hoped that they may effectually contribute to the improvement of the rising generation, by affording the opportunity of becoming familiar with the axioms and sentiments of renowned Christians, patriots, statesmen, philosophers, historians, and poets.

JUSTICE AND JURISPRUDENCE is intended to be a history, a hand-book, a primer to teach all races to uphold and perpetuate the reign of constitutional law. It is stored with sound principles, through which all classes may comprehend the true grounds of the authority of the Fourteenth Amendment, and of their obligation of obedience to its commandments. It teaches that the marvellous advancement of civilization over barbarism is owing to the conquest of the sottish prejudice, the ridiculous vanity, and the rude ignorance of mankind; that by enlargement of their reason and enlightenment of their conscience men come at last to discover that their own customs, manners and opinions, are not always the standards of right or wrong, of true or false;

that it is training, discipline, the efficacious art of instruction, which disinter the soul and fetch out its inherent beauties, regardless of the body which envelops it; that the education of an American citizen, to be worthy of the time, ought to include, in its wide compass, some knowledge of the true foundations upon which rests constitutional liberty.

Public instruction touching the principle of equality of rights by Due Process of Law, the significance of which ever demands to be anew inquired into and anew made manifest, is the great subsidiary purpose of the Brotherhood. The work admonishes those statesmen and jurists whose bent of mind is dogmatic rather than philosophic, that, instead of cultivating the growth of noxious herbs, they must be uprooted; that only when *they* begin to wither will nobler plants shoot up in their place. The author has ventured to suggest, that, unless the American tree of Jurisprudence be too matured to receive the scion engrafted by the Fourteenth Amendment, all its branches, if there be any affinity between the graft and the stock, will shortly bring forth noble fruit. He has also reminded their rulers that, as the American people stand upon the summit of a structure in the evolution of which centuries have been employed, they should be the possessors of the political wealth of all ages.

The foreign jurist, in the course of his inquiry concerning the limitations of the amendments, explores and exposes all the hidden recesses of the race-question. The intellectual acumen and the philosophic discrimination of the calm seeker after truth are nowhere displayed to so great advantage as in the following deductions and conclusions :

That every race owes something to the race beneath it; that the principle of equality of right, so congenial to the atmosphere of the Constitution, opens an ample highway for universal progress; that the educational advantages, since the readjustment of American society, which have wrought such a wondrous improvement in the colored man within twenty-five years, are the heralds of an incoming era in which the race-problem will be solved in a way not inconsistent with a republican form of go-'ernment; that should fomenters of a war of races hereafter appear, and should they pour forth their blood to *disenfranchise* this race even more freely than did a half-million of their fore-fathers to emancipate it, the problem would still remain unsettled, and could be determined only by law; that the repeal of the Fifteenth Amendment, and the placing of eight millions under the tutelage again of the general government, would destroy the material interests of the country, the industrial education of these producers, impede the moral development of both races, and, leading inevitably to the nullification of the amendments, and perhaps to the disintegration of the Constitution itself, would prove as threatening to the unity and happiness of the American people, as did the revolt of the Southern States against the government. That in this age neither social abhorrence of the colored population, nor unintelligent, retrogressive, pro-slavery heresies, obsolete views of a day that is dead, nor myopic, pride-begotten prejudices, can be substituted for the widening character and the growing force of American thought, the sublime mission of which is to restore peace and order to human hearts and human society, by the establishment of the fundamental principle of the civic equality of all American citizens; that, in the Atlantic States south of the thirty-sixth parallel of latitude, the relations of the races are interdependent; that eight millions of Afro-Americans can neither be annihilated nor transported.

The Brotherhood respectfully submit, that if the polity of Catholicism and the spirit of Catholicity, with a governmental control extending over the peoples of every nation of the earth, has preserved the unity of its flock, in spite of the vicissitudes of almost twenty centuries, surely the chosen guardians of the American republic may hope for all time to perpetuate and combine in perfect unity its diverse popular elements, by preserving inviolate the sanctity of that principle which has been rigidly enforced for centuries by the Roman hierarchy,—the catholic doctrine of liberty regulated by law, which is the essence of the spirit of equality of right by due process of law, which the Fourteenth Amendment proclaims; that the freedom of the whole American people is now imperilled by judicial interpretation rendering this beneficent maxim inoperative as to the immunities of the colored race; that juristic impairment of this organic law, emboldens those kites of commerce, whose despotic aggressions are destructive alike of national and individual values, and who are themselves a standing menace to the American doctrine of *equality of right* in every department of commercial enterprise; that compassing the defeat of the national polity in favor of their people has invited, stimulated, and popularized the lawlessness of race-antagonism, which is not less systematized by the industrial element North and East, than it is legitimated by popular opinion South and West.

The Brotherhood do not affect to suppress their anxiety lest their people should remain stationary in the midst of a rapidly advancing nation.

They believe that for the African just emerging from conditions which the barbarities of two centuries of slavery had established, and not yet lifted above the vices incident to that system; whose every step of progress has been antagonized and retarded; who is forever exposed to the malign influence of the intrigue and imposture of spoil-hunting political adventurers, the heavenly light of education, which teaches him to become an upright, valuable member of society, happy in himself and useful to others, is a Christian instrumentality which will prove in the end the most effective policy to fit him for a radically changed order of things, and for the true functions of American citizenship.

The Brotherhood insist that all the sectional evils attendant upon the change of the status of this race are owing to its state of transition, and that these drawbacks are but temporary and of far less magnitude than the sociological disabilities which slavery entailed upon the whole body politic. They invite attention to what such Southern authors as Thomas Nelson Page and Joel Chandler Harris have chronicled respecting the wonderful devotion and self-abnegation, the rare fidelity, the delicacy, the untaught chivalry, the noble virtues, of the old family servants who guarded the infancy and early youth of the Southron under the old *régime;* and they insist, that what the descendants of those trusty servants require to fit them for the new conditions of their high place as American citizens, is that which the greatest law-givers, statesmen, and political philosophers and the most illustrious champions of freedom have always preached,—the education of their people. They humbly crave leave to remind the American people that the State should take charge of the education of the people; that the first admonition of Penn, addressed to the colony which he founded, was, " Educate the people;" the unceasing exhortation of Jefferson was, " Educate the people," and the dying legacy which Washington bequeathed to the nation he had saved was, " *Educate the people.*"

THE BROTHERHOOD OF LIBERTY.

CONTENTS.

CHAPTER I.

CHAPTER II.

CHAPTER III.

CHAPTER IV.

CHAPTER V.

CHAPTER VI.

CHAPTER VII.

CHAPTER VIII.

CHAPTER IX.

CHAPTER X.

CHAPTER XIV.

CHAPTER XV.

CHAPTER XVIII.

Reappearance of the term "reasonable" in the closing paragraph of
Mr. Justice Clifford's opinion—Objectionableness of his use of
terms—Their generality opens the way to the subversion of the
amendment—This law invests the public servant with discretion,
which he may exercise to the best of his temerity, ignorance,
and prejudice—Extraordinary conglomeration of unintelligible
law-jargon introduced into the well-established doctrines of
bailees—Open to two constructions—They say to the public servant, The bands of obedience to the Fourteenth Amendment
are loosened—The term "discretion" as applied to civil rights
not to be taken as it has been since the Levitical and canon law
and *jus gentium*—The novelty of this law no more wonderful
than that of the creation of seven millions of citizens by a stroke
of the pen—The liberties of the African race effected by the
war-measures of the Republican party may be destroyed by the
subtle distinctions of the courts—The public servant may infuse
the same bigotry into his regulations as into his religion or
politics—He need have no superstitious veneration for the
fundamental law of his country—He may under this law
commit the old pro-slavery sin in the new Fourteenth Amendment, commercial, inaction-of-Congress, Hall-*v.*-DeCuir way—
The hoof of the unclean beast everywhere visible—This doctrine receives the *imprimatur* of the Supreme Court by their
affirmation of rules and regulations which on account of race
discriminated against a citizen of the United States—Authorities cited by Mr. Justice Clifford to maintain the latitudinous terms employed in his separate opinion do not support his
doctrine—Those decisions rendered at a period of bitter racial
excitement, under the high pressure of pro-slavery sentiment—
Those authorities are antiquities, pre-historic, in the light of
Strauder *v.* West Virginia—The "free-and-untrammelled-as-
far-as-practicable-reasonable-discretionary prerogative" of the
public servant abandoned by Mr. Justice Clifford at the end
of his opinion—This doctrine tenable only upon the exploded

CHAPTER XIX.

CHAPTER XX.

CHAPTER XXI.

CHAPTER XXIV.

The offence of railroad magnates, rank though it be, is whiter than wool contrasted with the subversion of the fundamental principles of the government—Other illustrations of the liabilities of individuals to damage by the altered conditions of society consequent upon the adoption of new laws for the common wellfare—The railroad interests and capital of $7,254,995,223 subject to the interstate-commerce decrees—Arthur Kill case—Kansas *v.* Herman Ziebold and others—Kansas Prohibition cases—The foundation-stone of these decisions is the sacrificial principle which runs through political society, traceable to the doctrines of Christianity—St. Augustine's view—Sacrificial view from state stand-point—The Interstate-Commerce Law operating against vested interests for the general good—Its almost unlimited powers—The Christian doctrine of sacrifice applicable in government—The existence of evil unavoidable—The public servant

CHAPTER XXVIII.

CHAPTER XXIX.

CHAPTER XXX.

CHAPTER XXXI.

CHAPTER XXXII.

CHAPTER XXXIII.

CHAPTER XXXIV.

CHAPTER XXXV.

CHAPTER XXXVI.

CHAPTER XXXVII.

CHAPTER XXXVIII.

CHAPTER XXXIX.

CHAPTER XL.

CHAPTER XLI.

CHAPTER XLII.

CHAPTER XLIII.

CHAPTER XLIV.

CHAPTER XLV.

Equality by due process of law does away with the tyranny of
opinion—Breaks down antiquated forms—Looses conventional
fetters—Elevation of lower stratum of society not degrading to
higher—Civic equality by due process of law as great an advance upon Dred-Scott inequality as *Magna Charta* upon the
primitive law of William the Conqueror—The amendments define the relation of every individual to the nation, and of the
nation to every individual—They place in eternal bondage the
ape and tiger element in the society of America—Civic equality
creates the positive right out of the natural right—Must necessarily have precedence over all other considerations of which
jurisprudence takes cognizance—The permanent maintenance of
the primal prerogatives of humanity, admeasured by the provisions of the amendments—Oriental immobility of American
jurisprudence—The development of the deeper unity of the
nation the task of the judicial, not of the legislative department
—Charm of old ritual of despotic power for jurisprudence—The
embodiment of the political wisdom of all ages contained in the
amendments—Jurisprudence declares them ideal abstractions
and political empiricisms—Their framers, according to Hall *v.*
DeCuir and the Civil-Rights Cases, blinkards and simpletons—
Gradual ascent of man in the scale of being—His advance
through conflict to the realization of freedom mere paltry pageantry—The shifting changes of political scenery—New foundation for the equality of the rights of mankind—Jurisprudence
and the leprosy of slavery—The dead-looking, pallid construc-

CHAPTER XLVI.

The civil rights of the citizens of African descent a great trial for Jurisprudence when the peers of race-prejudice thrust them into its face — The test taxed too heavily the candor of the court—It could not rise to the height of Christian or constitutional teachings — " Anything for the times : nothing for the truth"—" Vehement in words but not in things"—The right and truth of the amendments overturned by petty prejudices and cavils—The rights of no race safe if discrimination against one allowed—Impregnable truths at the bottom of the amendments—Refusing to take God's justice from a race which bears his image—Mankind not separated by any broader line of classification than environments have established—Whole question of civil rights discussed *ad nauseam* in Hall *v.* DeCuir, but no reference made to the Fourteenth Amendment—Veil of sanctimonious profession removed from the face of Jurisprudence— Jurisprudents need to look back over history—The law not to be interpreted to please the delicate tastes of powerful members of the state—The chain of equality on which the rights of all depend no stronger than its weakest link—The history of equality of right by due process of law the history of progressive liberty —Its overflowing records invite the fullest exercise of judicial perspicacity—Its pages the noblest and darkest in history—Its full, genuine, massive ring—Replete with the cultus and consistence of constitutional historical equality—Purpose of the framers of the amendments to introduce every member of the family of men to American civilization—They saw the necessity of a permanent addition to the political rights of all American citizens, and of imparting a continuous power, a living energy, to social development in America—They saw that the divine and human sides of equality of rights, like separate streams, had held divergent courses—They foresaw the " excellent foppery" and errors of Jurisprudence, and endeavored to guard against them—After Dred-Scott decision the doctrine of absolutism in America not superior in its primal tenets to those of the Suttee and the Thuggee—The civic whirlwinds which had swept away the short-lived freedom of other governments to be prevented from recurring in America only by the maintenance of the principle of the equality of right—The destruction of Liberty rendered impossible by the constitutional instalment of the sovereign

DEDICATORY ADDRESS.

"Then amidst the hymns and hallelujahs of saints some one may perhaps be heard offering at high strains, in new and lofty measures, to sing and celebrate thy divine mercies and marvellous judgments in this land throughout all ages; whereby this great and warlike nation, instructed and inured to the fervent and continual practice of truth and righteousness, and casting far from her the rags of her old vices, may press on hard to that high and happy emulation to be found the soberest, wisest, and most Christian people at that day, when thou, the eternal and shortly-expected King, shalt open the clouds to judge the several kingdoms of this world, and, distributing national honors and rewards to religious and just commonwealths, shalt put an end to all earthly tyrannies, proclaiming thy universal and mild monarchy through heaven and earth; where they undoubtedly, that, by their labors, counsels, and prayers, have been earnest for the common good of religion and their country, shall receive, above the inferior orders of the blessed, the regal addition of principalities, legions, and thrones into their glorious titles, and in supereminence of beatific vision, progressing the dateless and irrevoluble circle of eternity, shall clasp inseparable hands with joy and bliss, in overmeasure for ever."—MILTON.

"And do not those revolutions which cast down dynasties or even whole kingdoms into the dust, those huge wrecks which we fall in with in the midst of the sands, those majestic ruins which the field of humanity presents, —do not those cry loud enough, God in History?"—D'AUBIGNÉ.

"When Congress assembled a year ago the war had already lasted nearly twenty months, and there had been many conflicts on both land and sea, with varying results. The rebellion had been pressed back into reduced limits; yet the tone of public feeling and opinion, at home and abroad, was not satisfactory. With other signs, the popular elections, then just past, indicated uneasiness among ourselves; while amid much that was cold and menacing the kindest words coming from Europe were uttered in accents of pity that we were too blind to surrender a hopeless cause."
—LINCOLN.

1

"But the history of liberty—the history of men struggling to be free, the history of men who have acquired and are exercising their freedom, the history of those great movements in the world by which liberty has been established and perpetuated—forms a subject which we cannot contemplate too closely. This is tne real history of man,—of the human family,—of rational, immortal beings. This theme is one : the free of all climes and nations are themselves a people. Their annals are the history of freedom. Those who fell victims to their principles in the civil convulsions of the short-lived republics of Greece, or sunk beneath the power of her invading foes ; those who shed their blood for liberty amidst the ruins of the Roman republic ; the victims of Austrian tyranny in Switzerland and of Spanish tyranny in the Netherlands ; the solitary champions, or the united bands of high-minded and patriotic men, who have, in any region or age, struggled and suffered in this great cause, belong to that people of the free, whose fortunes and progress are the most noble theme which man can contemplate."—EVERETT.

"There has been in the historical course of the United States the higher development of the civil and political organization of society,—the commonwealth and the nation. Their sequence is not the mere accident of history, nor the induction of an arbitrary theory, nor the assumption of a legal formula ; but it has been justified in the reason of the state. It is an organization ampler and nobler than they who in the generations have builded in it could wholly comprehend ; and, working steadily and faithfully in their own day, they have wrought in the ages, building better than they knew. It has been vindicated in political science in the pages of its few masters. It fills the almost prophetic conception of Milton,—' not many sovereignties united in one commonwealth, but many commonwealths in one united and intrusted sovereignty.' "—MULFORD.

"After the performing so glorious an action as this, you ought to do nothing that is mean and little, not so much as to think of, much less to do, anything but what is great and sublime."—MILTON.

"To show as great justice, temperance, and moderation in the maintaining your liberty as you have shown courage in freeing yourselves from slavery."—ID.

"Of those who were slaves at the beginning of the rebellion, full one hundred thousand are now in the United States military service, about one-half of which number actually bear arms in the ranks ; thus giving the double advantage of taking so much labor from the insurgent cause and supplying the places which otherwise must be filled with so many white men. So far as tested it is difficult to say they are not as good soldiers as any. No servile insurrection or tendency to violence or cruelty has marked the measures of emancipation and arming the blacks. These measures have been much discussed in foreign countries, and contemporary with such discussion the tone of public sentiment there is much improved. At home the same measures have been fully discussed, supported, criticised, and denounced, and the annual elections following are highly encouraging to those whose official duty it is to bear the country through this great trial. Thus we have the new reckoning. The crisis which threatened to divide the friends of the Union is past."—LINCOLN.

" The inner life of man is manifested in the evolution of society; the love of the family passes into the love of the state, and the love of the state rises into the all-embracing love of humanity."—COMTE.

" Christianity, which has now taken possession of the portals of nations, which is at this moment reigning or wandering over all the tribes of the earth from the rising to the setting of the sun, and which incredulous philosophy herself is obliged to acknowledge as the spiritual and social law of the world."—D'AUBIGNÉ.

" To the eye of vulgar Logic, says he, what is man? An omnivorous biped that wears breeches. To the eye of Pure Reason what is he? A soul, a spirit, and a divine apparition. Round his mysterious Me there lies, under all those wool-rags, a garment of flesh (or of senses) contextured in the loom of heaven; whereby he is revealed to his like, and dwells with them in union and division; and sees and fashions for himself a universe, with azure starry spaces, and long thousands of years. Deep hidden is he under that strange garment; amid sounds and color, and forms, as it were, swathed in, and inextricably overshrouded: yet it is sky-woven, and worthy of a God. Stands he not thereby in the centre of immensities, in the conflux of eternities?"—CARLYLE.

" Where are we, fathers? Are these really religious, and priests, who talk in this manner? Are they Christians? are they Turks? are they men? or are they demons? And are these 'the mysteries revealed by the Lamb to his society?' or are they not rather abominations suggested by the Dragon to those who take part with him?"—PASCAL.

" If fugitive-slave laws, providing modes and prescribing penalties whereby the master could seize and recover his fugitive slave, were legitimate exercises of an implied power to protect and enforce a right recognized by the Constitution, why shall the hands of Congress be tied, so that, under an express power, by appropriate legislation, to enforce constitutional provision granting citizenship, it may not by means of direct legislation bring the whole power of this nation to bear upon States and their officers, and upon such individuals and corporations exercising public functions as assume to abridge, impair, or deny rights confessedly secured by the supreme law of the land?"—Mr. Justice Harlan, C.R.C.

" The names of those who are faithful in misfortune are sacred in the page of history."—Hazlitt.

" Ye will perhaps make answer, that, being persuaded already as touching the truth of your cause, ye are not to hearken unto any sentence, no, not though angels should define otherwise."—Hooker.

" The extremity of right or law is said to be, when a man ties himself up to niceties, dwells upon letters and syllables, and in the mean time neglects the intent and equity of the law ; or when a written law is cunningly and maliciously interpreted."—Milton.

" You that go about to pervert so sacred and so glorious a law, with your fallacies and jugglings; you who would have this supreme law, and which of all others is most beneficial to mankind, to serve only for the impunity of tyrants ; let me tell you,—let me, I say, be so far a prophet as to tell you,—that the vengeance of God and man hangs over your head for so horrid a crime."—Id.

" When the case happens I shall do that which shall be fit for a judge to do."—Mansfield.

" Hitherto thou hast but freed us, and that not fully, from the unjust and tyrannous claim of thy foes ; now unite us entirely, and appropriate us to thyself, tie us everlastingly in willing homage to the prerogative of thy eternal throne."—Milton.

" I think it absolutely certain that the rebellion can in no way be so certainly, speedily, and economically suppressed as by the organized military force of the loyal population of the insurgent regions, of whatever complexion. In no way can irregular violence and servile insurrection be so surely prevented as by the regular organization and regular military employment of those who might otherwise probably resort to such courses. Such organization is now in successful progress, and the concurrent testimony of all connected with the colored regiments in Louisiana and South Carolina is that they are brave, orderly, and efficient. General Butler declares that without his colored regiments he could not have attempted his recent important movements in the Lafourche region ; and General Saxton bears equally explicit testimony to the good credit and efficiency of the colored troops recently sent on an expedition along the coast of Georgia. Considering these facts, it seems to me that it would be best to omit from the proclamation all reference to military employment of the enfranchised population, leaving it to the natural course of things already well begun ;

or to state distinctly that, in order to secure the suppression of the rebellion without servile insurrection or licentious marauding, such numbers of the population declared free as may be found convenient will be employed in the military and naval service of the United States."—LINCOLN.

" In the long, fierce struggle for freedom of opinion, the press, like the church, counted its martyrs by thousands."—GARFIELD.

" With what astonishment and veneration may we look into our own souls, where there are such hidden stores of virtue and knowledge, such inexhausted stores of perfection ! We know not yet what we shall be, nor will it ever enter into the heart to conceive the glory that will always be in reserve."—ADDISON.

" There is not, in my opinion, a more pleasing and triumphant consideration in religion than this of the perpetual progress which the soul makes towards the perfection of its nature without ever arriving at a period in it. To look upon the soul as going on from strength to strength ; to consider that she is to shine forever with new accessions of glory, and brighter to all eternity ; that she will be still adding virtue to virtue, and knowledge to knowledge ; carries in it something wonderfully agreeable to that ambition which is natural to the mind of man : nay, it must be a prospect pleasing to God himself to see his creation forever beautifying in his eyes and drawing nearer to him by greater degrees of resemblance." —ID.

" Finally, I respectfully suggest, on an occasion of such interest, there can be no imputation of affectation against a solemn recognition of responsibility before men and before God ; and that some such close as follows will be proper :

" And upon this act, sincerely believed to be an act of justice warranted by the Constitution, and of duty demanded by the circumstances of the country, I invoke the considerate judgment of mankind, and the gracious favor of Almighty God."—CHASE'S AMENDMENT TO EMANCIPATION PROCLAMATION.

" Give unto us righteous laws, wisely interpreted and strongly enforced, and fill us more and more with brotherly kindness, peace, and good will. Bless the great people of this land in all their interests, and make our land Immanuel's Land. Thou hast exalted us among the nations of the earth : make us a pattern nation, O God, and let thy blessing rest on these, thy servants, who to-day hold a representative place in the great family of nations. Oh, that the kingdom of peace and righteousness may every-where prevail, and that the people of the nations may be made free with that freedom which Christ alone can give !"—CHAPLAIN BUTLER.

" We worship thee, God of our fathers, our covenant God and Father. We bless thee for all of truth and of righteousness embodied in the Constitution and laws of this republic. We thank thee for the faith of the fathers, and for the faith and piety and patriotism and wisdom of their sons. We bless thee for the rich heritage of freedom coming to us, and we thank thee, O God, that in all our history, thou hast guided and defended us."—ID.

To THEIR EXCELLENCIES, THE PRESIDENT AND VICE-PRES-IDENT OF THE UNITED STATES OF AMERICA; to the Honorable, the Governors of the States; to the illustrious Representatives of the American people, who desire the favor of the Almighty, and are awake to the honor and interest of the nation, whose measures and movements have been marked by a patriotic, sincere, steady, and active support of the soundest principles of constitutional liberty, and whose careers have exhibited that calm and unyielding determination which is always the fruit of mature thought and strong principle; to the Judges, Federal and State, the most glorious prerogative of whose exalted calling is to ensure the triumph of justice over violence, law over anarchy, and freedom over oppression; and to the Public Press and Clergy of America, to whom the nation looks with loyal trust, as the appointed guardians of the true interests of the country, " JUSTICE AND JURISPRUDENCE," an Inquiry concerning the Thirteenth, Fourteenth, and Fifteenth Articles of Amendment to the Constitution of the United States, is humbly dedicated, by " The Brotherhood of Liberty of the United States," in the sincere hope that it may, in some measure, aid them in the fulfilment of their noble mission.

They beg leave to submit herewith some reasons and considerations which have emboldened them to undertake this matter. They apprehend that the official and non-official representatives to whom they dedicate this work are not wholly irresponsible for the present condition of civil rights, and they hereby invoke their aid, believing them the fittest and best qualified to assist in the great work of firmly establishing the future legal status of the civil rights of the race to which these addressers belong, as well as those of all other races in America. The addressers freely magnify and are duly grateful for what has already been accomplished towards the full establishment of the civil liberty of their race by the efforts of those whose mission upon earth it apparently was to execute the grand plans of the Divine Architect of the stateliest temple of freedom, who gave it a place in America and put it upon an eminence by itself. But they respectfully submit, that much still remains to be performed before the imposing fabric erected, under the superintendence of Providence, by the love and labors of these authors, asserters, and recoverers of constitutional liberty, can be pronounced perfect and complete.

It appears to your addressers that civil-rights doctrines are still in an imperfect, unsettled, mischievous state, and that the decisions of the courts are involved in an intricate tangle of verbal mysticism, the unravelling of which puts to confusion the legal acumen of even the most learned and skilful expositors of jurisprudence. At least, it cannot be denied that interpreters of the amendments in different sections of the country, equal in ability and legal knowledge, perpetually contradict one another. It must further be admitted that such an inconsistent administration of justice has, and must have, a tendency to create two distinct civic classes under the same government,—a most pernicious result, and one which the noble framers of the amendments especially sought to avoid. Instead of sowing the seeds of harmony, charity, humanity, and compassion; instead of creating bonds which by deep, strong, fervent ties would unite this race to the others which compose the nation; the present legal condition of civil rights fills the community with rancor, strife, and virulence. It is apparent that no system more partial or tyrannical is conceivable, than that which gives to one class of citizens the general power of meting out the civil rights of another class, whom the former have been long accustomed to regard as objects of social and civil contempt. This arbitrary subjection of a whole class of citizens to discriminative treatment is *non-American* and *unconstitutional*. These addressers submit that, if their people are expected to make moral, material, and intellectual advancement, if they are to become patriotic, meritorious, and useful citizens, they must be surrounded with all the conditions indispensable to such progress.

The Providence which guides the destiny of mankind having solved the dark enigma of slavery in America, there is no longer any sound reason apparent to these addressers why the civil status of the newly-constituted member of the American state should not be recognized as equal to that of any citizen. They feel that the time has arrived when the old pro-slavery sentiments, judicial, civil, or political, should pass away, and that an enlightened public opinion should prevail in accordance rather with present than with past conditions. They think that not a flaw in the superstructure of liberty should be permitted to escape the penetrating eye and the vigorous intelligence of the American people, that it is for the interest of the whole nation that correct views prevail upon the momentous subject of the civil liberty of their race, and that the polity of the State should be in full harmony with the constitutional amendments. They contend that frequent resurveys of its landmarks are essential to the preservation of the territory of constitutional freedom; and beg leave to suggest that, inasmuch as slavery desecrated all those humanities of life which are the original inheritance of mankind, the public mind should ponder the circumstances of the national history of the colored citizen; believing that, if the people of the nation would study the beginning of the social anomaly of slavery in this free country, the thoughts thence arising must result in the creation of a popular intelligence to which these addressers could with greater confidence appeal, to throw off the horrid incubus which for centuries has hampered the nation's judgment.

They further submit that the legal status of the civil rights of *every* race in America is an important matter, well worth the consideration of men of wisdom and equity, and that they ought, therefore, to be heard with patience, and their complaints judged by the light of the sun of reason rather than by that of the satellite prejudice; that not until all grievances are dispassionately listened to, attentively considered, and thoroughly reformed, are the utmost bounds of civil liberty attained for which all true men look; that if complaints be not patiently heard, and the evils set forth proved and fully redressed, then the "bravery" of the words of the Fourteenth Amendment rather injures than promotes the cause of civil liberty.

In this presentation of the cause of their people they do not wish to heighten the difficulties of the situation, but simply to imitate the example of impartial justice, which, though forced to condemn, never exaggerates the fault of the wrong-doer.

These addressers do not regard themselves as innovators, dreamers, murmurers, or diffusers of civil discontent; nor are they ambitious to propose any visionary scheme of unattainable perfection. They only desire to see rigidly maintained the spirit of the Supreme Court's decisions in the civil-rights cases, that the "Fourteenth Amendment obliterated the race-line so far as all rights fundamental in a state of freedom are concerned." The following work, undertaken and written at their request, is intended to further this end; and it is hoped that it will have a tendency to check the fungus-growth of illicit constitutional construction which has already so emasculated the amendments, and that it may induce the guardians of jurisprudence to substitute a sound and robust method of interpretation, in the place of those metaphysical abstractions and subtle distinctions which have served no better purpose than to aid in the resurrection of some of the ceremonialisms of slavery long after its interment.

These addressers only claim liberty to exercise the superior right of thought,—that independent freedom of inquiry which so conspicuously distinguishes the present age and our country. They insist that the significance, dignity, and importance of the African race as a potent industrial and economic factor, and a valuable and reliable political force, in its relation to the American commonwealth, are susceptible of demonstration, without subtlety, florid eloquence, or the vehement asseverations of acrimonious debate. It is their purpose to endeavor to expose the crudities, and correct the antiquated but still vigorous errors, of race-prejudice; and they fully realize that they have to combat a strange mixture of prejudice and indifference, and the worst of all tyrants,—authority confirmed by long-continued

custom, whose yoke it is alike hard to break and wearisome
to bear.

It is also their opinion that in the recent civil-rights decisions
false refinement, obscurity, and injustice are inseparable companions; that the Fourteenth Amendment, which was designed
for the protection of the civil rights of the colored citizen, has
been interpreted against him by a construction too favorable to
those who are inclined to oppose his further progress and development; and that under the rulings of these decisions certain public servants and the monopolistic labor class practically exercise
the authority of making what rules and regulations they may
see fit.   They submit that no racial prejudice or sociological
argument should legalize customs which, besides being subversive of the Constitution as amended, are in their very nature
high treason against humanity and civilization; that law, which
is founded solely upon principles of reason and justice, should
in no way be subject to a bias which inclines its ministers to
favor the perpetuation of the ancient rites of the age of slavery
which sooner or later must be buried in the wrecks of time; and
that civil rights rest upon the foundation of mutual equity and
utility, of which the Fourteenth Constitutional Amendment is
declaratory as the measure of American public justice.   Inasmuch as they are subject to the burdens of the government,
they respectfully urge that they have the right to enjoy the
benefits of all the provisions of its laws.

These addressers desire to raise up a perpetual monitor in the
minds of all peoples and races against any encroachment or innovation upon the precepts of the Fourteenth Amendment.
They feel that, as it is the duty, it should also be the glory,
of the American people to cherish, and protect against all attacks,
the doctrine of the " Equality of Rights by Due Process of
Law," a fundamental principle which ought to be constantly and
solemnly asserted and claimed by all Americans.

They submit that the decision in Hall and DeCuir, in the
eyes of all men of candor and sense, confessedly operates as an
overruling of this sacred provision of the Fourteenth Amendment; that the separate opinion in that cause exhibits the hyp-
ochondriac alarm and valetudinary longevity of race-prejudice.

They fear, too, that some judges are unconsciously biassed and misled by the prejudices of early education, or by a deference to the opinions of others; and that, instead of mounting over the *débris* of the fallen institution of slavery to a higher level of knowledge, instead of elevating their judgments by contemplating the lofty standard of constitutional truth which the Fourteenth Amendment proclaims, they often are only too ready to adopt happy phrases, specious and ingenious but shallow sophisms, "nice, sharp quillets of the law" to support more ancient but now unsuitable customs. These judges seem altogether forgetful of the fact that, until correct determined rules of action are adopted with reference to civil rights, there can be no permanent settlement of the public policy ; which, to be stable, must be based upon the absolute moral, constitutional, civil, and political truths of the Fourteenth Amendment.

The complaint of these addressers is, that amidst the hosannas of the survivors of a drivelling generation of slavery-worshippers (who have not yet learned any wisdom greater than their own), race-prejudice, oftentimes, with only the conceptions and character of a peddler, exercises with impunity its tyrannous power, in all the departments of civic life. For the ordinary regulation of business pursuits, so far as our race is concerned, it adopts the motto of Danton, "*l'audace, l'audace, et toujours l'audace.*" It may honor the form, but it tramples upon the real substance of this fundamental law, and has now grown to be a monster, with the hands of Briareus and the head of Polyphemus. It is quick to execute the behests of slavery customs, but slow to carry out the requirements of the Fourteenth Amendment. In deference to a certain popular clamor, it formulates its rules and regulations for the enjoyment of civil rights by the colored race upon a tyrannical system of sheer blindness, obstinacy, unsteadiness, sophistry, fraud, and injustice. Instead of helping to dispel old prejudices, its vigilant and over-sagacious wits are occupied in bringing to light the little latent wisdom which slumbered in the antiquated slavery customs, with which its understanding was perhaps originally indoctrinated. It cannot altogether disassociate itself from the observance of the rites and ceremonies of the days of bondage, and seems to consider that the great truths of the Fourteenth Amendment should give way to treachery, cupidity, cruelty, and tyranny. What was meant for bread it appears to regard itself as authorized to turn into stone.

But to leave for the present this monstrosity of our civilization, your addressers conceive and respectfully set forth, that it requires no great understanding nor labor of thought to unfold those fundamental principles, which to every enlightened mind, imbued with the love of liberty, ought to be self-evident. It is apparent to the student of history, that American society, to be in conformity with the polity of this amendment, must submit to some radical changes; that new feelings and sensibilities must be introduced into the departments of industry; and that the effects of a different scheme of government and system of law, and superior methods of training and education, must eventually lead the citizens whom these addressers represent to a higher civic recognition. It appears to them, that the past and present attitude of classes in America, under a democratic government, presents an exterior structure similar to that of classes in Central Europe under feudalism. Although the American realization of constitutional government is set forth in the model principles of the amendments, which unite all the excellences found in different systems of ancient or modern liberties, nevertheless they are regarded by some statists as mere political theories inapplicable to their race. One of the main purposes of these addressers is to draw attention to the peculiar tenets of these jurists and statesmen, and to the difference between the abstract theories of jurisprudence and their practical administration of justice. The addressers submit, with great deference to the better judgment of their patrons, that there are judicial procedures the end of which is justice, but which are nevertheless a mere verbal identification of jurisprudence with justice; that the primitive element of justice in America is the conformity of the nation to the law of the Fourteenth Amendment; that its commandment was given because it was deemed just, but that jurisprudence seems to regard it as just only because it is commanded.

These addressers consider that the ancient system of slavery in America consisted of many parts, having a social, civil, political, and ecclesiastical character; that it withstood many shocks of awakened reason, with the greatest composure; and that its leaden mace still holds sway over the public mind; that the despotic system of the crafty chieftains of race-prejudice is artfully constructed, and great abuses are perpetrated by the lowest in its ranks. They earnestly plead for that national progressive justice, which will insure the African citizen's civil right to the exemption from industrial discrimination of strikes, boycotts, and class-labor, on account of color and previous condition. The ever-present discouragement of this antagonism prevails throughout all workshops, North, East, and West. For its warrant of authority, it has the example of, and is fostered by, the mighty precedents set for the defeat of civil equality, by constructions subversive of the letter and spirit of the Fourteenth Amendment. The laws on which its living progress and organic development depend cannot be violated without retarding the advance of our race. Industrial progress is made up of an ever-changing tissue of relations. It must be permitted to have all the benign influence evolved from new conditions, and must grow as a part of the warp and woof of current events. If its thread is unravelled and segregated the economic value of our race energies must, in the eternal nature of things, become atrophied.

In the present condition of affairs every door of industrial aspiration and advancement is barred against the African citizen. He can lease no house but in the vicinity of moral asphyxia. He pays the highest rent, yet receives the lowest wages. He is not admitted to learn trades in which skilled laborers are employed. If he applies to workshops, he is abruptly notified that " no colored man need apply." He has not the opportunity for self-respecting means of education. Civil right is denied him especially throughout the workshops of the North, East, and West. In short, he is debarred industrial progress, without regard to the question of his fitness. His development is confined to servile occupations. He can neither be a carpenter, type-setter, machinist, mason, or blacksmith, nor can he grow skilful in any of the multitude of manual arts. He is in these respects upon terms of civil equality with no other race. He is under the sceptre of an iron rule, which is unintelligent and revolutionary. By this retrogressive movement, solely on account of their color and previous condition, millions of our citizens are violently deprived of a most essential civil right,—the privilege of pursuing means of education upon terms of civil equality with all the other citizens. The fundamental law of the Fourteenth Amendment cannot free him from the merciless clutches of the monopolistic labor class, which has condemned him to the unremunerative pursuits of caterer, cook, coachman, porter, drayman, scrubber, carpet-beater, hod-carrier, stevedore, or bootblack.

The late decade has been a momentous era for classes and interests. A vast upheaval of industries has been evolved from different conditions, and is inspired by different purposes, North and South. In the political and industrial departments the invasions of majorities are as unlimited and unconscionable as their power over minorities is absolute. The plutocracy of money and the oligarchy of labor overwhelmingly repudiate the constitutional limitations whenever their interests can be promoted, apparently with the sanction of public opinion, certainly without the arrest of the law. The disasters which overwhelm our race's industrial factors touch the interests of the country at large. This result is the effect of the contagious example of these law-breakers in the formation of public opinion. The society of the state has not yet grown sufficiently enlightened to conform its opinion to its constitutional law. Instead of being a living force, the law has now grown to be a familiar skeleton, a mere scare-crow of retributive justice.

These addressers realize that it takes many blows of the hammer of advancing knowledge to awaken to full activity that thick-headed, mole-eyed, somnolent giant, the public. In behalf of their undertaking, they humbly implore the Supreme Lawgiver of the Universe to aid those Christian messengers who

"Celebrate the throne and equipage of God's almightiness"

in strains which angels pause to hear; who represent the reign of God and the reign of law on earth: those intrepid disciples

who are ever ready to buckle on the armor of truth and sally
out against the adversaries of Christianity and the forces of
wrong; who through centuries of bitter trial have ever been
the acknowledged champions of moral and intellectual superiority: those noble ecclesiastics who have so interwoven religion
with civil government that the soundest philosophic basis for
the state must be found in those divine truths which they proclaim, and which are indissolubly connected with all that is
great, good, and glorious in the destiny of the American people;
who have never basely descended to foster the seed or propa-
gate the germs of evils, which the teachings of their master and
the supreme law of the land alike seek to eradicate from the
breasts of the American people; who, by inculcating the practice of such principles of moral action as are conducive to
the highest, purest, and best interests of mankind, have laid the
foundations of the intrinsic grandeur and importance of the
American state: those ministers of Christ whose church has
been the natural companion of civil liberty throughout all its
conflicts, and whose religion is now become the sun of the state,
the source of its life and warmth, and the centre to which it
gravitates: the loving disciples who, having labored long and
earnestly to strike off the chains of slavery, now seek to
elevate seven millions of people prostrated by the degrading
despotism of centuries; who have dethroned oppression, extirpated fraud, and banished violence; whose weapons are not
carnal, and whose kingdom is not of this world: those evangel-
ists whose holy mission has been fulfilled through that progressive civilization of the church which has made an exquisite
adaptation of morality to the human heart: those subjects who
serve a Being able to crush all his adversaries; and who, having
sacrificed all worldly passions and interests, strive unceasingly to
prepare themselves for a future and higher life: the holy messengers who have proclaimed faith, hope, and charity to men;
whose duty it is to magnify goodness; whose teachings have promoted the happiness of mankind by inculcating that spirit of
mercy, moderation, and benevolence which has been most efficacious in the introduction of a better and more enlightened sense
of justice: these addressers invoke the blessings of the Supreme

Being upon all these followers of Christ who, however divided
in creed, yet join in one " sublime chorus to celebrate the truths
of Christianity, and lay upon its holy altars the never-fading
treasures of their immortal wisdom."

These addressers crave permission to remind that august, enlightened, and illuminating body, the Supreme Court of the
United States, the most illustrious of a judiciary where all are
illustrious, that unto jurisprudence, which is the natural, and
should be the true, auxiliary of Christianity, is committed the
rare and extraordinary authority of expounding that important
branch of the administration of government, upon the correct
application of the principles of which depends the happiness of
seven millions of human beings who are citizens of the United
States.   They make bold to bring to the remembrance of these
vicegerents of the Almighty, that their predecessors have never
failed in fidelity to the principles of liberty protected by law;
that the greatest triumph of their genius has been unfolded in
following and protecting the solid precedents of popular freedom,
by exact learning and profound reasoning; that these proud
memorials are a monument of fame more lasting and far exceeding in grandeur those of political or martial glory; that the
task of developing a system of law in full accord with the national polity in its true aspect has fallen to the lot of the present
and future courts of justice; that this development necessitates
the opposition of positive to negative tendencies in the administration of justice in civil-rights cases, and the exchange of
vague for fixed and settled rules, by means and instrumentalities
attainable only through the comprehensive medium of jurisprudence.   They beg to remind these supreme expounders of the
law, that the constitutional doctrines which the amendments introduced are for the building up of all the elements (lower as
well as higher) of the state; that they aim to deal with the entire body of the state in its progressive movement towards a
more advanced civilization than a pro-slavery constitution permitted; that the fate of the civil rights of the nation rests upon
the life-giving principles of these amendments, and that the duty
is incumbent upon the bench to see that the old dogmas are so
relaxed as to be adjustable to the altered conditions which the

late political revolution has wrought; that an open, honest endeavor to conform the rules of law to the amendments is an imperative necessity for the attainment of their grand purpose; that the varied forces which are ever acting and reacting upon each other, in the wondrous complication of the multiform elements making up the state, require reciprocal action between the principles of jurisprudence and the declared civil polity of the nation ; that the attitude of jurisprudence towards this great charter of freedom should be independent of the conflict between the old and the new form of political society ; and that the new-fashioned modesty, cold, coy, reserved, and doubtful, introduced since these amendments, should give way to a larger charity, a broader humanity, and a more decided juristic recognition of the new members of the state. It is indisputable that to be numbered among freemen but at the same time to be subjected to servile discriminations clogs the moral faculties, and reduces the conduct of the man to the standard of a beast, by compelling a degrading submission ; that the Dred Scott case demonstrated the fact that jurisprudence, even in a republic of republics, might be made a vehicle of tyranny ; that, when the old customs of slavery have a hiding-place in the heart of the public, its errors die hard; that its spirit, still possessed of vital force, may unconsciously incline the ministers of justice to create, within the circumference of a government professedly thoroughly constitutional, a despotism, which may remorselessly crush out all that is most precious and most essential to the enjoyment by this race of their new-born citizenship.

It must be apparent to all men of reflection, that, if the execution of the national purpose to endow this race with the immunities and privileges of American citizenship be committed to a judiciary which disapproves of the polity of the state, whose head and heart are against it (the spirit of liberty commanding only its hands), the revolution in favor of their civil rights will not be progressive. If the noble efforts of wisdom and equity which these amendments embody are intrusted to the management of monopolistic labor-caste and to the public servant, who are under the dominion of vulgar prejudices, jurisprudence is stripped of one of her most glorious prerogatives : she can no longer emulate the example of those brave spirits, broad in comprehension and rich in virtue, who have had the courage to extirpate the seeds by which the growth of slavery customs was propagated.   They respectfully submit, that the earlier civil-rights decisions bade fair to extend the blessings of this great liberty to their full limit, but the brighter effulgence which the gleams of the dawn seemed to promise has not yet shone upon the children of silence and sorrow ; that the earlier civil-rights decisions were in full accord with the magnanimity of those heroes who, bold in strife, were patterns of humility in peace, and who were bright exemplars of justice, integrity, disinterested patriotism, and humanity. These addressers fully realize, that the first and noblest of human sciences, which in its practical application requires a greater knowledge of mankind and a far more extensive comprehension of popular government than all others, " combining the principles of original justice with the infinite variety of human concerns," is the sole instrumentality by which American liberties can be preserved.   They exhort these administrators of justice, who by a long course of study have attained a wisdom greater than that of the majority of men, to emulate those venerable sages of the law whose careers afford brilliant examples of exact and profound justice. They humbly exhort them to remember that in the whole compass of human affairs there appears no nobler spectacle than that of jurisprudence engaged in extending the domain of justice, and contracting within the narrowest possible limits the dominions of brute force and arbitrary will.

It is not needful to remind American judges that the august image of their exalted wisdom in the administration of jurisprudence is a miniature of that eternal justice which presides in the dispensations of the Almighty ; that the wise men of the bench should not necessarily agree with the opinion of the mass of people ; that popular notions and circumstances which sway unofficial judgments are neither the standards of rectitude nor masters of the juristic conscience ; that jurists of substantial greatness must often look down with contempt upon the applause or censure of the multitude.

Finally, with confident assurance in its advocacy of the mag-

nificent principle of the Fourteenth Amendment, these addressers approach the first and greatest champion of civilization,
the defender which defies opposition and is itself indestructible.
They invoke the majestic name of the public press, that great
director of the course of human events whose sublime mission
it is to fight the battles of free thought and to guide the current
of public opinion.   Upon this noble benefactor of mankind de-
volves the pleasing duty of diminishing the power of evil and
increasing the dominion of good.   It is the most progressive,
the most expansive, the mightiest, widest, and most important
instrument of all our glorious civilization.   Accustomed to
grapple with difficulties, it is capable of unfolding the most
involved truths and exposing the most intricate and subtle
errors.   It imparts the hidden spiritual forces which cause the
steady progress and the eternal development of the human
mind.   By inculcating obedience to the voice of reason, from
what source soever it may proceed, and by affording a rational
amusement, it confers the greatest blessings upon society.   From
its lips fall diamonds, amethysts, rubies, emeralds, all the jewels
of truth; its thoughts are ever refulgent with reason, language
brighter than the stars, deeper than the seas, fairer than the
flowers.   It has established higher tests for national respect and
confidence, by substituting protracted and patient investigation,
as well as acute and severe analysis, in the place of passionate
declamation.   Its wealth of illustration and splendor of diction,
its variety of knowledge, its copiousness of style, by communicating the best ideas of the most qualified minds in the most
capable way, have elevated the tone of society and cultivated
popular sensibilities in the highest degree to noble and ennobling ends.   It has rendered knowledge what it ought to be,—
the great bulwark of civil tranquillity, the deep foundation of
social virtue, and the vital cause of human civilization.   Its
resources seem the measure and day-spring of the intellectual
wealth of the age: like Jeanne d'Albret, queen of Navarre,
who fought the battles of the Reformation, it empties its jewel-
rooms to win the richer jewel of liberty.   Like the fabled Grecian horse from the tread of whose hoofs sprung fountains of
living water, the press pours forth continuous and copious

streams which irrigate and keep green the broad fields of truth, justice, and freedom. The rod of its dominion stretches across the continents and oceans, and its voice is as terrible as an army with banners. It has built bridges of communication with all parts of the earth, and everywhere established reservoirs for the more abundant fructification of knowledge. As the dragon protected the fruit of the Hesperides, so its faithful sentinels, with sleepless vigilance, guard constitutional liberty. It possesses the liberty of discussing without fear or favor every subject within the compass of the human mind. In its mighty grasp it holds all the great problems of thought; upon its strong arm the nation has rested in the past, and will in the future lean for support when the great events now in the loom of time shall be fully developed.

It was chiefly through the agency of this mighty power that the conditions of the past were moulded and forced into the splendid liberal triumphs resulting in the amendments. Its vision first pierced the pitchy cloud of darkness which brooded over America in the days of human bondage. Its voice was first lifted up for the release of America from the shameful reproach of constitutional slavery; its efforts in her disenthralment from the slave-oligarchy have wonderfully stimulated and increased economic prosperity in America; and without its intelligent guidance, only imperfect results can be attained when the time arrives for the final adjustment of the great issues now rising before us. Upon the public press rests the obligation of extending the old and faithfully maintaining the new boundaries of freedom, by the thorough emancipation of the American people from that traditional spirit of evil which is even now striving to arise from the tomb in which slavery is buried,—a tomb which should be sealed for all time. It was the public press which first taught the necessity of the sacrifice of national prejudice to the national welfare. When impending changes in the polity of the nation encountered the scorn and hatred, as well as the purblind ignorance, the pompous vanity, and the pitiful sophisms of slavery, then the public press warned those feeble-minded and superficial observers that God's providence rules supreme over America, and that the deformed thing which they have worshipped had retarded their own civilization. Its sublime mission is to keep watch and ward that the stream of time may not be obstructed, or diverted from its true course.

"JUSTICE AND JURISPRUDENCE" is intended to be a defence of the civil liberty of the whole American people. It presents the claim of the African race with no fairer gloss than naked truth affords. It is especially designed to be a treatise on the true exposition of the noble principle of *equality of rights by due process of law*, which these addressers insist is the great seminal doctrine of the Fourteenth Amendment; and constitutes an impregnable foundation for the civil tranquillity, present and future, of a strong, proud, loving, and united people. The book is also intended as an unfolding of the true policy of the American state, and endeavors to demonstrate that the safety and uniformity of the constitutional liberties of the whole American people can rest upon no more solid foundation than is afforded by the rigid enforcement of the principle of the equality of the rights of all citizens by due process of law. They believe that the popular specious pretensions and perversions employed for the maintenance of a contrary doctrine by those false-hearted scribes and Pharisees who worship the graven images—the *dii inferni*—of slavery are factious, fallacious, and dangerous to the civil tranquillity of the whole people of the United States, and they strenuously maintain that the Constitution as amended by Article Fourteen is the most perfect work of political wisdom the world contains, fixed in perfect form by superintending Providence through the mighty efforts of gigantic minds. And if the principles of the Fourteenth Amendment be carried into every region of civil right, if its precepts are observed in sober verity and executed with due charity, even by magistrates of less mental stature and far feebler powers than the transcendent genius which framed that article, it will in time prove to be of the greatest advantage to the inseparable interests, the general happiness, and the practical prosperity of the whole American people.

May a wise, happy, and speedy settlement of this grave issue be soon realized. To the obtaining of this blessed Christian end, subservient alike to the teachings of the gospel of Christ and to the mandates of the Constitution of the United States as augmented by the Thirteenth, Fourteenth, and Fifteenth Articles of Amendment, may the sacred light of divine grace and power ever shine upon one and all their patrons! That the deep shadows of the past may fade away before the unutterable splendors of universal freedom in America, and that thy law, O Heavenly Father, "without whose help all labor is ineffective, and without whose grace all wisdom is folly," may be put in their inward parts and written in their hearts; that civil liberty, which the visible hand of thy providence has planted in America, may never be rooted out of the kindly soil of constitutional law; that their cup of gall and bitterness may pass altogether from the lips of seven millions of thy people; that those of this great multitude who have not known the full fruition of thy civil peace may speedily attain unto it as complete citizens of the American state; and that the interpretation of thy decrees, which are embodied in these amendments, may never hereafter be blemished with the stain of human infirmity, is the fervent prayer of seven millions of thy devoted people, in the dedication of this work to those faithful servants unto whom thou hast seen fit to commit the preservation of the pure spirit of that civil liberty which in the course of thy providence seems destined to enlighten and bless the civilized world.

THE BROTHERHOOD OF LIBERTY

TO THEIR BRETHREN THE CITIZENS OF THE UNITED STATES OF AFRICAN DESCENT.

"The shoemaker, in 'The Relapse,' tells Lord Foppington that his lordship is mistaken in supposing that his shoe pinches."—MACAULAY.

"For books are not absolutely dead things, but do contain a potency of life in them, to be as active as that soul whose progeny they are; nay, they do preserve, as in a vial, the purest efficacy and extraction of that living intellect that bred them. I know they are as lively, and as vigorously productive, as those fabulous dragon's teeth; and, being sown up and down, may chance to spring up armed men. A good book is the precious life-blood of a master spirit, embalmed and treasured up on purpose to a life beyond life."—JOHN MILTON.

"All history shows that reforms in government must not be expected from those who sit serenely on the social mountain-tops, enjoying the benefits of the existing order of things. Even the divine author of our religion found his followers, not among the self-complacent Pharisees, but among the lowly-minded fishermen."—TILDEN.

"Let wealth and commerce, law and learning, die. But give us back our old nobility."—LORD JOHN MANNERS.

"Truth wears no mask, bows at no human shrine, seeks neither place nor applause; she only asks a hearing."—RELIGIO-PHILOSOPHICAL JOURNAL.

"Take fast hold of Instruction; let her not go; keep her; for she is thy life."—PROVERBS.

"But the instant the world (that dread jury) are impanelled, and called to look on and be umpires in the scene, so that nothing is done by con-

23

nivance or in a corner, the reason mounts the judgment-seat in lieu of passion or interest, and opinion becomes law, instead of arbitrary will; and farewell, feudal lord and sovereign king."—HAZLITT.

"We stand in a region of conjectures, where substance has melted into shadow, and one cannot be distinguished from the other."—CARLYLE.

"Hear else what Cicero says in his Fourth Philippic: 'What cause of war can be more just and warrantable than to avoid slavery? For though a people may have the good fortune to live under a gentle master, yet those are in miserable condition whose prince may tyrannize over them if he will.' "—MILTON.

"There seems to be something in the institution of slavery which has at all times either shocked or perplexed mankind, however little habituated to reflection, and however slightly advanced in the cultivation of its moral instincts."—MAINE.

"In all governments, there is a perpetual intestine struggle, open or secret, between authority and liberty."—HUME.

"Everything that sets in motion the springs of the human heart engaged them to the protection of their inestimable privileges."—PATRICK HENRY.

"Sell all and purchase liberty."—ID.

"And can we imagine that the whole body of the people of a free nation, though oppressed and tyrannized over and preyed upon, should be left remediless?"—MILTON.

"Struggling, struggling like a mighty tree, again about to burst in the embrace of summer, and shoot forth frondose boughs which would fill the whole earth. A disease, but the noblest of all,—as of her who is in pain and sore travail, but travail that she may be a mother, and say, Behold, there is a new man born!"—CARLYLE.

"They might foresee a struggle, the last convulsive efforts of pride and power to keep the world in its wonted subjection; but that was nothing; their final triumph over all opposition was assured in the eternal principles of justice, and in their own unshaken devotedness to the great cause of mankind! If the result did not altogether correspond to the intentions of those firm and enlightened patriots who so nobly planned it, the fault was not in them but in others."—HAZLITT.

" It is the night of the world, and still long till it be day; we wander amid the glimmer of smoking ruins, and the sun and the stars of heaven are as if blotted out for a season; and two immeasurable phantoms, Hypocrisy and Atheism, with the ghoul, Sensuality, stalk abroad over the earth, and call it theirs: well at ease are the sleepers for whom existence is a shallow dream."—CARLYLE.

" All true men, high and low, each in his sphere, are consciously or unconsciously bringing it to pass; all false and half-true men are fruitlessly spending themselves to hinder it from coming to pass."—ID.

" All evil, and this evil too, is as a nightmare: the instant you begin to stir under it, the evil is, properly speaking, gone. Consider, O reader, whether it be not actually so. Evil, once manfully fronted, ceases to be evil; there is generous battle-hope in place of dead passive misery; the evil itself has become a kind of good."—ID.

" Yet I,
A dull and muddy-mettled rascal, peak,
Like John-a-dreams, unpregnant of my cause,
And can say nothing."—SHAKESPEARE.

" What posterity is likely to judge of these matters we may the better conjecture if we call to mind what our own age, within a few years, upon better experience, hath already judged concerning the same."—HOOKER.

" Perhaps there are individuals who will oppose fewer prejudices to the lessons of paganism than to those of Christianity."—D'AUBIGNÉ.

" These men's end in all their actions is distraction; their pretence and color, reformation."—HOOKER.

" Are we opossums? have we natural pouches, like the kangaroo? Or how, without clothes, could we possess the master-organ, soul's-seat, and true pineal gland of the body social,—I mean, a PURSE?"—CARLYLE.

" Yet if God wills that it continue until all the wealth piled by the bondsman's two hundred and fifty years of unrequited toil shall be sunk, and until every drop of blood drawn with the lash shall be paid by another drawn with the sword, as was said three thousand years ago, so, still, it must be said that the judgments of the Lord are true and righteous altogether."—LINCOLN.

" No race has ever shown such capabilities of adaptation to varying soil and circumstances as the negro. Alike to them the snows of Canada, the hard, rocky land of New England, or the gorgeous profusion of the Southern States."—H. B. STOWE.

"One thing remains yet to be done, which perhaps is of the greatest concern of all, and that is, that you, my countrymen, refute this adversary of yours yourselves, which I do not see any other means of your effecting than by a constant endeavor to outdo all men's bad words by your own good deeds."—MILTON.

"Yet, however blinded that assembly may be, by their intemperate rage for unlimited domination, so to slight justice and the opinion of mankind, we esteem ourselves bound, by obligations of respect to the rest of the world, to make known the justice of our cause."—DICKINSON.

"But time advances: facts accumulate; doubts arise. Faint glimpses of truth begin to appear, and shine more and more unto the perfect day. The highest intellects, like the tops of mountains, are the first to catch and to reflect the dawn. They are bright, while the level below is still in darkness. But soon the light, which at first illuminated only the loftiest eminences, descends on the plain, and penetrates to the deepest valley. First come hints, then fragments of systems, then defective systems, then complete and harmonious systems. The sound opinion, held for a time by one bold speculator, becomes the opinion of a small minority, of a strong minority, of a majority of mankind. Thus the great progress goes on, till school-boys laugh at the jargon which imposed on Bacon, till country rectors condemn the illiberality and intolerance of Sir Thomas More."—MACAULAY.

"Be of hope! Already streaks of blue peer through our clouds; the thick gloom of ignorance is rolling asunder, and it will be day. Mankind will repay with interest their long-accumulated debt: the anchorite that was scoffed at will be worshipped; the fraction will become not an integer only, but a square and cube."—CARLYLE.

> "Footprints that perchance some other
>   Struggling on life's stormy main,—
> Some forlorn and shipwrecked brother,—
>   Seeing, may take heart again."—LONGFELLOW.

"That it might flame far and wide through the earth, and many a disconsolately wandering spirit be guided thither to a brother's bosom!"—CARLYLE.

"The saddest of all words are, 'My people perish for want of knowledge.'"—CHATEAUBRIAND.

" We cannot read their book. They tell us different stories about what it contains, and we believe they make the book talk to suit themselves."— RED-JACKET.

" False rules prankt in reason's garb."—MILTON.

" Yea, I take myself to witness that I have loved no darkness, sophisticated no truth, nursed no delusion, allowed no fear."—EMPEDOCLES.

" I assured his honor, that law was a science in which I had not much conversed, further than by employing advocates in vain upon some injustices that had been done me : however, I would give him all the satisfaction I was able."—SWIFT.

" All true men in America pledged their lives, their fortunes, and their sacred honor to ' throw off the shackles of usurped control,' and in the outcome they did ' hew them link from link.' The friends of liberty in England sided with patriots here. Burke and Fox made the defensive sophistry of ministers contemptible ; Chatham declared that if Americans submitted they would become slaves themselves, and fit instruments to enslave others. ' I rejoice,' said he, ' that America resisted.' "—J. BLACK.

" So I hear in the dim distance the first notes of the jubilee, rising from the hearts of the nation ; soon, very soon, you shall hear it at the gates of the citadel, and the stars and stripes shall guarantee liberty forever from the lakes to the gulf."—PHILLIPS.

" Suspect every one who approaches that jewel."—PATRICK HENRY.

" What I intend now to say to you is, next to your duty to God and the care of your salvation, of the greatest concern to yourselves and your children : your bread and clothing, and every common necessary of life, entirely depend upon it. Therefore I do most earnestly exhort you as men, as Christians, as parents, and as lovers of your country, to read this paper with the utmost attention, or get it read to you by others."—SWIFT.

" I was born an American ; I shall live an American ; I shall die an American."—WEBSTER.

" The same deep-seated love of Liberty
    Beats in our hearts. We speak the same good tongue
    Familiar with all songs your bards have sung,
    Those large men, Milton, Shakespeare, both are ours."—STODDARD.

"Men of learning find nothing new in it; men of taste many things to criticise; and men without either, not a few things which they will not understand.   It will, nevertheless, be read and praised, and become a powerful engine in forming the public opinion."—MADISON.

"Stick to the bill: it is your Magna Charta and your Runnymede. King John made a present to the barons.   King William has made a similar present to you.   Never mind, common qualities good in common times. If a man does not vote for the bill he is unclean; the plague-spot is upon him: push him into the lazaretto of the last century, with Wetherell and Sadler; purify the air before you approach him; bathe your hands in chloride of lime if you have been contaminated by his touch."—SYDNEY SMITH.

"With malice towards none, with charity for all, with firmness in the right, as God gives us to see the right."—LINCOLN.

"Yesterday you wiped the tears from our eyes, that we might see clearly; you unstopped our ears, that we might hear; and removed the obstructions from our throats, that we might speak distinctly."—RED-JACKET.

"Republicanism says to every man: 'Let your soul be like an eagle; fly out in the great dome of thought, and question the stars for yourself.'" —INGERSOLL.

"Forasmuch as many have taken in hand to set forth in order a declaration of those things which are most surely believed among us, even as they delivered them unto us, which from the beginning were eye-witnesses, and ministers of the word; it seemed good to me also, having had perfect understanding of all things from the very first, to write unto thee in order, most excellent Theophilus, that thou mightest know the certainty of those things wherein thou hast been instructed."—ST. LUKE.

"They were not slaves, rising in desperation from beneath the agonies of the lash, but free men, snuffing from afar ' the tainted gale of tyranny.'" —EVERETT.

"Give me the liberty to know, to utter, and to argue freely above all liberties."—SUMNER.

"Hear me for my cause."—SHAKESPEARE.

"We shall this day light such a candle, by God's grace, in England as, I trust, shall never be put out."—LATIMER.

WE think, and appeal to the country for a justification of our opinion, that cases like those of the Norfolk Ferry-Boat, the Knights of Labor at Richmond, the William Lloyd Garrison Post, at Brooklyn, and countless others of daily occurrence, never meeting the public eye, but borne in silence and with that spirit of meekness and long-suffering which characterize our race, demand of us the gravest deliberation. We have further reached the conclusion that by placing within reach of the American public a concise summary of all the civil-rights adjudications since the emancipation proclamation, we may inaugurate a reform in public opinion which will correct the innumerable evils, and do away with the manifold abuses, from which our race grievously suffer east and west, north and south, which are particularly set forth in the foregoing dedicatory address.

The philanthropist and friend of civil liberty may look with sorrow upon the melancholy plight of African civil rights in America, but the far-seeing eye of the philosophic statesman can predict with certainty the period in the nation's history when the evolution of time will quietly, but surely, perfect that great picture of freedom, the canvas for which was stretched upon the pillars of the world, by the hands of the angels, at creation's dawn. The abolition of slavery in the British possessions, the manumission of the serf in despotic Russia, and the great emancipation amendment in this land of the free, were all the work of time. We need champions to combat the spirit of discrimination; inflexible, intrepid, fearless leaders of our own race; men of strength, grace, and wisdom, of unselfish love and purity; men who are able to tread the steep and arduous paths of duty; cool, prudent, and considerate, with gravity of character and of sound judgment. Night and day, in season and out of season, each of us, strong or weak, must make every effort to advance the standard of our constitutional rights, for we have found by experience that an obsequious subservience to race-prejudice seriously threatens their extinction. We must learn the eternal truth which Tacitus taught, " Oh, men! voluntary slaves make more tyrants than tyrants make involuntary slaves."

We must peaceably but firmly claim every jot and tittle to which we are entitled under the organic law of this great country, not permitting the spirit of the Fourteenth Amendment to be shaken by the coarse resistance of prejudice, or frittered away by the quibbles and hair-drawn distinctions of learned ingenuity, without earnest and united protestations and appeals on our part to enlightened public opinion. The two races must work out their destiny side by side, for they are indissolubly united by the triumph of the foremost civilization of the earth, which has at last established a government consecrated to the preservation of the equal rights of all its citizens, irrespective of race, color, creed, or previous condition; a government which recognizes no superior in the state but the caste of that justice, wisdom, and generosity which lifts up all the fallen and unfortunate of the family of mankind.

It is a cheering reflection that the American sense of justice, however long delayed, has never yet failed to recognize the constitutional rights of the masses against classes. We are convinced that American reverence for law, the great guardian spirit of every free country, is a potent factor, which it is not possible to overestimate. No civilized community can forever withstand just, enlightened, dispassionate, earnest presentations of great political truths. Statesmen and the public both know that the civil rights of American citizens, white or colored, are alike shaken, when by ingenious subterfuge the spirit of the law is frittered away. We believe that the most efficient, durable force in America is an awakened, enlightened public opinion. We feel that the changes wrought in our condition within a quarter of a century are signs that the complete attainment of our full civic capacity is drawing near.

We now represent upward of one hundred millions of taxable property. We have nineteen thousand teachers in the field; and in twenty years, at least in ten Southern States, shall have a majority of votes. The increase of the white population in the United States in the last ten years was thirty per cent.; nine per cent. of this was by foreign emigration, leaving but twenty-one per cent. of natural increase; but we have multiplied eight times in less than a century. We entered 1888 with seven millions; in 1900 we shall be twelve millions; in 1920, twenty-four millions; in 1940, forty-eight millions; in 1960, ninety-six millions, and in 1980, one hundred and ninety-two millions. We are convinced that the advancing column of our race, thirsting for some higher use of the nation's gift than invincible prejudice now tolerates, will never halt, until in the near future the politicians are driven to recognize the influence of a political power which they cannot safely disregard.

But if the bands woven of the strands of ancestral race-prejudice are wrapped round and round our race, every step of our way must be a triumph of will over circumstances. To the resolute, nothing is impossible. That, as Mirabeau said, "is a blockhead of a word; the stars in their courses are in league with him who is fully committed to duty; the cherubim are his allies; the angels have been commissioned to bear him on his way, and the pestilence flees at his approach." Defeat came not to Socrates in his cell, nor to Savonarola in the flames: this was their hour of triumph. Every year the Minotaur claimed its tribute of young men and maidens of Greece, until Theseus boldly entered the den of the monster and killed it. Every day the pro-slavery Minotaur—Race-Prejudice—demands, of our young men and maidens, that they shall fall down upon their knees, and, bowing low and humbly, surrender those pledges of civil rights which the mighty dead bequeathed them by the Fourteenth Amendment.

The imperative necessity of to-day is the sanitary influence of light, Justice herself holding aloft the torch. Is it not in the artificial world of civil rights as in the natural material world? When the clear beams pierce the clouds which envelop the mountain-top, its lofty peaks grow discernible to the eye of those in the vales below. The light of the primary, accurate, practical knowledge of our constitutional rights, and of the principles of the common law, will lift the dense fog and clear the murky atmosphere which hang over the valley of superstitious caste, wherein race-prejudice " genders and knots itself." The clarified atmosphere with healing on its wings will dispel the malarial poison which permeates the air within sight of the statue of Liberty Enlightening the World.

All men of sense recognize and cheerfully assent to the exigencies demanding the exercise of a reasonable discretion in adopting rules regulating industrial pursuits and the conduct of the servant of the public. But they regard with grave distrust the undermining policy of the courts, and the encroachment of the public servant. Our onward march must depend upon agitation, demonstration, protestation, and the stimulating of public thought. There is no power to solve the dark problems of the future except law,—in its highest essence, the soul of the universe—the will of God,—not silent, abstract, sleeping law, but law diffused like the fresh air permeating the hidden places wherein race-prejudice coils its dark and venomous folds.

The silent circumspection with which the courts have walked around the Fourteenth Amendment has not been unespied by the faithful determined friends who have the battle to fight with unfettered hands. We cannot stand idly by and permit a reactionary movement towards the mediæval regulations of slavery. We cannot suffer the doctrine of civic equality in the state to sink under the dark current of prejudice. Tyrannical proscription stalks abroad in the land, and the spectacle of civil rights drinking the hemlock of race-prejudice is daily witnessed in America. Its executioners, unlike the jailer who presented the hemlock to the great Greek, do not turn aside and weep at the sight. No lover of freedom can fail to view with ill-suppressed alarm the transformations of the jurisprudence of civil rights in America. The way to their destruction is easy : first one civil right is dispensed with on certain conditions, the observance of others is then rendered unnecessary, then technicalities represent the remainder, until at last all of their original elements pass out of sight.

One of two conclusions seems to us inevitable : either our ignorance upon the subject of civil rights is simply abysmal, or else jurisprudence stands accused. Is the tenure by which we hold these great guarantees merely permissive ? Are they only colorable civil rights, to be weighed as mere dust in the balance, beside the prejudice of by-gone slavery, to be determined only according to the best of the prejudices of our judges ? Can it be that the Constitution, repaired by the Fourteenth Amendment at the expense of thousands of millions, and cemented by such a profusion of the best blood of the nation, after the lapse of a quarter of a century, is a mere mouldy parchment?

A grave philosopher has declared, "The republic which sinks to sleep, trusting to constitutions and machinery, to politicians, statesmen, and courts, for the preservation of its liberties, never will have any." Eternal vigilance is the price of civil liberty. We do not believe that the grave problem of the enforcement of the rights of seven millions of citizens, which the Supreme Court has frequently declared to be one of the main objects of our national policy, can depend upon capricious judgment, or upon any transient phase of juristical faith or public opinion born of the hour. The best men in the country see that favoritism on the one hand, and oppression on the other, are inevitably the contagious result of the free and untrammelled discretion intrusted by the Supreme Court to a body dominated by class interests and instincts. They realize that the love of liberty, and of the civic equality of man, legitimate children of Christian thought and of the Christian religion, are fundamental political truths, which must triumph over the injustice of prejudice with every advance of civilization.

From our view, the points decided in Hall and DeCuir resemble the feudal-castle turrets of the old institution of slavery, which have again reappeared above the subsiding wave. They introduce the infectious example of a theory of discriminative civil rights, racial civil rights, which has led to organized, legalized injustice in civil life, to which the badge of sufferance must be added, and an arbitrary assortment of the civil rights of seven millions of citizens, according to race, color, and previous condition. Viewed in the light of this amendment and that of American history, can aught be more unconstitutional, falser in faith, or more infamous in theory and practice? This case says to the public, out of respect to white citizens, look upon colored citizens not as citizens; their right as citizens is a mere extravagant delusion, which your reasonable discretion enables you to dissipate.

This law-phrase, "reasonable discretion," thus interpolated to shield color-prerogative, sounds as if it meant something, but to us it seems used only to supply the place of a reason ; it keeps up an appearance in spite of the most abject mental poverty ; it asserts and insists, in spite of positive enactment, upon an unconquerable aversion to the civic equality of all races, as justifying the violation of the broad, deep, organic law. We feel that the fundamental maxim of a free government, wrought into the organic law, should have a more substantial solution than "*the free and untrammelled rules*" established by an unenlightened body of tradesmen, whose high standard of civil right accords with the scientific morality of their business code. All those grave questions which puzzled Webster, Calhoun, Hobbes, Bentham, and hosts of other eminent men, have been practically submitted to the enlightened perceptions of the servants of the public, and to the industrial labor-caste, which regulates all artisan vocations by guilds excluding our race from self-development in all their departments of handicraft, and each of them construing the Fourteenth Amendment in a manner closely resembling the doctrine of that profound political sophist of the beer-saloon, Most, who contends that political justice is a mere imposition of the legislative will, a tyrant, a creature which must be overcome by the propagandists of deeds.

Do these people not maintain that, the moral sense of one set of citizens being opposed to the practical principles of government, the government is a tyrant, a creature to be overcome by the propagandists " of a ' free and untrammelled authority' " ? Do they not reject with disdain Burke's theory, " That the nation would fall into ruin if the foundations of society rested upon having their reasons made clear and demonstrative to every person," and deny that the Fourteenth Amendment is mandatory legislation, that its rule for the decision of civil-rights controversies is the equality of all citizens before the law ?

They deem it a monstrous proposition, that a different set of principles, rules, or formulæ should not be applied to the colored citizen, from those by which the white citizen in general is held bound, and is habitually regulated in the enjoyment of his civil rights.

Against all such construction of the color-line let us declare war, war for ourselves and for our children and for our grandchildren; but let that war be constantly renewed, and urged before the courts, in the press, on the hustings, and before the public throughout our educational institutions.

The Dred Scott decision judicially doomed to slavery a vast empire of mankind. By the Fourteenth Amendment the nation released it, and that great organ of freedom, liberty, and truth cannot now be converted into an instrument for the public debasement of unprotected, helpless victims, at the very foot of the altar of justice, by the vesting of irresponsible powers in the public servants and labor-guilds of America.

The system of Hall and DeCuir, which licenses this spirit of tyranny, resembles the ancient judicial system of Athens far more than it does our American judicature. In Athens six thousand judges were chosen by lot, they had ten departments of justice, with five thousand judges, and a reserve force of one thousand. But the American dicastery is not chosen by lot. Our judges elect themselves, by taking out charters or licenses from the State and organizing guilds, unions, secret labor associations, boycotts, and strikes; they are not limited to six thousand nor six million of dicasts, but are divided into as many legions or departments as there are States, counties, cities, villages, hamlets, municipal or private corporations, and industrial employments, yet, according to Hall and DeCuir, the common notions of justice prevailing among this enlightened body of tradesmen are superior to the policy and wisdom of the Fourteenth Amendment. In spirit and letter these judges deny the verity of the common-law maxim *ubi jus ibi remedium*. They assert that the right may be given by the Fourteenth Amendment but the remedy can be refused by the public, and as we understand Hall and DeCuir, the courts of civil jurisdiction have only the office of affirming their discretionary arbitrament, as the Supreme Court did in that celebrated cause. Is it not manifest that rules of construction which it would be absurd to apply to white citizens are not less ridiculous when applied to others?

The Fourteenth Amendment requires in its interpretation a system of comprehensive principles, not a dispute about words or doctrines. The great governing, controlling law, which supplies the link in the change or transition from slavery to freedom, cannot be construed as a trivial parol contract between citizens; it must be expounded broadly, understandingly, and conscientiously, as a grave national compact of freedom with seven millions of adopted citizens.

On the continent of Europe, the colored man of pure morals and refined manners, with a gentleman's toilet and cultivated intellect, has found paths in pleasant places, and that, too, in countries where caste prevails. Have we not the right to be regarded and treated as citizens in America, as beings who have a high destiny? Have we not a right to every opportunity for self-development and gratification which produces no harm to others, and ought we not to be spared every mortification which produces no other good than to gratify prejudices which the laws of the country denounce? No race has appeared in history more obstinately tenacious of their civil rights than the Anglo-American. Why should it continue to view with profound indifference the extraordinary powers expressly conferred upon the public servant, usurped by labor-guilds, and habitually exercised not only without caution, moderation, or impartiality, but with despotic arrogance? The nation gave the coveted boon of citizenship, in order that character, intelligence, refinement, objects of ambition, property, all the gifts which dignify human nature, should be the goals at which the enfranchised black man might arrive; and do its statesmen, publicists, jurists, laymen, or tradesmen suppose that the narrow and single file, the exclusive solitary slave-path, which this decision marks out, can keep our people from the industrial progress of the great family of mankind?

The Fourteenth Amendment removed the obstructions to the free exercise of human rights and powers which the public servant and labor-caste struggle to re-establish. It intended to impart dignity of character, loftiness of sentiment, and to afford the opportunity for all those qualities and attributes that pronounce man a blessing to himself and society. It declared the chief prerogative and glory of man to be self-dominion; it said the oppression of arbitrary, capricious rules is terrible to sensitive, generous souls; its whole purpose was to shield from civic ostracism and contemptuous attacks an inoffensive, useful citizen, who in decorum, education, and natural nobleness might become the peer of any American citizen. The same love of freedom, the same hatred of oppression, the same recognition of the rights of humanity wherever the Christian religion has breathed and shown its force have inspired principles of action similar to this amendment. It is a vast, imposing national structure, builded by the people of the United States, and its nationality stands out and towers above all the petty attributes of caste ; it sowed a living seed, promising immeasurable good. It has long been known, all over the globe, to be a fundamental maxim of the American Constitution that every rank or character of citizen is equally subject to the laws,—can it be that that national maxim and the sublime principle underlying it may be overturned by the " reasonable discretion" of any class ? Must not all rational minds reflect that mutual toleration is one of the penalties of civilized, polite society ? That in church, state, business, and personal intercourse, toleration of others is the foundation of all individual, political, and civil social rights ? Is not that doctrine in full accord with the Declaration of Independence, " that all men are born free and equal" ? Political, civil, public rights are not to be misunderstood, as if they gave license for the indulgence of purely personal and private tastes, predilections, affinities, and attractions ; the two are not commingled ; they stand apart. The one is a civil, the other a social right. Can there be racial-political civil rights, racial public rights ? Are not all civil rights the same in America, independent of race or previous condition ?

This " reasonable discretion" of Hall and DeCuir authorizes discrimination, based on color, not on character. It does not pretend to bear any relation to moral worth or civic fitness, but insists upon treating this race as a fallen, degraded offspring of the nation, with whom the government and people of the country where it lives, must not sympathize, but whom they may lawfully ostracise ; it denies the existence in America, in so far as these citizens are concerned, of the indiscriminative, unchallenged constitutional freedom and privilege of citizenship.

Hall and DeCuir judicially determines that there is an unlimited power to oppress and wound color, upon the ground that it is color. "If this be freedom, it is the freedom of Nero." Can a citizen be daily excluded from paths of industrial progress and exposed to insults, hold his rights, immunities, and privileges at the mercy of a contemptuous public, and yet be a citizen of the United States? If this be a true exposition of constitutional law, the civil rights and the happiness of our race are alike words without meaning, only lofty phrases, mere declamation, and the Fourteenth Amendment is mere *brutum fulmen.*

There was a time when there were Catholic and Jewish disabilities; they have passed away, and now a more enlightened civilization has to encounter color disabilities. A citizen of color may be subjected to debasing restrictions and artisan discriminations, and, although constituting one of the people of a common country, must be stripped of a feeling of unity with those about him, and exposed to vulgar insults. Color is made a legal and industrial disability; it is subjected to contemptuous treatment, and told, that it is the reasonable right of the public to visit it with these contumelies because it makes other citizens more comfortable and prosperous in their vocations of trade.

Do not let us cease to remember that the innumerable stars of freedom that shine upon this world shine from other worlds; that it is only the bleared optic of prejudice which beholds all these worlds and is unable to perceive the beneficent uses for which they were placed in the firmament by their divine Creator. We are not unmindful that every advancing civilization which has touched the pride of race has encountered proscription, but for the dwellers in the calm realm of truth, whose habitation is not in strife, " the indifference of the great, the sneers and the enmity of the mass," have no terror. They well know that before the age when manuscripts were written with a pointed stick, centuries before the sea had abandoned the salt deserts of Iran and Chaldea, or the mud deposits of the Nile had joined lower Egypt to the plains of Memphis and Thebes, distinctions founded on wrong and injustice have endured for the night; but after the night of sore travail came the day in its glory.

We know that American civil rights cannot always be trampled under foot by the jurisprudence which has only a primitive conception of the justice and of the ethics of the Fourteenth Amendment. We know that the jurisprudence in Hall and DeCuir, which substitutes the " free and untrammelled discretion of the public to ostracise and disenfranchise the civil rights of any class of citizens" for *justice*, is a repudiation of the Fourteenth Amendment. The subject is too vast to admit of discussion in this address; it will furnish matter for a great and important work, involving the legal status of the civil rights of all American citizens. No matter how long enshrouded in the labyrinthine mazes of obscure decisions and jargon of words it may have slept, the absolute verity of the sublime truth will be in the fulness of time revealed: that the grand bond which unites American citizens, the glory of our common country, is the universality of that liberty which makes the meanest member of the state sacred in the glory of its reflected lustre, that liberty which abounds with pure and heartfelt love for the cause of humanity, regardless of class, color, race, creed, or previous condition; the Christian liberty which imposes the duty of universal benevolence and charity, because the soul of each human being is alike precious and immortal in the sight of the great Author of nature and government.

ORIGINAL LETTER

OF THE

BROTHERHOOD OF LIBERTY

TO

THEIR COUNSEL.

"Those who employ their pens on political subjects free from party-rage, and party-prejudices, cultivate a science which of all others contributes most to public utility."—HUME.

"The point of view from which jurisprudence regards the slave is always of great importance to him."—MAINE.

"Of all men that distinguish themselves by memorable achievements, the first place of honor seems due to *legislators* and founders of states, who transmit a system of laws and institutions to secure the peace, happiness, and liberty of future generations."—ID.

"The exchange of laws in practice with laws in device."—HOOKER.

"This is the design you aim at,—to restore our lost liberty."—PLINY.

"Another sort of men there are which have been content to run on with the reformers for a time, and to make them poor instruments of their own design. These are a sort of godless politics."—HOOKER.

"The cause we maintain is (God be thanked!) such as needeth not to shun any trial."—ID.

"On your shoulders is laid the burden of upholding the cause by argument."—ID.

"The reformation destroyed the illusions both of spiritual and of secular authority, by bringing them to the test of reason and conscience. The tiara and the crown lost their magnetic charm together. The domineer-

40

ing, supercilious pretensions of infallible orthodoxy and bloated power were inseparably linked together, and both gave way or recoiled under the shock and encounter of the common nature and the common understanding of man. The first step to emancipate the bodies of the enslaved people was to enfranchise their minds; and the foundation of the political rights and independence of states was laid in the ruins of that monster superstition that reared its head to the skies and ground both princes and people to powder. The first blows that staggered this mighty fabric were given and the first crash was heard abroad; but England echoed it back with 'her island voice,' and from that time the triumph of reason over pride and hypocrisy was secure, though remote and arduous."
—HAZLITT.

THE undersigned have already published, and distributed throughout the country, the legal paper prepared by you as counsel in certain civil-rights causes. · We felt that this declaration most forcibly presented in their constitutional aspect the true legal status of our civil rights as American citizens.

The civil-rights cases are scattered throughout various law reports, State and national, not readily accessible to the masses, who, therefore, are not in a position to form any proper estimate of the extent of the wreck of the Fourteenth Amendment, "freighted with the world's sublimest hope." We want all the opinions so collated and presented that he "may run that readeth."

What we desire is, not only a searching review of the most important decisions relating to this—to us—most vital subject, but a general discussion also, presenting the existing legal status of civil rights and an independent, broad, earnest, conscientious, critical survey of the legal relations between all classes of citizens and our race, particularly the social phenomena of the monopolistic labor-class, which, in spite of our civil equality, excludes the colored citizen from competition in all industrial arts. Fisher Ames expressed our meaning when he said, "We want the rights of man printed, that every citizen shall have a copy." The Hales, Mansfields, and Marshalls have all declared "justice to be the end and jurisprudence the means;" and if, as Lord Coke says, "The common law is nothing but reason;" if, as the highest authorities have always held, all laws, organic or otherwise, in their interpretation should be held subject to a reasonable intendment, we should like to know how much of Lord Coke's "reason" or what reasonable intendment marked the action of the courts which in substance have given to mere public servants and labor-classes "*free and untrammelled authority*" to construe the Fourteenth Amendment.

This subject requires heroic treatment. We are convinced that a vigorous, bold writer will put an end to the feeble, imperfect, cowardly, apologetic spirit of justice, which has completely abandoned the weaker citizen to the tyrannies of the stronger class.

We desire your opinion, whether the Fourteenth Amendment is sovereign, or whether citizen-kings in America have prerogatives superior to those dictates of reason and justice which it embodies. We demand to know whether there is not to be a grander solution of the problem of citizenship in America than the labor-kings, the public-servants, and the labor-classes, marshalled by Hall *v.* DeCuir, practically have evolved. What we earnestly desire is a comprehensive review of the jurisprudence of those motley bodies of legists whose decisions, since the Supreme Court in Hall *v.* DeCuir gave them " free and untrammelled authority to pass rules and regulations under State laws" for the conduct of the public business, constitute the practical, scientific, philosophic, historical, and commercial judicature of civil rights in America. By an intrinsic strength of social superiority they have ridden roughshod over the Fourteenth Amendment, and all the analogies and doctrines of the common law. The science of this branch of American jurisprudence, since left to their acute perceptions, is in an unsatisfactory condition, and we want a sober investigation and dissection of the decisions of our courts which have produced or suffered the present obscuration of the great political truths of the Fourteenth Amendment. We also desire a philosophic account of the jurisprudence of race-prejudice, and of the history of its lineal descent from the ancestral jurisprudence of slavery.

It may be permitted us, before you set about your work, to

remind you that Jefferson proposed a clause in the Declaration of Independence charging that George the Third was determined to keep open market where men could be bought and sold, and had resisted every legislative attempt to prohibit or restrain this execrable traffic; that so strong, North and South, was the feeling averse to slavery in the convention which framed the Constitution, that the word "slave" was not permitted to have a place in the fundamental law of the republic; that not until the cotton-gin enhanced the profit of slave-labor did a radical change take place in the South; and that it has been judicially determined, that among the "we, the people," who declared their independence were colored freemen in various States.

The only prerequisite for the performance of the great work assigned him is, that the author should be unencumbered with biassing influences or pre-engendered preferences and desires, and that he should be impelled solely by that unswerving love of truth and sense of duty which will guide him to a correct judgment commensurate with the grave issues involved.

THE BROTHERHOOD OF LIBERTY.

ANSWER OF COUNSEL

TO

ORIGINAL LETTER OF THE BROTHERHOOD.

"We find, in the case of political affairs, that the most servile submission to privileged classes, and the grossest abuses of power by these, have been the precursors of the wildest ebullitions of popular fury,—of the overthrow indiscriminately of ancient institutions, good and bad,—and of the most turbulent democracy, generally proportioned in its extravagance and violence to the previous oppression and previous degradation. And, again, we find that, whenever men have become heartily wearied of licentious anarchy, their eagerness has been proportionably great to embrace the opposite extreme of rigorous despotism ; like shipwrecked mariners clinging to a bare and rugged rock as a refuge from the waves."
—Whately.

"The democracy or community have all possible motives to endeavor to prevent the monarchy and aristocracy from exercising power, or obtaining the wealth of the community for their own advantage. The monarchy and aristocracy have all possible motives for endeavoring to obtain unlimited power over the persons and property of the community. The consequence is inevitable ; they have all possible motives for combining to obtain that power."—James Mill.

"In the cold-blooded reptile race, whose poison is exalted by the chemistry of their icy complexion, their venom is the result of their health, and of the perfection of their nature. Woe to the country in which such snakes, whose *primum mobile* is their belly, obtain wings, and from serpents become dragons. It is not that these people want natural talents, and even a good cultivation ; on the contrary, they are the sharpest and most sagacious of mankind in the things to which they apply."—Burke.

"Constitutions are in politics what paper money is in commerce. They afford great facilities and conveniences. But we must not attribute to them that value which really belongs to what they represent. They are

44

not power, and will in an emergency prove altogether useless unless the power for which they stand be forthcoming. The real power by which the community is governed is made up of all the means which all its members possess of giving pain or pleasure to each other."—MACAULAY.

" It is authority against authority all the way, till we come to the divine origin of the rights of man, at the creation. Here our inquiries find a resting-place, and our reason finds a home. If a dispute about the rights of man had arisen at the distance of a hundred years from the creation, it is to this source of authority they must have referred, and it is to the same source of authority that we must now refer."—PAINE.

" The learned have weighed it, and found it light ; wise men conceive some fear, lest it prove not only not the best kind of government, but the very bane and destruction of all government."—HOOKER.

" New Pilates and modern Herods, men devoid of justice, piety, and religion, who, while they see you robbed of your liberty and betrayed to your enemies, make not the slightest murmur of protest or disapproval, but, to hide or excuse their own cowardice, would have the world believe that the wrongs of the Holy See flow from what they call misfortune and the unhappy temper of the times."—CARDINAL GIBBONS.

> " Mulmutius made our laws ;
> Who was the first of Britain which did put
> His brows within a golden crown, and called
> Himself a king."—SHAKESPEARE.

> " A noble peer of mickle
> TRUST and POWER."—MILTON.

" The shadow takes the place of the substance till the country is left with only shadows in its hands."—PAINE.

" In this period of the world, in this decisive crisis between ancient and modern times, in this great central point of history, stood two powers opposed to each other. On one hand we behold the Roman emperors, the earthly gods, and absolute masters of the world, in all the pomp and splendor of ancient paganism, standing, as it were, on the very summit and verge of the old world, now tottering to its ruin ; and on the other hand we trace the obscure rise of an almost imperceptible point of light, from which the whole modern world was to spring, and whose further progress and full development, through all succeeding ages, constitutes the true purport of MODERN HISTORY."—SCHLEGEL.

" The giants, when they found themselves fettered, roared like bulls, and cried upon Setebos to help them."—TRAVAYLE.

" A husband and wife may be divorced, and go out of the presence and beyond the reach of each other; but the different parts of our country cannot do this. They cannot but remain face to face; and intercourse, either amicable or hostile, must continue between them."—LINCOLN.

" No; you dare not make war upon cotton. No power on earth dares to make war upon it. Cotton is king. Until lately, the Bank of England was king; but she tried to put her screws, as usual, the fall before the last, on the cotton crop, and was utterly vanquished. The last power has been conquered. Who can doubt, that has looked at recent events, that cotton is supreme?"—EVERETT.

" When . . . the pedigree of King Cotton is traced, he is found to be the lineal child of the tariff; called into being by a specific duty; reared by a tax laid upon the manufacturing industry of the North, to create the culture of the raw material in the South."—ID.

" Support the pillar of the Roman state,
   Lest all men be involved in one man's fate."—HORACE.

" Every epoch has two aspects,—one calm, broad, and solemn, looking towards eternity; the other agitated, petty, vehement, and confused, looking towards time."—CARLYLE.

" It might have been added, that, while the Constitution, therefore, is admitted to be in force, its operation in every respect must be precisely the same, whether its authority be derived from that of the people in the one or the other of the modes in question, the authority being equally competent in both; and that, without an annulment of the Constitution itself, its supremacy must be submitted to."—MADISON.

' Madness . . . invisible, impalpable, and yet no black Azrael, with wings spread over half a continent, with sword sweeping from sea to sea, could be a truer reality."—CARLYLE.

" ' The philosopher,' says the wisest of this age, ' must station himself in the middle.' How true! The philosopher is he to whom the Highest has descended, and the lowest has mounted up; who is the equal and kindly brother of all."—ID.

" I will not avoid doing what I think is right, though it should draw on me the whole artillery of libels."—MANSFIELD.

" I speak as but one poor individual, but, when I speak, I speak the language of thousands."—PATRICK HENRY.

" The people are a set of masters whom it is not in a man's power in every instance fully to please, and at the same time faithfully to serve. He that is resolved to persevere without deviation in the line of truth and utility must have learnt to prefer the still whisper of enduring approbation, to the short-lived bustle of tumultuous applause."—BENTHAM.

" Plain law and plain sense."—ID.

" Could the wand of that magician be borrowed, at whose potent touch the emissaries of his wicked antagonist threw off their several disguises, and made instant confession of their real character and design,—could a few of those ravens by whom the word *innovation* is uttered with a scream of horror, and the approach of the monster denounced, be touched with it,—we should then learn their real character, and have the true import of these screams translated into intelligible language."—ID.

" *Buller.*   Whom you crucify, like a very Czar of Muscovey !
" *North.*   No, sir, I only hang them up to air like so many pieces of old theatrical finery on the poles of Monmouth Street."—NORTH.

" It cannot be that you have acted wrong in encountering danger for the liberty and safety of all Greece.   No : by the generous souls who were exposed at Marathon ; by those who stood arrayed at Platæa ; by those who encountered the Persian fleet of Salamis—who fought at Artemisium ; by all those illustrious sons of Athens whose remains lie deposited in the public monuments."—DEMOSTHENES.

" When all the principal joists of a building have started, and all its stays and fastenings, from the roof to the foundation, have become loose, then will the first storm of accident easily demolish the whole structure, or the first spark set the dry and rotten edifice in flames."—SCHLEGEL.

" What would you do in my position ?   Would you drop the war where it is, or would you prosecute it in future with elder-stalk squirts charged with rose-water?   Would you deal lighter blows than heavier ones ? Would you give up the contest leaving every available means unapplied ?" —LINCOLN.

" Satire is the right hand of burlesque."—VOLTAIRE.

" Cervantes smiled Spain's chivalry away."—BYRON.

HEREWITH is presented a digest of the legislation and of all cases involving the civil rights of citizens of the United States under the Thirteenth, Fourteenth, and Fifteenth Articles of Amendment to the Constitution of the United States.

The object of this portion of the work is to state concisely, but substantially, the facts, and the principles of law which the learned courts have announced as controlling the judgment in each decision, and to bring together the various Federal and State enactments relating to this subject. The compiler of this summary has endeavored to conform to your views, and trusts it may not altogether fail to accomplish the purpose you intend, of affording the general public, without laborious research into text-books and law reports, the opportunity and means of becoming familiar with the facts to which principles of law have been applied, and upon which the vast array of civil-rights cases have been decided by the courts.

In the performance of the remainder of the undertaking which you have assigned him, constituting the main part of the work, the writer is free to confess, that at every step he has encountered all the extraordinary and particularly discouraging embarrassments which environ the natural and artificial status of civil rights.

Your court of final resort appears to the writer to be Public Opinion,—a tribunal whose verdict is consequent upon the educational status of the young men of the country. The public opinion of the future will depend upon the profoundness of their sympathy with the spirit of our institutions, the depth of their aspiration for the welfare and improvement of society, and the extent of their acquaintance with the enlightened and liberal laws of the land. These are the practical consummations most devoutly to be wished, by those whose struggles now deserve the applause which after-ages always bestow upon good and virtuous actions, as, when truth, having submitted to be obscured for a while, shall triumph over the delusions of error. As, when the sun has sunk below the horizon into the hemisphere of darkness, and the stars shine forth divinely clear, the darkness itself shows to greater advantage those eternal jewels of the sky, so the infinite resplendent images of truth are made more effulgent when they shine out amidst the black night of error. The removal of the opposition of race-obstructionists (who blemish all discussion by their partialities) to the prime requisites for the education of the rising generation, is an imperative preliminary condition to the success of any work in aid of your proposed gradual reform of a deep-seated, wide-spread evil.

That all sorts of partial affection may be laid clean aside in their consideration, those law points, the discussion of which constitutes the main work, are presented through the medium of an introductory conversation between the Chief Justice of the Supreme Court and a foreign jurist void of the intellectual bias generated by the civil and social environments of slavery. By this conception an attempt has been made to thrust that skeleton into temporary retirement at the inception of the argument. After seeking an acquaintance with and consulting the notable leaders of the press, the foreign publicist, who has completed the studies in American law recommended by the Chief Justice, proceeds to review the civil-rights cases, Hall and De-Cuir, and the Supreme Court's construction of the Thirteenth, Fourteenth, and Fifteenth Amendments.

The professional reader may perhaps find some cause of complaint in regard to the preliminary statement, which is occupied in part with the introduction of what a severe critic might deem extraneous matter. But he must be reminded that the latitude of counsel in opening may lawfully exert a direct and powerful influence in dispelling the falsehood and delusion which may have eclipsed, but not extinguished, "Truth, the daughter of Time." If, for example, it is clearly seen that in the course of political evolution, the ballots of those citizens to whom their full civil rights are now denied may be made conservative of the equilibrium of the American state, and that they themselves may become factors in our advancement towards the mighty goal of political progress, leaders of public thought and legislators may see the fitness of establishing, by State laws, that mutual limitation upon men's civil conduct which their coexistence as units in civil society under a constitutional government demands.

Whether the opening statement or the argument which follows may aid in the accomplishment of your purpose, all-trying time can alone determine. If the close mode of combat adopted shall be deemed in some quarters a transgression against conventional usage, this system of warfare has not been chosen without adequate motive or justifiable occasion.

Apparently your purpose is, by national education, to influence national character; to induce white American citizens to favor the declared policy of the nation, rather than to foster prevailing popular error. Assuredly, the subject is deserving of the gravest reflection by every citizen, who is truly anxious for the welfare of his country and the maintenance of her freedom. In its practical execution, this attempt at rudimentary political education, which you desire to see progress, has encountered many embarrassments. The measured movement of logic, which custom prescribes in arguments concerning matters governed by the exact science of the law, and an abstruse, profound, dry treatise would prove wearisome, if not repulsive, to the average reader unaccustomed to thought. If a discussion of civil rights can be made interesting to a larger number (who are able to grapple with more extended bearings and magnitudes than are afforded by strict, narrow issues of law, not always having a close connection with the specific subject), it appears to the writer that, as the avowed mode of accomplishing your great purpose is to educate the nation by the conversion of the individual citizen, conventional dignity could rarely be sacrificed with more advantage than in an undertaking of the proposed character.

However infelicitous to trained thinkers, long hackneyed in anatomizing legal distinctions, may be the general arrangement of this work and the frequent interpolation therein of apparently irrelevant matter, the hope is indulged that the plan adopted, even with its manifold imperfections, may prove less unattractive to the general reader, in whom it is your main purpose to stimulate thought.

The work is directed towards a practical end; and it is matter of regret, that the connection and drift of the argument, at times, has apparently not been clearly preserved nor the objective point kept immediately in view by a uniform scientific plan; but it is hoped that liberality and candor, which are the usual accompaniments of extensive information, will allow for the painful embarrassment of the undertaking, for the arduous task, which requires of the advocate an argument adapted to the lay as well as to the professional mind, upon most subtle and complex problems.

The gravest of all the difficulties encountered was the over-weight and copiousness of the matter, and the labor of its modification and connection by any comparatively lucid system. It is a matter of regret that the plan of the work made it necessary to avoid many authentications by notes and original references which, if full enough to be of value, would have made long and frequent interruptions without the advancement of its main object. Moderate success is as much as could be reasonably anticipated for limited abilities, in the brief space of time allotted for the performance of the work. Many errors and omissions might have been avoided had there been leisure for consideration of methods rather than results, since inaccuracies and incompleteness are unavoidable in a work executed with intermitted study, and by piecemeal, in moments snatched from anxious care of every-day professional life, often filled with deep solicitude.

The experienced trial-table lawyer, to whom has been given the understanding of many mysteries, is aware that in the presentation of an obscure cause it is frequently necessary to throw the great corrective force of light upon hidden truth by bold, characteristic, often grotesque, portrayal. Hamlet's delineation of his father as " Hyperion to a satyr," compared with his step-father, affords an apt illustration of the exaggerated representation of an advocate engaged in presenting the truth of a good cause in a strong light. It is only under such a combination of mirrors as apparently augment its dimensions that the real characteristics and the hidden " proper deformity" of error can be clearly discerned.

The practitioner will readily admit that both court and jury, in their daily routine, as a rule, are slow of heart to perceive, or to distinguish the true from the false; neither eats long of the same spiritual food, nor drinks often of the same spiritual drink.

The advocate's mission is that of an educator; and the education which is demanded is frequently to be effected only by a constant ringing of the changes, by "line upon line, precept upon precept: here a little, and there a little." It often happens, that what is exceedingly prolix to the court tends greatly to clarify the understanding of the jury, which may receive impressions from arguments (through the emotional nature of its members), which the court, as a trained scientist following the lead only of an artificial principle, might arbitrarily reject. If there is discovered in the arguments a frequent reiteration of the same line of thought, if through the various forms of language employed a frequent return to the same points is traceable, if the same issues are presented from various stand-points, it may be fairly urged in justification that human receptivities, old or young, ignorant or learned, have each a combination-lock, which does not open to the same pressure, and which is as mysterious in its construction as individual resemblances and differences.

Apparently the foreign reviewer, heretofore referred to, has profited by the rich wisdom of the Pauline educational system: "And unto the Jews I became as a Jew, that I might gain the Jews; to them that are under the law, as under the law, that I might gain them that are under the law; to them that are without law, as without law (being not without law to God, but under the law to Christ), that I might gain them that are without law. To the weak became I as weak, that I might gain the weak. I am made all things to all men, that I might by all means save some."

If the writer, in adopting the guise of a foreign reviewer, has gone beyond legitimate criticism of the treatment of civil-rights by the courts, it is with him a matter of deep regret. It must not be forgotten, however, that the domain of truth is not susceptible of partition by any treaty with error; that the intercourse of Despotism with Liberty is always parturient of an evil brood, which may increase and multiply by cohabiting together; and that the perpetuation of Freedom requires the extermination, *manu forti*, of the incestuous progeny.

The author found himself engaged in a struggle where the

general public was apathetic, and in a controversy which enlisted the sympathy of not a single friend. Deeply impressed with the painful consciousness of his inadequate qualification and of the responsibility of his undertaking, ever doubtful of the expedients of his unaided individual judgment, yet possessed with a profound and earnest desire, in a stern and truthful way, to perform a professional duty, by maintaining the free and absolute civic rights of a large body of citizens, under a civil contract which was compacted into the Constitution of a common country, it is not impossible that the wide and deep strokes of the discussion may have exceeded the narrow limitations within which legal controversies are ordinarily conducted. In an humble way he has striven to perform this—the highest and most unquestioned duty to his clients.

Any serious treatment of a broad subject, of such grave import, involving the national polity of the government, and the construction of articles of amendment upon which depend the right and title of seven million citizens to their constitutional estate of freedom, imposes upon one who speaks with the authority of many voices, the simple performance of duty. The fulfilment of his duty being the edict of God to man, "that strong-siding champion, conscience," will leave no place for fear in his quiet bosom. Being an authority over-ruling all other authorities, it imposes upon counsel engaged in such an undertaking as this, the grave professional obligation, not alone of investigating the rights of those who stand in a cliental relation, and exhibiting an abstract of their title to the enforcement of public justice, according to the judgment of the learned, but entails upon him the additional obligation, by independent original methods of inquiry and research, of exploring the recesses, and laying bare and criticising the internal motives and external measures, through which the universal equity contemplated by the Fourteenth Amendment (a law of justice and humanity of inestimable value to the whole family of mankind) has been practically annulled by an unjustifiable and alarming innovation upon the letter and spirit of its provisions.

This second American Bill of Rights having extended the authority of civil equality to all races, a momentary reflection will convince the simplest understanding, that, if the satanic profoundnesses of race-hatred are now to preponderate over the people's love and veneration for their Constitution, which pays no respect to persons, if Jurisprudence can with safety pluck Justice by the nose, and if the exclusive possession of constitutional right will once become subordinated to classes, then the rising flood of anarchy will soon weaken the pillars of the State; and its turbulent torrent, rushing with tumultuous uproar and quickly inundating the country, will eventually overturn our whole system of government.

It is demonstrable, that, if the gratification of the civic rights of one class, in consequence of their *previous condition of slavery,* can be avoided by the tyranny of this generation, in the to-morrow of the country, another class, by reason of their *previous condition of master, or rebel,* or of their existing beliefs, religious, aristocratic, political, civil, or other "natural and well-known *repugnances*" to still grander tyrants, under this precedent of arbitrary power, may be denied their constitutional rights.

The jurisprudence which tolerated the usurpation of justice in the case of the one class of citizens, would not be less anarchical in its tendency than that which justified the disfranchisement of it in the other; and thus the community of the present and future nation would be exposed to the dire peril of a governmental condition in which the measure of right might be the anarchy power. There would then follow that state of society in which oppression, terror, and confusion would not be limited by any other law than the aggressive, revolutionary, unreasoning mob-violence of popular opinion. The government having abandoned the impartial administration of justice, and the rule of no rule but the "bare-faced power" of unenlightened public opinion having been proclaimed, the mandate of that imperious anarch, whose charter is as large as the wind, would eventually be substituted for the Constitution itself.

It appears to the writer, that the invitement of your letter, respecting the structure, functions, and development of monopolistic labor caste, involves a discussion of many subjects unrelated to the legal status of civil rights. Any delineation of this department, to be of value, would require the treatment of a

collaborateur who fully comprehended the subject in its *ensemble.*
Literature is rich in treatises upon it, while the public press
teems with ingenious and plausible speculations respecting the
laws by which the social phenomena of capital and labor, as
mutually dependent parts of one great whole, should be regulated.   The autocracy of the labor class, the regulation of production by trusts, the control of wage-earners by artisan guilds
(each of which systems is maintained by a strong-armed despotic
majority) do not limit their exhibitions of arbitrary force to
special employments or classes, nor to present or past conditions,
colors, or races.   These kingly usurpers with fierce demeanor
set at defiance all limitations, precautions, and guards established by the community for the protection of individuals, other
than those which, in their ignorance or disregard of economic
conditions, they assume the necessities of trade to impose.   Their
sociological and jurisprudential tenets have no counterpart but
in the doctrine of the Dred Scott case.   In effect, they hold,
with Scott *v.* Sandford, especially north of Mason and Dixon's
line, not only that the African citizen has no rights which the
white citizens are bound to respect, but that no citizen, white or
black, has any rights unless he has the force of a majority in
numbers or values to support his claim to equality.   These
combinations are without color of lawful warrant or authority.
They pay no regard to the interdependence of human relations
in politic society.   The principia of their system rest upon
no known principle of social science.   The tendency of their
doctrine is to commit individual property to the custody and
protection of the commune.   Their theory has no comprehensive classification, utilities, statistics, solid data, or foundation
in law or equity.   One and all are alike unconstitutional, almost
regal usurpations of the civil rights of others.   They have created the present crisis in the science of political economy; and
they have disturbed the harmonious working and threaten to
overturn the organic provisions of our Constitution for the protection and enforcement of the equality of the rights of all
citizens by due process of law, irrespective of race or previous
condition.

The writer understands your special complaint and desire of

enlightenment to be in regard to the portentous struggle of your minority with this majority. Your grievance is, that, as an industrial factor, equal in fitness with others, your race represents as such factor no recognized value, especially in the North, East, and West; that your labor as a commodity, because it is excluded *manu forti* from just participation in industrial pursuits, represents neither its legitimate value to the nation nor to the individual possessor of the civil rights guaranteed by the Constitution. The czardom of Labor, which thus arbitrarily rejects as contraband the candidate of this race for industrial preferment, violates in principle the civil rights of every American citizen.

That the industrial value of this citizen has thus fallen an easy prey to the ferocious labor mastiff unquestionably results from a civic inferiority which renders him comparatively defenceless. It is the pitch of race-prejudice which, having daubed and defiled his civic equality and compelled it to most ignoble stooping in the high department of the State's Justice, has communicated its touch to inferior tyrants, who boldly refuse all recognition of the value of a national industrial factor in a realm where their sway seems absolutely independent of constitutional limitation. Example in the loftier stations of the government is a most seductive and generative school for the pupilage of tyrants in its lower departments. This result of a denial, to citizens of this race, of the communitive, distributive justice which others of different color enjoy in all their pursuits of life, affords an apt illustration of the contagion of example, and of the pernicious efficacy of the public opinion thus formed, which first suffers to be debased and finally destroys the enormous economic value to the nation of millions of citizens fit for industrial producers, who are thus excluded from opportunities accorded other citizens. That such an incalculable loss to the nation's resources should be tolerated under a government guaranteeing the enforcement of the equality of the right of all its citizens by due process of law is almost incredible. It matters but little to-day, for, thus far, the public or private interests of no class, majority or minority, has suffered so gravely as to arrest national attention; but this gradual undermining of the bases on which repose the equilibria of the government portends the violent upheaval of ground considered secure, threatens the disruption of all constitutional ties, and may ultimately lead to the overthrow of constitutional liberty in America.

No lover of " liberty regulated by law" can observe without alarm the stealthy approach of this revolutionary spirit, however it may be masked. If freedom is to survive, the fortress of constitutional liberty must be proof against the peril of infection within, as well as impregnable to the assaults of foes without. If the love of civic liberty be interwoven with every fibre of the American heart, if equality of right by due process of law is the birthright of every American citizen, then this eternal principle of right should be guarded by an ever-wakeful vigilance. Constructions subversive of the spirit of this great freedom may have the specious appearance of a rigid execution of justice, but they are in reality more to be dreaded than that violent seizure of right which threatens open-handed destruction by bloody insurrection.

In by-gone years, the "great northern confederacy," the Hartford-convention rebels, and the alien-and-sedition malcontents of 1798 in Virginia; later on, Dorr's Rhode-Islanders, South-Carolina Nullifiers, Slaveryites, King Cotton, Secession, and Rebellion struggled for royal supremacy over this sacred principle. Those discarded ancient and modern potentates, small and great, each in their turn have been urned in that sepulchre of time which has buried every error, covered every defect, extinguished every resentment, but traced no epitaph upon their tomb. Their fell spirits have now reappeared in formidable shape ; and to-day it may be fittingly asked, " Under what King Bezonian" shall our sociological development be marshalled? to what coronet shall the Constitution we have crowned, bend and bow ? If the assertion of power unlimited by law be indicatory of the future exercise of supreme authority, then the womb of America is teeming with a mighty brood of embryo kings. Shall the Electoral-Political Balance of Power, with its newly intrusted sceptre, whether Republican or Democratic, wrapped in the swaddling-clothes of yesterday's vote, be anointed and declared the rightful heir, and with its strong right hand pluck the royal diadem in the presence of an enfeebled minority? Is Protection or is Free Trade to wear upon its baby brow the "round and top of sovereignty"? Shall Transportation, the august grasping tyrant, who has immanacled and so "grievously ransomed" Trade ever since he has held dominion over her, when he seize advantage, not add the immortal title of king, with crown and coronet, to the sovereign greatness and authority of his empire in America? Why should the claims of the oligarch of Labor be overlooked, with his shreds and patches; with well-placed words and reasons not unplausible, but without broad-minded consideration for the interests of the greatest number; with fair pretence of friendly ends, but with stolid ignorance of the laws of industrial progress; with his implements of commercial war and subjugation, and with the solidarity of the labor vote in his favor,—why should the claims of an imperious oligarch be discarded who, under the sanctimonious veil of the Brotherhood of man, because this race antagonizes special labor classes, disfranchises the intelligence, character, and capacity of its seven millions of producers?—why should not this sun of glory, this light of men, aspire under combination of favoring circumstances to bear the "golden show"? Although "the conception of the national government as a huge machine, existing mainly for the purpose of rewarding partisan service," was "so alien to the character and conduct of Washington that it seems grotesque even to speak of it," does it need great forecast to predict the reign, in the near future, of the royal political plutocrats of the spoils system and practical politics?

With a title to kingly glory far exceeding in power and importance that of all these mighty Cæsars, came yesterday, a formidable shape, a hunched venomous creature, of savage temper and grim aspect, large-bodied and round-backed; "what seemed his head, the likeness of a kingly crown had on;" a pretender to the throne, resembling a huge industrious spider, spreading his web over every highway obvious to commerce. He has secured, by a combination of indirect, crooked ways and by-paths, a majority in numbers and values. His ravenous maw is filled with the vitals of trade. He never shuts his eye. His appearance turns values to stone. He utters vapid platitudes about productive co-operation, productive capital, the co-operation of labor, the ebb and flow of the tides of trade, and the survival of the fittest. He is stocked with the principles of political economy and the whole circle of its related sciences. He discourses learnedly about finance and economic laws. He indulges in magnificent speculations about the great advantages of massed capital and the subdivision of labor. He has promulgated sublime theories about lessening the cost to the consumer. Why should Trust,—

> " Abominable, unutterable, and worse
> Than fables yet have feigned or fear conceived,
> Gorgons and hydras and chimæras dire,"—

whose upward gaze is lovingly directed towards a golden uncontrolled enfranchisement, and to a regal state-cap dropping upon his head,—why should Trust, already " dazzled by visions of diadems, of stars and garters, and titles of nobility," not be proclaimed and installed king of values and reign over the American people?

These half-grown kings in wielding their mighty tridents have, one and all, stretched the sides of the Constitution. These ugly-headed monsters stand ready indirectly to subvert it. The sceptre of unlawful power has at times seemed almost within the fast hold of their ambition; and there can be no more fitting opportunity than is now afforded by the timely inquiry of your Order concerning the constitutional status of the civil rights of your race, to proclaim to this degenerate faction of covert traitors, that the majestic, all-powerful sovereign in America is the Constitution, and not a public opinion, which has the cowardice to recognize the usurpations of these embryo kings; and that the civil rights of all classes and interests, irrespective of conditions, are to be judged by this law of Liberty. It is the concealed, gradual, quiet approach of the civil polity which tends towards the creation of a novel and distinct classification of the civil rights of the whole American people,—it is this cloaked attempt to inaugurate an unconstitutional, arbitrary schedule for the arbitrament of civil rights,—as if this sacred and inalienable birthright were to be regarded as merchandise of an ascertainable value, as if this government were constitutional only in form,—

"Whose hollow womb inherits naught but bones,"—

it is this nefarious system, attempted to be executed through
fraud or force, which is not limited to color, race, or the previous
condition of any citizen,—it is this evil-disposedness of ever-
recurring turbulent, insidious, and covert factions, protean in
shape, which will not down at the bidding, which will not yield
to the authoritative force, nor recognize the "unblenched majesty"
of the Constitution, which calls with solemnity for a close scrutiny
into the working of the machinery of jurisprudence, in the administration of the justice of that grand pledge for the equality
of all men before the law, the Fourteenth Article of Amendment to the Constitution.

Although jurisprudence may be regarded in the nature of an
apparatus for the administration of justice, yet it is not a *machine*,
inert, and without natural power of self-propulsion, to be set in
motion either by the almighty fiat of party or by the gross delusion of popular opinion. So foul a blot, upon the escutcheon
of those who dispense justice for the state, as the bare suspicion that its mighty axe in their hands could cut two ways, that
its sharp edge could be bated by the foul breath of popular
opinion, or uplifted at the almighty fiat of party, would render
questionable, throughout all the departments of justice, the moral
parentage of the decrees of all her ministers. And a few such
precedents, of distorted birth but poor validity, would shortly
destroy the harmonious working and in time wither the strength
of our entire system of jurisprudence.

The question is not whether a juridical construction of the
Fourteenth Amendment which defeats its spirit, and deprives
the colored race of the authorities, rights, and liberties guaranteed under constitutional limitation, may not, in view of their
former condition and present relation, be the wiser course, and
be actuated by good will, benevolence, and a high moral consideration for the permanent advantage of the citizens for whose
betterment this amendment was made a part of the Constitution. The moral beauty and comeliness of so virtuous a
purpose could be safely admitted; but the objection is that it

involves the unconstitutional exercise of a terrific power, the boundaries of which are distant and shadowy, and not within sight of this constitutional limitation. Instead of fashioning an easy yoke for the neck of these citizens, what if this enlightened, beneficent, but experimental despotism, which substitutes the arbitrary decree of Jurisprudence in the place of a constitutional limitation, should in the end prove to be the setting of a precedent for the destruction of the civil rights of the last posterity of the Constitution? What if its prolific progeny shall hereafter claim constitutional primogeniture, and under the color of this legal precedent assert unlimited authority of less dubious utility in other directions? Future usurpations may not be prompted by the same large and far-seeing benevolence, nor be in quite so full accord with the social tone of other times, or as well assured of strong political support from the mass of the people. It may not be so possible hereafter, as it now is, to stay so dark a torrent from invading other constitutional domains, than the empty shadowy one which seven millions of citizens are forced now to occupy, under this unconstitutional curtailment of their civil rights. It may hereafter be the lot of the patrons of tyrannical right in America, who entertain contrary convictions, to discover the necessary political alexipharmac for this jurisprudential suicide.

The purpose of this " Inquiry concerning the constitutional limitations of the Thirteenth, Fourteenth, and Fifteenth Amendments" is to institute a general search and inquisition upon which presentment may be found against Jurisprudence: First, for deliberate, palpable, and persistent violation of the letter and spirit of the Fourteenth Amendment. Secondly, for the usurpation of colossal powers which aid, abet, and compass an abridgment of the substantial justice of *equality of right by due process of law,* in deference to the prevailing delusions of popular sentiment, so gross that it acquiesces in the formidable tyranny of civil discrimination against certain citizens because of their color, race, and previous condition ; notwithstanding the solemn guarantee of our Federal Constitution for the equality and universality of civic freedom, irrespective of race, birth, creed, color, or previous condition,—a delusion so monstrous, that it breathes defiance to the Constitution; so anomalous in its characteristics, that it regards as *brutum fulmen* grave penalties, civil and criminal, attached by the nation to those State agencies which disregard the sanctity of this great fundamental law; so universal, that with permissive passivity it suffers the individual citizen of the nation or State, the public servants, and the oligarchy of labor-caste, throughout the country, at their pleasure to invade and violate this constitutional limitation; from intrusion upon whose sacred boundaries *sovereign States* are constitutionally inhibited, even when in the exercise of their original, sovereign, and substantive powers to regulate the domestic concerns of their own citizens.

JUSTICE AND JURISPRUDENCE.

" Abstracts, abridgments, and summaries, etc., have the same use with burning-glasses,—to collect the diffused rays of wit and learning in authors and make them point with warmth and quickness upon the reader's imagination."—SWIFT.

" The wisdom of the wise, and the experience of ages, may be preserved by quotation."—DISRAELI.

" A reader must confine himself to certain limits, and select only the choice parts from those immense collections which the study of one person cannot possibly comprehend."—VOLTAIRE.

JUSTICE.

".Justice is the greatest interest of man on earth. It is the ligament which holds civilized beings and civilized nations together wherever her temple stands, and so long as it is duly honored there is a foundation for social security, general happiness, and the improvement and progress of our race. And whoever labors on this edifice with usefulness and distinction, whoever clears its foundations, strengthens its pillars, adorns its entablatures, or contributes to raise its august dome still higher in the skies, connects himself, in name and fame and character, with that which is and must be as durable as the fame of human society."—WEBSTER.

JURISPRUDENCE.

" There can be no less acknowledged of Law than that her seat is the bosom of God, her voice the harmony of the world ; that all things in heaven and earth do her homage, the very least as feeling her care, and the greatest as not exempted from her power ; both angels and men, and creatures of what condition soever, though each in a different sort and manner, yet all with uniform consent, admiring her as the mother of their peace and joy."—HOOKER.

"Mankind in general are not sufficiently aware that words without meaning, or of equivocal meaning, are the everlasting engines of fraud and injustice, and that the Grimgribber of Westminster Hall is a more fertile and a much more formidable source of imposture than the Abracadabra of magicians."—Epea Pteroenta.

" He finds the Republicans insisting that the Declaration of Independence includes all men, black as well as white, and forthwith he boldly denies that it includes negroes at all, and proceeds to argue gravely that all who contend that it does, do so only because they want to vote, eat and sleep, and marry with negroes! He will have it that they cannot be consistent else. Now, I protest against the counterfeit logic which concludes that, because I do not want a black woman for a slave, I must necessarily want her for a wife. I need not have her for either : I can just leave her alone. In some respects she certainly is not my equal ; but in her natural right to eat the bread she earns with her own hands, without asking leave of any one else, she is my equal and the equal of all others."—Lincoln.

" For the moment he [Lincoln] was dealing with two mighty forces of national destiny,—civil war and public opinion ; forces which paid little heed to theories of public, constitutional, or international law where they contravened their will and power. In fact, it was the impotence of legislative machinery, and the insufficiency of legal dicta to govern or terminate the conflicts of public opinion on this identical question of slavery, which brought on civil strife."—Nicolay and Hay.

" The vehemence and asperity, the downright bare-faced imposture, the alarming hypocrisy, the solemn restless grimace of jurisprudence, when it makes a convulsive backward step to give to party what was meant for mankind."—Bolingbroke.

" If this be not a sound construction of the Fourteenth Amendment, then that race is left, in respect of civil rights in question, practically at the mercy of corporations and individuals wielding power under the States." —Mr. Justice Harlan.

Dissenting opinion in Civil-Rights Cases, 109 U. S. Rep.

"I insist that the national legislature may, without transcending the limits of the Constitution, do for human liberty and the fundamental rights of American citizenship what it did, with the sanction of this court, for the protection of slavery and the rights of the masters of fugitive slaves."—Id.

EMANCIPATION.

" The way these measures were to help the cause was not by magic or miracles, but by inducing the *colored people* to come bodily over from the rebel side to ours."—Lincoln.

"I mean only in this form to express an earnest conviction that the court has departed from the familiar rule requiring, in the interpretation of constitutional provisions, that full effect be given to the intent with which they were adopted."—MR. JUSTICE HARLAN.

"But no human power can subdue this rebellion without the use of the *emancipation policy* and every other policy calculated to weaken the moral and physical forces of the rebellion. Freedom has given two hundred thousand men raised on Southern soil. It will give us more yet. Just so much it has subtracted from the enemy. . . . Let my enemies prove, to the contrary, that the destruction of slavery is not necessary to a restoration of the Union. I will abide the issue."—LINCOLN.

"The adoption of the Thirteenth, Fourteenth, and Fifteenth Amendments to the Federal Constitution closed one great era in our politics. It marked the end forever of the system of human slavery and of the struggles that grew out of that system. These amendments have been conclusively adopted, and they have been accepted in good faith by all political organizations and the people of all sections. They close the chapter. They are and must be final. All parties hereafter must accept and stand upon them ; and henceforth our politics are to turn upon questions of the present and the future, not upon those of the settled and final past."—TILDEN.

"Principles, it has been said, have no modesty. Their nature is to rule, and they doggedly insist on the privilege. If they meet in their path with other principles which dispute their ascendency, they give battle instantly ; for a principle never rests till it has conquered. Nor can it be otherwise. To reign is its life ; if it reigns not it dies."—D'AUBIGNÉ.

"When, early in the war, General Frémont attempted military emancipation, I forbade it, because I did not then think it an indispensable necessity. When, a little later, General Cameron, then Secretary of War, suggested the arming of the blacks, I objected, because I did not yet think it an indispensable necessity. When, still later, General Hunter attempted military emancipation, I again forbade it, because I did not yet think the indispensable necessity had come. When in March and May and July, 1862, I made earnest and successive appeals to the border States to favor compensated emancipation, I believed the indispensable necessity for military emancipation and arming the blacks would come unless averted by that measure. They declined the proposition, and I was, in my best judgment, driven to the alternative of either surrendering the Union, and with it the Constitution, or of laying strong hand upon the colored element. I chose the latter."—LINCOLN.

"You think you have power and impunity on your side ; and I think that I have the truth and innocence on mine. It is a strange and tedious war, when violence attempts to vanquish truth. All the efforts of violence cannot weaken truth, and only serve to give it fresh vigor. All the lights of truth cannot arrest violence, and only serve to exasperate it. When force meets force, the weaker must succumb to the stronger; when argument is opposed to argument, the solid and the convincing triumphs over the empty and the false; but violence and verity can make no impression on each other. Let none suppose, however, that the two are, therefore, equal to each other; for there is this vast difference between them, that violence has only a certain course to run, limited by the appointment of Heaven, which overrules its effects to the glory of the truth which it assails; whereas verity endures forever, and eventually triumphs over its enemies, being eternal and almighty as God himself."—PASCAL.

" Sir, when men have a great, benevolent, and holy object in view, of permanent interest, obstacles are nothing. If it fails in the hands of one, it will be taken up by another. If it exceeds the powers of an individual, society will unite towards the desired end. If the force of public opinion in one country is insufficient, the kindred spirits of foreign countries will lend their aid. If it remain unachieved by one generation, it goes down, as a heritage of duty and honor, to the next; and, through the long chain of counsels and efforts, from the first conception of the benevolent mind that planned the great work, to its final and glorious accomplishment, there is a steady and unseen but irresistible co-operation of that divine influence which orders all things for good."—EVERETT.

" I am naturally antislavery. If slavery is not wrong, nothing is wrong. I cannot remember when I did not so think and feel, and yet I have never understood that the Presidency conferred upon me an unrestricted right to act officially upon this judgment and feeling. It was in the oath I took that I would, to the best of my ability, preserve, protect, and defend the Constitution of the United States. I could not take the office without taking the oath. Nor was it my view that I might take an oath to get power, and break the oath in using the power."—LINCOLN.

" Who knows not, he exclaims, that Truth is strong! Next to the Almighty, she needs no policies, no stratagems, no licensings, to make her victorious. Though all the winds of doctrine were let loose upon the earth, so Truth be in the field, we injure her to misdoubt her strength. Let her and Falsehood grapple; who ever knew Truth put to the worse in a free and open encounter?"—MILTON.

" I could not feel that, to the best of my ability, I had even tried to preserve the Constitution, if, to save slavery or any minor matter, I should permit the wreck of government, country, and Constitution together."—LINCOLN.

" Truth, though now hewn like the mangled body of Osiris into a thousand pieces, and scattered to the four winds of heaven, shall be gathered limb to limb, and moulded with every joint and member into an immortal feature of loveliness and perfection."—BACON.

" Therefore the nation, as it has its end in the moral realization of the life of humanity, is to regard each individual person also as an end, for there is for each the infinite sacredness which is revealed in the Christ,— the life of humanity. The Christ who is declared to be the head of humanity ' is the head of every man.' In the Christ, there is the unity and foundation of humanity in its divine origin, and the realization of personality is in its redemptive life.

" In the Christ there is the revelation of the divine life of humanity. It is held in no abstract and formal conception as the evolution of a logical sequence; it is held in no vague and empty conception, as in an unhistorical existence; it is the resultant of no numerical estimate; it is no indefinite and unlimited being in which the consciousness of the individual is lost; but there is the revelation of humanity in its realization in personality, in its divine relations."—MULFORD.

" In the Christ, as the Prophet and Priest and King, there is alone the source of the prophetic and priestly and kingly powers in humanity. The comprehension of humanity in an isolated individualism is false and unreal. It is the source only of an evil egoism."—ID.

" The policy of emancipation and of employing black soldiers gave to the future a new aspect, about which hope and fear and doubt contended in uncertain conflict. According to our political system, as a matter of civil administration, the general government had no lawful power to effect emancipation in any State, and for a long time it had been hoped that the rebellion could be suppressed without resorting to it as a military measure. It was all the while deemed possible that the necessity for it might come, and that if it should the crisis of the contest would then be presented."— LINCOLN.

" The thought that every one, even the least, his welfare, his rights, his dignity, is the concern of the state,—that every one in his own personality is to be regarded and protected and honored and esteemed, without respect to ancestry or rank or race or gifts, if only he bear the human face and form,—this is the characteristic principle of the age, and its true distinction. This principle is alien to the earlier ages, and even to the age of the Reformation. It is first in the modern age that humanity in its full conception has become an energizing principle of right and duty, determining the whole order of society."—STAHL.

" The life of the nation, and the sacred obligations of its citizenship, which so inspire common men that they will die for them, and pass those gates of holy and willing sacrifice with the sacraments of the nation upon their lips, it regards only with moral indifference. If a people in a great crisis are redeemed from slavery, it sees not the glory of their deliverance. It heeds not the roll of the waves parted by the right hand of Majesty on high, but asks only that it still may catch the murmur of waters breaking on the shores of ancient wrong. It repeats its protest against sedition, conspiracy, and rebellion, but to their reality its conscience is dead. It asks, in the litany of human hopes and sorrows, for the unity of all nations, but for those who hold the unity of the nation as a divine gift it is silent and offers only the drowsy opiates of this world that drug the spirits of men."—MULFORD.

" When you labored under more sorts of oppression than one, you betook yourselves to God for refuge, and he was graciously pleased to hear your most earnest prayer and desires. He has gloriously delivered you, the first of nations, from the two greatest mischiefs of this life, and most pernicious to virtue,—TYRANNY and SUPERSTITION."—MILTON.

" Our commerce was suffering greatly by a few armed vessels built upon and furnished from foreign shores, and we were threatened with such additions from the same quarter as would sweep our trade from the sea and raise our blockade. We had failed to elicit from European governments anything hopeful upon this subject. The preliminary emancipation proclamation, issued in September, was running its assigned period to the beginning of the new year. A month later the final proclamation came, including the announcement that *colored men of suitable condition* would be received into the war service."—LINCOLN.

" Every step by which you have advanced to the character of an independent nation seems to have been distinguished by some token of providential agency."—WASHINGTON.

" I expect to maintain this contest until successful, or till I die, or am conquered, or my term expires, or Congress or the country forsake me."— LINCOLN.

" The struggle between the fury of despotism and the heroism of conviction, between executioners and martyrs, is worthy of eternal remembrance."—SISMONDI.

" Among the agencies he employed none proved more admirable or more powerful than this two-edged sword of the final proclamation, blending sentiment with force, leaguing liberty with Union, filling the voting armies at home and the fighting armies in the field. In the light of history we can see that by this edict Mr. Lincoln gave slavery its vital thrust, its mortal wound. It was the word of decision, the judgment without appeal, the sentence of doom."—NICOLAY and HAY.

"Between conquerors? no; the primary and secondary rights of patricians or plebeians? no; races? no; utilities? no; climates? no; aliens? no: but between citizens, whom the commonwealth has created. It is a question of the absolute duty of political society, through positive law, to restrain unconscionable invasions by the majority, which is now absolute in power, and capable of the greatest tyranny to the minority, because of a strong division prevailing throughout the province."—DIONYSIUS OF HALICARNASSUS.

"By this salutary sign, the genuine type of fortitude, I have liberated and freed your city from the slavish yoke of the tyrant; and have set at liberty the Senate and people of Rome, restoring them to their pristine splendor and dignity."—CONSTANTINE.

"I have descended into the field to which the narratives of our historians invited me, and there seen the actions of men and of states in energetic development and violent collision: of the clang of arms I have heard more than I can tell; but nowhere have I been shown the majestic form of the Judge who sits umpire of the combat."—D'AUBIGNÉ.

"Gold is a wonderful clearer of the understanding. It dissipates every doubt and scruple in an instant, accommodates itself to the meanest capacities, silences the loud and clamorous, and brings over the most obstinate and inflexible. Philip of Macedon was a man of most invincible reason this way. He refuted by it all the wisdom of Athens, confounded their statesmen, struck their orators dumb, and at length argued them out of all their liberties."—ADDISON.

"Let us have peace."—U. S. GRANT.

"My experience of men has neither disposed me to think worse of them, nor indisposed me to serve them; nor, in spite of failures which I lament, of errors which I now see and acknowledge, or of the present aspect of affairs, do I despair of the future. The truth is this; the march of Providence is so slow and our desires so impatient, the work of progress is so immense and our means of aiding it so feeble, the life of humanity is so long and that of the individual so brief, that we often see only the ebb of the advancing wave, and are thus discouraged. It is history that teaches us to hope."—R. E. LEE.

" But if it should fall out otherwise (which God forbid) ; if as you have been valiant in war you should grow debauched in peace, you that have had such visible demonstrations of the goodness of God to yourselves ; and that you should not have learned by so eminent, so remarkable an example before your eyes, to fear God, and work righteousness ; for my part, I shall easily grant and confess (for I cannot deny it), you will find in a little time, that God's displeasure against you will be greater than his grace and favor have been to yourselves, which you have had larger experience of than any other nation under heaven."—MILTON.

" Perhaps, too, there may be a certain degree of danger that a succession of artful and ambitious rulers may, by gradual and well-timed advances, finally erect an independent government on the subversion of liberty. Should this danger exist at all, it is prudent to guard against it, especially when the precaution can do no injury."—MADISON.

" The community that by concert, open or secret, among its citizens denies to a portion of its members their plain rights under the law has severed the only safe bond of social order and prosperity. The evil works, from a bad centre, both ways. It demoralizes those who practise it, and destroys the faith of those who suffer by it in the efficiency of the law as a safe protector."—PRESIDENT HARRISON.

" An unlawful expedient cannot become a permanent condition of government. If the educated and influential classes in a community either practise or connive at the systematic violation of laws that seem to cross their convenience, what can they expect when the lesson, that convenience or a supposed class-interest is a sufficient cause for lawlessness, has been well learned by the ignorant classes ?"—ID.

" A community where law is the rule of conduct, and where courts, not mobs, execute its penalties, is the only attractive field for business investments and honest labor."—ID.

" Anticipate the difficult by managing the easy."—LAO-TZE.

" No matter how unimportant the breach may seem ; though small at first, it will widen like a crevasse in the Mississippi, until the whole stream of arbitrary power goes rushing through it. Besides, the grade of a crime is not measured by the extent of the particular mischief. Forgery is forgery, whether the sum obtained by it be great or small, and murder is not mitigated by showing that the victim was short of stature."—J. BLACK.

> " 'Twill be recorded for a precedent ;
> And many an error, by the same example
> Will rush into the state : it cannot be."—SHAKESPEARE.

"It is by a simple rule I have studied the Constitution, which rule is, that no human being, no race, should be kept down in their efforts to rise to a higher state of liberty and happiness ; if any such would rise, I say to them in God's name good-speed."—SEWARD.

"Why may not illicit combinations for purposes of violence be formed as well by a majority of a state as by a majority of a country or a district of the same state ?"—MADISON.

"The Federalists of our time look to a single and splendid government, founded on banking institutions and moneyed corporations, riding and ruling over the plundered ploughman and beggared yeomanry."—JEFFERSON.

"Civil broils arise among them when it happens for one great bone to be seized on by some leading dog, who either divides it among the few, and then it falls to an oligarchy, or keeps it to himself, and then it runs up to a tyranny."—SWIFT.

"It is not to be denied that we live in the midst of strong agitations, and are surrounded by very considerable dangers to our institutions of government. The imprisoned winds are let loose. The East, the West, the North, the stormy South, all combine to throw the whole ocean into commotion, to toss its billows to the skies, and to disclose its profoundest depths."—WEBSTER.

"In proportion as governments rest on public opinion that opinion must be enlightened."—WASHINGTON.

"The result of the whole is, that we must refer to the monitory reflection that no government of human device and human administration can be perfect; that that which is the least imperfect is therefore the best government; that the abuses of all other governments have led to the preference of republican government as the best of all governments, because the least imperfect; that the vital principle of republican government is the *lex majoris partis*, the will of the majority ; that if the will of a majority cannot be trusted where there are diversified and conflicting interests, it can be trusted nowhere, because such interests exist everywhere ; that if the manufacturing and agricultural interests be of all interests the most conflicting in the most important operations of government, and a majority government over them be the most intolerable of all governments, it must be as intolerable within the States as it is represented to be in the United States ; and, finally, that the advocates of the doctrine, to be consistent, must reject it in the former as well as in the latter, and seek a refuge under an authority master of both."—MADISON.

CHAPTER I.

"It is impossible ever to effect any good for mankind till we are aware of the obstacles offered to it, and of the resistance we have to encounter from prejudice, pride, and interest."—HAZLITT.

"The difference, not between the old and new philosophy, but between the natural dictates of the heart and the artificial and oppressive distinctions of society, was so vast and obvious, that the people in general could not conceive it possible for any one to be sincere or merely mistaken in withholding their claims."—ID.

"It is to state and to defend what I conceive to be the true principles of the Constitution under which we are here assembled. I might well have desired that so weighty a task should have fallen into other and abler hands. I could have wished that it should have been executed by those whose character and experience give weight and influence to their opinion such as cannot possibly belong to mine. But, sir, I have met the occasion, not sought it; and I shall proceed to state my own sentiments, without challenging for them any particular regard, with studied plainness, and as much precision as possible."—WEBSTER.

"You might as well ask a people to punish one another for their complexion, the color of their hair, or the shape of their bodies."—BLACK.

> "My soul aches
> To know, when two authorities are up,
> Neither supreme, how soon confusion
> May enter 'twixt the gap of both and take
> The one by the other."—SHAKESPEARE.

"I believe, Mr. President, that I am about as likely to retract an opinion which I have formed as any member of this body, who, being a lover of truth, inquires after it with diligence before he imagines that he has found it."—PINCKNEY.

IT needs no argument to prove that, in comparison with the civil rights, privileges, and immunities enjoyed, without discrimination or qualification, by all white citizens, as artificers, machinists, and workers in all handicrafts, mechanical and industrial vocations, employments, or business, or in their pursuit of pleasure, the freedom of their person in travel, their public entertainment by inn-keepers and by the proprietors of places

72

of public resort for instruction or amusement, the civil rights, privileges, and immunities of American citizens of African descent have stood, in different sections of the country, and stand to-day, in a certain abeyance, notwithstanding "that series of constitutional amendments securing to them the full and equal enjoyment of all the civil rights which the superior (white) race enjoys." The Civil-Rights Bill of 1866, the Enforcement Act of 1870, and the Civil-Rights Bill of 1875, have been confessedly ineffectual in removing the disabilities which the colored race everywhere encounters.

However deeply experienced in disordering or destroying the framework of jurisprudence, however profoundly versed in the artificial reasoning and in the broad general principles of law, a foreigner, landing for the first time upon our shores, without experience of the chill blasts of racial adversity, and unacquainted with the long-established order of white civil rights in America, would be curiously perplexed at the anomalous status of the civil rights of our citizens of African descent. After acquainting himself with the national legislation upon this subject, he would learn that thus far the learned courts have discovered no solid ground for controversy respecting the interpretation of the terms employed by the national legislators, such as "citizens," "immunities," "civil rights," and "privileges;" and that the sovereign authority of the Supreme Court has again and again asserted the proposition, that in the equality of the civil rights, privileges, and immunities of all citizens lies the fundamental principle of all American liberty.

After a careful review of the comprehensive language used by the Supreme Court, in the legal construction of those constitutional amendments conferring civil rights and equality upon the citizens of the nation's adoption, such a stranger would rationally conclude that, in every lawsuit about the civil rights, immunities, and privileges of any American citizen, there would be for trial only the single issue of fact, whether or not these rights, privileges, or immunities had suffered unjust discrimination. He would be slow to understand why the color of the plaintiff's skin, whether copper-colored, pink, purple, white, black, bottle-green, blue, or resplendent with all the colors of the rain-

bow, should have any more relevancy to the question of. the infringement of his civil rights than the inquiries of a physiologist
concerning the fibre of his muscle or the texture of his brain, or
the speculations of a specialist regarding the physiognomy of the
plaintiff or the craniognomy of the defendant.   Under the oft-
repeated declarations of the Supreme Court, with entire confidence
that he was standing on solid ground, regardless of all discriminators, the foreigner would stoutly maintain that the plaintiff, if a
good citizen, a man of pure morals, well educated, and otherwise
gentlemanlike, had only to show that he was denied a civil right
enjoyed by all other citizens of the United States, and the controversy would be confined to the single and simple issue of fact,
whether or not the enjoyment or exercise of the plaintiff's civil
right *had been* invaded, questioned, or denied by the defendant
in his capacity of public servant or in his private duty as a citizen of the commonwealth.   He would declare that direct or
indirect reference in such trials to the plaintiff's skin could
have no more relevancy to the civil-rights issues, than it would
have as evidence of his guilt or innocence if he were on trial
for high treason, murder, arson, or larceny.

If, however, such a legal tactician as we will suppose our
foreign publicist to be, dexterous and versed in the legerdemain
of the law, should press his investigations a step further, and,
instead of surveying general doctrines, should apply himself to
the examination of special cases, he would discover (anomalous
as it must appear to him) that not a single controversy between
black-faced plaintiffs and black-faced defendants, or between
white-faced plaintiffs and white-faced defendants, on the question
of the infringement of their civil rights, could the books reveal ;
but he would find an endless amount of litigation in cases where
the plaintiff's cuticle was dark, and the defendant's of thinner
and more pellucid texture.   Stranger still would be his discovery that in every such controversy the learned court, the
counsel of the plaintiff and of the defendant, and the entire bar
had at the start unanimously declared that the doctrine of the
universality of civil rights was fundamental American law,
applicable to all citizens of the United States, irrespective of
their several cuticles.

Imagine the confusion of a patient searcher after truth at learning that the defendant of the pellucid skin, in an action brought against him by the darker-hued plaintiff, interposed certain pleas and defences which, while confessing the civil right of the plaintiff, avoided it by certain new matter of law, or of fact, not found in either the spirit or the letter of the constitutional amendments or of any subsequent legislation; that, by reason thereof, it not infrequently happened that a colored plaintiff was wholly denied the identical civil rights, privileges, and immunities accorded absolutely and without question to each and every other of the sixty millions of American citizens whose skin happened to be white; and that the records of the nation did not present a single instance in which a white-skinned man or woman had ever complained that he or she had been deprived of a civil right by the darker-skinned citizen, whilst the national and State dockets literally swarmed with controversies in which complaint was made by colored citizens that these very rights had been denied them by white citizens of the United States.

Before this dangerous anomaly in the administration and practical adjustment of civil rights, acting thus injuriously against one class of American citizens, can be removed, and the constitutional amendments, which form a part of the organic structure of American jurisprudence, cleared of all obscurity, evidently some unknown factor, as yet concealed, and operating in the dark, must be brought to light; for our investigator would learn that heretofore no white philanthropist, publicist, layman, or even common scribbler, had so far ventured to display either his temerity, his learning, or his ignorance as to attempt the solution of the white- and dark-skin rulings in the multitudinous array of the cases of Black Civil Rights *v.* White Civil Rights. However clear his discernment, he would have to confess himself puzzled by the mysterious workings of these rulings, and his confusion would be greatly increased when he learned that the judges who presided over the trials were never of the darker-skinned race, but were chosen by white and black voters because of the imposing splendor of their learning, the purity of their characters, their lofty patriotism, ample experience, and profound judgment.

CHAPTER II.

"Let me, disclaiming all such slavish awe,
Dive to the very bottom of the law;
Let me (the weak, dead letter left behind)
Search out the principles, the spirit find,
Till, from the parts made master of the whole,
I see the Constitution's very soul."—GOTHAM.

"Among the faithless, faithful only he;
Among the innumerable false, unmoved,
Unspoken, unseduced, unterrified,
His loyalty he kept, his love, his zeal."—MILTON.

"You tread upon the high places of earth and history; you think and feel as an American for America. Her power, her eminence, her consideration, are yours; your competitors, like hers, are kings; your home, like hers, is the world; your path, like hers, is on the highway of empires; your charge, her charge, is of generations and ages; her image, one immortal, golden vision on your eye, as our western star at evening rises on the traveller from his home."—CHOATE.

"Here my master, interposing, said 'it was a pity that creatures endowed with such prodigious abilities of mind as these lawyers, by the description I gave of them, must certainly be, were not rather encouraged to be instructors of others in wisdom and knowledge;' in answer to which I assured his honor 'that in all points out of their own trade they were usually the most ignorant and stupid generation among us, the most despicable in common conversation, avowed enemies to all knowledge and learning, and equally disposed to pervert the general reason of mankind in every other subject of discourse as in that of their own profession.'"—SWIFT.

To eliminate and lose sight entirely of the effects of two centuries of slavery; to divorce from our consideration the irrelevant issues usually entangled with every discussion of civil rights; and to present the question in its bare essentials, in the cold light of a dispassionate search after truth, striving at every step to distinguish the right from the wrong, the true from the false; it has occurred to the writer that it might serve the pur-

76

pose of a calm and impartial judicial inquiry, and tend at the same time to bring the subject within the range of vision of the non-professional reader, to assume an unbiased attitude, and follow steadily and closely the friendly inartificial dialogue which opens in this chapter between our unprejudiced student from abroad and the illustrious Chief Justice of · the Supreme Court. The former has already been introduced and described as having suddenly landed in our midst, without experience of the chill blasts of racial adversity, and being unacquainted with the long-established order of white civil rights in America.

" I am free to confess," said the Chief Justice, " that I am anxious to see in what light the question of civil rights presents itself to the dispassionate mind of one who is unfamiliar with our local institutions. Should you desire to glance at the decisions, permit me to explain, as a preliminary, that questions daily occur in the course of practice demonstrating the obscurity of the subject. Like the problems relating to the previous condition of slavery, the doctrines of civil rights and their enforcement puzzle the greatest adepts in jurisprudence and political science. The subject requires deliberation, patient investigation, and sound judgment; for it is a misfortune inseparable from human affairs that these mixed questions are rarely considered with that freedom from prejudice which is essential to a just estimate of their tendency to advance or obstruct the public good. I make no apology for not referring you to the decisions of the Supreme Court of the United States and to those of the various State courts; for you must bear in mind that, according to our form of procedure, we pass only upon such questions as the records of the causes tried by the inferior courts present, and are in nowise responsible for the issues thereby and therein raised, upon which questions of civil rights have been determined.

" A review of these cases will reveal the varied aspects in which the civil rights of our American citizens of African descent have been viewed by the courts throughout the country; and after a critical examination you cannot fail to surmise that some imperceptible mystery, preventing the enforcement of the Fourteenth Amendment, was at work beneath their sur-

face, which one of the litigants was ashamed or feared to urge
in his defence, and which was also perhaps too galling to the
sensibilities of the other to reveal; and that possibly the learned
courts, not unaware of the embarrassment of both suitors, and
of the sensitiveness of public opinion in reference to this concealed factor in the civil-rights cases, with the utmost tact and
delicacy, in a kindly spirit of fraternal charity for the plaintiff,
the defendant, and the fastidiousness of public opinion, aided by
the sublime proficiency of the special pleaders at the bar, had
permitted these civil-rights issues to be framed with such dex-
terity as to enable the question of " civil rights" to be decided,
not according to the Fourteenth Constitutional Amendment, but
in accordance with the paramount authority over that Constitutional Amendment which those public servants, the common
carrier, the inn-keeper, and the proprietor of places of public
resort for instruction and amusement, have been pleased to assert
for the protection and guidance of their vocation under the
authority, which the pleaders set up, of common-law rules applying to these vocations, which, they substantially insist, indirectly repudiate, repeal, and override the Constitution and the
declared civil policy of the nation in respect of these civil rights.
You will also note that the issues raised by these special pleaders
do not involve civil rights so much as the rights of race."

The ambitious student, who had been early introduced into
the aristocratic circle of learning, and had mingled freely in its
royal entertainments, was greatly impressed with the noble candor,
sublime simplicity, and the absence of illusory dignity in the
judicial bearing of our representative of American jurisprudence.

With that intellectual conscientiousness and balanced good
judgment which befit a jurist and statesman of lofty type, before opening further to the student the stores of his knowledge,
the Chief Justice continued,—

"Although, sir, it cannot dim the lustrous reign of those
sovereigns in jurisprudence to whose august throne I have succeeded, yet candor obliges me to confess, on behalf of the nation
whose judicial crown I wear, that, improbable to you as it may
seem, it is nevertheless true that Christian, liberty-worshipping
America, offering, as she does, an asylum for the oppressed of all

other lands, was the first government, from barbaric ages down, in which, by a solemn Constitution, slavery was encircled with, and maintained by, all the power of the state. You are perhaps unacquainted with the historical events preceding the Rebellion. Their dark shadow can be traced as far back as the invention of the cotton-gin. Time and opportunity will not permit me to dilate at length upon the statesmanlike policy which the leaders of the Republican party adopted in favor of the abolition of slavery, nor to recount to you in sufficiently glowing terms how that party rose with the battle-cry of freedom almost to imperial power. Hereafter I will direct your attention to the history of the Republican party as it has been faithfully recorded by one of her noblest sons."

The Chief Justice paused, and the student made a passing inquiry as to the immediate authors of the civil war. Considering a moment, and towering, as was his wont, far above the mere prejudices of the political rabble which infest the party-plains below, he exclaimed:

" Goaded nigh to madness by the irrepressible-conflict doctrines of the high-priests of the Republican party respecting the equality of man, North, South, East, and West sent up the cry, ' To arms! To arms!' Then, as if from infernal caverns, sprang civil war. In the midst of its bloody throes the Emancipation Proclamation was sent forth, and before the on-looking populations of the globe, which watched with breathless interest the unnatural strife, that crime against human nature, doomed slavery, met its fate,—

> ' Was, with its chains and human yoke,
>   Blown hellwards by the cannon's mouth,
>   While Freedom cheered behind the smoke.'

" But you are not to understand from this confession, sir, that slavery in the nineteenth century was an exclusively American crime," said the Chief Justice. " For, as a student of history, you must know that during the first ten years of this century, in the face of the civilized world, three hundred thousand Africans were conveyed in English bottoms across the Atlantic, fully one-half of whom perished from atrocious treatment during the voyage. It is an historical fact, also, that as late as 1815 an English wife, but one month married, was haltered by her husband, led to Smithfield, and there sold at auction. If my recollection serves me rightly, as late as the close of the eighteenth century slavery existed in England, in the colonies of France and Spain, in Scotland, Prussia, Hungary, Austria, and Russia."

As the conversation proceeded freely onward, the Chief Justice read that noble document, the Emancipation Proclamation, to our student, and he listened with reverent attention to that series of constitutional amendments which again declare " that all men are created equal; that they are endowed by their Creator with certain inalienable rights, the chief of which are life, liberty, and the pursuit of happiness ; and to secure these rights, governments are instituted among men."

When the Proclamation, the Thirteenth, Fourteenth, and Fifteenth Amendments, and the acts of Congress in pursuance thereof, had been read and the volumes were closed, the divine truth was revealed to the calm, dispassionate inquirer, and he exclaimed, with a warmth unusual with him, " After the lapse, then, of almost two centuries, the Republican party has rolled away the stone from the sepulchre of American Freedom !"

The Chief Justice, a devout believer in the Providence which directs the ways of empires, replied : " It seems to me as if, from the dawn of creation, the invincible spirit of liberty had brooded, with eternal vigilance, over the deeps of this infernal darkness ; that, with the Proclamation of Emancipation, which the patriot President sealed with his blood, the long, loud chants of freedom ascended on high, and were heard and regarded in the courts of heaven ; and that the auspicious rays of its celestial light still warm and illumine the last and noblest empire of time."

" If you will not consider it presumption in a foreigner to speak so despairingly of your countrymen," said the student, " I think they depreciate civil liberty itself when they nullify such integral parts of your Constitution as these amendments. Is it not highly probable that a broader discernment of their true nature, and a deeper and fuller conception of the spirit and meaning of the terms employed, may fundamentally modify the present attitude of thoughtful minds towards the subject of race rights? If some process could be suggested of removing the bandages from the eyes of the pseudo-conservative school, the obscurantist dissenting class of your people, they would soon discover, I think, what is so apparent to the rest of the world, that race-instincts in America involve only prejudice against the helplessness of a fellow-man.

"The glance I have had at the fundamental provisions you have so kindly read, clearly shows that their intention was, that your States and people should constitute a plural unit,—one country, one liberty, one destiny. I can realize, however, what a terrible social upheaval, what a moral earthquake it must have required to unfix and do away with that fossilized race-prejudice which the former institution of slavery had fastened upon the body-politic. I heartily concur in what you have said, that this civil and legal problem ought to be approached without pre-possession of any kind, in the same spirit of exact justice and unimpassioned inquiry which has heretofore enabled the bene-factors of mankind to solve many other problems not less closely involved in the institutions of their day nor less hotly contested.

"The question of the enforcement of the civil rights of Amer-ican citizens of African descent is a matter not only of the laws but also of the civil polity of your nation. Should I venture too far if I should assert (it may be in my ignorance) that only a limited class of your people stands in the way of the operation of those mighty instruments, the Thirteenth, Four-teenth, and Fifteenth Amendments, which, it seems to me, are intended to sweep away every vestige of the previous condition of those unhappy people? It appears to me, that these amend-ments to your Constitution were wrought out in the timing of the Almighty, not so much through the agency of the Republi-can party, as you think,—and I trust you will pardon my free-dom,—as through the instrumentality of Christian civilization. The color-caste philosophers of your country fail to realize the fact that they can no more frustrate this sublime decree of divine Providence, in behalf of a down-trodden race, than they can move from their orbits those heavenly luminaries which, in their ordered and majestic march through space, shed their be-nign light upon the darkling earth."

CHAPTER III.

"You, sir, are fully acquainted with this, and know that men generally judge of everything by prejudice, hearsay, and chance. No one reflects that the cause of a citizen ought to interest the whole body of citizens, and that we may ourselves have to endure in despair the same fate which we perceive, with eyes and feelings of indifference, falling heavily upon him. We write and comment every day upon the judgments passed by the Senate of Rome and the Areopagus of Athens, but we think not for a moment of what passes before our own tribunals."—VOLTAIRE.

"Hence our ancient and famous lawyer Bracton, in his first book, chap. viii., 'There is no king in the case,' says he, 'where will rules the roost, and law does not take place.'"—MILTON.

"Contempt for private wrongs was one of the features of ancient morals."—JAUBERT.

"Being imbedded in the Constitution, it cannot be destroyed except by force strong enough to overthrow the Constitution itself. Legislative enactments or judicial decisions are powerless either to strengthen or impair it. The legerdemain of law, craft, the catches of special pleading, the *snapperadoes* of practice, do not help us to decide a matter like this."—J. BLACK.

"My master was yet wholly at a loss to understand what motives could incite this race of lawyers to perplex, disquiet, and weary themselves, and engage in a confederacy of injustice, merely for the sake of injuring their fellow-animals."—SWIFT.

"It is not possible to found a lasting power upon injustice."—DEMOSTHENES.

"Right is the eternal sun; the world cannot delay its coming."—PHILLIPS.

"It is in the body politic, as in the natural, those disorders are most dangerous that flow from the head."—PLINY THE YOUNGER.

THE student, whom we have recognized as a man of so much ability and of so little pretension, with that artless simplicity which accompanies, with rare exceptions, all forms of true greatness, continuing his inquiries asked the Chief Justice,—

" Do the laborer, the common carrier, the inn-keeper, the proprietor of places of public resort, and the saloon-keeper, then, who have thus attempted a criminal repudiation of the Constitutional Amendments, enjoy the sympathy of representative men, and notable leaders with vast fortunes, the monopolists, millionaires, money kings, merchant princes, and railroad magnates ?"

In answer to this inquiry the Chief Justice, who was wakeful to the expediency of avoiding further reference to the *modus operandi* by which the jurisprudence of public servants had so far maintained a paramount authority over the Constitution, not without a transient flush upon his face, simply replied,—

" This *vulnus immedicabile* is rather in the lower than in the upper classes. The wealthy citizens, to whom you have referred, have partly attained their status in the commonwealth by reason of the absence of that narrow spirit of intolerance which tends to dwarf all men. From every stand-point *they* realize the advantages to be derived from keeping pace with the progressive liberal spirit of the age and maintaining constitutional authority. This view is firmly held by them, not because of their abstract reverence for law, but because their intellects are broad and deep enough to discern at a glance the manifold and material advantages which result to every member of the commonwealth from the legal maintenance of the letter and spirit of these amendments. Instead of being found in the ranks of these titled dignitaries of the country, the stabbers at the Constitution and its amendments are the under-strata of our society, who draw what is called a ' dead-line' or a ' color-line' across the face both of these amendments and of the acts of Congress passed in pursuance of their authority. Aided by the special pleaders of whom I have spoken, the public servants and labor tyrants have built a sort of Chinese wall around themselves and their private and public callings; and although their guilt is notorious, yet, since the Constitutional Amendments act only upon the States, and not upon individual aggressors, no way has been found to drag any of the criminals to justice. The Supreme Court, you will find, has determined that the amendments inhibited only unfriendly legislation by the States, and could not be construed to cover the wrongful individual acts of their citizens. We have already suggested that the responsibility and duty of altering this state of affairs rests upon Congress, not upon the courts; and Congress has not seen fit to remedy the evil through the medium of corrective legislation."

"But pray, sir," said the student, "will you be good enough to indulge me further, and explain, what possible motive the inferior class has in depriving the meekest of citizens of their immunities and privileges?"

"Except as their motives and intents are evinced by *actions*, the wrong-doers," answered the Chief Justice, "are rarely susceptible of judicial cognizance; they are offenders in the realm of conscience, and are responsible to the church and priest rather than to the state and court. I sometimes incline to the opinion, however, that there is an instinct in mankind similar to that which gives the lower order of animals a certain gratification in asserting the arrogance of their strength against 'the tainted wether of the flock, meetest for death.' To their deepest shame, I confess, observation leads me to the further lamentable conclusion, that this cowardly, invidious arrogance is oftenest exhibited, with entire impunity, towards a helplessly unfortunate fellow-man. It is true, sir, that the most aggressive enemies of civil rights in America are not confined to these public servants of whom I have spoken, but *their* hostility to our constitutional law and national policy is more open and avowed. In their interpretation of the terms 'citizen,' 'civil rights,' 'immunities,' and 'privileges,' in their gauging of constitutional law and of our national polity, these creatures of the State regard themselves as chartered libertines, to be guided by no loftier standard than dollars and cents can afford. They gravely urge that their business cannot be conducted in conformity with the civil-rights amendment—which they nevertheless confess is the supreme law of the land—without incurring the risk of losing those customers who in their hearts are opposed to the carrying out of this provision of constitutional law."

The student for some moments regarded the Chief Justice with impassioned, almost irrepressible earnestness, in a manner strangely at variance with his usual imperturbable demeanor; then, with heart-felt warmth, he exclaimed :

"The presumption, Mr. Chief Justice, of public servants in assuming the attitude of bold enemies to the Constitution of their country, surpasses the comprehension of a foreigner. If I may make so bold, sir, the '*vulnus immedicabile*,' of which you have spoken, is not an incurable wound in the breast of the supercilious *grands seigneurs* of the public service; it is the attempted overthrow of the Constitutional Amendments themselves. The Amendments are the organic law of the land ; and the impudent readiness of these people, upon any pretext whatever, to dethrone and usurp the civil rights of seven million of citizens thus sacredly secured, without any warrant, colorable or otherwise of law, except the unproved fact of injury to their business if they should conform to the declared will of the nation, is without a parallel in the constitutional history of the world. These high-flown *bourgeois gentilhommes* are guilty of impious and infamous tyranny against the civil rights of seven millions of people, on the simple ground of prospective business losses. These crows of the commonwealth forsooth must needs borrow hawk's wings to fly in the face of the American eagle, and insult the majesty of the nation by trifling with and evading its most sacred laws."

"The Fourteenth Amendment," replied the Chief Justice, "is the universal rule of action,—in fact, the supreme law. It has no relation, special or general, remote or proximate, to the interests of any person as respects his business or calling. For every citizen it provides a rule to which all private interests must be subordinate."

Continuing in the same vehement strain, the student said,—

"Gravely to maintain that there is any law, lawyer, logic, or logician, sufficiently powerful to defend and maintain their high and mighty arrogance in repudiating the Constitution, is treason against the human understanding. It is as unreasonable as to assert the philosophy of savages against the philosophy of *savants :* as degrading as to substitute the instinct of the herd of human cattle, for the rational judgment of the highest order of nature. A sadder travesty upon law, reason, philosophy, and constitutional liberty, I cannot well imagine. It is impossible, from the nature of things, by any metaphysical legerdemain to annihilate these Constitutional Amendments. It transcends the wildest extravagance of fancy to assert that any class may thus trample on justice and defile reason. The common understanding of the whole world revolts at the defence set up, that the principles of the common law, which are in force in America, regulating the rights and duties of the public servants, sanction a violation of the supreme law of the land. It appears to me that it does not require a very piercing glance to probe these arguments to the bottom. The clear atmosphere of the judicial mind, at least in the northern clime, must penetrate the fog; your courts must listen with impatient reluctance to dull stolidities, which no talent could make respectable; for there can be no reasonable reply to arguments of arrogant shallowness, breathing only defiance to the Constitution and the general voice of the nation.

" What possible benefit can these seven millions of enfranchised citizens derive from the comprehensive language of the Fourteenth Amendment, and the precise, specific, and general terms in which their civil rights are therein set forth, if common sense and plain reason are thus to be trampled under foot ? Is not the language of the Amendments to be understood as all language should be,—that is to say, as people generally understand it,—and not according to the fancy of the popular caprice, or the special interests of the public servants, mechanics, and artisans ? Is it not the grossest absurdity for lawyers to maintain that these Amendments are to be construed as if the States, Congress, the common law, or the public, had annexed to them a clause providing that ' nothing herein contained shall be so construed as to impair the emoluments which industrial orders, or which hotel-keepers, common carriers, or the proprietors of places of public resort for instruction or amusement may hereafter receive from citizens who repudiate these amendments ; and that in all cases in which it may prove to the interest of said mechanics or said public servants to foment discord, to foster and gratify race-prejudice by individual or class discriminations on account of color or of previous condition, then and in all such cases it may and shall be lawful for said public servants and said industrial orders to pass such rules and regulations as tend to establish and maintain a color-line; and it is further provided, that, whenever said rules and regulations are established for the benefit and commercial advantage of trades, and the comfort and convenience of one class of citizens, though in reality they may operate to the pecuniary loss, pain, humiliation, discomfort, and disfranchisement of the civil rights of another class, then and in all such cases said rules and regulations shall be deemed by the courts to be, and are hereby declared to be, "reasonable rules and regulations," anything in the letter or spirit of these Amendments to the contrary notwithstanding'?"

"There has never been any contention so farcical," answered the Chief Justice, "nor would any court tolerate such a burlesque upon the methods of constitutional construction. To maintain so monstrous an absurdity it would be necessary to advance very far into the region of vagaries. If the State should, through her Legislature, pass an act clothing the mechanics and public servants with authority to make such rules, that State enactment would be void, as we have decided in the famous civil-rights cases, and the public servants or others who attempt to enforce it would be liable to the gravest civil and criminal penalties."

"Would it not then follow," replied the student, "that rules, which are *reasonable* when adopted by artisans or the public servants, entail criminal and civil responsibilities if exercised under the broad sovereignty of the State?"

"To maintain that such rules and regulations based upon discriminations of color are reasonable rules and regulations," said the Chief Justice, "it is necessary to assert, that the invasion of the South by the North, the loss of hundreds of thousands of precious lives and millions of treasure, the Emancipation Proclamation and the Amendments of the Constitution (all uniting to compass the result of making people of African descent citizens of the United States, notwithstanding their color or previous condition), were each and all of them unreasonable in the view of the profound enlightenment of mechanics and the public servants."

"These Amendments," he continued, "granting civil rights to American citizens of African descent, involve the eternal difference between the rights of freedom and wrongs of slavery, and should never be subject to sectional bias, to the fluctuations of public opinion, to race-prejudice, nor to industrial, social, or individual idiosyncrasies and interests. In their workings these great principles of civil liberty must be immutable and independent of the public, corporate, or individual interests and prejudices, upon which it is assumed they produce hardships."

The Chief Justice, continuing, said, "The saviours of the nation, by the invention and enforcement of a rigorous system of taxation, produced the means to sustain the national credit; for at the commencement of the Rebellion our treasury was nearly empty. Billions were thus raised, entailing sacrifices upon the whole Union, and half a million of lives were lost to secure those very civil rights which it is asserted a two-penny public servant may now repudiate because he may lose a dime in his business if the civil rights of one class of citizens are not sacrificed to the objections of another class. Those illustrious friends of mankind who represented the Republican party were a noble band, now admired by men of every political faith. Wherever the language of civilization is spoken they are regarded as great teachers and thinkers; they are acknowledged to be the enlightened patriots, the earnest law-givers, and the true sages of the nineteenth century. In truth, the history of civil rights is their biography."

The student inquired, in a grave manner, whether it was possible to regard their great lives and works, and the civil rights of seven millions of people, purchased by a vast national debt, as trifles light as air, compared with the alleged loss to the public servants of the patronage of passengers whose sectional prejudice is opposed to the operation of these amendments, and who, in effect, repudiate and repeal them by their covert acts as much as if pro-slavery feeling in a State had, by hostile legislation, encouraged their violation. He continued,—

"I am not well versed in the history of American constitutional law, sir, but I venture to assert that the records of legal disputations furnish no parallel to such an unwarrantable conclusion. It is a startling doctrine that the public laborer and the public servants of any country may jeer and gibe like angry apes at the great work of its illustrious dead ; and that they may do so not only with legal impunity, but even with the pretended sanction of law ; that they have rendered, and still may render, void the Constitutional Amendments which the nation enacted for the emancipation of seven millions of freemen ; and that, too, upon the puerile pretext, not that their business *is,* but that it *may be* affected, if they conform it to the provisions of constitutional law and the existing policy of the nation."

"The bare assertion of power in a mere creature of the State," said the Chief Justice, "to overthrow the Constitution from which its breath of life proceeds, and that, too, through the agency of the professors of the common law, seems to me to rest not upon reason but rather upon the despair of the existence of reason itself."

"If this be true," said the student, "the public servant and the artisan in America must indeed be distinct creations and orders, not amenable to the Constitution. But, sir, may I venture to ask, to whom did the mighty dead of the Republican party, who amidst darkness and danger framed this broad charter of freedom, look for protection from its future enemies?"

CHAPTER IV.

"The mischiefs whereinto, even before our eyes, so many others have fallen headlong from no less plausible and fair beginnings than yours are; there is in every one of these considerations most just cause to fear, lest our hastiness to embrace a thing of so perilous consequence should cause posterity to feel those evils which as yet are more easy for us to prevent than they would be for them to remedy."—HOOKER.

"The best and safest way for you, therefore, my dear brethren, is, to call your deeds past to a new reckoning, to re-examine the cause ye have taken in hand, and to try it even point by point, argument by argument, with all the diligent exactness ye can, to lay aside the gall of that bitterness wherein your minds have hitherto overabounded, and with meekness to search the truth."—ID.

"That optical illusion which makes a brier at our nose of greater magnitude than an oak at five hundred yards."—BURKE.

"What if I should answer you thus? That words ought to give place to things; that we, having taken away kingly government itself, do not think ourselves concerned about its name and definition; let others look to that, who are in love with kings: we are contented with the enjoyment of our liberty."—MILTON.

IN answer to the question put by the student, at the close of the last chapter, the Chief Justice said,—

"The saviours of our nation, sir, commended it to a double care: first, to the Supreme Court of the United States, by virtue of the Constitution; and, secondly, they imposed upon the Congress of the United States in apt terms—'with power to enforce by appropriate legislation,' words full of legal significance —the solemn obligation of protecting the precious legacy of freedom bequeathed to seven millions of citizens whom the nation had adopted as the common children of one beneficent parent."

After a moment's consideration he continued,—

"I listened with impatient silence, sir, to your views respect-

90

ing the common-law theories of public servants in America, and their conflict with our Constitution, but your mind is as yet confused upon the subject. The common law is not the law of the government of the United States: we have decided to the contrary.[1] The Constitution and the acts of Congress passed in pursuance thereof are the laws which govern the United States of America, where there is a conflict between them and the common law."

" It would seem to me, a mere layman, Mr. Chief Justice," said the student, " if the common law is not the law of the United States, as you have explained, and if the supreme law of the nation is the Constitution, together with the acts of Congress passed in pursuance thereof, that the pretensions of the public servants are so much the more extravagant; for they seek to place the Amendments underneath and the common law uppermost, when they assert that the civil rights of these citizens are not to be judged by the Constitution as amended, but rather by their paramount authority."

" There can be no conflict," replied the Chief Justice, " between our constitutional law and the common law. The Constitution furnishes the inviolable and standard rule of right over the States and their citizens ; it is the supreme law of this country, and it imposes such restraints on the States, and on the actions of individuals, as are necessary for the safety and good order of the community at large. The States have manufactured their laws by Acts of Assembly, or they have adopted the English common-law and chancery principles ; and for the suitors in the State courts (and in the United States courts, by statutes of the United States, in common-law cases) these statutes and the common law furnish the artificial rules and precedents regulating the rights of persons and things which are founded on the law of reason, natural justice, and equity. By the common law no man is so low as not to be within the law's protection. That apparently is right reason. But this doctrine of the common law was not in force in America prior to the

---

[1] State of Pennsylvania *v.* William Bridge, 13 How. 519; Wheaton *v.* Peters, 8 Peters, 591, 659.

Civil War, which, as you will hereafter see, was a bloody arbitrament of this right reason, resulting in the restoration to the
law's protection of those who, according to the decision of the
Supreme Court in Scott *v.* Sandford, were situated so low as not
to be within the reach of its protecting arm. The States, by
the adoption of these Constitutional Amendments, incorporated
into the Constitution, as part of the organic law, the sound
proposition that no man is so humble as to be denied the law's
protection; and that the civil rights which any citizen enjoys
shall be possessed by all, freely and without price; this, however, not as a re-enactment of the common law, but as the assertion of an eternal and immutable rule of right for a free
people."

If then, by the common law, civil liberty and civil rights
were the inheritance of mankind, the student wondered how any
lawyer of sound judgment, even though he might sneer at the
lofty ethics of universal civil rights, could, without incurring the
guilt of warring against conscience, argue with gravity the abstract legal proposition, that, although the Rebellion, the Constitution, and the Amendments thereto had firmly established the
common-law doctrine of the equality of all men, yet wherever and
whenever the interests of public servants might be prejudiced by
conforming to that doctrine, *eo instanti* it ceased to act; that, as
the artisans and public servants were a superior order of the
State, the doctrine of civil rights did not apply to them; that
they might plead their privilege to disregard the constitutional as
well as the common- and statute-law provisions for the enforcement of the civil rights of any citizen, in case their business interests were favorably affected by depriving those citizens of their
civil rights, privileges, and immunities; and that such act was no
violation either of the Constitution or of the common law, but, on
the contrary, was privileged and licensed upon the express ground
that such action, in the judgment of the artisan and public
servant, tended to promote the general welfare of the public, and
private emolument in the public service. But he concluded at
that time to give no voice to these reflections. After a momentary pause in the conversation, he observed, that unless he altogether misunderstood the Chief Justice, the Supreme Court and

Congress had been placed by the framers of the Constitution and these amendments under the "noble necessity" of being true to their double trust; and, continuing their discourse, he expressed a desire to obtain a fuller comprehension of the meaning of the terms "civil rights," "immunities," and "privileges."

The Chief Justice inquired what works he had read. He replied, that he was not unfamiliar with the general doctrines contained in Cicero and Aristotle, Vattel, *Droit des Gens*, Lerminier, *Philosophie du Droit*, the Pandects, Grotius, Stoicesco, Gaius, Fœlix, Calvo (Ortolan), the provisions of the Civil Code of France, Zouche *De Jure*, Gutierrez, Codigos, *Derecho Civil Español*, Montesquieu, Savigny, Eichhorn, Schröder, Mommsen, Rudorf, and other treatises upon the philosophy of jurisprudence.

"These great authors," said the Chief Justice, "have prepared you for the course of study I was about to suggest. No foreigner can ever comprehend the meaning of the terms 'civil rights,' 'privileges,' and 'immunities,' in our republican acceptation of them, until he has spent his nights and days over Magna Charta, the Confirmatio Chartarum, the Statute of Treasons, the Petition of Right, the Habeas Corpus Act, the Bill of Rights, the Massachusetts Body of Liberties, the Declaration of Independence of the United States of America, the Declaration of the Virginia Bills of Rights, the Massachusetts Declaration of Rights, and that crowning glory among the memorable achievements of the human race, the Constitution of the United States, which, as you have already learned, bound in indissoluble union thirteen original States, and to-day is the central 'force which binds together the individual orbs of our stupendous American system,' superior, as experience has shown, to the wiles and forces of all enemies, within and without."

CHAPTER V.

" God has placed upon our head a diadem, and has laid at our feet power and wealth beyond definition or calculation. But we must not forget that we take these gifts upon the condition that justice and mercy shall hold the reins of power, and that the upward avenues of hope shall be free to all the people."—PRESIDENT HARRISON.

" The whole earth is the monument of illustrious men."—HUMBOLDT.

" Men of this character, stars of this lustre, are still stuck in good plenty up and down our hemisphere. The changes of the weather may sometimes hide but cannot extinguish them. Their short-lived obscurity is indeed their advantage; and by this we know what it is to want them and their influence. Their brightness is tried and distinguished from meteors and false fires. The regularity of their courses is more observed; and their glory, when it breaks out again, becomes more renewed."—CHOATE.

" I looked, and behold a pale horse; and his name that sat on him was Death."—REVELATION.

" And, again,—' I am apt to imagine that, were the imperfections of language, as the instrument of knowledge, more thoroughly weighed, a great many of the controversies that make such a noise in the world would of themselves cease; and the way to knowledge, and perhaps peace too, lie a great deal opener than it does.' "—TOOKE.

" I COULD but reflect, Mr. Chief Justice," said the student, " when recently witnessing the imposing ceremonies at the unveiling of the statue which now holds its silent vigil in the ocean highway of your great metropolis, how, by force of example, this constitutional bulwark of your civil rights is extending the great principles of American freedom over the whole globe; and how admirably the artistic genius of France has expressed the universal sentiment of the civilized world, when, as an enduring token of her heart-felt admiration for civil liberty, with an inspiration of sublime grandeur, she has im-

94

personated America, in the colossal statue of a goddess bearing on high a flaming torch, which she has fitly named 'Liberty Enlightening the World.'"

"I must warn you," said the Chief Justice, "in reference to your employment of terms, that, while you intended to say the 'bulwark of your civil liberty,' you said, 'civil rights': the former is to the latter as the genus is to the species, although the phrase 'civil rights' is in a manner *sui generis.* You will find my countrymen, especially in Georgia and Kansas, a little sensitive about it. When you have read the authors I have just recommended, I would suggest for your perusal the letters of Alexander Hamilton, John Jay, and James Madison, most of which appear in the 'Federalist,' and you might afterwards acquaint yourself with the letters of Helvidius, also by Madison, and of Pacificus, by Hamilton. Study these authors with the utmost deliberation along with a careful review of the contemporary debates upon the adoption of the Constitution, by the giants of those days, the glorious sovereigns of yore, who yet rule us from their tombs. To lay broad and deep your foundation of knowledge, go afterwards to those other storehouses of learning; and select from such statesmen, philosophers, patriots, and orators as Otis, Henry, Drayton, Warren, Livingston, Ames, Rutledge, Randolph, Hancock, Adams, Washington, Dickinson, Ramsay, Martin, Ellsworth, Morris, Harper, Emmet, Marshall, King, Bayard, Pinckney, Randolph, Dexter, John Quincy Adams, Clay, Burgess, Webster, Story, Wirt, Calhoun, Sergeant, Gaston, Hayne, Prentiss, and a host of others. When you have risen from this sumptuous entertainment, which, I promise you, will prove one of the most delightful feasts to be enjoyed in a scholar's lifetime, more charming than even Lucullus was wont to spread, and when you have taken leave of a company as illustrious as ever the sun shone upon, I shall ask your kind permission to discharge the last and most agreeable office I can perform, in presenting you in person to a most distinguished citizen of America, Mr. James G. Blaine, whose talents and fame are far from being circumscribed even by the broad limits of his own great country. If I may borrow from the bountiful imagery of Horace, this son of America, in his 'Review of the Events which led to the Political Revolution of 1860,' has completed, for his country and himself, 'a monument more lasting than bronze, and loftier than the royal elevation of the Pyramids, which neither the wasting shower, nor the raging north wind, nor the flight of seasons, shall be able to demolish.' Mr. Blaine, too, has been brave enough to measure out full and exact justice to his countrymen. In the work of this noble author you will find earnestness, sagacity, and manful worth, but no sectional rancor or bitterness. He has done justice to virtue, talent, courage, and patriotism, regardless of sectional lines. He has told the truth with studied candor and simplicity, and nowhere upon the pages of this fair history appear the footprints of the scavengers of the Civil War, with their long-accumulated stores of stale and loathsome calumnies; but he has left them to moulder in oblivion upon 'Carrion Heath.' On every page of the two volumes of his work—which, with exemplary modesty, the great author has presented to his country, under the simple title of 'Twenty Years of Congress'—you will find a substantial, systematic statement of events and facts of tragic interest fully unfolded, in which none of History's secrets are left unspoken. When you have diligently perused this faithful narrative of simple truths by this gentleman, statesman, and scholar, you will have advanced in your special study as far as American history goes, and will be thoroughly prepared by many noble paths to reach the goal, at which I understand you aim, of rightly discerning the legal status of the civil rights of citizens of the United States of African descent.

"Considerable time," continued the Chief Justice, "must be expended before you are prepared for the discussion of this grave subject, and before we meet again many varying phases of the question may be presented for determination to the Supreme Court and the State courts. May I suggest the expediency of your forming or giving expression to no opinion until you have diligently, patiently, and zealously completed the great course I have assigned you? When your work is done, I beg you will stand upon no ceremony, but seek me at once. The attitude of the labor-caste and the public servants towards the Constitutional Amendments may incline the courts of the country to disregard the narrow issues of special pleaders. I almost now foresee that in the near future grave political questions and weighty considerations of state may arise, rendering it as expedient in the civil-rights cases, as it was in the legal-tender decisions, to reverse our former rulings. Such action is often the result of political expediency, for public opinion may change as rapidly in the one as in the other case. This reversal of our former judgments may be upon those very issues which, as I have told you, our brethren at the bar framed with much adroitness to avoid the consideration of the constitutional construction of these amendments.

"Our discussion, though informal, has taken a much wider range," concluded the Chief Justice, "than I at first thought the subject might justify. The diversity and multiplicity of my labors render it impossible for me, without deliberate reflection, to state with accuracy the exact legal status of the civil rights of American citizens of African descent, but I have placed you in the way of preparation for the fullest attainment of this knowledge; and I look forward with pleasure to our future meeting, when you will have reached your conclusions and prepared your arguments in support of them."

After a momentary pause the Chief Justice—who

> "Walked thoughtful on the solemn, silent shore
> Of that vast ocean he must sail so soon,"

as if, indeed, approaching death had cast its shadow before the soul shortly to be released from the ligaments of the body—continued in a graver strain,—

"I often reflect with sorrow and astonishment on the little contests, disputes, debates, and competitions of mankind, when I consider the coming of that great day when all races must make their appearance together. It is the part of wisdom to provide beforehand for the emergencies of those we leave behind. We should strive to do our duty to those who come after us, before the veil of death is drawn over our senses. This thought habitually kept before us is well calculated to promote a state of preparedness for our setting out on the great voyage. The time of our departure from this world and entrance into the other is altogether uncertain; and, that they who come after you may have the full advantage of your labors, I would suggest that it would be your wiser course to prepare a work upon the subject of the Amendments. Present and future generations would thus be afforded the opportunity of viewing the questions relating thereto in the light in which they have presented themselves to a foreign jurist. In my opinion, it might be well for you to dedicate your labors to the judicial and political authorities of America, its clergy and public press. I must remind you, however, at the start, that this grave duty may in the end prove a cold, stern, uninviting thing, but it is one of those duties which are unavoidable and unimpeachable. It is an undertaking, also, which requires, as Lord Bacon once said, ' no patrons but Truth and Reason.' I need not warn you, for every man of wit perceives, that of all creatures in the universe the public is the most fickle and ungrateful. I most earnestly hope you will immediately set about your labors. Reform is the work of time. It required in free and enlightened America a violent, bloody revolution to eradicate the national error and deep-seated abuses of slavery. At the close of the Civil War the nation immediately embodied in the Constitution these very amendments, the proudest work of her power and wisdom. A quarter of a century has scarcely elapsed since their adoption, and yet some of our citizens, in the pride and narrowness of their understandings, stand ready to trample beneath their feet these manifold titles of the country's glory. Pardon my freedom in making another suggestion. The oracular, *ex-cathedra* style of discussion will not prove acceptable to Americans. Our public is used to severe analysis and solid argumentation. The majority of our citizens entertain no opinions which they would not at any time willingly exchange for exact knowledge and wise counsel, which they well know converge the rays of truth as lenses collect the scattered force of the solar beams. And yet you may fairly anticipate for your work at the outset an unfavorable reception. Innovations upon received customs and modes of thinking are always unpopular. They are regarded by many politicians as the visionary speculations of impractical theorists, and are always the lawful prey of those critics whose principal occupation is 'looking into everything and seeing nothing.' Every attempt at the removal from the national canvas, of the discoloration of slavery, will be sure to meet with the opposition of those who love its old faults.

"It was, I think, Milton who said, 'Long is the way and hard, that out of hell leads up to light.' The noisy, impotent, hot-brained sciolists of this generation, who have no reverence for the Constitution, require a scourge of merciless severity, for their pride and presumption are as great as their ignorance ; but your work is independent of their judgment or their edicts. It is also, I think, within its legitimate province, if you discover their internal monitors asleep, to touch and awaken the slumberous consciences of those ministers of our state, who have sworn with their mouths but not with their hearts to support the Constitution ; and remember that just in proportion as your work strengthens the hands of constitutional law, it tightens the cords which restrain despotic dominion. As your undertaking is in behalf of all races and classes, it deserves the gratitude, and in due season will reap the applause, of the nation."

"No honor," replied the student, "could be conferred on me, which I should value more highly than the kind consideration you have had the goodness to show me. I thank you heartily, sir, and I shall, so far as my poor ability extends, follow your instructions to the letter. I trust, indeed, the good fortune may be mine to meet you again in the near future. Until that time, I shall pray God to give you, for your own and your country's sake, strength and opportunity to continue to play well your great and noble part as Chief Justice of the United States."

CHAPTER VI.

" Notwithstanding the softness which it now assumes, and the care with which it conceals its giant proportions beneath the deceitful drapery of sentiment, when it next appears before you it may show itself with a sterner countenance and in more awful dimensions. It is, to speak the truth, sir, a power of colossal size,—if, indeed, it be not an abuse of language to call it by the gentle name of a power."—PINCKNEY.

" Sir, this was a single arch; it is rapidly becoming a combination of arches, and where the centre now is, whether in Kentucky or in Pennsylvania, or where at any given time it will be, might be very difficult to tell."—SERGEANT.

" I am not well versed in history, but I will submit to your recollection, whether liberty has been destroyed most often by the licentiousness of the people or by the tyranny of rulers. I imagine, sir, you will find the balance on the side of tyranny. Happy will you be, if you miss the fate of those nations who, omitting to resist their oppressors, or negligently suffering their liberty to be wrested from them, have groaned under intolerable despotism."—PATRICK HENRY.

" I conceive that the object of the discussion now before us is, whether democracy or despotism be most eligible."—MARSHALL.

" What does reason, what does argument avail, when party spirit presides? Subject your bench to the influence of this spirit, and justice bids a final adieu to your tribunals."—BAYARD.

" Ye gentle graces, if any such there be who preside over human actions, how must ye weep at the viciousness of man!"—PAINE.

" But my whole endeavor is to resolve the conscience, and to show, as near as I can, what in this controversy the heart is to think, if it will follow the light of sound and sincere judgment, without either cloud of prejudice or mist of passionate affection."—HOOKER.

" The American people owe it to themselves, and to the cause of free government, to prove, by their establishments for the advancement and diffusion of knowledge, that their political institutions, which are attracting observation from every quarter, and are respected as models by the new-born States in our own hemisphere, are as favorable to the intellectual

100

and moral improvement of man as they are conformable to his individual and social rights."—MADISON.

> " This is true liberty, when free-born men,
>   Having to advise the public, may speak free ;
>   Which he who can, and will, deserves high praise ;
>   Who neither can, nor will, may hold his peace :
>   What can be juster in the state than this?"—EURIPIDES.

" According to Johnson, 'the glory of every people arises from its authors:' yet our literary men are less honored than people of title; the writers of our leading journals are unknown ; and we see much more respect shown to a Rothschild, or a Baring, than to our Faradays and our Owens."—SPENCER.

" Such ministers will not suffer the law to be made the backsword of Justice which cuts only one way."—BOLINGBROKE.

" ' How do you find the government of the Great Mogul?' said the counsellor. 'Abominable,' answered the Brahmin: 'how can you expect a state to be happily governed by Tartars? Our rajahs, our omras, and our nabobs are very contented, but the citizens are by no means so ; and millions of citizens are something.' "—VOLTAIRE.

" Remember there was a fraud, and a very gross one, committed by one party or the other. If the State of Louisiana chose Kellogg and the other candidates on the Hayes ticket for presidential electors, and the Democratic politicians, knowing this, did, nevertheless, deny the truth and fabricate a false return for Tilden, which they persisted to the last in trying to pass for a true one, they were a combination of most redemptionless rogues ; and it will be recorded, as an aggravation of their crime, that, when the righteous majority of the Electoral Commission crushed out their falsehood, they turned about and, with calumnious accusations, charged their own guilt upon their innocent opponents. The converse of these propositions is also true. If the Tilden electors were duly chosen by the people, and the Republican leaders in and out of the State altered the returns, falsified the records, and constituted a counterfeit Electoral College, whereby the people of the State and the Union were cheated out of the President whom they had legally elected by a large majority, then it is only anticipating history to say that all who aided, abetted, and encouraged that offence ought to be classed among the worst malefactors of the age."—BLACK.

As iron sharpens iron, scholar sharpens scholar, so this dialogue had quickened the vision of the student. The love of study, ever a passion with him, received a fresh enthusiasm and derived new vigor from the daily exercise of his faculties in the

new field opened up before him by the Chief Justice. His mind
became more enlarged and liberal from contact with the lofty
types to which he had been introduced. There was an unspeak-
able charm in the life of this whole-souled student, pursuing the
even tenor of his way. He resolved to strengthen the sunken
piers, and erect a massive foundation destined for a bridge over
which all races might travel with safety. His studies, like
Circe's cup, bewitched him, and "his soul, like a star, dwelt
apart." From this his world of thought he banished all the
pleasures of idleness, and, possessed with a feeling of inspiration,
he seemed to become for the time being one of that illustrious
company of martyrs, statesmen, philosophers, patriots, and soldiers, to the study of whose grand teachings and deeds the Chief
Justice had kindly recommended him. He spent many hours,
days, and months in examining their luminous treatment of civil
liberty. In his mind's eye he saw, from day to day, these
mighty warriors of American liberty, as they seemed to sweep
along through the dim vista of the past. They grew as familiar
to him as the images of living men.

He realized the fact that their priceless stores of knowledge
and experience had been bequeathed to the world as a precious
heirloom ; that, as a wise parent in his will divides his property
among his children, so our divinely-inspired forefathers had by
the Constitution entailed civil liberty not only upon those then in
being, but in perpetuity upon countless millions yet unborn ; and
that their sons, who, inheriting under the Constitution, in their
day had enjoyed the royal patrimony of freedom, being charged
with the sacred constitutional obligation of preserving and transmitting it to their posterity, had left three codicils, the Thirteenth, Fourteenth, and Fifteenth Amendments, which, sealed in
blood, had been intended to secure to all mankind, as lawful
heirs and children of one Father, that noble birthright and
heritage. Throughout all his labors the one beautiful countenance, which had so early impressed him when unveiled by the
side of the sea, alone attracted the gaze of the ambitious student ;
and, as he sat in the solitude of study and reflection, he desired
and sought only the glorious manifestations of that truth which
her noble image portrays.

After many delightful nights and days spent in searching for the vantage-ground of truth, our indefatigable student descended from that clearer, rarer, and more serene atmosphere which surrounds the exalted temple of the wise, to launch himself into the madding crowd, and, with spirit purged and mental vision clarified, to discern more distinctly " the errors and wanderings, and mists and tempests in the vale below."

Not only had he completed the course the Chief Justice had marked out, but he had also carefully reviewed from first to last all the civil-rights decisions. This tour of inspection seemed to him to lead through a bewildering maze of crooked passages lying underneath the Temple of Justice, where the bones of its illustrious dead were deposited. From this labyrinth it was next to impossible to extricate himself. But once free from the vague, crude, and superficial opinions, colored by the many-hued prejudices of sectional feeling displayed in the cases, and having made good his escape from the subterranean passages which he styled the Funeral Departments of Justice, our student concentrated his energies on a close and steady pursuit of his object. He resolved to omit nothing essential to a clear under-standing of civil rights ; and, before reaching any conclusions of his own, he determined to consult all the available oracles of wisdom, and to present whatever truth he might glean from them to the consideration of the enlightened and statesmanlike understanding of the Chief Justice. He wisely concluded first to hold converse with the foremost thinkers, the real rulers of all nations, those calm and placid commanders who, when the strained masts begin to quiver, and its torn canvas flutters in the gale, safely guide the gallant ship of state through the winds and the waves of political factions.

In conversation with his familiar friends the student always spoke of the leaders of the press as the Napoleons of Peace, from whose proud dominions of intellect the winds of heaven daily scattered the seeds of science and truth, from which sprang trees of knowledge, like the banyan's branches, dropping shoots into the ground, and taking root only to bring forth new stocks, until their foliage encircled the globe. He thought al-ways with the greatest reverence of that lofty race of solitary

sages, eternally shut up in the closet of the editorial rooms. He
desired to learn of the wise men who from their own brains
seemed to materialize intellect and argument for the rulers of
the nation, and who were looked to for daily sustenance as
parents are by their children. Yet he was studious to avoid the
least contact with those feeble, maudlin, snivelling bits of frothy
daily vituperation, who now and then stole cold scraps from the
feast of learning which these bountiful providers sometimes
spread. He desired to hold communion only with the successors
of those lawful sovereigns of the journalistic world whose long,
fierce struggle for mankind had maintained civil rights as the
foundation of the American state. He wanted first to learn what
judgment these noble guardians of freedom pronounced over
the repudiation of civil rights ; above all, he waited with impatient anxiety to learn what light the Argus-eyes of the press
had discovered, and in what direction this hundred-handed
Briareus, whose proud conquest was liberty and whose offspring
was civilization, would hereafter lead the vanguard of emancipated thought.

Our student was courteously received by all the American
gentlemen whom he sought, and, after extended discussion with
the leaders of public opinion, he could discover no marked diversity among them in their attitude towards the question of the
civil rights of the adopted citizens. One of the profoundest
representatives of the press, whose treatment of the schemes of
political men seemed to our student to resemble a Bengal tiger
playing with mice, voiced the prevailing sentiment of his brethren of the press when, in explanation of its apathy upon the
subject of civil rights, he replied, with playful irony,—

" Each of our hands is as full as any ordinary school-master's.
The big and little children who are under our instruction cannot
be kept in order or under any discipline without continual individual watching. All of them are more or less engaged in a
variety of monkey-tricks for the applause of their fellows ; and
no sooner are their unruly sessions closed, and the doors locked
on them, than the surrounding country, which is their play-
ground, begins to resound with their canine eloquence.

" The management of the tariff, labor, land, and various other

schools that are being daily evolved," he continued, " imposes
the utmost vigilance upon the press, which has no means of dividing its higher duties.   In spite of the utmost caution, many
great and small offences, legal, executive, legislative, and judicial,
even now need the rod of correction ; but the wrong-doers often
make good their escape from deserved chastisement, by reason of
the multiplicity of the offenders and of their offences, which an ordinary lifetime would not afford the opportunity of investigating.
The many rods now in pickle are soaking in the brine, but are not
yet saline enough for those big scholars who are so far advanced
as to know better than the little ones, whom they call their con-
stituents, and upon whom they have the cunning to charge the
responsibility primarily resting upon their own inexcusable violation or non-observance of the fundamental rules which they
well know have been made for the government of all."

Continuing in the same caustic vein, the great reviewer laugh-
ingly exclaimed, " You cannot imagine how backward, considering their years and stature, some of these big ones are.   It seems
to me that in exact proportion to their imposing exterior is the
selfish littleness of their interior.   You do not know what a
thankless task it is to teach some of these plodding dunces, nor
the time it takes to lecture one set of offenders in private, and
another in public, and that, too, often without any result.   We
newspaper men thus have our hands full.   Providence will help
civil rights when it is strong enough to help itself.   The press
presents a variety of teachers, called organs, and each is charged
with the responsibility of keeping together its own flock, which
is scattered over a wide extent of country.

" You must see the injustice," he continued, " of fastening
upon the press what the Supreme Court charges Congress with
neglecting and what you charge the courts and the pleaders
generally with avoiding, by issues as feigned in substance as
John Doe *v.* Richard Roe was in form.   The daily and weekly
journals, the monthly and quarterly magazines, are beacon-lights
which guide the wandering minds of millions, and their lamps
must be kept trimmed and bright.

" Besides, you must bear in mind, that we have each our separate hospitals, wards, and sick-list, and that extreme caution

for the special and general welfare of the members of the various classes must be observed in the diagnoses of their complicated diseases and in their treatment. Sometimes our judicial doctors violently dispute about their prescriptions, which they call their ' opinions.' In one notable case we called in two consulting physicians, and, wonderful to relate, the patient, a full-grown sick man of the Republican class, nicknamed ' Legal Tender,' [1] was enabled to throw away the crutches upon which he had hobbled for years, simply by reversing the old-fashioned consti- tutional treatment, and substituting the new-fangled Republican materia medica.

" The Supreme Court decided that an obligation for the payment of money can be discharged by tender of notes or bills of credit of the government created as a means appropriate and defensi- ble as an exercise of the war-power, or of the power resulting from an aggregate of powers, to act by any means not prohibited in the Constitution for the preservation of the government; and that, too, in spite of those provisions of the Constitution which forbid the taking of private property without compensation; holding that the exigency to justify its exercise is a question for Congress and not for courts to determine, and that it makes no difference that its exercise may incidentally affect the value of private contracts.

" We had a still more dangerous pupil in Mr. Tilden; his class-mates called him ' Uncle Sammy;' since his death we all revere him as the ' Sage of Greystone.' When standing at the very head of his class he was taken down by a violent illness in the fall of 1876. Dr. Chandler, the regular family physician, called into consultation fifteen other doctors, who were styled the Electoral Commission. These doctors were to decide whether Republican or Democratic prescriptions were the safer to be given to the patient. It was determined that those very cele- brated physicians, Drs. Clifford, Miller, Field, and Strong, should consult with Dr. Davis, a regular Democratic practitioner, but an unlooked-for event summoned Dr. Davis, who was a surgeon of national repute, to another field of duty. Dr.

---

[1] 12 Wall. 457; id. 604; 15 id. 195; 110 U. S. 421.

Bradley, who was called in during Dr. Davis's enforced absence, agreed with the majority, that it was the wiser course to hypnotize the patient. During the trance Dr. Chandler introduced hypodermic injections of Republican concoction, the effect of which was that the patient expired in great agony, on the 5th of March, 1877.

"Imagine, if you can," he continued, "the grave responsibilities we are often obliged to assume. Surgeon-General Chandler and the Republican consulting physicians said, that Mr. Tilden's ailment was mortification from corruption, and that the herb never grew which by any possibility could cure him. The Democrats said that the Republican diagnosis was faulty, and that the noble patient had no fatal disease, but that the Republican prescription, like Lucretia Borgia's, was deadly and poisonous. While committees of visiting physicians were making their report upon the patient's condition, the disease proved contagious; it spread over all the country, and at one time it looked as if a national surgical operation was inevitable.

"An investigation of the causes which had brought about this grave condition became an imperative duty. After laborious researches, our leaders reported that several members of the Electoral Commission were obsessed and others were *hypnotists ;* that by the induction of a trance they could obtain as complete sway over their adversaries as a magnetizer who deprives his victim of his mind without leaving any trace of force upon his body ; that the press met similar obstacles, in its analysis of this strange power, as the chemist and physicist encounter in tracing animal magnetism in molecular solid, fluid, or gas; that this *occult* force resident in certain members of this commission was not unknown to scientists, ancient or modern ; that Kapila called it 'akasa'; the Theosophists, 'astral fluid'; the Biologists, 'psycholasm'; Baron von Reichenbach, 'brain-waves' or 'psych-aura'; Cope, 'æsthetophone' or 'bearer of consciousness'; and Coues, 'biogen'; that the presence of this '*nervaura*', in judicial, legislative, or political hypnotists, enabled them to become national mind-readers, clairvoyant, clairaudient, and to place the public into a somnambulistic trance whenever they desired to control a presidential election or to usurp unconstitutional powers; that, like the tinkling of the silver bell of the Theosophist, the American political hypnotist, by a Code of Signals at Washington, can alter at will an election return; and that the telepathic *rationale* by which Hayes appeared as President, and Tilden as a presidential ghost, was scarcely less marvellous than the occurrences reported by Madame Blavatsky or the London Society for Psychical Research in 'Phantasms of the Living.'"

CHAPTER VII.

"In short, sir, you are of opinion with Bayes,—'What the devil does the plot signify, except to bring in fine things?' "—WALTER SCOTT.

"The old notions of republican simplicity are fast wearing away."—STORY.

"Give me liberty, the greatest of all earthly blessings, and you may take everything else. But I am fearful I have lived long enough to become an old-fashioned fellow."—PATRICK HENRY.

"Like Alciphron we swing in air and darkness, and know not whither the wind blows us."—PUTNAM'S MAGAZINE.

"Others have applied to philosophy for the spirit which should give fruit to their labors. To facts they have united speculative views, instructive lessons, political and philosophical truths, enlivening their narrative by the language which they have made it speak, and the ideas which it has enabled them to suggest."—D'AUBIGNÉ.

"When that ancient equality was laid aside, and instead thereof ambition and violence took place, tyrannical forms of government started up, and fixed themselves in many countries."—MILTON.

"There can be no greater solecism in government than a failure of justice."—HALIFAX.

"I hope I may be pardoned, if these discoveries inclined me a little to abate of that profound veneration which I am naturally apt to pay to persons of high rank, who ought to be treated with the utmost respect due to their sublime dignity, by us their inferiors."—SWIFT.

"So close does falsehood approach to truth that the wise man would do well not to trust himself on the narrow ledge."—CICERO.

"A state is a corporation armed for the maintenance of peace. . . Its existence is bound up with all the other corporations; it lives and moves in them; they are its natural organs; and as soon as the state, whether with despotic or anarchical views, attempts to impede the natural functions of these organs, to disturb or derange their peculiar sphere of action, it impairs its own vital powers, and prepares the way sooner or later for its own destruction."—SCHLEGEL.

109

"All the space between my mind and the mind of God is full of truths waiting to be crystallized into law for the government of the masses."— T. Parker.

"In this country all men and all classes are equal. No man can lawfully say to another, 'Stand aside, I am holier than thou,' and push him from his place on the platform of the Constitution. Superior sanctity is not a thing to be safely believed : it is easily simulated ; it is often false ; and when it comes into politics, it is almost universally put on to cover some base and malicious design. The Scribes and the Pharisees were hypocrites."—J. Black.

"It is true, also, that court sycophants and party hacks have many times written pamphlets, and perhaps large volumes, to show that those whom they serve should be allowed to work out their bloody will upon the people. No abuse of power is too flagrant to find its defenders among such servile creatures. Those butchers' dogs, that feed upon garbage and fatten upon the offal of the shambles, are always ready to bark at whatever interferes with the trade of their masters."—Id.

"One melodious synopsis of man and nature."—Carlyle.

"Human error walks in a cycle, and reappears at intervals."—Id.

"All, too, will bear in mind this sacred principle, that, though the will of the majority is in all cases to prevail, that will, to be rightful, must be reasonable ; that the minority possess their equal rights, which equal law must protect, and to violate would be oppression."—Jefferson.

"I would hide the frailties and deformities of my political mother, and place her virtues and beauties in the most advantageous light. This was my sincere endeavor, in those many discourses I had with that monarch, although it unfortunately failed of success."—Swift.

————————

The student was somewhat puzzled to discover what relevancy the patients of political parties had to the question of civil rights, and the sarcastic reviewer, seeing a shade of doubt flit across his countenance, smilingly said,—

"You must pardon my mixed metaphors and apparent digressions. I wanted to explain to you that, if there is a sick patient in this country, in our opinion, it is the civil-rights man ; but, you see, he does not yet belong to any of the old nor is he a member of either of the modern great parties of the country, and therefore he cannot legitimately share in the treatment practised by their moderators. One party, for the time being, has placed him in quarantine, in one or another of its judicial harbors, to await the disinfecting process, or the expediences of the future. The other has banished him into an infirmary called the State courts. There he will either die an unnatural death, or if ever under their tyrannical treatment he recovers his health, he will be permitted without further molestation to take up his bed and walk, only because his recovery will be universally accepted as a miraculous interposition of Providence. The historical occurrences which I have related were intended to convince you that, although a great party may not lack defenders to maintain and perpetuate its power by thinly-disguised invasions of the Constitution itself, yet we must rationally anticipate, that the reverence of the entire American people for their Constitution will not always tolerate gross violations of its sacred provisions in favor of the civil liberty and civil rights of seven millions of American citizens of African descent. I could almost predict, so many are the new factors and forces which are asserting themselves as our civilization advances, that in the near future the political necessities of the rival factions will oblige their leaders to make the tardy yet marvellous discovery (to borrow the phraseology with which politicians commonly veil their ascent to power), ' that the advancement of the best interests of the nation imperatively demands that those salutary Constitutional Amendments, securing the civil rights of their fellow-citizens of African descent, should be enforced by all the power of the nation, executive, legislative, and judicial.'

" In my mind's eye," he continued, " I can see inserted in the Democratic platform, in the near future, the following plank : ' That the Trust Gorgons, Labor tyrants, common carriers, hotel-keepers, proprietors of places for public resort, and school commissioners, with whatever divine prerogatives the English common law may have endowed them, are the servants and not the masters of the great body of their wage-earning fellow-citizens ; that the prerogatives of public servants are subordinate and not paramount to the Constitution ; and that the decisions of the courts to the contrary are the result of balefully intolerant race-prejudice; that the patient endurance of those tax-payers, who are attached to the principles of the Constitution, cannot be sufficiently commended, and must be immediately expiated by the adoption of amendments to the several Constitutions of the States, or a further amendment to the Federal Constitution and to the Judiciary Act practically unseating the present color-line judges.' This legislation may be enacted upon some pretext, such as increase of business, or some technical justification. Some future convention I foresee pledging itself to fill the State courts with judges known to be free from race-prejudices, and to elevate some of the colored race to the bench, and re-solving ' that the majority of the present court is called upon by the party to exert their wisdom to the best of their preju-dices, and to enforce the civil rights of our American citizens of African descent;' and that a ' committee be appointed to frame State laws for the punishment of any future repudiator of these Constitutional Amendments, notwithstanding any quackery, cloudy subterfuge, jugglery, legal pretext, or flimsy refinements of law whatsoever, that may be pleaded in mitigation or justifi-cation of such high crime and misdemeanor.' "

The student laughed heartily at this ingenious farrago of sense and nonsense ; confessing, however, that it bore a very striking resemblance to the resolutions of representative statesmen.

" But may I not venture to inquire," he responded, " whether you cannot draw another picture equally diverting in the case of other political assemblies? Is your gift of prophecy unique, and exclusively confined to the workings of one great party?"

" By no means," was the reply; " without pausing to consider from what direction the bird takes flight, we shoot folly as it flies. A moment since, a fanciful conception of the great party of civil liberty and civil rights flitted across my brain. I can see in the act of rising, decorated with a strand of white lilies, a politician of the Mugwump faith, with a narrow, angular, highly-arched forehead. He approaches the speaker's stand, with a Pecksniffian curl upon his bloodless lips; and in a small, shrill voice, he declares ' that, as for civil rights, he begs permission to say, that upon this, as upon those other grave national issues, the tariff, trust, and monopoly questions, he proposes to follow the policy of negation; that the present attitude of the leaders of all parties upon these issues is quite mixed; that civil-service reform is a more important factor in politics, and a more favored subject than civil rights; that the position of the leaders upon this question has long ago convinced him that the greatest factor in modern civilization is the independent voter; that party-platforms are a mere substitute of words for things, a cloaking of the ignorance and aspirations of the leaders under a variety of ingeniously-devised word-fabrics of more colors than Joseph's coat, which those unfortunate and usually uninformed persons called *party* voters have the simplicity to regard as the Delphic oracles of the political campaign.' For these reasons, he submits to the convention the propriety of permitting the much-vexed civil rights to repose in that mausoleum of all dead promises, where the Fourteenth Amendment to the Constitution lies buried. He understands that the courts of final resort have determined the amendments to be ' self-executive ;' that this is assuredly a practi cal interment of Civil Rights with the most solemn and splendid ceremonies, after preparation extending over nearly a quarter of a century. ' If,' he argues, ' the Amendments permit no intervention of the courts, although every citizen in the State violates their letter and spirit, then, unless the States attempt to galvanize new life into the question by unfriendly legislation, which these very Amendments inhibit, the resurrection of that which is believed to be stone-dead can be productive of no good result to that race, or its baptismal sponsor, the Republican party ; that, although the nation's covenant has been sealed with the white and the black man's blood, yet surely the courts, if it so please them, can determine that our public servants are at liberty, if it be more agreeable to their interests or to the prejudices of their patrons, to override the spirit and letter of that solemn compact. That civil rights have since these decisions lost much of their importance in the eyes of the cultivated descendants of those who risked their all to rescue the nation from the jaws of bankruptcy, by accepting bonds at one-half their face value with a legal rate of interest, and with only the collateral security of the national credit in pawn,—a liberality which was repaid by the advance of the stock. That the principal of the debt is safe and above par, and that therefore these Amendments can no longer be regarded from their original stand-point, as a nation's guarantee of civil rights and civil liberty to every American citizen, but that they now afford agreeable material for curious scholastic inquiries or the elegant amusement of statesmen, similar to those which exercise the learned in their disputes concerning the Pandects or Jus Gentium.' Thanking the convention for its kind indulgence of his protracted remarks, the polished Athenian resumes his seat, without a voice of applause from the cold and critical audience, who thought, with Bassanio, that the wordy orator had spoken 'an infinite deal of nothing, and that his reasons were like two grains of wheat hid in a bushel of chaff.' "

No sooner had the great intellectual gymnast cut off this mellifluous flow of oratory, than his countenance assumed a more sedate expression, as he said to the student,—

"These gloomy extremes may appear to exceed the folly of any deliberative body, but I assure you they represent the average wisdom of the every-day convention. You can judge as well as I what the chances are of either party's action upon this subject. I have sometimes doubted the wisdom of making light of the gathering political clouds. Although there may be monotony in the repetition of this truth, yet it is always the part of wisdom to keep it before us. Eternal vigilance has been truly said to be the price of liberty, and wise men of all shades of opinion should look well to the political part which the American citizens of African descent are to assume in the coming struggle. But our leaders are often the last to anticipate and act in advance of grave results, which are thus often precipitated upon the country when it is too late to avert their consequences. The people are oftener the alarmists, and, like storm-petrels, give the warning to our fair-weather commanders.

"I think I see a brewing storm," he continued, in a ponderous, meditative way, with his broad forehead and piercing gray eye turned towards the sky. "I think I see a brewing storm, that by its hollow rustling in the leaves, foretells a tempest and a blustering day. When all the party convoys weigh anchor and set sail, new political elements may be loosened in the fierce tempest which follows. Great naval commanders may be transfixed each on his own rock, mighty lieutenants overthrown like trees, and popular opinion driven around like a whirligig. The color-line discriminators, who, you say, are now obliged to conceal their hostility to the Constitution under the *reasonable rules* of the common law respecting public servants, which I own are merely a tissue-paper mask for racial prejudice, will disband when the courts, with stern impartiality, rebuke their impudent attempts under this dupery to repudiate this Amendment. There are other and more portentous enemies than the color-caste, whose aim is not the limitation of the civil rights of any one class, but the overthrow of the civil rights of all classes, by substituting the trust values of the plutocrats or of the communistic principle of the State for the individual. These peculiar theorists, both of whom equally make the individual nothing, and the plutocrats or the State the reservoir, and eventually the representatives of plutocracy or communism or the national government a distributing depot for all civil rights, have proved the most formidable enemies of civil liberty. The history of the decline and fall of liberty everywhere proves that whenever this same horde of barbarians, differing through all ages only in surrounding conditions and in the assumption of mere names, have first invaded her fair dominions, after devouring and destroying her substance, they have reared alternately the thrones of anarchy and of despotism upon her ruins, and then, in the sheer helplessness of despair, have raised to royal power some bloody butcher tyrant or usurping despot."

" But," interrupted the student, " are not these public enemies whom you fear only a handful ?"

" It is evident," replied the journalist, " that this topic requires other treatment than the opportunities of a cursory conversation can afford. The subject is as illimitable as the universal history of the government of mankind when it is carried on not by fixed constitutional laws, but by the temporary substitution of human expedients.

" To unfold my meaning," continued the journalist, " would require volumes, but I may disprove your generalization by particularization. John Brown was a convict, and expired on the gallows. The Abolitionists originally did not number a corporal's guard.　The French Revolution was set in motion by the spawn of the sewers.　Without the previous environments of France these vermin would have festered and perished in their hiding-places.　But danger lurks also in a country conditioned like ours, and this danger consists in a mixed popular vote, in party-unions, and in combinations, formed for one object, under altered conditions becoming allied to others, which charlatans, for their own purposes, to borrow a modern political phrase, may 'capture.' By the political laws of natural attraction, the various quasi-political associations tend towards each other, and, like atoms propelled by natural affinities, attract and are attracted, each to its neighbor.　The lesser political body gravitates towards the larger, just as cattle herd together in the fields.　Every sportsman knows that a stray bunch of the infinite variety of trashy wild ducks invariably will 'decoy to' and light amidst a promiscuous 'rick' of canvas-backs, red-heads, bald-pates, mallards, or black-heads, and all of them will soon unite in one mighty chorus of quack, quack, quack.　The frogs observe and are governed by the same law, as their multitudinous self-complacent croaking abundantly proves.　There is an analogy between the gravitation of the political masses and the gravitation of matter which no reflecting mind can fail to recognize. Political parties gravitate towards the centre which attracts them by a sort of centripetal force.　Tariffism, free-tradeism, monopolism, trustism, socialism, raceism, stateism, landism, laborism, repudiating-amendmentism, public-servantism, and sectionalism,—each and all illustrate the centrifugal force or tendency of their adherents, to recede from the centre which is the Constitution.　These knots represent millions of voters.　Political philosophers cannot always comprehend the future varied bearings of the ballot-elements.　If they did, they could, like astronomers, calculate the time and condition of a political eclipse; their perceptions would grow so large that they might peer into ages of futurity.　The grand panorama of American history has not yet been unfolded.　There are many factors at work, from the lowest type of the socialistic labor-element, whose weapons are bombs and dynamite, to higher forms, which generate daily literature for the masses,—sincere zealots, no doubt, and therefore the more dangerous navigators, because incapable of taking the deeper soundings of the sea of civil liberty. They are daily steering millions of the hardy sons of toil, in the way they themselves would veer the ship of state, to dangerous coasts, strewn in by-gone centuries with the wrecks of civil liberty.

" It is true," he continued, " the general press follow in the broad deep channels as did our forefathers, who sounded all the depths and shoals mapped out in the Constitution for the pres-ervation of our American civil rights. But I also think, with you, that the courts, which ought to be calm and collected and in command when we are at sea, should not, in the face of such a multitudinous array of formidable public enemies of high and low degree as is daily gathering, be unguarded, or give any loose or equivocal construction to these Amendments, which construc-tions in the end may come back to plague the inventors. The descendants of the freedmen, whose birthrights as citizens you charge to-day are openly sold for a mess of pottage, may yet be called upon, as were their forefathers in the days just gone by, to stand between the Constitution and its ruthless invaders, ' to shield it and save it, or perish there too.' [1]

" In the mysterious workings of Providence, to whose inscru-table ways the wisdom of man is foolishness, it may transpire that the present agitation of the constitutional enforcement of civil rights in favor of American citizens of African descent, may be another instrumentality for the establishment of civil rights as distinguished from the communistic principle of equality of right in property and from the despotism of trusts, upon a solid constitutional foundation, for all our citi-zens, irrespective of the color-line caste, prejudice, or previous condition. The time has arrived when it is no longer desirable

---

[1] It is a curious matter of judicial history that the Supreme Court of the United States, in the famous Slaughter-House cases, 16 Wall. 36, use the following language : " When the armies of freedom found themselves upon the soil of slavery, they could do nothing less than free the poor victims whose enforced servitude was the foundation of the quarrel ; and, when hard pressed in the contest, these men (for they proved themselves men in that terrible crisis) offered their services and were accepted by thousands to aid in suppressing the unlawful rebellion."

that any class of citizens should be allowed to hoist their colors and fly their anti-constitutional flags in the face of the courts. Higher considerations than the significant factor of the colored man's vote and of his well-known loyalty to the Constitution and institutions of the country ought to influence the American people in the enforcement of the constitutional rights of all American citizens. It is to be remembered that we are manufacturing by the million each year, out of foreign material, citizens who do not regard the Constitution as the central orb around which we and they must continue to revolve, or fly off into chaos.

" Our Constitution, sir, was not the gift of man : it was the grant of Heaven. It is the natural luminary for whose rays the world should long. I confess it makes my cheeks burn when, in the warm radiance of its ever-beaming light, I see a meagre, ghastly, shrivelled relic of the Color-Line, or Squatter-Sovereign of Property Equality, political Pharisee of Trust, illiterate vagabonds and demagogues of Labor, sitting upon that sacred instrument, so dear to every American heart, and with brazen effrontery holding aloft their black, red, or mixed colors, with such mottoes as ' Our rules and regulations are paramount to the Constitution,' ' The right of private property is lodged in the State as a public trust, and land is the only public debtor,' ' To the chain-gang with co-educationists,' ' Human nature is human nature.' "

CHAPTER VIII.

" In all the declarations and allusions of the Eternal Truth this present earthly nature is spoken of as the battle-place of invisible powers, the debatable ground on which the two armies of good and evil spirits and elements are posted in hostile array against each other and perpetually coming into collision."—SCHLEGEL.

" The shadow of a dream."—SHAKESPEARE.

" In dreams we are true poets: we create the persons of the drama; we give them appropriate figures, faces, costumes; they are perfect in their organs, attitudes, manners; moreover, they speak after their own characters, not ours; and we listen with surprise to what they say."—EMERSON.

" A jewel in a ten-times-barred chest
Is a bold spirit in a loyal breast."—SHAKESPEARE.

"I have a thousand spirits in one breast, to answer twenty thousand such as you."—ID.

" Let us fear the native mightiness and fate of him."—ID.

" You fools,
I and my fellows are ministers of fate."—ID.

" A figure of sufficient impressiveness; not lovely to the man-milliner species, nor pretending to be so; massive stature; big massive head, of somewhat leonine aspect, 'evident workshop and store-house of a vast treasury of natural parts.' "—CARLYLE.

" And forasmuch as I suppose some strangers, who happily shall chance to read these writings, may wonder what should be the reason that when my style is diverted to show those things that were done in Rome I relate nothing but of seditions, taverns, and such like base matters, I will summarily touch the causes hereof."—AMIANE.

" These are the periods when fair-weather philosophers are willing to venture out, and hazard a little for the general good. But the history of human nature is so contrary to all this, that almost all improvements are made after the bitterest resistance, and in the midst of tumults and civil violence,—the worst period at which they can be made, compared to which

119

any period is eligible, and should be seized hold of by the friends of salutary reform."—SYDNEY SMITH.

"If this republic," said he, with great earnestness, "is not made to stand on solid principle, it has no honest foundation, and the Father of all men will still shake it to its centre. If we have not yet been sufficiently scourged for our national sin to teach us to do justice to all God's creatures, without distinction of race or color, we must expect the still more heavy vengeance of an offended Father, still increasing his afflictions, as he increased the severity of the plagues of Egypt until the tyrant consented to do justice, and when that tyrant repented of his reluctant consent and attempted to re-enslave the people, he filled the Red Sea with broken chariots and drowned horses, and strewed the shores with the corpses of men."—STEVENS.

" 'In what state, under what dominion, would you like to live?' said the counsellor. 'Under any but my own,' said his companion, 'and I have found many Siamese, Tonquinese, Persians, and Turks who have said the same.' 'But, once more,' said the European, ' what state would you choose?' The Brahmin answered, 'THAT IN WHICH THE LAWS ALONE ARE OBEYED.' 'That is an odd answer,' said the counsellor. 'It is not the worse for that,' said the Brahmin. 'Where is this country?' said the counsellor. The Brahmin, 'We must seek it.' "—VOLTAIRE.

" Serbonian bogs of sans-culottism, stretching sour and pestilential."—CARLYLE.

" It becomes the caricature of the state, moving with a deceptive pomp in a disastrous pageant."—MULFORD.

" Events are written lessons, glaring in huge hieroglyphic picture-drawing, that all may read and know them : the terror and horror they inspire is but the note of preparation for the truth they are to teach."—CARLYLE.

" Hell is empty and all the devils are here."—SHAKESPEARE.

" Woe to the earth and to the sea, because the devil is come down unto you, having great wrath, knowing that he hath but a short time."—APOCALYPSE.

" Those beings whom Heaven has cast out and Hell would not receive."—DANTE.

" The hydra, royalist, and sans-culottic has many heads."—CARLYLE.

" I have long been convinced that institutions purely democratic must, sooner or later, destroy liberty, or civilization, or both. . . . I have not the smallest doubt that, if we had a purely democratic government here, the effect would be the same [as in France in 1848]. Either the poor would plunder the rich, and civilization would perish, or order and property would be saved by a strong military government, and liberty would perish. You may think that your country enjoys an exemption from these evils. I will frankly tell you that I am of a very different opinion. Your fate I believe to be certain, though it is deferred by a physical cause. . . . The day will come when, in the State of New York, a multitude of people, none of whom has had more than half a breakfast, or expects to have more than half a dinner, will choose a legislature. Is it possible to doubt what sort of legislature will be chosen? On one side is a statesman preaching patience, respect for vested rights, strict observance of public faith. On the other is a demagogue ranting about the tyranny of capitalists and usurpers, and asking why anybody should be permitted to drink champagne and to ride in a carriage while thousands of honest folks are in want of necessaries? Which of the two candidates is likely to be preferred by a workingman who hears his children cry for more bread? . . . There is nothing to stop you. Your Constitution is all sail and no anchor." —MACAULAY.

" If the fundamental principles of American liberty are attacked, and we are driven behind the inner walls of the Constitution to defend them, we can repel the assault only with those same old weapons which our ancestors used a hundred years ago. You must not think the worse of our armor because it happens to be old-fashioned and looks a little rusty from long disuse."—BLACK.

" It is not quite impossible that the farmers and the promoters of the great mining and manufacturing enterprises which have recently been established in the South may yet find the free ballot of the workingman, without distinction of race, is needed for their defence as well as his own."— PRESIDENT HARRISON.

" For, unquestionably, it is one among the many problems of philosophy to establish a wise economy and prudent stewardship of that ever-shifting mass of incoming and outgoing thoughts which make up our intellectual estate and property."—SCHLEGEL.

" YOUR political speculations," replied the student, after pausing for some time to consider the views last set forth by his instructor, " recall to me the significant truth, that there is a constant warfare between the spirit of good and the spirit of evil,—that neither one of them is in perpetual ascendency over the other.

This, indeed, appears to be the course of God's moral government on earth, which it is the part of wisdom as well as piety to recognize, in contemplating the various factors for good and for evil which confront each other at this point of the history of civil liberty in America; and, since civil liberty and civil rights are among the noblest fruits of Christianity, that warning voice should ever be in the ears of His chosen disciples of the State, 'What I say unto one, I say unto all, Watch.'"

The student, who was scarcely less impressed by the humor than by the gravity of the seer with whom he was permitted to converse so freely, asked, after a moment's pause, whether the duties of the American press were usually of the grave character which his caustic wit, at the opening of their conversation, had rendered so amusing.

"Oh! no," was the reply, "I must relate, before we separate, a curious incident, in connection with the foremost man in the Republican class,—to follow my figure of the school,—who was about to graduate with its highest honors. One day he went to New York; and while in the society of his friends there, he received from a zealous advocate and admirer, who familiarly styled his old classmate the 'Plumed Knight,' a decoction of his own invention which he thought would operate as a sort of politico-Brown-Sequard elixir. Mr. Blaine, without noticing the label, swallowed the contents of the bottle. The next day, upon examining it, he discovered that it was labelled 'Rum, Romanism, and Rebellion.' He instantly feared that, in the condition of his own system and of the public atmosphere, this mixture would prove a deadly poison. It was such a whimsical compound, however, that we at first thought no harm could come of it. In a few days we saw our mistake. Mr. Blaine was taken desperately ill. We all got to work, and night and day we used stomach-pumps,—but to no purpose; the mixture had so completely paralyzed the unfortunate candidate for the first honors of the national class that we despaired of his political life. You now see how all the leaders of the press must be forever on the alert for their friends as well as against their enemies. But I must now say adieu. I shall endeavor to obtain the views of our brethren on the subject of the legal status of the civil rights of

American citizens of African descent. I am glad you have directed our attention to it, for I confess that the question is a grave one, which requires our serious investigation; and I trust to communicate to you hereafter the result of the judgment of several eminent journalists, whose conclusions in matters of national import, disconnected from party politics, frequently attract popular attention, and arouse the martial instinct of their clansmen of the press: men who, like Highland chieftains, light their fires upon the hill-tops of public opinion, and soon summon clans which thrill the country with the wild war-notes of its Donalds, Evans, and Lochiels. It cannot have escaped so close an observer as yourself," continued the journalist, " on presentment found by the body of the country, against its recent chief magistrate for national misdemeanor in his high attempt to restore the Confederate flags, how quickly the slogans of our Union army sent forth their shrill alarm."

The student inwardly thought it a matter for still graver speculation that moth-eaten flags should have kindled so much greater a flame among a liberty-loving people than their motheaten Fourteenth Amendment.

"I have no language," he replied, "which can sufficiently convey to you my appreciation of the favor you have already bestowed upon me, and I hesitate to tax your kind indulgence in the future. Your craft hold, indeed, the telescope of truth, which strips the distance of its phantasies. I am more than ever convinced of the difficulty of measuring the power and utility of the American press. Its generals, sir, are in command of the forces of civilization. Its staff appear to me to move about like field-marshals, directing the rank and file against what fortresses to move the battering-rams of truth, and whither to aim her javelins. The single journal of which you, sir, are the honored commandant can strike more terror into the hearts of the repudiators of the Constitutional Amendments, the betrayers of the civil rights of the American citizen of African descent and all others, than could ' the substance of ten thousand soldiers armed in proof,' with all the panoply of racial prejudice, its bucklers, and its shields."

It was not until this interview with the journalist, after the election of 1884, that the student became aware that the great historian of whom the Chief Justice had spoken in words of such honeyed commendation was the sick man of the journalist's playfulness. From how many windows, he thought, these many-sided men of daily, weekly, and monthly literature must look out, to be able so quickly to photograph the large figures and the small details which make up the whole of political life! With what marvellous skill do they review and present mankind in the ever-varying glory of their morning sun and evening shadow! The fate which had overtaken the career of Mr. Blaine, whom he knew through his "Twenty Years of Congress," long after the Presidential election of 1884, cast a gloom over his sensitive and sympathetic temperament, and only the sweet rest of deep sleep drowned his pensive thoughts.

After many hours his soul seemed to wake, refreshed by the body's rest. It had cast off the weight of sleep, which still rested upon his closed lids, and was astir. In a vision he saw, or thought he saw, the self-same lineaments which appear upon the frontispiece of that author's work. The noble face of nature's lion-hearted son, Mr. Blaine, seemed present in a condition of undisturbed repose like that of one who, after profound contemplation, had resolved upon his course and was at rest. The student in his dream thought he observed at a distance, approaching towards this incomparable statesman, with slow and measured steps, three indistinct figures, arrayed like inferior deities. Their forms were scarcely discernible in consequence of the murky clouds which enveloped them. They seemed to approach, and stand very near Mr. Blaine and himself, and, as the mists which at first had veiled them gradually rose and disappeared, the countenance of one proved exceedingly beautiful to behold. Golden tresses fell upon her bosom, and the texture of her half-closed eyelids was so fine that it scarcely concealed the orbs beneath. Her lips were so sweet that they seemed to breathe eloquence. She looked as if formed to allure mortals unconsciously; and yet she resembled not Fame, but rather an angel clad in light and strength. With a wave of her right hand fragrance was scattered, which, intoxicating his senses, lulled Mr. Blaine into a profounder slumber.

In the cold commanding gaze of the second figure there was a mightiness such as the student had never before beheld. She was of a colossal stature; her huge right hand held an unsheathed sword. She seemed to possess a giant's strength; her face was full of sky-aspiring thought—a picture of vaulting Ambition.

The eldest had a hollow look and withered mien, and the lustre of her eye seemed spent and faded. She looked like Destiny, the child of Earth's old age. "I heard," she said, "yon mortal's boast, that he had climbed in safety the slippery tops of human state, and reached at last its gilded pinnacle. 'Necessity and Chance approach me not, and what I will is fate.' Vain boast! Man is the sport of circumstance, when circumstance seems the sport of man. My summons monarchs must obey. Though mortal be horsed upon the swiftest couriers of the air, swifter my shafts and surer is their aim."

The youngest seemed moved almost to tears while the hands of the eldest glided over the historian, now wrapped in the depths of slumber. But Destiny was inexorable, and neither supplications nor reproaches availed to dissuade her from her predetermined course of countermanding the order of Mr. Blaine's political life. After chanting mysterious rites, and apparently concluding her midnight inquest, the eldest exclaimed, in an impatient tone, "Come! come! let me cut the thread and thrum." The youngest urged that to cut the thread so long spun upon her own distaff would be to loosen and unravel the brightest woof Fame had ever woven. But neither her supplications nor her reproaches availed; and, while Fame held the distaff and Ambition continued to spin, Destiny instantly cut the threads, which were no sooner loosened than she exclaimed, while Fame and Ambition stood by in silence,—

"The Fates, whose decrees are serviceable to wise purposes, see at one view all the threads of existence. Their sentences, which now appear but mutinous accidents, run forward into all the depths of eternity, and will be accomplished in due time according to the preordained plan and a design full of wisdom. His political life has a 'germinant, springing *accomplissement;*' it vanishes now, after the manner of the gods, only to appear again. The Fates will commit to your adjustment the height and fulness of his future attainment. Your power will begin in 1888. Take Time by the forelock ; remember, it is the cradle of Fame, but the grave of Ambition; the stern corrector of fools, the salutary counsellor of the wise ; Wisdom walks before it, Opportunity with it, and Repentance limps behind. See that his life be not an arrant spendthrift, and that Fame and Ambition die not bankrupts to Destiny."

In his dream, the student thought he recognized the presence of the Parcæ, and yet they seemed not the daughters of Night, to whom was allotted the decision of Fate. They wore neither chaplets of wool nor flowers of Narcissus.

The sleeper awoke to find the unsubstantial pageantry of dreamland faded, and, like Ferdinand before Prospero's cell, he thought it a most majestic vision, and magically charming. The actors of the political tragedy seemed like spirits who before the dawn of day had " melted into air, into thin air." So real was his dream that when he awoke the student wished he might sleep again, and in that gorgeous imagery, behold anew the sweet nymph and those weird women who seemed the fellows and ministers of the Fates.

In these days of thought and anxious interest he often entered nature's temple, and under her archways of silence and solitude which made the edifice more striking, as he gazed upon her magnificence in the most splendid regions of her boundless dominions he reflected upon the Constitution and these Amendments. They appeared to him to have no other exemplar than the shining luminary of day, that flowing, living fount of light, shedding its rays over shoreless seas, where through abysmal depths plummet-line could find no bottom, and lighting up the darkest corner of the most distant world.

While awaiting the deliberations of the sages of the press respecting the legal status of the civil rights of the citizens of the United States of African descent, he could but reflect upon the significant horoscope of the future parties which the great political astrologer of the press had cast; and in his solitary musings he, for the first time, realized that in the unfoldings of the future the colored vote might prove, in the evolution of parties, a most significant factor in the destiny of America.

The vagaries of any faction with reference to their version of the true purpose of the organization of the State mattered but little, he thought, under a republican form of government, without votes to carry them into effect. The bookish speculations of abstract scientists upon the Economy of Society, he clearly saw, were of no more importance than the predictions of the savants in Egypt, whom Napoleon ordered with the jackasses to the rear. He reflected that both of the great parties had usually relegated theorists to the rear; that neither of them was able to command the millions of voters (who set up their own crude notion of the solution of the grave problems of the future of America, respecting the distribution and employment of the vast wealth accumulated, and daily accumulating, through the industrial developments of a mighty nation, which she must protect in every branch); that the standing army of Knights had established a thoroughly equipped *trust* over vast realms of commerce, and had set up their philosophy of government, and had undertaken the rectification of supposed economic maladjustments. The danger, he anticipated, was not so much in their theories as from their ballots. In the multifarious products of our social evolution, he could not clearly discern any insuperable obstacle to the final conquest by unscrupulous political *agitators* of those estrays from the Constitution whose tendency now was towards a gradual consolidation which would loosen Labor from all constitutional moorings.

Notwithstanding the several interests of the separate schools were at first apparently or professedly antagonistic, and although discordant bodies to-day respecting remedial forces, he thought to-morrow these various orders might unite their separate organizations to reap advantages in which none could participate without the combined effort of the whole.

He reflected that, although there may be a lull in sociological agitations, the main question would in the future reappear, and with increasing strength force its solution upon the nation. He also perceived that the present clap-trap arguments of their apostles aimed at a pretended justice above law, and had reared Labor to an equal height with thrones. The federation of the labor party, in all its departments, he saw, sympathized with anarchistic theories, if not with bombs. Their organs had daily published shallow, vapid, frothy, and impertinent defiance to the decrees of the law-courts, with the solid labor class for sympathizers and the freedom of the ballot for their fulcrum in all political agitations. The simple trades-unions of yesterday had already established a crude centralized despotism over the general business of to-day, and were no respecters of the civil rights of employers. The edicts of the monopolist and the " corners" of life's staples, throughout America, were not graver commercial despotisms than the iron-handed, arbitrary, and coercive decrees of the executive boards of the Knights of Labor, who to-day talked platitudes about the brotherhood of man and the fatherhood of God, and to-morrow ordered boycotts and strikes, and the confiscation of the civil right to the daily pursuits of labor and happiness which the Constitution guarantees to all,—even to the " scab,"—thus upsetting, with legal impunity, the calculations of manufacturers and the tariff of prices and destroying business interests in general.

In this view he thought of the following strange utterance : " Now mark my words, for I am speaking with some knowledge of the subject we are dealing with : the time will come when all these several divisions of the labor movement will unite, and we will have one grand reform organization." He reflected that, when this grand organization was ripe for action, the civil liberty, civil rights, political orthodoxy, and capital of the American people would have to contend with an assembly of Brutuses, who would be ignorant enough to believe it as easy for them to shatter the republic as to smash porcelain. He knew that Communism would dart on treasure like a bird of prey ; that its elements were hunger, envy, death, and legalized plunder ; that idlers were ever willing to contribute their penny to pocket labor's sovereign. He remembered the time when Cæsar or Communism was Rome's only alternative.

His imagination pictured vagabond politicians, the beggars of yesterday ; visionary dreamers ; men who, having failed in all other business, therefore felt themselves qualified to tinker with the Constitution ; the bandits of the slums, idlers, and loafers, assuming important airs ; all the representative spirits of disorder; bankrupts; apostates and scoffers at religion and morals, devoid of all noble instincts and manly virtues, gathered in one heterogeneous mass, whose crimson banners bore such mottoes as "Education for organization,"—"Capitalistic classes will not give up what they have peaceably,"—"Put down the rebellion of the capitalistic classes,"—"The tiger is never so dangerous as when he is hungry,"—

> "Rulers we detest;
> Freedom we request:
> To be equals we aspire.
> We will win or we'll expire."

When this hydra-headed despot of the Grand Reform Organization, he thought, is on the throne, and strong enough, in spite of his gasconade and pompous ignorance, he will control with his rough grasp the discordant elements of millions of voters. Was it not clearly discernible in the dim future, when the one hundred and sixty acres of land now open to every citizen should give out, what progeny would be born of the parentage of *Trustism*, Anarchism, Communism, Socialism, Trades-unions, and Knights of Labor; what throned monarchs might not spring from the "practical politics" of the bosses, national and State heelers, who by the mysterious workings of their criminal arcana already had seated in the United States Senate, and upon the governing boards of the country, the vulgar representatives of plutocracy? When the crude jumble of political leaven began to work and national fermentation commenced, he reflected, it would be then seen that there is no force in this country like votes.

Our student discerned clearly to how little purpose they had read history who suppose that millions can play with the ballots for the selection of a governing class, and attempt to establish their own scientific republic, without establishing anarchy first and despotism afterwards. It would not be difficult, he saw, to enact the necessary legislation in America, where, as Mr. George says, "the power is in the hands of the working class. When they choose to exercise it they can write the laws as they please. We have not to begin a revolution; we do not need to take up arms; but we can make a revolution through the ballot-box. We are citizens; we are voters. We have in our hands the sovereign power, and if there is injustice here we are responsible for it. No man can escape that responsibility. You know that in this city thousands of human beings die every year before their time, because they have not air and room enough; because, in this world overflowing with wealth, they are denied the necessaries of life. But the great laboring masses have at last got tired of this sort of thing. We now want something for ourselves, something for our wives and children, and what we want for ourselves we want for everybody else. We want to vote to make work plentiful, wages higher, house-rent cheaper; to make it easier for every man to get a home for himself and family. We want to vote to abolish this great injustice."

The student could not cease to wonder that neither the Republican nor the Democratic party had yet seized the golden opportunity which the abject condition of their civil rights now afforded of attracting to either fold the American citizens of African descent. If not from considerations of patriotism or regard for constitutional law, surely from motives of self-preservation in the coming struggle with *King Mob, King Trust, King Labor, et id omne genus,* threatening the subversion of all constitutional civil rights in America, our student thought the great constitutional-liberty-loving parties of the country, at no distant day, would each emulate the other in attracting the voters of seven millions of their fellow-citizens, by favoring the enforcement of those civil rights which were guaranteed by these Constitutional Amendments.

CHAPTER IX.

"Discomfort guides my tongue
And bids me speak of nothing but despair."—SHAKESPEARE.

"In the meantime, as Durandarte says in the Cave of Montesinos,
'Patience, and shuffle the cards.'"—BYRON.

"The silver-footed queen."—MILTON.

"Now glowed the firmament with living sapphires:
Hesperus, that led the starry host, rode brightest,
Till the moon, rising in clouded majesty, at length,
Apparent queen, unveiled her peerless light,
And o'er the dark her silver mantle threw."—ID.

"While overhead the moon
Sits arbitress, and nearer to the earth
Wheels her pale course."—ID.

"A work, concludes the well-nigh enthusiastic reviewer, interesting
alike to the antiquary, the historian, and the philosophic thinker."—CARLYLE.

"His attitude, we will hope and believe, is that of a man who had
said to Cant, Begone; and to Dilettanteism, Here thou canst not be; and
to Truth, Be thou in place of all men; a man who had manfully defied
the 'time-prince,' or devil, to his face; nay, perhaps, Hannibal-like, was
mysteriously consecrated from birth to that warfare, and now stood
minded to wage the same, by all weapons, in all places, at all times. In
such a cause, any soldier, were he but a Polack Scytheman, shall be welcome."—ID.

"A wreath, twine a wreath for the loyal and true
Who, for the sake of the many, dared stand with the few."—MORSE.

"The dreadful Sagittary
Appalls our numbers; haste we, Diomed,
To re-enforcement, or we perish all."—SHAKESPEARE.

"Since the time of John Milton, no braver heart had beat in any English
bosom than Samuel Johnson now bore. No Giant Despair appalls
this pilgrim; he works resolutely for deliverance, in still defiance steps
resolutely along."—CARLYLE.

SINCE our student's interview with one of the leading representatives of American journalism, several months had elapsed; but as yet there had been no fulfilment of the journalist's promise to communicate the result of his conference with the other leaders, to whom he had proposed to submit, for general consideration and future action, the legal status of the civil rights of American citizens of African descent. From this prolonged delay the student began to fear, as thousands of these very citizens in the hopelessness of their despair had anxiously feared, that the enormous shadow of race-prejudice, which had cast its dark form over the fresh clear glance of many lovers of civil liberty in America, might also dim the bright and shining lights which the great luminary had gathered around himself. Like many of our citizens, he began at last to indulge in gloomy forebodings respecting the course of the American press; for the unbounded radiance of hope which had dawned anew with the freshness of each morn, at length began to fade. The worshipper at the shrine of civil liberty had awaited for the summons " to-morrow and to-morrow and to-morrow," until hope deferred had made his heart sick, and the melancholy doubt crept over him, whether it might not transpire that, after all, even the leaders of the press were but weak and degenerate beings. As he sat in the dim loneliness of twilight which brought no tidings of good cheer, it, too, seemed to forebode that " the darkness of the dead deep," with its night of despair, was gathering, and would soon settle down upon the fair morn of civil liberty which had arisen in America.

One evening he walked forth to hold his customary communion with nature, and listen to her ever-varied language; and as he gazed, with his majestic forehead and royally-arched temples, " a very palace of thought," with his serene face raised in the attitude of prayer, and looked steadfastly upon the " floor of heaven thick-inlaid with patens of bright gold," and watched the golden candles in the cloudless canopy of blue, so far, far away, lit silently, one by one, by the hand divine which had fixed them in the air, all these gloomy forebodings vanished; and he seemed to behold, in the starry firmament, the express image of Civil Liberty looking down upon the earth with all her eyes, guarded by the innumerable hosts of Heaven. This was but for a moment; and then, arrayed in all her magnificence, she appeared to descend from her high eminence, and beckon to her natural guardians in this nether world.

However imaginary the skyborn revelation of the preceding evening, it proved to the student, the next morning, to be not all a dream; for the impossible had happened, as it often does, when least expected. The message came. The journalist excused the seeming delay, saying that a wider range of representatives of the press had united in the discussion than he had at first proposed; several of whom considered the subject an unprofitable one for their business relations; others thought that it was not altogether the time to entertain too liberal opinions about civil rights; and some noodles had only a chuckling grin or a sarcastic leer to contribute to grave and vital questions touching seven million American citizens. He explained further that after their late interview he thought it wiser to feel the pulse of this class of editors, and see beforehand in what direction their course tended. If they proved unruly, it would be necessary hereafter to put bearing-reins upon them. The friends upon whose sagacious co-operation implicit reliance could be placed, he stated, had arrived at a joint judgment; but in the meantime, as the student was in full sight of the unprogressive workings of that jurisprudence which maintained the foundation of caste in America by establishing distinctions and conferring privileges upon classes *as* classes, he proposed that the student should submit to the press for its analysis not a dry legal review of cases, but a philosophical generalization of the result of the decisions, and an exposure of the viciousness of a system which by legal casuistry so unmercifully abased and scourged seven millions of the society of the American state; a work which should also embody the writer's view of the constitutional status of the civil rights of our American citizens of African descent.

"But for the concise and able summary of the civil-rights cases," he remarked, "which you kindly placed at our disposal, our labors would have been still further protracted. Future investigators will be greatly facilitated in their researches by this compilation. This collation has brought to light a heterogeneous mass of the charred remains of race-prejudice, with its accumulation of black wrappage, dust, and dingy cobwebs, a parlous heap of trash, through which the moles of the law have been burrowing for a quarter of a century."

The character of the work suggested by the representative journalist harmonized in part with the course which the Chief Justice had recommended. After mature deliberation, the student resolved immediately to set about its accomplishment, through an argument which should combine a review of the legal status of civil rights, and an exposure of the unconstitutionality of those adjudications which had laid the foundation for caste in America by their interpretations of the Fourteenth Amendment. The result of his labor in carrying out this resolution is the following argument, which presents the foreign student's review of the constitutional status of the civil rights of African citizens. It begins in the following chapter.

CHAPTER X.

" Christianity is part of the law of England."—LORD ELDON.

" Liberty is part of the precious heritage which our God brought down with him from heaven to the earth and left to us, his sons. Let no one, therefore, marvel that we should hold it beyond all price, dearer to us than our lives."—CARDINAL GIBBONS.

" Holy Scripture comprehendeth history and prophecy, law and ethics, the philosophy of life that is to come."—POTTER.

" The world's history is a divine poem, of which the history of every nation is a canto and every man a word. Its strains have been pealing along down the centuries, and though there have been mingled the discords of warring cannon and dying men, yet to the Christian philosopher and historian—the humble listener—there has been a divine melody running through the song which speaks of hope and halcyon days to come."— GARFIELD.

" Nations in their loftiest successes, in their purest forms of civilization, are but travelling towards the ideal presented in Scripture, and as new phases of society appear that Scripture will be found adapted to each, so far as it may be legitimate, and be calculated to advance each to new glory and perfection."—POTTER.

" Whilst just government protects all in their religious rites, true religion affords government its surest support."—WASHINGTON.

" Without religion there can be no democratic society. Religion is the common source of all the benevolent ideas that exercise influence on mankind. The American people are religious by their origin, by conviction, and by democratic principles."—POUSSIN.

" Between these two corporations—the family, that deep, solid foundation of the social edifice below, and the church, that high, expansive, and illumined vault above—stands the state."—SCHLEGEL.

" There can be no political happiness without liberty, there can be no liberty without morality, and there can be no morality without religion." —RAMSAY.

"For if we seek the first origin and ultimate foundation of all right and all justice, we must seek it in God alone, who is the eternal Arbiter of the world of states and nations as well as of individuals, and who well knows how to requite every great political injustice on His appointed day of retribution, to visit it with unexpected punishment, and to reduce it to its own nothingness by an often fearful award. But so soon as man, or any earthly power, presumes to lay its hand upon this work—to propose to itself absolute justice, to judge and regulate all things by that standard, and to model the world in conformity to it—the consequence is a total revolution in all the relations of society."—SCHLEGEL.

"It was the discovery of Jesus Christ that gave John Müller, the prince of modern historians, his knowledge of history. 'The Gospel,' he says, 'is the fulfilment of all hopes, the finishing-point of all philosophy, the explanation of all revolutions, the key to all the apparent contradictions of the physical and moral world.' "—D'AUBIGNÉ.

"History has been robbed of her divine parent, and now, an illegitimate child, a bold adventuress, she roams the world, not well knowing whence she comes or whither she goes."—ID.

"In the earlier ages a national spirit has had an apparent influence in politics and the formation of the state. But in none has it wrought with the conscious energy of this age. Clearly discerned as the guiding-star of coming political life, appears the highest conception of humanity."— GESCHICHTE DES ALLGEMEINEN STATSRECHTS UND DER POLITIK.

"Immediately were brought by Mercury three large volumes in folio, containing memoirs of all things past, present, and to come. The clasps were of silver, double gilt, the covers of celestial turkey leather, and the paper such as here on earth might pass almost for vellum. Jupiter, having silently read the decree, would communicate the import to none, but presently shut up the book."—SWIFT.

"The people had now to see tyranny naked. That foul Duessa was stripped of her gorgeous ornaments."—MACAULAY.

"The language of passion, the language of sarcasm, the language of satire, is not on such occasions Christian language; it is not the language of a judge."—SYDNEY SMITH.

"He humbly gave the modern generals to understand that he conceived, with great submission, they were all a pack of rogues and fools and confounded loggerheads and illiterate whelps."—SWIFT.

"Whatever they did, the Elysians were careful never to be vehement." —BEACONSFIELD.

" Oh, intemperate, peppery Thomas Scott, and ye other constitutional patriots! is there no sense of truth in you, then? no discernment of what is really what?" —CARLYLE.

" Nor can you change the nature or lessen the degree of the wrong by your own contemptuous feeling for the object. He may be altogether unworthy of your favor, but you owe him *justice*, and you must pay the debt to the uttermost. A legal right is, in and of itself, a very respectable thing, however much you may hate and despise the man, or body of men, that set it up."—J. BLACK.

A PHILOSOPHICAL review of the political events which preceded the adoption of the Thirteenth, Fourteenth, and Fifteenth Amendments to the Constitution of the United States would involve the history of Civil Liberty from the dawn of its earliest star in Bethlehem of Judæa, when it led the wise men to the place where its first great teacher, wrapped in swaddling-clothes, was lying in a manger. If the Gospel of Saint Luke be accepted as a true version of the facts, by the jurisprudents whose watch is over our flock, suddenly an angel appeared, saying, " I bring you good tidings of great joy, which shall be"—not to Jew or Gentile, bond or free, but—" *to all people;*" and suddenly there appeared with the angel a multitude of the heavenly host proclaiming glory to God in the highest and on earth peace, good-will toward—not white, or black,—but *toward men.* Almost nineteen centuries after this historical occurrence, the cool-headed, representative statesmen of America, who had been conspicuous for their early, continued, and effectual labors for the universal freedom of man, whose fame will endure as long as the love of liberty animates the hearts of the American people, and whose feet had never been defiled by the slime of race-prejudice, laid the foundations of the civil rights of the descendants of the African race: they determined to follow the precedent set by the great law-giver of the enslaved Israelites. After grave deliberations, aided by the national counsellors of all the parties to this compact, who were properly regarded as the oracles of the country, and with the constitutional consent of the white American people, they carefully put three rolls, containing the law, inside the Constitution, that ark of God's

convenant, that this race might find a resting-place, and among
His chosen people have a witness of civil and religious liberty.
These three rolls, thus lodged in the ark of the covenant of
civil liberty, declared, among other things,—

First, Neither slavery nor involuntary servitude, except as a
punishment for crime, whereof the party shall have been duly
convicted, shall exist within the United States, or any place
subject to their jurisdiction.[1]

Secondly, All persons born or naturalized in the United
States, and subject to the jurisdiction thereof, are citizens of the
United States and of the States wherein they reside. No State
shall make or enforce any law, which shall abridge the privileges or immunities of citizens of the United States, nor shall
any State deprive any person of life, liberty, or property without due process of law, nor deny to any person within its jurisdiction the equal protection of the laws.[2]

Thirdly, The right of citizens of the United States to vote
shall not be denied or abridged by the United States, or any
State, on account of race, color, or previous condition of servitude.[3]

An abstract inquiry concerning the legal status of the civil
rights, in general, of this race of American citizens, apparently
involves a sound, broad, fundamental interpretation of these
special charters of liberty and equality, viewed from the loftiest
national stand-point. The intention of their framers and of the
States which adopted them was that they should operate to convey to the emancipated race the civil liberty guaranteed by the
Constitution, as thus amended, to the American people, as long
as that Constitution should survive in its integrity. To whatever extent controversies have heretofore arisen, and are now
daily arising and engaging the attention of the courts throughout the country, respecting the legal status of the civil rights
of these citizens, the abridgment of their privileges and immunities as citizens, and the denial to them of the equal protection
of the laws; there has never been, nor can there be, any dis-

---

[1] Thirteenth Amendment.   [2] Fourteenth Amendment.
[3] Fifteenth Amendment.

agreement upon the notorious matter of fact that these citizens
are denied the equal protection of the laws; that their privileges
and immunities, when measured by and contrasted with the
privileges and immunities (commonly called civil rights) enjoyed
without discrimination or qualification, by all other American
citizens in their industrial business, pursuit of pleasure, "liberty" of their person in travel, public entertainment by inn-
keepers and proprietors of places of public resort for instruc-
tion or amusement, are denied, abridged, and subjected to onerous
conditions; that this denial of the equal protection of the laws
and this abridgment of their rights and privileges is solely because
of their race, and not for reasons by law applicable to citizens
of every race or color, regardless of any previous condition of
servitude; and that their enjoyment of these civil rights has
been, and now is, subject to conditions, rules, and regulations,
prescribed by public servants, and all other classes, which are
solely applicable to the citizens of this race and color by reason
of, and for no other reason whatsoever than, their race, color,
and previous condition of servitude.

The three great Constitutional Amendments first breathed into
this oppressed race the breath of that real life, and bestowed
upon it that true living soul, which only can exist in an atmosphere of pure and perfect justice, liberty, and equality. That
their purpose to make this race rank as citizens should not be
defeated, the wise originators of these latter Amendments gave
Congress the power, and imposed upon it the duty and obligation, of carrying out the provisions of each of these articles by
appropriate legislation. It is a remarkable fact which seems
to have escaped general observation, that, notwithstanding the
momentous nature of the first twelve Amendments to the Constitution, the framers of those Amendments conferred no authority upon Congress to enforce them. The grave constitutional lawyers who prepared them did not adopt the far-sighted
policy of clothing the legislative department of the government
with authority to enforce their provisions.[1]

The Civil-Rights Bill of 1866, the provisions of which are

---

[1] Brigg *v.* The Commonwealth, 16 Peters, 559.

familiar to all, was the first exercise of the authority conferred by the Thirteenth Amendment. It operated to enforce absolute and universal freedom in America. There seems to have been no dispute, nor is there even ground for debate, that Congress could legislate as it did by this act, in a direct and primary way, to secure to citizens of every race and color those fundamental rights which are the essence of civil freedom. If any such question could have arisen, it was effectually dissipated and laid to rest by the adoption of the Fourteenth Amendment. After the latter became a constitutional provision, the Civil-Rights Bill of 1866 was re-enacted, with the modifications of the Enforcement Act of 1870. Subsequently "An act to protect all citizens in their civil and legal rights," passed in 1875, gave rise to the famous Civil-Rights Cases,[1] in which Mr. Justice Bradley, delivering the opinion of the Supreme Court, declared that the provisions of the first and second sections of this act, which are familiar to all, were unconstitutional and void. This decision, as we shall hereafter show, was (somewhat prematurely) regarded by the pro-slaveryites as a decisive victory over the Fourteenth Amendment.

By that adjudication Jurisprudence, upon apparently constitutional grounds, had endeavored to put to the sword the entire childhood of African Civil Rights, and to pillorize six millions of its full-grown subjects. By this judgment of the Supreme Court, Jurisprudence, with dry eyes, and with all the precision and stateliness of constitutional argument, had essayed to demonstrate that the key-stone of the arch upon which rested those guarantees of civil liberty to humanity of all colors in America, henceforth and forever was defective in three great points,— the beginning, the middle, and the end. The Congress which enacted this Civil-Rights Bill was composed mostly of the members of the Congress which had proposed the Fourteenth Amendment. The first and second sections, declared to be unconstitutional, were as follows:

Section 1. That all persons within the jurisdiction of the United States shall be entitled to the full and equal enjoyment

---

[1] 109 U. S. Reports, p. 11.

of the accommodation, advantages, facilities, and privileges of inns, public conveyances on land or water, theatres, and other places of public amusement; subject only to the conditions and limitations established by law, and applicable alike to citizens of every race and color, regardless of any previous condition of servitude.

Section 2. That any person who shall violate the foregoing section by denying to any citizen, except for reasons by law applicable to citizens of every race and color, regardless of any previous condition of servitude, the free enjoyment of any of the accommodations, advantages, facilities, or privileges in said section enumerated, or by aiding or inciting such denial, shall, for every such offence, forfeit and pay the sum of five hundred dollars to the person aggrieved thereby, to be recovered in an action of debt, with full costs.

The fact that the authors of the Fourteenth Amendment and of the Civil-Rights Bill were one and the same individuals was well known to the court, and in the opening of their opinion in the Civil-Rights Cases they say,—

" The principal arguments adduced in favor of the Civil-Rights Bill were such as were advanced whilst the law [Civil-Rights Bill] was under consideration. We have carefully considered these arguments, as was due to the eminent ability of those who put them forward."

It turned out in the end, however, that these laudatory commendations were merely colorable, and without other warrant than is usual from the courtesy of the bench; for at the close of this now famous decision, it cannot escape observation, that their well-known patriotism, their eminence, the gravity of their reputation as statesmen and constitutional lawyers, saved neither the authors and advocates of the Civil-Rights Bill, nor their argument in the civil-rights cases, from the playful irony of the court, underneath which lurked a deep seriousness of purpose not only to rebuke, but to place upon record the rebuke, —that their eminences, like guilty reprobates, " *were running the slavery argument into the ground.*" The agitation in the breast of the court, its hostile flashes, were regarded as unusual as its display was unwarranted by judicial precedent. If the arguments of these illustrious lawyers proceeded from the false fire of their overheated minds, the representatives of American judiciary should have viewed with pity and indulgence the infirmities and delusions which they have thus judicially decorated with their self-complacent censure. This chastisement was regarded by the public as carrying judicial pleasantry a little too far. The dignity and gravity of the Supreme Court of the United States, it was thought, could be displayed to more advantage in a frame of mind less emotional. The hotness of the ashes smouldering underneath this judicial opinion is quite perceptible on top when the court, losing sight of the constitutional abstractions which they had argued uncommonly well, departed entirely from the record to deliver a grave moral lesson, to utter a pious homily, to school and discipline colored humanity in the doctrines of humility; to caution it in the assertion of its civil rights, exhorting it not to walk erect, but more in accordance with the mediæval gait of Dred Scott.

When it is recalled that the Dred Scott decision was resisted by the law department of the United States in 1862[1]; that Mr. Chase, who took his seat as Chief Justice, soon afterwards admitted to practice a counsellor of African blood; that Mr. Buchanan, in his account of his administration, declared that the Republican party and the Douglas-Democrats, the two constituting a large majority, west, east, and north, repudiated the Dred Scott doctrine: that the Supreme Court twenty years thereafter should, in the face of the awful revolution which it precipitated, hold up Dred Scott as a mirror of civil rights, would not be readily believed without reading the opinion in the Civil-Rights Cases (109 U. S. p. 51); where the court, turning from the cold constitutional issues presented by the record, excitedly exclaim,—

" There were thousands of free colored people in this country before the abolition of slavery, enjoying all the essential rights of liberty, life, and property, the same as white citizens, yet no one at that time thought that it was any invasion of his personal status, as a freeman, because he was not admitted to all the

---

[1] General Bates's opinion, November 29, 1862.

privileges enjoyed by white citizens, or because he was subjected to discrimination in the enjoyment of accommodations in inns, public conveyances, and places of amusement."

The court thus drew a line across, what seemed to them, the extravagant legislation of Congress in placing American citizens above degradation. They instituted a comparison between the civil rights of 1875 and ante-bellum freedom. Justice to the great framers of the Amendments and of the Civil-Rights Bill imperatively demands an answer to the question, What were the civil rights of free colored people according to the ante-bellum code? They were judicially expounded by the Supreme Court in Scott *v.* Sandford, concerning which case, Mr. Lincoln said, in speaking of a proposed measure, " it fits exactly the niche for the Dred Scott decision to come in and to declare the perfect freedom no freedom at all." In that pro-slavery opinion of Judge Taney it is declared that " neither the class of persons who had been imported as slaves, nor their descendants, whether they had become free or not, were acknowledged as a part of the people, nor intended to be included in the general words used in the Declaration of Independence ;" that " they had for more than a century before been regarded as beings of an inferior race, and altogether unfit to associate with the white race, either in social or political relations ; and so far inferior that they had no rights which the white man was bound to respect, and that the negro might justly and lawfully be reduced to slavery for his benefit ;" that he was bought and sold, " and treated as an ordinary article of merchandise and traffic, whenever a profit could be made by it ;" and that " this doctrine was at that time fixed and universal as an axiom in morals as well as in politics, which no one thought of disputing or supposed to be open to dispute ; and men in every grade and position in society daily and habitually acted upon it, in their private pursuits, as well as in matters of public concern, without for a moment doubting the correctness of this opinion."

CHAPTER XI.

"If your Constitution cannot resist reasoning like this, then indeed it is waste paper."—BAYARD.

"Nations fall where judges are unjust, because there is nothing which the multitude think worth defending; but nations do not fall which are treated as we are treated, but they rise as we have risen, and they shine as we have shone, and die as we have died, too much used to justice, and too much used to freedom, to care for that life which is not just and free."—SYDNEY SMITH.

"But when a man's fancy gets astride of his reason; when imagination is at cuffs with the senses; and common understanding, as well as common sense, is kicked out of doors; the first proselyte he makes is himself, and when that is once compassed the difficulty is not so great in bringing over others; a strong delusion always operating from without as vigorously as from within. For cant and vision are to the ear and the eye the same that tickling is to the touch."—SWIFT.

"Fierce, fiery warriors fight upon the clouds."—SHAKESPEARE.

"Throw aside all these quibbles: a mighty work is before us."—PHILLIPS.

"Like the immortal Dexter, he had breasted that mighty torrent which was sweeping before it all that was great and valuable in our political institutions."—HAYNE.

"On that, the proudest day of his life, like a mighty giant, he bore away upon his shoulders the pillars of the temple of error and delusion, escaping himself unhurt, and leaving his adversaries overwhelmed in its ruins."—ID.

"Sure, it was the roar of a whole herd of lions."—SHAKESPEARE.

"But a community which has heard the voice of truth and experienced the pleasures of liberty, in which the merits of statesmen and of systems are freely canvassed, in which obedience is paid not to persons, but to laws, in which magistrates are regarded not as the lords but as the servants of the public, in which the excitement of a party is a necessary of life, in which political warfare is reduced to a system of tactics,—such a community is not easily reduced to servitude."—MACAULAY.

" As for those whose minds are blinded with superstition, magnanimity
and true liberty do not appear so glorious to them as they are in themselves ; it will be in vain to contend with them, either by reason and arguments or examples."—MILTON.

" The great, fundamental, and long-established principles of toleration."
—SCHLEGEL.

IN grave contrast with the old pro-slavery version of civil
rights, which the Supreme Court thus quotes with approval in
the Civil-Rights Cases, is the refreshing new version of constitutional civil rights, by the greatest of all the great expounders
of our Constitution, Justice Story, who, in his treatise on the
Constitution, quotes and adopts, as a sound exposition of constitutional law, Sumner and Everett's interpretation of the spirit
of American constitutional liberty, which lifts human consciousness out of the dust into dignity, and, instead of relegating
seven millions of people to the outer darkness of Scott *v.* Sandford, sheds upon their civil rights a more benign and genial
light.   Says this great authority upon constitutional law :[1]

" Such are the privileges and immunities of citizens of the
States: to be protected in life and liberty, and in the acquisition
and enjoyment of property, under equal and impartial laws,
which govern the whole community.   This ' puts the state
upon its true foundation : a society for the establishment and
administration of general justice,—justice to all, equal and fixed,
recognizing individual rights and not imparting them.'   It
recognizes ' the important truth—in a republican government,
the fundamental truth—that the minority have indisputable and
inalienable rights; that the majority are not everything and
the minority nothing ; that the people may do what they please,
but that their power is limited to what is just to all composing
society.'   The people of the States, in framing their several
Constitutions, have undertaken to secure these fundamental
rights against invasion : sometimes by particular enumeration ;
more often by general words ; always in some form of language
supposed to be completely effectual ; and we may, with the ut-

---

[1] Story on Constitutional Law, 4th ed., vol. ii. sec. 1936.

most propriety, apply to their several guarantees as they now stand what has so justly been said of one of them :[1] 'These are not vain words. Within the sphere of their influence no person can be created, no person can be born, with civil or political privileges not enjoyed equally by all his fellow-citizens, nor can any institution be established recognizing distinction of birth. Here is the great charter of every human being drawing vital breath upon this soil, whatever may be his condition and whoever may be his parents. He may be poor, weak, humble, or black; he may be of Caucasian, Jewish, Indian, or Ethiopian race; he may be of French, German, English, or Irish extraction; but before the Constitution all these distinctions disappear. He is not poor, weak, humble, or black, nor is he Caucasian, Jew, Indian, or Ethiopian; nor is he French, German, English, or Irish: he is a Man, the equal of all his fellow-men. He is one of the Children of the State, which, like an impartial parent, regards all its offspring with an equal care. To some it may justly allot higher duties according to higher capacities; but it welcomes all to its equal hospitable board. The State, imitating the divine justice, is no respecter of persons.' We take the liberty to quote somewhat from Mr. Everett on the same general subject.[2] 'Grant that no new benefit—which, however, can by no means with truth be granted—be introduced into the world on this plan of equality, still it will have discharged the inestimable office of communicating, in equal proportion, to all the citizens, those privileges of the social union which were before partitioned in an invidious gradation, profusely among the privileged orders, and parsimoniously or not at all among the rest.' 'The people of this country are, by their constitutions of government, endowed with a new source of enjoyment, elsewhere almost unknown,—a great and substantial happiness. Most of the desirable things of life bear a high price in the world's market. Everything usually deemed a great good must, for its attainment, be weighed down in the opposite scale with what is usually deemed a great evil,—labor, care, danger. It is

---

[1] Charles Sumner's Argument on Equality before the Law, Speeches, xi. 341.

[2] Everett's Orations, i. 122, 123.

only the unbought, spontaneous, essential circumstances of our nature and condition that yield a liberal enjoyment. Our religious hopes, intellectual meditations, social sentiments, family affections, political privileges,—these are springs of unpurchased happiness; and to condemn men to live under an arbitrary government is to cut them off from nearly all the satisfaction which nature designed should flow from those principles within us by which a tribe of kindred men is constituted a people.' " [1]

Except for the better understanding of the law, as it has been expounded in the decision of the Civil-Rights Cases, and in the dissenting opinion, it can serve no other than an historical purpose at this late day to stir the dust of those cases. In substance, the majority of the court held, that, until some State law has been passed, or some State action through its officers or agents has been taken, adverse to the rights of citizens sought to be protected by the Fourteenth Amendment, no legislation of the United States under said Amendment, nor any proceeding under such legislation, can be called into activity, for the prohibitions of the Amendment are against the State laws, and acts done under State authority. Legislation may and should be provided in advance to meet the exigency when it arises; but it should be adapted to the mischief and wrong which the Amendment was intended to provide against; and that is, State laws, or State action of some kind, adverse to the rights of the citizen secured by the Amendment. Such legislation cannot properly cover the whole domain of rights appertaining to life, liberty, and property, defining them and providing for their vindication. That would be to establish a code of municipal law regulative of all private rights between man and man in society. It would be to make Congress take the place of the State legislatures, and to supersede them. It is absurd to affirm that, because the rights of life, liberty, and property (which include all civil rights that men have) are by the Amendment sought to be protected against invasion on the part of the State without due process of law, Congress may therefore provide due process of law for their vindication in every case; and that, be-

---

[1] Story, Const., 4th ed., ii. p. 658, note 1.

cause the denial by a State to any persons of the equal protection of the laws is prohibited by the Amendment, therefore Congress may establish laws for their equal protection. In fine, the legislation which Congress is authorized to adopt in this behalf is not general legislation upon the rights of the citizen, but corrective legislation,—that is, such as may be necessary and proper for counteracting such laws as the States may adopt or enforce, and which, by the Amendment, they are prohibited from making or enforcing, or such acts and proceedings as the States may commit or take, and which, by the Amendment, they are prohibited from committing or taking. It is not necessary for us to state, if we could, what legislation would be proper for Congress to adopt. It is sufficient for us to examine whether the law in question is of that character.

The dissenting opinion of Mr. Justice Harlan in the Civil-Rights Cases may well challenge comparison in the history of constitutional debate. It is a massive structure; and yet acute perspicacity, delicate discrimination, lucidity, and comprehensiveness in the argument are everywhere apparent. In his exposition of the canons of constitutional construction, the resources of the lawyer and statesman seemed inexhaustible. In the unusual fearlessness of his freedom, Mr. Justice Harlan transgressed, or perhaps extended, the time-worn and long strictly-observed rules of judicial decorum. That sensitive judicial circumspection which often surmounts and dwarfs the opinions of the minority of the court did not seem to hamper his movements. With a proud and imposing air of superiority, armed with a magnificently stern array of precedents and authorities, he marched like a warrior into the camp of the majority of the court with the avowed object of demonstrating " that the opinion of the majority had proceeded upon grounds entirely too narrow and artificial, which had sacrificed by subtle and ingenious verbal criticism the substance and spirit of the law," which he explained by the remark, " It is not the words of the law but the internal sense of it that makes the law : the letter of the law is the body : the sense and reason of the law is the soul." On page 26, C. R. C., Mr. Justice Harlan says :

" Constitutional provisions, adopted in the interest of liberty, and for the purpose of securing through national legislation, if need be, rights inhering in a state of freedom, and belonging to American citizenship, have been so construed as to defeat the ends the people desired to accomplish, which they attempted to accomplish, and which they supposed they had accomplished, by changes in their fundamental law. By this I do not mean that the determination of these cases should have been materially controlled by considerations of mere expediency or policy. I mean only, in this form, to express an earnest conviction that the court has departed from the familiar rule requiring, in the interpretation of constitutional provisions, that full effect be given to that intent with which they were adopted."

In this dissenting opinion Mr. Justice Harlan sends forth the lion-roar. He does not seem anywhere to conceal or suppress his earnest conviction that Civil Liberty was being strangled at its birth, by the decision of a majority of the court; that the canons of constitutional construction established during the pro-slavery contests, which led to the adoption and enforcement of the civil rights of the slave-power under the fugitive-slave bill, had been revolutionized and overturned when invoked to maintain civil rights of African citizens under the Fourteenth Amendment. If the object of the majority of the court had been an attempt to annihilate the justice of God by judicial subtilties, the mission of this dissentient would seem to be to re-establish it upon a solid constitutional foundation, through the fearless exercise of the pure and Heaven-sent gift of right reason. The court having adjudicated that Congress had no authority to establish such regulations as the first and second sections of the Civil-Rights Bill of 1875 provided for the primary enforcement of the civil rights therein enumerated, Justice Harlan cites Section 2, Article iv. of the Constitution. He says :

" Before considering the language and scope of this Amendment, it will be proper to recall the relations subsisting, prior to their adoption, between the national government and the institution of slavery, as indicated by the provisions of the Constitution, the legislation of Congress, and the decisions of this court.

In this mode we may obtain keys with which to open the mind of the people, and discover the thought intended to be expressed. In Section 2, Article iv. of the Constitution, it was provided that ' no person held to service or labor in one State, under the laws thereof, escaping into another, shall, in consequence of any law or regulation therein, be discharged from such service or labor, but shall be delivered up on claim of the party to whom such service or labor may be due.' Under the authority of this clause Congress passed · the Fugitive-Slave Law of 1793, establishing a mode for the recovery of fugitive slaves, and prescribing a penalty against any person who should knowingly obstruct or hinder the master, his agent, or attorney, in seizing, arresting, and recovering the fugitive, or who should rescue the fugitive from him, or who should harbor or conceal the slave after notice that he was a fugitive.

" In Prigg *v.* Commonwealth of Pennsylvania, 16 Pet. 539, this court had occasion to define the powers and duties of Congress in reference to fugitives from labor. Speaking by Mr. Justice Story, it laid down these propositions : ' That a clause of the Constitution conferring a right should not be so construed as to make it shadowy, or unsubstantial, or leave the citizen without a remedial power adequate for its protection, when another construction equally accordant with the words and the sense in which they were used would enforce and protect the right granted ; that Congress is not restricted to legislation for the execution of its expressly granted powers ; but, for the protection of rights guaranteed by the Constitution, may employ such means, not prohibited, as are necessary and proper, or such as are appropriate, to attain the ends proposed ; that the Constitution recognized the master's right of property in his fugitive slave, and, as incidental thereto, the right of seizing and recovering him, regardless of any State law, or regulation, or local custom whatsoever ; and that, the right of the master to have his slave, thus escaping, delivered up on claim, being guaranteed by the Constitution, the fair implication was that the national government was clothed with appropriate authority and functions to enforce it.' The court said : ' The fundamental principle, applicable to all cases of this sort, would seem to be that when the end is required the means are given, and when the duty is enjoined the ability to perform it is contemplated to exist on the part of the functionary to whom it is intrusted.' Again, ' It would be a strange anomaly and forced construction to suppose that the national government meant to rely for the due fulfilment of its own proper duties, and the rights which it intended to secure, upon State legislation, and not upon that of the Union. *A fortiori*, it would be more objectionable to suppose that a power which was to be the same throughout the Union should be confided to State sovereignty which could not rightfully act beyond its own territorial limits.' The act of 1793 was, upon these grounds, adjudged to be a constitutional exercise of the powers of Congress. It is to be observed from the report of Prigg's case, that Pennsylvania, by her attorney-general, pressed the argument that the obligation to surrender fugitive slaves was on the States, and for the States, subject to the restriction that they should not pass laws or establish regulations liberating such fugitives; that the Constitution did not take from the States the right to determine the status of all persons within their respective jurisdictions; that it was for the State in which the alleged fugitive was found to determine through her courts, or in such modes as she prescribed, whether the person arrested was, in fact, a freeman or a fugitive slave; that the sole power of the general government in the premises was, by judicial instrumentality, to restrain and correct, not to forbid and prevent in the absence of hostile State action; and that for the general government to assume primary authority to legislate on the subject of fugitive slaves, to the exclusion of the States, would be a dangerous encroachment on State sovereignty. But to such suggestions this court turned a deaf ear, and adjudged that primary legislation by Congress to enforce the master's right was authorized by the Constitution. We next come to the Fugitive-Slave Act of 1850, the constitutionality of which rested, as did that of 1793, solely upon the implied power of Congress to enforce the master's rights. The provisions of that act were far in advance of previous legislation. They placed at the disposal of the master seeking to recover his fugitive slave, substantially the whole power of the nation. It invested commissioners, appointed under the act, with power to summon a *posse comitatus* for the enforcement of its provisions, and commanded all good citizens to assist in its prompt and efficient execution wherever their services were required as part of the *posse comitatus*. Without going into the details of that act, it is sufficient to say that Congress omitted from it nothing which the utmost ingenuity could suggest as essential to the successful enforcement of the master's claim to recover his fugitive slave. And this court, in Ableman *v.* Booth, 21 How. 506, adjudged it to be ' in all of its provisions fully authorized by the Constitution of the United States.' "

However diversified may have been the gifts and endowments of the framers of the " Civil-Rights Bill," the spirit of prophecy would certainly appear not to have been included among the number; for if it had been, their prescience would surely have foreseen, and, since " forewarned is forearmed," carefully provided, that its salutary provisions should not be frittered away, or lost, amidst the contradictory elements of the human mind or the wandering mazes of subtle constitutional disputation. Undoubtedly these statesmen believed that an embodiment and unification of the principles of the common law, by a declaratory statute of the United States,—the Civil-Rights Bill,—would be a great and substantial security against the infringement of its general rules, in the mixed and altered condition which the introduction of seven millions of citizens, formerly slaves, had necessarily created in American civil life. Mr. Sumner thought the Civil-Rights Bill "invincible, impassive to the · blows of fate, and proof against the machinations of men." Neither he nor his associates, the illustrious friends of the Civil-Rights Bill, any more dreamed that civil rights would be defeated in the Supreme Court, than the Child of the Revolution, whose footsteps, like theirs, " had an audible echo through the world," could have augured the burning of Moscow.

CHAPTER XII.

"Nor yield I now: my rage shall burn the same;
Eternal wrongs eternal vengeance claim;
Still will I rise a more inveterate foe,
And, dead, pursue them from the shades below."—TASSO.

" The assassination of two Presidents, one inaugurated at the beginning, the other at the close of this period, while a cause of profound national grief, reflects no dishonor upon popular government. The murder of Lincoln was the maddened and aimless blow of an expiring rebellion. The murder of Garfield was the fatuous impulse of a debauched conscience if not a disordered brain. Neither crime had its origin in the political institutions or its growth in the social organization of the country. Both crimes received the execration of all parties and all sections. In the universal horror which they inspired, in the majestic supremacy of law which they failed to disturb, may be read the strongest proof of the stability of a government which is founded upon the rights, fortified by the intelligence, inwrought with the virtues of the people. For, as it was said of old, wisdom and knowledge shall be stability, and the work of righteousness shall be peace."—BLAINE.

" The true question is, shall the judiciary be permanent, or fluctuate with the tide of public opinion?"—BAYARD.

"Behold (she cried) what power is in my hand!
I rule your fates with uncontrolled command:
My will can keep you from ethereal light,
The hapless prisoners of eternal night."—TASSO.

"Immortal light beams struggling through the black vapors of death."
—CARLYLE.

" I wish your example in tracing our constitutional history through its earlier periods could be followed by our public men of the present generation. The few surveyors of the past seem to have forgotten what they once knew, and those of the present to shrink from such researches, though it must be allowed by all that the best key to the text of the Constitution, as of a law, is to be found in the contemporary state of things, and the maladies or deficiencies which were to be provided for."—MADISON.

" The national government has in these twenty years proved its strength in war, its conservatism in peace. The self-restraint which the citizens of the republic exhibited in the hour of need, the great burdens which they bore under the inspiration of patriotic duty, the public order which they maintained by their instinctive obedience to the command of law, all attest the good government of a self-governing people. Full liberty to criticise the acts of persons in official station, free agitation of all political questions, frequent elections that give opportunity for prompt settlement of all issues, tend to insure popular content and public safety. No government of modern times has encountered the dangers that beset the United States, or achieved the triumphs wherewith the nation is crowned."—BLAINE.

" May it please your honors, you know, and I know, and everybody else knows, that it was the intention of the men who founded this republic to put the life, liberty, and property of every person in it under the protection of a regular and permanent judiciary, separate, apart, distinct, from all other branches of the government, whose sole and exclusive business it should be to distribute justice among the people according to the wants of each individual."—J. BLACK.

" To argue otherwise, is to take up the Machiavelian position, that it is right for the legislature to be an imposture, an 'organized hypocrisy' ; that it is necessary for a nation to be cheated by the semblance of virtue when there is no reality ; that public opinion ought to be founded in error rather than in truth ; or that it is well for the people to believe a lie."— SPENCER.

IT is matter not wholly unrelated to the issue, and of curious note in connection with the awful fate which, as we have just seen, overtook the Civil-Rights Bill, that just sixteen years before the 17th of July, 1881, one of these great law-givers,— fresh from the scene of the attempted assassination of William H. Seward, that aged civil-rights crusader, whose life was a continuous assertion that the conflict between freedom and slavery was irrepressible,—while standing over the bloody bier of the great father of civil rights, who had issued in her darkest hour her famous monitory Proclamation of Emancipation, spoke, in a clear and impressive voice, these remarkable words : "Clouds and darkness are about Him ; His pavilion is dark waters, and thick clouds of the skies. Justice and judgment are the establishment of His throne ; mercy and truth shall go before Him. God reigns, and the government at Washington still lives." These historical occurrences, preceding and following the Civil-

Rights Bill, seemed ominous of its fate. The author of the bill had been stricken down in the Senate Chamber from the rear, by a valorous champion of the "Crime against Kansas," who boasted that "a blow struck by him would be followed by a revolution." On the 17th of July, 1881, just sixteen years after the memorable words of Garfield had been pronounced over the martyred President, the utterer of those famous words was himself dying from the bullet of an assassin. Too faint for utterance, he wrote on a piece of paper his name, followed by "*Strangulatus pro republica.*" These were his last words. What was thus spoken by the martyr-President Garfield over the body of the martyred Lincoln, and the words written of himself on his death-bed, linked together by the chain of destiny, seemed, in the mysterious mechanism of events, to be almost a prediction of the fate which overtook the Civil-Rights Bill, the favorite daughter and reputed heiress of the Republican party, for whose life these martyrs and hundreds of thousands more had laid them down to their last sleep on many a hard-fought battle-field.

The lowering face of Jurisprudence in the Civil-Rights Cases at first plunged the hopes of the African race into outer darkness; but when the smoke of the great Civil-Rights contest had cleared away from this temple of the giants, and when at last the morn of reason dawned and smiled upon this "grim-looked night," the dark-skinned children of the sun, who had kept watch, saw that this decision had not condemned their race to a kingdom of perpetual night, for the Fourteenth Amendment was still standing, *in proprio vigore.* And as the fiery cross appeared to Constantine in the noonday sky, so, in their journey towards their land of promise, the luminous sign of Civil Rights shone upon their sorrow-stricken vision, and they read in the Fourteenth Amendment, as if the words had been placed there by the nation, "*In hoc signo vinces.*"

The Supreme Court had adjudged, in the Civil-Rights Cases, that the Fourteenth Amendment clothed Congress with no authority to adopt a civil code for the regulation of the conduct of individuals in the States in their corporate or personal capacity. It had decided that the Fourteenth Amendment is a prohibition upon the States only; and the legislation authorized to be adopted by Congress for enforcing it is not direct legislation on the matters respecting which the States are prohibited from making or enforcing certain laws, or doing certain acts, but is corrective legislation, such as may be necessary or proper for counteracting and redressing the effect of such laws or acts;[1] that this inhibition contained in the amendment has exclusive reference to State action, and means that no agency of the State, or of the officers or agents by whom its powers are exerted, shall deny to any person within her jurisdiction the equal protection of the laws.[2]

The Fourteenth Amendment, therefore, comprehensive and "as broad and general as the casing air," stood, after this decision, and stands now, as the supreme law of the land, fitly joined to and compacted with the Constitution. This amendment declares, and embraces under general terms, the whole body of the advanced rights, public and private, which constitute the charm of modern civilized life to all citizens of the United States. It is an integral part of the Constitution, operating, like the other parts, on the State sovereignties as well as on the people. It laid the foundation of, and defined, the individual rights of the adopted citizen, which neither the law-power of the United States nor that of the States could infringe or curtail. This great superstructure of law, embodied in the Constitution, followed after a tremendous internal struggle for the attainment and preservation of freedom; and constituted for the African race the formal acknowledgment of, and their muniment of title to, the rights, liberties, immunities and privileges of American citizenship.

Although the Civil-Rights Cases decide that Congress cannot "step into the domain of local jurisprudence," and that the Fourteenth Amendment does not invest Congress with power to legislate upon subjects which are within the domain of State legislation; although it does not authorize Congress to create a code of municipal law for the regulation of private rights, yet, says the court, " It had a deeper and broader scope: it nullifies and

---

[1] Civil-Rights Cases, 109 U. S. 3.
[2] *Ex parte* Virginia, 100 U. S. 339; Strauder *v.* West Virginia, ib. 302.

makes void all State legislation, and State action of every kind, which impairs the privileges and immunities of citizens of the United States ; or which injures them in life, liberty, or property without due process of law ; or which denies to any of them the equal protection of the laws. It not only does this, but, in order that the national will, thus declared, may not be mere *brutum fulmen*, the last section of the Amendment invests Congress with power to enforce it by appropriate legislation ; to adopt appropriate legislation for correcting the effects of such prohibited State laws and State acts, and thus to render them effectually null, void, and innocuous."

It seems indisputable to an impartial and clearsighted mind, that this Amendment was not only a muniment of the title of these citizens to the same privileges and immunities as those possessed by the citizens of the several States, but that under article four, section two, the Constitution, which provides that " the citizens of each State shall be entitled to all the privileges and immunities of citizens in the several States," also conferred absolute authority upon the judicial department of the government, independently of the action of Congress, to enforce the provisions of this Amendment by nullifying any action of the individuals of the States which encroach upon or violate its provisions, under and by virtue of the decisions of State courts, based not only upon inimical State statutes, but upon the common law, or customs prevailing in such States, having therein the force of law.[1]

It also seems undeniable, that the judgment of a State court, establishing rights arising from the contracts of its citizens professedly founded upon a treaty, alliance, or confederation secretly made by that State with a foreign power, or upon a State grant of letters of marque and reprisal, or for the coinage of money, or upon an *ex-post-facto* law, or law impairing the obligation of contracts, would not be more unconstitutional and void (even in the absence of *congressional legislation*), by virtue of constitutional provisions inhibiting State action respecting the exclusive powers of the general government, than would be the enforce-

---

[1] Strauder *v.* West Virginia, 100 U. S. 310.

ment by process of law of any judgment of the State which in effect abridged the privileges or immunities of citizens of the United States, or deprived any person of life, liberty, or property without due process of law,[1] no matter upon what foundation such a judgment professedly rested.

Is it not a grave misconception *to assume* that *in the absence of appropriate congressional action*, under the Fourteenth Amendment, any violation, infringement, or encroachment upon the letter or spirit of that amendment (which is the supreme law of the land) is not equally void and unconstitutional, whether such violation, encroachment, or infringement necessarily results from the decision of a State court, based upon any customary usage, common-law principle or precedent, in force in such State, or any other prevailing State custom which has the force of law? Is the repudiation of the supreme law of the Fourteenth Amendment upon such grounds more justifiable than if in fact based upon a State statute inhibiting or abridging the rights, privileges, and immunities of the citizens secured by the Fourteenth Amendment?[2] The provisions of section two of article six of the Constitution—which are " that the Constitution, and the laws of the United States which shall be made in pursuance thereof, and all treaties made or which shall be made under the authority of the United States, shall be the supreme law of the land, and the judges in every State shall be bound thereby, anything in the Constitution or laws of any State to the contrary notwithstanding"—would seem to demonstrate it to be the sound construction of the Fourteenth Amendment, that, in the absence of congressional action to enforce the provisions of the Fourteenth Amendment, all judgments of State courts which tolerated an infringement of the provisions of the Fourteenth Amendment by the act of the individual, of the State or otherwise (although there was no such State law authorizing such encroachment), would be void, as much as if such violation of

---

[1] Story on the Constitution, 4th ed., c. 47.

[2] Washington A. G. Railroad Co. *v.* Brown, 17 Wall. 445; Virginia *v.* Rivers, 100 U. S. 313; Strauder *v.* West Virginia, 100 U. S. 303: Neal *v.* Delaware, 103 U. S. 370; Yick Wo *v.* Hopkins, 118 U. S.; *Ex parte* Yarborough, 110 U. S. 651, 28, 274.

the provisions of the Fourteenth Amendment were authorized by any State Constitution, law, or custom. In the midst of the throes of our civil war, the Supreme Court confirmed this construction, and, speaking in emphatic tones, it declared that the Constitution is " a law for rulers and people equally in war and in peace, and covers with the shield of its protection all classes of men at all times and under all circumstances." [1] Since the first Wednesday of March, 1789,[2] when the Constitution took effect, this interpretation has been practised under and acquiesced in, and has remained unquestioned. The all-absorbing, vital, and important question, therefore, which survived the downfall of the Civil-Rights Bill, and must survive as long as the Fourteenth Amendment and the Constitution itself survive, is *whether or not the individuals of the State* can be constitutionally inhibited by congressional legislation, under the Fourteenth Amendment, or *whether or not* they can be constitutionally authorized by jurisprudence to break through the " cobweb chains of this paper Constitution," whenever popular opinion favors the disfranchisement of a disfavored class of their *constitutional* rights. Upon the solution of this grave question of constitutional justice depends the legal status of the civil rights of citizens of the United States of African descent. If private citizens of the States be permitted to violate this solemn constitutional compact, no matter under what forms of jurisprudence, the framers of the Fourteenth Amendment, who also framed the Civil-Rights Bill, have labored in vain to follow the example of those able English statesmen and profound lawyers who, after the revolution of 1688, deemed it important (notwithstanding the Great Charter with its restrictions and guarantees was acknowledged as the law of England) that a declaratory bill of rights, enumerating their civic rights, should also be promulgated.

Irrespective of the power to enforce by appropriate legislation the provisions of the Fourteenth Amendment, or of its exercise by Congress, the following substantive affirmations unquestionably represent the constitutional status of the civil rights of American citizens of African descent.

---

[1] *Ex parte* Milligan, 4 Wall. 120, 121.
[2] Ownings *v.* Speed, 5 Wheaton, 420.

1st. The Fourteenth Amendment is a valid, subsisting compact between the sovereign people of the United States and the citizens of African descent of its adoption.

2d. That, from and after its adoption, freedmen born or naturalized in the United States, and subject to the jurisdiction thereof, were citizens of the United States and of the States wherein they resided.

3d. That no State can make any law which shall abridge their privileges and immunities as citizens of the United States; nor deprive them of life, liberty, or property, without due process of law; nor deny them the equal protection of the laws.

4th. That, by the adoption of this compact, the Fourteenth Amendment to the Constitution became *the supreme law of the land,* and that under article six, section two of the Constitution, the judges in every State were thereby bound, *notwithstanding anything in the Constitution or laws of any State to the contrary.*

5th. That, at the time of the adoption of this compact by the sovereign people of the United States with these citizens of African descent, the privileges and immunities of which "citizens in the several States" were in the full enjoyment were those which are fundamental, and constitute the essence of the republican citizenship in or under free republican government, such as are and have been common to citizens in the several States under their Constitutions and laws.

6th. That the privileges and immunities of citizens of the United States of African descent are the privileges and immunities of citizens of the several States, which are in their nature fundamental, and which belong of right to the citizens of all free governments, and which have at all times been enjoyed by the citizens of the several States composing this Union, from the time of their becoming free, independent, and sovereign States; those fundamental principles being subject, nevertheless, to such restraints as the government may justly prescribe for the general good of the whole,—to use the expressions of the preamble of the corresponding provision in the old Articles of Confederation, —"the better to secure and perpetuate mutual friendship and intercourse among the people of the different States of the Union."[1]

7th. That the citizens of the United States of African descent, under this constitutional grant, became *eo instanti* entitled to all the privileges and immunities of citizens in the several States, coming within the legal interpretation of section two of article four of the Constitution,—to wit, "The citizens of each State shall be entitled to all privileges and immunities of the citizens in the several States."

8th. That by no qualification or discrimination on account of their race, color, or previous condition of servitude, and for no other reasons than by due process of law, or according to the law of the land, which shall be applicable alike to every other of the sixty millions of citizens and to the most favored, by reason of any common law, custom, or State enactment, can the citizens of the United States of African descent be constitutionally deprived of the full and unqualified enjoyment of all such civil immunities and privileges.

9th. That the citizen of African descent, by virtue of being a citizen of the United States, is clothed with immunity from, and protection against, all discrimination on account of his race, color, or previous condition; and, as a citizen of the United States, he is entitled in the several States to all the privileges and immunities which are accorded therein to their most favored citizens as fundamental rights of citizenship.

10th. That under the Fourteenth Amendment, by virtue of section two of article four of the Constitution, the civil rights, immunities, and privileges of American citizens of African descent are not *constitutionally* subject to any limitations, provisions, requirements, conditions, abatements, rules, regulations, encroachments, or infringements which, in substance or form, directly or indirectly, remotely or proximately, obstruct, interfere with, encroach upon, curtail, infringe, limit, or abridge their immunities and privileges, no matter whether they be promulgated or adopted under color of any law, by any individual, corporation,

---

[1] Coonor *v.* Elliot, 18 How. 591; Ward *v.* Maryland, 12 Wall. 418; McCreart *v.* Virginia, 94 U. S. Rep. 391.

or association whatsoever, provided such abridgments, limitations, etc., are made or are solely applicable to citizens of the United States of African descent, by reason or in consequence of their race and previous condition, and for no other reason, cause, pretence, or ground whatsoever than their color, race, or previous condition of servitude, and are not limitations, provisions, requirements, conditions, abatements, rules, regulations, encroachments, or infringements, applicable alike to all citizens of the United States by the supreme law of the land, or are in conformity therewith.

11th. And that, among divers other privileges and immunities, the citizens of the several States of the United States were and have been since the first Wednesday of March, 1879, and now are, in the free and uninterrupted enjoyment of the privilege and immunity of engaging in all industrial pursuits, and in a free and equal enjoyment of all the accommodations (upon the same terms as they are enjoyed by the citizens of each State), advantages, facilities, and privileges of inns, public conveyances on land or water, theatres and other places of amusement, subject only to the conditions and limitations established by law, and applicable alike to all citizens of the United States and of every State.

12th. That the words used in section first of the Civil-Rights Bill of 1875, "without due process of law," and "the equal protection of the laws," are words of limitation, and their apparent purpose is the individual protection of these citizens, and they are also a limitation upon the usurpation of individual power, which in any form should seek to oppress them; that the meaning of these legal phrases is identical and is aptly illustrated in the famous provision, that " no freeman shall be taken, or imprisoned, or disseized, or outlawed, or banished, or any ways destroyed, nor will the King pass upon him, or commit him to prison, unless by the judgment of his peers, or of the law of the land." That said words, " law of the land," as used in this section, and " due process of law" are to be interpreted in behalf of the liberties, rights, and freedom of these citizens, as legal writers and jurists have interpreted " law of the land" as used in the celebrated twenty-ninth chapter of King John, where it was promised as the security of freemen.

In connection with these twelve propositions, defining the legal status of the civil rights of these citizens, a momentary departure may be pardoned, to note that the three amendments to our Constitution first transplanted England's civil rights upon American soil, by the "law of the land," and that nowhere in judicial literature can a more profound or comprehensive interpretation of the Thirteenth, Fourteenth, and Fifteenth Amendments be found than in the brilliant eloquence with which the wandering, meteor-like genius of Curran nobly depicted the spirit of Anglo-Saxon liberty, when he exclaimed,—

" I speak in the spirit of the British law, which makes liberty commensurate with and inseparable from British soil; which proclaims, even to the stranger and sojourner the moment he sets foot upon British earth, that the ground on which he treads is holy, and is consecrated by the genius of UNIVERSAL EMANCIPATION. No matter in what language his doom may have been pronounced, no matter what complexion, incompatible with freedom, an Indian or an African sun may have burnt upon him, no matter in what disastrous battle his liberty may have been cloven down, no matter with what solemnities he may have been devoted upon the altar of slavery; the first moment he touches the sacred soil of Britain, the altar and the god sink together in the dust, his soul walks abroad in her own majesty, his body swells beyond the measure of his chains that burst from around him, and he stands redeemed, regenerated, disenthralled, by the irresistible genius of Universal Emancipation."

Well, indeed, after they had slept unhonored in a foreign land for a quarter of a century, might the awakened spirit of civil liberty bear the sacred remains of her loving son to their last resting-place, upon her own soil, where they now repose under a noble pile of granite.

CHAPTER XIII.

" And may it not be fairly left to the unbiassed judgment of all men of experience and of intelligence to decide which is most to be relied on for a sound and safe test of the meaning of a Constitution,—a uniform interpretation by all the successive authorities under it, commencing with its birth, and continued for a long period through the varied state of political contests,—or the opinion of every new legislature, heated, as it may be, by the strife of parties, or warped, as often happens, by the eager pursuit of some favorite object, or carried away, possibly, by the powerful eloquence or captivating address of a few popular statesmen, themselves perhaps influenced by the same misleading causes? If the latter test is to prevail, every new legislative opinion might make a new Constitution, as the foot of every new chancellor would make a new standard of measure." —MADISON.

" Must these rules of construction be now abandoned? Are the powers of the national legislature to be restrained in proportion as the rights and privileges, derived from the nation, are valuable? Are constitutional provisions, enacted to secure the dearest rights of freemen and citizens, to be subjected to that rule of construction, applicable to private instruments, which requires that the words to be interpreted must be taken most strongly against those who employ them, or shall it be remembered that a constitution of government founded by the people for themselves and their posterity, and for objects of the most momentous nature, for perpetual union, for the establishment of justice, for the general welfare, and for a perpetuation of the blessings of liberty, necessarily requires that every interpretation of its powers should have a constant reference to these objects?"—JUSTICE HARLAN, CIVIL-RIGHTS CASES.

" No interpretation of the words in which those powers are granted can be a sound one which narrows down their ordinary import so as to defeat those objects."—STORY.

" But though Barrière succeeded in earning the honorable nicknames of Witling of Terror and the Anacreon of the Guillotine, there was one place where it was long remembered to his advantage that he had, for a time, talked the language of humanity and moderation."—MACAULAY.

" What is oppression? Power misapplied to the prejudice of some individual. What is that a man has in view when he speaks of oppression? Some exertion of power which he looks upon as misapplied to the preju-

164

dice of some individual,—to the producing on the part of such individual some suffering, to which (whether as forbidden by the law or otherwise) we conceive he ought not to have been subjected."—BENTHAM.

" Belief always bears the impress of character,—is, in fact, its product. Anthropomorphism sufficiently proves this. Men's wishes eventually get expressed in their faiths,—their real faiths that is ; not their nominal ones. Pull to pieces a man's theory of things, and you will find it based upon facts collected upon the suggestion of his desires. A fiery passion consumes all evidences opposed to its gratification, and fusing together those that serve its purpose, casts them into weapons by which to achieve its end. Perhaps the slave-owner's assertion that negroes are not human beings, and the kindred dogma of the Mahometans, that women have no souls, are the strangest samples of convictions so formed."—SPENCER.

" I possess dignity and power, which ignorance and credulity have founded. I trample on the heads of men prostrated at my feet; if they should rise and look me in the face, I am lost ; they must, therefore, be kept bound down to the earth with chains of iron."—VOLTAIRE.

" Shall the prejudices and paralysis of slavery continue to hang upon the skirts of progress ? How long will those who rejoice that slavery no longer exists cherish or tolerate the incapacities it put upon their communities?"—PRESIDENT HARRISON.

" Surely there is some tender chord, tuned by the hand of its Creator, that struggles to emit in the hearing of the soul a note of sorrowing sympathy."—PAINE.

" It is the nation in its organic and moral unity, which acts as a power in history, and not a race in its special and separate physical character. The fact in correspondence with this has always been, that the nation has been rent and broken in its strength and swept from the foundation on which it alone can subsist, when it has assumed to identify itself exclusively with a race or to build upon the distinction of races. It has no longer a moral foundation nor a universal end when it asserts as its ground the rights of a race, and not the rights of a man ; and the government which no longer recognizes justice as necessary, nor subsists in the sovereignty and freedom of the people in a moral organism, but is in identity with a race, is the sign of an expiring civilization."—MULFORD.

" I know it is said that it is impossible to civilize Africa. Why? Why is it impossible to civilize man in one part of the earth more than in another? Consult history. Was Italy—was Greece—the cradle of civilization ? No. As far back as the lights of tradition reach, Africa was the cradle of science, while Syria and Greece and Italy were yet covered with darkness. As far back as we can trace the first rudiments of improvement, they came from the very head-waters of the Nile, far in the interior of Africa; and there are yet to be found, in shapeless ruins, the monuments of this primeval civilization. To come down to a much later period, while the west and north of Europe were yet barbarous, the Mediterranean coast of Africa was filled with cities, academies, museums, churches, and a highly civilized population. What has raised the Gaul, the Belgium, the Germany, the Scandinavia, the Britain, of ancient geography, to their present improved and improving condition? Africa is not much lower than most of those countries were eighteen centuries ago; and the engines of social influence are increased a thousand-fold in numbers and efficacy. It is not eighteen hundred years since Scotland, whose metropolis has been called the Athens of modern Europe, the country of Hume, of Smith, of Chalmers, of Scott, of Brougham, was a wilderness, infested by painted savages. It is not a thousand years since the north of Germany, now filled with beautiful cities, learned universities, and the best-educated population in the world, was a dreary, pathless forest."— EVERETT.

" Granted that we are chiefly interested in ascertaining what is relatively right, it still follows that we must first consider what is absolutely right; since the one conception presupposes the other."—HUTTON.

"The mystic cord of memory, stretching from every battle-field and patriot grave to every living heart and hearth-stone all over this broad land, will yet swell the chorus of the Union, when again touched, as surely they will be, by the better angels of our nature."—LINCOLN.

" This is our only revenge, that you join us in lifting to the serene firmament of the Constitution, to shine like stars forever and ever, the immortal principles of truth and justice, that all men, white or black, shall be free and stand equal before the law."—GARFIELD.

" The difference between equality and privilege, between civil rights and capricious favors, between freedom of conscience and persecution for conscience' sake, were not matters of moot debate or abstract conviction with our countrymen."—EVARTS.

" She views him, not simply as man, but as the image of the God whom she adores. She feels for every one of the race a holy respect, which imparts to him, in her eyes, a venerable character, as redeemed by an infinite price, to be made the temple of the living God."—PASCAL.

" Equal protection by 'due process of law,' or by the 'law of the land,' should become a pledge of the protection of equal law for indestructible ' vested rights' created by that indestructible charter, that ' every citizen shall hold his life, liberty, property, and immunities under general rules which govern society.'"—WEBSTER.

"'Thank God,' he exclaimed, 'that I should have lived to witness a day in which England is willing to give twenty million sterling for the abolition of slavery!'"—WILBERFORCE.

BEFORE the embodiment of these mighty provisions into the Constitution by the Fourteenth Amendment, Mr. Justice Johnson, in construing the words of Magna Charta,—"No freeman ought to be taken or imprisoned," etc., "or deprived of his life, liberty, or property, but by the judgment of his peers or by the law of the land,"—declared, after volumes had been spoken and written with a view to their exposition, "The good sense of mankind has at length settled down to this, that they were intended to secure the individual from the arbitrary exercise of the powers of government, unrestrained by the established principles of private right and distributive justice;" which only can be in conformity with due course of legal proceedings, according to those rules and forms established for the protection of private rights by the supreme law of the land.[1]

From an historic stand-point, the philosophic reviewer of American jurisprudence will hereafter naturally turn with profound interest to the judicial interpretation placed by the Supreme Court upon the grand provisions of this new charter of Universal Emancipation, which first made liberty in America commensurate with and inseparable from American soil. Upon a close examination of the earliest decisions of the Supreme Court, declaratory of the civil rights of American citizens of African descent (under the provisions of the Fourteenth Amendment), it will become apparent, that the foregoing twelve law propositions, defining the constitutional status of the civil rights of the citizens of the United States of African descent, place them upon a more solid and substantial although a less lofty basis than do the earlier Supreme Court decisions.

The enthusiastic judges of the Supreme Court forced the tri-

---

[1] Bank of Columbia *v.* Oakley, 4 Wheaton, 235.

umphal march of these citizens. In an imposing array of words gleaming with the purple and gold of glittering generalities, the court made sudden haste to destroy every vestige which remained of the ancient landmarks of slave-power, and, wheeling about, pressed the advance-guards of Liberty into the very heart of the nation, never pausing until, with high-sounding, lofty manifestoes, the boundaries of civil rights had been extended throughout the mighty borders of the republic dedicated anew to the universality of freedom. Recognizing at a glance the sublime civic principle and purpose of these amendments,—that they breathed a new and more beautiful form of civil life into America, and that they had banished from the country the moral turpitude by which one man asserts dominion over the civil rights of another,—the Supreme Court spoke in the tones of fearless truth. To the nation, and to the great political party which had risen to almost imperial power, and grown fat upon the doctrine of the equality of man before the law, —throughout its exposition of these amendments, the Supreme Court substantially declared: At last we have recognized the African race before God and men as a member of the great human family, bound by a common interest, and by the indissoluble laws of equity and charity which these amendments seek to enforce; they were not artfully-contrived, splendid baubles of State, nor a *brutum fulmen* of the national will; but a solemnly-pronounced conviction of duty, and solemnly-pledged vindication of man's rights, recognizing no privileged order of white or black; and an indelible infamy attaches to the nation, and, it may with truth be said, to the Republican expounders of the Constitution, if they forsake this outpost of civil freedom. It declared to the color-caste constructionists, Here is an ignorant, weak young race; out of it we must make men of stature and force, men of moral and intellectual energy.

The recorded decisions of the Supreme Court again and again substantially proclaim, that the chief prerogative and glory of man is self-dominion, and that this directly tends to increase his dignity of character and loftiness of sentiment,—all that makes man a blessing to himself and civil society; that these amendments are imposing national structures, built by the people of the United States for the accommodation of the newly-adopted citizens; that they who had been inferior under the Constitution are now, by these amendments, equals in the eyes of the law; that the nation henceforth recognizes only individual rights and merits; and that the new system throws citizens upon their own resources, irrespective of color, starting them unhandicapped in the race of life.

The judgments of the Supreme Court, recorded with an iron pen, and indelibly engraved on American Jurisprudence, declare that caste-constructionists must not forget, that before these amendments, citizens of African descent had the rights, immunities, and privileges of freedom; that long before charters and communities the rights of man existed; that these rights, immunities, and privileges are not conventional, and not revocable except by a violation of those natural laws which are as eternal as the right to exist; that the citizen is not the creature of the state, that he is older than nations and will survive when they perish; that the law of humanity is more primeval than the law of these amendments; that the former condition of slavery was incapable of being introduced into our civil society (until the invention of the cotton-gin made slave-labor valuable) on any reason economic, moral, or political, but only by and through absolute fraud; that by natural, revealed, civil, and common law, the stigma of color is no stigma fixed upon the soul; and that if it be a stigma, if it be a brand of discrimination, it is a stigma or brand which attaches to the "figure of God cut in ebony."

Upon every page of these imperishable decisions does this august tribunal record that his color does not reach the soul, the mind, or the heart of the new citizen; that civilization and intelligence are only what the race requires to fit it for high places; that, although nature has marked God's children from Africa "with the shadowy livery of the burnished sun," they must nevertheless go forth to connect themselves with other citizens, to form alliances by means of trade and business, and that their property, life, liberty, and pursuit of happiness are involved in the unrestricted privileges of civil intercourse; that their rights of labor and education, of purity and refinement, are of little value if the accident of color can subject them to marks of degradation in public; that the fruits of the whole earth to a citizen refused his civil rights are of no appreciable value; that color-caste constructionists should remember how every living thing —man, beast, bird, or insect—delights in absolute freedom; that the elements of life are no dearer or more inestimable than the right of free and unrestrained action in the business and pleasures of life; and that a limitation or discrimination imposed upon one class of citizens, and not upon another, is destructive of the happiness of the class thus deprived of natural liberty. The color-line constructionists must remember that there is a deep instinct of the soul, founded in man's physical and spiritual nature, which calls for personal liberty; that it matters not that fetters are woven of silk: as chains they are iron; that these citizens thirst for personal freedom; that the desire for exemption from any form of bondage is breathed by the Creator into every human soul, white or black; and that their whole nature is on fire to escape from invidious distinctions.

To those nursed and brought up to look upon their fellow-beings as an inferior race, whose inborn, innate instincts, traditions, associations, and education take from them the possibility of realizing that the once inferior creature of the state has become a full-grown citizen, the earlier decisions say, in unmistakable tones,—"like a flash of lightning from a dark cloud,"—The work of force and bloodshed is over; you cannot now sin against light. The virtuous, elevated minds who consecrated their lives to this work; who desired to waken America, South and North, East and West, to the rights, capabilities, purposes, and greatness of human nature, whether clad in a black or a white skin; and whose main object in framing these amendments was to give stability to freedom, by clothing it with civil rights, so that it might be carried forward to fulfil its destiny,—embodying the voice of Anglo-Saxon liberty in these amendments, say to Christian America, Why should these men live under that withering curse, the contempt of their fellow-men? Why should not the paths of honor and gain, education, morals, and civic usefulness be opened to a suffering race rocked in the cradle of slavery for two centuries? Let them be viewed in the light of the spirit of Christianity, of which these laws, after all, are only an assertion. Remember that human liberty, in individuals as in societies and governments, implies the necessity of conforming to a supreme national law, which emanates from the Creator. Let it be borne in mind that the greatest and wisest statesmen, worthy to live forever in the memory of mankind, gave their profoundest consideration to the subject of civil rights, and then framed these three memorial monuments to themselves; insisting that it was the gravest of errors to regard the aversion between the races as irreconcilable; that the whole experience of mankind as jurors, legislators, voters, and tax-payers disproves this assumption; that, the adopted citizens being under the same government, and having the same language, manners, learning, faith, and worship as those of longer standing, the object of this legislation was to better our civil institutions by establishing upon an eternal foundation the civil rights of a class of people, not fierce, savage, or indomitable, but rather the most sensitive, modest, inoffensive, good-hearted, simple, affectionate, truly loyal race on earth, who were now declared to be citizens; and who were closely connected with the rest of the community by a common religion, language, and literature, by common interests and a concern for one another's fate, property, and happiness, and by varied associations which, subjecting them to the discipline, fitted them to be competitors in the active arena of life.

But aside from these amendments, independent of their spirit and the spirit of the earlier decisions of the Supreme Court which is clearly discernible in every line of its recorded wisdom, who is so pitifully ignorant of the mighty drama enacted upon the theatre of time, " with suns for lamps, and eternity for background," as not to know, that the white, not the black skin, was formerly the badge of human bondage; and that, as late as the period when Charles V. took Tunis, he released twenty thousand white Christian slaves? Those who read history with the discrimination of Christian philosophers can see clearly, that, as Charles released these white Christian slaves, so do these Amendments operate to release seven millions of black Christian slaves. If men would make philosophical inquiries respecting the annals of the past, what lessons could be learned! Look for a moment into the times of yore, and in imagination mingle in the silent, mournful procession of the bereaved of olden ages! There you will behold the cultivated Greek slave and the rude Cappadocian chained hand to hand. Race-discriminationists would discover by history that slaves have been of all colors, hues, creeds, and faiths in the earlier days of antiquity. They would learn that in the most boasted civilization of the ancient world, when the Roman Empire was at its height, Britain, Gaul, Scandinavia, Sarmatia, Germany, Dacia, Spain, the different countries of Africa from Egypt to the Troglodytes of Ethiopia, the Western Mediterranean Islands, Sicily, Greece, Illyria, Thrace, Macedonia, Epirus, Bithynia, Phrygia, and Syria furnished the bloody butchers of mankind, in ancient days, with their contingent of human flesh, regardless of age, sex, color, faith, race, or previous condition of civilization, refinement, crime, or barbarism.

CHAPTER XIV.

"O merciful God, what man's wit is there able to sound the depth of those dangerous and fearful evils, whereunto our weak and impotent nature is inclinable to sink itself, rather than to show an acknowledgment of error in that which once we have unadvisedly taken upon us to defend, against the stream, as it were, of a contrary public resolution?"—HOOKER.

"For my purpose herein is to show, that, when the minds of men are once erroneously persuaded that it is the will of God to have those things done which they fancy, then opinions are as thorns in their sides, never suffering them to take rest till they have brought their speculations into practice. The lets and impediments of which practice, their restless desire and study to remove, leadeth them every day forth by the hand into other more dangerous opinions, sometimes quite and clean contrary to their first pretended meanings."—ID.

"The hardest that men of sound understanding conceived of them was but this, '*O quam honesta voluntate miseri erant!*' With how good a meaning these poor souls do evil!"—ID.

"But if the skilfullest among you can show that all the books ye have hitherto written be able to afford any one argument of this nature, let the instance be given."—ID.

"Ye go about to destroy a thing which is in force, and to draw in that which hath not as yet been received; to impose on us that which we think not ourselves bound unto, and to overthrow those things whereof we are possessed."—ID.

"Howbeit, better it was in the eye of his understanding that sometime an erroneous sentence definitive should prevail, till the same authority, perceiving such oversight, might afterwards correct or reverse it, than that strifes should have respite to grow, and not come speedily unto some end."—ID.

> "That proud honor claimed
> Azazel as his right, a cherub tall:
> Who forthwith from his glittering staff unfurled
> The imperial ensign, which, full high advanced,
> Shone like a meteor streaming to the wind,
> With gems and golden lustre rich emblazed,
> Seraphic arms and trophies."—PARADISE LOST.

" Nature will be buried a great time, and yet revive upon the occasion of temptation ; like as it was with Æsop's damsel, turned from a cat to a woman, who sat very demurely at the boards until a mouse ran before her."—BACON.

" Each successive result becomes the parent of an additional influence, destined in some degree to modify all future results. No fresh thread enters into the texture of that endless web, woven in ' the roaring loom of Time,' but that more or less alters the pattern. It has been so from the beginning. As we turn over the leaves of the earth's primeval history, as we interpret the hieroglyphics in which are recorded the events of the unknown past, we find this same ever-beginning, never-ceasing change." —SPENCER.

" I must take the liberty to assert, that, if this be law, it is not that sort of law which Hooker speaks of when, with the splendid magnificence of eastern metaphor, he says, that ' her seat is the bosom of God, and her voice the harmony of the world.' Such a chimera can never be fashioned into a judicial rule fit to be tolerated or calculated to endure. You may, I know, erect it into a rule : and when you do, I shall, in common with others, do my best to respect it ; but, until you do so, I am free to say, that, in my humble judgment, it must rise upon the ruins of many a principle of peculiar sanctity and venerable antiquity, which ' the wing of Time has not yet brushed away,' and which it will be your wisdom to preserve and perpetuate."—PINCKNEY.

" In the universal convulsion and overthrow of society, many things have come to light on this mysterious and esoteric clue in modern history, things which when combined together furnish us with a not incorrect, and a tolerably complete, idea of this mighty element of the Revolution, and of illuminism both true and false, which has exercised so evident and various an influence on the world."—SCHLEGEL.

" Oliver Twist in the parish workhouse, Smike at Dotheboys Hall, were petted children when compared with this wretched heir-apparent of a crown."—MACAULAY.

THE Sanhedrim of political race-propagandists profess to regard much of the phraseology in the earlier civil-rights decisions of the Supreme Court and the other courts, which followed the precedents it established, as pompous partisan rhapsodies, and an unauthorized departure from the concise gravity which should mark a well-formulated judicial opinion. If many of the passages, in the earlier decisions of the courts, which justify those broad, sagacious, and Christian constructions universally attributed to them, and which have filled the professional mind with admiration and wonder, shall prove in the end to have been only the diplomacy of juristic partisans, veiled under hyperbolical metaphors ; and if those passages were merely the fashionable embroidery of a new garb, presented by the Republican court at the birth of Civil-Rights, the High Priest of slavery, with his " iron eye and cold sneer," might indeed find ample food for a hearty repast. Time, the sole test of truth, will determine if the spirit which breathes so fervently throughout many of these decisions was only the falling down of the Republican Party before the newly-born Amendment. But neither the Mephistopheles of pro-slavery, nor his lineal descendant, the color-line obstructionist of constitutional liberty, can deny, that, whether or not the declarations in these opinions were merely whiffs of political incense, " the perfume and suppliance of a moment," the sweet, but ephemeral extravagance of a party, flushed with triumph, assuredly those noble sentiments reflect truly the radical changes in the thought and feeling of the American people, which the great revolution had wrought. Lord Bigot's cynical sneers and snarls at the spirit of the earlier decisions will not prove more acceptable to the pro-slaveryites than to the rest of the world appears the lofty smile with which Christian Philanthropy, arrayed in the awful garb of constitutional law, greeted the long-lost Child of Humanity, saying, You have found favor in our sight ; the sunshine is upon your path. It does not admit of serious confutation, that, in their wide range, the earlier decisions have taken in the past, present, and future condition of the citizens of the United States of African descent ; and that, by the law of the land, they have established upon a foundation of adamant the irrevocable doctrine of the equality of civil rights, which must endure so long as the gorgeous ensign of the Republic floats over the broad dominions of Civil Liberty.

It may prove not only an interesting, but a very useful labor, to gather some of these scattered sweets ; to stir the pure odor of these judicial findings, and preserve, by way of remembrance and grateful acknowledgment, the essence of their extracts.

Amidst the embarrassment of riches, it is difficult to make selections. A few of the precious stones and jewels, some of the broken fragments of the ivory and porphyry in these vessels of silver and gold, may serve as illustrations of the whole, and prove just as competent and sufficient legal witnesses to show the spirit of the earlier civil-rights construction of the Supreme Court, as if the whole mass of their adjudications had been "heaped up, Ossa on Pelion."

On April 14, 1872, Mr. Justice Miller says,—

"We repeat, then, in the light of this recapitulation of events, almost too recent to be called history, but which are familiar to us all ; and on the most casual examination of the language of these amendments, no one can fail to be impressed with *the one pervading purpose found in them all, lying at the foundation of each, and without which none of them would have been even suggested ;* we mean *the freedom of the slave-race, the security and firm establishment of that freedom,* and the protection of the newly-made freeman and citizen *from the oppressions of those who formerly exercised unlimited dominion over him.*   It is true that only the Fifteenth Amendment, in terms, mentions the negro, speaking of his color and his slavery.   But it is just as true that each of the other articles was addressed to the grievances of that race, and designed to remedy them, as the Fifteenth."   And quoting from the language of Chief-Justice Taney, in another case, the court said, "*that, for all the great purposes for which the Federal government was established, we are one people, with one common country, we are all citizens of the United States ;*" "*and it is as such citizens that their rights are supported in this court.*" [1]

Mr. Justice Field, same case, says, "The fundamental rights, privileges, and immunities which belong to him" (*i.e.*, the colored man) "as a free man and a free citizen, now belong to him as a citizen of the United States, and are not dependent upon his citizenship of any State.   The exercise of these rights and privileges, and the degree of enjoyment received from such exercise, are always more or less affected by the conditions and the local institutions of the State or city or town where he resides.   They

---

[1] Slaughter-House Cases, 16 Wall. 71-79.

are thus affected in a State by the wisdom of its laws, the ability of its officers, the efficiency of its magistrates, the education and morals of its people, and by many other considerations. This is a result which follows from the constitution of society, and can never be avoided, but in no other way can they be affected by the action of the State, or by the residence of the citizen therein. They do not derive their existence from its legislation, and cannot be destroyed by its power.

"But if the amendment refers to the natural and inalienable rights which belong to all citizens, the inhibition has a profound significance and consequence." [1]

"That amendment was intended to give practical effect to the declaration of 1776 of inalienable rights, rights which are the gift of the Creator, which the law does not confer, but only recognizes." [2]

"That only is a government free, in the American sense of the term, under which the inalienable right of every citizen to pursue his happiness is unrestrained, except by just, equal, and impartial laws." [3]

Justice Bradley, same case, quotes Sharswood's "Blackstone," 127, note 8: "Civil liberty, the great end of all human society and government, is that state in which each individual has the power to pursue his own happiness according to his own views of his interest, and the dictates of his conscience, unrestrained, except by equal, just, and impartial laws." [4]

"A citizen of the United States has a perfect constitutional right to go to and reside in any State he chooses, and to claim citizenship therein, and an equality of rights with every other citizen ; and the whole power of the nation is pledged to sustain him in that right. He is not bound to cringe to any superior, or to pray for any act of grace, as a means of enjoying all the rights and privileges enjoyed by other citizens. And when the spirit of lawlessness, mob violence, and sectional hate can be so completely repressed as to give full practical effect to this right, we shall be a happier nation, and a more prosperous one than we now are. Citizenship of the United States ought to be, and,

---

[1] 16 Wall. 95, 96.   [2] P. 105.   [3] P. 111.   [4] P. 111.

according to the Constitution, is, a sure and undoubted title to
equal rights in any and every State in this Union, subject to
such regulations as the legislature may rightfully prescribe.   If
a man be denied full equality before the law, he is denied one
of the essential rights to citizenship as a citizen of the United
States."

"The first political act of the American people, in their independent sovereign capacity, lays the foundation of our national
existence upon this broad proposition : ' That all men are created
equal ; that they are endowed by their Creator with certain inalienable rights ; that among these are life, liberty, and the pursuit of happiness.'   Here again we have the great threefold
division of the rights of freemen, asserted as the rights of man.
Rights to life, liberty, and the pursuit of happiness are equivalent to the rights of life, liberty, and property.   These are the
fundamental rights which can be taken away only by due process of law, and which can be interfered with, or the enjoyment of which can be modified, only by lawful regulations,
necessary or proper for the mutual good of all ; and these rights,
I contend, belong to the citizens of every free government."[1]

"It is pertinent to observe that the clause of the Constitution
referred to, and Justice Washington in his comment on it, both
speak of the privileges and immunities of citizens *in* a State, not
of citizens *of* a State.   It is privileges and immunities of citizens
—that is, of citizens as such—that are to be accorded to citizens
of other States when they are found *in* any State; or, as Justice
Washington says, ' privileges and immunities which are, in their
nature, fundamental : which belong, of right, to the citizens of
all free governments. ' "[2]

"The mischief to be remedied was not merely slavery and its
incidents and consequences ; but that spirit of insubordination
and disloyalty to the national government, which had troubled
the country for so many years in some of the States ; and that
intolerance of free speech and free discussion, which often rendered life and property insecure, and led to much unequal legislation.   The amendment was an attempt to give voice to the

---

[1] 16 Wall. 112, 113, and 116.   [2] P. 117.

strong national yearning for that time and that condition of things in which American citizenship should be a sure guarantee of safety, and in which every citizen of the United States might stand erect on every portion of its soil, in the full enjoyment of every right and privilege belonging to a freeman, without fear of violence or molestation." [1]

In same case, Justice Swayne, dissenting, says, " Fairly construed, these amendments may be said to rise to the dignity of a new Magna Charta. The Thirteenth blotted out slavery and forbade forever its restoration. It struck the fetters from four millions of human beings and raised them at once to the sphere of freemen. This was an act of grace and justice performed by the nation." [2]

" Life is the gift of God, and the right to preserve it is the most sacred of the rights of man. Liberty is freedom from all restraints but such as are justly imposed by law. Beyond that line lies the domain of usurpation and tyranny." [3]

" These amendments are all consequences of the late civil war. The prejudices and apprehension as to the central government, which prevailed when the Constitution was adopted, were dispelled by the light of experience. The public mind became satisfied that there was less danger of tyranny in the head than of anarchy and tyranny in the members. The provisions of this section are all eminently conservative in their character. They are a bulwark of defence, and can never be made an engine of oppression. The language employed is unqualified in its scope. There is no exception in its terms, and there can be properly none in their application. By the language ' citizens of the United States' was meant all such citizens ; and by ' any person' was meant all such persons within the jurisdiction of the State. No distinction is intimated on account of race or color. This court has no authority to interpolate a limitation that is neither expressed nor implied. Our duty is to execute the law, not to make it. The protection provided was not intended to be confined to those of any particular race or class, but to embrace equally all classes, races, and conditions of men. It is objected that the

---

[1] 16 Wall. 123.   [2] P. 125.   [3] P. 127.

power conferred is novel and large. The answer is that the novelty was known and the measure deliberately adopted. The power is beneficent in its nature, and cannot be abused. It is such as should exist in every well-ordered system of polity. Where could it be more appropriately lodged than in the hands to which it is confided? It is necessary to enable the government of the nation to secure to every one within its jurisdiction the rights and privileges enumerated, which, according to the plainest considerations of reason and justice and the fundamental principles of the social compact, all are entitled to enjoy. Without such authority any government claiming to be national is glaringly defective. The construction adopted by the majority of my brethren is, in my judgment, much too narrow. It defeats, by a limitation not anticipated, the intent of those by whom the instrument was framed and of those by whom it was adopted. To the extent of that limitation it turns, as it were, what was meant for bread into a stone. By the Constitution, as it stood before the war, ample protection was given against oppression by the Union, but little was given against wrong and oppression by the States. That want was intended to be supplied by this amendment. Against the former this court has been called upon more than once to interpose. Authority of the same amplitude was intended to be conferred as to the latter. But this arm of our jurisdiction is, in these cases, stricken down by the judgment just given. Nowhere, than in this court, ought the will of the nation, as thus expressed, to be more liberally construed or more cordially executed." [1]

On March 27, 1876, Mr. Chief-Justice Waite, construing the Fourteenth Amendment in its relation to a conspiracy to prevent certain persons in Louisiana from enjoying equal protection of the laws,[2] says, "The Fourteenth Amendment prohibits a State from depriving any person of life, liberty, or property, without due process of law; but this adds nothing to the rights of one citizen as against another. It simply furnishes an additional guarantee against any encroachment by the States upon the fundamental rights which belong to every citizen as a mem-

---

[1] 16 Wall. 128, 129.   [2] United States *v.* Cruikshank, 92 U. S. Rep. 554.

ber of society. As was said by Mr. Justice Johnson, in Bank of Columbia *v.* Okely, 4 Wheat. 244, it secures 'the individual from the arbitrary exercise of the powers of the government unrestrained by the established principles of private rights and distributive justice.'"

In the United States *v.* Rives,[1] the Supreme Court say,—

"The plain object of these statutes, as of the Constitution which authorized them, was to place the colored race, in respect of civil rights, upon a level with whites. They made the rights and responsibilities, civil and criminal, of the two races exactly the same. The provisions of the Fourteenth Amendment of the Constitution, which we have quoted, all have reference to State action exclusively, and not to any action of private individuals. It is the State which is prohibited from denying to any person within its jurisdiction the equal protection of the laws, and, consequently, the statutes partially enumerating what civil rights colored men shall enjoy equally with white persons, founded as they are upon the amendment, are intended for protection against State infringement of those rights. Section 641 (R. S.) was also intended for their protection against State action, and against that alone. It is doubtless true, that a State may act through different agencies, either by its legislative, its executive, or its judicial authorities; and the prohibitions of the amendment extend to all action of the State denying equal protection of the laws, whether it be action by one of these agencies or by another. Congress, by virtue of the fifth section of the Fourteenth Amendment, may enforce the prohibitions whenever they are disregarded by either the legislative, the executive, or the judicial department of the State."

On the first of March, 1880, Mr. Justice Strong delivered the opinion of the Supreme Court in Strauder *v.* West Virginia.[2] In construing the Fourteenth Amendment in connection with a West Virginia statute, which denied to its citizens the right and privilege of participating in the administration of justice by being jurors, Mr. Justice Strong says,—

"This is one of a series of constitutional provisions having a

---

[1] 100 U. S. Rep. 318.   [2] 100 U. S. pp. 306, 307, 308.

common purpose,—namely, securing to a race recently emancipated, a race that through many generations had been held in slavery, all the civil rights that the superior race enjoy. The true spirit and meaning of the Amendments, as we said in the Slaughter-House Cases, 16 Wall. 36, cannot be understood without keeping in view the history of the times when they were adopted, and the general objects they plainly sought to accomplish. At the time when they were incorporated into the Constitution, it required little knowledge of human nature to anticipate that those who had long been regarded as an inferior and subject race would, when suddenly raised to the rank of citizenship, be looked upon with jealousy and positive dislike; and that State laws might be enacted or enforced to perpetuate the distinctions that had before existed. Discriminations against them had been habitual. It was well known that, in some States, laws making such discrimination then existed, and others might well be expected. The colored race, as a race, was abject and ignorant, and in that condition was unfitted to command the respect of those who had superior intelligence. Their training had left them mere children, and as such they needed the protection which a wise government extends to those who are unable to protect themselves. They especially needed protection against unfriendly action in the States where they were resident.

" It was in view of these considerations the Fourteenth Amendment was framed and adopted. It was designed to assure to the colored race the enjoyment of all the civil rights that under the law are enjoyed by white persons, and to give to that race the protection of the general government, in that enjoyment, whenever it should be denied by the States. It not only gave citizenship and the privileges of citizenship to persons of color, but it denied to any State the power to withhold from them the equal protection of the laws, and authorized Congress to enforce its provisions by appropriate legislation.

" To quote the language used by us in the Slaughter-House Cases, ' No one can fail to be impressed with the one pervading purpose found in all the amendments, lying at the foundation of each, and without which none of them would have been suggested; we mean the freedom of the slave race, the security and

firm establishment of that freedom, and the protection of the
newly-made freemen and citizens from the oppressions of those
who had formerly exercised unlimited dominion over them.'
So again : ' The existence of laws in the States where the newly
emancipated negroes resided, which discriminated with gross
injustice and hardship against them as a class, was the evil to be
remedied, and by the Fourteenth Amendment such laws were
forbidden. If, however, the States did not conform their laws
to its requirements, then, by the fifth section of the article of
amendment, Congress was authorized to enforce it by suitable
legislation.' And it was added, ' We doubt very much whether
any action of a State, not directed by way of discrimination
against the negroes as a class, will ever be held to come within
the purview of this provision.'

"If this is the spirit and meaning of the amendment, whether
it means more or not, it *is to be construed liberally,* to carry out
the purposes of its framers. It ordains, that no State shall
make or enforce any laws which shall abridge the privileges or
immunities of citizens of the United States (evidently referring
to the newly-made citizens, who, being citizens of the United
States, are declared to be also citizens of the State in which they
reside). It ordains that no State shall deprive any person, within
its jurisdiction, of life, liberty, or property without due process
of law, or deny to any person the equal protection of the laws.
What is this but declaring that the law in the States shall be the
same for the black as the white ; that all persons, whether colored or white, shall stand equal before the laws of the States ;
and, in regard to the colored race, for whose protection the
amendment was primarily designed, that no discrimination shall
be made against them by law because of their color? The words
of the amendment, it is true, are prohibitory, but they contain a
necessary implication, of a positive immunity, or right, most
valuable to the colored race,—namely, the right to exemption
from unfriendly legislation against them distinctively as color ;
exemption from legal discriminations, implying inferiority in
civil society, lessening the security of their enjoyment of the
rights which others enjoy, and discriminations which are steps
towards reducing them to the condition of a subject race."

" The very fact that colored people are singled out and expressly denied by a statute all right to participate in the administration of the law as jurors, because of their color, though they are citizens and may be in other respects fully qualified, is practically a brand upon them, affixed by the law, an assertion of their inferiority, and a stimulant to that race-prejudice which is an impediment to securing to individuals of the race that equal justice which the law aims to secure to all others."   " By their manumission and citizenship the colored race became entitled to the equal protection of the laws of the States in which they resided ; and the apprehension that, through prejudice, they might be denied that equal protection,—that is, that there might be discrimination against them,—was the inducement to bestow upon the national government the power to enforce the provision that no State shall deny to them the equal protection of the laws.   Without the apprehended existence of prejudice, that portion of the amendment would have been unnecessary, and it might have been left to the States to extend equality of protection." [1]

" Its aim was against discrimination because of race and color. As we have said more than once, its design was to protect an emancipated race, and to strike down all possible legal discriminations against those who belong to it.   To quote further from 16 Wall. (*supra*) : ' In giving construction to any of these articles [amendments], it is necessary to keep the main purpose steadily in view.'   ' It is so clearly a provision for that race and that emergency, that a strong case would be necessary for its application to any other.'   We are not now called upon to affirm or deny that it had other purposes.   The Fourteenth Amendment makes no attempt to enumerate the rights it designed to protect.   It speaks in general terms, and those are as comprehensive as possible.   Its language is prohibitory ; but every prohibition implies the existence of rights and immunities, prominent among which is an immunity from inequality of legal protection, either for life, liberty, or property.   Any State action that denies this immunity to a colored man is in conflict with the Constitution." [2]

---

[1] 100 U. S. 319.   [2] P. 310.

On May 2, 1881, Mr. Justice Harlan, in Neal *v.* Delaware,[1] in construing the Fourteenth Amendment, says, " The question thus presented is of the highest moment to that race, the security of whose rights of life, liberty, and property, and to the equal protection of the laws, was the primary object of the recent amendments to the national Constitution."

In United States *v.* Harris,[2] decided at October Term, 1882, Mr. Justice Woods, speaking of this amendment, says, " The language of the amendment does not leave this subject in doubt. When the State has been guilty of no violation of its provisions ; when it has not made or enforced any law abridging the privileges or immunities of citizens of the United States ; when no one of its departments has deprived any person of life, liberty, or property without due process of law, or denied to any person within its jurisdiction the equal protection of the laws ; when, on the contrary, the laws of the State, as enacted by its legislative, and construed by its judicial, and administered by its executive departments, recognize and protect the rights of all persons, the amendment imposes no duty and confers no power upon Congress."

Mr. Justice Bradley, in the Civil-Rights Cases, decided at October Term, 1883, in construing the Civil-Rights Bill of 1875, says, " This abrogation and denial of rights, for which the States alone were or could be responsible, was the *great seminal and fundamental wrong which was intended to be remedied.*"[3] " Positive rights and privileges are undoubtedly secured by the Fourteenth Amendment."[4]

Again, in same case, Mr. Justice Harlan, dissenting, says,—

" But what was secured to colored citizens of the United States—as between them and their respective States—by the national grant to them of State citizenship? With what rights, privileges, and immunities did this grant invest them? There is one, if there be no other,—exemption from race-discrimination in respect of any civil right belonging to citizens of the white race in the same State. That, surely, is their constitutional privilege when within the jurisdiction of other States ; and such

---

[1] 103 U. S. 389.   [2] 106 U. S. 639.   [3] 109 U. S. 18.   [4] P. 11.

must be their constitutional right in their own State, unless the recent amendments be splendid baubles, thrown out to delude those who deserved fair and generous treatment at the hands of the nation. Citizenship in this country necessarily imports at least equality of civil rights among citizens of every race in the same State. It is fundamental in American citizenship that in respect of such rights there shall be no discrimination by the State, or its officers, or by individuals or corporations exercising public functions or authority, against any citizen because of his race or previous condition of servitude."[1]

" They are not to be sustained, except upon the assumption that there is, in this land of universal liberty, a class which may still· be discriminated against, even in respect of rights of a character so necessary and supreme that, deprived of their enjoyment in common with others, a freeman is not only branded as one inferior and infected, but, in the competitions of life, is robbed of some of the most essential means of existence; and all this solely because they belong to a particular race which the nation has liberated. The Thirteenth Amendment alone obliterated the race-line so far as all rights fundamental in a state of freedom are concerned."[2]

" It was undoubtedly the object of the clause in question to place the citizens of each State upon the same footing with citizens of other States, so far as the advantages resulting from citizenship in those States are concerned. It relieves them from the disabilities of alienage in other States; it inhibits discriminating legislation against them by other States; it gives them the right of free ingress in other States and egress from them; it insures to them in other States the same freedom possessed by the citizens of those States in the acquisition and enjoyment of property and in the pursuit of happiness, and it secures to them in other States the equal protection of their laws. It has been justly said, that no provision in the Constitution has tended so strongly to constitute the citizens of the United States one people as this."

" Otherwise, it would be in the power of any State, by dis-

---

[1] 109 U. S. 48.   [2] Pp. 39, 40.

criminating class legislation against its own citizens of a particular race or color, to withhold from citizens of other States, belonging to that proscribed race, when within her limits, privileges and immunities of the character regarded by all courts as fundamental in citizenship; and that, too, when the constitutional guarantee is that citizens of each State shall be entitled to 'all privileges and immunities of citizens in the several States.' No State may, by discrimination against a portion of its own citizens of a par-ticular race, in respect of privileges and immunities fundamental in citizenship, impair the constitutional right of citizens of other States, of whatever race, to enjoy in that State all such privileges and immunities as are there accorded to her most favored citizens. A colored citizen of Ohio or Indiana, while in the jurisdiction of Tennessee, is entitled to enjoy any privilege or immunity, fun-damental in citizenship, which is given to citizens of the white race in the latter State. It is not to be supposed that any one will controvert this proposition." [1]

" The one underlying purpose of congressional legislation has been to enable the black race to take the rank of mere citi-zens. The difficulty has been to compel a recognition of the legal right of the black race to take the rank of citizens, and to secure the enjoyment of privileges belonging, under the law, to them as a component part of the people for whose welfare and happiness government is ordained." [2]

" I hazard nothing, in view of former adjudications, in saying that no State can sustain her denial to colored citizens of other States, while within her limits, of privileges, immunities, funda-mental in republican citizenship, upon the ground that she ac-cords such privileges and immunities only to her white citizens and withholds them from her colored citizens. The colored citizens of other States, within the jurisdiction of that State, could claim, in virtue of section 2, article 4, of the Constitution, every privilege and immunity which that State secures to her white citizens."

" If the constitutional amendments be enforced, according to the intent with which, as I conceive, they were adopted, there

---

[1] 109 U. S. 47, 48.   [2] P. 61.

cannot be in this republic any class of human beings in practical subjection to another class, with power in the latter to dole out to the former just such privileges as they may choose to grant. The supreme law of the land has decreed that no authority shall be exercised in this country upon the basis of discrimination, in respect of civil rights, against freemen and citizens because of their race, color, or previous condition of servitude. To that decree—for the due enforcement of which, by appropriate legislation, Congress has been invested with express power—every one must bow, whatever may have been, or whatever now are, his individual views as to the wisdom or policy, either of the recent changes in the fundamental law, or of the legislation which has been enacted to give them effect."[1]

The foregoing extracts abundantly establish all that the friends of civil rights have claimed for the earlier decisions of the Supreme Court. That milk-white hind,—Civil Liberty,—doomed to death, but fated never to die, had taken sanctuary under the broad shadow of the Supreme Court. We have seen that the Supreme Court continued, with richest hands, to rain its pearls and gold upon the pathway of Civil Rights, until the 14th day of January, 1878. Thereafter the generous shower suddenly abated.

---

[1] 109 U. S. 62.

CHAPTER XV.

"Fierce as a vulture rushing on its prey."—TASSO.

"Away! these trappings to the rabble show:
Me they deceive not; for your soul I know,
Within, without."—PERSIUS.

"There is, sir, a magic in this arrangement, which is not friendly to justice."—BAYARD.

"A great nation must not be impaled upon a pin's point."—J. BLACK.

"And then the justice,
In fair round belly, with good capon lined,
With eyes severe, and beard of formal cut,
Full of wise saws and modern instances.
And so he plays his part."—SHAKESPEARE.

"The dew of justice which did seldom fall,
And when it dropped, the drops were very small."—BEAUMONT.

"Words are grown so false I am loath to prove reason with them."—SHAKESPEARE.

"Vossius is indeed a great authority; but, when he has nothing to justify a useless conjecture but a similarity of sound, we ought not to be afraid of opposing an appearance of reason to him."—TOOKE.

"If they could only have understood that, in a free country, liberty and law are inseparable, they would have been enrolled among our greatest benefactors, for they would have added strength and grandeur to our institutions. But they could not come up to the height of the great subject."—BLACK.

"While the beacon-fire blazed its brightest, the watchman had quitted it; that no pilgrim could now ask him, Watchman, what of the night?"—CARLYLE.

"Under this double trust, then, from the past and for the future, let us take heed to our ways, and, while it is called to-day, resolve that the great heritage we have received shall be handed down through the long line of

189

the advancing generations, the home of liberty, the abode of justice, the stronghold of faith among men, 'which holds the moral elements of the world together,' and of faith in God, which binds that world to His throne."—Evarts.

"There were giants in the earth in those days."—Genesis.

"I have a large acquaintance among the most exalted classes of men; but you are the only human being for whom I ever feel an awful reverence."—Wilberforce.

"I fancy he had been looking this long time to give it up whenever the commander-in-chief requested; to quit his laborious sentry place; honorably lay up his arms, and be gone to rest,—all eternity to rest."—Carlyle.

"I take the liberty to introduce your august and immortal name in a book I send you."—Wilberforce.

"The fervid genius which has cast a sort of shade upon all the works of man."—Erskine.

"Like the setting of a great victorious summer sun, its course now finished."—Carlyle.

"A few feet under the ground reigns so profound a silence, and yet so much tumult on the surface!"—Victor Hugo.

"In the democracy of death all men, at least, are equal. There is neither rank nor station nor prerogative in the republic of the grave. At that fatal threshold the philosopher ceases to be wise and the song of the poet is silent. At that fatal threshold Dives relinquishes his millions and Lazarus his rags. The poor man is as rich as the richest, and the rich man is as poor as the pauper. The creditor loses his usury, and the debtor is acquitted of his obligation. The proud man surrenders his dignity, the politician his honors, the worldling his pleasures. Here the invalid needs no physician, and the laborer rests from unrequited toil."—Ingalls.

"And with the setting sun,
Dropped from the zenith like a falling star."—Milton.

"'Stop, stop, sir. Not so hasty, I beseech you. Let us leave the Swedes and the Russians and the Greeks and the Romans out of the question for the present; and confine yourself, if you please, as in the beginning you confined my inquiry, to the English only. Above two hundred instances, do you say, produced by Johnson as proofs of at least forty-six different meanings of this one preposition "*for*," when Harris will not

allow one single meaning to all the prepositions in the world together.' "
—Epea Pteroenta.

"Ali Baba, when he entered the cave of the Forty Thieves, could not
have been more amazed by the wealth of its contents than some people
will be when they read it."—Putnam's Magazine.

"It is likewise to be observed, that this society has a peculiar cant and
jargon of their own, that no other mortal can understand, and wherein
all their laws are written, which they take special care to multiply;
whereby they have wholly confounded the very essence of truth and falsehood, of right and wrong."—Swift.

> "The earth hath bubbles, as the water has,
> And these are of them."—Shakespeare.

"Your demurrer is a preposterous sham, and you must answer over."
—J. Black.

"A man must be not only well practised, but even hackneyed, in our
courts of justice to discover the above description of my crime in the prepositions '*of*' and '*concerning.*'" —Mansfield.

"Having at the same time a kind of obscure signification,
And yet having neither signification nor no signification,
But a middle something between signification and no signification,
Sharing the attributes both of signification and no signification,
And linking signification and no signification together."
—Epea Pteroenta.

"It is necessary to insist upon this; for upon sacks of wool, and on
benches forensic, sit grave men, and agricolous persons in the Commons,
crying out 'Ancestors, ancestors! hodie non! Saxons, Danes, save us!
Fiddlefrig, help us! Howel, Ethelwolf, protect us!' Any cover for nonsense, any veil for trash, any pretext for repelling the innovations of conscience and of duty!"—Sydney Smith.

The opinion in Hall *v.* DeCuir was filed on the 14th day of
January, 1878. It was the first of the succession of legal wounds
from which the prostrate form of Civil Rights never rallied.
Upon the lost tribe of freedom, upon the startled ears of the
sable children of sorrow and darkness, its echoes pealed, like
the reverberations of Sumter's guns upon Mr. Webster's land

of "Liberty and union, now and forever, one and inseparable."
It filled the newly-adopted citizens with alarm. In their agony,
men and women sat down and wept. The exaggerations of
fear hurried them to erroneous conclusions; and even before they
had examined the decision, they had feared that grave and
learned legal opinions would be only the diplomatic artifices of
subserviency, to undermine the sanctuary to which they had
fled, and in which they had hoped to find eternal protection.
The more enlightened reflected, that after a vast and sudden
national change, judges must, as men, be liable to be unconsciously swayed by the general current of the feelings and actions
of the individuals and communities around them, who had not
accommodated themselves to the reformation contemplated by
the war amendments and as yet accomplished only on paper.
Time has justified their apprehensions; the natural progeny
of this decision was the race-antagonism which now fills the
country with the same agitation as did slavery. The eye of the
vulgar (which looks only at results) quickly saw that the Civil-
Rights Cases had in effect decided that civic inferiority on account of color had not been removed even by an act of Congress;
that the Civil-Rights Bill was constitutional only in so far as it
inhibited discrimination by the *States* on account of color, but
was unconstitutional and void when it prohibited the *citizen* of
the State from treating the African as if he had rights which
the white man was bound to respect. In fact, the unlearned
could not draw the distinction between this decision and that
of Scott *v.* Sandford, which suggested that the African had no
rights which the white citizen was bound to respect. The industrial classes construed the judgment in the Civil-Rights Cases
as a license for the indulgence of their prejudices to the utmost
of their caprice. The ferocious Labor Mastiff, "Tray, Blanche,
Sweetheart, the little dogs and all," which up to this period had
been securely chained to their kennels under the authority of
this act of Congress, were immediately loosened, and have ever
since unceasingly kept up a furious barking at every African
citizen who dared approach any avenue of distinction leading to
the royal reservations of the aristocracy of Labor. At this time
all the great luminaries of "Civil Liberty" had set; those great

lights, Lincoln, Greeley, Sumner, Seward, who for a long period shone so auspiciously in the country's firmament, had "dropped from the zenith like falling stars." The sudden eclipse of Civil Rights in the case of Hall *v.* DeCuir was viewed with abject terror; and in this reign of darkness the decision could not be regarded as dispassionately as hereafter it may be viewed, under the steady light of that large clear star, the philosophic historian of the future, when the dust of both races will have been mingled in one common soil. It was not strange that this suffering, benighted race—which could not be sure, that resistless destiny, in the march of illimitable progress, would eventually work out in America the civic equality of all men before the law—should feel that the covenant of their freedom had been violated in its chosen sanctuary; and should fear that they would now be subjected to the most odious of all tyranny,—that of the myrmidon Labor-tyrant and public servant.

The African race looked then, and looks now, upon the decision in Hall *v.* DeCuir as an attempt to perpetuate the rites of slavery. In vain, they thought, had civil war severed the head of slavery from its trunk, if its mortal poison still lurked in the veins of the commonwealth. Civil Rights once smothered, though with roses, the gentleness of the process made little difference to them. They felt as if with naked feet they were treading upon snakes. It seemed to them, that robust legal organisms had taken the infectious disease; that ere long, resounding glen, rock, and cavern would give back the deep-mouthed baying of the Cerberus of race-antagonism. All these gloomy forebodings, though not more rational, were far more excusable, than the inflammatory chaff, the Murat-Halstead-Foraker pure and unadulterated dry rot, that "the war amendments might be repealed," "the South indemnified for emancipated slaves," "the Confederate soldiers pensioned," and "slavery reestablished under the ante-bellum black code," if the political antagonists of this class of sturdy and belligerent statesmen should control the government.

An explanatory retrospection may well be pardoned before approaching the Sumter-gun of Hall *v.* DeCuir, from which the smoke has not yet rolled away. The history of the Civil-Rights

Bill is almost a biography of Charles Sumner,—orator, scholar, philanthropist, statesman,—who, unfortunately for the cause his martyr-life espoused, was, nevertheless, neither a Napoleonic commander in the field of national politics, nor a constitutional nor *nisi-prius* lawyer. The enlightened publicists who believed slavery a divine institution regarded him as a gladiator who fought in the arena for public entertainment, a knight-errant searching for adventures in which he might exhibit his prowess. To the chosen disciples of Civil Liberty throughout the world, he was the morning sun, shining in all the strength of an advancing civilization, the resplendent illuminator of the Western hemisphere; a dignified, majestic, natural king among men, whose words were the divinity of human reason. Great lawyers, before the evil days, when the simple process of complaint and answer places ignorance upon equality with learning, that breed of soaring eagles (now hawked at by mousing owls) who telescoped their quarry from the lofty solitary peaks of learning, —men of gold-coin mintage, like Webster, Pinckney, Choate, Cushing, O'Connor, Carpenter, Reverdy Johnson, Black, Frelinghuysen, Evarts, Brewster, Garland, and hosts of others, whose splendid fame at the bar, like Mr. Sumner's in the Senate, will always "form a part of the true glory of the nation,"—the men who had sat at trial-tables for a quarter of a century, day in and day out, who were always serene and profound,—saw further into its evolution than did the author of the last Civil-Rights Bill. And yet the amplitude and activity of his intellect were never more wonderfully illustrated than in that "historic review of the foundation of republics," in his speech upon the basis of representation, filling forty-one columns of the *Congressional Globe*, and closing with these memorable words:

"Show me a creature with erect countenance, and looking to heaven, made in the image of God, and I will show you a man who, of whatever country or race, whether darkened by equatorial sun or blanched with the northern cold, is an equal with you before the heavenly Father, and equally with you entitled to all the rights of human nature. You cannot deny these rights without impiety. God has so linked the national welfare with national duty that you cannot deny these rights without peril to the republic. It is not enough that you have given liberty. By the same title that we claim liberty do we claim equality also. . . . The Roman Cato, after declaring his belief in the immortality of the soul, added, that if this were an error it was an error that he loved ; and now, declaring my belief in liberty and equality as the God-given birthright of all men, let me say in the same spirit, if this be an error it is an error which I love, if this be a fault it is a fault which I shall be slow to renounce, if this be an illusion it is an illusion which I pray may wrap the world in its angelic form."

Profound constitutional lawyers like Senators Anthony and Fessenden perceived that the Civil-Rights Bill was only a re-enactment by Congress of the Fourteenth Amendment, and that civil rights were safer under this amendment than under any act of Congress passed to enforce its provisions ; and when Mr. Sumner complained of the emasculation of his Civil-Rights Bill, which had taken place during his enforced absence, he was gravely reminded that, as originally framed, it was doubtful law. These great legal instructors of their kind had more enlarged practical experience in solving the legal uncertainties attending developments of great constitutional reformations than Mr. Sumner ; and when, on the afternoon of the 14th day of January, 1878, they read the opinion and the concurring judgment in Hall *v.* DeCuir, their blood almost ran cold, they turned pale, for they saw at a glance that defeat had again happened in the history of the civil rights of these American citizens. It had many times before chanced in their great battles that a diminutive creature, like Titmouse, " on the other side," a simple-looking old rodent, with gray beard, sleek skin, long tail, and sharp teeth, had gnawed away the meshes in which a Numidian lion lay toiled.

It is one of the most touching events in the historical literature of civil rights, that for almost fifteen years before the eventful fourteenth day of January, 1878, Life and Death had been disputing for victory over Mr. Sumner. During this period the " fell sergeant, who is strict in his arrest," had more than once, with his dread summons, appeared to the great American ; but he always felt powerless to serve the writ of Hades when this noble weary spirit, this latter-day Cato, uniformly sighed forth, from the depth of a suffering heart, the mournful reply: "If the publication of my works were complete.l, and my Civil-Rights Bill passed, no visitor could enter the door that would be more welcome than Death." At last, upon midnight of Tuesday, March 10, 1874, Mr. Sumner distinctly felt God's finger touch him; he knew his angel was there; it stood so near him, he could hear the beatings of its wings; and when, on the afternoon of the next day, the solemn messenger, showing him "the golden key that opens the palace of eternity," kindly beckoned him away, the watch-worn, weary sentinel signified his willingness to lay aside his armor and be at rest. The royal spirit had passed through the eternal gates, but his mighty work survived.

Let us turn from the mere shadow, the man, to the great living reality, his work, and mingle with those hard-headed, common-law, common-sense lawyers, cold as Alpine glaciers and as immovable, who, as the assayer weighs gold, weighed every word of the opinions which Mr. Chief-Justice Waite and Mr. Justice Clifford had filed on the fatal 14th day of March, 1878, in the momentous case of Hall *v.* DeCuir. It will be remembered that Mr. Justice Clifford had dissented from the construction his brethren had placed upon the Fourteenth Amendment, in the famous case of Strauder *v.* West Virginia. This was a decision which excited the admiration and wonder of the American people; not only because it was judicially adverse to the pagan theology of the Dred-Scott case, and was the revelation of a new and more beautiful form of life and doctrine in America, but because it carried also the imperishable charm of a determination by the Supreme Court to maintain, as the American Gospel under the new dispensation of the Fourteenth Amendment, that the first duty of God's ministers of justice was to free his subjects from any restriction upon the inalienable rights of humanity. Mr. Justice Clifford not only concurred with the court in the case of Hall *v.* DeCuir,[1] but also delivered with great force his separate opinion,—more properly an invaluable treatise, a masterpiece of learning and ingenuity, upon miscella-

---

[1] 95 U. S. 485.

neous subjects ; such as the exclusive authority of Congress to regulate interstate commerce, the enrollment and licensing of common carriers, the color-line discrimination in public schools, and other not less interesting though not quite kindred legal topics, inasmuch as the sole question presented by the record involved the constitutionality of a Louisiana statute, and of that only in so far as it assumed the right of regulating the business of common carriers by water beyond the State limits of Louisiana. A natural deference for extraordinary ability, well-known patriotism, strict impartiality, and exalted station, scarcely concealed the wide-spread solicitude that the all-embracing mind of Mr. Justice Clifford, throughout the wide range of this constitutional, foreign and domestic excursion, should not have paid even " the cold tribute of a passing glance" to the Fourteenth Amendment, and to its constitutional and commercial bearing upon the rights, immunities, and privileges of American citizens who were subjected to the rules and regulations of public servants. Mr. Chief-Justice Waite delivered the opinion of the court, defining the prerogative of the public servant, with a more guarded and abundant caution. Professional expectation, however, was doomed to deplore the absence in his opinion also of any reference to the bearing of the Fourteenth Amendment upon these grave questions. The conspicuous absence in both these judgments of any reference to the commercial aspect of civil rights under this amendment might, in law phrase, be appropriately classed under *casus omissi ;* but the American citizens of African descent uniformly regarded it as a pregnant coincidence.

The Louisiana act, stripped of its technical verbiage, enacted substantially the provisions of the Civil-Rights Bill of 1875. The facts in Hall *v.* DeCuir were these: Mrs. DeCuir, a citizen of African descent, took passage, on a regular packet for transportation of persons between New Orleans and Vicksburg, for Hermitage, an intermediate point; and, being refused, on account of her color, the cabin accommodations especially set apart for white persons, brought an action for damages for her mental and physical suffering.

The defendant maintained that he, as owner, had by law the

right to prescribe rules and regulations for the accommodation of passengers on his steamer. The sole questions presented by the record were, first, whether State legislation which seeks to impose a direct burden upon interstate commerce, or to interfere with its freedom, encroaches upon the exclusive power of Congress ; secondly, whether the Louisiana act of February 23, 1869, regulating the business of carriers of passengers, so far as it has effect upon foreign and interstate commerce was unconstitutional. Speaking of the general authority of the public servants to adopt regulations for passengers, Mr. Chief-Justice Waite said: [1]

" This power of regulation may be exercised without legislation as well as with it. By refraining from action, Congress, in effect, adopts, as its own regulations, those which the common law, or the civil law, where that prevails, has provided for the government of such business, and those which the States, in the regulation of their domestic concerns, have established affecting commerce, but not regulating it within the meaning of the Constitution; in fact, congressional legislation is only necessary to cure existing laws, as they are discovered, and to adapt such laws to new developments of trade. As was said by Mr. Justice Field, speaking for the court in Welton *v.* Missouri, 91 U. S. 282, ' Inaction (by Congress) is equivalent to a declaration that interstate commerce shall remain free and untrammelled.' Applying that principle to the circumstances of this case, congressional inaction left Benson at liberty to adopt such reasonable rules and regulations for the disposition of passengers upon his boat, while pursuing her voyage within Louisiana or without, as seemed to him most for the interest of all concerned. The statute under which this suit is brought, as construed by the State court, seeks to take away from him that power so long as he is within Louisiana ; and, *while recognizing to the fullest extent the principle which sustains a statute, unless its unconstitutionality is clearly established, we think this statute, to the extent that it requires those engaged in the transportation of passengers among the States to carry colored passengers in Louisiana in the same cabin with whites, is unconstitutional and void.*"

---

[1] 95 U. S. 490.

That the unprofessional reader may more clearly discern the veiled sophistry by which Jurisprudence in this case thus triumphed over the *Justice* of the Fourteenth Amendment, it is necessary to scrutinize more closely the false assumption in the premises upon which the conclusions of the court rest; and it will be seen that the major and the minor terms and the conclusion were falsely derived. It is true, that the rules of carriers for the transportation of passengers between the States may be a regulation of commerce between the States. It is also true, that Congress has constitutional authority to regulate such interstate commerce. It is true that Congress has not seen fit to legislate upon the subject of that species of commerce between the States which consists in the transportation of citizens between the States; but it is *equally true*, that, independent of the legislation of Congress upon the branch of commerce which embraces transportation of citizens through the States, the right, privilege, and immunity of citizens of the several States to be transported throughout the United States without being subjected to regulations of the carrier which discriminate against them on account of their color, is also secured by the constitutional guarantee of the Fourteenth Article of Amendment to the Constitution.

The vice in the logic applied by the court to the "circumstances of this case," and the fault of its syllogism is discoverable in the very important omission of the guarantee contained in the prohibitive provisions of the Fourteenth Article of Amendment to the Constitution. That guarantee was not affected by the inaction of Congress, and it was assuredly as potential as either the "*action*" or the "*inaction*" of Congress. The court seems not to have heard the voice of the Fourteenth Amendment. The regulations of the master of transportation in this case which authorized discrimination on account of color in the commerce between the States, which consists of the transportation of citizens, could no more repeal this prohibitive guarantee than could Congress and the Supreme Court repeal the Constitution.

That is to say, the court decides, that the Fourteenth Amendment being the supreme law, and the acts of Congress to enforce its provisions having been declared *void*, in so far as it operated to prevent individual or corporate discrimination on account of color in the enjoyment by a citizen of the United States of her civil rights, it could be fairly maintained, that this "*inaction*" by Congress—that is, the passage of the Enforcement Act of 1866—was equivalent to a declaration by Congress, and an adoption as its own regulation, *that interstate commerce*— that is, the *exercise of her civil rights by Mrs. DeCuir* to travel on a steamboat—shall remain free and untrammelled, which means shall be *subject* to those regulations which the common or civil law of the State provided for the government of such business ["such business" meaning the exercise of a civil right of a citizen of the United States], and those which that State, in the regulation of her domestic concerns (that is, the authorization of *discrimination by their common carriers' rules and regulations on account of color*), have established respecting *commerce*, —that is, by the term COMMERCE meaning the *enjoyment of their civil rights, by citizens* of the United States of African descent, to travel upon a steam vessel.

Mr. Justice Clifford, after discussing[1] the authority of the public servants under this particular statute, returns to the general subject, and says :

"Such proprietors have not only that right, but the further right to consult and provide for their own interests in the management of the vessel as a common incident to their right of property. They are not bound to admit passengers on board who refuse to obey the reasonable regulations of the vessel, or who are guilty of gross and vulgar habits of conduct, or who make disturbances on board, or whose characters are doubtful, dissolute, suspicious, or unequivocally bad. Nor are they bound to admit passengers on board whose object it is to interfere with the interests of the patronage of the proprietors on board so as to make their business less lucrative or their management less acceptable to the public. (Jencks *v.* Coleman, 2 Sumn. 221.) Corresponding views are expressed by the Supreme Court of Michigan in an analogous case, in which the distinction of the right of an applicant to be admitted on board, and his claim to

---

[1] 95 U. S. 552.

dictate what part of the vessel he shall occupy, is clearly pointed out. Referring to that subject, the court say the right to be carried is one thing, and the privilege of a passenger on board as to what part of the vessel may be occupied by him is another and a very different thing; and they add, that it is the latter and not the former which is subject to reasonable rules and regulations, and is, where such rules and regulations exist, to be determined by the proprietors. Damages were claimed in that case for refusing the plaintiff the privilege of the cabin, but the court held that the refusal was nothing more or less than denying him certain accommodations from which he was excluded by the rules and regulations of the steamer. (Day *v.* Owen, 5 Mich. 520.) Proprietors of the kind may make rules and regulations, but they must be reasonable; and the court held in that case, that to be so they should have for their object the accommodation of the passengers, including everything to render the transportation most comfortable and least annoying, not to one, two, or any given number carried at any particular time, but to the great majority ordinarily transported; and they also held, that such rules and regulations should be of a permanent nature, and not be made for a particular occasion or emergency.

"Special and important duties indubitably are imposed upon carriers of passengers for the benefit of the travelling public, but it must not be forgotten that the vehicles and vessels which such carriers use do not belong to the public. They are private property, the use and enjoyment of which belong to the proprietors. (Ang., Carriers, 5th ed., sec. 525.) Concede, what is undoubtedly true, that the use and employment of such vehicles and vessels, during the time they are allowed the privileges of common carriers, may be subjected to such conditions and obligations as the nature of their employment requires for the comfort, security, and safety of passengers, *still the settled rules of constitutional law forbid that a State legislature may invade the dominion of private rights by arbitrary restrictions, requirements, or limitations, by which the property of the owners or possessors would be virtually stripped of all utility or value if bound to comply with the regulations.* (Jencks *v.* Coleman, *supra.*) Both steamboats and railways are modern modes of conveyance, but Shaw, Ch. J., decided that the rules of the common law were applicable to them, as they take the place of other modes of carrying passengers, and he held that they have authority to make reasonable and suitable regulations as regards passengers intending to pass and repass in their vehicles or vessels. (Commonwealth *v.* Power, 7 Met. 601; Hibbard *v.* R.R. Co., 15 N.Y. 405; R.R. Co. *v.* Whittemore, 43 Ill. 420.) 'They are,' said the Chief Justice, in that case, 'in a condition somewhat similar to that of an inn-keeper, whose premises are open to all guests. Yet he is not only empowered to make such proper arrangements as will promote his own interests, but he is bound to regulate his house so as to preserve order and, if practicable, prevent breaches of the peace.' (Vinton *v.* R.R. Co., 11 Allen, 304.)

" Cases of like import are quite numerous, and the Supreme Court of Pennsylvania decided directly that a public carrier may separate passengers in his conveyance; and they deduce his power to do so from his right of private property in the means of conveyance, and the necessity which arises for such a regulation to promote the public interest. Speaking to that point, they say that ' the private means the carrier uses belong wholly to himself;' and they hold the right of control in that regard as necessary to enable the carrier to protect his own interests, and to perform his duty to the travelling public. His authority in that regard, as that court holds, arises from his ownership of the property, and his public duty to promote the comfort and enjoyment of those travelling in his conveyance. Guarded by those views, the court held that it is not an unreasonable regulation to seat passengers so as to preserve order and decorum, and to prevent collisions arising from natural or well-known repugnances which are likely to breed disturbances, where white and colored persons are huddled together without their consent. (R. R. Co. *v.* Miles, 55 Pa. 209.)

" Where the passenger embarks without making any special contract, and without knowledge as to what accommodations will be offered, the law implies a contract which obliges the carrier to furnish suitable accommodations according to the room at his disposal; but the passenger in such a case is not entitled to any particular apartments or special accommodations. Substantial equality of right is the law of the State and of the United States, but equality does not mean identity; as in the nature of things identity in the accommodation afforded to passengers, whether colored or white, is impossible, unless our commercial marine shall undergo an entire change. Adult male passengers are never allowed a passage in the ladies' cabin, nor can all be accommodated, if the company is large, in the state-rooms. Passengers are entitled to proper diet and lodging; but the laws of the United States do not require the master of a steamer to put persons in the same apartment who would be repulsive or disagreeable to each other. Steamers carrying passengers as a material part of their employment are common carriers, and as such enjoy the rights and are subject to the duties and obligations of such carriers; but there was and is not any law of Congress which forbids such a carrier from providing separate apartments for his passengers. What the passenger has a right to require is such accommodations as he has contracted for, or, in the absence of any special contract, such suitable accommodations as the room and means at the disposal of the carrier enable him to supply; and, in locating his passengers in apartments and at their meals, it is not only the right of the master, but his duty, to exercise such reasonable discretion and control as will promote, as far as practicable, the comfort and convenience of his whole company."

CHAPTER XVI.

"Divers philosophers hold that the lips are parcel of the mind."—
SHAKESPEARE.

"To whom the double blessing does belong,
  With Moses' inspiration, Aaron's tongue."—ANONYMOUS.

"O Physics, beware of Metaphysics!"—NEWTON.

"But hell's dire fiend, who saw the tumults cease,
  And every vengeful bosom calmed to peace,
  Still unrestrained, by Stygian rancor driven,
  Opposed the laws of fate and will of Heaven."—TASSO.

"In general, I adhere to the remark, that the proper way to understand our novel and complex system of government is to avoid, as much as may be, the use of technical terms and phrases appropriate to other forms, and to examine the process of its formation, the peculiarity of its structure, and the limitation and distribution of its powers."—MADISON.

"It is the record of the revelation through history of the divine economy. It is not to construe the polity of one age, but of the ages. There is the unfolding of principles which are deeper than a formal order and a formal organization. They are not concluded in the transient and local. In the succession of events they do not become isolated, and in the changes of time they do not become obsolete. They are the revelation of an authority which no tyrant can suspend and no anarchy subvert."—MULFORD.

"Let me ask if this was not a vicious construction of a court of the highest authority and greatest importance in the nation,—in a court from which no one had an appeal, and to whom it belonged to establish the leading principles of national jurisprudence?"—BAYARD.

"It withdraws particular facts from their historical connection, and holds them up as the centre and term of a system, without any limitation, and without any regard to historical circumstances."—SCHLEGEL.

"Your objection is like that of the ancient Pistol to the word 'steal,' for which he wished to substitute 'convey.'"—J. BLACK.

204

"Our fathers long ago cast them both aside among the rubbish of the Dark Ages; and they intended that we, their children, should know them only that we might blush and shudder at the shameless injustice and the brutal cruelties which they were allowed to perpetrate in other times and in other countries."—ID.

"'I fancy,' said the Brahmin, 'that we should find very few republics on earth. Men are seldom worthy to govern themselves. This happiness should only belong to little people, who conceal themselves in islands or between mountains, like rabbits who steal away from carnivorous animals, but at length are discovered and devoured.'"—VOLTAIRE.

THE profound jurisconsult, Mr. Justice Clifford, in the opening of his concurring opinion, broadly announces that "common carriers" by water may adopt "rules and regulations for the management of their business not inconsistent with the State Constitutions and enactments of the State legislatures." The civil and common-law courts, in an unbroken current of decisions from the earliest period of commerce, have uniformly declared that such "rules and regulations" must be "reasonable" and tend to promote the general welfare of the public. It is the absence of the primal condition, "*reasonable*," annexed by the law to all the rules and regulations of common carriers as a condition precedent to their validity, which makes Justice Clifford's opinion anomalous.

Chief-Justice Waite, delivering the judgment of the court, had quoted with approval the language of Justice Field in Welton *v.* Missouri:[1] "Inaction (by Congress) is equivalent to a declaration that interstate *commerce shall remain free* and untrammelled." He continues: "Applying that principle to the circumstances of this case, congressional inaction left Benson (the master of the steamer upon which Mrs. DeCuir had taken passage) free to adopt such 'reasonable' rules and 'regulations' for the disposition of his passengers upon the boat, while pursuing her voyage within Louisiana or without, as seemed to him most for the interest of all concerned."

The *rationale* of Mr. Justice Clifford's opinion, therefore, is,

---

[1] 91 U. S. 282.

that, wherever the State Constitution or legislature has *not* imposed limitations upon the authority of the public servants, such "inaction" is equivalent to a declaration that commerce—which involves the public service, and its rights, privileges, and immunities—called civil rights—shall be "free and untrammelled," and that mere public servants are invested with discretionary powers to establish just what rules and regulations they may see fit, without right of appeal, whether or not said rules and regulations are "*reasonable*," provided they seem to them to promote the comfort and general convenience of the public. This is a most extraordinary doctrine. If fully carried out, it would make the public servant entirely irresponsible. The traditionary lore of the centuries may be ransacked in vain for a more scientific plan by which one class of the community is authorized to tyrannize over another. It is difficult, in an age when the enjoyment of almost every civil right is dependent upon the REASONABLE nature of these very rules, to conceive of a more absolute systematized despotism, or of one less incapable of recognition according to any established principles of judicial practice and procedure.

The legal signification of the phraseology "free and untrammelled," as thus applied for the first time to the grave duties and extraordinary responsibilities which the civil and common law impose upon the vocation of public servants in the commerce of common carriers,—mere bailees for hire,—is extremely obscure; nor is it at all clarified by the Chief Justice's annexation to these mysterious words of the significant legal term "reasonable." If the Chief Justice by the term "reasonable" intended to impose a limitation upon the words "free and untrammelled," Mr. Justice Clifford has rejected the qualification—paradoxical at best—by omitting the word "reasonable" from the text in this part of his concurring opinion. It was certainly not intended to assert, nor can it be maintained, that State or interstate commerce, by the "inaction" of Congress under its authority to regulate commerce, was left "free and untrammelled" from the operation of the Fourteenth Amendment.

This curious phrase, "free and untrammelled," thus employed in connection with the commerce of bailees for hire, originated, and was first introduced into the jurisprudence of this country, in defining the commercial law of bailment in its application to a citizen of the United States of African descent asserting her privileges and immunities from discrimination on account of color under the Fourteenth Amendment. Her civil right, enabling her to travel, was as such an adjunct and necessary incident to commerce, and subject to the regulation of Congress like all interstate traffic.

It may be observed that the construction thus placed, for the first time, upon the "inaction of Congress," by apparently enlarging the authority and lightening the responsibility of a common carrier for hire, by indirection, most directly afforded the opportunity, which the public servant, always on the alert to pander to popular prejudice, was not slow to perceive and improve, of establishing sham "rules and regulations" which should at his pleasure defeat the title of citizens of African descent or any others, to their estate of freedom, by depriving them of one of its most beneficial uses, privileges, and immunities,—freedom from discrimination, as individuals or as a class. If public servants may adopt any rules in a State, where the Constitution or legislature have imposed no restrictions upon their commerce (and it is believed that no State Constitutions or legislative enactments contain such inhibitory provisions), it would seem that the license of the public servants, under this definition of the law, exceeds the summary power which the poet has bestowed upon the judge of the lower world,—

> " *Gnosius hæc Rhadamanthus habet durissima regna,*
> *Castigatque auditque dolos, subigitque fateri.*"

If this doctrine be sound law, the public servants in America, like the Brahmins, are the "chief of all creatures, with the universe held in charge. for them;" the public, merely Sudras, "who simply have life through the benevolence of other divinities." If this doctrine be valid,—if the public servants have, "by the law of the land," full discretion to adopt such "rules and regulations" as they may see fit, without regard to their reasonableness, they may enact under such rules and regulations masterpieces of injustice, inequality, and wholesale discrimination. Such a construction of the law would

confer upon the public servant of America a not less absolute
and despotic authority than was exercised by the feudal barons
of the Rhine, those iron-handed, primitive masters of transportation, whose "free and untrammelled" commercial "rules and
regulations" for the travelling public of the Rhine provided:
first, that any baron could establish and alter from time to time,
as he saw fit, a tariff of rates; secondly, that appellants from
his discretionary judgments should incur the pains of instant
death, or a prolonged detention in his dungeons, at the election
of the master of transportation; thirdly, that the first accumulated cost of transportation should be a debt, upon which annual
interest should be paid by the public; fourthly, that the right
to discriminate in reference to precedence, place, previous condition, or race of the passenger, should be sacredly reserved to
the master; fifthly, that "by the law of the land" or by "due
process of law" should be intended the grim, satanic will of the
saturnine baron.

What is still more marvellous than these monstrous results—
the inevitable legal and logical outgrowth of a doctrine which
clothes the public servants with such extraordinary authority—is
the open-mouthed, bare-faced truth, that, in order to strike down,
circumvent, undermine, and overthrow the letter and the spirit of
this American Magna Charta, it is an imperative necessity to reverse and overrule civil- and common-law decisions which, from
the time of Grotius, Vattel, and Puffendorf, Sir William Jones,
Lord Mansfield, and Mr. Justice Story to Hall *v.* DeCuir, have
remained both unquestioned and undisturbed. To compass and
accomplish the wholesale destruction of the civil rights and immunities of seven million citizens of the United States, it is indispensable to go to the extreme length of deciding the law to be (as it
has actually been laid down by Mr. Justice Clifford in Hall *v.*
DeCuir): That the common carrier, and his fellow-servants the
inn-keeper and the proprietors of places of public resort for
amusement or instruction, have "free and untrammelled authority," in their *commerce*, to adopt such "rules and regulations" as they may see fit; and that, too, without the common-
sense limitation, which the civil and common law impose upon
the "rules and regulations" of all public servants,—namely,

that they shall be "reasonable." To assail the doctrine of the equality before the law of all American citizens in this regard, it is necessary to declare the law to be: That the public servant is clothed with plenary power to prescribe such discretionary "rules and regulations" as he may see fit to adopt; that there shall be no appeal from his prescription; and that these "rules and regulations" shall not be subject to any such absolute limitation, as that they shall be "*reasonable* rules and regulations," conducive to the comfort and well-being of the public, of which these seven millions form a constituent part, and by whose authority, through charter or license, the public servant is alone authorized to conduct his business.

When the result of this decision of Mr. Justice Clifford was announced by the grave lawyers who interpreted it, the leading citizens of the African race, possessed of cultivation and wealth, when time had calmed their fears, openly declared that the common sense of all mankind rebelled at such a conclusion. This decision, they said, strips us of self-respect,—a more valuable privilege than property. Its tendency is to relegate our race back to the status of barbarism; it is not the kind of teaching by which we must train our children for the discharge of the duties which await an American citizen. It showed, they said, the littleness of the influential class, and how slow the conscience of advancing civilization was in awakening to the injustice of their situation. And, lastly and chiefly, they grounded their indignant protest upon the fact, that it was un-American, and opposed to the spirit of our institutions, which fostered *equality* of chance for every citizen to rise and advance himself and his family, and promised him protection in his struggle to elevate himself and maintain a noble position in the battle of civil life. Records, they said, as old as the history of human thought, could afford few illustrations of a position so glaringly contradictory to long-established and well-settled principles; and those who could not see this could see nothing. It was Russian, not American, doctrine, and the noisome pestilence that walketh in darkness was no greater scourge than this exhalation of color-caste; there was not a fibre of legal truth in these arguments; they proclaimed that as yet the court was too weak to nourish the roots of civic liberty for six millions of free, vigorous plants which the Fourteenth Amendment had firmly fixed in the American soil!

As the common carrier's obligation attaches to all responsible transportation, they thought it must be in accord with his public profession; discrimination and partiality in the exercise of a public vocation both the common and civil law abhorred; and the recent declaration of an English journal, that the United States is an American heptarchy, ruled by seven railroad kings, each district having a separate monarch, they thought was in their case fully realized by this ruling. They argued with Job, that those who decided the contrary, " are those that rebel against light; they know not the ways thereof, nor abide in the paths thereof;" and that if this government had no power to defend its citizens, and allowed the public servants to violate its laws with impunity, " it carried the seeds of destruction in its own bosom;" and contended that, if the courts only saw fit to afford efficient legal protection, they possessed a complete panoply of defensive armor against civil discrimination; but the tribunals of justice seemed to them rather to sympathize with those who were bent on crushing the hope, pride, and manhood of their race into the dust, just as if they, or their ancestors, were in any way responsible for the black cloud of ignominy which had overshadowed their previous condition. Some, however, maintained that the intellectual revolution which was sweeping over the country would sooner or later dissolve the foundations of constitutional historical slavery, and break down established opinions in America; that it would grind to powder every die used to stamp the burdens, badges, disabilities, and essential incidents of slavery, which were now again attempted to be fastened with the iron grasp of a czar upon the emancipated race.

CHAPTER XVII.

" These be our nimble-spirited Catsos, that ha' their evasions at pleasure, will run over a bog like your wild Irish; no sooner started, but they'll leap from one thing to another, like a squirrel. Heigh! dance and do tricks in their discourse, from fire to water, from water to air, from air to earth: as if their tongues did but e'en lick the four elements over and away."—BEN JONSON.

" We have blind, one-eyed, cross-eyed, and squinting people; visions long, short, clear, confused, weak, or indefatigable. All this is a faithful image of our understanding; but we know scarcely any *false* vision: there are not many men who always take a cock for a horse, or a coffee-pot for a church. How is it that we often meet with minds, otherwise judicious, which are absolutely wrong in some things of importance? How is it that the Siamese, who will take care never to be overreached when he has to receive three rupees, firmly believes in the metamorphoses of Sammonocodom?"—VOLTAIRE.

" I have avoided Ay and No, because they are two of the most mercenary and mischievous words in the language, the degraded instruments of the meanest and dirtiest traffic in the land."—PURLEY.

" The history of this Parliament is not edifying to constitutional men."
—CARLYLE.

" But what is there—I will not say, in man, but in all heaven and earth—more divine than reason? which, when it has arrived at maturity, is properly termed wisdom."—CICERO.

" A sable cloud
Turns forth her lining on the night."—SHAKESPEARE.

" They that dally nicely with words."—ID.

" But his lordship and his fautors will do well to contend stoutly and obstinately for their doctrine of language, for they are menaced with a greater danger than they will at first apprehend: for if they give up their doctrine of language, they will not be able to make even a battle for their metaphysics; the very term metaphysics being nonsense; and all the systems of it, and controversies concerning it, that are or have been in the world, being founded on the grossest ignorance of words and of the nature of speech."—TOOKE.

"I could sooner believe with Lord Monboddo, that there are men with tails like cats, as long as his lordship pleases, and conclude with him, from the authority of his famished friend, that human flesh (even to those who are not famished) is the sweetest of all viands to the human taste, than admit that ' every kind of relation is a pure idea of intellect, which can never be apprehended by sense ; and that those particularly which are expressed by cases are more abstract and metaphysical than the others.' " —ID.

> "Antipholus of Ephesus, Antipholus of Syracuse,—
> . . .   the one so like the other
> As could not be distinguished but by name."—SHAKESPEARE.

"If any minister, or any king, in war or in peace, had dared to punish a freeman by a tribunal of his own appointment, he would have roused the wrath of the whole population ; all orders of society would have resisted it ; lord and vassal, knight and squire, priest and penitent, bocman and socman, master and thrall, copyholder and villein, would have risen in one mass and burned the offender to death in his castle, or followed him in his flight and torn him to atoms.   It was again trampled down by the Norman conquerors ; but the evils resulting from the want of it united all classes in the effort which compelled King John to restore it by the Great Charter."—BLACK.

"The case was of such magnitude, in the scope given to it, as to call, if any case could do so, for the views of the subject separately taken by them.   This might either, by the harmony of their reasoning, have produced a greater conviction in the public mind, or, by its discordance, have impaired the force of the precedent, now ostensibly supported by a unanimous and perfect concurrence in every argument and dictum in the judgment pronounced."—MADISON.

WHEN we reflect that the rights and immunities of seven millions of these citizens hung trembling in the balance, it does not seem unreasonable that hosts of them should regard the ultimate ascent from the fathomless abyss, into which they feared this fatal decision had suddenly plunged them, with the same terror and forebodings as did Æneas the obstructions in the way of his return from the lower regions, "*Hic labor, hoc opus est.*" The more they examined this decision, the more it confounded and confused them. They fancied, however, that, by reading between the lines, they saw a helpless, uncertain, straggling way, on the part of Jurisprudence, of getting out of the enforcement of the Fourteenth Amendment. This opinion was in marked contrast with the gigantic powers which characterized the judgments of the illustrious jurisprudent, Mr. Justice Clifford, in questions not involving the unsavory odorousness of race-prejudice. To the vulgar understanding this opinion seemed to be a narrow, backstairs way of escaping grave constitutional responsibility, by expounding the law in accordance with party or popular feeling, and not by the plain standard and constitutional canons of interpretation. To their sensitive race-instinct, this opinion did not have the ring of genuine deep conviction. It did not admit of a face-to-face, heart-to-heart, deep-seated, deeply-thought explication; but wherever the modest stillness and humility of wisdom prevailed, the most enlightened citizens of the suffering race revolved in silence the thought that they were "like lambs dumb before their shearers, and opened not their mouths."

The composure of a majority of their clergy was unruffled. They chose to suffer contumelious indignities rather than make complaint. They preached, and prophesied with childlike simplicity, that the "Sun of righteousness, with healing in his wings," was about to arise; "that the flock shall pass through the sea, with affliction, and shall smite the waves in the sea, and all the deeps of the river shall dry up, and the pride of Assyria shall be brought down;" "that his feet shall stand that day upon the Mount of Olives, which is before Jerusalem on the east; and the Mount of Olives shall cleave in the midst thereof toward the east, and toward the west, and there shall be a very great valley; and half of the mountain shall remove toward the north, and half of it toward the south." These sermons and prophecies of the good shepherds of the colored race exercised an unusually sobering influence upon their affrighted flocks. They remembered what George Cranmer said to Richard Hooker, in the days of old when uniformity of ecclesiastical polity was not less hotly debated than in these times is equality before the law: *Vincit qui patitur,*—"He is victor who suffereth."

Justice Clifford, by eliminating the word "reasonable" from the rules established by public servants, and the Chief Justice, by prefixing it to them, alike conducted Mrs. DeCuir, and seven millions of her race relations, by separate ways to the goal at which the great Captain Benson, that worshipful, impartial expositor of the canons of constitutional construction, proposed that she and they should arrive. That is to say, it was decided by both judges: first, that this Louisiana statute, to the extent that it required those engaged in the transportation of passengers among the States to carry colored passengers in Louisiana in the same cabin with whites, is unconstitutional and void, because such a statute could not have an extra-territorial force, as it invaded the government's exclusive authority to regulate commerce between the States; secondly, that, by the application of Mr. Justice Field's doctrine of "inaction" by Congress to the State of Louisiana, its "inaction" (or unconstitutional action), applied to the "*circumstances*" of Mrs. DeCuir's case, left Benson's delicately acute and profoundly discriminative sagacity at liberty to adopt such *reasonable* rules for the disposition of his passengers as seemed to him most for the "interest of all concerned"; and, in the exercise of this mighty prerogative, the conclusions at which he arrived were that the inhuman policy of "organized, legalized incivility" was a "reasonable" regulation in the transportation of all citizens of African descent; that it was "reasonable" to impose invidious restraints and discriminations derogatory to womanhood and manhood on account of color and previous condition, discriminations which would be resented by blows if an attempt were made to enforce them against other citizens.

By this canon of construction, that was a "*reasonable rule*" which set up the old-time privilege of a separate legal status, as contradistinguished from the equality of legal status, and defiantly refused to recognize the difference between existing institutions and those of the black code of slavery, now relegated to the "dark backward and abysm of Time." It was a "reasonable rule" which, like the plague of Zechariah, left the public servant "free and untrammelled" so to smite his fellow-citizens with a plague that "their flesh shall consume away while they stand upon their feet." It was a "reasonable rule" which sullied humanity, and made it contemptible and base before all people; saying "whither thou goest, I cannot go; where thou lodgest, I cannot lodge; thy people are not my people, and thy God is not my God."

Under the Bensonian "Reasonable Rule" seven millions of the travelling public were and are to be forcibly dissevered from the other sixty millions, and on all public and private occasions to be assigned to separate and exclusive apartments, where dignity of mind and a feeling of individual respectability cannot be maintained; as if they were not citizens, but rather outcasts, the base objects of civil contempt and reproach. Under this very "reasonable rule," that ineffaceable desire of man for the esteem of his fellows, without which no possession of the earth affords real comfort or happiness, was ruthlessly trodden under foot. This "reasonable rule," which asserts the permission of the greatest baseness on the part of one citizen in trying to humiliate another, is pronounced to be a proper regulation for public guidance. This "reasonable rule" renewed the list of burdens and disabilities which attached to the previous condition of servitude; its "reasonableness" consists in maintaining that the substance and visible form of slavery still subsist and are the portion of freemen and citizens. M. Turgot has declared that such a "reasonable rule" as this, which subjects citizens to the tyranny of the people, is the most cruel and intolerable, because it leaves the fewest resources to the oppressed. A despot, he says, "is restrained by a sense of his own interest; he is checked by remorse, or public opinion; but the multitude never calculate; the multitude are never checked by remorse, and will even ascribe to themselves the highest honor when they deserve only disgrace."

This "reasonable rule" is obstructive of substantial progress towards broad and enlightened views of human right and equality. Is it a "*reasonable* rule" which says that, on account of color, and for no other reason than color, *Learning, Gentlemanliness,* and *Moral Superiority,* alike consistent with all colors, must stand apart, since under the ban of race-prejudice the blood of the colored man is attainted? Is it a "*reasonable* rule" which, in the language of Judge Harlan in the famous "Civil-Rights Cases," "at every step confronts the nation with class tyranny: of all tyrants the most intolerable, for it is ubiquitous in its operation, and weighs heavily upon those whose obscurity and distance would withdraw them from the notice of a single despot?"

If the "congressional-inaction" doctrine of Mr. Justice Field, as applied by Chief-Justice Waite to "the civil rights, immunities, and privileges of Mrs. DeCuir," which the Chief Justice terms in Hall *v.* DeCuir the "circumstances of this case," involves this unreasonable consequence, it demonstrates either the unfitness of the learned court's application, or the unsoundness of the doctrine. It is submitted, with great deference, that the source of this fruitful error can be readily traced to the wholly distinct and different constitutional meaning of the term "commerce," as employed in the case of Welton *v.* State of Missouri, and the term "commerce," or "circumstances of the case" (civil rights, immunities, and privileges), as employed in Hall *v.* DeCuir. The "regulation of commerce" within the meaning of the construction in Welton's case, and the "regulation of commerce" ("civil rights"), which are used as common terms, and intended to convey one and the same meaning, in Hall *v.* DeCuir, represent wholly disconnected and unrelated legal entities. In Welton *v.* Missouri it was determined, that a statute of Missouri which requires the payment of a license-tax from persons who deal in the sale of goods, wares, and merchandise which are not the growth, produce, or manufacture of the State, by going from place to place to sell the same in the State, and requires no such license-tax for persons selling in a similar way goods which are the growth, produce, or manufacture of the State, is in conflict with the power vested in Congress to regulate commerce with foreign nations and among the several States. That power was vested in Congress to insure uniformity of commercial regulation against discriminating State legislation. It covers property which is transported as an article of commerce from foreign countries, or among the States, from hostile or interfering State legislation, until it has mingled with and become a part of the general property of the country; and protects it, even after it has entered a State, from any burdens imposed by reason of its foreign origin. In this connection, it was determined that "congressional *inaction*" in interstate commerce,

" WHEN CONSIDERED WITH REFERENCE TO ITS LEGISLATION
WITH RESPECT TO FOREIGN COMMERCE, IS EQUIVALENT TO
A DECLARATION THAT INTERSTATE COMMERCE SHALL BE
FREE AND UNTRAMMELLED."

Commerce in Welton *v.* Missouri, and the misnamed theoretical " commerce" imported by the Chief Justice into DeCuir's
case, are not correlated, nor have they the same legal parentage or
significance. The theory of the " inaction of Congress" leaving
interstate commerce " free and untrammelled," under the regulations which the common or the civil law of the State " had
provided" in Welton's case, was in no sense, under the Fourteenth Amendment, " equivalent" to a declaration, that " Benson
should remain free and untrammelled" to adopt such " reasonable"
rules and regulations, and discriminate on account of their color
as he saw fit, respecting the immunities and privileges of passengers upon his boat. The promiscuous terms " circumstances
of the case," employed by the Chief Justice, in Hall *v.* DeCuir,
do not express the legal meaning of " commerce" as used in
Welton's case. This verbal expression, " circumstances of the
case," is obscure, ambiguous, and of indeterminate import ; and
has led to the gravest legal misunderstanding by employing
the same legal terms to represent as similar, things which, as
matter of fact and matter of law, are entirely dissimilar. The
transportation of Mrs. DeCuir was not, in the sense of commerce,
the transportation of a live cargo, which had no civil rights,
immunities, or privileges in the sense of the civil rights, immunities, and privileges attaching to the person of an American
citizen. Under the provisions of the Fourteenth Amendment,
civil rights are no more subject to rules which infringe or usurp
the immunities of citizens of the United States in transportation,
than a cargo would be subject to regulations of State laws or
customs which deteriorate its value, or bring about its confiscation. Admit that the Louisiana statute was void because it was
an invasion of the exclusive authority of Congress to legislate
respecting interstate commerce, it did not follow that a master
of transportation, because Congress had taken no action upon
the subject of the interstate transportation of citizens of the
United States, could make void the Fourteenth Amendment

by rules which discriminated in such transportation on account of color.

But the law had yet another hold upon Benson, which neither the Chief Justice nor Mr. Justice Clifford apparently perceived. The Fourteenth Amendment was a constitutional *action,* not "*inaction.*" The nation had expressed itself by this amendment, and Congress had spoken audibly upon the subject by the first Civil-Rights Bill. The supreme law of the land did not leave Benson "free and untrammelled": it bound him with chains of adamant. Although, when the cause of action in Hall *v.* DeCuir arose, the Civil-Rights Bill of 1875 was not in operation, the act of 1866 was. The Civil-Rights Bill of 1875 was pending before Congress, and had not been regarded by its opponents as unconstitutional. There was therefore *no* "inaction," of the nation or of Congress, in respect of the "circumstances" of Mrs. DeCuir's case. They were governed by the Fourteenth Amendment, and the declared policy of the first Civil-Rights Bill. To demonstrate the constitutional unfitness of the application of the "congressional-inaction" theory of Welton's case to the civil rights "circumstances" of Mrs. DeCuir's case; to show that the term "commerce," as construed in Welton's case, had not the remotest resemblance to the legal signification of the terms "civil rights" and "circumstances of the case," as employed in Hall *v.* DeCuir, suppose the common or civil law prevailing in some States in regard to interstate commerce to be subversive of the fundamental rights secured by the Fourteenth Amendment. Would not the "national will" be a mere "*brutum fulmen*" if Benson, by the "inaction of Congress respecting such interstate commerce laws," and in spite of its positive enactments, and also of the Fourteenth Amendment, was left "free and untrammelled," under such common or civil law prevailing in such States, to impair the "privileges and immunities" of citizens of such States by the adoption of any rules and regulations which he might regard as "reasonable," notwithstanding they denied to those citizens "due process of law" or the "equal protection of the supreme law" of the land, because of color and previous condition? It is only necessary to read from the decision of Welton *v.* Missouri to demonstrate the soundness of this criticism. Says the court in Welton's case : [1]

"Commerce is a term of the largest import. It comprehends intercourse for the purposes of trade in any and all its forms, including the transportation, purchase, sale, and exchange of commodities between the citizens of our country and the *citizens* or *subjects* of different States. The power to regulate it embraces all the instruments by which such commerce may be conducted. So far as some of these instruments are concerned, and some subjects which are local in their operation, it has been held that the States may provide regulations until Congress acts with reference to them ; but *where the subject to which the power applies is national in its character*, or of such a nature as to admit of *uniformity of regulation*, the power is exclusive of all State authority. It will not be denied that that portion of commerce with foreign countries and between the States which consists in the transportation and exchange of commodities is of national importance, and admits and requires uniformity of regulation." The very object " of investing this power in the general government was to insure this uniformity against discriminating State legislation. The depressed condition of commerce and the obstacles to its outgrowth previous to the adoption of the Constitution, from the want of some single controlling authority, has been frequently referred to by this court in commenting upon the power in question. The fact that Congress has not seen fit to prescribe any specific rules to govern interstate commerce does not affect the question. Its inaction on this subject, *when considered with reference to its legislation with respect to foreign commerce*, is equivalent to a declaration that interstate commerce shall be free and untrammelled. As the main object of that commerce is the sale and exchange of commodities, the policy thus established would be defeated by discriminating legislation like that of Missouri."

But aside from the Chief Justice's version of Welton's case, is it entirely clear, under the exposition of Mr. Justice Field, that the provisions of the Fourteenth Amendment are not " in-

---

[1] 90 U. S. 349, 350.

cidental to, or connected with commerce" and its subject, and "national in their character"? and does not the "*subject*" of commerce, to which "civil rights" applies, "admit of uniformity of regulation," by due process of law, or the law of the land? If this be conceded, what becomes of Benson's "free and untrammelled" authority, under Mr. Justice Field's doctrine, representing the concurring wisdom of the Supreme Court? If the State provides no statutory regulation, and the common and the civil law allow the servant to adopt "reasonable rules," and Congress does not formulate "uniformity of regulation," or, as in the Civil-Rights Bill, its attempt proves abortive, does the common law of the State, or the rules of the public servant in pursuance thereof, where the "subject is national in its character," and is exclusive of all State authority, if repugnant to constitutional civil rights, "override the supreme law of the land, which has ordained the universality of civil rights, privileges, and immunities?" Where the "subject of commerce is national and admits of uniform regulations," is the common law, or the Constitution, the supreme law of the land? Does the common or civil law unhandicap race-prejudice, and give it unqualified liberty to establish such a "uniformity of regulation" as Benson's, and thereby defeat the supreme law of the land? or is the contrary doctrine the truth,—namely, that the Fourteenth Amendment unhands every citizen, commercially and otherwise, from the common or civil law of the State, giving him free course to enjoy the privileges and immunities of all citizens "*free*" *from* "*and untrammelled*" *by* the rules and regulations formulated to pander to race-antagonisms?

The subject of commerce in its relation to civil rights, to which *the power of Congress applies*, is beyond all peradventure "*national in its character*," and of such a nature as to admit of "*uniformity of regulation*." The uniform regulation is provided by the Fourteenth Amendment. If this supreme law of the land is uniformly obeyed, no further or more certain regulation could be formulated, as is conclusively shown by the absence of national or State action to secure "uniformity of regulation" where white civil rights are involved. In this event, says the Supreme Court in Welton's case, the power to regulate commercial civil rights is exclusive of all State authority. If this is not so, what is the meaning of Mr. Justice Field when he declares the " very object of investing this power in the general government was to insure this uniformity against discriminating State legislation ?" The difference between this power vested in Congress to "*regulate commerce,*" referred to in Welton's case, and its applicability to the commercial side or phase of civil rights, as illustrated in Hall *v.* DeCuir, is, that, instead of "*vesting Congress with the power to secure uniformity of commercial regulation in respect*" of commercial civil rights, the Fourteenth Amendment itself declared the universality of a fundamental law. It did not say that Congress should have power to regulate civil rights, immunities, or privileges, when they involved interstate-commerce regulations, but declared that they were the common privilege of every citizen of the United States, and that Congress might intervene, provided any State laws were subversive of the fundamental rights specified in the Fourteenth Amendment, by subjecting its violation to severe civil and criminal penalties. That the first or second section of the act of 1875 was void, or voidable, proves only that Congress overstepped the limitations the Fourteenth Amendment imposed upon it; but not that because of its " inaction"—under this constitutional proviso—the fundamental law which decreed civil rights is less in force, or that Benson was at liberty to act without regard to it. Benson could not invalidate one of these constitutional rights because Congress had not spoken and said, " You shall not imprison on one part of your boat a citizen of African descent; you shall not refuse to entertain or lodge a citizen of African descent, for any reason which would not be applicable to any other citizen, irrespective of color or previous condition." The civil right, immunity, and privilege of being carried without unlawful discrimination is guaranteed by the Fourteenth Amendment.

Whether the ground upon which the majority of the court were content to rest their judgment in the Civil-Rights Cases, as Mr. Justice Harlan in his separate opinion charges, " is more ingenious than solid," is unimportant; for the Civil-Rights Bill only re-enacted the Fourteenth Amendment. All that the Civil-Rights Bill attempted, the Fourteenth Amendment had already accomplished by the establishment of a rule of civil conduct prescribed by the supreme power of the Constitution, no matter what statute, common or civil law, or custom, there was to the contrary in any State. The Chief Justice in Mrs. DeCuir's case maintains that the omission of Congress " *uniformly to regulate*" this commerce (the exercise of this vested right which Congress could no more add to or take from than it could add to or take from the Constitution itself) left the commercial construction of the Fourteenth Amendment to the wisdom of Benson, guided by the common or civil law of Louisiana. The mere statement of this proposition conclusively shows it to be a grave misconception of the scope of the Fourteenth Amendment, by which " *positive rights and privileges* were undoubtedly secured," as has been determined in the Civil-Rights Cases.

The right to travel, with all privileges incident to and inseparable from its full enjoyment, subject only to such rules as were alike applicable to all travellers without regard to color or previous condition, itself constituted one of the immunities granted by the Fourteenth Amendment; this was one of those civil rights which contains the " essence of citizenship," and the enjoyment or deprivation of which " *constitutes one of the essential distinctions between freedom and slavery.*" When, however, Congress, by the Civil-Rights Bill of 1875, undertook to " establish uniformity of regulation" in respect of the civil rights, immunities, and privileges of all American citizens,—the broadest illustration of a " subject national in its character,"—the Supreme Court, instead of recognizing this act as a constitutional exercise of its power to regulate interstate commerce, then said, " Congress has overstepped the limitations of the Fourteenth Amendment, which operate only as an inhibition upon hostile State legislation, by creating a code of municipal law for the regulation of private rights." But Welton's case decided, that, where the subject of commerce is national and admits of uniformity, the power of the government is exclusive of the civil or common law of the States. By the decision in DeCuir's case, in spite of the commercial aspect of civil rights,—a subject of national power and character and not local, and admitting of " uniformity of regulation"; in spite of the " inaction" of Congress (the passage of the Civil-Rights Bill) and of the "*positive immunities and privileges undoubtedly secured by the Fourteenth Amendment;*" in spite of the exclusive power of the government over commerce relating to the subject; Benson was left at liberty to adopt in reference thereto such "reasonable rules" as he saw fit, under the guidance of the common or civil law prevailing in Louisiana. The Civil-Rights Cases decide that the Civil-Rights Bill to establish uniformity of regulation (by stepping "into the domain of local jurisprudence" upon a national subject in regard to which the power of the government was exclusive of all State authority, its prevailing customs, and of the common or civil law) exceeded the authority conferred by the Fourteenth Amendment, and consequently sections one and two were void.

Thus does it demonstrably appear that, by a canon of constitutional construction, legitimately employed in Welton *v.* State of Missouri, but erroneously applied to the "circumstances of the case" in Hall *v.* DeCuir, these subtle dialecticians ingeniously substituted the one term for the other: that is to say, the term "circumstances of the case" was expounded in Hall *v.* DeCuir in the same sense as the term "commerce" in Welton *v.* State of Missouri. The court thus rightly applied a canon of constitutional construction in Welton's case, but wrongfully converted and misapplied it to the "circumstances of the case" in Hall *v.* DeCuir. But the arguments by which they maintained the rightful application in the one case, and the wrongful application in the other, seemed to themselves equally powerful and apparently as convincing; and thus by the wrongful application of this canon they succeeded in overturning the Fourteenth Amendment. Some thick encircling darkness seems to have blinded their vision to the true meaning and scope of that great comprehensive factor—that Magna Charta—which, like the sun, shines with impartial light upon all men. From the decision of the court in Hall *v.* DeCuir it would seem as St. Augustine hath said: "There is great difference between the judgments of men; some half-waking, and others not yet thoroughly awake in the light of a true understanding."

CHAPTER XVIII.

"How unequal is the contest between honesty and reason on the one part, and sinister interest in or out of office on the other! How hard the lot of the advocate on the honest side! On the part of sinister interest, a short phrase composed of falsehood and nonsense is thrown out, and this is to be accepted as a reason—as a reason, and that of itself a conclusive one—on which the whole difference between good government and bad government—in this country, and thence perhaps in every other—at this time, and thence perhaps at all times—is to depend."—BENTHAM.

"In truth it is a sad sight for any one who has been, what Bacon recommends, 'a servant and interpreter of nature,' to see these political schemers, with their clumsy mechanisms, trying to supersede the great laws of existence."—SPENCER.

"Their golden visions have been far from realized, however. Slave countries are comparatively poverty-stricken all over the world. Though Jamaica at one time sent us a few overgrown nabobs, yet West-Indian history has been a history of distresses and complainings, in spite of continual assistance and artificial advantages."—ID.

"But, sir, of all descriptions of men, I consider those as the worst enemies of the Union who sacrifice the equal rights which belong to every member of the confederacy to combinations of interested majorities, for personal or political objects."—HAYNE.

"The primitive Christians, a whimsical set of people, when they came into power took it into their heads, evidently out of a spirit of oppression, to 'administer justice upon all days alike.' In the eyes of Blackstone, neither of these courses coinciding with existing practice, both it seems were wrong: the *dies fasti* and *nefasti* made an extreme; and justice upon all days alike, a sort of confusion of all order, made 'a contrary extreme.' "—BENTHAM.

"This is the common argument of men who, being in reality hostile to a measure, are ashamed or afraid of appearing to be so. It is the same sort of quirk as a plea of abatement in law,—which is never employed but on the side of a dishonest defendant, whose hope it is to obtain an ultimate triumph, by overwhelming his adversary with despair, impoverishment, and lassitude."—SYDNEY SMITH.

224

" What he shows us through his telescope is a *fata morgana*, and not the promised land. The real haven of our hopes dips far down below the horizon, and has yet been seen by none. It is beyond the ken of seer, be he never so far-sighted. Faith, not sight, must be our guide. We cannot do without a compass."—SPENCER.

' Snail's-pace argument.—' One thing at a time! Not too fast! Slow and sure! Importance of the business,—extreme difficulty of the business,—danger of innovation,—need of caution and circumspection,—impossibility of foreseeing all consequences,—danger of precipitation,—everything should be gradual,—one thing at a time,—this is not the time,—great occupation at present, wait for more leisure,—people well satisfied,—no petitions presented,—no complaints heard,—no such mischief has yet taken place,—stay till it has taken place !' Such is the prattle which the magpie in office, who, understanding nothing, yet understands that he must have something to say on every subject, shouts out among his auditors as a succedaneum to thought."—SYDNEY SMITH.

" In such passage, unhappily too rare, the high Platonic mysticism of our author, which is perhaps the fundamental element of his nature, bursts forth, as it were, in full blood ; and, through all the vapor and tarnish of what is often so perverse, so mean in his exterior and environment, we seem to look into a whole inward sea of light and love ; though, alas ! the grim coppery clouds soon roll together again, and hide it from view."—CARLYLE.

" Error, on the other hand, is always unhistorical ; the spirit of time almost always passionate ; and both, consequently, untrue."—SCHLEGEL.

" If, sir, the people, in these respects, had done otherwise than they have done, their Constitution neither could have been preserved, nor would it have been worth preserving. And, if its plain provisions shall now be disregarded, and these new doctrines interpolated in it, it will become as feeble and helpless a being as its enemies, whether early or more recent, could possibly desire."—WEBSTER.

" Not daring to trust ' heaven's first law' to itself, they wish to help it by artificial classification. They fear that the desired ' order' will not be maintained unless it is looked after ; and so these ' greater than the rest' are picked out by official divination, ranged in tiers, and ticketed with their respective values."—SPENCER.

" LAW—the absolute justice of the State, enlightened by the perfect reason of the State. That is law."—CHOATE.

" As a citizen may not elect what laws he will obey, neither may the executive elect which he will enforce. The duty to obey and to execute embraces the Constitution in its entirety and the whole code of laws enacted under it. The evil example of permitting individuals, corporations, or communities to nullify the laws because they cross some selfish or local interests or prejudices, is full of danger, not only to the nation at large, but much more to those who use this pernicious expedient to escape their just obligations or to obtain an unjust advantage over others."—PRESIDENT HARRISON.

"I see, therefore, that this has been the idea of the wisest, that law has not been devised by the ingenuity of man, nor yet is it a mere decree of the people, but an eternal principle which must direct the whole universe, ordering and forbidding everything with entire wisdom."—CICERO.

"This country, with its institutions, belongs to the people who inhabit it."—LINCOLN.

"A grisly law Pluto, and dark law monster, a kind of infernal king, chief enchanter in the domdaniel of attorneys; one of those frightful men who, as his contemporaries passionately said and repeated, dare to 'decree injustice *by a law.*' "—CARLYLE.

"One after another they have closed the heavy iron doors upon him; and now they have him, as it were, bolted in with a lock of a hundred keys, which can never be unlocked without the concurrence of every key; the keys in the hands of a hundred different men, and they scattered to a hundred different and distant places; and they stand musing as to what invention, in all the dominions of mind and matter, can be produced to make the impossibility of his escape more complete than it is."—ID.

"I shall do all I can to save the government, which is my sworn duty as well as my personal inclination. I shall do nothing in malice. What I deal with is too vast for malicious dealing."—LINCOLN.

"Was not this a task which Destiny, in any case, had appointed him; which having now done with, he sees his general day's-work so much the lighter, so much the shorter?"—CARLYLE.

IN the *closing* paragraph of Justice Clifford's extended review of the prerogatives of the public servant, the following words occur: "It is his duty to exercise such *reasonable* discretion and control as will promote, as far as practicable, the comfort and convenience of his whole company."

The "free and untrammelled" exercise by a public servant of

" such reasonable discretion and control" as will promote the comfort of guests as far as practicable, is an elastic, insubstantial, untechnical definition of long-established, characteristic, broad, and comprehensive rules of action, which, as will hereafter appear, had been vigorously imposed upon the calling of the public servant in all its branches and ramifications by public policy and by the civil and the common law. Mr. Justice Clifford, as we have already seen, at first conspicuously omitted from the rule of action which he advanced, the term *"reasonable,"* which term makes its appearance only in the closing paragraph of this remarkable opinion.

The words "control," "reasonable," "discretion," "practicable," coupled with the expression "free and untrammelled," as used in the last clause of Mr. Justice Clifford's opinion, are not less objectionable in substance than in form. The relativity of these terms is obvious; they are dependent upon the conscientiousness, good faith, loyalty, breadth, experience, and intellectual development of the public servant. If the law invests him with discretion, and he exercises it to the best of his temerity, ignorance, and prejudice, upon what theory, pray, is he then responsible? Under the lax rule of a "free and untrammelled," "reasonable discretion and control," Benson flagrantly violated the fundamental provisions of the Fourteenth Amendment, by establishing an arbitrary regulation not applicable to all citizens alike, but applicable exclusively to colored citizens,—a regulation which on account of color, and for no other reason than color, and the previous condition of which it was a badge, openly denied Mrs. DeCuir the equal rights, privileges, and immunities of all citizens of the United States.

But what is the legal import of these terms? Why is an extraordinary conglomeration of unintelligible law-jargon introduced for the first time into the well-established doctrine of bailees for hire? "Free and untrammelled," "reasonable," "discretionary control" are words which palter in a double sense. They are open to two constructions: a lawful one; *and* an oppressive, arbitrary interpretation, incompatible with that spirit of legal liberty which the Fourteenth Amendment breathes. Under their comprehensive generalities, regulations subversive of the Fourteenth Amendment can readily be framed. Indeed, the door to their admittance is thrown wide open. In the introduction of these terms the court travelled widely out of the record of Hall *v.* DeCuir, which really presented only the question of the legality of the Louisiana statute. Jurisprudence extra-judicially volunteered the information to the Public that the bands of obedience to the law of the Fourteenth Amendment were loosened. It said, in effect, You are now at liberty to establish rules which are applicable solely to this race, although every American citizen of common right should be freed from all discriminations, restrictions, or disqualifications which are not by law applicable uniformly to the status of American citizenship. If the scales of civil equality are not justly poised under this rule, your discretion may take shelter in the shallow artifice, more cunning than capable, that *"the natural and well-known repugnance"* [1] of the color-line to the Fourteenth Amendment justifies the public servant in establishing a rule which renders transportation less repulsive to the natural feelings, long-established customs, and prejudices of the white American citizens, as *"there is no principle of law, human or divine,"* [2]—*except the Fourteenth Amendment,*—which requires all men, in their pursuit of commerce or pleasure, to be thrown into that hotchpot of humanity which is called equality before the law. Your discretion is *"free and untrammelled"* under the common and civil law, and the term *"discretion"* is not to be taken as it has been ever since the prevalence of the Levitical and canon law and *jus gentium,*—*Discernere per legem quid sit justum.* A new law we present unto you, says Hall *v.* DeCuir, which absolves your discretion. It need no longer be guided by certain positive rules and well-known principles. *Quicquid judicis auctoritati subjicitur novitati non subjicitur,*— Whatever has been decided by the authority of the judge is not open to new interpretation,—has not guided Jurisprudence in this decision.

Jurisprudence substantially said, the novelty of the principle we have adopted is not more wonderful than the novelty of the

---

[1] Miles *v.* P. Railroad Co.   [2] Id.

creation of seven millions of citizens by a stroke of the pen! The amendments were unlike the forms of religion: they were not established for substance; they were only artificial contrivances to lift from the republic the load of shame which the African slave-traders, and their accessories before and after the fact,—the American people,—had suffered to accumulate for two centuries. This ruling in Hall *v.* DeCuir assumes, if it does not directly state, that the liberties of this race were invented by nice, subtle, distinctions of the Republican party. They can be destroyed in the same way. For does it not allow the public servant to deceive by chicanery and hypocrisy, and to be treacherous without art? By any pitiful quibbling, evasion, or catching at forms, ostensibly established under his "free and untrammelled" authority, is he not at liberty to remove the landmarks established by former decisions, and to invent different laws for white and black citizens when both require his services upon the same occasion and are engaged in the same rights of commerce, life, liberty, or the pursuit of happiness?

Does not this ruling say, You are at liberty on all such occasions, Mr. Public Servant, and Mr. Labor Tyrant, to infuse the same amount of bigotry into the regulations of your business as you may have injected into your religion or your politics; and whenever the double-distilled and trebly-refined sentimentality of White Civil Rights is brought into the presence of Black Civil Rights, a regulation which provides that Black Civil Rights are to suck the poison of asps is within your "free and untrammelled discretion." Whenever it promotes the comfort of the claimants of White Civil Rights, then and in all such cases it is within your "free and untrammelled discretion" to establish such a rule, because by its *inaction* Congress has intrusted the exposition of a reasonable rule to your discretion, regulated by the customs and the common or civil law of your State, which may be *reasonable* and yet *opposed* to the supreme law of the land and to the declared Christian and political polity of the United States. Discriminate on all occasions against Black Civil Immunities, when in public they confront or interfere with the enjoyment of White

Civil Rights. That the civil rights of both races are precisely the same and annexed by a living charter to American citizenship appears only from these three perfunctory Amendments. You need have no superstitious veneration for the fundamental law of your country. Your business vocation does not require you to assist in preserving civil liberty; it simply imposes upon you the loftier obligation of putting money in your pocket.

As a public servant your rules may be steeled against all other considerations. You are *not* obliged to bear in mind that every American citizen, whether he be a self-constituted patrician, distinguished for his blood, brains, property, and place in society, or a poor, suffering, shoeless plebeian, is entitled under the provisions of the Fourteenth Amendment to the full, free, and equal enjoyment of all the rights and privileges of an American citizen. Remember, when you formulate your rules, that the right of every citizen of African descent to be treated with decency and propriety, in the enjoyment of his civil rights, is at all times subject to the presumption, insolence, meanness, ignorance, and rancor of race-prejudice! Your discretion need not consider that decency, propriety, and courtesy in the discharge of your duties, are the civil rights equally of the white and the black patron! You are not supposed to be familiar with the events preceding the Rebellion, which ought to be engraved on every loyal American heart! You are not supposed to have read the speeches of the great men who took part in the discussion when the subject of civil rights was debated. You are not, at this late day, to recall how they stood in the breach, and, with arguments and eloquence more than human, defeated the pernicious attempts of the representatives of race-antagonism of that time to maintain the impious and unconstitutional doctrine, that all men were not born " free and equal"! You have forgotten the preamble to the Civil-Rights Bill: " We recognize the equality of all men before the law, and hold that it is the duty of government, in its dealings with the people, to mete out equality and exact justice to all, of whatever nativity, race, color, or persuasion, religious or political."

It is not, therefore, surprising if, with all the politeness imaginable now and hereafter, the present or future public servant should perchance arrive at Benson's method of committing the old pro-slavery sin in the new Fourteenth-Amendment-inaction-of - Congress -Welton-*v.*-State-of- Missouri - commercial way; for Benson, before the promulgation of the rule in De-Cuir's case, filled with the spirit of wisdom, had anticipated its suggestion. The hoof of the unclean beast of slavery is everywhere visible in these regulations, which violated the statute of Louisiana and its common and civil law. This monstrous injustice, under the shadow though not in accordance with the spirit of the law, was nevertheless wrought under a form or figure of law into Justice by the *imprimatur* of Jurisprudence.

No one of the authorities cited by Justice Clifford sanctions the latitudinous terms he employs, " discretionary," " control," "reasonable," "as far as practicable," etc. Although Day *v.* Owen and Miles *v.* P. R.R. Co. are his main supports, and extended the authority of the public servant beyond any precedent, these obscure State decisions were rendered at a period of bitter racial excitement, and under pressure of the pro-slavery sentiment then prevailing. Those cases may now justly be regarded as antiquities of the Dred-Scott period. They are almost prehistoric in the light of the Fourteenth Amendment and of the subsequent doctrines of the Supreme Court, notably in Strauder *v.* West Virginia. Day *v.* Owen was decided in 1858, when the political pulse of the Democratic party and the people was at fever-height, and in Miles's case, just prior to March 2, 1867, it arose still higher; but no such terms as "discretionary," "as far as practicable," "free and untrammelled," "control," appear in these decisions. On the contrary, throughout them stands in bold relief, with all its legal significance unshorn, the term "reasonable." Benson's regulation, under the sanction of the Supreme Court, left at the mercy of the public servant the indestructible rights of citizens of the United States established by an indestructible charter. Yet, wonderful as it must appear, this " free-and-untrammelled-as-far-as-practicable-reasonable-discretionary-control" prerogative of Benson was not, after all, in the opinion of Justice Clifford or of the court, a sound pivotal point for the affirmation of Benson's right to annul the Fourteenth Amendment. Abandoning the whole of this *terra incognita* of the law, Justice Clifford finally does not maintain the lawfulness of Benson's ruling because it was in the exercise of the " free and untrammelled" prerogative of a public servant, with which public policy, the civil and common law of Louisiana, and " metaphysical aid" had crowned him withal ; but he is forced to abandon and fly from this ground, which throughout his opinion he had valiantly but vainly struggled to hold, by fairly, flatly, and squarely admitting at the end that Benson's repeal of the Fourteenth Amendment was allowable upon the already exploded doctrine of the " inaction" of Congress, although Congress had spoken its opinion in the Civil-Rights Bill of 1866, and was by no means guilty of this inaction. For, says the Justice,—

" Governed by the laws of Congress [*i.e.,* its inaction], it is clear that a steamer carrying passengers may have separate cabins and dining-saloons for white persons and persons of color, *for the plain reason that the laws of Congress contain nothing to prohibit such an arrangement.* Steamers carrying passengers for hire are bound, if they have suitable accommodation, to take all who apply, unless there is objection to the character or conduct of the applicant. Applicants to whom there is no such valid objection have a right to a passage, but it is not an unlimited right. On the contrary, it is subject to such reasonable regulations as the proprietors may prescribe for the due accommodation of passengers, and the due arrangement of the business of the carrier."

The judgment of the judicious reader, upon whom modesty sits well in the presence of this august tribunal, is left no other choice or alternative, however, than to conclude from this opinion,—

First, that, " for the plain reason that the acts of Congress contain nothing to the contrary," the public servant is at liberty to turn the Fourteenth Amendment round-about and upside-down as he pleases, and thus land himself in a safe position to violate all the sacred principles and just claims it was intended to enforce, as " to him seemeth best" ; in order that he may place himself in a secure and advantageous situation, and for no other reason whatever.

Secondly, that the "inaction" of Congress upon the subject of interstate commerce, *ipso facto*, authorizes the public servant to repeal that part of the Fourteenth Amendment which provides that "no State shall make any law (common, civil, statutory, or customary) which shall abridge the privileges or immunities of citizens of the United States, nor deny to any person within its jurisdiction the equal protection of the law."

Thirdly, that the establishment of a rule of action applying to seven millions of citizens, on account of color, and not applicable to a single one of the other fifty millions, a rule which abridges the immunities and privileges of these seven millions of citizens by stamping upon them a brand of discrimination and inferiority, is justifiable for the singular reason that the laws of Congress contain nothing to prohibit such an arrangement.

Fourthly, that for the plain reason that the laws of Congress contain nothing to prohibit robbery, mayhem, or manslaughter, under the "free and untrammelled" license of public servants, some "reasonable" rule favoring robbery, mayhem, or manslaughter, if tending to promote the comfort, as far as practicable, of all concerned, might be ordained with legal impunity; provided it discriminated against, and was applicable, on account of their color, race, and previous condition, *solely* to these citizens.

Fifthly, that the public servant is the monarch, and the public His Majesty's liege subject.

Sixthly, that, under this capacious, self-adjusting machinery, the public servant may accommodate the discharge of his public duties to the weakness or wickedness of his patron, without offence to his license, his conscience, or the Fourteenth Amendment. He may be ever so guilty in the practice and fact of violating the fundamental law of the country, and yet in theory be innocent.

A more cynical and cutting irony upon the Fourteenth Amendment cannot well be imagined than the laxity in which this doctrine indulges itself.

Under this readily-adjustable garment, leaving right out of the question, the highest pitch of piety could not say, that in "feeding fat" the ancient antipathies of clamorous race-harpies, the public servant, as a conservator of justice, striving to serve the public, is not at liberty conscientiously to stiletto the civil rights of a colored citizen, upon the plausible, if not justifiable, ground of "well-known and natural white race-repugnance" to any and all the civil rights accorded these citizens. If this be true of the most exalted and sanctified of the tribe of public servants, it is matter which deserves still graver consideration, when it is reflected that the civil rights of these citizens may be lodged in the hands of devotees of race-prejudice,—blind, sordid, feeble-minded tyrants, who, with the ancients, are ready to exclaim, *Omnia pro tempore, nihil pro veritate.* By this "free and untrammelled" authority, civil rights rest upon a very precarious and slippery footing. If, in place of the rigid and impartial enforcement of the wholesome restraints of positive law, the public servant is allowed to substitute his "free and untrammelled" discretionary regulations wherever the civil rights of these citizens are involved, what more effectual mode of repealing the Fourteenth Amendment can be suggested?

CHAPTER XIX.

" Like tumbler pigeons, it makes all sorts of summersaults and evolutions of figures."—BOLINGBROKE.

" This piebald, entangled, hyper-metaphorical style of writing."—CARLYLE.

" Earth, water, nature, they may subdue, but truth they cannot subdue. Subtle and mighty, against all efforts and devices, it fills every region of light with its majestic presence."—SUMNER.

" Luminous and lofty eloquence."—SCHLEGEL.

" I will throw you a great many barleycorns if, in ransacking this book of yours, you can show me one jewel."—MILTON.

" Abraham Lincoln saved for you a country; he delivered us from bondage, according to Jefferson, one hour of which was worse than ages of the oppression your fathers rose in rebellion to oppose."—FREDERICK DOUGLASS.

" But now behold the change: the judgment of the present hour is, that, taking him for all in all, measuring the tremendous magnitude of the work before him, considering the necessary means to ends, and surveying the end from the beginning, Infinite Wisdom has seldom sent any man into the world better fitted for his mission than Abraham Lincoln."—ID.

" The Emancipation Proclamation did not draw its breath in the serene atmosphere of law. It was born in the smoke of battle, and its swaddling clothes were rolled in blood."—WELLING.

> " Upon his back a more than Atlas load,
>   The burden of the commonwealth, was laid;
>   He stooped and rose up to it, though the road
>   Shot suddenly downwards, not a whit dismayed.
>   Hold! warriors, councillors, kings! All now give place
>   To this dear benefactor of the race."—STODDARD ON LINCOLN.

"I might call him a thing divine, for nothing natural I ever saw so noble."—SHAKESPEARE.

" The Declaration of Independence, the Constitution, were each the work of bodies of men. The Proclamation in this respect stands alone.

235

The responsibility was wholly upon Lincoln, the glory chiefly his. No one can now say whether the Declaration of Independence or the Constitution of the United States or the Proclamation of Emancipation was the highest, best gift to the country and mankind. In the presence of slavery the Declaration of Independence had lost its power: practically it had become a lie. In the presence of slavery, we were to the rest of mankind, and to ourselves, a nation of hypocrites."—BOUTWELL.

" To be President, to be king, to be victor, has happened to many: to be embalmed in the hearts of mankind through all generations as liberator and emancipator has been vouchsafed to few."—LOVEJOY.

" In those deep, mournful eyes, which are always full of noble, silent sorrow, of affection and pity, what a depth to-day of thoughts that cannot be spoken !"—CARLYLE.

" That they had no law to protect them, no sanctuary to betake themselves to ? Can we think that they were delivered from the bondage they were under to the Egyptian kings, to be reduced into a worse to one of their own brethren ?"—MILTON.

" It appears to me, as it does to you, that the occasion did not call for the general and abstract doctrine interwoven with the decision of the particular case. I have always supposed that the meaning of a law, and, for a like reason, of a Constitution, so far as it depends on judicial interpretation, was to result from a course of particular decisions, and not those from a previous and abstract comment on the subject."—MADISON.

" And why ? Because this country is a country of the law ; because the judge is a judge for the peasant as well as for the palace ; because every man's happiness is guarded by fixed rules from tyranny and caprice."—SYDNEY SMITH.

" An actual flesh-and-blood fact, with color in its cheeks, with awful, august, heroic thoughts in its heart, and, at last, with a steel sword in its hand."—CARLYLE.

EVERY great political question may be viewed in many ways ; and we may look at this subject of civil rights with a scant, sidelong glance, or we may examine it with a keen, searching, face-to-face inspection. With our imperfect mental and physical equipment, much that is presented to percipience takes its stamp from the profoundness or picayunishness of the percipient. It would take a long process of Republican

acclimation for a dyed-in-the-wool, hickory Democrat to conclude, with Mr. Justice Miller, in *Ex parte* Yarborough,[1] that
the bare question of the authority of the Supreme Court to restrain the Ku-Klux from intimidating a Republican voter of
African descent, was " *a proposition so startling as to arrest attention and demand the gravest consideration.*" To the standing
army, national and State, of great and small Jeffersonians,
the intimidation of a " darky," a " fourteenth amendment," a
" coon," a " black fellow," a " servant," about to deposit a Republican ballot, would seem a " trifle light as air"; and when
they heard of Mr. Justice Miller's profound and eloquent vindication of the powers and purposes of this government in his
behalf, they would exclaim, " Can anything be more justly due
to the vanity and weakness of this opinion than laughter?"
The " Jackson and Liberty" followers, a hundred thousand
strong, would cry out *uno flatu,* " Come, let us reason out Mr.
Justice Miller's profundity!" Let us see : The right to vote
comes from the State, but *State discrimination* between its voters
is prohibited by the Fifteenth Amendment. Let us read what
the court does say. It uses the following language :

" The government of the United States was created by the
free voice and joint will of the people of America, for their
common defence and general welfare. Its powers apply to those
great interests which relate to this country in its national capacity, and which depend for their protection on the consolidation of the Union. It is clothed with the principal attributes
of political sovereignty, and it is justly deemed the guardian of
our best rights, the source of our highest civil and political
duties, and the sure means of national greatness.[2] It is as essential to the successful working of this government, that the
great organisms of its executive and legislative branches should
be the free choice of the people, as that the original form of it
should be so. In absolute governments, where the monarch is
the source of all power, it is still held to be important that the
exercise of that power shall be free from the influence of extraneous violence and internal corruption. In a republican

---

[1] 109 U. S. 166.   [2] 1 Kent's Com. 201.

government, like ours, where political power is reposed in representatives of the entire body of the people, chosen at short intervals by popular elections, the temptation to control these elections by violence and corruption is a constant source of danger. Such has been the history of all republics, and, though ours has been comparatively free from both these evils in the past, no lover of his country can shut his eyes to the fear of future danger from both sources. If the recurrences of such acts as these prisoners stand convicted of are too common in one quarter of the country, and give omen of danger from lawless violence, the free use of money in elections, arising from the vast growth of recent wealth in other quarters, presents equal cause for anxiety. If the government of the United States has within its constitutional domain no authority to provide against these evils, if the very sources of power may be poisoned by corruption or controlled by violence and outrage, without legal restraint, then, indeed, is the country in danger, and its best powers, its highest purposes, the hopes which it inspires, and the love which enshrines it, are at the mercy of the combinations of those who respect no right but brute force, on the one hand, and unprincipled corruptionists on the other."

As he proceeded to consider this opinion, the ablest debater, the clearest thinker, the most powerful intellectual giant, of the " Jackson-and-liberty" " Bread-and-meat" brigade, in spite of his prejudices, would be hurried along by the sweep and majestic strides of the massive thought ; his contemptuous smile, at doctrines which before reading them he regarded as ridiculous sky-soarings, would quickly give way to an attentive gaze, a rapt contemplation of Mr. Justice Miller's glowing picture, and the exceeding fineness of a finish painted with

> " Carraccio's strength, Correggio's softer line,
> Paulo's free course, and Titian's warmth divine."

Mr. Justice Miller's examination into *Elective Franchise Civil Rights* in Yarborough's case was *not* with a scant, careless, sidelong glance. The intimidation of this " darky," " coon," " fourteenth amendment," " black fellow," about to deposit a Republican ballot, had touched mightily the conscience of the court. But there is

another aspect of civil rights which does not involve solely the
right to vote, by the side of which Mr. Justice Miller's magnificent political pageantry, like a dissolving view, fades away
into comparative nothingness. Let the reader slowly avert his
gaze from Ku-Klux intimidation, the classic subject of the
Supreme Court's political and poetical jurisprudence, and fix
his eyes upon civil rights when disconnected from party politics.
Upon the historical background of Constitutional Civil Rights,
still wet with the blood of the nation, let him regard in mournful
silence the revered shade of the immortal Lincoln; his face like
the first martyr's, "as it had been the face of an angel," laden
with the inspiration of woe and surrounded by the grim, tattered remnants of Gettysburg, Manassas, and the Wilderness,—
and in the foreground, gorgeous with the crimson and gold of
its coloring, the Fourteenth Amendment,—that stupendous
and beautiful fabric, unsurpassed in natural grandeur,—by
which seven millions of people were raised to unqualified
freedom through the generous philanthropy of a Christian
nation.

Here is a great and commanding picture, representing the
liberty and equality of all mankind, which ought to inspire
loftiest thoughts,—"thoughts that breathe and words that
burn." But civil rights, unless presented in the fascinating
aspect of a voter, have never caused the heart of the Court to
swell with awe-struck admiration. It strangely happens that the
public servant and his pigmy patron, the sham public, although
they voted for the Fourteenth Amendment, are themselves independent and careless of the civil rights bestowed by it, but
not politically regardless of Ku-Klux "intimidations." The
Olympian Joves of the Republican party, floating midway
betwixt heaven and earth, in the empyrean heights of "high
moral ideas," already monarchs of all they had surveyed in
political America, greeted the Yarborough protectorate and perpetuation of their power with precisely the same shout which
was called forth from the leaders of race-mania, with their rank
and file of discriminationists, by the doctrine of Hall *v.* DeCuir.
Both of these deluded political schools were blind leaders of the
blind, and fell into the self-same ditch.

The pro-slavery opinion in Hall *v.* DeCuir says, in effect, Can anything be more justly due to the vain show and weakness of the Fourteenth Amendment than laughter? What can be more absurd than that " a colored fellow," " coon," " darky," " domestic," should be manufactured into a citizen of the United States, with all the privileges and immunities of the superior race, by the mere parchment authority of the Fourteenth Amendment? It is absurd to claim for this " fourteenth amendment" that personal liberty, which consists, says Blackstone, " in the power of locomotion, of changing situation, or removing one's person to whatever places one's own inclination may direct, without restraint, unless by due course of law." It is folly and weakness and vanity in this paper man, this stuffed, saw-dust specimen of the legislation of sagacious Republican trimmers, who only sought to perpetuate their political supremacy by means of his vote, to expect to stand in public assemblies for instruction or amusement by the side of the superior race, or to expect by the " commercial regulations" of the public servant to be placed upon substantial equality of rights with white citizens.

" I don't want any civil rights on my boat, and I won't have them," says Benson. What says Hall *v.* DeCuir? " These questions of *commercial* civil rights" are unlike those presented by the convicts of record in Yarborough's case. The " circumstances of the case" in Hall *v.* DeCuir are not propositions " so startling as to arrest attention and demand the gravest consideration." We leave all those questions to the public servants, with " free, untrammelled, and discretionary control under the common or civil law of the State." We leave " colored fellows," these " fourteenth amendments," these " darkies," to " the mercy of the combinations of those who respect no right but brute force," disguised though it may be under simulated law forms, which palter in a double sense with the civil rights, immunities, and privileges of citizens of the United States, " keeping the word of promise to the ear, but breaking it to the hope." The intimidation of a citizen of the United States of African descent about to cast a Republican ballot is a proposition so startling it asphyxiates thought; but the assertion in Hall *v.* DeCuir, of the lawful authority of all *classes*, throughout the United States, to strike down and trample upon the Fourteenth Amendment, is a "trifle light as air." The "*inaction of Congress*" has left the civil rights of seven millions of citizens to the mercy of these venal and prejudiced judges and executors of their own decrees.

"The country is in no danger," although "its best powers, its highest purposes, the hopes which it inspires, and the love which it enshrines," are at "the mercy of the combinations of those who respect no right but brute force," and that brute force is engaged in toppling over this great monument to freedom! There is nothing in this assault upon the Fourteenth Amendment "so startling as to arrest attention and demand the gravest consideration," contrasted with the heinous national crime of intimidating this race as voters, for the commission of which Yarborough may be lawfully made a convict of record. Although that "brute force" daily loads seven million people with chains which deprive them of the full enjoyment of their intellectual, moral, and personal emancipation; refusing them, under "free and untrammelled," "discretionary rules," their constitutional rights, and the tender sympathy and safeguard of the nation; although that "brute force" denies them the simple, natural gratifications which produce no harm to others; and by an arbitrary rule,—no matter how respectful or dignified their individual demeanor or how perfect their decorum,—subjects them, *as a race*, to mortifications abhorrent to refined, generous, sensitive, inoffensive citizens, who, though often ignorant of the rights and privileges of their new citizenship, add to all the natural freshness of a child, the depth of men and women of most earnest upright souls.

Why are the intimidation of a colored Republican in the exercise of his civil right to vote, and the deprivation of a citizen of the United States of African descent of any other civil right, two different questions? "Change places, and, handy-dandy, which is justice and which is the thief?" The triumphant Democracy, in its campaign hallelujah, says, "Yarborough's crime is Justice striving to defeat the Republican party;" while the Republican party, like a Janus-faced, gaping monster, with deep intent, half-veiled and half-shown, hiding one

thing in its heart and uttering another, cries out in its plat-
forms and upon the hustings, "Benson, the denier of civil
rights, is the thief. Away with him! torture him! He is
undermining the Constitution itself; he is the old sleeping
Samson of slavery, with his treacherous arms grasping the pillars of the State. Beware of the Democratic separate opinion
in Hall *v.* DeCuir!" A moment's reflection will convince any
admirer of the noble family of Truth, that neither of these
factions is her offspring, nor can either justly lay claim to any
of her virtues. Which one of them, courting, as they both do,
the favor of the venal harlot, Political Power, and alternately
receiving her promiscuous favors, dares look fully into the face
of the noble matron, Truth?

There was no race-blindness in Yarborough's case. The court
declared, "Although the Fifteenth Amendment gives no afirm-
ative right to the citizens to vote, yet there are cases in which
it is substantially conferred; and, in construing the Constitution, the doctrine that what is implied is as much a part of
the instrument as what is expressed, is a necessity by reason of
inherent inability to· put all powers into words." It was considered "a waste of time to seek for specific sources of the power
to pass these [Ku-Klux] laws."

An almost imperceptible political and civil right, reposing
in the ample bosom of the Constitution, was brought to attention and made quite visible to the naked eye of the most vulgar
understanding, by the shining luminaries of Jurisprudence. It
was shown in Yarborough's case, as in the famous Legal-Tender
Decisions, that the Constitution covers an infinite sphere, of which
the centre is everywhere, the circumference nowhere. When, as
in Yarborough's case, the pathway of a Republican member of
the national Congress on his way to Washington was ambuscaded
by the Ku-Klux, the Constitution was an Eternal Lamp, making
light the hidden places of constitutional obstructionists; but not
a single ray of that holy light penetrated the darkness of the
Mississippi Valley on the night of the eventful voyage from
New Orleans to the Hermitage, which gave birth to the case of
Hall *v.* DeCuir. A citizen of the United States, standing erect,
with the broad and ample folds of the Fourteenth Amendment

round about her, in the peace of God and of the State of Louisiana, obnoxious neither in word nor deed, neither in law nor fact, to any constitutional objection, was so defenceless, in consequence of her status as an African, that the mere vermin of the public service swarmed over her civil rights, immunities, and privileges, as if she were attainted or her civil rights merely "commerce" or merchandise, subject as such by the "inaction" of Congress, to the rules, regulations, and vicissitudes of a "free and untrammelled discretionary control," and to the brute force of the master of transportation. And why? Because of her color, and not for any reason or rule by law alike applicable to every other citizen, no matter what his nativity or his previous or present condition, whether of debasement, ignorance, crime, or squalid moral and physical degradation.

And yet in Yarborough's case Jurisprudence with trumpet-tongue proclaims that the principle of political ethics in the Fourteenth Amendment is the dignity of man; that it is "essential to the successful working of the government that the great organs of its executive and legislative branches should be the free choice of the people," who "*should be free from the influence of extraneous violence.*" The burning, fiery eloquence of Justice Miller in Yarborough's decision swept before it all difficulties in the way of a recognition of the legal rights of the black race when the Ku-Klux finger of intimidation was pointed at that race as voters. Is there any special divinity, *outside party politics,* under the Constitution, which hedges in a colored citizen's civil right to vote that does not equally protect the civil rights of a colored traveller in the pursuits of his life, on a steamboat, ferry, railway, or when he is located in an inn, or a place of public resort for business or pleasure? Why should there be any more insuperable obstacle in compelling a "recognition of the legal rights of the black race" in the one case than in the other?

Mr. Justice Harlan, in the Civil-Rights Cases, speaks of "the difficulty of the legal right of the black race to take the rank of citizens, and to secure the enjoyment of privileges belonging under the law to them as a component part of the people." Why should this difficulty be so easily overcome when the black race "takes the rank of citizens" to *vote?* "The privilege of voting" equally belongs to them, under the law, as a component part of the people, for whose welfare and happiness "government is ordained." In voting, do they not take the rank of citizens? The "enjoyment of this privilege, belonging to them under the law, as a component part of the people," has been effectually secured by enforcement of the several penalties provided against individuals who obstruct or discriminate against it.

This question is one of constitutional law. Why is there a constitutional power to prohibit, by the Enforcement Acts, an *individual* of the State from discriminating against the civil right of this race to vote, but not to prevent an individual or corporation in the State from discriminating against all the other civil rights, immunities, and privileges of this race under the Civil-Rights Bill? This distinction is anomalous: it requires an explanation, which cannot be found in the Constitutional Amendments. When the Ku-Klux lays the weight of his finger upon the timid black of the South, or the practical "boss" tempts with gold and silver the droves of purchasable political cattle throughout the country, they commanded that the great furnace of Justice should be heated seven times more than it was wont to be heated; whilst these criminal classes were told, in blood-curdling tones, "The true Shekinah is man. There is but one temple in the universe,—the body of man; nothing is holier than that high form"—*engaged in the exercise of the elective franchise;* "in bending before men is the reverence done to this revelation in the flesh; we touch Heaven when we lay our hands upon a human body"—*in the act of voting.*

The transcendent admiration which Mr. Justice Miller and his brethren entertained for the Constitution, when the civil right of voting was slightly interfered with, overcame all constitutional impediments. The illustrious Republican court, with a tread not to be mistaken, "*stepped into the Ku-Klux State domain,*" and showed no desire to evade, but a determination to recognize and enforce by all the power of the government, the stupendous force of the Fifteenth Amendment, when the "*in-*

dividuals of the State" (*not the State*) showed the whites of their eyes or upturned their noses at the exercise by a " black fellow" at the South, of the fundamental civil right, immunity, and privilege of voting which was accorded alike to all other citizens, irrespective of previous condition.

There was no masquerading with this civil right of the ballot in the case of Yarborough; there was no talk about " Congress being clothed with no authority to adopt a civil code for the regulation of the conduct of individuals in the State in their corporate or personal capacity." These individual State offenders were made to feel the penalty of outraged law; they were made convicts of record; they were told, one and all, " It is not in the power of such vermin as you to undermine this new pillar of the State." The court, with a noble, grave aspect, in an earnest, sternly-impressive manner, told unscrupulous dissemblers, political despots, usurpers, and " bosses," " Your chief material is fraud and falsehood, but this government shall henceforth be administered not for you or your partisans, but by due process of law, for the enforcement of this civil right of all its children."

There was no toying or paltering about this civil right to vote, in Yarborough's case; no equivocating sibylline answer. The decision said to the wild boars of the national forest, " You may break through the local State cobwebs of the law, but the toils of the nation's court are made of sterner stuff. Justice shall reign among men. The fundamental law of the nation declares that you shall not tamper with this civil right of every subject. The rainbow stretched across our sky reflects all colors, and proclaims to the world that the black tempest has subsided, and that ' equality before the law' is henceforth the watchword of the republic." The great question at the outbreak of the Rebellion was, Shall we have equality of law for all men, and risk the life of the republic to attain it ? All the people said, " Freedom, due process of law, equality according to the law of the land, or the death of the republic." The opinion of the Supreme Court in Yarborough's case lacked no heartiness : it had a rugged homeliness, a directness of purpose, a robust simplicity which filled the nation with admiration. Justice walked with a velvet tread, but it struck with a hand of steel, and awed back the robber chieftains North and South.

From this pleasing and refreshing spectacle, let us turn back to Hall *v.* DeCuir, the last peak of the submerged world of slavery, with the hope that the swell of the incoming tide of civilization will shortly entomb it in the fathomless abyss of Scott *v.* Sandford. The gaps of centuries seem to intervene between the civilization of Yarborough's case and the retrogression of Hall *v.* DeCuir. Between the fate of civil rights in the two cases as great a gulf is fixed as that which after death was found to separate a " certain rich man which was clothed in purple and fine linen and fared sumptuously every day" and "a certain beggar, named Lazarus, which was laid at his gate, full of sores, and desiring to be fed with the crumbs which fell from the rich man's table." From the *terra mobilis* of Hall *v.* DeCuir, let us challenge a closer combat upon the *terra firma* of the Fourteenth Amendment.

CHAPTER XX.

" Reason eclipsed by that strangely artificial and seemingly most profound formula."—Hegel.

" A spurious impartiality, little better than a culpable indifference to questions the most important that can agitate our own generation and all humanity, or the discriminating contempt of an arrogant superiority, still more offensive and baneful to truth."—Schlegel.

" And I hope I may now be permitted to have done with etymology : for though, like a microscope, it is sometimes useful to discover the minuter parts of language which would otherwise escape our sight ; yet it is not necessary to have it always·in our hands, nor proper to apply it to every object."—Tooke.

" Ay. So he tells us again that right is—' not wrong,' and wrong is— ' not right.' But seek no further for intelligence in that quarter ; where nothing but cant and folly is to be found,—misleading, mischievous folly ; because it has a sham appearance of labor and learning."—Id.

" A yellow ant in a nest of red ants, a butcher's dog in a fox-kennel, a mouse in a beehive,—all feel the effects of the intrusion."—Sydney Smith.

" Let us always reflect, that the first law of the empire of Russia, which is greater than the Roman empire, is the toleration of every sect."—Voltaire.

" ' Do you believe,' said the European, ' that laws and religions can be formed for climates, the same as furs are required at Moscow, and gauze stuffs at Delhi ?' ' Yes, doubtless,' said the Brahmin ; ' all laws which concern physics are calculated for the meridian which we inhabit ; a German requires only one wife, and a Persian must have two or three.' "—Id.

" What is toleration ? It is the appurtenance of humanity. We are all full of weakness and errors ; let us mutually pardon each other our follies,—it is the first law of nature."—Id.

" If I should labor for any other satisfaction but that of my own mind, it would be an effect of phrensy in me, not of hope ; since it is not truth, but opinion, that can travel the world without a passport."—Id.

" There is, in a certain school, a tendency to refer the whole course and development of civilization to races, and to regard separate races in their racial character, as the integral powers in history. In this assumption the history of the world is apprehended as consequent not from the special and physical properties of the soil, the climate, and the like, but from the properties of races. The development of history is presumed in the institution of the power and supremacy of a race. The most complete construction of history is traced through the suggestion of names in ancient genealogical records, and the most elaborate and far-reaching theories are literally built upon no other foundation than the scattered bricks of the ruins of the tower of Babel, in whose hieroglyphics modern philologists decipher the whole course of history, and find the key that opens all its changes."—MULFORD.

" The nation, on the contrary, comes forth in the realization of the life of humanity. The life of humanity is not a restriction, as in some external limitation to the nation as a moral person, but its fulfilment is in the nation as a moral person. It is thus that there is in the nation a constant exclusion of a selfish egoism instead of a construction of society out of it."—ID.

" It is thus also that it cannot be retained in the exclusive claim of a family or a race. In its work for humanity, and its fulfilment in its divine origin and relations, the nation has been formed in the modern world."—ID.

HOWEVER imposing its exterior, candor will oblige the impartial reviewer to confess that the inner fabric and the main pillars which underprop Mr. Justice Clifford's stately edifice of theoretical jurisprudence in Hall *v.* DeCuir are flimsy and insubstantial. That jurist's delineation of the prerogatives of the public servants, and of the duties and obligations which the community owe to these creatures of the State, stripped of the luxuriance of its verbal foliage, presents as the outcome of his understanding of the law of civil rights (concerning which, ever since the passage of the war amendments, two distinct orders of society have involved the courts in endless litigation) the general propositions that the public servant is under no lawful obligation to admit, receive, entertain, or transport—

1st. Those who may refuse to observe the *reasonable* rules of the service.

2d. Those who may be guilty of gross and vulgar acts of conduct.

3d. " Those who may make disturbances."

4th. Those " whose characters may be doubtful, dissolute, suspicious, or unequivocally bad."

5th. Those whose object may be to injure his business, by making it less lucrative, and the management less acceptable to the public.

6th. That the public servant is authorized to establish a legal quarantine, to be rigidly enforced, against one portion only of the society of the State ; and if, at the expiration of forty days of fumigation, it shall appear, upon due inspection, that the legal and moral preliminary jurisdictional conditions (arbitrarily established) have been fully complied with, such of the obnoxious class as still possess their souls in patience, may claim the civil rights, immunities and privileges which *all* citizens of the United States and of the several States, according to the law of the land, are entitled to enjoy without let or hinderance.

7th. That one portion of the society of the state may be subjected to limitations upon and restrictions of its civil rights, which are never imposed upon the other.

8th. That the proprietors of these public institutions " have the right to consult and provide for their interests in their management, as that is a common incident to property."

9th. That these public institutions " do not belong to the public ; they are private property, the use and enjoyment of which belongs to the proprietors."

10th. That these public institutions may be subjected to " such conditions and obligations as the nature of their enjoyment requires, for the comfort, security, and safety of passengers."

11th. That, notwithstanding this concession, " the settled rules of constitutional law forbid State legislatures to invade the dominions of private rights, by arbitrary restrictions, requirements, or limitations," conforming the business of the public servant to the supreme law of the land ; by which the property of owners or possessors " would be virtually stripped of all utility or value."

12th. " That the right [of the carrier] to separate his passengers grows out of his right of private property, and the necessity of regulations promoting the public interest."

13th. " That the right of control in that regard springs from the private means he employs; and it is necessary to protect his own interest, and to perform his duty to the travelling public,—which is, to promote the comfort and enjoyment of those who exercise this civil right;" provided, color or previous condition can be discriminated against in the case of travellers of African descent.

14th. That the passenger is not entitled to any particular apartment or special accommodation.

15th. That "substantial equality of right" is the law of the State and of the United States; but " *equality* does not mean *identity,*" as, "in the nature of things, *identity* in accommodation of passengers, whether white or black, is impossible."

16th. That the laws of the United States do not require persons to be put in the same apartment who would be repulsive or disagreeable to each other, provided such repulsiveness is because of color or previous condition.

17th. That there is no law of Congress which forbids "separate apartments" for citizens of the United States, although by *separate apartments* is meant *discrimination* on account of color.

18th. That in locating the public in apartments, or at meals, it is not only the right, but the duty, of the public servant to exercise such reasonable discretion and control as will promote, as far as practicable, the comfort and convenience of the whole company, more especially if it can be done by discrimination upon the ground of color.

19th. That the right of the public to entertainment is one thing, and its claim to dictate after it is admitted to the right is a very different thing, particularly in the exercise by these citizens of their civil rights.

20th. That it is the *public*, particularly the African part of it, and not the *public servant*, which is subject to reasonable rules; and such rules and regulations are to be determined by the proprietor.

The origin of this legal philosophy is obscure. From its nebulous aspect it may be inferred, according to fashionable Jurisprudence, that the *Jus Civile, Jus Gentium, Jus Commune,* and *Jus Singulare* still prevail among the various State tribes in the primeval forests of America; and that the *lex scripta* or *non-scripta*, foreign or domestic, regulative of their rights, justifies such limitations and restrictions upon the exercise by one portion of the State of the civil rights which the other enjoys without controversy. A cautious analysis of this tangled mass of verbal growth will reveal at a glance, that its mixed and muddled postulates present only generalizations, which, like all generalizations, contain some obviously sound abstractions; that these twenty tables in their every-day practical workings, instead of affording a philosophic plan of administering public law so as to protect the weaker element of the State, can be readily transformed, by the shrewd, conscienceless cunning and selfish thrift of the charlatans of the color-line, into self-adjusting engines of oppression.

Justice Clifford's " law of the Twenty Tables," if not exactly a weak, is certainly not a strong attempt to handle a weighty subject. Each one of the vast horde of petty, pelting tyrants understands these rules as he pleases, and applies them as he sees fit. Instead of securing equality of right for the weakest, they introduce into jurisprudence for the first time the doctrine of the survival of the fittest,—that is, of the strongest element of the state. Except in pith and brevity, they are not unlike the Visigothic code: " Thou shalt be king if thou doest right, and if thou doest *not right thou shalt not be king.*" This code substitutes for the sharply-defined specialization of the Civil-Rights Bill a mere air-drawn form of words; mere legal generalities, having no stern, sound, legal signification, that " free and untrammelled authority" may not, with average craft, defeat. For positive law it substitutes the general conscience of that motley-minded gentleman, the public servant. It nowhere asserts, that the rights of each individual must stand or fall by the same rules of law that govern every other member of the body politic under similar conditions and circumstances. It denies that legal liberty which consists in every man's security against wrong. It ignores the doctrine of Lieber, that " the liberty of social man consists in the protection of unrestrained action, in as high a degree as the same claim of protection of each individual admits, or in the most efficient protection of his rights, claims, interests, as a man, or citizen, or of his humanity manifested as a social being." It substitutes the will of the public servant for the State and its government. It enables him to say, "The State and I are one,"—"*L'état, c'est moi.*"

It is not in accord with Hooker, "the law which doth assign to each thing the kind, that which doth moderate the force and the power, that which doth appoint the force and manner of working the same." This "law of the Twenty Tables" may be described as the despair of *Justice.* It proclaims that divine Providence has endowed the public servant with a scientific and unerring knowledge of the principles of equality before the law, and declares that the hopeless enigma of black civil rights in the history of American *Jurisprudence* must be solved by that pure legist. The Fourteenth Amendment, which is the expression of the will of the sixty million sovereigns who compose the American state, is subjected under these tables to the scientific morality and theoretical jurisprudence of the Public Servant; whose constructions may be outside of the law, against the law, and yet according to the law : *Fuera de la ley, condra de la ley, y segun la ley.*

The history of civil rights and the evidence in the cases, with rare exceptions, incontrovertibly prove that the Machiavellis of the public service manifest a constant and perpetual will to deprive these citizens of their equality before the law, to hurt every one of them, when they can, and to give to no one of them his due, by laying down one-sided rules and regulations, under the general abstractions of the Twenty Tables, ostensibly established for the enforcement of the equality before the law of the weaker race. The difficulty which the civil rights of one portion of the society of the state encounters is met on the very threshold. It has its root in the application of Justice Clifford's generalities to the special circumstances of each case. If the oligarchy of caste is authorized to issue its royal mandate, to mount and range its guns, the surrender of Black Civil Rights, under the practical working of his "law of the Twenty Tables," is sooner or later inevitable. The elastic conscience and the "free and untrammelled discretion" and "authority" of the crafty proprietor, who is from motives of self-interest a natural panderer to caste, can readily adjust these general rules to individual cases in such a manner as apparently to obey their letter while violating their spirit. Thus the system of the Twenty Tables is made a purveyor to discrimination, invites race-antagonisms, and facilitates, under color of lawful warrant, both public and private imposition upon Black Civil Rights. "The voice is Jacob's voice, but the hands are the hands of Esau."

The exposition of the rules governing common carriers with reference to the civil rights of persons, as announced by Mr. Justice Clifford in Hall and DeCuir, is in marked contrast with those universally acknowledged, acted upon, and daily received, as we have already seen, before the science of black civil rights made its appearance in this department of the law. The letter and the spirit of the law, and the former interpretation of the obligations of this branch of the public service respecting the rights of persons, are as far removed from the interpretation embodied in these tables as are the poles. The stringency of the law which measures the commercial obligation of the public servant is apparent when it is remembered that before the period of Sir William Jones, from Coggs *v.* Bernard[1] until to-day :

1st. The common carrier was and is regarded as an insurer of goods against all casualties, except those which arise from the act of God or the public enemy.

2d. By "the act of God" was intended anything in the production of which man has no agency, immediate or remote.

3d. Inevitable accidents—the *vis major, casus fortuitus*—can alone exempt this public employment. Indeed, so stringent is the rule that to excuse the carrier, the injury must in no degree be connected with human intervention, or human neglect ; this rule applies to hackney-coaches, cabs, carmen, express companies, barges, transportation companies, ferrymen, truckmen, wagoners, drivers, stage-coaches, railroads, steamboats, navigation warehousemen, forwarding merchants, toll-bridge-keepers, innkeepers, etc.

4th. The impolicy of allowing these servants to limit their liability has been gravely discussed and variously determined.

---

[1] 2 Lord Raymond's Reports, 951.

5th. In cases of personal injuries, brought about by a combination of the heedlessness of passenger *and* carrier, the contributory negligence of the passenger does not excuse the carrier, if by the exercise of ordinary care the defendant might have avoided the injury.

An estimate may be formed of the extensive controversies to which the application of these doctrines has given rise in the commerce of the country, when it is reflected that the laborious author of Wood's Railroad Law has collated upwards of twenty thousand recent cases, between white citizens; not one of which, however, involves the civil rights of the white portion of the State, whose equality before the law has either never been questioned or has remained so long undisturbed and settled as not to admit of disputation. The calling of the public servant, which has recently become a subject of great magnitude, was, prior to the passage of the war amendments, that of a simple bailee. The rational grounds for holding the carrier to the strictest discharge of his duties are founded upon public policy.

CHAPTER XXI.

" The advocate of reason sets himself to work : he displays the nothing-ness, he detects and exposes the fallacies. What is he the better? The exposure is turned aside from : the compound of falsehood and nonsense continues to be delivered, with the same effrontery and the same intolerant arrogance as ever. Even were that abandoned, some other phrases of the like material would be employed instead of it : the same work would be to do over again and with equal fruit."—BENTHAM.

" Their ignorance and idleness make them contented with this vague and misapplied metaphorical language : and if we should beg them to consider that words have no locomotive faculty, that they do not flow like rivers, nor vegetate like plants, nor spiculate like salts, nor are generated like animals ; they would say, we quibbled with them ; and might perhaps in their fury be tempted to exert against us ' vigor beyond the law.' And yet, until they can get rid of these metaphors from their minds, they will not themselves be fit for etymology, nor furnish any etymology fit for reasonable men."—DIVERSIONS OF PURLEY.

" Now your honor is to know, that these judges are persons appointed to decide all controversies of property, as well as for the trial of criminals, and picked out from the most dexterous lawyers, who are grown old or lazy ; and, having been biassed all their lives against truth and equity, lie under such a fatal necessity of oppression, that I have known some of them refuse a large bribe from the side where justice lay, rather than injure the faculty by doing anything unbecoming their nature or their office."—SWIFT.

" The point where sense and nonsense join."—PAINE.

" And now, after this long interval of time, we behold our greatest right—the right on which all other rights depend—successfully assailed in our own Congress with the same small weapons that Grenville used. If brute force had crushed it out, we might have borne the calamity with fortitude ; but to see it circumvented by knavery and pettifogged to death, is too much to be endured with any show of patience."—J. BLACK.

" And the manifold evils which have filled the world for these thousands of years ; the murders, enslavings, and robberies ; the tyrannies of rulers, the oppressions of class, the persecutions of sect and party ; the multi-form embodiments of selfishness in unjust laws, barbarous customs, dis-

255

honest dealings, exclusive manners, and the like, are simply instances of the disastrous working of this original and once-needful constitution, now that mankind have grown into conditions for which it is not fitted,—are nothing but symptoms of the suffering attendant upon the adaptation of humanity to its new circumstances."—SPENCER.

" The Royal Psalmist hath foretold for your comfort and that of all the just, that God will in his own time arise to judge your cause and to scatter and destroy your enemies. He will awake as from sleep, and will cover them with everlasting shame. He will arise and will have mercy on Sion, which the wicked have made their spoil. Meanwhile, we, your sons, relying on these sacred oracles and on the promises of our Saviour Christ, will from our inmost soul most fervently pray that the time so long looked for may swiftly come, in which you may with entire freedom rule over the whole church, having changed even the wolves now raging about the fold into the lambs of the flock."—CARDINAL GIBBONS.

LONG ago Lord Holt[1] declared, " This is a politic establishment controlled by the polity of the law for the safety of all persons, the necessity of whose affairs obliges them to trust these sort of persons, that they may be safe in their ways of dealing. For else these carriers might have an opportunity of undoing all persons that had any dealing with them," etc. The exceptions which public servants, exercising a public vocation, may make are well recognized. They may discriminate against suspicious persons, or persons with infectious diseases, or in cases where the service is professedly special and limited exclusively to invalids, drovers, or any other class. But this authority cannot be extended so as to thwart public policy ;[2] the obligations of which require them (to the extent of their accommodations) to entertain all suitable persons who may apply for entertainment or transportation. As in America the principle of individual liberty undoubtedly fosters the growing sense of the personal importance of each member of the society of individuals which constitutes the state, it would seem to require exceptional temerity to assert, that the would-be potentate of the public service is clothed with authority to curb the rights of persons,

-----

[1] Coggs v. Bernard, 2 Lord Ray. 909, 918.
[2] Marklam v. Brown, 8 N. H. 523.

although he is bound hand and foot respecting the rights of things.

The complaint of the citizen of African descent is, that the decay of "natural and well-known repugnances" creating civic discrimination cannot be expected, so long as the judicial interpretation of our laws, directly encourages the supremacy of one class of citizens over another in the every-day, joint and several enjoyment of those civil rights, immunities, and privileges which the supreme law of the land declares shall be the equal heritage of all classes in the state. The African citizens protest and claim that a uniform, precise, and fixed regulation of the sov-ereign rights of all the individuals who now compose the state, in accordance with the letter and spirit of the law of the land, would put an end to the bickerings, rancor, and discord which foment race-antagonisms throughout the land. They say truly, that the vexatious litigation between the races incontestably establishes, what is too notorious for question, that the more numerous and powerful body in the state daily trample under foot the civil rights of a minority,—of a sensitive, peaceful, unresisting, helpless, and useful portion of the civic society ; that the state now requires the repose which the amendments to the Constitution contemplate ; that this anarchistic force in the state must be curbed, controlled, and counterbalanced by the law of the land ; that an amphibious code of crude, contradictory textual rules, instead of repelling insolent despotism, encourages the spirit of race-antagonism to enter fresh fields, and, with new allies under its command, to commit new depredations upon all the other civil rights of these citizens ; that their general civil right to engage in all departments of industry requires something more for its protection than a mere grammatical construction of the words employed in the Fourteenth Amendment, and an ambulatory parade around the amendment itself, with an army of pretentious learning,—an imposing array of deceptive dialectical subtleties ; that to meet the race-perils which confront the state, in the present condition of civil rights, there is an imperative need either of new legislation, or of the enforcement of the existing law by rules which will protect, on life's common way, the lowliest child of the state's adoption, making him feel that he is a man, majestic and free : rules of such strength and grandeur that they will inspire each member of the state with awe and reverence; so clear, uniform, stern, and unrelenting in their character, that the most profligate or powerful member of the state will not dare to evade or dispute their authority.

They claim that, in direct conflict with all this, the infant science of civil rights has been smothered under the loose generalities of the doctrines promulgated in Hall *v.* DeCuir, which are as muddy, muddled, and misty as race-antagonism could desire ; that the true solution of this branch of the science of civil rights lies in that specialization which the national Civil-Rights Bills presented to the public of America, and the Louisiana Civil-Rights Bill to its citizens. They claim that in that special branch of their immunities the Civil-Rights Bill is a specialization and realization of the equality before the law, which the Fourteenth Amendment contemplates; and that, in effect, these " Twenty Tables" substitute " free and untrammelled authority" for the true intention of that body of reasoned truths which the Civil-Rights Bills announce. The citizens of African descent cheerfully concede all the authority that the law asserts for the discretion of the servant of the public in the bestowal of his passengers under general, reasonable, and just rules, which are made applicable to the whole public alike, without the invidious distinctions of color or previous condition. They insist, however, that, to be just and reasonable, these rules should have for their object the accommodation not only of the white public, but also of the public whose complexion has the tinge of the Fourteenth Amendment, " including everything to render the transportation most comfortable and least annoying," not solely " to the great majority ordinarily transported," as Mr. Justice Clifford declares, but to each and every individual, irrespective of race or color.

They claim that this doctrine of Hall *v.* DeCuir licenses Labor-Caste and the intolerance of race-antagonism, and deprives the minority of the state of its constitutional rights ; upon the ground, that the deprivation of the minority of their civil rights [which, if granted, would render their daily pursuits comfortable and enjoyable], and the imposition and enforcement of rules most annoying and destructive to their peace and happiness, degrading them in their own and the public estimation, may be a regulation of civil rights *most enjoyable to the great majority* of Race-Caste, whenever the pursuits of the latter bring them into the presence of what is (in their opinion) the inferior order of the State, but that it is a doctrine directly contrary to the object and intent of the Fourteenth Amendment.

The spirit of "equality of civil rights" refuses to acquiesce in the ruling of Justice Clifford, that there are "well-settled rules"—or any rules whatever—"of constitutional construction, which forbid a State legislature from the invasion of private rights, by arbitrary restrictions and requirements or limitations by which the property of the owners would be virtually stripped of all utility or value," if, by "arbitrary restrictions, requirements, or limitations," etc., Justice Clifford intends (as his contention manifestly is) that rules of such "settled constitutional construction" are applicable to the legislation by the States which restricts and limits private rights, and the owners of public or private property in its use, to a substantial, wholesome compliance with the letter and spirit of the Fourteenth Amendment, the declared policy of the American nation. When, in their anxiety to solve the pressing race-problems which loomed up so threateningly in the then disordered condition of the sovereign State of Louisiana, a few of her citizens, who were strenuous toilers after liberty, with disinterested zeal for the oppressed and poor, the weary, doubtful, plodding "seekers after light," foresaw that if the sensitive plant of civil-rights, recently transplanted to the soil of Louisiana, depended for its nourishment upon State jurisprudence, it would ere long sicken and die, they quickly resolved to anticipate the apathy of jurisprudence by some decided action. They accordingly hastened to adopt in Louisiana the code recommended by those eager and loving disciples of liberty, who stood in the front ranks of the nation's new civilization. On the 23d of February, 1869, they enacted in their State a Civil-Rights Bill, the main provisions of which were afterwards incorporated into the national Civil-Rights Bill, the object of which was to specialize the general rights conferred by the Fourteenth Amendment and to conform them to the supreme

law of the land by asserting that the enjoyment of the civil
rights thus specially enumerated partly constituted the equality
before the law provided for by the Fourteenth Amendment. It
is the provisions of the Civil-Rights Bill of Louisiana—similar to the provisions of the national Civil-Rights Bill which
was subsequently passed by Congress when it was composed of
the individual legislators who had formulated the war amendments—that Mr. Justice Clifford declares to be void by " the
settled rules of constitutional law," because " they [the provisions of the Louisiana bill] were invasions of private rights,
which virtually stripped the owners of property of all its
utility."

With this averment of fact Civil Rights joins issue. It
denies, as a matter of fact, that the duty of compliance with the
supreme law of the land, embodied in a State statute, would in
any wise " depreciate the value of private rights or property in
its public or private employment." It demurs to the law of the
supposed " settled rules of constitutional construction," which
forbid State legislatures, courts, juries, public or private corporations, or their special agencies, to carry out the provisions of the
Fourteenth Amendment in State or in interstate commerce involving the right of transportation of citizens of the United
States. It contends that, even if it had been established by
competent proof, or could be in any way shown, that constitutional legislation did incidentally operate to " divest private
property of its value" or strip it of all its utility, such loss
would be *damnum absque injuria*.

All history disproves the allegation that business and the
institutions of commerce will be stripped of all utility and
become valueless if the civil rights of every citizen of the
State are protected and enforced with uniform impartiality.
Rome was the residence of promiscuous aliens gathered from all
countries and all climes. Nevertheless, these discordant, belligerent elements became citizens and equals before the Roman
law, notwithstanding the bitterest antagonisms of barbarism,
previous conditions, skin, race, birth, religion, and " natural and
well-known repugnances," together with all the concomitants
and ingredients which fill to the brim the poisoned chalice of

race-prejudice. The difference between the Roman and the American systems is, that the policy of the latter invites, encourages, aids, and abets race-antagonisms, while the former sunk all racial differences in the State, by the rigid, impartial, and stern enforcement of its laws, in letter and spirit.

It was not until internal corruption and "the free and untrammelled" brutal race-antagonisms of barbarism overcame the fundamental law of the Roman Empire, that it began to decline and fall. At the beginning of the fourth century the issue was still between the prejudices of barbarism and the faith of Christ. Up to that period all save four of those loving disciples who represented the Holy See of St. Peter had laid down their lives to maintain it; afterwards the Papacy and the Church passed through persecutions without parallel in the history of the world's horrors for the maintenance of that principle which has borne its noblest flower and fruit in the American Constitution. It was not until the Bishop of Rome dispensed laws to Christendom, from the Capitol where pagan prejudice had fulminated its edicts against Christianity, not until the Crescent of Mohammedanism gave place to the Cross of Christ at Lepanto, that the dark shadows of despotism were dispelled, and the celestial morn of civilization began to dawn on earth. When the grandeur of the Roman state was at its height, she acknowledged the supremacy of law, and, as the Fourteenth Amendment freed all American citizens on paper, the Roman law freed all Roman citizens in fact.

Under the Laws of the Twelve Tables, there was no provision for recalcitrant race-tricks. There was no public servant's "free and untrammelled authority" to regulate the civil rights of the citizens of Rome. Every citizen of all classes was free and proud to utter the boast, *Civis Romanus sum ;* every citizen could ask, with Paul, "Is it lawful for you to scourge a man that is a Roman and uncondemned?" The Apostle did not (as the African for two centuries has done in America) unavailingly fall upon his knees, and, in the sad voice of stricken humanity, imploringly ask, "Am I not a man, and a brother?" On the contrary, when the judge—the high priest—commanded those that stood by to smite him on the mouth, because he said, "I have lived in all good conscience before God," this Roman citizen—an inferior in the state, by birth a Judean, contending with the all-powerful majority of his countrymen—did not speak to his judicial oppressor with bated breath, nor in a bondsman's key, but in the fearless tones of truth. He said, "God shall smite thee, thou whited wall: sittest thou there to judge me after the law, and commandest thou me to be smitten contrary to the law?" These citizens of the United States cannot say, with Paul, " I was free *born.*" But they can declare, with the chief captain, to " private rights," to the " owners and possessors of property," and to these construers of " settled rules of constitutional construction," "With a *great sum* obtained I this freedom :" with bonds of the United States payable in gold coin, piled mountain-high; and with rivers of the nation's precious blood which flowed in crimson torrents over the Southron's soil, leaving in its dark red track half a million dying heroes, who, with supreme and steadfast courage, faced death, in the honest conviction that they were maintaining their vested rights under settled rules of constitutional construction.

CHAPTER XXII.

" A law is the deed of the whole body politic, whereof if ye judge yourselves to be any part, then is the law even your deed also."—HOOKER.

" This necessity, however, exists; and the problem to be solved is, not what form of government is perfect, but which of the forms is least imperfect; and here the general question must be between a republican government, in which the majority rule the minority, and a government in which a lesser number or the least number rule the majority."—MADISON.

" It has been justly said to be ' a settled principle, growing out of the nature of well-ordered civil society, that every holder of property, however absolute and unqualified may be his title, holds it under the implied liability that his use of it shall not be injurious to the equal enjoyment of others having an equal right to the enjoyment of their property, nor injurious to the rights of the community. All property . . . is held subject to those general regulations which are necessary for the common good and general welfare.' And ' it must, of course, be within the range of legislative action to define the mode and manner in which every one may so use his own as not to injure others.' Illustrations might be given indefinitely of the proper use and employment of this power in such manner as, though lawful, may greatly circumscribe the use and reduce the value of some one or more species of property, and in some cases even practically annihilate it."—STORY.

" If there be not the consciousness of the unity and sovereignty and freedom which subsist in the organic being of the people, then all argument is empty, and all inquiry is vain. The realization of history can be determined by no political abstractions, and events conform to no individual preconceptions. Facts do not defer to theories ; in the strong image of the poet, ' Words are men's daughters, but God's sons are things.' "—MULFORD.

" The absurdity is in supposing that by some ingenious artifice we may avoid the consequences of our own natures. The civil power no more does what to the careless eye it seems to do than the juggler really performs his apparent miracles."—SPENCER.

" In this sense the restraints on men, as well as their liberties, are to be reckoned among their rights."—BURKE.

LET us assume the mere apprehension of Mr. Justice Clifford to be established by incontrovertible proofs ; let us grant that the ebb and flow of the tides of commerce will be affected ; that Caste would deny itself the consolation of religion, food, drink, raiment, travel, and amusement, because its avenues to these pursuits were opened to the newly-adopted citizens ; let us assume the result predicted, that, if each citizen of the state is obliged to acquiesce in the fundamental law of the land, and in the acknowledgment of the civil rights, immunities, and privileges of every other citizen, the churches, railways, steamboats, hotels, opera-houses, theatres, and saloons would, like exposed mummies, crumble into dust ; that " arbitrary restrictions, requirements, and limitations," which the Fourteenth Amendment imposes upon property, its owners and possessors, " virtually strips it of all its utility or value," because it binds all to a compliance with the doctrine of the equality of all men before the law : we still ask what settled rule of constitutional construction forbids a State to pass and enforce a law, following hard upon the footsteps of the Fourteenth Amendment, the supreme law of the land ?   If, peradventure, such devastation should happen to follow, upon what principle of " settled constitutional construction " can the public servant claim specific compensation for such injury to his rights ?   If sacrifices are, by the law of the land, generally demanded for the benefit of the entire community, why is he an exception to the universally understood, necessary condition upon which men enter into political society and establish governments ?   His assent to the workings of the State system, like that of every other member of the organic whole, is implied.   Public servants' peculiar rights, unlike the rights or property of other citizens, did not exist prior to constitutions and states.   On the contrary, the public servant is an institution of a ripe civilization.   The birth of his employment and the rights and property appertaining to it are only coeval with the establishment of commerce.   In a condition of natural law his employment had no place.   It was as great a stranger to primitive society and primeval law as any other offspring of civilized society.   If the Odyssey of Homer is authority, any idea of commerce must have been foreign to the individ-

uals of a primitive race, who "had neither assemblies for consultation, nor *themistes,* but every one exercised jurisdiction over
his wife and children, and they paid no regard to one another."
The "public servant" of modern civilization had no type in
archaic society. The patriarchal condition had no more conception of him than of the submarine cable.

If, then, he had neither a cognate nor an agnate relationship
to "special rights" in a state of natural law, if his connection
with rights of property is only contemporary with commerce,
when, under the equality of the law in America, the citizens
(whose rights as *men* antedated all charters and civilization)
claim his services,—as their civil right, their personal property,
their vested right, their public privilege under the law of
nature, and the law of the Fourteenth Amendment,—what
champion of race-prejudice can indicate the "settled rules" of
constitutional law which permit the public servant to invade
the "private and personal civil rights" of these citizens by his
"arbitrary restrictions, requirements, or limitations," when by
these restrictions this property of these owners and possessors
of civil rights is virtually "stripped of all utility or value, if
they are bound to comply with *his* regulations"? Do these
"settled rules of constitutional construction" place the public
servant's rights on a higher plane, or a less precarious footing,
than the rights of person and property thus doubly secured by
the natural law and the amendment? What right has the
public servant superior to the rights of any other individual
or institution of the state? Are not his and theirs, both being
the rights of persons, simply civil rights in the generic sense
of the term,—a species of property? and as such recognized and
protected by the awful majesty of the state, which guards, by
due process of law (the law of the land) and the sword of Justice, civilization and its countless myriads?

The learned author of Cooley's "Constitutional Limitations" [1]
recognizes the principle that private interest may become subordinate to public good when he says,—

"In organized society every man holds all he possesses, and

---

[1] 4th ed., p. 444.

looks forward to all he hopes for, through the aid and under the protection of the laws. But as changes of circumstances and of public opinion, as well as other reasons affecting the public policy, are all the while calling for changes of the laws; and as these changes must influence more or less the value and stability of private possessions, and strengthen or destroy well-founded hopes; and as the power to make very many of them could not be disputed without denying the right of a political community to prosper and advance; it is obvious that many rights, privileges, and exemptions which usually pertain to ownership under a particular state of the law, and many reasonable expectations, cannot be regarded as vested rights in any legal sense. In many cases the courts, in the exercise of their ordinary jurisdiction, cause the property vested in one person to be transferred to another, either through the exercise of a statutory power or by the direct force of their judgment or by means of compulsory conveyances. If in these cases the courts have jurisdiction, they proceed in accordance with ' the law of the land,' and the right of one man is divested by way of enforcing a higher and better right in another. Of these cases we do not propose to speak. Constitutional questions cannot well arise concerning them, unless they are attended by circumstances of irregularity which are supposed to take them out of a general rule. All vested rights are held subject to the laws for the enforcement of public duties and private contracts and for the punishment of wrongs; and if they become divested through the operation of those laws, it is only by way of enforcing the obligations of justice and good order."

" The office of an attorney is property, and he cannot be deprived of it except for professional misconduct or proved unfitness. A person has no property, no vested interest in any rule of the common law: rights of property which have been created by the common law cannot be taken away without due process; but the law itself, as a rule of conduct, may be changed at the will or even at the whim of the legislature, unless prevented by constitutional limitations." [1]   " The State may take away rights

----

[1] Munn *v.* Illinois, 94 U. S. Rep. 113, 134; Railroad Co. *v.* Richmond,

in a public fishery by appropriating the water to some other use." [1]

With a stern acknowledgment of her allegiance to a true recital of the course of events, History records, on every page of her story of advancing civilization, the impairment, often the total destruction, of the property rights of whole communities. This waste has often proved essential to the maintenance, preservation, and promotion of the general welfare of the civil society of particular states; and the public servant should not be an exception to the general rule, even if the assumption that the Fourteenth Amendment, in its workings, imposes hardship upon his business should be sustained by substantial proof.

There is no end to the examples which may be cited to illustrate the many-sided restrictions of individual rights in civil society. The very object of government is to impose upon every citizen's action whatever is necessary to the free exercise of every other citizen's rights. "In a state of nature the individual finds, in the enjoyment of his own rights, that he transgresses the rights of others." But the fundamental rule of all civilized government is well expressed by the civil law,—*Sic utere tuo ut alienum non laedas.* It is the law of every well-ordered society that the good of the individual must yield to the good of the whole community. Take the vast array of cases in which public policy steps in, and restrains individual rights in alienations; discriminating contracts; contracts in restraint of trade, destructive of competition and promotive of monopoly; and contracts limiting or waiving legal rights. The Fourteenth Amendment is a limitation, imposed by the Constitution of the United States, upon any State action which interferes with what are called natural rights. The amendment is prohibitive of that which the community of States says is hurtful to society. *Salus populi suprema lex* is the well-recognized maxim upon the principle of which individual rights must give way to the paramount claims of society. It is difficult to declare where the police power may

---

96 U. S. 521; Transportation Co. *v.* Chicago, 99 U. S. 635; Newton *v.* Commissioners, 100 U. S. 384.

[1] Howes *v.* Grush, 131 Mass. 207.

not enter, or what the omnipotence of a State Legislature may not do.

The Constitution draws a circle around the public servant's vested rights. He is not an exception to the working of this universal rule, to which every other individual is subject. The exemption of the public servant was first discovered and announced in Hall v. DeCuir, when his property, as Justice Clifford apprehended, was likely to be "stripped of all its utility." Supposing that apprehension to be well grounded, would he not still have the abiding consolation that his loss resulted from his conformity, as a member of the State, to the law which his representatives had established? He should reflect that all a man holds is rendered secure by the protection of the law, and that reasons of public policy are always calling for changes which influence the value of private property. If the Fourteenth Amendment does operate injuriously upon the vocation of the public servant, that unavoidable result surely should not release him from obedience to its obligations. The civilization which gives to each privileges requires sacrifices from all of its members. There is nothing in the Constitution, civil, or common law which exempts his business from the burdens incident to government.

Strange it seems, and strangely it sounds, that the jurisprudence of Mr. Justice Clifford, and the primitive condition of mankind, are both in accord with the theory of the great modern philosopher and his followers. According to Justice Clifford's legal philosophy, it is with civil rights, in the full stature of civilization, as it was with the childhood of savagery,—" the survival of the fittest,"—that is, the survival of the strongest. The primitive man's so-called rights existed only so long as they could be maintained *vi et armis;* and the public servant must remember that every form of government known to mankind is an attempt, through the combined power of its society, to solve the problem of the equality before the law of each of its members. The State undertakes, if it does not always accomplish, the restoration and preservation of the equilibrium of each individual's right.

The definition of a despotic government is the exercise by

one, or by a plurality, of the legislative, executive, and judicial functions of the State; and this result is precisely what these "settled rules of constitutional construction" have accomplished for the public servant. He is one of a plurality which repeal the Fourteenth Amendment, by usurping under "free and untrammelled" rules and regulations the legislative, judicial, and executive departments of the State. The smallest and weakest, "the tainted wether" of the civic flock, gathers courage in the majestic presence of the State, and takes refuge in her sheltering arms. In civil society, the strength, safety, and happiness of the individual consist in the equality before the law of every member of the commonwealth. The combined force of the State supplies the civic equipoise, and the pernicious doctrine of the "survival of the fittest" in reference to civil rights has no place in a free government. It is the doctrine of anarchy, despotism, and revolution.

The order of God's moral government on earth seems a succession of good and evil alike to states and men. His rain falleth upon the just and the unjust: no rules of constitutional construction have hitherto thrown their beacon-light upon the inscrutable ways of Providence; which has not seen fit to exempt the public servant, in his rebellion against its decree of the Fourteenth Amendment, from the business loss with which Justice Clifford apprehends a just and true allegiance thereto threatens him. These "settled rules of constitutional construction" do not exempt this magnificent member of the State from the evils to which all others are subject. The public servant, in the hour of his sore travail, must rely either upon the sympathy of Providence, or upon the "settled rules" of an earthly tribunal, whose recorded wisdom is liable at the next term of court to be upset. The reversal of the Legal-Tender Cases in the interest of vast corporations enabled them to discharge in paper debts originally payable in gold coin, when the difference between the two payments involved an immense loss to private interests.

It has happened, in the course of human events in America, that the Supreme Court, acting the part of a political body, by the exclusion of proffered testimony showing fraud in several

States, overturned a presidential election. By its installation of Mr. Hayes, the bureaucratic "vested rights" of a standing army of Democratic office-seekers to the emoluments and perquisites of the national offices in America, founded upon the long-established doctrine that "to the victors belong the spoils," and the political right of every Democratic voter in America to see Mr. Tilden installed, were "stripped of all utility," without any compensation whatsoever.

CHAPTER XXIII.

" Private property which is affected with a *public interest* ceases entirely to be *juris privati*."—MUNN *v.* ILLINOIS, 94 U. S. 113.

" A political community implies a sacrifice of individual right for the benefit of the state, often for a cause in which they have no personal interest. In obedience to the laws of Sparta, three hundred members of that body politic laid down their lives in the pass of Thermopylæ."—STORY.

" The supreme object of the government is to care for the preservation of the nation. In this end it is justified, in its necessity, in the suspension of the ordinary procedure of its law and order, which then becomes the assertion of its higher law, and the maintenance of its enduring order. The principle of action is then, *salus populi suprema lex*."—EVERETT.

" Of all free governments compact is the basis and the essence, and it is fortunate that the powers of government, supreme as well as subordinate, can be so moulded and distributed, so compounded and divided by those on whom they are to operate, as will be most suitable to their conditions, will best guard their freedom, and best provide for their safety and happiness."—MADISON.

" You Southern men will soon reach the point where bonds will be a more valuable possession than bondsmen."—LINCOLN.

" Mill-fires were lighted at the funeral pile of slavery. The Emancipation Proclamation was heard in the depths of the earth, as well as in the sky : men were made free, and material things became our better servants."—PRESIDENT HARRISON.

" The Constitution of the United States being established by a competent authority, by that of the sovereign people of the several States, who were the parties to it, it remains only to inquire what the Constitution is ; *and here it speaks for itself*."—MADISON.

" Of all institutions, therefore, which the imperfect man sets up as supplementary to his nature, the chief one must have for its office to guarantee his freedom."—SPENCER.

" An incarnation of fat dividends."—SPRAGUE.

271

EARTH's finite stranger, peering darkly through the glass of nature into the arcana of the infinite, finds the providence of the Almighty mysteriously veiled. It has not been permitted him to break the eternal seal of the purpose of the Everlasting, or fully to understand the "ways" of the Divinity that shapes his ends. The poor child of doubt and fear, doomed for a time to walk the earth, holds life itself by a tenure so frail that the spider's most attenuated thread is cord and cable to the tie. His ancestral parents, by an act apparently not *malum in se,* but *malum prohibitum,* forfeited the beatific rights of Paradise. In the inscrutable order of Providence the history of human suffering begins with Adam's banishment from Eden. His disobedience to the command of his Creator and Law-giver entailed upon his limitless posterity a life of sacrifice. There is no stability in human affairs. Civilized society does not huddle like sheep in a fold : it marches on with vigorous strides, and to-day overflows the boundaries of yesterday. Like an impetuous torrent, it is constantly shifting its course.

According to Cicero, "Civil society, whose agent is government, consists of a multitude of people united by common interest, and by common laws to which they submit with one consent." This theory the public servant repudiates. He says, My rules and regulations are the rules of the common law, to which those members of the civil society who are of the African race must submit, without their own assent or the consent of the Fourteenth Amendment.

Locke[1] says, "When any number of men have consented to make a community or government, they are thereby presently incorporated and make one body politic, wherein the majority have the right to act and conclude the rest." The public servant says, This original compact, whereby *myself* and others have been incorporated into one society, signifies nothing, and is no compact at all. The majority who passed the Fourteenth Amendment had not, under *my* rules and regulations, the right to act and conclude me, or my business, which I do not see fit to conduct in accordance with this action of the constitutional ma-

---

[1] Book ii., ch. viii., sec. 95.

jority of the States. It is true, that if my rules and regulations are carried out the Fourteenth Amendment is no compact at all; but, even if it be, I will eliminate from its operation those citizens whom it was especially designed to protect. The simple question then is, shall these adopted citizens be divested of the rights which cost the government millions to establish, because it is alleged, but not proved, that, if their rights are preserved and enforced, some public servant's business, perchance, may suffer a diminution of its profits?

Mr. Burke, in his "Reflections on the Revolution of France," says of the social compact, "Its ends cannot be obtained in many generations: it becomes a partnership not only between those who are living, but between those who are living, those who are dead, and those who are not born; each contract of each particular State is but a clause in the great primeval contract of eternal society linking the lower with the higher natures, connecting the visible with the invisible world according to a fixed compact, sanctioned by the unavoidable law which holds all physical and all moral natures, each in their appointed place."

Christ's entire life furnished the noblest example which ever illuminated the earth of the atoning efficacy of sacrifice. The Man-God mournfully said, "The foxes have holes, the birds of the air have nests, but the Son of Man hath not where to lay his head." All history, and particularly the history of judicature, long before its black-lettered nomenclature, is conversant with the rights and wrongs of persons and things. At every epoch it affords analogies illustrative of the injuries to the individual's absolute or relative rights, for which, from causes arising from the nature of government, no specific compensation can be provided.

The theory of a remedy for every wrong, in the sense of specific compensation, is the closest approach which the common law makes to the preservation of the civic equilibrium. But unfortunately it is an abstraction. The artificial principle is founded in wisdom and justice, but the remedial forms often prove delusive. Either the injuries are not susceptible of retribution in gold, or the "cry is so far" that the enforcement of the remedies by an appeal to the courts is too costly. The text-books on nuisances are filled with illustrations of the diminution and destruction of individual rights, especially by municipal corporations, frequently irremediable by proceedings at law. The police power may authorize a statutory nuisance: no man may use his freehold estate in such a way as to injure any other citizen, though that use might be a valuable right of property to such owner of the fee.

The State, by paying for the ground, the brick and the mortar, may, under its power of eminent domain, invade and destroy the sanctity of the ancestral home. The original framers of the Constitution of the United States inserted in it a clause to protect and enforce, as sacred, the rights of property in man, and by the "settled rules" of constitutional construction they were vested rights. But when the revolt against slavery came and the Republican party, with its recruits from Whigs, Free-Soilers, and War Democrats (under the lead of such earthly deities as Lincoln, Seward, Stanton, Chase, and Grant), reversed, by force of arms, these "settled rules of constitutional construction," the result was, that those individuals of the state who engaged in battle to sustain and enforce these "settled rules of constitutional construction" perished upon the field; their homes were burned, their landed estates made howling wildernesses, and their wives and children beggars, because they were simple enough to rely upon the Supreme Court's "well-settled rules of constitutional construction."

The angels who wept and the devils who laughed over *ante-bellum* "settled rules of constitutional construction" may now be weeping and laughing over the latter-day construction of the Fourteenth Amendment. But Truth, the daughter of Time, not of Prejudice, with her rosy fingers is already unbarring the gates of light. All things come at last to those who watch, wait, and suffer.

The Civil-War sacrifice of one portion of the country for the good of the whole, and the providence of the God of battles in overruling the Supreme Court's "settled rules of constitutional construction," have received an ample vindication in the increased value of property and the general prosperity and further civilization of the damaged members of the Republic:

all resulting from the establishment of the efficacious and benefi-cent doctrine of the equality of all men before the law.

A boundless field for juridical science has been opened by Mr. Murat Halstead, of radiant and perfumed memory, in his irre-pressible anxiety to discover by what rules, settled or unsettled, constitutional or political, the repeal of the war-amendments, and specific compensation in gold coin can be effected, for the Thirteenth-Amendment invasion of private rights, which vir-tually stripped the South, after the war, of $1,250,000,000 of "vested rights" under the Constitution, to personal property, in the men, women, and children who have since grown into full-fledged citizens of the United States. The distinguished author of the separate opinion in Hall *v.* DeCuir had never discovered any such rules, but the distinction the eminent jurist makes between this construction of the Thirteenth Amend-ment, and a State statute carrying out in good faith the provi-sions of the Fourteenth Amendment, is not so apparent to the uneducated perception of a less profoundly sagacious and dis-criminating understanding.

In 1860 there was $1,250,000,000 of this private property in slaves. After the passage of the Thirteenth Amendment it disappeared from the national assets, and from the private pockets of the Southern members of the Union. By the Murat Halstead constitutional construction, this property, "stripped by the Thirteenth Amendment of all its utility," should be repaid in kind. Mr. Justice Clifford, and Mr. Justice Halstead, in whatever else they may agree to disagree, apparently approach close enough for the eclipse of one or the other luminary. They certainly seem to cover the same point, and the largest disk may claim the victory. If the statute of Louisiana for the enforce-ment of civil rights guaranteed by the Fourteenth Amendment operates to "strip of its utility the private property" of the public servant, it is void, says Justice Clifford ; but, says Justice Halstead, the Thirteenth Amendment was the forerunner of civil rights under the Fourteenth Amendment.

If obedience to the supreme law of the land and of the State subjects the common carrier to the displeasure of those citizens whom the Thirteenth Amendment deprived of their "vested right," and if their disfavor strips the common carrier's private property of all its utility, then the statute enforcing obedience to the supreme law of the land is void. But how can this Louisiana statute, which is the legal evolution of the Fourteenth Amendment, be void, and yet the Thirteenth Amendment and its incidental but absolute deprivation of those displeased citizens of their property, at the same time be valid?

In a time of profound peace the Fourteenth Amendment was adopted by a constitutional majority of the States then composing the federation of the United States. If the law of Louisiana which maintains within her borders the supremacy of the national law is void, because its observance threatens to strip a class of her citizens of a minimum of their property, how is the national law of the Thirteenth Amendment, which at one fell swoop annihilated vested rights to the amount of $1,250,000,000, valid? Says Jurisconsult Halstead, In reality we agree: Mr. Justice Clifford's "settled rules of constitutional construction" and mine lead to the same result. The Thirteenth Amendment abolished slavery ; Justice Clifford abolished a statute of Louisiana declaratory of the Fourteenth Amendment, which amendment evolved the freedman into a citizen of the State. The statute is void because, by commanding a recognition of his equality before the law, the common carrier may lose the patronage of those members of the State who prior to the Thirteenth Amendment claimed as their vested right of property the whilom slave, now a citizen.

This Clifford-Halstead constitutional imbroglio is not apparently susceptible of clarification. The amendments are unlike the stars in this, that they do not differ in brilliancy : the glory of the Thirteenth Amendment is the same, in the firmament of American jurisprudence, as that of the Fourteenth Amendment. The Thirteenth Amendment said to the slave, " You are a freedman." The Fourteenth Amendment said to the freedman, "You are a citizen." The statute of the State of Louisiana said to her citizens, in the words of the Apostle to the Gentiles, "Take heed to yourselves and to the whole flock ;" allow these new citizens the same rights in Louisiana which the supreme law of the land accords them in America.

"If your doctrine is sound," says Jurisconsult Halstead, "I am still puzzled, for how can you consistently maintain it in reference to the Louisiana statute, and deny mine with regard to the repeal of the war-amendments? The Thirteenth Amendment made the freedman by stripping the South of $1,250,000,-000 of her ' vested rights,' out of which property the Fourteenth Amendment made the new citizen. Your ' settled rules of constitutional construction,' therefore, Mr. Justice Clifford, authorize the South to demand compensation for the raw material, valued at $1,250,000,000, out of which a constitutional majority of the States, by an invasion of the private rights of the· Southern people in and to the same (which, according to your doctrine, the settled rules of constitutional construction forbade), manufactured seven millions of freemen in America, and breathed into their nostrils the breath of civic life."

Let us inquire a little further about this novel doctrine of the Supreme Court, that a State law conforming its internal polity to the supreme law of the land is void because it may strip the property of a private citizen of its utility. Let us test its soundness by other analogies affecting the total collective wealth of the nation. Take the many-sided questions concerning the effect of the tariff upon the great staples of production and manufacture. Are the " vested rights" of certain favored classes more inviolable, under " settled rules of constitutional construction," than the national vested interests of domestic and foreign commerce, some branches of which have languished for years under tariff invasions of the invested capital of individuals, corporations, and communities, while others equally vast are threatened with extinction to maintain the equality of the commercial interests of the whole American people? Why should not public servants bear their share of the burden of a more solid, sound, and matured civilization, now rapidly developing? The national revenue and its burdensome taxation, the " vested rights" of producers, manufacturers, and capitalists seem to be the legitimate subject of legislative regulation. The serene intelligence of the defenders of the " vested rights" of public servants, while keenly alive to the sensibilities of race-prejudice, seems profoundly dumb and unable to discover any " settled rules of constitutional construction" which prevent the wholesale invasion of private rights by economic dabsters and unscrupulous, sagacious political trimmers.

Why should the public servant complain that his private rights are invaded by the Fourteenth Amendment when other citizens of the state have complained with equal justice, that upon June 30, 1888, one hundred and forty millions of the people's money was piled up in the United States treasury, idle and useless? It is only the apprehended, not the actual, loss of the public servant which filled the Supreme Court with alarm and caused them to resist as unconstitutional the enforcement of the Fourteenth Amendment in Louisiana. In his message of 1887, President Cleveland declared, " It is not the apprehended but the *actual* condition [the accomplished fact], which has overtaken the values of commerce vested in the other members of the state." That worthy Chief Magistrate recognized the sacrificial liability to civic martyrdom which private interests of individuals must suffer, and which no " settled rules of constitutional construction" can prevent, when he said, " Relief should be devised with special precaution against imperilling the existence of our manufacturing interests." He significantly adds, " The fact is not to be overlooked, that competition among our domestic producers sometimes has the effect of keeping the price of their products below the highest limit allowed by such duty. But it is notorious, that this competition is too often strangled by combinations quite prevalent at this time" (organized under " well-settled rules of constitutional construction"), " frequently called *trusts,* which have for their object the regulation of the supply and price of commodities, made and sold by members, for any consideration in the operations of these selfish schemes."

The vested rights of individuals in all national industries, heretofore fostered and protected, are confessedly the legitimate subjects of congressional legislation, if, in the opinion of the national legislature, the common interests of the whole country can thereby be promoted. Are these great commercial interests of the nation " trifles light as air," when contrasted with the fare of a local steamboat company, which may or may not be prejudiced by conforming its public business to the supreme law of the land? It is the legitimate exercise of constitutional power to divest individual or national industries of all their utility, when necessary, for the welfare of the country; but a State may not conform the traffic of a steamboat company to the supreme law of the United States lest, peradventure, here and there a fare may be jeopardized! Are the national finances, revenue laws, commercial and mercantile pursuits, to be subjected to empirical economic laws, whose effect upon commerce and the national welfare is as yet a matter of open discussion? Are the many vested rights of communities and individuals affected by the disputed policy of protection mere bagatelles, beside the so-called "vested rights" of a public servant, not in constructive, but in actual and open rebellion against the supreme law of the land?

Another example: take the recent Report of the Congressional Committee upon the Western Pacific roads. In the face of these "settled rules of constitutional law," this committee has had the temerity to suggest the unsettlement of every "vested right" of the brilliant railroad financiers who regulate the transportation companies of the West. Those royal burglars, as public servants, expended $96,000,000 to build six roads. They shingled those roads with bonds to the extent of $268,000,000, and forced certain other members of the state, called shippers, to pay interest to the amount of $140,000,000, and dividends to the amount of $63,250,000 upon this investment. Their Royal Highnesses offered the United States $36,000,000 for its debt of $122,000,000, explaining that $25,000,000 had been paid for rebates and pools (to the imperial dignitaries themselves), and $5,000,000 for legal expenses, they having "dissipated" only $107,000,000. They confessed to having contracted with themselves for construction and supplies; and, to avoid the State tax, they had *prudently* neglected taking out patents for millions of acres.

Say these majestic lords of the public service: "Our accumulations are gigantic. Besides money spent in elections, State and national, which we controlled, we have billions upon billions. We have cornered all the staples of life. With the possession of a monopoly of oil, we have at last cornered light. All that is left free is the air, which we flatter ourselves our presence invigorates and purifies. While one foot is on the sea, the other is upon the land; we plough the former with steam plows, and we have occupied the latter with our steel rails. Cormorant-like, we have devoured the substance of the country. Our well-planned robberies of yesterday are become the sacred ' vested rights' of to-day. We confess to have broken through the laws, as spotted leopards may break through cobwebs, and by this means to have acquired individual, colossal fortunes, which have now become consecrated,—inviolable constitutional rights vested in us as public servants, under national charters, which we cannot but confess to have forfeited. As for your poor outside public, which composes the balance of the country, it simply holds our repudiated bonds, watered stocks, and depreciated values."

It would sound strange to argue gravely, that, inasmuch as these public robbers are *public servants,* the "settled rules of constitutional construction" encircle them and protect their booty as a vested right. But these malefactors, if national justice is sufficiently strong, are in a fair way to be dragged before the bar of the nation's Representative House and the courts, and to be forced to restore their ill-gotten gains to the treasury; so that the "settled rules of constitutional construction," which inhibit a sovereign State from compelling the obedience of her citizens to the supreme law of the land, have no application even to these great robber kings, and do not prevent the national Congress or the courts from exhausting their remedies by due process of law to enforce the restoration of the rights of the other citizens who compose the body politic. And yet these great railroad criminals made no assault upon the fundamental principles of the government; their attack was merely upon the wealth of the nation, and the only penalty they can be made to suffer is a disgorgement of millions of stolen property. There are no "settled rules of constitutional law" to prevent a divestiture of the vested rights of the public servants who maintain that capital is bound to respect no public right if it can avoid it by knavish expedients.

Under well-settled rules of constitutional construction, then, the highest malefactors of the age are amenable to the law which says, "Thou shalt not steal;" but when the lowest of the tribe violate the supreme commandment of the nation, their robbery of seven millions of citizens of that which is more precious than hecatombs of gold is authorized by "settled rules of constitutional construction," which forbid a State to enforce obedience to the national commandment because, peradventure, it may strip private property of its utility.

CHAPTER XXIV.

"In settling the question between these rival claims of power, it is proper to keep in mind that all power in just and free governments is derived from compact; that when the parties to the compact are competent to make it, and when the compact creates a government, and arms it not only with a moral power, but the physical means of executing it, it is immaterial by what name it is called. Its real character is to be decided by the compact itself; by the nature and extent of the powers it specifies, and the obligations imposed on the parties to it."—MADISON.

"Hence Cicero, in his *Oratio pro Flacco*, 'Our wise and holy ancestors,' says he, 'appointed those things to obtain for laws that the people enacted.' "—MILTON.

"As though, when public consent of the whole hath established anything, every man's judgment being thereunto compared were not private, howsoever his calling be to some kind of public charge. So that of peace and quietness there is not any way possible, unless the probable voice of every entire society or body politic, overrule all private of like nature in the same body."—HOOKER.

"Call to mind the sentiments which nature has engraved in the heart of every citizen, and which take a new force when they are solemnly recognized by all."—PAINE.

"This can only be done by a power out of themselves, and not, in the exercise of its function, subject to that will and to those passions which it is its office to bridle and subdue."—BURKE.

"Be admonished by those words of Oriental piety,—'Beware of the groans of the wounded souls. Oppress not to the utmost a single heart; for a solitary sigh has power to overset a whole world.' "—SUMNER.

"In the absolute spirit of our age, and in the absolute character of its factions, there is a deep-rooted intellectual pride, which is not so much personal or individual as social, for it refers to the historical destiny of mankind, and of this age in particular."—SCHLEGEL.

"Carbuncled noses, cadaverous faces, fetid breaths, and plethoric bodies meet us at every turn; and our condolences are perpetually asked for headaches, flatulence, nightmare, heartburn, and endless other dyspeptic symptoms."—SPENCER.

" Cripples, with aches and with age oppressed,
Crawl on their crutches to the grave for rest."—ELIZA.

" When will man cease his frantic pretension of scanning this great
God's world in his small fraction of a brain ; and know that it has verily,
though deep beyond his soundings, a Just Law ; that the soul of it is
good ; that his part in it is to conform to the law of the Whole, and in
devout silence follow that, not questioning it, obeying it as unquestion-
able?"—SPENCER.

" The permission of evil is the immediate consequence of the creation
of free beings."—SCHLEGEL.

" The half of human life on this side of the grave cannot be understood, unless we contemplate at the same time its second half, on the
other side of the tomb, as its complement, and as a necessary element
towards the elucidation of the whole."—ID.

" The battle-place and debatable ground of the still undecided, or, rather,
not as yet terminated, struggle between the good and the evil powers."—
ALTERTHUMSWISSENSCHAFT.

" Even mythology might teach the sages of our day."—D'AUBIGNÉ.

" The irony of fate is refuted. The wrongs of time are redressed and
injustice is expiated. The unequal distribution of wealth, of honor,
capacity, pleasure, and opportunity, which make life so cruel and inex-
plicable a tragedy, ceases in the realms of death. The strongest has there
no supremacy, and the weakest needs no defence. The mightiest captain
succumbs to that adversary who disarms alike the victor and the vanquished."—INGALLS.

" It is the morning-star itself that shall expand into the full sun, and
illuminate the whole world with its light."—SCHLEGEL.

" But this divinity of pagan antiquity is only a dim reflection, a flicker-
ing shadow of the Eternal Jehovah."—D'AUBIGNÉ.

" The nation may break down the division and antagonism of races, in
a moral order and organism, but this principle is wanting in the empire,
and thus it can only embrace subject races as inferior. It is this which
tends always to bring the empire into alliance with slavery. The government is not formed in the institution of rights, since no rights are recognized beyond the imperial will ; nor in freedom, since only the will of
the imperator is allowed freedom ; nor is it in the protection of the weak
and poor, but it is the sign of their subjection to the strong. It compre-

hends the people not as integral in the state, but as masses and fragments, and sects and parties of races, and in these conditions they are subject, and the government is an external affair."—MULFORD.

"Intelligence, patriotism, Christianity, and a firm reliance on Him who has never yet forsaken this favored land, are still competent to adjust, in the best way, all our present difficulty."—LINCOLN.

"And so, by a strange law of 'pre-established harmony,' the anti-Christian poet and these anti-Christian thinkers unexpectedly meet together at the point of a spurious sublimity."—SCHLEGEL.

"It also conversely remains, that in the destruction of the nation there will appear anarchy, violence, slavery, and the want of a continuity of purpose,—that is, the extinction of civilization, whatever be the racial capacities and characteristics of men."—MULFORD.

"The conception also of a power whose strength is in a race, and whose distinction is in the separation of a race, does not represent the hope which is moving in history, and is in direct antagonism to the historical course of the modern world."—ID.

THE question is not, to what branch of the public service does either of the offenders belong, but whether or not they have violated the supreme law of the land, which inhibits railroad peculations by a public servant less strongly than it inhibits a denial to any citizen of his equal civil rights. The offence of these magnates of the public service, rank though it be, is whiter than wool compared with that of the legal subversions of the fundamental principles of the government by the authoritative decrees of its loftiest tribunals. The taking away, against the will of the owner, of any portion of his civil rights, immunities, and privileges, is robbery in the sight of the Fourteenth Amendment, just as much as the taking of public lands without compliance with the terms of a charter is a gross violation of the rights of the nation.

Take another example of the individual damage resulting from altered conditions of society consequent upon its adoption of new laws, from which Mr. Justice Clifford strives to exempt the public servant. The total railroad mileage in the country is

137,986 miles; twelve hundred railroads are operated by five hundred corporations. The cost of construction and equipment of the 137,986 miles of road is estimated at $7,254,995,223, and the funded debt of the companies at $3,882,966,330. Interest was paid by the companies for the last fiscal year to the amount of $187,354,540, and the aggregate payment to stockholders in dividends was $80,094,138. These vast interests are subjected to the provisions of the Interstate-Commerce Law. From reasons of general expediency, the government has imposed upon this private property obligations, the performance of which these corporations complain " strips their private property of much of its former utility." The Interstate-Commerce Commissioners may by their decrees lawfully regulate this national public servant, representing an investment in construction and equipment of $7,254,995,223. Though they may alter the entire money values of national commerce, and disastrously depreciate the investments of capital in railroads, yet a sovereign State, with the duty and obligation resting on her of conforming her commerce to the law of the land, is forbidden, by " settled rules of constitutional construction," from enacting, through her legislative authority, rules of civil action in conformity with the supreme law of the land, because the conformity of her internal system of laws to the supreme law of the country may, peradventure, affect her citizens' property.

This is a most extraordinary doctrine. The Interstate-Commerce Commissioners may by their decrees incidentally alter the value of the " vested rights" of these American robber-kings and their stockholders, and upturn their kingdom itself, and yet there are " settled rules of constitutional construction" which forbid a sovereign State, under the Fourteenth Amendment (which imposes a profound obligation upon every State to conform its internal government to this law of the land) to compel its local institutions and creatures to obey this constitutional commandment. In strict accordance with this most curious doctrine, a law of the State of Louisiana requiring a steamboat captain to conform his rules and regulations to the supreme law of the Fourteenth Amendment has been determined to be unconstitutional since, by so doing, he may incur the displeasure of some disloyal citizens who may deprive him by withdrawing their patronage of some small portion of his vested rights.

The regulation of the freight rates of the mammoth national commerce ; the correction of evil railroad practices notorious in the railway service before the passage of the Interstate-Commerce Act; the establishment of rules of equality and justice between carriers and shippers ; the readjustment of unjust and unreasonable rules of discrimination and undue preferences,—is the assertion of a most extraordinary jurisdiction over the private interests of these kings of the public service. It is such a universal invasion of the "vested rights" of capital throughout the commercial, manufacturing, and industrial centres of the nation as extends almost beyond the boundaries of fiction, turning the world of trade upside down. Under their delegated authority, this board may deprive shippers and carriers of great natural and capitalistic advantages, almost eliminate competition, and, by an exercise of sovereign legislative power, establish a new tariff of rates throughout the whole country.

The inviolable sanctity of the public servant's calling (*whenever the issue of black civil rights presents itself*), which Mr. Justice Clifford strives so valiantly to maintain, apparently was not one of those superstitions entertained by the Congress which passed the Civil-Rights Bill of 1875, nor the Interstate-Commerce Bill of 1886. The spirit of the age obviously repudiates this dogma, for these Interstate-Commerce Commissioners, in their first report, suggest to Congress that it might possibly be within the competency of legislative power to prescribe for the several interstate railroads equal mileage-rates for the whole country. This, if enforced, would put an end to competition as a factor in making rates, and, to a very large extent, deprive the great business centres of the country of their several natural advantages, and also of the benefit of expenditures made by them in creating for themselves new channels of trade. "It would, in fact, work a revolution in the business of the country, which, though it might be greatly beneficial in some directions, would be fearfully destructive in others." The Interstate-Commerce Commissioners have also suggested amendments to the present law. They say:

" Especially ought the laws, as we think, to indicate, in plain terms, whether the express business and all other transportation by the carriers named in the act shall be governed by its provisions. The provision against the sudden raising of rates ought to be clearly made applicable to joint rates as well as to others. The Commission ought also to have the authority and the means to bring about something like uniformity in the method of publishing rates, which is now in great confusion; and to carefully examine, collect, and supervise the schedules, contracts, etc., required by the law to be filed, as well as properly to handle the mass of statistical information called for by the twentieth section."

Justice Bradley recently held that an act of Congress authorizing the construction of a bridge over and across the Arthur Kill was constitutional. New Jersey was striving to maintain upon her soil the termini of all the railroads which connect the whole country to the south and west with the great port of New York, from which her citizens had derived a vast revenue. The court said, that, if that State had riparian rights and a power of eminent domain over lands under water, those rights and that power cannot stand in the way of the exercise of the authority of the United States in a matter in which its jurisdiction is supreme and absolute. If it is necessary for it to exercise a power of eminent domain higher than that of the State, in order to carry out its purposes in pursuance of its authority to regulate commerce, it can exercise that power.

The Supreme Court of the United States recently rendered an opinion in the case of the Minneapolis and St. Louis Railway Company, plaintiff in error, *v.* Oliver Beckwith, in error to the Circuit Court of Kossuth County, Iowa. This was an action brought to recover the value of three hogs run over and killed by an engine of the railroad company. Under the law of Iowa, railroad companies neglecting to fence their road are liable for damages for stock injured through such negligence, and if they refuse to pay the value of the damage done within thirty days the owner of the stock may recover double damages. Counsel for the railroad company contended that these provisions are unconstitutional, on the ground that they deprive the company of property without due process of law, and deny them the equal protection of the laws. Justice Field says that this does not withhold the equal protection of the laws. The "clause in the Constitution is not designed to limit the police power of the States, and it has been repeatedly held, that, where a business is attended with unusual danger, the States may properly impose restrictions upon the business, the only condition being that *all those engaged in the same pursuit shall be subjected to the same restrictions.*" As to the allowance of double damages being unconstitutional, the court says that it is the duty of the railway company to keep its track free from animals, and that its neglect to do so by adopting reasonable means for that purpose justly subjects it to punitive damages where injuries are committed by reason of such neglect. The imposition of punitive or exemplary damages *cannot be held to be a deprivation of property without due process of law.* It is only one mode of imposing a penalty for the violation of duty, and its propriety and legality have been recognized by repeated judicial decisions for more than a century.

The Supreme Court, in the famous cases of the State of Kansas *v.* Herman Ziebold and others, known as the Kansas Prohibition Cases, decided at the close of 1887, afford a notable illustration of the "well-settled rules of constitutional law" which do in certain cases "strip private property of its utility." Justice Harlan, delivering the opinion of the court, says:

"It had been held repeatedly, that the right of a State to regulate the sale of liquor did not invade the constitutional rights of the citizen. It was contended, however, that no legislature had a right to prohibit any person from manufacturing liquor for his own use or for export, for the reason that it was an invasion of the personal liberty inherent in citizens. It must be observed, however, that the right to manufacture drink for one's own use is subject to the restriction that it shall not injuriously affect the public. The right to determine what was injurious had to exist somewhere, and the right of determining what measures are necessary for the preservation of the public morals, health, and safety had been vested in the States by the constitutional right given them under the police power to regulate their own internal concerns. While this police power could not be abused, and must only be exercised for objects of real merit, this court would certainly not say that the liquor traffic was not one which the State could lawfully prohibit, because it was well known that the abuse of intoxicants was productive of pauperism and crime. The next ground of contention," the Justice said, " was that the breweries had been erected prior to the passage of the prohibition law, and, as they were of little use except as breweries, their property was taken without due process of law, in violation of the Constitution. But all property, under our form of government," he held, " is subject to the obligation that it shall not be used so as to injuriously affect the rights of the community, and thereby become a nuisance. The State of Kansas had a right to prohibit the liquor traffic. It did not thereby take away the property of the brewers: it simply abated a nuisance. The property is not taken away from its owners; they are only prohibited from using it for a specific purpose which the legislature declared to be injurious to the community."

Although it does not cite the text, the foundation-stone of this judgment rests upon the doctrine of Christianity. This opinion says, with the Apostle, " For as we have many members in one body, and all members have not the same office : so we, being many, are one body in Christ, and every one members one of another." It says, in effect, that, although society must do good to its fellow-creatures, and must take care of their private good, yet the eternal vital principle which belongs to it, and holds it together, imposes upon it the duty and obligation of the preservation of all its members, although that principle may entail some hardship upon an individual. It says, in the sublime words of St. Augustine, " The family of men, living by faith, use the goods of the earth as strangers here, not to be captivated by them, or turned away by them from the goal to which they tend, which is God, but to find in them a support which, far from aggravating, lightens the burthen of this perishable body which weighs down the soul."

The law which Mr. Justice Harlan decides is indeed briefly comprehended in this saying, " Thou shalt love thy neighbor as thyself." Upon what other foundation can a government, formed after the doctrines of Christ, rest than his teachings? Upon what permanent foundation can the American society of Christians rest, except upon one which is analogous to and framed in accordance with God's moral government, as exhibited by the workings of His providence? May not the same sort of difficulties which are encountered in the course of nature be reasonably anticipated to exist in a government resting upon the revealed will of the Architect of nature? And what does that revealed will discover but the sacrificial principle in the life of men? In response to the negation of self which government requires, piety and wisdom also teach that the plan of life here is so connected with the life hereafter, that the course and constitution of God's government of the earth is perfectly in accord therewith, though it may be imperfectly comprehended. It seems a system of rewards and punishments, productive of the moral and material advancement of the individual, wherein many of the laws are as steadfast in their working as that of gravitation. From the state stand-point, as well as from that of a future world, civic life is a condition of probation; the vicissitudes, trials, exposures, dangers, and self-denials which environ mankind in the civilized state tend towards the establishment of his moral and intellectual discipline. The unvarying testimony of history shows that man's amelioration through sacrifice is gradual, dependent upon his energy, moral culture, foresight, and labor, and that sacrifice and virtue are the factors of a progressive humanity.

The system which Christ proclaimed, and upon which our Constitution and government really rest, teaches the doctrine of individual sacrifice; which, according to Mr. Justice Clifford, "well-settled rules of constitutional law" in America repudiate. The Justice maintains that the public servant's property will be "stripped of all its utility" unless he disobeys this fundamental law of Christianity evolved in the form of the Fourteenth Amendment. And for what purpose but to give license and indulgence to clamorous race-harpies, craving their accustomed gratification? The answer to this juristical fallacy is contained in hosts of decided cases, and is written on every page of nature and of history. All civilized life abounds with illustrations of it. The examples of sacrifice in private life and under all forms of government are scattered throughout the records of the past. The civil and ecclesiastical polity of the world, poetry and prose, novels and newspapers, unceasingly offer their evidence of it. Even literature has oftentimes the appearance of repeating the lamentations of Job. What else but evidential facts, establishing the liability of man's vested rights to be "stripped of all their utility," are Tennyson's last cry of despair, Turgéneff's bold characters, and Ruskin's teachings? Mr. Justice Clifford's separate opinion constitutes the sole exception to this doctrine. He alone maintains the doctrine, that the public servant is exempted from liability to any sacrifice of his vested rights in his property, even although public interests require it.

Of the contrary opinion are Adam Smith, Turgot, Malthus, Sismondi, Droz, Rossi, Léon Fancher, and Roschers,—those rare masters who have contributed out of the abundance of their positive riches to the historical development of economic society, and who have each taught the philosophy of sacrifice. It can be truly affirmed of these great writers, that the noblest teaching of the science they have illustrated and adorned, is the "economy of sacrifice," "binding the present to the future, widening the horizon of thought, inspiring foresight, lengthening the lever of human activity by providing it with new instruments." Their starting-point is the numberless wants of man, physical and intellectual. The philosophy they advocate deals with the science of public and private economy, the factors of production, productive co-operation, the community of goods, their circulation, distribution, and consumption; all of which political economy, in the widest sense, teaches as the exalted lesson of the eternal relations resulting from the nature of things, which the rights of every individual in society, vested, relative, absolute, or conditional, sustain to the rights of every other member of the community.

To deny this law is to deny the chief corner-stone upon which Christianity rests. Throughout the Middle Ages it required the combined efforts of the church and the state, in many bloody struggles, to maintain this doctrine, which Hall *v.* DeCuir now repudiates. The law of sacrifice is the eternal basis on which human society reposes. It is the law of the Great Architect. It was not made by man, nor can it be unsettled by his "settled rules of constitutional law." It is natural jurisprudence, and is founded upon natural justice.

The destructive chimeras of Mr. Justice Clifford in Hall *v.* DeCuir exempt from martyrdom (?) the " vested rights" of the public servants, by exposing to martyrdom the " vested rights" of seven millions of the other citizens of the State. The observing, penetrating eye, looking backward behind the Constitution, and the woolsack, which Mr. Justice Clifford surely adorned, perceives that the sacrifice of individual rights in a civilized state involves more than any rule of constitutional construction can satisfactorily explain. The problem presents an abstract inquiry concerning the origin, nature, and presence of the huge mass of evil existing under every form of government; and a principle works, unseen though it may be, for the ultimate deliverance and triumph of imprisoned *Justice.*

The choice disciples of philosophy, " finely touched to fine issues," have not penetrated beyond the confines of the realms of silence and mystery. Explorers throughout the centuries, whose research promised noble service, return with the same report: " We waited until the day should break and the day-star arise ; but we find the *Spirit of Evil* coy, haggard, and wild ; its dwelling-place is amidst thick clouds and darkness, and no light shineth in the darkness ; we cannot tell whence it cometh or whither it goeth." With Solomon, each of them has declared, " When I applied mine heart to know wisdom, *and to see the business that is done upon the earth :* then I beheld all the work of God, that a man cannot find out the work that is done under the sun ; because, though a man labor to seek it out, yet he shall not find it; yea, further, though a wise man think to know it, yet shall he not be able to find it."

The laboratory of *Evil,* and the mixed ingredients of its caldrons, were hidden from the searching eyes of the ancient, as to-day they are concealed from those of the modern sage. Long before the hand of war had established the universal empire of Rome, and the Romans had attained their greatest power

and civilization; long before Christianity began its slow conquest of the Roman empire; when morality, religion, politics,
and philosophy had attained their highest dominion over mankind; countless ages before Confucius, Buddha, Jesus, Mohammed, and Savonarola, under every form of government and
religious creed, in the by-gone ages, as in the nineteenth century,
swarming in their abodes of squalid huts or tenements, sub-
mitting to the law of sacrifice, pinched with cold and hunger,
perishing from heat or pestilence, with pallid, sunken cheek and
hollow eye, that inhabitant of the earth,—

> " Like some ill-destined bark that steers
>   In silence through the gate of tears,"—

the degraded *nullius filius,* offspring of the state, lived and
breathed,—close to his lordly legitimate brother, residing in a
vast palace of civilization, with all the romance of charming
pageantries and ceremonies; its chambers hung with purple
and golden upholsteries; surrounded with colleges and libraries,
rich with the bequests of dead sovereigns, and filled with
sculptured pediments, gleaming marble, speaking statues; the
intermixture of splendor, genius, and taste; a marvel of all that
was attractive, mystic, and imaginative; temples, saloons of
luxury, academies of science, conservatories of music, and
flowers; his sons and daughters, amidst the splendors of this
world, with all the youthful freshness and color of life, leading
enchanted lives, ascending and descending golden stairways,
listening to the sweet music of adulation, and pledging each the
other with enchanting cups of intellectual and material enjoyment which intoxicate as they sparkle on the brim.

But when the Greek philosophers had exhausted themselves
in worthless speculations, when Jehovah had delivered the un-
believing Jew to his idols, when the Pharisaic code of Caste
prevailed; when luxury, tyranny, murder, poison, usury, robbery, the worst form of slavery, and the wild beast and gladiator of the arena had made life, except to the favored few, a
living death; there was heard a voice which has pealed in clarion
tones down through the ages. It said, with the old prophet,
" Wash you, make you clean." To the State it said, " Follow

thou me; government means justice, love, order, humanity, equality." The Son of the living God, who proclaimed this doctrine of "good will" in the midst of this den of wild beasts of the Old World, standing upon the moral wreck and ruin of society, stretching forth his arms towards heaven, cried, to all weary toilers seeking death as a respite from a life of living torture, "Come unto me, all ye that labor and are heavy-laden, and I will give you rest." To his disciples he said, "Feed my lambs"; to his heralds, "Go ye and preach my kingdom"; "Go ye and teach all nations." Since then countless myriads have lived and died in the religion of Jesus, that religion which first fitly bore the flower and fruit of a universal philanthropy. The doctrine which, in the days of Tiberius Cæsar, He preached at Capernaum was in the fulness of time transported to the wilds of America; and having, according to the will of His Father, first received a baptism of blood, was at last incorporated into the Constitution of the United States of America.

Yet even then the veiled *Spirit of Evil*, in the shape of Slavery, walking by the side of the *Spirit of Liberty*, forced its way into the Constitution (that ark of the covenant), and there the "foul fiend" remained until exorcised by the God of battles. On January 14, 1878, almost a quarter of a century afterwards, comes Hall *v.* DeCuir, worshipping the idol the nation had so strenuously overthrown, and proclaiming that, unless the state partly rehabilitates the old rites of slavery in America, well-settled rules of constitutional construction are violated, because, forsooth, an individual's vested right to a dime may be sacrificed. The religion of human brotherhood, justice, and truth in their widest sense, which the doctrines of Christianity and the Fourteenth Amendment proclaim, welcomes to "equality of rights" all men of all races in America to-day, with the same indifference to rank and caste which the holy Nazarene preached and practised in Northern Palestine. And there is no "settled rule" of religion or "of constitutional construction" or of civilization in America which gainsays this equality except the interpretation in Hall *v.* DeCuir of the Fourteenth Amendment.

CHAPTER XXV.

"The nation can meet the forces with which it has to contend only as it realizes its own moral being, and recognizes its origin and end in God. If it be held in a merely material conception, it can bring no strength to the real battle of history, where moral forces contend. If it be regarded as only formal, it will be broken by that held in a subtler bond. The nation is called to a conflict in every age, where the result does not depend upon the strength of its chariots, nor the swiftness of its horses. It is to contend with weapons wrought not alone in earthly forges: it is to go forth clothed with celestial armor and of celestial temper. It is to fulfil a divine calling. It is to keep a holy purpose. It is to enter the battle of righteousness and freedom. It is to contend through suffering and sacrifice, with faith in the redemption of humanity, for the rights of humanity,—rights given to it by Him whose image it bears."—MULFORD.

"In all such cases it is only the false light of some internal *ignis fatuus* that produces this illusion of the unintelligible, or rather of nonsense."—SCHLEGEL.

"The love of power, and the desire to display it when it can be done with impunity, is inherent in the human heart. Turn it out at the door, and it will in again at the window. *Power is displayed in its fullest measure, and with a captivating dignity, by restraints and conditions.*"—PINCKNEY.

"The thinking separately of the elements of a proposition is mistaken for the thinking of them in the combination which the proposition affirms."—MARTINEAU.

"If we express this relation between two parts in the one, and the corresponding parts in the other, by the formula A is to B as a is to b; if we otherwise write this, A to B $= a$ to b; if, consequently, the fact we prove is that the relation of A to B equals the relation of a to b; then it is manifest that the fundamental conception of similarity is equality of relations."—SPENCER.

"Lord Mahon will find, we think, that his parallel is, in all essential circumstances, as incorrect as that which Fluellen drew between Macedon and Monmouth."—MACAULAY.

"The internal difference between right and wrong does not fluctuate: it is immutable."—PATRICK HENRY.

" But the equality and rights of men here contemplated are natural, essential, and unalienable, such as the security of life, liberty, and property. These should be the firm foundation of every good government, as they will apply to all nations, at all times, and may properly be called a universal law."—BOUDINOT.

" But while the constitutional compact remains undissolved, it must be executed according to the forms and provisions specified in the compact. It must not be forgotten that compact, express or implied, is the vital principle of free governments as contradistinguished from governments not free ; and that a revolt against this principle leaves no choice but between anarchy and despotism."—MADISON.

THE unflinching friend of civil liberty cannot look upon the decision of Hall *v.* DeCuir but with profound melancholy. Admitting the opinion of Justice Clifford to be innocent of dishonest error, its infirmity, laxity, and bias are so marked that it is difficult, in spite of the primacy of his legal genius and upright intention, to avoid the conclusion that his judgment was not independent of a desire, in the midst of the sunshine of liberty and progress, to cling to the authority of antiquated proslavery predilections. In forcibly thrusting back this race into its old trammels, in ignoring the historic and constitutional relation of the Fourteenth Amendment to elementary American civil rights, his opinion betrays the parentage of Caste.

The sovereign necessities of truth will throb with the daily life, and beat with the heart-throes of the great masses of mankind ; who will not fail to recognize that all conditions of civic life, when divorced from humanity, produce no generous fruit, but grow barren and cumbersome. The next generation in America, from whose eyes the scales of caste shall have fallen, will view the society of the state in a fresh, unprejudiced, original way ; as it actually exists, lives, moves, and has its being, in the wide, free, untrammelled world of men and things about them. The Supreme Court of the future will wonder how the civil rights of any American citizen could have been so debased by juristical casuistry. The coming race will relegate the erroneous judicial expositions in Dred Scott and Hall *v.* DeCuir to the limbo of race or political prejudice, and these judgments in other ages will stand as stand to-day the feudal laws of the old barons.

Although, as has been stated, Mr. Justice Clifford, in the opening of his opinion in Hall *v.* DeCuir, would seem to have rejected the term " reasonable" as inapplicable to his hypothesis of the doctrine of " Civil Rights" ; yet is he afterwards forced to admit, what indeed is hornbook law, that the public servant, as carrier, inn-keeper, or proprietor of places of public resort, is bound " to adopt such *reasonable* rules and regulations, and generally to exercise such *reasonable* discretion, as will promote, as far as practicable, the comfort and convenience of his entire company." Does it not then follow that, in any civil-rights case, the sole question and issue of law involved must be, whether the discriminating rule or regulation of the public servant is reasonable or unreasonable? But how can that proposition be determined otherwise than by ascertaining, whether or not the rule or regulation complained of conforms to the organic law of the nation? The Fourteenth Amendment furnishes the universal, authoritative standard of recognition for a principle or rule of action for the States. Is that then a reasonable regulation of the public service which challenges and contradicts this organic law?

If the State of Louisiana had by its Legislature adopted the opinion of Mr. Justice Clifford in Hall *v.* DeCuir, by the decision of the Supreme Court in the Civil-Rights Cases, such statute would be void; and the judge or officers of the State who attempted its enforcement would render themselves liable to indictment, fine, and imprisonment. But, according to Justice Clifford (inasmuch as the Fourteenth Amendment operates as a deterrent not on individuals, but only upon States), a rule or regulation which would, by the law of the nation, be a high misdemeanor if adopted by a State in its sovereign character, and would be void and inoperative to affect the civil rights of any citizen, becomes a reasonable rule and regulation if adopted by any individual member of that State. A law which is unconstitutional, criminal, and void if passed by any member of the confederation of the United States, is yet a reasonable rule and regulation if adopted by a public servant; although it subjects one whole portion of the society of the State to limitations and restrictions of its civil rights, which are never imposed upon, or enforced against, any other portion. The public servant, then, has "the right to consult and provide for his interests as a common incident to property," by making a rule which it is criminal for the Legislature of his State to enact; and this rule of the public servant is reasonable.

The reasonableness or unreasonableness of the rule, in the altered condition of the United States, does not depend upon the inconveniences that may result to either the white or black society of any State. That was an argument used by the enemies of the Fourteenth Amendment; which, after mature deliberation, the nation overruled by the adoption of that amendment as its fundamental law. It is true that no *individual,* white or black, is entitled to any particular or special accommodation; the great provision being that the public service shall be conducted under the guidance of general rules, operating alike upon both classes. It is equally true, as Mr. Justice Clifford asserts, that neither the Constitution nor any statute of the United States "requires persons to be put in the same apartment who would be repulsive or disagreeable to each other." But how can a regulation, which denies that *substantial equality* (upon which the Fourteenth Amendment so strongly insists) on account of color, race, or previous condition, be said to be a reasonable rule and regulation, when such rule overturns, repeals, and defeats the spirit, purpose, and intent of the national legislation? A State statute declaring that the seats in cars, hotels, theatres, and the like, should not be accessible except under limitations applying only to one class of citizens, on account of their color or previous condition of servitude, would be *ipso facto* void, criminal, and unconstitutional. By what system of legal legerdemain, then, can the rules of a public service, devised to effect the same result, be judicially determined to be reasonable rules and regulations; by any constitutional, moral, natural, sensible, common or statute-law definition of the term reasonable?

The term "reasonable," in its legal signification, as applied to the regulations of the public service, must be construed in the light of the Fourteenth Amendment; and, in order to determine whether a regulation of the public service is reasonable, it is obviously necessary to consult the Supreme Court decisions construing this organic law. The patient reader who examines the interpretation of Mr. Justice Clifford, and then is at the pains to consult the earlier decisions of the Supreme Court, will be struck with the vast disparity in learning, wisdom, legal acumen, common sense, judgment, sound knowledge, and all the qualifications and attributes distinguishing the true from the false, which operate in favor of the latter against the former. He will discover the difference between the wind and the weathercock, the creature and the creator. God lent his noblest intellects for the exposition of this fundamental law, and only in their sunlight can the rules of Hall *v.* DeCuir be rightfully adjudged. Throughout the pages of the earlier Civil-Rights Cases, the faithful expositors of the Fourteenth Amendment proclaim, with Selden, " Before everything, liberty ;" " Equality of rights." Says Jurisprudence in Hall *v.* DeCuir, " Truth, legal truth, is not one and the same, forever, eternal and absolute; it is one-sided, half-way, all awry, when applied to a skin not of a white color." For a reasonable rule Hall *v.* DeCuir substitutes, against Justice, the iron despotism, the selfish and calculating apostasy of the public servant. The Fourteenth Amendment and Hall *v.* DeCuir are in open conflict. Can that be a reasonable rule which, in the exposition of Civil Rights, substitutes the dead rinds of yesterday for the living fruits of to-day !

Although the events which gave rise to Hall *v.* DeCuir occurred prior to the passage of the Civil-Rights Bill in 1875, and were not therefore affected by it; yet Mr. Sumner's bill stood unshorn of its constitutionality at the time when Justice Clifford declared that the " laws of the United States did not require persons to be put in the same apartments who were repulsive to each other," because of the guilty color of the " man and brother's" skin. Such was substantially his contention. The Civil-Rights Bill, then in full force, commanded that the " accommodations, privileges, and facilities of public conveyances, inns, and places of public amusement," should not be refused on account of color. Five years later, when the Supreme Court, as we have seen, decided the Civil-Rights Cases, this doctrine of Justice Clifford was abandoned. It is true, the first and second sections of the Civil-Rights Bill, which, in effect, provided that equality of right should not be denied because of the "repulsiveness" of a black skin, were declared to be unconstitutional, but the majority of the court in the Civil-Rights Cases say, "Positive rights and privileges are undoubtedly secured by the Fourteenth Amendment." If this be conceded, how can that be a reasonable rule of the public service which gives the form of equality but withholds its substance?

All these decisions, *uno flatu*, say, that the power of Congress does not extend to the passage of laws for the suppression of crime within the States. This is a duty which the general legislative body of the country is not required or authorized to perform. It is one which the great guarantee, the Fourteenth Amendment, supposes to be the office of the State itself, and which it commands the State to fulfil.

CHAPTER XXVI.

"Unless the force and manner of signification of words are first well observed, there can be very little said clearly and pertinently concerning knowledge."—TOOKE.

"VALIANT.—I am of Darkland, for there I was born; and there my father and mother are still. GREAT-HEART.—Darkland, said the guide; doth not that lie upon the same coast with the city of Destruction?"—BUNYAN.

"I shall allege other and greater arguments."
"What! greater arguments than what the law of God and nature afforded? Help, Lucina! the mountain Salmasius is in labor!"—MILTON.

"Without dispute,
Through all the realms of Nonsense, absolute."—DRYDEN.

"The artillery of words."—SWIFT.

"The vanity of human wisdom, and the presumption of human reason, are proverbial. This vanity and this presumption are often neither reasonable nor wise. Humanity, too, sometimes plays fantastic tricks with power. Time, moreover, is fruitful in temptations to convert discretionary power to all sorts of purposes."—PINCKNEY.

THE duty of protecting all their citizens in the enjoyment of an equality of rights was originally assumed by the States, and with them it still remains. "The Fourteenth Amendment simply furnishes an additional guarantee against any encroachment by the States upon the fundamental rights which belong to every citizen as a member of society.[1] It [the Fourteenth Amendment] is a guarantee against the exertion of arbitrary and tyrannical power on the part of the government and legislature of the States." All the Supreme Court decisions deny the power of Congress, under the amendments, to pass any act regulating the conduct of persons in the States. They decide

---

[1] United States v. Cruikshank, 92 U. S. 542.

that political rights are derived from the Constitution and laws of the State. " Civil rights are the absolute rights of persons, which, according to the fundamental principles underlying the American government, are inalienable."

In Strauder *v.* West Virginia,[1] a case which involved the construction of the Fourteenth Amendment as applied to a West Virginia statute authorizing only white citizens to act as jurors, the Supreme Court emphatically states : " The spirit and meaning of the amendment is to be literally construed, to carry out the intention of its framers. The words of the amendment, it is true, are prohibitory, but they contain a *necessary implication of a positive immunity or right, most valuable to the colored race,*—the right to exemption from unfriendly legislation, against them distinctly defined; exemption from *legal discriminations implying inferiority in civil society, lessening the security of their enjoyment of the rights which others enjoy.* It [this act allowing white persons only to act as jurors] is practically a brand upon them, an assertion of their inferiority, and a *stimulant to that race-prejudice which is an impediment to securing to individuals of the race that equal justice which the law aims to secure to all others.*" Says Justice Davis, in the same case, " The apprehension that *through prejudice* they might be denied that *equal protection*—that is, that there might be *discrimination against them* —was the inducement to bestow upon the national government the power to enforce the provision, that no State shall deny to them the equal protection of the laws."

Again it is said,[2] " Its aim was *against discrimination* because of race and color, *to strike down all legal discriminations and protect an emancipated race.* In giving construction to any of these articles [amendments] it is necessary to keep the *main purpose steadily in view.* The Fourteenth Amendment makes no attempt to enumerate the rights it designed to protect. It speaks in general, comprehensive terms. Its language is prohibitory; but every prohibition implies the existence of rights and immunities, prominent among which is an immunity *from inequality of legal protection.*"

---

[1] 10 Otto, 303.   [2] Id. p. 310.

It has been held,[1] that a State judge who refused or failed to select jurors of color was exercising ministerial functions, and was indictable if he violated the constitutional inhibition, because he was the agent of the State. Mr. Justice Field, construing the provisions of the first section of the Fourteenth Amendment, which declared, " No State shall deny to any person within its jurisdiction the equal protection of the laws," said, in distinguishing between political and civil rights, " it [the Fourteenth Amendment] secures[2] to all persons their civil rights upon the same terms." It rests upon positive law; it does not refer to social rights and duties, though they are potential in controlling the intercourse of individuals; "civil rights," he says, "are absolute and personal."

It was declared in Prigg v. Pennsylvania,[3] as to the construction to be put on constitutional amendments, "That a clause of the Constitution conferring a right should not be so construed as to make it shadowy or unsubstantial, or leave the citizens *without the remedial power of its protection, when another construction, equally accordant with the words and sense in which they were used, would enforce and protect the right granted.*" The Supreme Court has determined, that "The one great purpose of these amendments was to raise the colored race, from that condition of inferiority and servitude in which most of them had previously stood, into perfect equality of civil rights with all other persons within the jurisdiction of the States. They [the amendments] were intended to take away all possibility of oppression by law because of color. They were intended to be, what they really are, limitations of the power of the States and enlargements of the power of Congress." Again, it has been decided, that "The design of the amendments was not only to guarantee, in the largest sense, to every citizen of the United States, a sacred right of equality, under the law, throughout the whole land, but also to protect from invasion the essential rights that belong to the citizen and flow from the Constitution."[4] "The main purpose of the amendments was to establish the citizenship of

[1] *Ex parte* Virginia, 10 Otto.   [2] 10 Otto, 367.
[3] 16 Peters, 539.   [4] Hebbs *v.* Johnson, 1 Wood, 537.

the race of people who had not heretofore been citizens of the United States or the State;[1] and, though in form prohibitions, they imply immunities such as may be protected by congressional legislation."[2] " The object of the civil-rights statutes, as of the Constitution which authorizes them, was to place the colored race, *in respect of civil rights, upon a level with the white;* they made the *rights and responsibilities, civil and criminal, of the two races exactly the same.*"[3]

" The fundamental idea and principle prevading these amendments is an *impartial equality of rights* and privileges, civil and political, to all citizens of the United States." " Equality of rights, privileges, and capacities is a condition of all citizens, established by these organic laws."[4]

" The amendment did not add to the privileges and immunities of a citizen. It simply furnished a protection to such as he already had."[5]

" The Fourteenth Amendment is one of a series of constitutional provisions having a common purpose; securing the race, recently emancipated, all the civil rights which the superior race enjoy," "all the civil rights which are enjoyed by white persons."[6] " What is this but declaring that the law in the States shall be the same for the black as for the white ?"

" Equal protection of the laws means equal security *under* them, to *everything* on similar terms, in one's life, liberty, property, and in the pursuit of happiness."[7]

" It [the amendment] not merely requires equality of privileges, but it demands that the privileges and immunities of all citizens shall be absolutely unabridged and unimpaired."[8]

" The object of the amendments, and of the statutes, is to relieve the citizens of the black race *from the effects of prejudice,* to protect them in person and property from its spirit. We are

---

[1] Marshall *v.* Donovan, 10 Bush, 681.
[2] *Ex parte* Virginia, 100 U. S. 339, 344. 345.
[3] Virginia *v.* Rives, 100 U. S. 313, 318.
[4] Donald *v.* State, 48 Miss. 675.
[5] Barbinger *v.* Jona, 18 Wall. 129.
[6] Strauder's case, 100 U. S. 303.   [7] Fox Cases, 8 Saw. 261.
[8] Slaughter-House cases, 16 Wall 36.

disposed to construe these laws according to their very spirit and intent; so that equal rights, and equal protection, shall be secured to all, regardless of color." [1]

If the Fourteenth Amendment "imposes the duty and obligation upon the States of preventing discrimination because of color," how can that be a reasonable rule or regulation which discriminates wherever and whenever color is disagreeable or "repulsive"? If the Fourteenth Amendment furnishes an additional "guarantee against encroachment" by the States upon the rights of these citizens because of their color, how can that be a reasonable regulation which, because of color, deprives these citizens of "the fundamental rights which belong to them as members of society"? If the Fourteenth Amendment is a guarantee against the exertion of arbitrary and tyrannical power on the part of the government and legislatures of the States, because of color, race, and previous condition, by what process of abstract logic can it be decided, that a rule which exerts arbitrary and tyrannical power because of color, race, and previous condition, is reasonable? If the "amendment contains a necessary implication of a positive right and immunity" (in spite of color); "if the right of exemption from unfriendly legislation against them is distinctly defined;" if "exemption from legal discrimination, implying inferiority in civil society, lessening the security of their enjoyment of the rights which others enjoy," is guaranteed to them; how is a rule which, on account of color, subjects them "to legal discrimination, implying inferiority in civil life and lessening the security which others enjoy," a "reasonable rule"?

If it be judicially determined, that "discrimination, on account of color, is a brand upon this race, and a stimulant to that race-prejudice which is an impediment to securing to individuals of the race that equal justice which the law aims to secure to all others," how does it happen that a regulation framed to accomplish just this result is nevertheless, in the eyes of the law, to be deemed a reasonable rule? If the inducement of the nation to "bestow on the national government power to

---

[1] Coger *v.* N. W. Co., 37 Iowa, 155.

enforce the provisions of the Fourteenth Amendment was to prevent State enactments denying the equal protection of the law," is that rule reasonable which defeats the provisions of this grant by the refusal of such equal protection? If " civil rights are absolute and personal," if " they rest in positive law," if " they are secured upon the same terms," is that rule reasonable which allows the exercise of absolute and personal civil rights only upon invidious discriminations based upon color alone?

How is that a reasonable rule which repeals " an inalienable right "? If the Fourteenth Amendment be " one of a series of constitutional provisions, having the common purpose of securing to the·race recently emancipated all the civil rights which the white race enjoy," and if " this is the same as declaring that the law in the States shall be the same for the blacks as for the whites," must not that be an unreasonable rule which is formulated for the express purpose of exciting race-antagonisms, and which has the iniquitous " purpose" of depriving the recently emancipated race, because of its color, of the very rights which the white citizen fully enjoys?

If, as the Supreme Court declares, " the one great purpose of these amendments was to raise the colored race, from that condition of inferiority in which most of them had stood, into perfect equality of civil rights with all other persons ;" if " that one great purpose was to do away with all possibility of legal oppression because of color ;" and if " impartial uniformity in the administration of justice be the great end of civil society ;" who is profound enough in counsel to discover that to be a reasonable rule of the public service, the one great purpose of which is to degrade and oppress the colored race, to maintain that condition of inferiority, and to prevent that equality of civil rights, all because of color? If " equal protection of the laws means equal security under them to every one, in life, liberty, and the pursuit of happiness," can that be a reasonable regulation of the public servant which makes equality conditional upon color?

If " the object of the amendments is to relieve citizens of the black race from the effects of prejudice and to protect them from its evil spirit," it would require a most extraordinary exercise of jurisprudential subtlety to decide that to be a reasonable rule which utterly defeats their purpose. The most optimistic believer in the perfectibility of juristical human nature would pause in his opinion were it incontestably proved, that the court had held a rule to be reasonable " which guaranteed a sacred right of equality," *provided the citizen were white,* when the same court had declared, that the main purpose of this organic law was to establish citizenship and guarantee a sacred right of equality throughout the whole land, and to protect the essential rights belonging to *black citizens,*—rights which flowed from the Constitution, equally for blacks and whites. The most blatant intolerance blared by a devil's trumpet cannot have the temerity to argue that, "if the object," the fundamental idea and principle, of this amendment is, in the court's language, an *impartial* equality of rights and privileges [that " equality of rights and privileges is a condition of all citizens, established by these organic laws"], a rule emanating from the will of a public tyrant, whose mental vision is distorted by race-prejudice, shall nevertheless be construed as " reasonable," although the fundamental idea and principle pervading such rule be an equality of rights, privileges, and capacities conditioned upon the *color* of the applicant.

A symbol of universal justice, an inflexible rule of natural right, incorporated into the organic law may be overturned by an inferior class in the State, and yet the instrumentality through which its overthrow is effected can be judicially determined to be a " reasonable" rule! The iron hand of the Czar could stretch no further to transgress principles of justice! Rules conformable to the necessities of right reason, which appear to be recognized among all men, are to be violated, in order that the unhallowed banquet of *muckworms* on the remains of the Fourteenth Amendment may not be rudely disturbed by the enforcement of a constitutional law! There is no depth, strength, apprehension, or acuteness in the mind of man sufficient to solve so hopeless an enigma in the history of jurisprudence, as the " *reasonableness*" of the rule in Hall *v.* DeCuir.

CHAPTER XXVII.

"In mathematics he was greater
Than Tycho Brahe or Erra Pater."—HUDIBRAS.

"See, then, our predicament. We can think of matter only in terms of mind. We can think of mind only in terms of matter."—MARTINEAU.

"Cæsar and Tacitus, writing at the distance of two centuries, two of the finest geniuses of antiquity, historians without rivals and without models, have recorded no subtle mechanism more illustrative of the fertility of human genius."—HAZLITT.

"How is this to be accounted for? Do you suppose he was unacquainted with the opinions of grammarians, or that he despised the subject?"—TOOKE.

"The reason, indeed, which supplied these weapons was not one scientifically cultivated and morally regulated, but thoroughly sophistical and wholly perverted, which, however, put into requisition all the weapons of a brilliant but sceptical wit, and moved in the ever-varied turnings of a most ingenious and attractive style."—SCHLEGEL.

"Protection,—this is what men seek by political combination; and whether it be against internal or external enemies matters not."—SPENCER.

"Oh! for a muse of fire, that would ascend
The brightest heaven of invention."—DRYDEN.

"A violation of constitutional law is not an offence which is ever made venial by the occasion. You cannot do evil that good may come. The evil is there, and the good never comes."—J. BLACK.

"Let us exalt patriotism, and moderate our party contentions. Let those who would die for the flag on the field of battle give a better proof of their patriotism, and a higher glory to their country, by promoting fraternity and justice."—PRESIDENT HARRISON.

"If civil society be made for the advantage of man, all the advantages for which it is made become his right. It is an institution of beneficence; and law itself is only beneficence acting by a rule."—BURKE.

308

" Among the means best calculated to diminish the risk which threatens an interruption of these blessings, is a cordial union of every description of citizens in supporting their government in its necessary authorities, and in promoting the execution of the laws with an exemplary vigilance. Nothing, therefore, could be more reproachful than efforts to open one of the most baneful sources of discord, by arraying the interest of one section of our country against that of another ; nor would anything be more to be dreaded than such efforts, were not so effectual an antidote to the poison to be found in that liberal spirit, that brotherly disposition, and those comprehensive views, which pervade our fellow-citizens at large, and of which so honorable a sample is now before me."—MADISON.

" I do not doubt that if those men in the South who now accept the tariff views of Clay and the constitutional expositions of Webster would courageously avow and defend their real convictions, they would not find it difficult, by friendly instruction and co-operation, to make the black man their efficient and safe ally, not only in establishing correct principles in our national administration, but in preserving for their local communities the benefits of social order and economical and honest government."
—PRESIDENT HARRISON.

" Consider, then, before, like Hurlo-Thrumbo,
      You aim your club at any creed on earth,
      That, by the simple accident of birth,
 You might have been high-priest to Mumbo-Jumbo."—HOOD.

" Reason is that human faculty which is conversant with grammatical construction, logical inferences, dialectic contests, systematic arrangement ; and in practical life it serves as the divine regulator, in so far as it adheres to the higher order of God. But when it refuses to do this, and wishes to deduce all from itself and its own individuality, then it becomes an egotistical, over-refining, selfish, calculating, degenerate Reason, the inventress of all the arbitrary systems of science and morals dividing and splitting everything into sects and parties."—SCHLEGEL.

" Blockheads, who have never been able to render a pure worship to the God who made you ! Wretches, whom the example of the Noachides, the Chinese *literati*, the Parsees, and of all the wise, has not availed a guide ! Monsters, who need superstitions just as the gizzard of a raven needs carrion ! We have already told you,—and we have nothing else to say,— if you have two religions among you, they will massacre each other ; if you have thirty, they will live in peace. Look at the Grand Turk : he governs Guebres, Banians, Christians of the Greek Church, Nestorians, and Roman Catholics. The first who would excite a tumult is empaled ; and all is tranquil."—VOLTAIRE.

" Sir, are they not words of brilliant, polished treason, even in the very Capitol of the Republic?"—BAKER.

" The lion of England and the lilies of France have appeared upon the same royal escutcheon."—McCARTEY.

FROM the time of Edward the First, when the reign of the common law commenced, we may look in vain through the works of Vacarius, Bracton, Britton, Thornton, Glanville, Fleta, the German legislation which was the *corpus juris*, the foundation of our comprehensive, scientific jurisprudence, for a parallel to this doctrine of the reasonableness of such a rule. The rule in Hall *v.* DeCuir is not a reasonable rule. It is rather an imperial law; it is absolutism, Cæsarism; it is autocratic Russianism; it is anarchy in jurisprudence; it is *Jurisprudence* without the semblance of *Justice.* From the discovery of the first perfect copy of the Pandects at Amalphi, the searching eye of the historian may ransack the literature of law in vain for an example of similar judicial misinterpretation.

The Duns Scotuses, Aquinases, and all the doctors of the Middle Ages, with all their talent for subtle dialectic ratiocination; the repertory of all the metaphysicians who have ever lived and died, whose understanding was profound even to intuition; all the extraordinary mystics, with their arts of divination, from Jacob Boehm down; all the speculations of the pagan mind from the days of Plato,—cannot with their united forces prove such a rule to be reasonable. Their vocabularies and brains would prove as barren, for such a purpose, as would the science of the law even if ransacked by an analyst of mature jurisprudence, conversant with all its speculative amplitude.

The term "reasonable," as applied to such a rule, is a solecism in jurisprudence and in justice, unless it be claimed that these amendments are not the fully-developed plants of civil liberty, but immature, unhealthy germs, which have sprung up out of the blood of half a million citizens. Is not the term "reasonable," as applied to the regulations of the public servant, to be interpreted in the light of American history?—in the light of the history of the origin and development of the Abo-

lition party; of the history of the events which led to the Rebellion of 1860; of the history of the Civil War, resulting in
the passage of these very amendments; of the history of their
construction by the Supreme Court; of the history of the Civil-
Rights Bill of 1866, the Enforcement Acts of 1871, and the
Civil-Rights Bill of 1875?

If these adamantine links forged in the furnace of civil war
indissolubly bound civil rights to these citizens, is that a reasonable rule which seeks to dissolve the mighty bonds? Is that
a reasonable rule which forgets, that the law of the amendment
overleaps all the boundaries of slavery, and, showing no desire
to compromise with existing prejudice, seeks to stamp it out?
If by a reasonable rule be intended that which accords with the
perfection of legal construction, can that be construed as " reasonable" which does not adhere to the ground-plan laid out by
the framers of the amendments, but by a subtle perversity of
construction attains antagonistic conclusions apparently without
departing from the literal plan?

The rule ordained by Benson, and construed by Hall *v.* De-
Cuir to be " *reasonable,*" in so far as it tended morally to degrade *one* citizen on whom the same duties were imposed, and
to whom the same rights belonged, as attached to the collective body of citizens, was in itself an outrage, but its true
significance cannot be fully realized until it is reflected, that,
when the Supreme Court refused the intellectual sanction of its
supereminent wisdom to the repeal of Benson's pro-slavery
modification of universal liberty, this judgment of the court
degraded seven millions of citizens and became the sin of the
whole community of individuals which it represents. This
august tribunal refused to repudiate, as unreasonable, a rule
of the public servant which affirms that the modern society of
America is not composed of inextinguishable individual units,
a rule which insists that the individual sovereign lacks moral
elevation, which insists upon trying to topple over the edifice
of freedom which the nation has erected, and upon damming up
a current of seven millions of people, seeking to find their way
onward and outward into the sea of universal liberty and enlightenment, by chaining them down to those views of civil life

and civil conduct which prevailed during the by-gone ages of slavery.

A similar great division upon the construction of civil rights once existed in France. The irrepressible conflict between the law of the amendments, and the Bensonian law adopted by the Supreme Court as the law of the land, is as great as that between the *Pays du Droit Écrit* and the *Pays du Droit Coutumier;* as vast and irreconcilable as that which was carried on between Cujas and Montesquieu, Desmoulins and D'Aguesseau.

If the Fourteenth Amendment, which to those agencies of good government — education, industry, and suffrage — adds civil rights, is a mere shell, if that mighty instrument is only a metaphysical conception under a legal aspect, undoubtedly the exercise of a "free and untrammelled" authority by the public servant, in the usurpation of the civil rights of these citizens, is reasonable. If the nation has determined to close the storehouse of civil rights, and is prepared to say to this race, Do not make ready to take your place amidst our civilization; instead of upward and onward, your march must be downward and backward,—then the best interests of the nation do require the substantial defeat of civil rights in the enlarged progressive sense of that term. If the juristical oligarchy in America may lawfully oppose to the Fourteenth Amendment the same resistance which the ancient oligarchical depositaries of Roman law offered to the codes for the protection of plebeian rights, then the Bensonian theory is in accord with right reason. If in America is to be repeated the history of Greece, Italy, and the Hellenized seaboard of Western Asia, where the privileged oligarchies, who were the depositaries of the law, upon their mere *ipse dixit*, without judicial precedent, formulated and determined the reasonable rules on which depended the civil rights of the inferior classes, Benson's construction of the Fourteenth Amendment was and is " reasonable."

If the rules and regulations of the most disastrous and blighting of all human institutions are to be maintained, after the institution itself has been undermined, exploded, and blown up; if its forms are preferable to the spirit of the laws and the spirit of Christianity, which teaches the world to look for its goal not to the past, but forward to the joy and gladness of an advancing civilization which unbars the way to human progress, the Bensonian code is superior to the code of the Fourteenth Amendment! But unless the institution of slavery has a super-sensible perfection (as precious and as fleeting as that of the lost arts), which America must enshrine and cherish by its decisions; unless the subtle essence of this prized civil treasure must be religiously preserved in the archives of the Supreme Court; unless, to be consistent with her past in the drama of history, the courts deem it necessary to darken the future of America; unless American self-respect demands that, in her rules and regulations for the public servant, regarding the rights of these citizens, the courts must have a care by nothing they do to con-fess that slavery was even a doubtful virtue, and must hold that it is an institution from which they cannot divorce themselves without blushing for their loss of consistency and dignity,—then, Benson's repeal of the Fourteenth Amendment was unreason-able. By no other devices which are not a diabolic mockery of civil rights and Christianity can the rules in Hall *v.* DeCuir be maintained.

The significant question which presses for solution to-day in America—aroused from the deadly lethargy of slavery—is, whether it is more reasonable that the old stereotyped, fixed, Bensonian rules and regulations which constitute the badges and ceremonials of slavery should be established; or that the sacer-dotal order of race-discriminationists, like all other aristocracies, should disappear or fade into the insignificance of a shadowy individual assertion, and whether the effort of the juristical oligarchy to perpetuate the reign of slavery is not an unreasona-ble exercise of a despotic power under the guise of a constitu-tional construction.

Has the day, indeed, arrived when the Fourteenth Amend-ment, like the Hindoo code of Manu, represents a set of rules never actually observed? Is it only an ideal picture of what, in view of the war and the agitation for a half-century preceding it, ought to be the law? Supereminent fraud, force, and vio-lence, from the commencement of history, clothed the slave-oligarchy with what was claimed to be the divinely-given prerogative of enslaving human beings. Until very recent years it was regarded as an evidence of the loftier nature, the greater wisdom, courage, and virtue, of a superior race. This monstrous delusion was a part of the religion of caste; and the question now is, whether the tribunals of justice shall not decree the total overthrow of this superstition, its rights and ceremonials; whether rules and regulations regarding civil rights, which advance step by step with the martial music of the Republic dedicated anew to liberty, which follow the noble conceptions of those leaders of public thought who formulated the mighty instruments of freedom, are not "*reasonable*" in the highest legal sense of that term?

To construe the rules of Hall *v.* DeCuir as reasonable under any interpretation of that term, presents a curious historical anomaly; for the Fourteenth Amendment, and this decision purporting to construe it, are as opposite poles. Instead of a reasonable rule, Benson's regulation was clearly the result of a vicious bias, traceable to slavery, the coarse palpable badges of which were only slightly disguised.

The reader of history grows familiar with the extraordinary vitality of errors of heredity, and this attempt to establish per-perpetual curtailment of the "perfect liberty" bequeathed by the Fourteenth Amendment is an illustration in the nineteenth century of the extraordinary vitality of the errors of slavery in America. Benson-like regulations prevailed during the dark age of Dred Scott, and the rules which Hall *v.* DeCuir sanction had prevailed since the primitive ages of slavery. Is it reasonable, after this long-suffering race have been released from their calamities, that their progress shall be arrested by the application to them, in a state of liberty, and as citizens of the United States, of any of the discriminative conditions which existed while they were in the bonds and fetters of slavery?

One of the almost insuperable obstacles to the perfect recognition of their civic rights undoubtedly consists in the difficulty of dissociating from the mind of the individual public and the judges of the courts, the inherited social prejudices and slavery bias of the man; a civic and political, from a social right; the legal, from the social personality of the African; the political and civic right of this race, from what the white race regard as an invasion of their exclusive personal and social privileges : the white race cannot separate and distinguish in their minds the negro slave from the American citizen ; the present citizen, from the former slave. The ancient white *régime* adheres with great stubbornness to the old classification of quasi-social civil rights and its grades of distinction. It says, this amendment is only a phantasm,—a legal fiction,—and must be construed not in conformity to constitutional rules of construction, but in accordance with usages respecting the exercise of civil rights by colored people which long prevailed in America. *Our* civil rights, they insist, stand conventionally higher than the civil rights of those citizens whose adoption was brought about by an innovation upon our more dignified caste. But no mere fiction of law can alter the superior status of our civil rights. The fetters which slavery imposed upon your race, citizens of African descent, you are relieved from, but the *sacra* of our old race-code demand that the jurisprudents who are to construe the Fourteenth Amendment emphasize the *lower order* of the civil rights which belong to your so-called citizenship. This " reasonable" rule says, Man's original rights depended on his being a member of a certain group. He was originally of the order of aristocrat or proletariat, patrician or plebeian, free or slave, nor can you by any " reasonable rule" be deemed to be what God made you long before the amendments were passed—a man.

Instead of being reasonable, such a rule must be relegated to the *leges barbarorum.* It insists upon patching the new dress of American citizenship with the worn-out colors of the ancient institution. Like the " *sacra*" or family rites, these badges of slavery are sacrifices which must be made by the new American citizen to commemorate and perpetuate the *manes* of defunct slavery. Rules are reasonable, forsooth ! which require that on all prominent occasions the continuous existence of race-antagonism may be insured. The ancestor is dead, but by the laws of succession the right to the observance of this formula of the slave-owning family still exists. Like the Hindoo law, the slave-power obliges the adopted citizen to provide the funeral cake, the water, and all the solemn sacrificial array for his own immolation.

The white allodial proprietors of civil rights in America can find no precedent for the reasonableness of these rules outside of the customs of barbarians; nor should they be strengthened or allowed to stand through the feebleness and unresisting imbecility of the courts. Are the co-heirs of liberty and citizenship in America peasantry or serfs? Is there a caste of *grands seigneurs* here, who may demand of this race a variety of symbolical acts, in their pursuit of business or pleasure, in the highest degree ceremonial? Can Civilization be as much wedded to her idols as Barbarism, and still boast that she is a superior creature?

Many things well known and pleasing to scholars are extremely problematic and distasteful to caste. The Greek states, Rome, the Teutonic aristocracies in Ditmarsh, the Celtic clan tribes, the Slavonic, Russian, and Polish nationalities were founded by aliens in race, color, and blood. The proud Caucasian of caste should know that his blonde and brunette types, if traced back through the gaps of by-gone ages, are but an outcome of the admixture of races. If the genealogy of races as thus traced presents the fact, to which the Fourteenth Amendment is the testimonial of America, that the family of man is as broad as mankind, how can it be gravely contended that the rule in question is " reasonable"?

Although Europe is known to have been originally populated chiefly by whites, every shade is now represented there, from the fairest Swede to the dark-skinned inhabitants of the Mediterranean coast, only a shade lighter than the Berbers on the opposite side of that sea. Tacitus speaks of "black Celts." Upon the whole, it seems that the distinction of color, from the fairest Englishman to the darkest African, has no hard-and-fast lines, but varies gradually from one shade to another. The cultured reader, and every educated mind with any breadth of survey, must find a vast array of examples throughout history, to show that the adaptation, accommodation, and assimilation of races to the requirements of new systems, is only a question of time. How, then, can a rule which retards this result, in any sense, be said to be reasonable, from a political, economic, constitutional, or common-law stand-point?

Alteration in the political and social condition of classes is nothing new in the world's history. Greece, Italy, and Asia Minor had dominant orders which likewise laid claim to a sacred character. Their assumed sanctity and superiority, in the first struggle with popular opinion, were as completely overthrown as the doctrine of the divinity of human slavery. The Germany of Tacitus is full to repletion of the barbarism, the lofty contempt and indifference of race for race. But in time, when it was found that the difference between the one and the other was more in their surroundings, and in their interests or prejudices, than in heredity, there came the final triumph of civilization over all these barriers.

CHAPTER XXVIII.

"As well might we seek to light a fire with ice, feed cattle on stones, hang our hats on cobwebs, or otherwise disregard the physical laws of the world, as go contrary to its equally imperative ethical laws."—SPENCER.

"Those who consider the periods and revolutions of human kind, as represented in history, are entertained with a spectacle full of pleasure and variety, and see with surprise the manners, customs, and opinions of the same species susceptible of such prodigious changes in different periods of time."—HUME.

"History should be made to live with its own proper life. God is this life. God must be acknowledged—God proclaimed—in history. The history of the world should purport to be annals of the government of the Supreme King."—D'AUBIGNÉ.

"It is the burden of the prophets borne through all the ages of their history."—MULFORD.

"But if you insist to know, 'by what right, by what law;' by that law, I tell you, which God and nature have enacted,—viz., that whatever things are for the universal good of the whole state, are for that reason lawful and just. So wise men of old used to answer such as you."—MILTON.

"During the civil commotions in England, which lasted from the beginning of the reign of Charles I. to the revolution of 1688, the best men and the purest patriots that ever lived fell by the hand of the public executioner. Judges were made the instruments for inflicting the most merciless sentences on men the latchets of whose shoes the ministers that prosecuted them were not worthy to stoop down and unloose."—BLACK.

"And as for you, Isaac Newton; Frederick the Great, king of Prussia and Elector of Brandenburg; John Locke; Catherine, Empress of Russia, victorious over the Ottomans; John Milton; the beneficent sovereign of Denmark; Shakespeare; the wise king of Sweden; Leibnitz; the august house of Brunswick; Tillotson; the Emperor of China; the Parliament of England; the council of the Great Mogul; in short, all you who do not believe one word which I have taught in my courses on divinity, I declare to you that I regard you all as pagans and publicans, as, in order to engrave it on your unimpressible brains, I have often told you before."
—VOLTAIRE.

" I believe it the only one where every man, at the call of the laws, would fly to the standard of the law, and would meet invasions of the public order as his own personal concern."—JEFFERSON.

" Our whole age has learned dearly enough the lesson, that this dogma, practically applied on a large scale, may indeed lead to a despotism of liberty, and to the lust of conquest, but can as little effect the re-establishment of a true civilization as it can bring back the state of nature."—SCHLEGEL.

" There is in the progress of the nation the ampler recognition of its calling. It was to bear witness to a divine King and Deliverer and Judge, against those who would subject the spirit of man to the things which are seen. It was to bear witness to righteous Will, which would establish righteousness on the earth, against those who assumed only a momentary and transient will, or the self-will of men. It was to bear witness to Him and His righteousness against those who corrupted society, those who took bribes, those who removed landmarks. The nation was the witness that these could not have their own way on earth, that there was a righteous Will which would regard them. And if the people were in complicity with these, the judgments they had uttered against others were to fall upon themselves. There was then for them a plague of fire and a plague of blood ; that two-handed engine at the door which smites once and smites no more."—MULFORD.

" The nation is the work of God in history. Its unity and its continuity through the generations is in Him. He is present with it as with the individual person, and this is the condition of its being, as a moral person. Its vocation is from God, and its obligation is only to God, and its freedom is His gift. The transmitted purpose which it bears in its vocation, is in the fulfilment of His will. The procession of history is in the life of nations, and in the perfected nation is the goal of history."—ID.

" Scattered fragments of the tomb of Romulus, reliefs of Marcus Aurelius, busts of Cicero and Virgil, statues of Cæsar and Augustus, trophies of Trajan, and steeds of Pompey, shall not we discover amid all ruins, and recognize as the hand of our God ?"—D'AUBIGNÉ.

Is the Fourteenth Amendment incapable of enforcement in America by the application of reasonable rules ? When Grotius wrote that marvellous book, *De Jure Belli et Pacis*, the condition of the public law of nations was no more chaotic, and apparently not less capable of practical solution, than is the law of civil rights under the Fourteenth Amendment to-day. Their enforcement by reasonable rules requires only the same wisdom and persistence of purpose as that which sketched the ground-plan and built this great constitutional edifice. The race-antago-nism of the age of Grotius between separate nations was as great as that which crops out now between distinct races in the same States in America.

But what, after all, are the qualities of any race but such as its predecessors have transmitted under the modifying causes which accompany them? The instincts of freedom and a sturdy spirit of independence created the Constitution of America, and finally these amendments. The savage blight of slavery produced the semi-barbarous condition of the enslaved. But, nevertheless, science has traced the relationship of races appa-rently the most dissimilar, in similarities of language,—common inheritances in words and in grammatical structure. Science —the great leveller—insisting upon identity of form, structure, and power, points unmistakably to the brotherhood of man. The manners, institutions, strangeness, uncouthness, and inde-cencies of barbarous races, through the instrumentality of law and organized society, have undergone changes so swift and rad-ical that they stagger belief. American civilization, north, south, east, and west, is marvellously dissimilar even among the white race. Climate, local causes, accident, soil, difference of pursuits, —all have dealt with the nature of man, as if it were as clay in the hands of the potter. In the "*Esprit des Lois*" this same view is presented under a name as great as that of Montesquieu. Is that rule reasonable which rejects the truths which the history of all mankind incontrovertibly proves?

But is it possible that a rule can be reasonable which forcibly thrusts back the race into its old courses on account of its color, and for no other reason than that previous condition which color symbolizes? The wise and noble men who framed the Four-teenth Amendment found in the bold and fearless spirit of lib-erty an ever-propelling inspiration. Broad, deep students of this department of philosophic inquiry, they concluded, at the end of their laborious researches, that the science of man was as ap-plicable to this as to all other races; that the existing differences between this race and others in America were in a great measure owing to the conditions engendered by slavery from which the black race was slowly emerging. These great thinkers all saw alike ; and they said, that caste-prejudice against civil rights is the blindness of a monstrous ignorance to which the votaries and victims of race-feeling have voluntarily condemned themselves, in spite of the lessons of history and of the influence of a nobler civilization which, like a fructifying stream, now permeates America.

But caste will not be at the pains to familiarize itself with the philosophy of liberty ; its squeamish appetite takes a delicate dislike to the whole subject of black civil rights.   In its analysis of political society in its reorganized condition in America, it refuses to follow the course of the well-informed specialist. Instead of taking a blind neighbor for its instructor, it should call to its assistance History ; it should confess, By reason of my inherited blindness, I am incapacitated to inquire into the civic conditions brought about by the amendments, so much do they differ from that to which I have been accustomed.   Instruct me, History ; Philosophy, lead me, I pray ye, to a rational, reasonable rule of action in my novel, bewildered new position. It prefers not to regard the subject of civil rights even as one of ontological inquiry.   Instead of a body of reasonable rules, it prefers to accept the ready-made, easily-adjustable, peculiarly plastic and novel terminology, the plentifulness of words, and the confused bulky conceptions, which are the singularly exclusive productions of the discussion in Hall *v.* DeCuir.   It proclaims that to be a reasonable rule which refuses to communicate the tinge of liberty to the black skin in America unless it also attaches the earmarks of slavery.

If the sojourners in the cloudy tabernacle of caste have not the courage or amplitude of mind to grapple with the perplexities and entanglements of an altered condition of the country ; if they refuse to read rightly the history of human events and destinies ; if they cannot perceive the advantage which the law of humanitarianism has over the archaic law of slavery ; if they cannot comprehend the difference between the past and the present ; still, they may be able to understand the proposition, that, in determining the question of the obligation of this *Supreme Law,* there are three words which, unless the Fourteenth Amendment is crumbling away, like Baalbec and Palmyra of old, should silence all objection and quickly dispose of the abundant, gratuitous, technical evasions and verbal avoidances introduced by the discussion in Hall *v.* DeCuir,—"*Ita scriptum est.*"

Is the spirit of slavery so deep-rooted in America that whoever discusses civil rights must have the courage to encounter the base barbarities of race-bigotry? Shall it be said that the "strong lance of Justice hurtless breaks" when couched against this base pretender? In determining what is a reasonable rule of action for the sixty millions of people who constitute the nation, are the bloated pride of obscure, complacent vulgar ignorance, the feeble gibberings of presuming folly, or the tattered rags and sophistries of the doctrinaires of race-mania, to be preferred to the profound reflection, the extensive knowledge, and the acute observation of historical occurrences by experienced statesmen, and jurists who are superior to the prejudices of the age in which they live, and whose cultivated intellects are strong enough to grasp great principles, and courageous enough to follow them in all their results? To be rational, must not the reasonableness of a rule involving this vast subject be determined in accordance with the philosophy of history? What other lamp has jurisprudence to guide its footsteps but the experience of the past?

Is the rule unreasonable in America in the nineteenth century which was reasonable in the revolution of 1688? Thoughtful Englishmen of the middle classes asked for political and spiritual representation; they revolted against the "free and untrammelled" intolerance of the church and the state. They compelled the class-instinct of that age of bigoted caste to drop its prejudices and hatreds. What slavery in America was to the soul and body of the slave, the Established Church and the state, in those days, were to the conscience and civil rights of the middle class of Englishmen. The downfall of the Stuarts accomplished for them what the war amendments performed for the liberated slaves. The revolutions of 1776 and 1861 alike left arbitrary power prone in the dust. The revolution of 1861 wrought a change in the hearts of the American people; a radical change also in opinions, principles, duties, and obligations. It drew the sword with visible reluctance, only after the deliberate calculation of half a century. When the task of cleansing through blood was done, it calmed down, and its work was completed by the insertion into the Constitution of the Thirteenth, Fourteenth, and Fifteenth Articles of Amendment.

Whoever studies the phenomena of the war amendments historically, as a statesman, philosopher, or philanthropist, will perceive that these great movements were in a direct line of progression from the sixteenth century downward. What the revolution of 1688 did for England, the revolution of 1776 did for America. It transferred sovereignty from the throne to the people; it abolished absolutism over civil rights, and gave a constitutional government of reasonable rules. From Pym's Parliament to the achievement of the independence of the United States, these two developments mark the history of religious and civil freedom, and the abolition of that spirit of intolerance and of political and civil tyranny out of whose ruins sprang popular sovereignty. What the revolutions of 1688 and 1776 accomplished for the slaves of the church and state who were deprived of their rights of conscience, their civil rights and political powers, the last American revolution accomplished for those who had been held in bondage by the whole power of the American state.

In a few simple words of surpassing weight, the Fourteenth Amendment repealed the iniquitous laws which had subverted in America the divinely-established relations of humanity. It overturned the tradition, prejudice, habit, and fashion of the state. This coronal of civil liberty is a spectacle for the world, for angels, and for men to look upon. The eternal principles of justice which it established breathe only conciliation and benevolence. Its broad statesmanship, its luminosity, strong apprehension, and keen appreciation of the national environment of slavery, laid down one universal fundamental rule.

This beneficent rule every class of the pro-slavery rump of race-tyrants would repeal to-morrow. By cunningly devised law-fables, they are industriously striving to rehabilitate the old customs which prevailed before the nation's emergence from slavery to freedom. Instead of inclining towards the new, they look back longingly to the old order of the state. Their pride and self-importance incline them to sacrifice the civil rights of the new citizens, and, whenever and as best they can, to sap their legal foundation. They would adapt the law to the spirit of the ninth, not to that of the nineteenth century. They are ready to compromise the eternal principle of natural justice embodied in this amendment, which, clearly recognized as the essential rule of right action, is one of the most glorious achievements of Christianity. They are prepared to substitute for its right reason the unreasonable rules in Hall *v.* DeCuir. They declare that to be a reasonable principle of interpretation which affirms that time and experience demonstrate that the progress of this race is but an illusion, that the "equality" before the law which the Fourteenth Amendment secures is not the harmonious expression and type of civic unity in America.

Nothing in the annals of mankind has equalled America's coronal of civil rights. The sceptre of slavery had now departed, and everything in the Fourteenth Amendment seemed the fruit of profound, tranquil, disinterested meditation. The mission of its civilization was to blend into more harmonious civic relations all Americans. It reared a throne of Justice in the midst of the poor, the sorrowful, and the heavy-laden; the offspring of generations of dense ignorance and superstition, many of them wholly illiterate, and, except certain *white* foreigners, the lowest stratum of society. There was heard throughout America, as it were, the echo of that voice which said in the beginning of time, " Let there be light" ; and, the light having dissipated the darkness, behold, the gift of simple justice and freedom had crowned each citizen with individual sovereignty throughout a glorious republic ! Its heralds proclaimed, in accordance with the revealed law of Christianity, which is the foundation of all laws, and according to the natural law and the *Jus Gentium*, that the Fourteenth Amendment declares the central figure in government to be man ; that, since Americans have been made one *gens*, there should hereafter be no separate race-rights, the rights of the community of men being blended into one, with the same privileges and immunities.

Justice was by this amendment more in accord with the progress of the societies of mankind. To all people naturalized or born in America, it declared that a universal succession of civil rights should be their portion. This proclamation of civil liberty said to the whole American people, For two centuries you have borne the burden of this shameful error, which you ignorantly worshipped and clung to as if it were a blessing. I declare unto you, that this slave was your brother in disguise. That which your Fugitive-Slave Law treated as inanimate property has now been animated with civil life in conformity to the law of nature, which gave the same soul to the slave as to the master.

It is the single and simple ingredient of liberty according to the law of nature which this amendment reveals to both white and black. It has given birth to civil rights according to the law of nature. Its chief function, principle, and postulate was the declaration of this natural law, and its binding force on the States, that the citizens thereof should be absolutely equal ; that they should stand related as sovereign to sovereign, the difference in the pigment of their skins having no more effect upon their civic right than the fashion or fabric of their garments. As sovereign States stand to sovereign States, under the doctrines of international law, this redeemed race, newly admitted into the family of man, stands to the originally exclusive proprietors of civil rights in America.

For him, whoever he may be, who bears the imprint of the Creator's hand, it provided opportunities for the highest and best attainments. It opens for him the grandest civilization, just as much as for the heaven-anointed slave-power of the color-caste. The principles upon which it rests declare, there is no clan or tribe so degraded that it has not some acquaintance with the rights of man. The altar of that eternal rule of natural justice which is now established by the Fourteenth Amendment is older by innumerable æons than the doctrines of states or of men ; the ancient society which was founded upon slavery is abolished in the American state ; its laws, customs, rites, and ceremonies must cease to operate. The new-comers by adoption are one of the component parts of the state; the political dogmas of slavery have crumbled into dust, and upon their ruins the law of nature asserts itself. It introduced under auspices most favorable to its development a primitive society; and it said to the pride of race, Recognize the laws of God and nature by which you have ascended from naked barbarians to your present height in the scale of being. In time, the law which has altered your status will alter that of those beneath you. Show your gratitude to the bountiful Provider by helping upward those of His creatures whom your civilization has ground into the dust for two centuries.

CHAPTER XXIX.

"We here highly resolve that these dead shall not have died in vain; that this nation, under God, shall have a new birth of freedom; and that a government of the people, by the people, and for the people shall not perish from the earth."—LINCOLN.

"It is rather for us to be here dedicated to the great task remaining before us, that from these honored dead we take increased devotion for that cause for which they gave the last full measure of devotion. It is for us, the living, rather to be dedicated here to the unfinished work which they who fought here have thus far so nobly advanced."—ID.

"If we shall suppose that American slavery is one of these offences which, in the providence of God, must needs come, but which, having continued through His appointed time, He now wills to remove, and that He gives to both North and South this terrible war as the woe due to those by whom the offence came, shall we discern there any departure from those Divine attributes which the believers in a living God always ascribe to Him?"—ID.

"The movement of the progressive societies has been uniform in one respect. Through all its course, it has been distinguished by the gradual growth of individual obligation in its place. The individual is steadily substituted for the family as the unit of which the civil law takes account."—MAINE.

"I plant myself on the ancient ways of the Republic, with its grandest names, its surest landmarks, and all its original altar-fires about me."—SUMNER.

"In this idea I saw no narrow advantages merely for individuals or classes, but the sovereignty of the people, and the greatest happiness of all secured by equal laws."—ID.

"Such a law you declare to be constitutional and valid. There is not a half-grown boy in the country of average understanding that does not know better. I cannot help but believe that a little reflection would have saved even you from the shame and folly of making an assertion so destitute of all sense and reason."—J. BLACK.

"I will continue to cherish the belief, that, although, like all other human institutions, it may for a season be disturbed, or suffer momentary

327

eclipse by the transit across its disk of some malignant planet, it possesses a recuperative force, a redeeming energy in the hearts of the people,
that will soon restore it to its wonted calm, and give it back its accustomed
splendor."—PINCKNEY.

"As all governments in this world, good and bad, liberal or despotic,
are of men, by men, and for men, this new State, having no *castes or rank*,
or degrees discriminating among men in its population, becomes at once a
government of the people, by the people, and for the people."—EVARTS.

"Even Napoleon, after his seeming success, his triumphs, his profound
statesmanship, his far-seeing 'policy,' ended in the belief that 'There is
no power without justice.'"—SPENCER.

"Work that is true and will last through all eternity."—CARLYLE.

THE framers of the Fourteenth Amendment did not dream
that after the grave civil commotion the imperial power of race-
opinion would resist through the courts, even in theory, the
solemn mandates of constitutional law. Those profoundly
acute, analytical, legal philosophers, peerless in the realm of
thought, and filled with the spirit of practical wisdom, said,
with Lord Coke, "The principles of natural right are perfect
and immutable; but the condition of human law is ever
changing, and there is nothing in it which stands forever.
Human laws are born, live, and die."

Those great masters reflected, that the unnatural rule of "might,
not right," had passed away, and they asked, how can the law of
race-antagonism hope to survive? When the conditions which
created it had ceased, they had hoped it would die amidst its
worshippers. Yet they knew that the snaky sorceress Slavery
still sat at the gate of hell, holding the key, and was in league
with the foul fiend to let forth anew upon the earth the imprisoned spirits of evil. To defeat her wiles, they established,
by the Fourteenth Amendment, no uncertain juridical rules for
human conduct, the operation of which judges might defeat if
America's citizens should remain imbued with race-prejudice.
This amendment was the embodiment of broad, deep ethical
precepts of national morality, for the enforcement of which no
more coercive measures should be necessary than for the enforcement of the worship of the Creator by His creatures. To the

keeping of the Supreme Court and the Congress of the United States, they committed the sublime truth they had embodied in this amendment, with an unquestioning faith that, through an everlasting past to an everlasting future, " The eternal years of God were hers."

This sublime trust, bestowed on America, has not been fulfilled by its Congress or its courts. Eminent persons deny that the necessities of the civilization which it proclaims require the equality of rights it commands. The united brotherhood of race-devotees, like the enthusiastic worshippers of the sun, moon, stars, and a multiplicity of gods and demons, insist that it is reasonable to view the white color-line as did the heathen their divinities, and that " as far as practicable" they should have " free and untrammelled authority" by their own " reasonable rules" to compel the black race to worship it, and " as far as practicable" to confer celestial honors upon it. These crazy-headed, fantastical coxcombs and their followers, the pontiffs, priests, and ministers who indulge in this pagan worship by taking the chief part in stirring up race-controversies, have no just notions of Christ's doctrine, nor of obedience to any law, human or divine, which interferes with the genius and spirit of race-antagonism. They insist upon regarding as unreasonable all regulations in civil society which interfere with the observance of race-rites, because such rules do not permit them in America to worship their idol according to the dictates of their enlightened consciences.

Devout zealots in by-gone ages erected shrines not to white, yellow, brown, or swarthy skins, but to the skies, mountains, trees, rivers, and winds. This worship was practised even in the Augustan age, the most polite and learned the world has ever seen, when the love of literature was a universal passion. But the wiser part of those pagans looked upon that religious system just as sensible citizens regard the exclusive worship of their idol according to the rites of the color-line. The politic pagans of that age, like those of this generation, agreed that the decree to abolish human sacrifices, and to do away with sacred religious rites and mysteries, which had so long marked their ascendency in the state, was unreasonable in any reorganization of political society; that the instrumentalities by which

Hadrian undertook to overthrow these rites operated upon the " States as political entities, but not on their population in whole or part," who were at liberty by " reasonable rules" to overthrow and repeal them.   The true worshippers of that, as of this age, repealed those decrees by the same " reasonable rules" by which Hall *v.* DeCuir overturned the Fourteenth Amendment.

The rites appointed by Moses were not to the chosen people more sacred and inviolable than are the precepts of Scott *v.* Sandford to the color-line brigade.   The learned among the Hebrews defended their tenets with the same zeal and pertinacity as race-discriminationists maintain their unreasonable rules of civic inequality.   They are to-day just as much opposed to the civil rights of the black race as were the ancient Jews to the Samaritans.   With the same urbanity and unanimity, the Pharisees and Essenes excluded all nations from the hope of eternal life, as Hall *v.* DeCuir, by its reasonable rules, excludes citizens of the United States from the privileges and immunities exclusively enjoyed by the white Pharisees and Essenes of America.   The inferior priests of the race *sacra,* who are dissolute and abandoned so far as the keeping of the new commandment is concerned, openly confess that these amendments are like the religion of the Persians and the Egyptians.   They were only " forms of policy," to do away with the more obnoxious parts of slavery-paganism in America, to extend the supremacy of party and to maintain its royal authority.   Beyond the attainment of these results the enforcement of these rules, in their opinion, is unreasonable.

The soft-tongued, lynx-eyed race-Pharisees will not regard as a reasonable rule, the determination, which this amendment affords, of a sociological question, which pressed for solution half a century prior to the war.   Deaf to the voice of the dread whirlpool of time, at the bottom of which lay the ruins of centuries piled upon centuries, saying to them, with a sullen roar, Equality of law is the destiny of man ; at that time they replied, The abolition of slavery is unconstitutional ; reasonable rules of constitutional construction forbid it ; and their descendants to-day claim *that* rule to be " unreasonable" which, like the dews, and the rain, and the sun, would take in all the world.

The reasonable rules of the Fourteenth Amendment affirm, and their unreasonable rules deny, that the plan of the world, material and moral, seen and unseen, is adjusted to man and to the fulfilment of his destinies.

Invisible Providence stepped across the water and planted an upward-growing glorious tree, under the shade of which this weary humanity might rest. A voice whispered to His torn and defaced image in America, saying, Humanity itself, deeply considered, touches the boundary of the superhuman. Remember, the power of Rome endured for twelve centuries. But the "Eternal City" of to-day is built upon its own accumulated destruction. So, though men may come and go, and states, constitutions, and laws crumble, yet the same equality of right remains. The all-seeing Eye beheld the defaced image of this race, and an audible voice called to it, Come up a little higher. Whatever has been your actual place, "the place of potential man in the hierarchy of creation is a very high one." You may not be merely an automatic man. You are, "in form and moving, express and admirable," permanent, indestructible; and have a positive influence upon the political condition of the country, which is advanced by your advancement. Against manifest destiny, against this decree of the Holy One, the little impious hand of Race-Antagonism is now raised up, and his mouth is opened to declare that "well-settled rules of constitutional construction" determine that His great commandment is unreasonable!

As we have seen, the decisions of the American courts, volume after volume, page after page, line after line, substantially declare that the human imagination cannot conceive a greater height of God-like power than lifting from the dust of ages seven millions of human beings and making of them citizens. In the trail of heavenly light which ushered in the morning, under the open sky, amidst their brakes and cotton-fields, the innocent, helpless band thought they saw in these decisions the opening of their gate to heaven. They are now citizens; and yet they are to be told that the Color-Line, like a vulture roaming far and wide bent on its prey, bars the way. By sly circumspection the Labor Tyrant and all other classes have power to deprive these

redeemed people of the rights, immunities, and privileges which
all other citizens may freely enjoy.   They all have now free
and untrammelled authority, not according to the Fourteenth
Amendment, but according to the old customs which prevail in
the State in spite of it, to adopt such " reasonable rules and regulations" as they, in their discretion, may see fit ; and if those rules
repeal the Fourteenth Amendment, and strangle civil rights in
their birth, they are not unreasonable, because " well-settled
rules of constitutional construction" prevent the State from
legislation " which strips private property of all its utility."

If this " kingly palace-gate" of humanity can thus be shut ;
if the ascent of this race to and through this magnificent structure,
erected by the joint hands of Christianity and Civilization, can
thus be barred ; it will not be through the *reasonable* rules of the
common law, but through the hypocrisy which defeats the letter,
spirit, and true intent of the Fourteenth Amendment: hypocrisy,—that sin which neither man nor angel can discern,—

> " Hypocrisy, the only evil that walks alone
> Invisible except to God above,
> By his permissive will through heaven and earth."

If this be true, the fresh stream of Civil Liberty has been again
poisoned at its fount.   The rights of man have not been restored ;
he cannot in America stand

> " God-like, erect, with native honor clad."

The sly enemy of the human race has renewed in America his
old argument in Eden, insinuating that " public reasons just"
have overthrown the Fourteenth Amendment.   These " *public
reasons just* " compass no less than the re-installation in America
of the *dii inferni* of " the lost cause."   It can no longer be concealed that under the disguise of constitutional construction, in
the shape and form of *Justice*, the foul spirit of banished slavery
has re-entered America, and is now pursuing the politic course
of Satan in Paradise, as depicted by Milton :

> " Thence up he flew, and on the tree of life—
> The middle tree, and highest there that grew—
> Sat like a cormorant ; yet not true life
> Thereby regained, but sat devising death
> To them that live."

CHAPTER XXX.

" They were considered of the irrevocable class,—a kind of law over which the dead only were omnipotent, and the living had no power. Frost, it is true, cannot be put off by act of Parliament, nor can spring be accelerated by any majority of both houses."—SYDNEY SMITH.

" It was high time: for in truth the Hydra, on every side, is stirring its thousand heads."—CARLYLE.

" Forgive me for presuming to intimate, that if, after you have achieved it, you pronounce the notion to be correct, you will have gone a great way to prepare us, by the authority of your opinion, to receive as credible history the worst parts of the mythology of the pagan world."—PINCKNEY.

" Oh! Sir Harry Vane! Thou, with thy subtle casuistries and abstruse hair-splittings; thou art other than a good one, I think! The Lord deliver me from thee, Sir Harry Vane."—CROMWELL.

" To say that a law is contrary to natural liberty, is simply to say that it is a law: for every law is established at the expense of liberty—the liberty of Peter at the expense of the liberty of Paul. When a law is reproached as hurtful to liberty, the inconvenience is not a particular ground of complaint against that law,—it is shared by all laws. The evil which it causes in this manner,—is it greater than the good which it does in other ways? This is the only question to be examined."—BENTHAM.

" What warrant was there for the confidence that upon these plain precepts of equality of right, community of interest, reciprocity of duty, a polity could be framed which might safely discard Egyptian martyrs, and Hebrew reverence, and Grecian subtlety, and Roman strength,—dispense, even, with English traditions of

' Primogeneity and due of birth,
Prerogative of age, crowns, sceptres, laurels' ?"—EVARTS.

" He surely has not reflected upon the magnitude of the principle contended for, or he would have perceived at once the utter insignificance of all objects of factious and party contest, when compared with the mighty interests it involves. It concerns ages to come, and millions to be born. We who are here, our dissentions and conflicts, are nothing, absolutely nothing, in the comparison: and I cannot well conceive that any man, who is capable of raising his view to the elevation of this great question, could suddenly bring it down to the low and paltry consideration of party interests and party motives."—JOHN SERGEANT.

" Abandoning its own proper region, it either soars up to heaven to weave there its fine-spun webs of dialectics, and to build its metaphysical castles in the air, or else, losing itself on the earth, it violently interferes with external reality, and determines to shape the world according to its own fancy, and to reform it at will."—SCHLEGEL.

" I never could see why the whole community should not be bound by as strong an obligation to do justice to an individual, as one man is bound to do it to another."—BAYARD.

" It is the nature and essence of a compact, that it is equally obligatory on the parties to it, and, of course, that no one of them can be liberated therefrom without the consent of the others, or such a violation or abuse of it by the others as will amount to a dissolution of the compact."—MADISON.

" We are all children at the foot of an infinite mountain, glowing with a hallowed light inviting us upward. Our world is touched as never before by the infinite sea, sobbing and sighing from the eternal shore. We bathe in its rivers of light and hear the echoes of the long ago translated in the souls that speak again from the lips long silent."—HOWE.

" I count all the follies and failures indispensable factors in the evolution of truth."—ID.

" As with all progress worth fighting for, the contest is stubborn and resolute. Delays and defeats are inevitable, but temporary. The advance is sure."—CURTIS.

IF law is rational in its nature, there should be a multitude of tests to determine whether a rule is agreeable to reason, whether it conforms to those principles which reason supports and justifies. The bull of Alexander the Sixth divided the undiscovered countries of the world between the Spaniards and the Portuguese, by a line drawn one hundred leagues west of the Azores. By some it was regarded at the time as a reasonable exercise of papal authority ; by others as an extravagance of exceeding absurdity. The coming generation of America will not regard that bull as a more extraordinary example of the unwarrantable usurpation of power, and the perversion of reason, than is afforded by the decision of the Supreme Court that a State statute, requiring the conduct and the business of its citizens to conform to the supreme law of the land, is void, because obedience to the provisions of that supreme law (which the State is obliged to enforce either by her statutes or by the courts —her State agencies) may excite the displeasure of citizens disloyal to the Fourteenth Amendment, who may see fit to withdraw their patronage from a public servant's business conducted in conformity with the supreme national and State law. The impartial historian of the future will perceive at a glance, that, far from being reasonable in any sense of that much-abused term, the decision of the court was as absurd and unwarrantable a usurpation of the judicial authority as Alexander's edict was of the papal power.

The calling of the public servant is carried on by the express authority of the State, which gives it certain rights and imposes upon it certain salutary restraints, prohibitive of all discrimination. Every branch of this calling either exists by virtue of a charter, or is licensed, or a privilege. Innumerable rights are derived from the State by the incorporation of individuals under private charters, or by payment for a license for the conduct of private business. Has it ever entered into the most extravagant conception of their powers, by the individuals so incorporated or licensed, that their right to conduct their private business in their own way is independent, indefeasible, absolute, and beyond all constitutional or legal limitation? Has such a paradoxical assumption ever before been dreamed of, as that they may violate the written law of the Constitution and the declared policy of the nation; upon the ground, that, owing to a condition of sickly sentimentality in some sections of the country, the observance of its mandates in the conduct of business would imperil the profits of a calling which it has voluntarily assumed with full knowledge of that public sentiment and of certain constitutional or legal provisions? The familiar law maxim says, they are not injured who consent.

Jurisprudence upholds no legal relations peculiar to such social phenomena. Its phases are ephemeral, and cannot be indulged to the extent of repealing this organic law,—the Constitution. This amendment provides rules of civic action, to which all ranks, classes, and conditions of citizens must conform both their lives and their business. How else could its workings be uniform and universal? The injury resulting from obedience to the law is, however, unproved, and asserted hitherto without a single evidential fact to support it. But were it admitted that the business of the public servant would be diminished if the civil rights guaranteed to all were granted to this class of citizens; upon what legal analogy, rule, or principle could a discrimination be authorized, which sets the Fourteenth Amendment at defiance either by direct evasion, or by such a qualified satisfaction of its provisions as made that one class an object at which the slowly-moving finger of scorn could point as a degraded race, in spite of its emancipation from all thraldom and class-distinctions?

The obvious answer to this argument is, that these vocations can be exercised only in accordance with and never in violation of constitutional prohibitions. Inasmuch as the right to engage in the calling is subject to the limitations of constitutional law, if obedience to the constitutional mandate is demanded of every public servant and enforced, how can the private property of any individual engaged in these vocations be stripped, in any legitimate sense, of any portion of its utility? The public travel by land and by sea, and frequent places of instruction and amusement, in spite of various annoyances which are hard to bear, and which they may regard—not as public or private nuisances, of which the law takes cognizance—but as a quasi-social nuisance, of which the law takes no note. Until Lord Campbell's comparatively recent act, death by the default, neglect, or omission of the public servant, or private citizen, was not actionable, and there was no civil remedy for such injuries; the rule being that personal actions die with the person. The public servant could thus annihilate the pecuniary value of life with impunity from civil damage by the law of the land. Upon what reasonable theory can he complain, that obedience to the law of the Fourteenth Amendment operates, in an altered condition of the State, against his former rights under Scott *v.* Sandford? He might with as much reason complain that by Lord Campbell's act, a right of action survived to the husband, wife, parent, or child, in the event of a death caused by his neglect or default; and that this act had violated the common law which provided that personal actions should die with the person. Travellers in America encounter daily peril by sea and peril by land, almost as frightful to contemplate and front as the color of this race! Yet they are not thereby deterred from entering public assemblies, or from traversing space for purposes of business or pleasure.

The decision in Hall *v.* DeCuir gratuitously assumes that a conformity of the public servant's business to constitutional law may strip his property of all its utility. Is it *reasonable* to complain that conformity to organic law may strip property of its utility, when this would be impossible provided there were a universal enforcement of its provisions? It might as rationally be contended that, by enforcing the observance of the Commandments, the interests of the church might suffer, because if its members should not be allowed to worship the graven images of this world; if they were obliged to remember the Sabbath day and keep it holy; if they were prohibited from killing, committing adultery, stealing, bearing false witness, and coveting their neighbor's goods, much of their private property would be stripped of its utility, and many of their darling inclinations abridged. The clergy of all denominations, on the other hand, would unanimously declare, that the Commandments must be enforced, since they constitute the foundation-stones of Christianity. The guardians of the church would stoutly maintain that the Commandments were delivered by the great Jehovah to Moses for all times and for all people; and the great leaders of thought would undoubtedly concede that the history of ecclesiastical and of civil polity alike incontrovertibly establish the great truth, that the permanence and stability of church and state equally depend upon the rigid enforcement of these fundamental laws which, as a rock of ages, underlie these glorious superstructures of advancing civilization. All denominations of men of catholic culture would perceive that the violation of these sacred commandments by some of their members afforded no "justifiable, reasonable rule" for their non-enforcement by the church, still less for the promulgation of a loose textual code of discretionary, absolving rules for the gratification of the inordinate desires of certain of its members, who, notwithstanding the uncleanness or dark ribaldry of their private lives, outwardly professed a belief in the abstract theory of the organic laws of the church. These grave expositors of ecclesiastical .polity would insist that this diseased condition of the church only proved that some of her branches were rotten and cumbersome. And aroused Christendom would sustain this faithful construction of the doctrines of the church ; with no less fervor than it will hail with delight the auspicious day, when the faithful, unperverted, rigid enforcement of this amendment against the royal *lanistae* of caste in America shall strip the mask from those fraudulent pretenders whose cunningly-devised and subtly-forged rules and regulations, in spite of their sworn allegiance to the Constitution of their fathers, are standing menaces to that lofty standard of political reason and truth, the Fourteenth Amendment,—the practical fulfilment in America of a great political reformation which has eluded the grasp of the philosophic statesmen of past ages.

But are these rights of property of the public servant any more sacred than that vast, innumerable host of properties which civilization daily multiplies and the state respects and protects ? The vocation of the public servant is subject to no other hardships or exactions (if observance of law be one) than the property of private persons daily encounters in the pursuits of business. American competition as the destroyer of every branch of commerce is the most revolutionary factor of the age. Securities of every description may be stripped of all their utility by laws of finance, which the Wall-Street magnates have established and which they claim to be wise and just laws of trade, and which are as immutable in their workings as the ebb and flow of the tide. Since the business of the public servant in all its branches and departments is authorized by virtue of State charters, State or municipal license, or other public authority, it follows that, although private capital is invested in its stock, the vocation itself is in no sense a private business, because the authority to exercise it is derived wholly from the public.

The courts have sometimes gone to the most extraordinary length in stripping this private capital so invested of its utility; especially when the calling is pursued in such a way as to deprive less-favored citizens of rights which they ought to be entitled with all others to enjoy. The Interstate-Commerce Law is the outgrowth of this salutary doctrine, and is a simple declaration by Congress, that this class of public servants shall conform their business to the organic law engrafted upon the Constitution.

If impartial treatment of all citizens is imposed upon public servants, they must carry on their business under impartial regulations; and if their regulations are based upon color as a ground of distinction, they cease, *eo instanti,* to be reasonable. The well-known repugnance of some citizens to the color and race of Chinamen cannot justify as reasonable a regulation based upon considerations of their color and race, when such regulation conflicts with the paramount authority of the law of the land.

Throughout Christian countries that system of reasoning which takes up arms against the truths of God has been justly held to be as far from reasonable as the nadir from the zenith. If the rights of seven millions of citizens be narrowed down to the compass of the term "reasonable," as all the disputants seem to admit, it is manifest, that every avenue of approach to the "reason" should be thoroughly explored. The artificial machinery of the State—its wheels and cogs so closely interwoven—ought to be carefully overhauled. Search ought to be made with untiring diligence throughout the *corpus juris,* for the true interpretation of the term "reasonable rules," applied in the exposition of the Fourteenth Amendment. The theories of flimsy, dexterous political dabsters; the superficial attenuations, all the "evanescent lines" and cobwebs of race-antagonism, ought to be swept away without ceremony. The reasonableness of a rule when so explored covers vast ancient and modern fields of religious, sociological, political, constitutional, and economic inquiry.

To be reasonable, such a rule must stand stringent tests. A rare combination of national reasons must unite to establish it. It should be nobly comprehensive, taking in the whole round of civil existence; harmonious, kind, and true. It should also be framed

with the remembrance that " we are laborers together with God";
it should be free from selfishness and prejudice; its continuous
aim should be, individual improvement.   In its working it must
have practical simplicity, so as clearly to guide the citizen amid
the multitude and minutiæ of matter involved in the pursuits
of daily life of which it is regulative.   Such a rule, to be reasonable, must not only be in contact with the constitution of
American society, but must take accurate cognizance of the
magnitude of the civil and political evils which the Fourteenth
Amendment was intended to wipe out.   It must look at the real
bonds of society, the laws of its progress, the philosophic basis
of civil rights, and the mutuality of the relations of the individual social units which compose American society; it must be
acquainted with the operation of new civil laws and the equilibria
of social life.   It must bear in mind, that, although what the
courts call a "natural and well-known repugnance" has been
created on the part of white citizens against those of African
descent by reason of their color and previous condition, nevertheless, this race should have all possible opportunities to fit
itself for independent responsible action in the situations brought
out by vast civic changes.   We have seen that Hall *v.* DeCuir
allows the public servant to formulate " discretionary, reasonable
rules"; but how should the people engaged in the public service
know anything about "reasonable rules" when they are no more
versed in the requisite fields of knowledge than the beasts of
burden which perform the chief part of their service?   Is it
rational to expect their rules to be reasonable?

CHAPTER XXXI.

" The spirit of toleration and desire for exact justice, which are necessary to harmonious social life, and are the distinguishing features of an advancing civilization. . . . How far we are from that result at present may be seen by any one who considers how few among so-called civilized people have that high regard for the essentials of justice that must lie at the foundation of any civilization that aims to make of men and nations true brothers in heart and sentiment."—THE BALTIMORE SUN.

" To go to the bottom of the subject, let us consult the theory which contemplates a certain number of individuals as meeting and agreeing to form one political society, in order that the rights, the safety, and the interest of each may be under the safeguard of the whole."—MADISON.

" Political reason is a competing principle,—adding, subtracting, multiplying, and dividing, morally, and not metaphysically or mathematically, true moral demonstrations."—BURKE.

" The life of the nation was through a course of moral conflict and endeavor. It was not—as in the civilization of the Philistine—an animal existence, with faith only in visible things and sunk in the worship of animal forms. It was through unceasing wrestling with evil that its advance lay. It was not formed in moral indifference. The awful gates of the mountains were open before it, and through them its journey led. It was tried in great crises. 'The Lord hath taken you and brought you forth out of the iron furnace.' "—MULFORD.

" Whereas, on the other side, domestical evils, for that we think we can master them at all times, are often permitted to run on forward, till it be too late to recall them. In the mean while the commonwealth is not only through unsoundness so far impaired as those evils chance to prevail ; but farther, also, through opposition arising between the unsound parts and the sound, where each endeavoreth to draw evermore contrary ways, till destruction in the end bring the whole to ruin."—HOOKER.

" I have touched, therefore, upon the traits that determined this national life as to be of, from, and for the people, and not of, from, or for any rank, grade, part, or section of them. In these traits are found the ' ordinances, constitutions, and customs,' by a wise choice of which the founders of States may, Lord Bacon says, ' sow greatness to their posterity and succession.' "—EVARTS.

"Let us have no partial freedom; let us all be free; let the reversion of our broad domain descend to us unencumbered and free from the calamities and the sorrows of human bondage."—SEWARD.

"'Nephew,' said Algernon Sidney in prison, on the night before his execution, 'I value not my own life a chip, but what concerns me is that the law which takes away my life may hang every one of you, whenever it is thought convenient.'"—SUMNER.

"What are the favorite maxims of democracy? A strict observance of justice and public faith, and a steady adherence to virtue. These, sir, are the principles of a good government. No mischief, no misfortune, ought to deter us from a strict observance of justice and public faith."—MARSHALL.

THROUGHOUT Christendom Jurisprudence proclaims that at the creation of man it was written by his Creator upon the tablets of nature that all men are equal (*Jura naturalia sunt immutabilia*). This *lex aeterna*, declaratory of a principle of natural justice, is embodied in the Fourteenth Amendment, that American Magna Charta—

> "'Neath whose sheltering wings
> Kings are but subjects, subjects kings."

Is this fundamental principle—the definitive command and expression of the sovereign will—a reasonable rule? If so, it should be enforced in spite of all the repugnances, natural or artificial, which it may encounter. According to the elegant definition of Celsus, "Justice is the art of the good and equal" (*Ars boni et aequi*). The reasonable rule of this amendment has one prescript: it commands the public to hurt no one, and to extend to every one the same rights, privileges, and immunities. Surely that only is a reasonable regulation which conforms to this fundamental principle. The powers of the public servants are defined and limited by this organic law, and its dictates are unquestionably supreme. How can those rules be reasonable which refuse to conform to the expressed will of the highest power in the State? If civil rights are created by the will of the government, how can they be reasonably subjected to the will, whims, or discretion of any of its individual citizens? If the amendment is the standard of right, it must be necessarily paramount and exclusive of any other authority. There can be no question of right or wrong, justice or injustice; its mandate must be obeyed. The only reasonable rule is that which conforms the public to this standard of right.

Here, then, is nothing indefinite or uncertain. This *is* a practicable and a reasonable rule; for the government must be the sole and supreme judge of what the law of utility may require. Aristotle says,[1] "Moreover, he who bids the law to be supreme makes God supreme; but he who intrusts man with supreme power gives it to a wild beast; for such his appetites sometimes make him; passion, too, influences those who are in power, even the very best of men; for which reason the law is intellect free from appetite."

The national enactment having laid broad and deep the foundation of an imprescriptible right of citizenship in this race, the rules of the public servant, to be "reasonable," must conform to its mandate, in letter, spirit, and truth. With the policy or impolicy of its provisions neither a State, political division of a State, corporation, citizen, or citizens are any more concerned than with the policy or impolicy of the ordinances of Caracalla, after the *Lex Julia municipalis* had extended Roman citizenship to all Italy. It would be more reasonable, and far less injurious, to institute at this day an inquiry concerning the just and enlightened sense of expediency, and consideration for the welfare of the people and the best interests of the country, embodied in that potent instrument the Declaration of Independence, than to question the deliberate determination of the whole people to place, by constitutional enactment, such a limitation upon the action of all citizens, as would prevent discrimination against the black race on account of their color or previous condition of slavery.

In Neal *v.* Delaware[2] the Supreme Court declared that this amendment "was designed, primarily, to secure to the colored race, thereby invested with the rights, privileges, and responsibilities of citizenship, the enjoyment of all civil rights that under

---

[1] Politics, l. iii. c. 16.   [2] 103 U. S.

the law are enjoyed by white persons." That court has repeatedly declared, that no authority shall be exercised in this country discriminating, in respect of civil rights, against freemen and citizens because of their race or color.

In England we have seen a king deposed, and the succession altered, on the ground, that, by "unreasonable rules," "the king had endeavored to subvert the constitution of the kingdom, by breaking the original contract with the king and the people, and had violated the fundamental laws." Can the violation of the supreme law be less perilous in America than in England? The law of England favors civil liberty, but America has enthroned it. America has made the private right of each citizen (subject to the public or State right) absolutely sovereign; and the question is, whether the assertion of an unequal and extraordinary restraint, derogating from the free and untrammelled exercise (by one class of citizens) of rights freely accorded to all others, is a reasonable rule.

Reason places the burden of proof upon the representatives of the State's justice—their courts—to justify this extraordinary and exceptional distinction of the color-line. They should assign some ground why that which is accorded to all other citizens should be refused to any "under substantially similar circumstances and conditions." It is confessed that this inequality in the administration of law is attributable to the repulsive color of the dark citizen, the equilibrium of whose rights is thus disturbed; and the question is, whether the difference of color, which alone gives rise to this inequality, can make the rule reasonable. The amendment authorizes no comminuible justice by the public in dispensing with the civil rights of any citizen. Is it not reasonable to suppose that the expressed will of the American State is the true moral, as well as the paramount, standard of legal civil rights?

The law authorizes these citizens to exact from the public servant the specific duty of forbearance from any act which, on account of color, discriminates against their race. The supreme political authority says to these colored citizens, We vest you with this control over the action of the public. Can its refusal to acquiesce in this right be a reasonable rule of action? The force of government is its justice, which is not a sentiment, but a severe uncompromising master. It is the omnipotence of the state which is thus violated. Can any morbid tenderness of Jurisprudence deem this violation reasonable?

The changes of time and public feeling, policy or impolicy, can by no *reasonable* rule alter a constitutional commandment. Is there a more reasonable standard, and a safer basis, for judicial decision than the enforcement of principles which are immutable, and in no wise dependent upon changes of time or fluctuations in public opinions? The question involves the civil rights of all American citizens, claimed under the Constitution. It is not a question of White or Red Roses, of theatric Neri and Bianchi, of Democratic or Republican parties. The reasonableness of the rule involves the fundamental provisions of a constitutional law, which cannot with safety, or without peril to the liberties of others, be denied upon any pretext to any citizen. If their violation is a crime against all American citizens, and if the legal excuses, as Mr. Sumner said, "are the apology tyrannical, the apology imbecile, the apology absurd, the apology infamous; if tyranny, imbecility, absurdity, and infamy unite to dance like the weird sisters about this crime," in what way is a rule which is a departure from this law reconcilable with right reason?

If civil rights are the same to all citizens, are rules born of a resolution to support, by hook or by crook, the conduct of those who are determined, in spite of the Constitution, to maintain and preserve discriminations reasonable? This charter of freedom swept away color as a factor in the national life; and the civic right of citizenship, irrespective of color, is now as fundamental as the Constitution by virtue of which the nation exists. It would seem a waste of time to argue that such a rule could be reasonable. A special plea, which justifies discrimination because of color, race, or previous condition, would be clearly demurrable. How, then, can the rule be reasonable if the defence of it is demurrable?

If discrimination in civil rights be allowable, it can obviously be supported only upon some ground, some principle, some policy, some lawful police regulation, or, lastly, some commercial reason which the law recognizes as just and equitable, founded in a salutary public policy, which does not contravene the voice of the nation as expressed in the amendments to the Constitution of the country. If interpretations hitherto placed by the Supreme Court upon these amendments are sound expositions, the rules of the public servant, to be reasonable, must conform to these interpretations and to the principles of the common law.

The common law includes all those rules of civil conduct which, originating in the common wisdom and experience of society, have by long usage become established customs, and have finally received judicial affirmance in the courts of highest resort. The written law comprises those rules of civil conduct which have been prescribed in so many words by the supreme power of the state itself. So that the common law, in its highest and widest sense, comprehends all those written (*lex scripta*) and unwritten usages, rules, and privileges (*lex non scripta*) laid down for the guidance of the community. The only difference between the written and the unwritten law is that every member of the community is regarded as having given his approbation and consent to the written, and is virtually a party thereto; which is exactly the relation that the American people (public servants included) occupy to these amendments. In their interpretation various recognized rules of construction have been adopted, too familiar to require explanation. One of the longest-established canons lays down four rules to be observed in the construction of acts of Parliament,[1] whether they be penal or beneficial, restricting or enlarging the common law: 1st. What was the common law before the making of the act? 2d. What was the mischief and defect against which the common law did not provide? 3d. What remedy the Parliament hath resolved and applied to cure the disease of the commonwealth. 4th. The true reason of the remedy.[2]

The common law, as prevailing in this country before the amendments, permitted the degradation of the black race by segregating them, on all occasions, from the white, in much the same

---

[1] Heydon's case, 3 Reports, 7.
[2] Broom's Common Law, p. 6, note S.

fashion as live-stock. The mischief and defects of slavery against which the common law in America did not provide are events too recent to constitute history : they involve all the horrors of the Civil War. The remedy to cure this disease of the common-wealth is contained in this amendment; and the true reasons for and application of the remedy have been explained by the Supreme Court in a multitude of causes, already referred to, wherein they have decided that the aim and object of this amendment was to do away with all legal discrimination because of race, color, or previous condition ; " their one great purpose being to raise the colored race from inferiority into perfect equality of civil rights with all other persons, and that the law of civil rights should be the same for the black as for the white." Can it be gravely contended, such being the purpose of the new constitutional provisions, that rules which in their cruel absurdities are mere mockeries of the amendments, regulations which reinstate and restore in most vital particulars the law as it was before the amendments, which tend to re-enact those " defects of law" and re-establish the old mischief, are reasonable, within the meaning of that term according to the canon of construction laid down in the celebrated common-law decision in Heydon's case ?

Numerous legal analogies could be produced to illustrate the meaning of a term of such national importance as " reasonable," when employed to define civil rights, immunities, and privileges. To avoid copiousness of legal analogy, definitive of that rational law termed a reasonable rule, let us take a universally-established principle applicable to the entire civic life under the system of municipal corporations in America : let us take the familiar illustration of the working of a reasonable rule as furnished in the " by-laws" of a public and municipal corporation. This example affords a striking analogy, and is the most far-reaching, since it governs these artificial creations throughout America. It is well known that, to be reasonable, a " by-law" must be uniform in its workings ; not inconsistent with the Constitution of the United States, or with the charter of the corporation, or with any statute of the State where it exists or carries on its business, or with the general principles of the common law, particularly those having relation to the liberty of the individual.[1]

Can the public servant, under his charter from the State, or license from a municipal corporation acting as a political agency of the State, have a greater authority than the sovereign—the State itself? Can any *one* of the fifty or more millions of white do, with impunity, to seven millions of black citizens, what the whole of the fifty millions could not attempt through the sovereign powers of their States? That is to say, thirty-nine States, representing fifty or more millions of citizens, cannot, by their combined sovereignty, accomplish what an individual tomtit is justified in doing by what he insists is, nevertheless, a reasonable law! No matter how profound their contempt of the amendment, sober second thought must convince the color-line, that such a monstrous doctrine cannot in any rational sense be deemed a reasonable rule.

A rule of a municipal corporation which was based upon color would be clearly unreasonable, arbitrary, oppressive, and partial. A rule founded upon such discrimination is void, because it must proceed from enmity, prejudice, favoritism, race-ism, color, previous condition, or other improper source. Its unreasonableness becomes apparent when a moment's consideration is given to the subject. Can a rule which makes arbitrary and unjust discriminations founded on difference in race, which makes unequal and oppressive distinctions between persons otherwise in a similar situation as citizens, be reasonable, because the makers of the rule are incorporated or licensed by the state? Does not the same principle govern, in the interpretation of the term reasonable, in all the agencies and instrumentalities employed in the administration of the government, whether superior, subordinate, legislative, executive, or judicial? How, then, can that which is unreasonable when applied to the other great instrumentalities of the state be reasonable when applied to those lesser creatures of its charter or license?

---

[1] Dillon on Muni. Cor., 3d ed., 319, and cases cited in notes.

CHAPTER XXXII.

" Equal and exact justice to all men, of whatever state or persuasion, religious or political."—JEFFERSON.

" But as the objects in view could not be attained if every measure conducive to them required the consent of every member of the society, the theory further supposes, either that it was a part of the original compact, that the will of the majority was to be deemed the will of the whole, or that this was a law of nature, resulting from the nature of political society itself, the offspring of the natural wants of man."—MADISON.

" Presume not, ye that are sheep, to make yourselves guides of them that should guide you ; neither seek ye to overslip the fold which they about you have pitched."—HOOKER.

" The illegal murder of one man by a tyrant is more pernicious than the death of a thousand by pestilence, famine, or any undistinguishing calamity."—HUME.

" Always towards perfection is the mighty movement,—towards a complete development and a more unmixed good ; subordinating in its universality all petty irregularities and fallings back, as the curvature of the earth subordinates mountains and valleys."—SPENCER.

" The very idea of the power and right of the people to establish government presupposes the duty of every individual to obey the established government."—WASHINGTON.

" Strange ! this interposition of God in human affairs, which even pagans had recognized, men reared amid the grand ideas of Christianity treat as superstition."—D'AUBIGNÉ.

" Which is the properest day to do good ? which is the properest day to remove a nuisance ? We answer, the very first day a man can be found to propose the removal of it ; and whoever opposes the removal of it on that day will (if he dare) oppose it on every other."—SYDNEY SMITH.

" Of all the great rights already won, they threw not an atom away. They went over Magna Charta, the Petition of Rights, the Bill of Rights, and the rules of the common law ; and whatever was found there to favor individual liberty they carefully inserted in their own system, improved

by clearer expression, strengthened by heavier sanctions, and extended by a more universal application. They put all those provisions into the organic law, so that neither tyranny in the executive nor party rage in the legislature could change them without destroying the government itself."
—J. BLACK.

A RULE which refuses to recognize the tie making this race an integral part of the human family, and disfigures the Fourteenth Amendment, is not a reasonable rule, for how can that be reasonable which overturns the foundation-stones of a newly-created, beautiful civil life, of individual honor, self-respect, sympathy, comfort, luxury, and all the finer environments of civic relationship? Civilized life cannot afford, under the mask of a reasonable rule, to contemn lawful power. The Fourteenth Amendment is the cardinal trust on which the very foundation of reorganized society in America reposes. If there is impatience of its authority and control; if that wicked disposition, like a pestilential virus, is creeping into the vital organs of American political society; does not the only safeguard of the state rest in the strict observance of its laws, popular or unpopular?

When the sublime conception, that all men are free and equal, which had shown its face for a moment, in the poetic abstraction of the Declaration of Independence, had at last descended to earth to dwell among men in the divinely illuminated actuality of the Fourteenth Amendment, the lofty rhetoric of the Supreme Court, transcending the usual grandiloquence of American oratory, drew perforce the minds of all men unto itself. It may be justly observed, that, if, in view of their former doctrines, the present opinions of any set of men are the lawful subjects of reproach, this fact goes far to show that such opinions are not conformable to right and reason. The drift and purpose of the Fourteenth Amendment are to be sought by reason, but that reason is no child of to-day's or yesterday's birth. At the advent of Civil Rights, the recorded wisdom of this household of liberty contained no hint of their present doctrine of the " free and untrammelled" "discretionary authority" of " reasonable rules" laid down by the public servant; and it is necessary to ransack every nook and corner of the universe of letters to discover wherein a rule not derived from the good and perfect laws of the Father of light, a rule which says, " Do not as thou wouldst be done by," is reasonable.

Some principles of reason are themselves so self-evident, that they universally obtain the recognition of all men in civil society; to deny them would be a palpable absurdity. One is, that the very soul of a political body—the force by which it is animated, set to work, and held together—is its government. No life fit for the dignity of man, no politic society, can exist without government. This very necessity of government presupposes the will of some members to be obstinate, rebellious, brutish, averse to all obedience, little better than a wild beast's. But it is the duty of government so to frame its laws that these members shall not destroy the common good, the peace and tranquillity, for which political society is instituted. Is the obstinate, rebellious member, who ordains rules violating the letter and spirit of the laws of government, reasonable?

Is it not clear, that nothing can be thoroughly understood, or soundly judged, until the first causes and principles from which it derives its value shall be brought to light? To judge soundly of the reasonableness of a rule is a weighty undertaking; and, if ripeness of judgment and patient labor of thought are required to interpret the meaning and intent of a statute, are they not infinitely more necessary in the discovery of reasons which shall set private regulations above the supreme law of the land?

Can there be *any* private reason in civil society for violating a public law? Is not the public power above every soul in the same society? Can the common law disregard those dictates of the Christian religion which are embodied in the Fourteenth Amendment? What is the meaning of the divine decree, " Let every soul be subject to the higher powers?" In the absence of any authority, it would seem that the Christian society of America, to be reasonable, must be guided by the spirit of Him who declared, " I am the way." " By me kings reign, and by me princes decree justice."

The state speaks audibly in this amendment, but that majestic creature, the *Public*, slots his ears, closes his eyes, and declares his own rules to be reasonable though they countermand the decree of the government under which he lives. That *jure-divino* monarchist, *the Public* in America, asserts with entire impunity the superiority of his private reason over the public law. Those great officials, the Cancellarius Magnus, the Lord Keeper of the Privy Seal, the Lord High Executioners of Civil Rights — the labor oligarchs and the public servants — have declared from their lofty seats, the highest sacks in the parliament of the republic, that the transformation of freedmen into citizens has only the colorable warrant of a constitutional amendment. The great civilians to whom the Supreme Court have intrusted the construction of the Fourteenth Amendment say, It is surely not one of the greatest events which has occurred in America. Grant that it has been worshipped at first by the Supreme Court as a god; whose front, like the giant's of the poet, was among the stars; that day could not weary him nor night arrest his progress. We have discovered that his limbs are paralytic. He is benighted, groping, weary, and ready to sink under the pillars of the temple of oppression which he has grasped.

Analogies and comparisons of many kinds disclose with tolerable clearness results which unite in the support and verification of the deductions of the true and clear principles of a rational law, and discover the meaning of a reasonable rule. But a momentary departure, to listen to the deep rich melodious voice of Mr. Gladstone, may here not be amiss. In an article in the *North American Review* for December, 1887, the great premier says,—

" Whatever be the place of actual man, the place of potential man in the hierarchy of creation is a very high one. History, complex and diversified as it is, and presenting to our view many a ganglion of unpenetrated and perhaps impenetrable enigmas, is not a mere congeries of disjointed occurrences; but is the evolution · of a purpose steadfastly maintained and advancing towards some consummation, greater probably than what the world has yet beheld, along with the advancing numbers, power, knowledge, and responsibilities of the race. That purpose is not always and everywhere alike conspicuous; but is it not like the river in the limestone tract, which vanishes from the surface and works its way beneath, only to reappear with renovated force? Or like the sun, which returns to warm us after the appointed space of night—

> ' And tricks his beams, and with new spangled ore
> Flames in the forehead of the morning skies ?'

Its parts are related to one another. The great lines of human destiny have every appearance of converging upon a point. As the Mosaic writer at the outset of Genesis declares the unity of the world, and as Doctor Whewell, in a passage of extraordinary magnificence, countersigns this testimony by predicting its catastrophe in the name of cosmic science; as, again, the mind of an individual, by the use of reflection, often traces one pervading scheme of education in the experiences of his life: so, probably, for the race, certainly for its great central web of design which runs unbroken from Adam to our day, there has been and is a profound unity of scheme well described by the poet Tennyson,—

> ' Yet I doubt not through the ages one increasing purpose runs,
> And the thoughts of men are widened with the process of the suns.'

" ' At sundry times, and in divers manners,' sometimes by conscious and sometimes by unconscious agency, this purpose is wrought out. Persons and nations who have not seen or known one another nevertheless co-operate and contribute to a common fund, available for their descendants and themselves. That, together with powers and resources, responsibilities must increase, is almost a truism. That there is such an increase in the sum total of powers and resources extraneous to ourselves appears also undeniable. It seems, then, as if the Almighty Ruler were now raising His claims upon His creatures, and demanding at last the larger usury which these larger gifts should earn. Whether there is a corresponding increase in the available brain-forces of the world and in its moral energies is a question perhaps only to be answered with some qualification, even some misgiving. But it will have been usefully put if it lead us to bow ourselves down as in the dust and ashes before the one Source of Strength, and if it remind us that the *humblest man* should also, under the *Christian dispensation,* be the *strongest man,* though it is in a strength not his own."

But to resume our argument. "It is one of the noblest properties of the common law that, instead of moulding the habits, the manners, and the transactions of mankind to inflexible rules, it adapts itself to the business and circumstances of the times, and keeps pace with the improvements of the age."[1] Must not a rule, to be reasonable, be in accord with this progressive spirit of the common law?

Reasonable rules, applied to civic rights, ignore present or previous conditions, intellectual training, habits, fashions, and all associations which engender civic, religious, social, or political antagonisms. The Abolitionist, the Free-soiler, the Union-shrieker, the Republican, the Secessionist, in their turn have been the subjects of social ostracism ; but no rule which discriminated against their civic equality in consequence of their political status would or could be deemed reasonable. The Protestant mutters between his teeth his contempt for what he regards as the mummeries of Rome, while the undoubting, demure believer in the successor of Saint Peter views with ill-suppressed disdain that shallow, reckless, heretical empiric in religion. But neither have ventured in America to maintain that rule to be reasonable which would discriminate against the immunities of either as a citizen.

The enlarged cautious minds of practical ability which construed the rudimental words of our Magna Charta measured all the profound depths of these sociological questions. They did not intrude upon their grave debates verbal cavils that had no more connection with fundamental expositions than the musty parchments or the ·black-letter *diablerie* of dusty, by-gone centuries. With broad, statesman-like views of reasonable rules, and an absence of all subtlety in their reasoning, ever leaning to the practical side of civil rights, after long and intense application, they exposed with consummate skill all the vulnerable points of their contemporaries who then took the same stand that the color-line brigade now insists upon establishing in America.

---

[1] Gibson, C. J , in Lyle *v.* Richards, 9 G. & R. 351.

Like William of Orange, they had a vocabulary no larger than was necessary for the transaction of business. But it embraced all the public rights of the citizens, and enabled those clear-minded, iron-handed jurists to find a broad and noble path to civil liberty by this amendment.

Civil liberty encountered in England the same antagonisms, on account of previous condition, as civil rights now encounter in America. Both were fashionable only in the more cultivated society of broader-minded constitutional lawyers. The leaders of that fashion in England and America were the patriots, statesmen, philosophers, and warriors who formulated its reasonable rules. And while the great masters of lingual fencing are rattling the dry bones of dead slavery in Hall *v.* DeCuir and the Civil-Rights Cases, reminding this race of the limited supply of civil right doled out to them during the reign of terror which preceded the outer darkness of Scott *v.* Sandford, the natural leaders of the state are watching in silent rumination the growth of this great plant of civil liberty. Like the fabled Igdrasil, it takes root in the soil of liberty, its trunk reaches upward towards the sky, its boughs are destined to cover the whole American race, while at its foot sit the Fates, watering its roots from the sacred well of civil liberty.

The letters-patent for universal emancipation from civil discrimination; the title-deeds to all the blessings of civil rights, free from encroachment, must be construed liberally in favor of the grantees. Any other rule bears upon its face the stigma of injustice. The tests which solve the reasonableness of the rules of the public must be those proposed and acted upon by the founders of civil liberty all over the world. But in effect the reasonable rules of the color-line brigade operate like the coercion acts of the English Tory ministry. They bring the national policy into disrepute, they tend to exhibit it as an utter failure, and they show that our great judicial magistrates have not comprehended the grandeur and majesty of the Fourteenth Amendment.

CHAPTER XXXIII.

" Sir, there have existed, in every age and in every country, two distinct orders of men,—the lovers of freedom, and the devoted advocates of power."—HAYNE.

" Try, therefore, the effect of such a gift; fling into the pre-existing caldron the whole list of recognized elementary substances, and give leave to their affinities to work."—MARTINEAU.

" If it be adjudged that the obligation to protect the fundamental privileges and immunities granted by the Fourteenth Amendment to citizens residing in the several States rests primarily, not on the nation, but on the States; if it be further adjudged that individuals and corporations, exercising public functions, or wielding power under public authority, may, without liability to direct primary legislation on the part of Congress, make the race of citizens the ground for denying them that equality of civil rights which the Constitution ordains as a principle of republican citizenship; then not only the foundation upon which the national supremacy has always securely rested will be materially disturbed, but we shall enter upon an era of constitutional law when the rights of freedom and American citizenship cannot receive from the nation that efficient protection which heretofore was unhesitatingly accorded to slavery and the rights of the master."—MR. JUSTICE HARLAN, C. R. C.

" Whoever, by virtue of public position under a State government, deprives another of property, life, or liberty without due process of law, or denies or takes away the equal protection of the law, violates the constitutional inhibition, and, as he acts under the name and for the State, and is clothed with the State's power, his act is that of the State. This must be so, or the constitutional prohibition has no meaning. But the constitutional amendment was ordained for a purpose. It was to secure equal rights to all persons, and, to insure to all persons the enjoyment of such rights, power was given to Congress to enforce its provisions by appropriate legislation."—ID.

" It is a maxim among these lawyers, that whatever has been done before may legally be done again; and, therefore, they take special care to record all the decisions formerly made against common justice and the general reason of mankind. These, under the name of precedents, they produce as authorities to justify the most iniquitous opinions; and the judges never fail of directing accordingly."—SWIFT.

356

" The characteristic excellence of the political system of the United States arises from a distribution and organization of its powers, which, at the same time that they secure the dependence of the government on the will of the nation, provide better guards than are found in any other popular government against interested combinations of a majority against the rights of a minority."—MADISON.

" The object and end towards which the people have moved has been the realization of a common end, and that the end of the being of the nation, the realization of freedom. The aim has been to place beyond all aggression the inalienable right of personality, the freedom of conscience and of thought, and to embody in more enduring institutions the rights of man ; and this in the course of the people has been increasingly apparent. The end was not the false and negative conception of what is called freedom, which was to exist only in their relative independence in respect to each other, a freedom of alienation and division ; but there was the unity of a moral aim, and for this the toil and conflict and sacrifice of years have been offered, and this has been given to the people."—MULFORD.

" And yet in all the movements of nations, there is a living principle which emanates from God. God is present on the vast stage on which the generations of men successively appear. True, He is there a God invisible ; but if the profane multitude pass carelessly by, because He is concealed, profound intellects, spirits which feel a longing for the principle of their existence, seek Him with so much the more earnestness, and are not satisfied until they are prostrated before Him. And their inquiries are magnificently rewarded. For, from the heights which they must reach in order to meet with God, the history of the world, instead of exhibiting to them, as to the ignorant crowd, a confused chaos, is seen like a majestic temple, on which the invisible hand of God himself is at work, and which, from humanity, as the rock on which it is founded, is rising up to His glory."—D'AUBIGNÉ.

" At her right hand sat Ignorance, her father and husband, blind with age ; at her left, Pride, her mother, dressing her up in the scraps of paper herself had torn. There was Opinion, her sister,—light of foot, hood-winked, and headstrong, yet giddy and perpetually turning. About her played her children, Noise and Impudence, Dulness and Vanity, Positive-ness, Pedantry, and Ill-manners. The goddess herself had claws like a cat ; her head and ears and voice resembled those of an ass ; her teeth fallen out before ; her eyes turned inward, as if she looked only upon herself ; her diet was the overflowing of her own gall ; her spleen was so large as to stand prominent, like a dug of the first rate ; nor wanted excrescences in form of teats, at which a crew of ugly monsters were greedily sucking ; and, what is wonderful to conceive, the bulk of spleen increased faster than the sucking could diminish it."—SWIFT.

"When, three years hence, we welcome that world upon our shores to another competition of proficiency in these arts, shall we be content with industrial superiority and material splendor? While our inventive genius, our swift civilization of a continent, may stir the wonder of a world, shall it not be our proudest boast, that, as the material miracle has been wrought under popular government, our greatest achievement is the moral miracle of the constant purification of that government by the virtue and intelligence of the people?"—CURTIS.

AT the institution of commonalties in the twelfth century, their charters contained immunities and privileges which formed the basis of their law and order, and introduced regular and equitable means of maintaining natural and political rights; and it is not extravagant to assert that they exhibited a moderation, impartiality, and deliberation, and an acquaintance with the human heart, which the "reasonable rules" of Hall *v.* DeCuir nowhere display. The question is not, whether the sovereign State through its executive, legislative, and judicial departments may defeat the provisions of the Fourteenth Amendment; but whether by any custom, rule, or regulation, which may yet be "*reasonable,*" an *individual* of a State can accomplish this result.

Such a primary juristical truth as that the law is deemed reason itself is undemonstrable. Therefore it follows that the law which the nation ordains must without demonstration be regarded as reasonable. So long as the law remains in existence, that without question must be held to be reasonable which the nation says a citizen must do or refrain from doing.

The amendment, voicing the convictions of the North, South, East, and West, granted this race freedom, and, creating them American citizens, gave unto them, and their descendants, the same constitutional immunities and privileges which the rest of the people constituting the nation enjoyed. Upward of forty millions of Americans executed the agreement. It was reduced to writing, and made part of their organic law. Is the intention of the millions who endorsed this national compact, through the constitutional majority of the States acting by their legislatures, to be defeated by the unreasonable rules of a minority so small that it is hardly capable of being rated? If, as the Supreme Court declares, "the Fourteenth Amendment can add nothing to the fundamental rights of a citizen, beyond the protection of those citizens in the enjoyment of an equality of rights," how, by any construction whatsoever, can the rule be deemed reasonable which deprives any citizen of his fundamental rights *as* a citizen?

A moment's calm analysis will show, that, instead of making the law sovereign, the unreasoning doctrine of Hall *v.* DeCuir surrenders its iron sceptre to every petty tyrant who may wield it, under the limitation solely of his discretion, to the full bent of his arbitrary will. This principle has clothed the public servant in America with the attributes of ancient royalty, for, according to Sallust, "To do whatever one has a mind to do, without fear of punishment, is to be a king." Conceive of the power thus committed to the public servant, whose name in America is Legion! Think of intrusting the construction of a constitutional amendment to a standing army of pigmy law-makers animated by the bitterness of race-grudge, sometimes without the understanding and frequently with more than the malice of an ape!

The doctrine of the rule is unreasonable because it confers upon the mere individual, jurisprudential power, and oftentimes places duty and interest in opposition to each other, thus leading into temptation those whose desires are influenced solely by their interests. It is difficult to conceive of a system more directly inviting the perpetuation of gross abuses, by its doors of subterfuge opening everywhere, than one which allows those who regard the profits of their business before everything to be party, judge, witness, jailer, and executioner.

Can any rule which thus puts into vogue the practices of ancient tyrants, which treats civil rights in the hands of one class of citizens as a base coin, be reasonable under the true construction of any provision of our American common law? When men are clothed with authority whose interest and chief study is simply how they can overthrow, not maintain, the law of the land, we ask, what ampler field for malpractice can partiality, injustice, pride, and tyranny desire? How can any system be reasonable in America which is so un-American? These people act as law-givers, without any code of well-reasoned truths, or formulated rules of action defining their authority.

The "*reasonable* rule of their free and untrammelled discretion" depends upon the levity, ignorance, and want of foresight of the maker. A rule so dependent is uncertain, precarious, and fluctuating ; and has left civil rights at the mercy of the temperament, character, and understanding of public servants who exercise a supreme authority over their fellow-citizens' public privileges, rights, and immunities.

Each of these Solons is an avowed assailant of constitutional liberty. The tranquillity of civil society, in his opinion, does not admit of equality and fraternity even among that portion of the family of mankind who compose one nation. On the contrary, he regards as more *reasonable,* just, politic, and wise those regulations which perpetuate between citizens of the same commonwealth a perennial internecine feud respecting the measure of their civil rights; in the view of the race legist, a rule which dethrones the Constitution, which displaces the written law, and makes the regulation of a mere creature of the law superior to the law itself, is reasonable ! If the sulks of race-prejudice regard the Fourteenth Amendment as ever so much a hateful innovation upon their received ideas, does that justify as reasonable a rule which commits the civil rights of seven millions of people to the discretion of those whose keenest sense of justice is stifled by an ingrained hatred of a race which they deem inferior, and who obstinately refuse to pave the way for the newer and more righteous system adopted by the American sense of justice?

Since the advent of Hall *v.* DeCuir, the science of Black Civil Rights throughout America has had no other nomenclature than the terms which this case affords. Since the publication of this code, under the shadow of the great name of Justice Clifford, there have been found no dikes or barriers to stem the torrent of illiterate prejudice which, like an insolent despotism, bears down all before it. Supported by this authority, the public servants of high and low degree impudently usurp and overturn the civil rights of these people, as if there were no Fourteenth Amendment. After a while, no doubt, they will have the temerity to assert that their immemorial usages, rights, and customs of adopting " reasonable rules," and " discretionary authority" in regard to African civil rights, are so ancient, that they require neither precedent, example, nor authority to justify them first in disregarding, and afterwards in abrogating, in part and in whole, the sacred provisions of the Fourteenth Amendment.

Would it not be as *reasonable*—and a more expeditious method of accomplishing their designs—to adopt a sixteenth amendment conferring upon the public servant in America the *Jura Regalia* of African civil rights? If they have such a supremacy over Justice as enables any tyrant to claim and usurp almost royal prerogatives, the public dominion over this race is little less extensive than that of the robber-chieftains under that able marauder, William the Conqueror. Which one of his brigands and bandits, savage in manners, debased in morals, and degraded in all his surroundings, could excel in barbarity the brainless, soulless, heartless atrocity of race-antagonism?—which, closing the heart to the gentle, piteous, humble human being bending under the accumulated weight of two centuries of oppression, illustrates the "free and untrammelled authority" of race-tyranny, when, in the ante-bellum jargon of a drunken demon, it interposes in mitigation and as an apologetic plea to the charge of manslaughter, "So help me God, sah, I never killed a nigger in my life, sah,—'ceptin' I war in liquor."

Though the opinion of the Supreme Court, and the separate opinion of Mr. Justice Clifford in Hall *v.* DeCuir, contain no more reference to it than to the edicts of the Prætor, the Stoic philosophy, the Twelve Tables, or the prophecies of the Apocalypse, they are in reality the far-reaching constructions which practically repeal the Fourteenth Amendment, by indirectly giving the public undefined supremacy over it. But all-powerful, unchangeable race-antagonism fails to discern that such a decision is a declaration of war against the essential truths of the Fourteenth Amendment, which are the only bulwark of civil rights, and a deterrent power from that scourge and pestilence of popular liberty,—the prevailing gross errors of the *ignobile vulgus*, which lead them to assail and jeer at the primal truths of a nation's polity. The skilled sophists of race-prejudice argue that such a rule may be *reasonable;* and that, if it involves discrimination in respect of the equality of civil rights, that result necessarily follows in part from a circumstance over which they have no control,—that manhood cast in the American mould cannot rise, as regards a purely civil right, above the ground-floor of race-prejudice.

Thus this demon of race-pride is perpetually pretending not to observe the approaches of reason and truth, although they are in sight. Its brood of hungry devils are daily eating out the life of American civilization. Its ignorant conceptions resemble the errors of the childhood of savagery. Cæsar and Tacitus tell us that according to the rules of primitive jurisprudence the principal persons of each district distributed justice as they fed chickens or pigs. The public at will throughout America are subjecting seven million citizens to the rules of slavery. Before Germany became a great nation, the Frank was judged by the law of the Frank, the German by the Germanic code. So it is to-day in America: the civil rights of citizens of African descent are judged by the customs of the separate States. If this system of Hall *v.* DeCuir is suffered to prevail, America shortly will resemble Italy, when there was an established Roman law, the Lombard law, the Riparian law, the Bavarian law; or the Eastern Empire, where the Hindoo law, Mohammedan law, Parsee law, and English law prevailed in different localities.

The defeat of civil rights by the manœuvre which gave to these servants the exposition of the law, because Congress had passed no act to enforce a civil right to travel in or between the States, bears a close analogy to the juristical hypocrisy by which the defeat of the English Statute of Entailment was effected. Judges who had prejudices against perpetuating landed estates eluded those statutes by the fiction of a common recovery. They practically ruled, like American courts in regard to this amendment, that, no statute of the English Parliament having forbidden the adoption of the rule of common recovery, the court was left free and untrammelled in its discretion to adopt any reasonable rule for the purpose of defeating the law of the land.

The great lawyers who flourished from Coke downward never conceived a more ingenious method of evading its provisions by leaving the construction of a great charter, which was the evidence of the good-will and of the national polity towards a newly enfranchised race, to the crooked and mischievous machinations, the cruel mutilations, and arbitrary encroachments of the public servants and labor classes, perhaps the most greedy and unscrupulous portion of the American people,—the very tyrants from whose dominion the amendment had sought to emancipate them. The savage irony of that explanatory jurisprudence which leaves the interpretation of this article not to legists or statists, but to illiterate, prejudiced classes, can find no parallel in the history of the jurisprudence of the nineteenth century. In fact, the edicts of the Roman tribunals whose incompetency led to proscriptions, and suspended law to glut the savage instincts of race-vengeance, are the only counterpart of the doctrines which in America to-day keep civil rights in abeyance.

Modern Jurisprudence under the Fourteenth Amendment, by ingenious devices, is succeeding in re-establishing the ancient rules of the ante-bellum code. The old-fashioned sin is being committed over again, in the new American way. Nor are historical parallels wanting. In the distinction and criteria established by the Roman church is to be seen much the same system of tactics as that which defeats civil rights: under the former there was no system of classifying venial and mortal sins but one of evasion, escape, and avoidance upon "reasonable rules." It is equally clear that caste-instinct during the reign of the later Stuarts flagrantly perverted justice by rules no less "reasonable" than those which now regulate civil rights in America.

The student of American political history must perceive at a glance, that theological influence has made itself felt throughout America never more than in the Fourteenth Amendment; that it was provided with a plastic, partly Christian, partly common-law terminology; that originally the Republican party was connected by ties of intellectual and moral environment with Christianity, and was in close communion with its principles, articles of faith, and creed; that the moral theology of the church gave birth to that party, just as the moral theology of the Reformation gave birth to Civil and Political Liberty. In the old world the moral theology of the Roman Catholic church, melting into casuistry, closely resembles the subtlety of the legal sophistry of Scott *v.* Sandford, Hall *v.* DeCuir, and other civil-rights cases.

CHAPTER XXXIV.

"The judges are not a privileged order: they have no shelter but their innocence."—BAYARD.

"My master was yet wholly at a loss to understand what motives could incite this race of lawyers to perplex, disquiet, and weary themselves, and engage in a confederacy of injustice, merely for the sake of injuring their fellow-animals."—SWIFT.

"The independence of the judiciary was the felicity of our Constitution. It was this principle which was to curb the fury of party on sudden changes. The first movements of power gained by a struggle are the most vindictive and intemperate. Raised above the storm, it was the judiciary which was to control the fiery zeal and to quell the fierce passions of a victorious faction."—ID.

"Political writers have established a maxim that in contriving any system of government, and fixing the several checks and controls of the Constitution, every man ought to be supposed a knave, and to have no other end in all his actions than private interests."—HUME.

"Why, Anaxagoras had to fly his country for having blasphemously asserted that the sun was not the chariot of the deity Helios."—SPENCER.

"How wicked (it is frequently said), how absurd and hopeless the enterprise, to make war upon *opinions!*"—BENTHAM.

"Slow are the steps of Freedom, but her steps never turn backward."—LOWELL.

"Grand as was the historical act of signing his decree of liberation, it was but an incident in the grander contest he was commissioned and resolved to maintain. That was an issue, not alone of the bondage of a race, but of the life of a nation, a principle of government, a question of primary human right."—NICOLAY AND HAY.

"That past which is so presumptuously brought forward as a precedent for the present, was itself founded on an alteration of some past that went before it."—DE STAËL.

"Of this kind were Epicurus, Diogenes, Apollonius, Lucretius, Paracelsus, Descartes, and others; who, if they were now in the world, tied
364

fast, and separate from their followers, would, in this our undistinguishing age, incur manifest danger of phlebotomy and whips and chains and
dark chambers and straw. For what man, in the natural state or course
of thinking, did ever conceive it in his power to reduce the notions of all
mankind exactly to the same length and breadth and height of his own?
Yet this is the first humble and civil design of all innovators in the empire
of reason."—SWIFT.

" We extol Bacon, and sneer at Aquinas : but if the situation had been
changed, Bacon might have been the Angelic Doctor."—MACAULAY.

" Alexandre Dumas the elder was of African descent. He was born on
July 24, 1802, in the village of Villers-Cotterets. His grandfather, a
Frenchman, the Marquis de la Pailletrie, was governor of San Domingo,
and married a negress named Tiennette Dumas."—BREWER.

IT is a matter of curious note, that the same absence of delicate sensitiveness and shrinking which marks the maturity of
the reign of jurisprudence in despotic ages and countries, is apparent in the jurisprudence of both Hall *v.* DeCuir and the
Civil-Rights Cases. To what but this absence of sensitiveness
and this blindness can defective jurisprudential vision be justly
attributed? It is well known to scholars that philosophy and
science are inhospitable to caste-prejudice. It is an unintelligent,
vagabondish vice. It has no vernacular, no speech, no mental
energy, thought, or depth. It does not require a severely-trained
mind to note that the intellectual diathesis which inclines to caste-
prejudice throws its film over all the faculties. This diseased
mental condition deprives the most advanced stage of intellectual
development of its normal power. The disputations of the
victims of this monstrous delusion are as absurd as those of
blind men respecting color.

They deal in wild speculations about what they see not ; and
reason, instead of being the moderator in their fantasies, stands
wholly apart. How are the blind to see? The novel set of
legal postulates introduced in Hall *v.* DeCuir, which completely
override the Fourteenth Amendment, and the older jurisprudence
of common carriers, illustrate this abnormal condition of blindness in the mental faculties, which cannot perceive that regulations in accord with the expansive ethical progress of the country

afford more rational rules of action than do the ancient dusty and sable-colored Dred-Scott regulations.

Nor is there any general, underlying, universal truth, upholding the scientific exercise of this prejudice, which by any reasonable principle or motive of action justifies the actual or constructive curtailment of the civil rights of this race.

That blindness is hopeless which does not perceive that civil degradation is not removed by insisting upon the observances which perpetuate it, and that the time has come when to maintain American institutions in their integrity the living principle of liberty must be planted in the breast of every citizen.

It seems clear, that the nation cannot afford always to keep this race infants under the pupilage of the jurisprudents of Hall *v.* DeCuir; that they must be made to advance concurrently with the other citizens, and be made producers and contributors to the common stock of the nation.

And great indeed must be the blindness which neither a bloody revolution nor the national sentiment can dissipate; which does not foresee that these retardations, instead of making civil rights stationary, or actually comatose, are the very means which will in a few years give additional definitiveness to the new and more progressive morality now prevailing in the ordering of the state, enlivening civilization, and giving it a fresher, quicker impulse.

To mental blindness what is true in the abstract is false in the concrete; what it assents to in theory it dissents from in fact. It is ready to agree with the language of the Republican party-platform of 1888, that "The name of American applies alike to all citizens of the Republic, and imposes upon all alike the same obligation of obedience to the laws. That citizenship is and must be the panoply and safeguard of him who wears it, and must protect him, whether high or low, rich or poor, in all his civil rights; that in a republic like ours, where the citizen is the sovereign and the official the servant, where no power is exercised except by the will of the people, it is important that the sovereign—the people—should possess intelligence"; when, however, it comes to practice, the Republican "color-line" is not willing to grant to the colored citizen any of the assistance and encouragement which this language implies and requires.

Civil rights are incapable of recognition wherever this mental blindness prevails. In fact, if not in theory, it is in America much the same as in the Congo State. The criminal nullification of the Fourteenth Amendment here is as open as the violation by Tippoo Tib of the laws of the nations against the slave-trade. The power of the one nullifier is, it seems, as incapable of physical, as is the other of legal limitation. The power of this savage over the slave-trade is not more absolute and unlimited than is the tyrannical authority exercised by the public in America over the civil rights of these citizens of the United States.

While national jubilees are being chanted in Brazil, and titles of nobility conferred on the prominent persons connected with the propagation and enactment of the measures which secured freedom to the slave ; while congratulations upon the auspicious event have flowed in from the whole civilized world ; Tippoo Tib, the extraordinary master of slave-transportation, reigns supreme in Congo, defying England and the civilized nations in league with her to their very face, by supplying the greater part of the Mohammedans with ship-loads of slaves whenever required, and in America the rights of freemen and citizens are being daily overridden by the pro-slavery rules of Hall *v.* De-Cuir and the Civil-Rights Cases which practically defeat the Fourteenth Amendment.

It is just as difficult to lower the crest of the color-line, and drive these simpletons from their fool's paradise in America, as it is for the thunder of the English guns to disturb that famous harpy who daily sits down to his unhallowed banquet upon human souls in Congo. To both these devotees of color-caste, slavery is an Elysium " empurpled with celestial roses." The American system of Hall *v.* DeCuir is only a new phase of the old Congo problem as now solved by Tippoo Tib.

The " reasonable rules" in Hall *v.* DeCuir declare, that this poisonous drug of hell shall not be banished ; that, in spite of the broad and expansive charter for all citizens, the white alone shall drink of heaven's sweet cup of liberty. These " reasonable rules" proclaim the survival and reorganization of much that seemed buried in the tomb of Civil War.

The mental blindness of race-antagonists cannot perceive that this pusillanimous surrender of civil rights reflects upon America but little less than slavery itself. In the by-gone days the portals of this great country shone forth to all, and shine to-day, inimitable on earth; but the foul stain remains upon the emblazonry of the land, by the attempt to perpetuate the degradation of this class of her citizens.

If they cannot perceive and feel this shame, they cannot see the blazing light of the sun throned on his meridian tower. Because they turn their backs upon civil liberty, they suppose that the brightness of that immortal " Amaranth"—

> " A flower which once in Paradise,
> Fast by the tree of life, began to bloom"—

has been swallowed up in the darkness of these days. Going back to the ideas and prejudices of the times of slavery, ignorance, and sloth, with all the contagious fervor of Asiatic paganism and bad enthusiasm, the color-line is deep in the work of the assassination of the Fourteenth Amendment. The goodly ornature of well-apparelled words and legal precedents under which the public servants masquerade are only the disguise of the fraudulent, foul impostors who bar the way to the just construction and true interpretation of the organic laws conferring civil rights.

Weaknesses in great minds often repeat themselves. It is remarkable that an intellect so profound as Bacon's should have doubted the rotation of the earth on its axis, after it had been affirmed by Copernicus, Kepler, and Galileo: so is it matter of wonderment that the wise and illustrious jurisconsult Taney, the meek, loving Christian, "about whom all the sanctities of heaven stood thick as stars," should have denied the doctrine of the inherent rights of man? The rankest weeds of prejudice grow in the richest soil; Copernicus himself, the boldest of theorists, believed in the most absurd contrivances of the Ptolemaic scheme. Is it not obvious that the erring judgments of these learned and enlightened men were the necessary sequences of prejudice? Still more remarkable is it, that, with the sun of civilization at its noonday splendor, mistakes not less extraordinary than the blunders of the Baconian age should be produced in America. It is still more startling, that these extraordinary anomalies of ignorance should have been received, accepted, and acted upon with the profoundest belief, as if they were truisms, and that too by the leaders of public thought in the Old World, as well as in the latest offspring of Time, the Republic just consecrated anew by a baptism of blood to the liberties of mankind.

A state of affairs analogous to the present demoralized position of civil rights in America has repeatedly shown itself, as all educated men know, in the history of every similar legal reformation. Asiatic paganism has exhibited the same exorbitant pretensions, the same antagonisms of privileged classes, which the color-line maintains in America. Can there be more serious controversy respecting the reasonableness of the modern than of the ancient caste-rules? Have not the pretensions of the ancient rules to reason long since been relegated by the historian of advancing civilization to the limbo of exploded errors, the vices and prejudices of barbarism? Are not both children of the same parents?

The rules of caste, new and old, if reintroduced, must ever refuse a cheerful recognition of humanity. Let the heathen idiot, with all his trumpery, bow down and worship these relics of the past, protean in form and shape—

> "If shape it might be called, which shape had none
> Distinguishable in member, joint, or limb,
> Or substance might be called, that shadow seemed."

But let the man of to-day, dwelling in the broad fields and "pastures green" of a higher civilization, slough off all the worn-out notions and distinctions of a world the fashion of which has passed away, and stand forth, the assertor and defender of the equality of civil rights for all men of all races.

And yet some of the professed followers of Christ in America are as wedded to their dark idolatry as any Asiatic. Devout worshippers in gorgeous temples forget the brotherhood of man

proclaimed by Him who preached in the open air to whoso-
ever would hear, and whose place of prayer was the wilderness
or the garden of Gethsemane. These mistaken followers of
the Man who died for all men regard the civic rights of the new
citizen of America as the legitimate subject of legal sophistry.
Sending missionaries to convert Islam, they have not yet learned
that charity begins at home.

It is indeed strange, but it is indisputable, that in the nineteenth century jurisprudence arrayed with all the technology and
dialectics with which the separate opinion in Hall *v.* DeCuir
abounds, should be able to afford no adequate conception of the
philanthropic principle and conception of the Fourteenth Amendment. Mr. T. U. Dudley fittingly and feelingly invokes that
spirit of Christianity-loving, liberty-loving America, which is
embodied in the Fourteenth Amendment, when, in the spirit
alike of the constitutional amendment and of Christianity, he
exclaims,—

"Still the problem remains, how shall these alien races dwell
in safety side by side, each free and unhampered in the enjoyment of life and liberty and in the pursuit of its happiness?
They are the descendants of one father, the redeemed children
of one God, the citizens of one nation, neighbors with common
interests ; and yet are separated by the results of centuries of
development, physical, mental, and moral,—separated by inherited traditions, by the spirit of caste, by the recollection of
wrongs done and suffered, though it may be, in general as innocent in the perpetrator as in the sufferer. How shall the rights
of all be duly guarded ? How shall the lower race be lifted up
to higher stages of human development?—for only so can the
rights of the superior race be made secure for the present and
for the future, and this is the chiefest right of them who are
now cast down.

" White men of the South" (and of the North, with equal
truth the learned writer might have added), " what answer shall
we, the intelligent, the cultured, the powerful, the inheritors of
noble traditions and of splendid ideas,—what answer, I ask in the
name of the God of freedom and of humanity, shall we make to
these men ? The solemn sanctions of the organic law are thrown

around about this liberty, and the robe of citizenship, full, perfect, and complete, with never seam nor rent, has been put upon it. The courts have declared its inviolable character, and this decree affirms the negro, the liberated slave, a citizen." " Declared Christians, as declared citizens, they need help—personal, individual, tender, persistent—to enable them to become such in any true sense." It is too obvious for serious controversy that, as it received its figure from the original architect, the Fourteenth Amendment must stand in the temple of American liberty, unmutilated, or fall " majestic in its ruin" under the inexcusable blows of the portentous barbarism of race-rancor, " fierce as ten furies, terrible as Hell."

CHAPTER XXXV.

"But on the part of an aristocratical body, of the surrender of any the minutest particle of power which they were able to retain, where is there as much as any one example to be found?"—BENTHAM.

"Perhaps, sir, you will permit me to remind you, that it is almost always in company with those considerations that interest the *heart* in some way or other, that encroachment steals into the world. A bad purpose throws no veil over the license of power. It leaves them to be seen as they are. It affords them no protection from the inquiring eye of jealousy. The danger is when a tremendous discretion like the present is attempted to be assumed, as on this occasion, in the names of pity, of religion, of national honor and national prosperity; when encroachment tricks itself out in the robes of piety, or humanity, or addresses itself to pride of country, with all its kindred passions and motives. It is then that the guardians of the Constitution are apt to slumber on their watch, or, if awake, to mistake for lawful rule some pernicious arrogation of power."—PINCKNEY.

"It is the course of principalities and powers, not of the government of freemen."—MULFORD.

"This freedom in every field is the condition of moral strength. In it the bondage of the animal is overcome, and 'the ape and tiger' die."—ID.

"The Constitution regulates our stewardship: the Constitution devotes the domain to union, to justice, to welfare, and to liberty."—SEWARD.

"Mankind, considered as brethren, should be dear to each other; but fellow-citizens who have together braved the common danger, who have fought side by side, who have mingled their blood together, as it were in one rich stream, who have labored and toiled with united efforts to accomplish the same glorious end, must surely be more than brethren: it is a union cemented by blood."—BOUDINOT.

"Do you rely on that popular will which has brought us frail beings into political existence? That opinion is but a changeable thing. It will soon change."—GOUVERNEUR MORRIS.

"What idols may successively be worshipped by the changing spirit of time, which easily bounds from one extreme to another, cannot be determined beforehand."—SCHLEGEL.

372

"If it was possible for men who exercise their reason to believe, that the divine Author of our existence intended a part of the human race to hold an absolute property in, and an unbounded power over, others, marked out, by his infinite goodness and wisdom, as the objects of a legal domination never rightfully resistible, however severe and oppressive, the inhabitants of these colonies might at least require from the Parliament of Great Britain some evidence that this dreadful authority has been granted to that body."—DICKINSON.

"Liberty which must be guaranteed not only by the letter of the law, but by real, effective, and practical measures."—SCHLEGEL.

"These considerations should lead to an attentive solicitude to keep the pure, unadulterated principles of our Constitution always in view."—BOUDINOT.

"By the new amendments to the Constitution the freedmen became a part of the people, and all the purposes for which it was made and established are to be deemed to have them in view, and to contemplate their protection and benefit as a part of the body politic."—COOLEY.

"The equality of rights, which includes an equality of burdens, is a vital principle in our theory of government, and its jealous preservation is the best security of public and individual freedom."—RUFUS KING.

"From none was this patriotic spirit more to be looked for than from those who, knowing most, experimentally, the price paid for our independence, must be the last to suffer its attributes to be impaired in its descent to their posterity. A free people, firmly united in a just cause, can never despond either of inspiring respect for their rights, or of maintaining them against hostile invasions."—MADISON.

"Be not you of so mean a soul as to fear the downfall of grammar and the confusion of the signification of words to that degree as to betray the liberty of mankind and the state, rather than your glossary should not hold water. And know for the future, that words must be conformable to things, not things to words. By this means you will have more wit, and not run on *in infinitum*, which now you are afraid of."—MILTON.

"False images from the tinsel kingdom of sophistry."—BACON.

MORE than three-fourths of the States of the Union having ratified the Fourteenth Article of Amendment to the Constitution, and empowered Congress to enforce its provisions by appropriate legislation, in execution of the authority thus conferred (which must be construed to mean duty and obligation), Congress, by a series of enactments, undertook to enforce its original principles of liberty, justice, and right. The object of the Civil-Rights Bills and Enforcement Acts was to put the State upon its true foundation,—a society for the establishment and administration of justice, equal and fixed, to all ; recognizing individual rights, not imparting them. Congress, having in mind these ends, sought to remove every obstacle which impeded, impaired, or diminished the usefulness of the colored race as citizens. It declared that they should not remain in a condition of permanent disability. The national legislature by broad rules endeavored to insure impartial legal protection. It declared that all American citizens were embraced in this amendment, and were equally entitled to the paternal consideration and protection of the government: that any other construction of the amendment would turn this part of the Constitution into mere nonsense, falsify long-established rules of interpretation, and assail the very foundation of a government whose fundamental idea was the equality of all its citizens.

The Civil-Rights Bill of 1875 declared that discriminations against persons, based upon grounds purely arbitrary and not recognizable by law, made solely because of certain physical characteristics, which in no way affected their capacity or fitness for the privileges and immunities of citizenship, were unlawful violence, and made them statutory crimes, inhibited by penalties of fine and imprisonment. Its aim was to compass the overthrow of all unbridled authority and of that arbitrary power which sought in any form to deprive these citizens of their civil rights. Its chief postulates were, that no particular color, religion, rank, nor class was exclusively entitled to occupy one or the other side of the edifice of Freedom ; that the royal patrimony—the inheritance of equality of right—was not susceptible of partition or diminution by rules based upon invidious distinctions ; that impartial legal protection was the right of every individual, whose life was interwoven with the civil fabric of the State; that the welfare of the nation required that the benefits of the general laws which govern society should be portioned out in equal shares to every one of its individual members; and all the congeries of hereditary tendencies begotten of slavery—its feelings, passions, and heart-burning jealousies—were declared to be not only *mala prohibita* but also *mala in se.* Those powerful factors of strife under this law represented no longer a scintilla of legal right.

By a prohibition as fundamental and decisive as that which prevented the territorial expansion of slavery, this legislation obliterated the arbitrary 36° 30' line of the slavery-caste, and extended throughout the continent the doctrine of the equality of man, notwithstanding his color. It destroyed every vestige of those images of pro-slavery worship whose feet had been worn by the kisses of the faithful; it buried in the outlying dumps of civilization its foul, fetish creeds, relics, and rituals, and, consigning to eternal oblivion its Baal and Moloch, it interred forever the remains of slavery in the sealed chamber of silence.

We have already seen that the Supreme Court, by a dash of its pen, has in effect erased this beneficent legislation from the statutes at large of the United States. A divided court determined that its self-evident postulates of freedom exceeded the line of constitutional limitation. The philosophic sages of Hall *v.* DeCuir, who out of the abundance of their legal stores contributed so largely to the learning of the profession in their researches beyond the record, did not with circumambulating caution travel backward, however, to investigate how far the Emancipation Proclamation overstepped the boundaries of the Constitution; nor to inquire whether the payment of the national debt, either in coin or in legal-tender paper, transcended constitutional limitation. They did not go the length of determining that the five hundred thousand and more of the country's bravest and best, who, noble and dauntless as the immortal three hundred at Thermopylæ, freely gave their lives that the nation might live, had *died unconstitutionally*, because the doctrine of the equality of man, for which they had contended and perished, was impossible of enforcement in America "unless" (according to Hall *v.* DeCuir) "our commercial marine shall undergo an entire change." Nor did the learned justices consider how far in excess of constitutional authority pensions were voted to save the grim, scattered remnants of our veterans from begging their bread "through realms their valor saved."

Be all this as it may, upon the memorable voyage from New Orleans to the Hermitage, the Supreme Court gave its sign-manual to the death-warrant of Civil Rights. It exculpated the hireling assassin of Civil Rights, who did the deed, upon the special plea, as we have seen, that he was a magnate of the realm, and, though a public servant, was as such justified under the common or civil law prevailing in the State. In this decision the judicial magistrate of the government reproaches the legislative department. He makes Congress, as we have seen, by reason of its inaction accessory, before and after the fact, to a criminal nullification of this Article.

The supreme judicial magistrate of the nation was in grave doubt, whether in fact any crime had been committed by the public servant of which, under constitutional limitation, his court could take cognizance; subsequently, in the Civil-Rights Cases, the jurisdiction of the court under this act of Congress, because it stepped into the State domain, was denied. The court, indeed, was at some pains to prove, that the *ex-parte* arraignment, trial, and execution of Civil Rights by Benson, the master of transportation, without due process of law, was not a foul betrayal of the spirit and letter of this Article. The grave argument is that the assassin cannot be indicted " unless the whole merchant marine undergoes a change" of those rules which obtained during the Dred-Scott *régime;* that this " is impossible;" that the public servant is not obliged by constitutional law to conquer his prejudices, but that he is authorized by the inaction of Congress to blink at and purposely disregard the amendment, without being guilty of a criminal assault upon Civil Rights; because this Article was not intended, as generally supposed, to guarantee a negation of arbitrary power which, in any form, should result in a deprivation of the civil rights of any citizen.

The Supreme Court at the time of this decision favored a departure from the spirit of this provision, as interpreted when " Civil Rights" was a more fashionable and a more presentable personage at the Republican Court. Its purpose is too plain to admit of doubt. By accrediting the public servant with extraordinary, far-reaching, all-pervading powers, fundamental in character, it has enabled him to attain " free and untrammelled authority," " by reasonable rules," and in his discretion, radically to change the legal status of Civil Rights, the latest-born, fairest daughter of the Republican party, to whom the nations of the earth brought gifts, and whom America gladly accepted, and, placing upon her brow what seemed to them a queenly crown, fell down and worshipped.

Although the rules of the common law governing common carriers favor equality of rights, and are in singular accord with the simple, majestic provisions of this Article; although both recognize the same equality of right, it cannot have escaped observation that, throughout this strange decision, any reference to the Fourteenth Amendment, or to a definition of the term " reasonable," as in accord with a Christian, constitutional, political, economic interpretation of the same, has been scrupulously avoided. As we have seen, this Article provides, that " All persons born or naturalized in the United States, and subject to the jurisdiction thereof, are citizens of the United States. No State shall make or enforce any law which shall abridge the privileges or immunities of citizens of the United States, nor deprive any person of life, liberty, or property without due process of law, nor deny to any person within its jurisdiction the equal protection of the laws." And Article IV., Section 2 of the Constitution provides, that " the citizens of each State shall be entitled to all privileges and immunities of citizens in the several States."

The issue was thus broadly presented; and apparently, the terms being so plain, there should and could be no suppression or avoidance of the real question, which involved the constitutional exercise of a civil right to travel between the States. The naked question thus presented is ably stated by an eminent publicist, Mr. Cable, who says,—

" Yet, with all the facts behind us, we cannot make and enforce that intelligent and approximately just assortment of persons in public places and conveyances on the merits of exterior decency that is made in all other enlightened lands. On such a plea are made a distinction and separation that not only are crude, invidious, humiliating, and tyrannous, but which do not reach or come near their ostensible end ; and all that saves such a plea from being a confession of drivelling imbecility is its speciousness. It is advanced sincerely ; and yet nothing is easier to show than that these distinctions on the line of color are really made not from any necessity, but simply for their own sake ; to preserve the old arbitrary supremacy of the master-class over the menial, without regard to the decency or indecency of appearance or manners in either the white individual or the colored. It insists upon the time-worn formula that expediency makes a more imperative demand than law, justice, or logic, and demands the preservation of the old order." "Somebody must be outraged, and if not the freedman then it must be a highly refined and enlightened race of people constantly offended and grossly discommoded, if not imposed upon, by a horde of tatterdemalions, male and female, crowding into a participation in their reserved privileges."

The specialization of Mr. Sumner's Civil-Rights Bill, which had at the time the authority of a statute of the United States, though its construction was not involved in the case, was yet before the court. His bill had solved in 1875, in the same way as had the framers of the Massachusetts Body of Liberties in 1641, the great issues which were presented, in words full of justice and wisdom,—

"The free fruition of such liberties, immunities, and privileges as humanity, civility, and Christianity call for as due to every man, in his place and proportion, without impeachment or infringement, hath ever been and ever will be the tranquillity and stability of churches and commonwealths ; and the denial or deprival thereof, the disturbance, if not the ruin, of both."

The stupendous issue presented in Hall v. DeCuir then pressed upon advancing civilization in America for solution, and confronts it to-day ; just as freedom and slavery confronted each other during the "irrepressible conflict" in the days of bondage. This grave issue, we say, hung trembling in the balance of Hall v. DeCuir, when, by a verbal contrivance of but little real enlightenment, Mr. Justice Clifford avoided it, and delivered Civil Rights, bound hand and foot, into the camp of the Public Servant of America. The capture was effected through an avoidance, and the avoidance was in the nature of a special demurrer, which, confessing the law of the "equality" of rights, privileges, and immunities, denied that *equality* of right, privilege, and immunity meant "*identity*" of right, privilege, and immunity.

As this special demurrer mounts up to the first fault in the long musty records of freedom, if sufficient in law, it strikes a blow so terrible, it must shake from foundation-stone to turret the superstructure of Civil Rights, and imperil Civil Liberty itself in America, through a grammatical or etymological controversy respecting the import of the word "equality"; which, far from being of uncertain etymology, or of shadowy or fugitive sense, is an organic term of noble lineage, a term which has attained, by universal consensus, a deep, rich, politico-civil and ethical significance (as if its very texture had been woven in the loom of heaven), which the household of Liberty, from prehistoric ages downward, has adopted, as having a meaning as expansive, everlasting, infinite, deep, and immeasurable as the soul of man itself. In fact, the word "equality" is the most auspicious in the historical life of the world, a truly royal word which has been formative and representative in the maintenance of freedom, in the development of the historical process, and in the progress of nations. It is a revelation of truth in the light of a clear understanding, and embraces all the knowledge of freedom which the sons of men have gathered through the cycles of time.

Rejected in all its aspects, grammatical, civil, political, and etymological, by the governments of the Old World, it was brought by the Pilgrim Fathers in the Mayflower to the New, and, having always (in the slow and long advance of humanity) been identified in America with civil and religious freedom, it suggested to her statesmen, on the eventful day of the Declaration of Independence, the doctrine, that "all men are born free and equal." Its latest, best meaning was well illustrated in America by the breaking down of the barriers of that opprobrious scheme

of shame—slavery—and taking from it the keys of Death and
Hell. In the American Civil War it became the watchword
of that mighty phalanx of kindred spirits, which, like a bright
constellation of stars moving in the same direction, and impelled
by the same cause, seemed to reflect on earth the thought of
God in heaven. That illustrious assemblage of the friends of
mankind first drew aside the curtain of time, and showed to
an admiring world the sublime picture of American Equality,
purchased by blood. Thenceforth, and until the coming of
Hall *v.* DeCuir, this word, "equality," had been the foundation and the chief corner-stone of the national edifice; but if
Mr. Justice Clifford's demurrer shall be sustained, the American
doctrine of "equality before the law" will stand, like the obe-
lisks and pyramids, a silent mystery for future generations to
ponder.

It is too obvious for controversy, that civil rights, agreeably
to the doctrine of Hall *v.* DeCuir, must stand or fall in America
according to the interpretation of the word "*reasonable*" as applied to the regulations of the public servant, and the meaning
of the word "*equality*" as definitive of the rights, privileges,
and immunities of American citizens. There is a recognizable
coherence in this word, which renders its scientific decomposition,
by any judicial process of volatilization, beyond the most subtle
action of the intellectual battery. Through the noblest and
darkest pages of history, the philosophic seer can discern the
principle of "equality" wrestling like a giant, in the arena of
intellect, with the thoughts of mankind.

CHAPTER XXXVI.

" John Hampden's motto was, *Vestigia nulla retrorsum :* so let ours be in this momentous time,—No step backward, but on, on ; in the field and in the senate ; in our aims and in our acts ; in our national rights and duties, calling and justice ; in all the work before us and around us."—LIEBER.

" Liberty is slow fruit."—EMERSON.

" The original proclamation has no constitutional or legal justification, except as a military measure. The exemptions were made because the military necessity did not apply to the exempted localities. Nor does that necessity apply to them now any more than it did then. If I take the step must I not do so without the argument of military necessity, and so without any argument except the one that I think the measure politically expedient and morally right ? Would I not thus give up all footing upon Constitution or law ? Would I not thus be in the boundless field of absolutism ? Could this pass unnoticed or unresisted ? Could it fail to be perceived that, without any further stretch, I might do the same in Delaware, Maryland, Kentucky, Tennessee, and Missouri, and even change any law in any State ?"—LINCOLN.

" Happily, there is a conservative and patriotic public intelligence which is the sure and invincible bulwark of popular institutions, because it saves popular impulse from its own excesses. When that intelligence fails, the republic ends. But that it is not failing our recent history shows."—CURTIS.

" Liberty is no negation : it is a substantive, tangible reality."—GARFIELD.

" Nothing that the worst men ever propounded has produced so much oppression, misgovernment, and suffering as this pretence of State necessity. A great authority calls it ' the tyrant's devilish plea,' and the common honesty of all mankind has branded it with everlasting infamy."—J. BLACK.

" I will only give you one instance of the use and the abuse of words, and leave it with you for your entertainment : from which you will draw a variety of arguments and conclusions.

> ' And soft he sighed, lest men might him hear.
> And soft he sighed, that men might not him hear.
> And soft he sighed, else men might him hear.

    Unless he sighed soft, men might him hear.
    But that he sighed soft, men might him hear.
    Without he sighed soft, men might him hear.
    Save that he sighed soft, men might him hear.
    Except he sighed soft, men might him hear.
    Outcept he sighed soft, men might him hear.
    Outtake he sighed soft, men might him hear.
    If that he sighed not soft, men might him hear.
    And an he sighed not soft, men might him hear.
    Set that he sighed not soft, men might him hear.
    Put case he sighed not soft, men might him hear.
    Be it he sighed not soft, men might him hear.' "—TOOKE.

" O ridiculous birth! a mouse crept out of the mountain! Help, grammarians! one of your number is in danger of perishing! The law of God and of nature are safe, but Salmasius's dictionary is undone."—MILTON.

"I decline to use the word 'impossible,'—that *bête de mot* with which that other stupid word 'incredible' might fitly be run, in couples."—ALEXANDER.

" In metaphysical controversy, many of the propositions propounded and accepted as quite believable are absolutely inconceivable. There is a perpetual confusing of actual ideas with what are nothing but pseudo-ideas. No distinction is made between propositions that contain real thoughts, and propositions that are only the forms of thoughts. A thinkable proposition is one of which the two terms can be brought together in consciousness under the relation said to exist between them."—MARTINEAU.

" *Shepard.*—Wull a' the metaphizzians in the warld ever expound that mysterious monosyllable?
" *Tickler.*—Monosyllable, James, did ye say?
" *Shepard.*—Ay, monosyllable; does na that mean a word of three syllables?
" *Tickler.*—It's all one in Greek, my dear James."—NORTH.

" That Chance ('high arbiter,' as Milton calls him), and his twin-brother, Accident, are merely the participles of *Escheoir, Cheoir*, and *Cadere*. And that to say, 'It befell me by chance, or by accident,' is absurdly saying, 'It fell by falling.' "—TOOKE.

"I was never so bethumed with words, since first I called my brother's father dad."—SHAKESPEARE.

"You must borrow me Gargantua's mouth first; 'tis a word too great for any mouth of this age's size."—ID.

" There may be in the physical distinction of races the elements of diversitude, and of an ampler and more opulent culture and character, and the physical laws and properties of races are to be studied and not to be disregarded ; but to assert the identity of the nation with a race is to assume for it a physical foundation, and involves the denial of its moral unity and moral order. If the utmost that language and architecture and every mode of culture may indicate, be allowed to racial characteristics, the conclusion yet remains, which has the universality of a law, that there may be the widest possible contrast in respect to civilization in the same race, alike in the same age, or in mainly the same condition of soil and climate in succeeding ages, and that this contrast will be in exact proportion to the development of the life of the nation."—MULFORD.

" I stand upon all just principles of law and reason."—PINCKNEY.

" And in another place, to the herald of Thebes, 'In the first place,' says he, 'you begin your speech, friend, with a thing that is not true, in styling me a monarch : for this city is not governed by a single person, but is a free state ; the people reign here.' "—MILTON.

" To advise your client, it was less important to be skilled in the books than to be acquainted with the character of the judge who was to preside. When the term approached, the inquiry was, what judge are we to have?" —BAYARD.

" Power is irresponsible when it acts upon those who are defenceless against it ; who cannot check it, or contribute to check it, in its exercise, who can resist it only by force."—PINCKNEY.

" I know only one country and one sovereign,—the United States of America and the American people."—SEWARD.

" In pleading, they studiously avoid entering into the merits of the cause, but are loud, violent, and tedious in dwelling upon all circumstances which are not to the purpose. For instance, in the case already mentioned, they never desire to know what claim or title my adversary has to my cow ; but whether the said cow were red or black, her horns long or short, whether the field I graze her in be round or square, whether she was milked at home or abroad, what disease she is subject to, and the like ; after which they consult precedents, adjourn the cause from time to time, and in ten, twenty, or thirty years, come to an issue."—SWIFT.

" Where the spirit of the Lord is, there is liberty."—EPISTLE TO THE CORINTHIANS.

" It is as plain as the noonday sun that without constitutional morality every pretence of patriotism must be false and counterfeit. The man who says he loves his country, and yet strikes a fatal blow at the organic law upon which her life depends, shows his sincerity as Nero proved his filial affection when he killed his mother and mutilated her body."—J. BLACK.

"With disputations as subtle and abstract as those of an Angelic doctor on a theological mystery."—BROUGHAM.

"The cold impartiality of a neutral judge."—BURKE.

IT cannot escape the critical observer, that the language of this demurrer has not a full, deep, noble, earnest ring about it. The words, "equality is not identity," are neither pertinent nor pungent. This obvious negative truism, "Equality does not mean identity," inserted in a judicially-formulated opinion, is rather thin and pale; as if the changing of phrases could alter the real nature of principles! But, although in itself, from every standpoint, an expression of ephemeral triviality, it has yet been fraught, as we have seen, with deepest consequence. So fateful an hallucination cannot be met without astonishment, or left without disapproval. Viewed as an argument of spectacles in which there are no glasses, it borders upon the ludicrous, having an unconscious irony not infrequent in learned, deep, thoughtful minds, which overshoot the mark; it would be laughable were its consequences less lamentable.

It is alike curious and interesting to note, in this connection, that since the confusion which has resulted from Mr. Justice Clifford's interpretation of the words "identity" and "equality," certain followers of a German Roman-Catholic priest, the Rev. Father Johann Martin Schleyer, of Constance, Baden, gravely argue, it is said, in favor of the adoption, in America, of Volapük, as a language better adapted to the purposes of common sense than the English: and not without some show of reason; since they insist that the rights of seven millions of Americans have been held in degradation on account of the uncertain meaning of the word "equality," and of its liability to confusion with that of "identity." They contend that this proves the English to be less certain than the Chinook jargon, compounded of English, French, possibly Russian, and the Si-wash dialect. They argue that in clarification, majesty of style, and elevation of thought, " *Mayed stula e subin tikas alegaloms, de Hall v. De-Cuir,*" compares favorably with the phraseology, " Equality does not mean identity ;" that the disastrous consequences which have resulted to seven millions of people from the confusion of these terms demonstrate the superiority of Volapük " *Aluato,*" or " *Pasi Linqua,*" over the incomprehensible English terms employed in Hall *v.* DeCuir ; and that the Volapük dictionary contains but thirteen thousand words, a lesser number than was actually employed in the unprofitable diligence of Mr. Justice Clifford's opinion. They argue, that this confusion in the meaning of terms proves the need of the more simplified and categorically regular Volapük language. Its disciples insist that the regular formation of adjective, verb, and adverb from a substantive root by certain definite terminations, allowing no exceptions, and the perfect regularity of the artificial language in other ways, render it impossible that the civil rights of a kitling, defined in Volapük, could be exposed to the grievous peril of a construction by the Supreme Court of the United States of those runic enigmas, " *equality and identity.*"

The *imprimatur* of the Supreme Court has been given to this doctrine as a sound exposition of our Constitution and of the law of common carriers. The inferior courts have followed it ; and it needs no argument to show that it has been the fruitful source of all those dire evils which have overtaken civil rights since their passage over the Red Sea of civil war. To whatever parentage this misbegotten progeny of Hall *v.* DeCuir may legitimately be traced, certain it is that it did not spring from the loins of the Constitution, nor was it the lawful issue of that noble sire of Civil Liberty, " Equality according to the Law of the Land." Whoever is familiar with the features of this illustrious family will find no trace of resemblance in them to those of this fruitful Mother of Evil, from whose Pandora-like box Hope fled at last. The dullest perception will readily observe that there is not the slightest similarity in their mien, air, or aspect. On the contrary, the experienced guardians who keep watch over the standards of Civil Liberty, all over the world, will at a glance discern, both in the mother and her

fatal brood, who stand alike ready to devour Civil Rights, a
marked family likeness to the Porteress of the dread abyss, and
to her offspring, as they appear surrounded with lurid light on
the dark canvas of Milton's Hell.

> " Before the gates there sat
> On either side a formidable shape ;
> The one seemed woman to the waist, and fair,
> But ended foul in many a scaly fold,
> Voluminous and vast, a serpent armed
> With mortal sting ; about her middle round
> A cry of hell-hounds never ceasing barked,
> With wide Cerberean mouths full loud, and rung
> A hideous peal ; yet, when they list, would creep,
> If aught disturbed their noise, into her womb,
> And kennel there, yet there still barked and howled,
> Within unseen."

The doctrine that " Equality does not mean identity," opened
the door which the Fourteenth Amendment, the Civil-Rights
Bill, and the Enforcement Acts had striven to close forever.
The significance of this decision cannot be exaggerated. Ever
since the promulgation of its doctrines, the public servants daily
throughout the land, by subjecting them in the exercise of *one*
civil right to humiliating discriminations, thereby attach to the
enjoyments of this race of their every civil right, privilege, and
immunity, upon both private and public occasions, the very same
conspicuously humiliating badges, the degrading customs and provisions, ignominious marks, conditions, and ceremonials, which
under the ante-bellum black code were notoriously constituent,
visible signs, and significant brands, definitive of the immeasurable distance which separated equality of right, privilege, and
immunity, inherent in the illustrious state of freedom, from the
inferior, debased, low, and sunken inequality of the same right,
immunity, and privilege legally attaching to the status or condition
of slavery.   Thus the public servant is enabled to enforce his
tyrannical usurpation over " equality" of right, privilege, and
immunity, under the specious doctrine, as we shall hereafter see,
that " Equality does not mean identity."

The practical, natural, and necessary outcome of the doctrine,
that " Equality does not mean identity," has been to re-enact, in

America, wherever and whenever a civil right, immunity, and privilege is exercised by this race, the Louisiana black code, which says, "that free people of color ought never to presume to conceive themselves equal to the white, but, on the contrary, that they ought to yield to them on every occasion, and never speak to or answer them but with respect, under the penalty of fine or imprisonment, according to the nature of the offence." The "equality-not-identity" theory is aptly illustrated by Mr. Cable, who says,—

"We allow the man of color to go and come at will, only let him sit apart in the place marked off for him. But marked off how? So as to mark *him* instantly as a menial. Not by railings and partitions merely, which, raised against any other class in the United States with the same invidious intent, would be kicked down as fast as put up, but by giving him besides, in every instance and without recourse, the most uncomfortable, uncleanest, and unsafest place. It is no longer a question of endurance between one group of States and another, but between the moral *débris* of an exploded evil, and the duty, necessity, and value of planting society firmly upon universal justice and equity."

This specious verbal sophism, "Equality is not identity," has disseminated far and wide the seeds of judicial error. Dressed up in the garb of antithetical phrase, it wears the semblance of profound wisdom, of coy impartiality, and seems the key of approaching knowledge, but its immediate effect was to set on sharper edge the teeth of the lion which lay across the path of Civil Rights. It introduced a vicious system of evasions and mental reservations; which provoked the public servant to harass, oppress, pain, humiliate, and enforce with unyielding, exasperating austerity, shameless and disgraceful practices, covert and wicked contrivances for the odious public ostracism and practical outlawry of this race, under the pretence of affording them equality, which, he claimed, did not mean identity of right. The rules and regulations of these despicable tyrants were and are personally degrading to free men and citizens; who neither in word nor deed were offensive to their fellow-citizens, and who, in moral character, extent of learning, personal deportment, dignity and decorum, cleanliness and freshness of person, refinement and taste in toilet, uniform gentlemanliness, courtesy, and politeness, were often the peers of any American citizen. To the silence of abject submission has the construction placed upon this phraseology condemned and abandoned such manly exemplars of civic fitness as are given in the foot-note.[1]

---

[1] "The Underground Railroad," "The Struggles for the Rights of the Colored People," etc., Wm. Still; "Autobiography," "Bondage and Freedom," Frederick Douglass, United States Minister to Hayti, etc.; "Lectures and Addresses," John M. Langston, LL.D., lawyer, minister-resident and consul-general, president of the Virginia Normal and Collegiate Institute; "Black and White," T. Thomas Fortune; "Music and Some Highly Musical People," James M. Trotter; "Tanner Outlines," Rev. T. B. Tanner; "The Rising Sun," "Sketches of Places and People Abroad," "The Black Man," "The Negro in the Rebellion," "Clotelle," "The Escape," "The Dough Face" (Dramas), "Mirala; or, the Beautiful Quadroon," Wm. Wells Brown; "Liberia," T. McCants Stewart, LL.B.; "Bond and Free," J. H. W. Howard; "Amanda Smith," Rev. Marshall W. Taylor, D.D., editor of *Southwestern Advocate;* "Church Polity," H. M. Turner, D.D., LL.D., Bishop A. M. E. Church; "Benjamin Banneker," Martha E. Tyson; "Principia," Martin R. Delaney; "Autobiography," A. W. Wayman; "Greatness of Christ," "Africa," Alexander Crummell; "Americus Moor," E. W. Williams; "Greek Text-Book," "Birds of Aristophanes," W. S. Scarborough; "The Colored Soldier," J. T. Wilson; "Forest Leaves" (Poems), Frances E. W. Harper; "Autobiography," Henry Bibb; "Memoirs of Phillis Wheatley, and her Poems," "Volume of Poems," Addison Bell; "Past, Present, and Future" (Poems), Clark; "A Man and Not a Man," A. A. Whitman; "Apology for Methodism," Rev. B. T. Tanner, A.M., D.D., editor of *A. M. E. Review;* "Toussaint L'Overture," D. Augustus Straker; "Selika Galop," "Arneaux March," "Excelsior," Craig; "The Negro Race," "Life and Time of Captain Paul," D. B. Williams; "Truth in a Nutshell," L. T. Smith; "Advice on Morals," R. H. Outerbridge; "Richard III." (Adaptation), J. A. Arneaux; "Sketch of Prominent African-Americans," Wm. J. Simmons, D.D., president of State University, Louisville, Ky.; "Negro Soldiers," George W. Williams; Rev. Harvey Johnson, D.D., author of "The Theophanies of the Old Testament Scriptures," "The Equality of the Father and Son," "Secret Disciples," and "The Hamite;" Granville T. Woods, electrician, mechanical engineer, manufacturer of telephone, telegraph, and electrical instruments; Wm. C. Chase, editor of *Washington Bee;* Rev. James W. Hood, Bishop of A. M. E. Zion Church, and Assistant Superintendent of Public Instruction; Samuel R. Lowery, silk-culturist, lawyer, and editor; Prof. J. W. Morris, A.M., LL.B., president of Allen University, Columbia, S.C., professor of languages; Robert Smalls, congressman; Rev. John Bunyan Reeve, D.D., professor of theology, Howard University, Washington, D.C.; Rev. Nicholas Franklin Roberts, A.M., professor of mathematics, president of Baptist

Their number is being daily multiplied throughout the land under the auspicious reign of individual freedom, by such representative men as Mr. Revels, Mr. Bruce, Mr. Rapier, Mr. Rainey, and Mr. Lynch.

It will be remembered, that, when the bill to remove the politi-

---

State Convention, N.C., moderator of one hundred thousand colored Baptists; Prof. J. E. Jones, A.B., professor of homiletics and Greek in Theological Seminary, Richmond, Va., corresponding secretary of Baptist Foreign Mission Convention; Prof. John C. Crosby, A.M., principal of North Carolina State Normal School; Rev. Charles L. Purce, D.D., president of Selma University, Selma, Ala.; Rev. E. K. Love, D.D., editor of "The Centennial Record of Georgia;" Samuel Allen McElwen, A.B., LL.B., lawyer, legislator, president of the Tennessee Fair Association; Wm. H. Steward, editor of *American Baptist;* Rev. Rufus L. Perry, Ph.D., D.D., editor of *National Monitor*, and author of "The Cushite;" Prof. James M. Gregory, A.M., dean of the College Department of Howard University; General T. Morris Chester, phonographer.; Charles B. Purvis, A.M., M.D., surgeon in charge of Freedmen's Hospital, Washington, D.C.; Rev. J. C. Price, A.B., president of Livingstone College; Prof. J. C. Corbin, A.M., linguist,—master of Latin, Greek, French, Spanish, Italian, German, Hebrew, and Danish,—mathematician, and musician; Henry Williams Chandler, A.M., member of State Senate of Florida, capitalist, lawyer, city clerk, and alderman; J. R. Clifford, editor and lawyer; Prof. John H. Burrus, A.M., president of Alcorn University, professor of mental and moral philosophy and constitutional law, teacher of political economy, literature, and chemistry; John Mitchel, Jr., editor of *Richmond Planet;* Prof. Richard Theodore Greener, LL.D., chief civil service examiner, lawyer, metaphysician, logician, and orator, prize essayist, dean of the Law Department of Howard University; Prof. Wm. Hooper Council, president of State Normal and Industrial School, Huntsville, Ala., editor and lawyer; Rev. James Poindexter, D.D., director of the Bureau of Forestry; Rev. B. W. Arnett, D.D., editor of the *Budget*, legislator, author of the bill wiping out the "Black Laws" of Ohio; John W. Cromwell, editor of *The People's Advocate*, Washington, D.C.; Rev. E. M. Brawley, A.M., D.D., editor of *Baptist Tribune*, president of Selma University, author of "The Baptist Pulpit;" Rev. B F. Lee, A.B., D.D., editor of *Christian Recorder*, president of Wilberforce University; Rev. E. H. Lipscombe, president of the Western Union Institute, Asheville, N.C., editor of *The Mountain Gleaner;* Robert Pelham, Jr., editor of Detroit *Plaindealer;* Prof. B. T. Washington, principal of the Tuskegee Normal School; Prof. C. H. Parrish, A.B., author of "What We Believe," professor of languages in Kentucky State University; Rev. D. A. Payne, D.D., LL.D., Senior Bishop of A. M. E. Church; Rev. W. J. White, editor of *Georgia Baptist;* Edward E. Cooper, editor of *The Freeman;* Rev. A. Brown, editor of *Baptist Messenger*.

cal disabilities imposed by the third section of the Fourteenth Amendment, known as the Amnesty Bill,—which included large classes of citizens of the revolting States, notoriously members of Congress and all those citizens who had been executive and judicial officers or members of their State legislatures,—was before the House of Representatives, the Democrats were un-willing to accept amnesty if they were to be subjected to the obligation of freeing those very colored representatives, and their race, from the odious personal discriminations at which Mr. Sumner's Civil-Rights Bill was aimed. It required only a majority of votes in the House to pass the Civil-Rights Bill, which was then pending; but it required a majority of two-thirds to pass the Amnesty Bill, which was also then on its pas-sage. But the Amnesty Bill was passed by the aid of the five above-named colored representatives who were in that Congress, without even the demand of a division of the vote. While these colored representatives, who had been slaves, freely voted to release their late masters from every form of disability, the latter, notwithstanding this magnanimity, refused on their part to vote for the civil enfranchisement of these their former bonds-men. The author of "Twenty Years of Congress," [1] referring to this subject, says of these colored representatives,—

"They were, as a rule, studious, earnest, ambitious men, whose public conduct—as illustrated by Mr. Revels and Mr. Bruce in the Senate, and by Mr. Rapier, Mr. Lynch, and Mr. Rainey in the House—would be honorable to any race. Coals of fire were heaped on the heads of all their enemies, when the colored men in Congress heartily joined in removing the disabilities of those who had before been their oppressors, and who, with deep regret be it said, have continued to treat them with injustice and ig-nominy;" "and so far as chivalry, magnanimity, charity, and Christian kindness were involved, the colored men appeared at an advantage."

This act of these colored representatives was an illustration of the effect of the grand code of "Equality"; it was an event in the historical life of humanity. Seldom or never, from the

---

[1] Blaine, vol. ii. p. 515.

disturbed fountain of human nature, has there flowed so pure a stream of harmony, fraternity, peace, cordiality, and the brotherly feeling of reconciliation. Its reflection of equality of rights is as clear, shining, unstained, and eternal as the stars in the firmament which looked down upon it.

What a lesson was this noble act! The soul-part of human nature, which is of the same color everywhere, pavilioned in tabernacles where just principles and true humanity reign, lost sight of external color, which is, after all, nothing but the result of environing conditions, and, rising to the sublime height of the magnificent opportunity, tore away from prejudiced statesmen and truculent politicians their veils of sanctimonious profession, and restored the boundless freedom of material, spiritual equality before the law, revealing the real altar of humanity. It crushed with the grasp of a Titan all the strange errors of the infatuated self-love of race, and, annihilating its past history, afforded the world an illustration (when illustration was most needed) of the colossal grandeur of the spirit of the Fourteenth Amendment, embracing, in its ample folds, the whole family of mankind. It threw open to the hereditary master and oppressor, at a time when this very master and former oppressor, by continuing a system of public discrimination and personal debasement, insisted upon remanding this race to the limitations of the days of slavery, all those rich treasures of liberty from which a political oligarchy of his white conquerors was seeking to exclude him, and which they then held under their exclusive and unlimited constitutional dominion by the law of the land. This act must live forever as one of the most glorious incidents in the annals of mankind, and, however its lustre may be obscured by the efforts of the intolerant bigotry of to-day, to the next generation, when this race shall be viewed with calmer, clearer vision, this simple and sublime exhibition will shine forth more resplendent, like the lamps of the early believers, illumining the tombs of these American martyrs to race-prejudice.

Although to-day the proposition "Equality does not mean identity" casts its film over the judicial eye, and keeps its view obscured by the imperceptible, unrecognized clouds of prejudice, to-morrow, as soon as Dikê, Irênê, and Eunomia, the lovely

Horæ, have unfolded the gates of dawn and "purged the visual ray," this construction of Hall *v.* DeCuir will be regarded as a most ingenious sophism of a foolish past, wholly subversive of the revealed truths of the Fourteenth Amendment. Beyond all question, as a shield for race-discriminationists, the doctrine that "Equality does not mean identity" has proved more protective of race-antagonisms than the famed buckler covered with ten bull-hides, which Ajax exchanged with Tychius of Hyle for the superb relic of Vulcan. Since it is impossible that we should thoroughly understand the nature of the signs unless we first properly consider and arrange the things signified, it becomes necessary to examine in its entirety this new-fangled phraseology.

No metaphysician engaged in the investigation of the profound philosophy of language, could ever have dreamed of a classification of ideas in which the word "equality" is synonymous with "identity." A clear perception of the relation which these terms, "equality" and "identity," bear to their corresponding ideas, show that they stand wholly apart, and exclude any process of reasoning based upon their similarity. It would, indeed, be a crude but bold effort of genius which, considering a subject so vast as that of the national polity in reference to civil rights, should seek to solve or settle the grave problem by a rule of construction based upon a purely gratuitous assumption of a similitude in the signification of terms.

The tortuous circumlocution and complication of this curiously fabricated mechanism of thought finds no justification in the language of the Constitution. There is a simplicity and felicity of diction in the words which it employs closely accessible to the understanding—and to the heart—which do not present any such dim, uncertain vista of ideas, as is involved in the mystification of equality with identity, and identity with equality. There is no warrant in the Constitution, or the amendment, for such a recklessly coined mintage. The words of recognized constitutional legitimacy, as we have seen, are in the most homely verbal garb : " The citizens of each State shall be entitled to all privileges and immunities of citizens in the several States. No State shall make or enforce any law which shall abridge the privileges and immunities of citizens of the United States, nor deprive any person of life, liberty, or property without due process of law, nor deny to any person within its jurisdiction the equal protection of the laws."

The threatened overthrow of a great principle underlying the national polity is thus clearly traceable to the erroneous negation that equality does not mean identity ; which negation, in the public mind, is accepted and followed as the affirmation by the Supreme Court of a principle definitive and regulative—but, in reality, destructive—of the rights of seven millions of American citizens. This mystifying construction affords another illustration in the bosom of American society—where least it would be looked for—of the truth of the philosophic reflection of that eminent representative of foreign statecraft, who said that " The verbal sophisms of partisans, and the subtle jugglery of a misapprehended term, adopted by adroit, unscrupulous agitators, have given rise to interminable national disputes, decided political questions of the deepest significance, kindled the flames of war, and even changed the destiny of empires."

Before the broad, grave, and sublime historico-legal significance of the provisions of Article IV., Section 1, of the Constitution, taken in connection with those of the Fourteenth Article of Amendment, can be legitimately understood, clearly discerned, and appreciated, it is imperatively necessary to realize the formidable and phenomenal results which the doctrine, " Equality does not mean identity," has compassed. These are not susceptible of exact admeasurement, but may be certainly regarded as a hinderance to progressive civil rights, scarcely less portentous than that which the institution of slavery opposed to the institutions of freedom.

To speak with accuracy, " identity" is rather a relation between our recognition of things, than between the things. As an abstract postulate, that " Equality does not mean identity" is as true of civil rights as that equality of the right to light, air, and water does not mean the right to the enjoyment of the same, identical light, air, and water. The proposition that " Identity does not mean equality" is not more tenable than its converse, that equality does not mean identity—exact unison between the two terms with respect to the properties each represents. Identity cannot express or compare the suitable relation, the just proportion, or the degree, nor be predicated of the evenly-balanced state of equality, in respect of constitutional right, immunity, or privilege, according to the genius of the nation's polity, as expressed in its written laws. As Lord Coke puts it, *Nullum simile est idem,*—nothing which is alike is identical. Identity excludes mere resemblance. He says, *Nullum simile quatuor pedibus currit.* It is clear, that in their unclarified and obscure sense, as employed in Hall *v.* DeCuir, both of these terms represent unascertained quantities. The actual effect of the doctrine of Hall *v.* DeCuir, that "Equality is not identity," was the authorization of the public servant, to observe the letter but to defeat the spirit of the Fourteenth Amendment while ostensibly conforming thereto.

That decision established the precedent which the inferior courts have since uniformly followed, that, as the equality of a civil right was separable from its identity, the avoidance of the spirit of the law, provided its letter was satisfied, was legitimate, upon the theory advanced by this precedent, that equality of right did not involve an identity of privilege. This, as we have seen, was the vehicle by which Mr. Justice Clifford journeyed in safety to the conclusion, that discrimination on account of color was justifiable upon this ground. The proposition that equality of right does not mean identity of immunity and privilege is startling; it " demands the gravest consideration ;" it arrests civil rights like a sheriff's writ, and asphyxiates perfect liberty. The point is not whether there is afforded a civil right which is identical, superior, or inferior in kind, but whether, irrespective of inferiority or superiority, the privilege of public accommodation accorded to any class to which it may belong involves an invasion of the constitutional immunity of this race from discrimination on account of race or color. The result of Hall *v.* DeCuir, as accepted by the inferior courts, is, that this doctrine operates as a limitation of the rights of citizenship, and that these people are citizens only in name, and incapable of the full attainment of the citizenship created by this amendment.

As Aristotle asked in the days of yore, so in America it may be inquired to-day, "Is not he justly a citizen who is created such by the act of the commonwealth?" The theory, that equality of right does not involve identity of privilege, may seem a kind of phosphorescent construction which plays harmlessly about those words, but in reality it is a grave constitutional construction which, undermining the Fourteenth Amendment, has upset this vast apparatus of government, and crippled the machinery by which it sought to grind into atoms the hardened crust of a fossilized institution.

It is not at all an unusual occurrence, to a mind observant of historical judicature, to find eminent judges, possessed of enlightened faculties, engaged in disputations merely concerning words (which a grammarian could more readily have settled), which they mistake for an able argument upon a controversy of the utmost gravity to the state. Of this calamitous, but not uncommon frailty, the judge in Hall *v.* DeCuir affords a signal illustration.

It is apparent, that a capricious discrimination on account of nationality, color, race, social position, political or religious belief is forbidden alike by the letter and spirit of the Constitution; whose conditions, limitations, and requirements now aim at the attainment of the highest degree of civil, social, political, and moral development, the highest possible end which the rightful use of the individual's natural faculties allows, and which is at the same time consistent with the right of all other citizens to a similar development. This doctrine stirred the blood and thrilled the whole being of the American nation, which pleaded for the embodiment of this spirit of truth and justice in a fourteenth amendment. America, like Icarus soaring upward, was thus driving straight to the sun. But these golden days of freedom, fruitful of all golden deeds of civilized liberty, had scarcely commenced, when the myrmidons of raceism—men whose masculine understandings, whose genius and virtue were the glory of the church and state; distinguished lights of science, inured to rigid habits of thought; in all other intellectual departments men of philosophic, profound, and serene wisdom—determined (wonderful to relate), at the first opportunity, to back the wheels of the state, and press downward the fundamental political

Christian principle thus embodied in the Constitution, by the gravitating force and degrading tendency which in Hall *v.* DeCuir, under the appearance and show of coy impartiality, defeated the beneficent purposes of America, by legitimating a rule of construction which tolerates an avoidance of the spirit, while it professes a desire to conform to the letter, of this great law.

Throughout American jurisprudence it has not before been found necessary to interpret the words " identity" or " equality," as applied to any other race,—swarthy or fair, whether indigenous or not to American soil. Certainly their constitutional construction has not hitherto been inquired into, in any controversy respecting the rights, immunities, and privileges of the imported Chinaman, Socialist, Nihilist, Pole, or those of the Mormon, boss, bummer, pauper, or criminal classes, against each of which a " natural and well-known repugnance," and a psycho-physical aversion exists throughout the civilized world, but in spite of which these offcasts, dregs, and cankers of the state, provided they are " white persons," are daily " huddled together indiscriminately" with the great masses of American citizens, by the promiscuous sociality of the public servant's rules, without regard to the import, so far as their civil rights are concerned, of the terms " equality" or " identity." It requires no copious or subtle argument to prove that neither of the terms " equality" and " identity" was suspected of having an interwoven, mysteriously correlated constitutional sense which required a Supreme-Court decision to disentangle; except when application to the rights, privileges, and immunities of citizens of the United States of African descent brought them into collision with race-antagonism.

If the accommodation of civil rights and privileges accorded this race was confessedly superior in all its particulars and qualities, in its internal and external conditions, under substantially the same situation and circumstances, but with peculiar slavery ceremonials thereto attached, which evaded the spirit of equality of right, by conspicuously preserving the spirit of discrimination on account of color which it was the object of the constitutional amendment to wipe out, such material superiority in the accommodation would constitute a more violent, vicious, palpable, obnoxious, and notoriously unconstitutional violation of both. the letter and spirit of this amendment, than if the accommodation was of such a degrading character, so uncomfortable and inferior in its kind and classification, and so substantially shorn in every respect of every value as to constitute it a mere burlesque in contrast with the comforts of the accommodation afforded the other race. In both instances the inward, solemn, burning conviction of America, and its outward expression through this amendment, are grossly disregarded and trampled upon. The purpose of the amendment obviously was that this branch of the society of the state should not thereafter be subjected by any mark, badge, sign, device, or token to civil ostracism ; that it could not be loaded with moral or personal chains without the commission of a grave crime against the state. The question substantially is, whether, through the " identity" loophole, the spirit of this grand work of patriots, philosophers, statesmen, and philanthropists can be evaded and shorn of its mightiness, by reason of the court's instituting an inquiry, and formulating a precedent upon an artificial distinction having no more solid foundation than a play upon the words, " equality" and " identity."

The doctrines of the Christ of history, events like Marathon and Thermopylæ, the American Revolution, the Civil War, and the Fourteenth Amendment, cannot be estimated by narrow rules of construction. The strait-jacket of legal formulæ is more readily adjustable to the littleness of every-day business, in which it might, with more candor, perhaps, but scarcely with less professional ability, be maintained, that *Equality in bulk does not mean identity in kind.*

CHAPTER XXXVII.

"This motion is a bold and original stroke in the noble science of defence. It marks the genius and hand of a master."—WIRT.

"There are those who never understand a word, nor learn to talk of a whole proposition, out of nature's strangely-sounding and most difficult language of hieroglyphics."—BOECKH.

"If others, of a more elegant taste for fine writing, are able to receive either pleasure or instruction from such truly philosophical language, I shall neither dispute with them nor envy them: but can only deplore the dulness of my own apprehension, who, notwithstanding the great authors quoted in Mr. Harris's treatise, and the great authors who recommend it, cannot help considering this 'perfect example of analysis,' as—an improved compilation of almost all the errors which grammarians have been accumulating from the time of Aristotle down to our present days, of technical and learned affectation."—TOOKE.

"We find the value of x in terms of y; then we find the value of y in terms of x; and so on we may continue forever, without coming nearer to a solution."—MARTINEAU.

"You do not produce the right Samuel, but such another empty shadow as was raised by the witch of Endor."—MILTON.

"I think that language ought not to be considered as mere arbitrary sounds; or anything less than a part, at least, of that living soul which God is said to have breathed into man."—ROULAND JONES.

"You, sir, are fully acquainted with this, and know that men generally judge of everything by prejudice, hearsay, and chance. No one reflects that the cause of a citizen ought to interest the whole body of citizens, and that we may ourselves have to endure in despair the same fate which we perceive, with eyes and feelings of indifference, falling heavily upon him. We write and comment every day upon the judgments passed by the Senate of Rome and the Areopagus of Athens, but we think not for a moment of what passes before our own tribunals."—VOLTAIRE.

"But when power to act is under discussion, I will not look to the end in view, lest I should become indifferent to the lawfulness of the means."
—PINCKNEY.

398

" See this old marquis treating us
    As if a conquered race:
His raw-boned steed has brought him back
    From distant hiding-place.
With sabre brandished o'er his head
    That never dealt a blow,
The noble mortal marches on,
    And seeks his old château.
Hats off, hats off! near and far,
Bow to the marquis of Carabas."—BÉRANGER.

" The Chinese mandarins were strongly surprised, and almost incredulous, when the Jesuits showed them how small a figure their empire made in the general map of the world."—BOLINGBROKE.

" Sir John Hawkins, in honor of his having been the first to commence the slave-trade, received the addition to his coat of arms of ' a demi-moor proper, bound with a cord.' "—SPENCER.

" In the South slavery had taken up arms to assert its nationality and perpetuity; in the North freedom had arisen first in mere defensive resistance; then the varying fortunes of war had rendered the combat implacable and mortal. It was not from the mouldering volumes of ancient precedents, but from the issues of the present wager of battle, that future judges of courts would draw their doctrines to interpret to posterity whether the Edict of Freedom was void or valid."—NICOLAY AND HAY.

" Nor could we, in the nineteenth century, find a match to that German captain of mercenaries, who in silver letters labelled himself, Duke Werner, Lord of the great Company; the enemy of mercy, of pity, and of God." —SPENCER.

No obscuration of the single, certain, and material issue (which lies in a narrow compass) ought to be tolerated by the introduction of such irrelevant matters as Mr. Justice Clifford's *obiter dicta* obtrude into the controversy; as, for example, " whether a passenger is entitled to any particular apartment" or " special accommodations;" whether the public servant has authority to preserve decorum and prevent collisions; nor respecting his " authority to separate persons," or " to regulate his business so as to preserve order;" nor " whether the vehicle of transport belongs to the public or to the public servant;" nor " what part of a public institution a citizen may occupy;" nor " that the public servant is not bound to accommodate people of gross habits or suspicious characters;" nor whether "the right be political or civil;" provided, underlying these propositions, the rules are regulative of the *public* rights in these regards; are not made for a particular occasion or class; and are equally applicable, under substantially similar circumstances and conditions, to all citizens, irrespective of race, color, creed, class, or caste. There never has been, and there never can be, any reasonable contention about these postulates. They are self-evident truths. Their introduction into the opinion, however, was a dull contrivance, which served a not more useful purpose than a temporary obscuration of the real issue; and ever since their appearance in Hall *v.* DeCuir, although immaterial, these questions are resurrected and dragged into every civil-rights cause, as if they tendered some issue with which the spirit of the provisions of the Fourteenth Amendment was at variance. Those weapons indeed belong to the antiquated artillery of the past; they serve the purposes only of such valiant warriors as will neither fight nor fly, take ground nor abandon it; whose courage and candor will not permit of a closer mode of combat than hovering over and concealing the real issue.

It is demonstrable that the civil-rights cases, decided after Hall *v.* DeCuir, have taken their cue, not so much from the opinion of the Chief Justice as from the *obiter dicta* of the separate opinion of Mr. Justice Clifford. The cases of the Steamer Sue,[1] Council *v.* Western and Atlantic R.R. Co.,[2] and William H. Heard *v.* Georgia R.R. Co.,[3] amply illustrate the tendency of the modern decisions to maintain the doctrine that " *Equality of rights does not necessarily imply identity of rights.*" From the plastic legal fiction, that equality of right is separable from identity of immunity and privilege, the courts, by some strange process of cerebration, have drifted unconsciously into the anomalous assertion that differentiated classification of persons may lawfully be made, in the equalization of civil rights, solely on account of race, color, or the previous condition of which color

---

[1] 22 Fed. Rep. 843.   [2] Interstate-Com. Rep. 339.
[3] Interstate-Com. Dec., February 15, 1888.

is a symbol; provided, the public servant, in good faith, furnishes " substantial" equality in his " accommodation."

Say the Interstate-Commerce Commissioners : [1] " So long as its rule separating passengers is maintained, its duty is to furnish for all passengers paying the same fare cars in all respects equal and provided with the same comforts, accommodations, and protection for travellers." The judges argue that the same rule of differentiation would be alike applicable to Irish or German skin, provided the " huddling together" of this foreign but American-ized skin interfered with the comfort (that is, the gratification of the race-prejudice) of the individuals who monopolize the benefits of all class-distinction, which they claim to be naturally sequent on their self-assumed civic superiority, or on account of their white garniture. This argument insists that the acknowl-edged superiority of rank of these dignitaries, and the admission of the sacred exclusiveness of their immunities, legitimately con-tribute and are necessary to their comfort, and to the enjoy-ment of their civil rights and privileges, which cannot be grati-fied otherwise than by the subordination of the civil rights of the other class through certain restrictions, constituting the primal symbol of the superiority of the white and the inferiority of the black race.

Froissart, speaking of the royal habiliments of Arteville, chief of the revolted Gantese, illustrates the point, where he says, " He was clothed in sanguine robes of scarlet, like the Duke of Brabant and the Count of Mainit." Just so must our Dukes of Brabant and Counts of Mainit wear the sanguine and scarlet robes to distinguish their immunities from those of other citi-zens. This doctrine would lead America backward towards the barbarism of primal savagery. Its parallelism can be found only among the Fiji, where hammocks and umbrellas are monop-olized by the king, and cannibalism is a right restricted to the chiefs and gentry ; or the Ioloffs, where the " mosquito-curtain is a royal prerogative ;" or in San Salvador, where the " prime men and notable soldiers alone can drink chocolate ;" or Peru, where a draught of coca is a royal privilege ; or mediæval

---

[1] Heard *v.* Georgia R.R. Co., 1 Interstate-Com. Rep.

France, where scarlet and purple were worn exclusively by the princes and knights. The American courts, fortunately for the cause of civil liberty, are not confined in their view of civil rights to the abstractions of the *obiter dicta* of Mr. Justice Clifford, but are bound by the concrete law of the Fourteenth Amendment, in its solidarity.

Whether, under this principle of differentiation, which is the genesis of the theory that equality is separable from identity, in the near future, the emigrant skin, and lastly Americans themselves, shall not be required at some future period, in addressing these sovereign creatures, the most worthy and worshipful public servants of America, to adopt some such salutatory, laudatory prefixes as those in which the subject in the East salutes his master, as "The Shadow of God," "Son of Heaven," "The Master of Life," "Behold the Moon and Stars," or others perhaps more in accord with the primeval civilization of our aboriginal Indian tribes, "has not, to our knowledge, been decided in any court;" or, as the learned judge in the Steamer Sue case said, in reference to discriminative differentiation on account of color, "the assertion by the public servant of a right"—to insist upon such salutatory prefixes—is "one which, it must be confessed, goes to the very limit of his right to regulate the privileges" of native-born or of naturalized skins.

But since America has paid in gold and blood the debt accumulated during two centuries of bondage, and by a constitutional amendment has sought to emancipate the new citizens from differential discrimination in their civil rights on account of skin and color, by what logic-chopping process is their constitutional emancipation from this very discrimination now brought into question? Has this curious result been attained by the judicial strategy which, first overturning the Fourteenth Amendment through the legal fiction that "Equality does not mean identity" of civil rights, has completely outgeneralled the serried column of advanced ideas in America? Either the inferior courts have misapprehended the legal drift and trend of the *obiter dictum* of Mr. Justice Clifford, or it is the manifest purpose of the Supreme Court to say in unmistakable tones to Civil Rights, "The amendments to the Constitution must yield something to the *vox populi;* we have limited your advance; thus far shalt thou go and no further."

The question is not merely what constitutional relation identity of civil rights bears to equality of civil rights, nor how far they are separable; but whether, in view of the historical aspect as reflected in the oft-repeated construction of the Fourteenth Amendment by the Supreme Court, the purpose of that noble instrument was not to wipe out every trace of slavery-distinction in civil life which implies the subordination or inferiority of this race on account of color, and to favor the growth of individuality, by such an equalization of the privileges and immunities of civil rights, as shall wholly obliterate every vestige of those degrading and harsh distinctions which in the past ages of slavery were ceremonials indicative of the inferiority of this race in civil society. The question relates to the construction of the doctrine of equality of the Fourteenth Amendment, in its bearing upon the lives, and education of the habits, of seven millions of men, women, and children in America; whether the civil rights bestowed in name and form can by a legal fiction be taken away; whether seven millions of people can be pillaged of their prerogatives; whether galling adamantine fetters can be clinched and riveted upon this race while Jurisprudence is nodding and napping; whether, in short, a metaphysical falsehood can subvert a divine truth.

The Fourteenth Amendment is a peremptory, decisive, special, and definitive governmental command to the courts and the people to uproot the ceremoniousness and punctiliousness of observances, which ever have been and now are manifestations of the distinction between the free and the slave class, and of the domination of the former over the latter. This grave and great command was as prohibitive to the American people, against the observance of slavery customs and usages, as was the second commandment to the Israelites against genuflexion in the presence of the graven images of idolatry; or as the teaching of our advanced civilization, which commands the laying aside of that formal prostration, cringing, and crouching, which marked the social subordination and personal inferiority of a mediæval serf, and was symbolic of the reverence which the inequality of the peasant owed to the superiority of the prince. Two centuries of slavery had developed and crystallized the symbolization of the inferiority of this race. These ceremonial controls were arbitrarily fixed to denote inequality and inferiority; they were signs of inequality and inferiority which marked the respect and homage due by the inferior to the superior race. Wherever its despotism was most unmitigated and unrelenting in America, the subjection of the slave to the master was expressed in ways too numerous to require illustration, and implied throughout all its forms a spirit of helplessness, profound homage, deference, cringing obeisance, and a reverent prostration. The pride and policy of the smaller specimens of the superior class aimed always to emphasize its contact with the slave by these instrumentalities. Examples of ceremonials indicative of inferiority and degradation were furnished them by Dahomey, whose abject subject, " when approaching Royalty, crawls like a snake, or shuffles forward on his knees;" or by Loango, " where the wives dare not speak to their husbands but upon their bare knees, and in meeting them must creep upon their hands." The " superior race" followed the example of the " superior" coast-negro,—whose descendants they held in bondage,—who exacted from his slave, as a sign of submission, that " before speaking he should fall on his knees and three times kiss the earth." In Mexico they had seen that cowering was a token of respect, and in Java they had learned that an inferior must move forward with his hams upon his heels until he is out of his superior's sight. In America they did not exact these precise forms of obeisance, but the vanishing shape of this savagery—its " double"—is clearly reflected in the long-acknowledged customs which sanctified the barbarous ceremonialism of American slavery, by a series of humiliating observances, which were signs of degradation, inferiority, and inequality, and a confession of submission by the slave to the master. Undoubtedly all of the American observances of slavery were derived from the primitive state of savagery where the conquered humbly prostrated themselves before their conqueror.

The Supreme Court in all of its constructions of the Fourteenth Amendment, even in those cases where, as we have seen, it invalidated a part of the Civil-Rights Bill and Enforcement Acts, substantially determined that the object of the amendments was to "wipe out" the spirit of haughty mastery which had characterized the conduct of the "superior" race; and had generated with multiplicity, definiteness, and conspicuousness, all those servile badges, ceremonials, and restrictions which distinguished the former slave from the free citizen, and branded the race as one of civil inferiority. The court, again and again, have substantially decided, that the Fourteenth Amendment commanded the total annihilation of "each, every, all, and singular" of those regulations, prescriptions, marks, and badges which were the essential accompaniments of the superior rank of the master in the exercise of his civil rights. Notwithstanding these decisions, upon the specious pretext that "natural and well-known repugnance" between the races—where white and colored are "huddled together" without their consent—justifies it, the handcuffs of slavery again threaten civil rights in America; and many of the very same ceremonials and restrictions,—the identical concomitants of slavery,—the same public class-distinctions, regulations, prescriptions, marks, and badges, are sought to be re-established, legalized, sanctioned, adopted, and rigidly enforced, whenever an attempt is made to exercise the civil rights, privileges, and immunities of this race in the presence or company of the other.

This shallow view was first suggested in Miles *v.* R.R. Co., which Mr. Justice Clifford's citation and quotation in Hall *v.* DeCuir stamped with the quasi-approval of the Supreme Court. Since then, as a principle and precedent, the doctrine has prevailed; until it has now attained the importance and gravity of a well-defined, settled rule of law, that there may be made a differentiation between the civil rights of this race and the privileges and immunities which the other race is entitled to enjoy under precisely similar circumstances and conditions. That is to say, that the equality born of the Fourteenth Amendment is separate from, and not identical with, the privileges and immunities of the inferior race; from participation in which equality the inferior race may be debarred by the perpetuation and enforced maintenance of the ceremonials of slavery. This modification of equality, or rather this reversal and denial of equality, has but one interpretation : it is, at most, but a base counterfeit of the genuine equality intended by the amendment.

The method of construction we have been considering introduces a novel system which confuses the civil rights granted by the Fourteenth Amendment with the pro-slavery social regulations which are now (and to the same extent as prior to the war) indicative of the inferiority, in civil society, of this race; and are to-day expressive of the very same utter disregard for the thoughts, feelings, and individualities of these citizens. If this fundamental distinction between a state of freedom and a state of bondage can be maintained and perpetuated, the ante-bellum insignia of slavery have been only seemingly laid aside, and the substantial civil and political attainments of the Fourteenth Amendment have effected no further change than to transform this race into citizens, and then deform the transformed citizens and relegate them to the status of inferior freedmen, little better than serfs, and this, too, by the law of the land, which, according to Mr. Justice Clifford's *obiter dicta*, authorizes the deepest political class-distinction and supremacy, placing the civil rights of this race at the mercy of the other, whose authority is executive, legislative, and judicial, and to whose decrees this race must bow in abject submission, wearing without a murmur the degrading badges which signify that at the close of the nineteenth century the primitive characteristics of slavery have been only slightly obscured in America.

CHAPTER XXXVIII.

"Where are my authorities? They are everywhere. Common sense is authority enough upon such a point."—Pinckney.

"Great is the danger when, in a vindictive spirit of reaction, a revolutionary conduct is adopted by the party of legitimacy; when passion itself is consecrated into a maxim of reason, and held up as the only valid and just mode of proceeding."—Schlegel.

"I throw into the same scale the venerable code of universal law, before which it is the duty of this court, high as it is in dignity, and great as are its titles to reverence, to bow down with submission. I throw into the same scale a solemn treaty, binding upon the claimant and upon you."—Pinckney.

"The true foundation and the right of things in the history of society, as in the lives of individuals, cannot thus be severed from their historical connection and their place in the natural order of events."—Schlegel.

"A clothed, nay sometimes a quilted dialect."—Carlyle.

"If the blacks, strongly marked as they are by physical and lasting peculiarities, be retained amid the whites, under the degrading privation of equal rights, political or social, they must be always dissatisfied with their condition, as a change only from one to another species of oppression; always secretly confederated against the ruling and privileged class; and always uncontrolled by some of the most cogent motives to moral and respectable conduct."—Madison.

"Truth loves an appeal to the common sense of mankind. Your unperverted understandings can best determine on subjects of a practical nature. The positions and plans which are said to be above the comprehension of the multitude may be always suspected to be visionary and fruitless. He who made all men hath made the truth necessary to human happiness obvious to all."—Adams.

"If the understanding power or faculty of the soul be (saith the grand Physician) like unto bodily sight, not of equal sharpness in all, what can be more convenient than that, even as the dark-sighted man is directed by the clear about things visible; so, likewise, in matters of deeper discourse the wise in heart doth show the simple where his way lieth?"—Hooker.

THE general history of human disenthralment from despotism shows, that, after freedom has been attained by force of arms, the natural sequence of civil rights can be maintained only by the repetition of the same arguments, with precision and emphasis, which were used before the arbitrament of the sword. And yet it seems absurd, a mere waste of time, to discuss this branch of the subject in view of the radiant light thrown upon it by the earlier decisions of the Supreme Court. The modern decisions, that "accommodation" "substantially equal" (which is the natural genesis of that *equality which is not identity*) satisfies the law, can be legitimately traced to the indefiniteness of the animated and ingenious volubility of Hall *v.* De-Cuir, which has tended to unsettle, if not to mislead, the inferior courts in the interpretation or application of its principle. But, however seemingly oracular may be the indefiniteness of Hall *v.* DeCuir, an unbroken current of Supreme Court decisions has so illumined the construction of the Fourteenth Amendment, that he that runs may read, that the equality of right it bestows is not separable from any immunity or privilege which a citizen of the United States may, in the exercise of his civil rights, enjoy, although the same physical accommodation may be afforded in fact; because the Fourteenth Amendment, as will hereafter appear, provides not less for the substantial "accommodation" in the material matters and conditions which environ his civic life, than for the conservation and advancement of the individual's spiritual existence.

To make good this assertion it is only necessary to refer again briefly to the decisions of the Supreme Court. In the Slaughter-House Cases[1] the following language is used,—

"On the most casual examination of the language of these amendments, no one can fail to be impressed with the one pervading purpose found in them all, lying at the foundation of each, and without which none of them would have been even suggested; we mean the freedom of the slave race, the security and firm establishment of that freedom, and the protection of the newly-made freeman and citizen from the oppressions of

---

[1] 16 Wall. 36.

those who formerly exercised unlimited dominion over him."
" But if the amendment refers to the *natural and inalienable rights which belong to all citizens, the inhibition has a profound significance and consequence.*"

" A citizen of the United States has a perfect constitutional right to go to, and reside in, any State he chooses, and to claim citizenship therein ; and an equality of rights with every other citizen ; and the whole power of the nation is pledged to sustain him in that right. He is not *bound to cringe to any superior, or to pray for any act of grace, as a means of enjoying all the rights and privileges enjoyed by other citizens.*"

" The Fourteenth Amendment prohibits a State from depriving any person of life, liberty, or property, without due process of law; but this adds nothing to the rights of one citizen as against another. It simply furnishes an additional guarantee against any encroachment by the States upon the fundamental rights which belong to every citizen as a member of society." [1]

Strauder *v.* West Virginia declares, " It" (the amendment) " was designed to assure to the colored race the enjoyment of all the civil rights that under the law are enjoyed by white persons, and to give to that race the protection of the general government in that enjoyment, whenever it should be denied by the States."

" The words of the amendment, it is true, are prohibitory, but they contain a necessary implication of a positive immunity, or right, most valuable to the colored race, the right to exemption from unfriendly legislation against them distinctively as colored ; exemption from *legal discriminations, implying inferiority in civil society, lessening the security of their enjoyment of the rights which others enjoy, and discriminations which are steps towards reducing them to the condition of a subject race.*"

" And the apprehension that, through prejudice, they might be denied that *equal protection,*—that is, that there might be *discrimination against them,*—was the *inducement to bestow upon the national government the power to enforce the provision that no State shall deny to them the equal protection of the laws.*"

" Its object is to place citizens of each State upon the *same*

---

[1] United States *v.* Cruikshank, 92 U. S. 542.

*footing with citizens of other States, and inhibit discriminative
legislation against them by other States."*

" This abrogation and denial of rights, for which the States
alone were or could be responsible, was the great seminal and
fundamental wrong which was intended to be remedied." [1]

The overwhelming testimony of these royal witnesses proves
that the constitutional provisions of the Fourteenth Amendment
are universally destructive of every vestige of the multiplied
encroachments, solemnities, conventional distinctions, and artificial ceremonials which the diseased pro-slavery social condition
had introduced into America as definitive of the status of the
slave. A modicum of penetration will show, that, if these decisions are to be overruled by the *obiter dicta* of Mr. Justice
Clifford's opinion, American jurisprudence will be forced into a
serious dilemma, from which its extrication will be difficult.

If the object of the "inhibition" of the Fourteenth Amendment, and the "pervading purpose lying at its foundation," "without which it would not have been suggested, was the security of
the liberated race in the enjoyment of freedom ; the protection of
the newly-made freeman and citizen from the oppressions of those
who formerly exercised dominion over him ;" if it has a " profound significance and relation to the natural and inalienable
rights which belong to this race as citizens ;" if " it furnishes an
additional guarantee against encroachment by the States upon
the fundamental rights which belong to every citizen as a member of society ;" if " it was designed to assure to the colored race
the enjoyment of all the civil rights that under the law are enjoyed by white persons ;" if its words are " not only prohibitory,
but contain a necessary implication of a positive immunity or
right most valuable to the colored race ;" if " the apprehension
that through prejudice there might be discrimination against
them was the inducement to bestow upon the national government power to enforce its provisions ;" if its object was to grant
their right to " exemption from legal discrimination implying inferiority in civil society, lessening the security of their
enjoyment of the rights which others enjoy," and " exemption

---

[1] Civil-Rights Cases, 109 U. S. 36.

from discriminations which are steps towards reducing them to the condition of a subject race;" if its design was to do away with all solemnities, ceremonials, conventional distinctions, humiliations, or badges of what kind soever, suggestive of personal degradation, implying subjugation by legal discrimination, and that "inferiority in civil society" which formerly authorized the public servant with an iron hand to oblige this race to "cringe to him," and "pray for permission" to enjoy any civil right (as a most condescending act of grace upon the part of the public servant); if the "whole power of the nation is pledged to sustain him in the equality of right;" if he is not now bound to "cringe to any superior, or to pray for any act of grace as a means of enjoying all the rights and privileges enjoyed by other citizens," and if it can with entire confidence be asserted, that these recorded constructions of the Fourteenth Amendment rest upon an undecomposable basis: may it not with entire safety be affirmed, that the combined power of every faculty of the human mind of which reason takes cognition will be incapable, by any recognized canon of jurisprudence or common sense, to prove that the doctrine of Mr. Justice Clifford is not utterly subversive and destructive of all just interpretation of the letter and the spirit of the Fourteenth Amendment?

Has not the establishment of that artificial and artful distinction between the equality of civil rights and their identity, which assumes, as a matter of fact, that substantial equality in "accommodation" satisfies the letter and spirit of the law, notoriously enabled the public servant to enforce with despotic power all the conspicuous pro-slavery ceremonials, the very same conventional distinctions, the same humiliating solemnities, which constituted the badges anciently attached to the civil status of the slave? Has not this vicious doctrine enabled him to perpetuate, through these slavery customs, "the great seminal and fundamental wrong which it was the object of the Fourteenth Amendment to correct"? Has it not prevented the colored race from enjoying "those very immunities from this sort of encroachment and discrimination which, under the law, are enjoyed by all other citizens"?

Has not this anomalous theory of equality given the public

servant " unlimited dominion over the rights of this race"? Has it not enabled him " to encroach upon their fundamental rights"? Has it not " deprived this race of many immunities which are enjoyed by the white race"? Has it not enabled the public servant to enforce legal " discriminations implying inferiority in society, lessening the security of their enjoyment of rights which others enjoy"? Has it tended to secure, or to destroy, " that one pervading purpose found in all the amendments, lying at the foundation of each, without which none of them would have been suggested"? Has it " protected the newly-made freeman and citizen from," or does it expose him to, the " oppressions of those who formerly exercised unlimited dominion over him"?

What " natural and inalienable right," of " profound significance," has it not strangled in its birth? Where has it ever recognized the " fundamental rights which belong to every citizen as a member of society"? On the contrary, has it not uniformly denied, by " legal discrimination on account of color, the very civil right of exemption from discriminations that under the law is enjoyed by all" other races in America? What doctrine could tend more effectually to " lessen the security of their enjoyment of the rights which other races enjoy," and better enable their " oppressors to enforce discriminations which are steps towards reducing them to the condition of a subject race"?

Is not this doctrine a substantial realization of " the apprehension that through prejudice they might be denied that equal protection which constituted the inducement to bestow upon the national government the power to enforce the provisions" of this amendment? Does not this extraordinary and phenomenal distinction between equality and identity, in spite " of the whole power of the nation being pledged to sustain" this race " in the enjoyment of their civil rights," oblige them, one and all, to " cringe to a superior" constituted by the Supreme Court's fiat? If there were no Supreme Court decisions construing the Fourteenth Amendment, could the clumsy mechanism of an impracticable mode of reasoning infringe or curtail the universal freedom of this gracious patent, by any such legal fabrication as that a " substantial equality" in the " accommodation" satisfies its provisions; and that this equality is separable from the identity of privilege and immunity of those very citizens of the State for the equalization of whose rights the Fourteenth Amendment was passed?

That the object of this amendment was the equalization of the civil rights of this race with the others is one of those historical facts which are beyond contradiction. To deny that the circumference, top, bottom, and middle portions of constitutional liberty are homologous, would be as absurd as a denial of the axiom, "that the whole is greater than its parts," or "that things which are equal to the same thing are equal to each other." The assertion of special privileges in the equalization of civil rights results from an "anarchical, capricious principle, founded solely upon internal and peculiar feelings;" and it may be added that whenever this principle has attained a locus in the State, it has always been destructive of its equity, freedom, and safety.

The oracular expression of the *obiter dictum*, "Equality is not identity," is either meaningless, or it signifies an infringement upon a rule of right. For the equality of the amendment, it substitutes its "moral sense," which denies "the fundamental truth of which the amendment is declaratory;" that first and all-essential law, that "the liberty of each is limited only by the like liberty of all;" it denies that equity, which (derived from the root of *equal*) literally means equality. But an equality in what? In those instinctive, individual, personal rights the universality of the assertion of which requires no greater evidence than the prevalence of courts, law-books, governments, arms, weapons, and the art of self-defence: each of which institutions and instruments incontrovertibly proves these instinctive feelings and personal rights to be inherent in mankind. This doctrine destroys this individualistic, humanistic feeling which, Mr. Herbert Spencer asserts, "leads him" (man) "to claim as great a share of natural privilege as is claimed by others,—a feeling that leads him to repel anything like an encroachment upon what he thinks his sphere of original freedom entitles him to claim." [1]

---

[1] Social Statics, p. 108.

The odious discrimination, to which this race is unlawfully subjected, itself constitutes an inferiority of privileges and immunities. It matters not that the public servant gives a "substantial accommodation," if it takes from the adopted citizen the right to do all he would and wishes to do, even though by so doing he does not infringe upon the equal freedom of any other citizen. And this is just what all other citizens have the full privilege of doing. They have full and free play for the gratification of all their individualistic desires, subject only to this limitation,—that in the exercise of their privileges they infringe not upon the equal freedom of any other citizen. It follows, therefore, that identity, as used in the postulate "Equality is not identity," is a negation of the equalness of freedom. If the privileges are equal in this sense, they are substantial; but if they are not equal, the two classes cannot substantially have the same rights. They have no rights which are identically the same or equal. This is a most serious dilemma. It involves the repudiation of Section 2, Article IV., of the Constitution, which provides that the "citizens of each State shall be entitled to all privileges and immunities of citizens in the several States."

This negation of the equalness of freedom affords a ludicrous illustration of insubstantial equality by authorizing the public servant to pick out, arrange, ticket, mark, stamp, brand, and label, on account of their color, the very class of citizens the recognition of whose equality of right and privilege, without regard to color, according to the Supreme Court, "all the power of the government is pledged to enforce." It contents itself with saying, We have afforded you a "substantial accommodation," although it is so conceded as clearly to show you disentitled to identity of right and privilege; and subjects you to the proscription and coercion from which the superior race is exempt, on account of the difference between its color and yours, which is emblematic of your previous condition.

The intolerance and the repressiveness of the "moral sense" (race-prejudice) of Hall *v.* DeCuir, thus disguised, abates the growth of free institutions in order to gratify all that remains of the hereditary instincts of by-gone slavery. The vanity and frippery which parade their ·tattered, faded rags and mouldy trappings, besmeared with the nation's blood, mock and burlesque the broad, plain, substantial, equality of this amendment; which is certainly not satisfied by an equality in "accommodation" afforded under such brutalizing conditions, and civilly more degrading to the race to-day than were slavery's clanking chains a century ago.

CHAPTER XXXIX.

"A great revolution has happened,—a revolution made, not by chopping and changing of power in any of the existing States, but by the appearance of a new State, of a new species, in a new part of the globe. It has made as great a change in all the relations and balances and gravitations of power as the appearance of a new planet would in the system of the solar world."—EVARTS.

"Oppression is but another name for irresponsible power, if history is to be trusted."—PINCKNEY.

"I could sooner believe with Lord Monboddo, that there are men with tails like cats, as long as his lordship pleases, and conclude with him, from the authority of his famished friend, that human flesh (even to those who are not famished) is the sweetest of all viands to the human taste, than admit that 'every kind of relation is a pure idea of intellect, which can never be apprehended by sense; and that those particularly which are expressed by cases are more abstract and metaphysical than the others.'"
—TOOKE.

"The doctrine, that 'all men are naturally equal' (of course, only in so far as their claims are concerned), has not only been asserted by philanthropists like Granville Sharpe, but, as Sir Robert Filmer, a once renowned champion of absolute monarchy, tells us, 'Heyward, Blackwood, Barclay, and others that have bravely vindicated the rights of kings, . . . with one consent admitted the natural liberty and equality of mankind.'"
—SPENCER.

"And possibly he will anticipate the further inference that this first and all-essential law, declaratory of the liberty of each, limited only by the like liberty of all, is that fundamental truth of which the moral sense is to give an intuition, and which the intellect is to develop into a scientific morality."—ID.

"It is a generalization of experience, too wide in its range to be taken in by a superficial observation, but which may, nevertheless, be laid down as a maxim of universal application, both to the individual and to the state, that in the long run morality is more convenient than convenience itself. And as to the familiar argument that breaches are so natural and so common and so hard to prevent and punish, there is this much to be said—the flag must be kept flying in high places. To accommodate private

416

appetite we must not scale down the standard of public morality. The state must not teach her own children object-lessons in vice."—JUDGE C. E. PHELPS.

" Men have such a propensity to divide into personal factions that the smallest appearance of real difference will divide them. What can be imagined more trivial than the difference between one color of livery and another in horse-races? Yet this difference begot the most inveterate factions in the Greek empire, the *Prasini* and *Veneti,* who never suspended their animosities till they ruined that unhappy government."—HUME.

" Should a state of parties arise founded on geographical boundaries, and other physical and permanent distinctions which happen to coincide with them, what is to control those great repulsive masses from awful shock against each other?"—MADISON.

" That the Christian religion cannot exist in this country with such a fraternity will not, I think, be disputed with me. On that religion, according to our mode, all our laws and institutions stand, as upon their base. That scheme is supposed in every transaction of life; and if that were done away, everything else, as in France, must be changed along with it. Thus, religion perishing, and with it this Constitution, it is a matter of endless meditation what order of things would follow it."— BURKE.

" Among the many difficulties that you find in expressing the heinousness of so incredible a piece of impiety, this one offers itself, you say, which is easily said, and must often be repeated,—to wit, that the sun itself never beheld a more outrageous action."—MILTON.

" Those who thrust temporal sovereignty upon her treat her as their prototypes treated her author. They bow the knee, and spit upon her; they cry ' Hail !' and smite her on the cheek; they put a sceptre in her hand, but it is a fragile reed; they crown her, but it is with thorns; they cover with purple the wounds which their own hands have inflicted on her; and inscribe magnificent letters over the cross on which they have fixed her, to perish in ignominy and pain."—MACAULAY.

THE title of the superior class to constitutional immunities and privileges under the " moral sense" of the " equality-not-identity" principle is no whit stronger than Attila's, who conceived himself " to have a divine claim to the dominion of the earth." The annexation of the artificial emblems of slavery constitutes in itself a substantial inequality between the races, because it transgresses freedom by compelling one portion of the society of the State, in its pursuits of life, liberty, and happiness, to exercise in a way not in accordance with its own volitions those immunities and privileges which are accorded the other race without restriction or limitation, and by permitting this constitutional right to be exercised by the inferior race, only in accordance with the condition that the same be enjoyed subject and subservient to the gratification of the capricious peculiar prejudices of the other race.

When it is reflected that the Supreme Court has declared that this grant of constitutional equality was a guarantee of the immunity of this race " from all legal discrimination indicative of inferiority in civil society;" that this grant of immunity must be construed liberally in conformity with the intention of the grantors, who designed thereby to express and enforce the doctrine of the universality of civil freedom for the express purpose of establishing upon a constitutional foundation the equality of the civil rights of this race : the subsequent promulgation of a theory, that, in the constitutional interpretation of this grant, a distinction must be observed between the identity and the equality of civil rights,—that equality does not include identity; that the consequence of the dissimilarity should authorize a system of constitutional inequality, indicative of the inferiority of the civil rights of this very race, by the re-institution and enforcement against it of well-recognized signs of its former subservience and inferiority in civil society,—would seem to afford a phenomenal illustration of the paradox mountainous, the paradox colossal, which, it is believed, is not equalled in all the records of historical jurisprudence.

That rule cannot work a substantial equalization which abrogates in respect of one race, even partially, the privileges and immunities which the other enjoys. To obtain such a consequent, the abrogation in respect of such privileges and immunities must necessarily be the result of restrictions and conditions, imposed in general rules equally applicable, under like circumstances and conditions, to both races. In the complex and highly-organized American civilization, the working of the rules which secure equality, in the every-day correlation of the civic life of the two races, should be free, easy, elastic, and natural.

No difficulty whatever, in the application of this highly simple and comprehensive principle, perfectly adaptable to the philosophy of liberty, has been so far encountered in the equalization of the civil rights of the superior class; and it is only necessary to enforce the very same rules and regulations which have heretofore obtained in the department of America's historical equality, before the admission of this race to American citizenship was made by the provisions of the amendment.

This rule of "equality-not-identity" and of "substantial accommodation," etc., instead of repealing all limitations on actions other than such as are necessitated by the coexistence, as equals, of the individual units of the society of the state, authorizes the imposition and enforcement of restrictions and limitations upon one class, the legal imposition of which upon any other is wholly omitted. Instead of bringing about that civic state of equilibrium which tends to direct both races in their onward march of progress, it segregates and isolates this one race from the other, and consequently retards the progress of both towards the one common goal of civic equality contemplated by this constitutional amendment.

Why should the "Equality-not-identity" legal fiction be allowed to limit the civil rights of men to mere physical "accommodation"? Is not this a purely gratuitous, arbitrary boundary line, located without warrant of law, divine or human? This limitation of civil rights to physical, substantial accommodation is in strict accord with the long-cherished theory of mediæval slavery, that the African citizen was not a human being. The semi-reptile purpose lurking beneath the sinuous folds of this doctrine is upon closer inspection entirely apparent. But the civil rights of an American citizen, who is now discovered to be a human being, embraces more than a particular quality, kind, and description of provender or apartment. He is not to be fed and stabled as cattle. This dumb, driven offspring of slavery cannot be led to the trough and chained by the halter of serfdom, even though the food and the accommodation should be finer. While the Fourteenth Amendment stands, the semi-savage spirit of slavery cannot thus lock the gates of the temple consecrated to Liberty. It cannot exorcise the spirit of Freedom by this sorcery of words. It cannot restore slavery's broken altars. Its dying worshippers might as well attempt to perpetuate its dark rites by sounding brass or clanging cymbal. Those living forces, the souls of this race as " human beings," constitute factors which the Christian state, by this amendment, recognizes before God and man. The doctrine that " Equality does not mean identity" removes from the consideration of jurisprudence the immortal part of man, which came from heaven and at last is to return thither. It is entirely oblivious of that within us which is so restless in its desires for the attainment of a higher good. This doctrine defaces the image of God in man, —richer than all worlds. It takes from the subject, who owes only his duty to the state, the aspirations of the soul which rules and moulds his existence.

Under this amendment the territory of civil rights is co-extensive with the domain of civilization, and the citizen of a Christian state never again can be subjected to ignominious indignities; restricted, imprisoned, isolated, branded, badged, classified, marked, or discriminated against by the formularies, ordinances, and ceremonials of primitive barbarism. It now appears (phenomenal as it may seem in Christian America), that the divine key-stone in the arch of universal Liberty—the soul of man—has escaped the attention of the ministers of justice; the sentient, immortal, intelligent, immaterial part of man, that which feels, thinks, doubts, moves, worships, loves, weeps; the vital force and energy which impart inspiration and aspiration ; the something unearthly which never dies, but returns to the God who gave it when dust returneth to dust: this part of the being of man—to whom civil rights were granted, for the exercise of his God-given functions—has, it appears, entirely escaped the juristical observation of the chief ministers of state seated, as the vicegerents of the Almighty, in the Supreme Court of America, with the general authority and jurisdiction, under the Fourteenth Amendment, of administering the heaven-born justice of equality, which the Declaration of Independence proclaimed.

In this extraordinary omission consists the fundamental defect of the startling creed that "Equality does not mean identity." Its postulate loses sight of the absolute and infinite ; it shuts its juristical eye to the bed-rock of the historic fact, that the foundation of the American state is to be traced nowhere else than to the doctrines of the Christ of history. This maxim loses sight of the historic fact, that, if Christian civilization means the gradual, progressive, indefinite improvement of man, his civil rights must, therefore, be adaptable to the wants and necessities of man's internal nature, his higher destiny, his endless perfectibility, and are not to be tortured into an instrumentality for his debasement. Thus American civil rights are intimately associated with man's true nature, his real inward essence, as it stands correlated to the physical. The doctrine that civil rights concern only the physical wants—in law-jargon, the "accommodation" of man—is stone-blind to the great political truth, that the Christian state is built upon the foundation of the equality of all men before the law, and other foundation can no man lay than that which is laid. The postulate of American equality must necessarily assume the divine origin of man.

The boldest defender of juristic race-despotism, and the whole venomous brood of sneerers at what they call the sentimentalism of the religious philosophy of the equality of man, cannot deny the historical truth, that the accepted principle of American equality by the law of the land is founded upon the doctrine of the Christ of history, and that from the Christian stand-point one of the main results of the bestowal of civil rights was the restoration of the mutilated, defaced, and half-obscured image of the spiritual man in the colored American. If this be not the true interpretation of the Constitution and this Article, the sun of Christian liberty must either wane, set, or swerve off into some eccentric Ingersollian course, condemned, like that lost star, through clouds and darkness forever to sweep onward into "unexplored infinity," and the State itself depart from the true purpose of its origin and foundation.

Whoever turns over the pages of history, and traces with attentive eye the mysterious clue of divine Providence in the American state, will see that it deals with the high destiny of man, the full rights and prerogatives of the spiritual relations of his being. His civil rights are not confined, as matter of law, to the accommodation of his physical wants. Every historical event in the onward march of the Anglo-Saxon, which preceded and led up to the Declaration of Independence and evolved the American Constitution, postulated man's likeness to God as a fundamental principle. Through his title to Christian freedom, which deals with internal factors, their structure and function, and whose aim it is to sustain and elevate man, he became endowed with the rights of a sovereign unit in the Christian state, by the very system of equality of civil rights which has heretofore developed the highest type of civilization of an American citizen.

Civil rights relate to what may be classified under the head of moral, emotional, and intellectual wants (not less than those which may be described and included under the law-term "accommodation"); signifying in their most comprehensive sense those refined appointments, adjuncts, and luxuries which minister to the happiness of daily life and have now grown to be necessities in America. Rightly considered as an assured truth and instrumentality of Christianity, their mission is to awaken, exalt, and illumine man's moral sense, impart warmth and energy to his daily pursuits, and stimulate a noble ambition for the attainment of every excellence in his civic, intellectual, political, and moral life in this world, which, according to the teachings of Christ, is a probationary state, in which this being, who has been created heir to the immortality and bears the image of his Maker, shall attain his highest development and preparation for a future and nobler existence.

If the Fourteenth Amendment is the very spirit of Christian justice engrafted upon the Constitution; if the genius of Christianity stands as a competent witness for the divine origin of liberty and equality in America; if equality means freedom from compulsory, unlawful restraint, exemption from interference, with full, equal, lofty, and universal right to do what the law allows; if it means the safe, unmolested enjoyment, in a quiet, sovereign, and continuous way, of those privileges and immunities which are the common liberties of the nation, which the whole society of the state—upper, middle, lower, social, capitalistic, and labor classes alike—daily enjoy, and freely as the air they breathe: then, according to the law of the land and the hypothesis of Christianity, the consequent is demonstrable: that deprivation of this natural liberty, by the open, notorious, deliberate, unnecessary, wilful civic debasement of any human being, be he originally Greek, barbarian, Scythian, bond or free, is a crime alike against the State and the Author of government.

It is apparent that the doctrine of "substantial accommodation," which, as we have seen, is the genesis of the "Equality-not-identity" theory, has no fitting place in the judicial administration of a free representative government. It is not a regulator or equalizer of human condition, but it is a begetter of those gross, corrupting, and degrading inequalities which are indicative of the lowest type of social life. It is equally apparent that this principle disregards the pure and spiritual foundation of the state, and that it daily turns away from the great fountain of Civil Liberty thousands who are sorely athirst for the waters of life. It has closed the great sanctuary of freedom to a people weary and heavy-laden, asking to worship at the common altar of humanity, pleading in vain for communion with their fellow-man in America, upon conditions which are not degrading, but befitting, to the divinity which stirs within them.

With cold judicial formalism Jurisprudence—in this instance a mere mockery of justice—turns aside and permits the spirit of man to be brutalized. by the sly public servant. The modern sectary of civilized savagedom seeks to perpetuate the previous condition of the slave by enforcing the observance of ceremonials and distinctions peculiar to slavery. Instead of abrogating antiquated customs, backed by all the power of the state, he is continually reburnishing those shackles and patching the barbaric dress and coverings which this amendment struck and tore from the freedman. He compels the new citizen to wear the habiliments of the old slave, and daily forges and fastens upon Civil Rights the newly-gilded chains which now manacle them with their base indissoluble bonds.

In vain do seven millions of men, women, and children cry

out, "See! the beast of slavery, from whom I fled; save me! for every vein and pulse throughout my frame, she had made tremble!" The "fell monster with the deadly sting" has indeed, with all the glorious circumstance and pomp of barbaric slavery, reappeared, disguised under this ugly mask, not unlike his counterpart, described in Dante's "Inferno,"—

> "His head and upper part exposed on land,
> But laid not on the shore his bestial train;
> His face the semblance of a just man's wore,
> So kind and gracious was its outward cheer;
> The rest was serpent all."

It is a curious historical matter, worthy of observation, that the "Equality-not-identity" fiction, which is the parent of the heresy, "Substantial equality in accommodation," in the features of its historic physiognomy closely resembles those of the famous English Historic Trust, of which it has been said, "It had for its mother Force and Fraud, and for its nurse a Court of Conscience." In the mean time, the illustrious sages of the law content themselves with the vague suggestion that the exorcism of the evil spirit is a matter over which Congress alone has exclusive jurisdiction.

Almighty Justice in America, with eminent authority, seldom speaks, contenting herself with enlarging her borders and making broader the phylacteries of her judicial robe. By abstract constitutional construction she pays—the lip-service—the "tithe of mint, anise, and cumin" to Civil Rights; but the weightier matters of the law—judgment and mercy unto seven millions of human beings, to free them from the burning shame of slavery's degrading ceremonialism—she omits. Whilst the myrmidons of race-prejudice are lifting up their voices, shouting, as of old, "Let them be crucified," supreme Justice, packed in the ice of conventional form, and too eminently decorous to exhibit human emotion, with averted eye stands aloof, utterly unconcerned at the dramatic scenes daily enacted in America, where hordes of semi-civilized barbarians appear plucking from the grasp of Civil Rights the glorious sceptre and the golden crown. Others strip her of that noble cloth of state woven in the mighty loom of the Fourteenth Amendment, the richest garment ever worn at the Republican Court. Some, again, have tattooed her limbs, in all the variegated hideous colors of the primitive barbaric age, whilst others hold infernal, exultant orgies over her prostrate form, while they plat a crown of thorns with which to bind her temples, and erect bitter crosses with this superscription (taken from the letter and spirit of the law of Hall *v.* DeCuir), " This is Civil Rights." " Equality of civil rights does not mean identity of immunity, and privilege from legal discrimination on account of color."

CHAPTER XL.

"Hence, though advanced ideas, when once established, act upon society and aid its further advance; yet the establishment of such ideas depends on the fitness of the society for receiving them."—COMTE.

"As, then, the disability of the savage to perceive the elementary truths of number is no argument against their existence, and no obstacle to their discovery and development, so, the circumstance that some do not see the law of equal freedom to be an elementary truth of ethics, does not prevent its being one."—SPENCER.

"But how am I to prove the existence of these rights? I do not propose to do it by a long chain of legal argumentation, nor by the production of numerous books with the leaves dog-eared and the pages marked. If it depended upon judicial precedents, I think I could produce as many as might be necessary. If we claimed this freedom under any kind of prescription, I could prove a good long possession in ourselves and those under whom we claim it. I might begin with Tacitus and show how the contest arose in the forests of Germany more than two thousand years ago."—J. BLACK.

"That men, yea councils, may err; and that, unless the judgment given do satisfy your minds, unless it be such as ye can by no further argument oppugn; in a word, unless you perceive and acknowledge it yourselves consonant with God's words; to stand unto it, not allowing it, were to sin against your own consciences."—HOOKER.

"It is thus that in imperial ages there may be a higher culture and structure of the civil order, as in France under the empire. It is thus, also, that the study of the civil law of itself has the attraction only of external symmetry, and impresses one only as a formal system and as a cold and lifeless anatomy. It has not the spirit of an historic power. The genius of the great masters of the Justinian era can throw over it only a faint glow, and the energy of a living spirit is wanting in the most splendid development of the civil organization of society."—MULFORD.

"We should not forget that our country is large, and our fellow-citizens of different manners, interests, and habits; that our laws, to be right, must be equal and general. Of course, the differing interests must be combined, and brotherly conciliation and forbearance continually exercised, if we will judge with propriety of those measures that respect a nation at large."—BOUDINOT.

426

" This is the age of freedom and political equality, not of privilege and oppression."—O'DONAHUE.

" The aim of the statesman is no longer the conformance of legislation to a divine law of righteousness, and the end of the state is no longer the fulfilment of an order which he did not create, but whose principle he is to obey. The faith of the people, the fulfilment of its work through all the trials of its years, the very devotion and sacrifice of its children, the wisdom and courage of its leaders, have no real moral significance, but are only the continuance of a sacrilegious course, the circumstances of a profane history."—MULFORD.

" It was a tremendous proclamation. Philosophy shrinks and shrivels before it. All ethical speculations are concluded by the one maxim, that God's commands are to be obeyed ; all metaphysical speculations are silenced by the shout of a host, ' He is, and we are sent to establish his authority over the earth.' "—ID.

" Their emancipation will sooner result from the mild and melting influences of Christianity than from the storm and tempest of fiery controversy. This influence, though slow, is sure. The doctrines and miracles of our Saviour have required nearly two thousand years to convert but a small portion of the human race, and even among Christian nations what gross errors still exist! Let us leave the progress as well as the result in the hand of Him who sees the end, who chooses to work by slow influences, and with whom a thousand years are but as one day."—GENERAL LEE.

" I said, there was a society of men among us, bred up from their youth in the art of proving, by words multiplied for the purpose, that white is black, and black is white."—SWIFT.

THE sudden re-arrangement of American society upon a pure principle of equality, before the moral perfection of jurisprudence was sufficiently advanced to admit the doctrine of equality in the distribution of civil rights, accounts for the unsympathetic and antagonistic tendencies, otherwise unintelligible, which have resulted in the formulation of the legal fiction, that " Equality does not mean identity ;" and the development of its natural corollary, that the substantial accommodation which satisfies the requirements of the law does not deny the right of the public servant to discriminate on account of color. The still-lingering savageness of the old conditions of pro-slavery jurisprudence could not immediately rise from its low instincts to the loftier, intrinsic ethical conceptions of the new institution. The Supreme Court have obviously regarded the political reorganization of the American state, upon the more elevated plane of the Fourteenth Amendment, as a movement in advance of the requirements of the civilization of the age, and wholly beyond the capabilities of the race to whose hitherto dormant faculties it afforded the possibilities and opportunities of future development.

From this false premise, it was an easy step to the conclusion that it was not only within the province, but that it was the manifest duty, of the judicial department, from motives of high moral and social expediency, to formulate a system by which the modification and curtailment of the practical working of the new institution could be accomplished, under the color of the lawful authority of the State. Significant evidential circumstances, clearly corroborative both of the motive and of the object had in view in the formulation of this " legal fiction," are furnished by the Supreme Court in the famous Civil-Rights Cases, where, as we have seen, that illustrious body, in its judicial opinion, warned the advocates of civil rights, that " they were running the slavery" (*i.e.*, equality of civil rights) "argument into the ground ;" and when the new citizen of the State, clamoring for a liberal and spiritual construction of his broad charter of freedom, declared to the court, " I was anterior to all this; I existed previously, in virtue of other titles; society belonged to me; I was a part of it, before this state of violence and struggle in which you meet with me; I was legitimate, but others contested and seized my rights ;"—when he exhorted the Supreme Court to rise above the fleeting passions and prejudices which agitate society ; to abandon a policy without principle and without banner, made up of expedients and pretexts ; ever tottering; leaning on every side for support, and advancing in reality towards no good object,—a policy which foments and aggravates that uncertainty of men's minds, that loss of heart, that want of faith, of consistency, perseverance, and energy, which cause disquiet to the country,—the Supreme Court contented itself with the stolid reply in the Civil-Rights Cases: " There were thousands of free colored people in this country

before the abolition of slavery, enjoying all the essential rights
of liberty, life, and property, the same as white citizens ; yet no
one at that time thought that it was any invasion of his personal
status as a freeman, because he was not admitted to all the privileges enjoyed by white citizens or because he was subjected to
discrimination.''

The judicial branch of the government, by this language of
grave import, admonished the country, that, according to the
moral sense of the theorists and ideologists of the court, it was
not expedient to conform American jurisprudence to the exalted
standard of morality which had been proposed by the nation,
and which the political reformation of the Fourteenth Amendment sought to enforce. As we have already seen, the appearance of this handwriting on the wall of the Supreme Court,
somewhat suddenly abated the severe rigor of the partisan eti-
quette which political policy had hitherto exacted whenever
Civil-Rights was presented in public.

It is now plain to the most unobservant that these tributes
to Civil-Rights were merely an ointment of precious words, the
lip-homage of a gross flattery, equally devoid of truthfulness,
fidelity, generosity, and honesty. And accordingly, since this
singular effort of judicial genius which attempted to relegate
Civil-Rights to the Dred-Scott status of a liberated slave, the
arbitri elegantiarum upon questions of civil rights have disappeared from the Imperial Republican Court. The abolition of
this judicial dilettanteism, after the ghastly foregone conclusion
that Civil-Rights was doomed in that august tribunal, tended
in a marked degree to restore national self-respect. Ever since
the promulgation of this lofty, high-sounding, and domineering
juristical pronunciamento, the advocate, and his pale, feeble
client, Civil-Rights, have stood trembling in the presence of
the courts ; and barbarizing race-antagonism has increased and
multiplied, until the features of its physiognomy are indelibly
engraven upon the hearts and minds of the public.

The inferior State courts, quoting the text of the decisions of
these justiciars of the Supreme Court, and following in their
course, have everywhere stereotyped their incompetency to recognize, that the appointed purpose of the spirit of " civic equality

before the law" was the adaptation of the humanity of this race
to the altered conditions of the civilization of which that civic
equality is the loftiest and most benign type.   Ever since the
solemn affirmation of the ante-bellum code in the Civil-Rights
Cases, " that it was no invasion of the status of a citizen of this
race, if he was not admitted to all the privileges enjoyed by
white citizens," and " was subjected to discrimination" by reason
of his color, American Jurisprudence has stood under the shadow
of the δαίμων of this darkened " moral sense," which illustrates
its unfitness to march in the triumphal procession of " equality
before the law," by its invention of that double-dealing legal
fiction, that " Equality is not identity," that "substantial accommodation" in form—which is substantial inequality in mind,
soul, spirit, heart, and feeling—satisfies the letter of the great
constitutional commandment of the Fourteenth Amendment;
that civic equality—the equality which implies immunity from
legal discrimination upon grounds which are equally applicable
to all citizens, under like circumstances of situation and conditions—is only the prerogative of the permanently privileged
class; that, provided " substantial accommodation" is afforded,
immunity from the legal discriminations of the ceremonialisms
of slavery which the superior race enjoys is not the privilege
of the inferior race.   This spirit of barbarism despiritualized
American civilization of its divine ideal, civic equality, by a
legal fiction which is utterly foundationless.   Thus ideas thought
to be obsolete have been reincarnated, and jurisprudence, by
the adoption of an utterly baseless semblance, has attempted to
retard and set back the growth of American civilization.   Either
as a premise, proposition, or conclusion of law, " Equality does
not mean identity" and " substantial accommodation" assert no
definite postulate.

Can any process of reasoning be conducted with obscure
terms which are left without definition ?   What conclusion can
be predicated of a premise which employs no well-known or
explainable terms, which omits all necessary principia, which
puts forth no axiom that is evident in itself or susceptible of
demonstration, and which involves mentally-substituted definitions that mislead by their ambiguity ?   Does either of these

propositions assert any axiom self-evident or demonstrable? Is it more or less than putting forth an ambiguous proposition, and taking advantage of its double-meaning terms, "equality," "identity," "substantial," by failing to produce definitions which explain them?

The superstructure of American equality rests upon no such fantastical basis as these factitious creations—mere legal fictions —gratuitously assume. That civic reorganization in America which gave each citizen of the State assurance of "equality before the law" has its foundation in the universal, broad, deep, vital regeneration of the nation. Its noble groundwork and superstructure afford problems and propositions, historical, ethical, constitutional, and economic, many of which are susceptible of a demonstration almost mathematical. The designers of American equality have furnished abundant supplies and fitting materials for solid, vigorous, convincing argumentation, by immutable rules of reasoning, well known to the lofty and logical minds of great publicists, constitutional lawyers, historians, and political economists.

The march of Providence does not restrict itself by the stationary, narrow limitation of the etymological definitions of the language of man. The postulate of Providence culminating in the Fourteenth Amendment does not trouble the nation with the consideration of any "fiction" which may spring out of social expediences, political lucubrations, or the *obiter dicta* of courts.

The problems presented by the Fourteenth Amendment of the Constitution reached their destination through time "as the gods of Homer strode through space." They looked forward to that development of man which was most precious and profitable to the whole society of the state. They sought, through the disenthralment of a down-trodden and shackled race and the restoration of all its primal manhood, the development of the true grandeur of the State. The propositions present no such absurd query as the question, how far equality could be transformed into inequality and yet remain substantial equality. On the contrary, they stretched to the sublime height of having for their object the development and ennobling of the faculties, sentiments, and ideas of the internal and external man. These propositions comprehend nothing less expansive and immense than the intellectual and moral development of the human species. Their framers saw that the treasures of a universal civilization, in all their lustre and grandeur, were now within the grasp of the American people, provided, by a reformation of the state, the cardinal fundamental principles of truth, right, and justice could be incorporated into their Constitution, and those of force, fraud, and falsehood forever eliminated.

Their objective point was not verbal captiousness, as Mr. Justice Clifford's *obiter dicta* might lead us to suppose; but the recognition of the great humane principle that all men in the state stand upon terms of civic equality; that the differences between races, in a great measure, result from the accidents of time and environment; and that the African, having the same right as the white man to claim Adam as his great first father, by the laws of nature and nature's God, and by all the charities of our divine religion, is entitled to the same opportunities of pleasure, education, and protection as are offered to the rest of mankind. The main postulate of this amendment undoubtedly is, the purification of America from the alloy of slavery; instead of dull, stupid selfishness, instead of the brutalizing instinct of physical force over the soul and body of man, its moral propositions afford an inspiration, throughout the wide borders of America, which invite that nobler sense of individual independence, the attainment of the full fruition of the pleasure " of feeling one's self a man, and the sentiment of personality, of human spontaneity, in its full development."

The prophetic gaze of the statesmen who framed this great measure foresaw the future admixture and coexistence, and the " *huddling* together" under one government, of various races and peoples, with narrow hereditary prejudices, and with ideas, habits, social manners and customs utterly diverse. They saw the vast career of continuous progress which lay in the pathway of American civilization. What they did not foresee was the overthrow and nullification of the organic law of the land by the juristical sophistries of its appointed guardians; and in their sanguine hopefulness, and trust of the future, destined so soon

to be disappointed, they enacted and confirmed, they thought,
by every sanction the broad provisions for that grand future
which are incorporated in the Thirteenth, Fourteenth, and Fifteenth Articles of Amendment to the Constitution, whose import
is as follows :

Thirteenth Amendment.—That " neither slavery nor involuntary servitude, except as a punishment for crime, whereof the
party shall have been duly convicted, shall exist within the
United States or any place subject to their jurisdiction."

Fourteenth Amendment.—That " no State shall deprive any
person of life, liberty, or property without due process of law,
nor deny to any person the equal protection of the laws." [By
Section 2 of Article IV. of the Constitution, it had been already
provided, that the " citizens of each State shall be entitled to
all privileges and immunities of citizens in the several States."]
That representation in the national government should be ap-
portioned among the several States according to their respective
numbers ; that if the right to vote of any individual male citizen
being twenty-one years of age was abridged, except for participation in rebellion or crime, the basis of representation should be
reduced in the proportion which the number of such citizens
whose right to vote was thus abridged should bear to the whole
number of male citizens twenty-one years of age. That the
validity of the " public debt," incurred for the payment of pensions and bounties, and for military services rendered in the suppression of the insurrection and rebellion against the doctrine
of equality before the law, which resulted in the recognition, re-
establishment, and enforcement of the equality of the rights of
mankind in America, should never.be questioned. That neither
the United States nor any State should assume or pay any claim
for loss, by emancipation from slavery, of a human being made
in the image and express likeness of his Maker ; nor pay any
debt or obligation incurred in aid of the insurrection or rebellion to overthrow that natural and revealed law of equality—
civil rights—of this part of the great family of mankind, who,
by reason of the *casus omissus* in the Constitution of a provision for " due process of law" (according to the historical and
political significance of those terms), had been held in bondage

as a mere chattel, by another and more favored class of the human species.

Fifteenth Amendment.—To prevent any curtailment whatever of political rights, it was further stipulated that " the right of citizens of the United States to vote should not be denied or abridged, by the United States or by any State, on account of race, color, or previous condition of servitude." To make assurance doubly sure, Congress in these three amendments was also invested with full power and authority to enforce, by the law of the land, these all-embracing and beneficent provisions for the fundamental incorporation in the American Constitution of the cardinal principle of the equality before the law of all American citizens. Such a provision had never before been thought essential either to the perpetuity of, or to the transmission of the title to, the royal patrimony of American freedom, in the preceding twelve amendments to the Constitution.

CHAPTER XLI.

"Progressing civilization, which is of necessity a succession of compromises between old and new, requires a perpetual readjustment of the compromise between the ideal and the practicable in social arrangements: to which end, both elements of the compromise must be kept in view."—HUTTON.

"Let us follow this luminous thread of plausible error, which pierces into the very marrow of humanity."—HEGEL.

"It entangles itself at last in a labyrinth of irreconcilable contradictions."—DESCARTES.

"It may never wholly cease until the end of history. The *confederacy* —Southern—is the embodiment of the evil spirit in which there is the destruction of the being of the nation, the organic and moral unity and continuity of society, and the subversion of the whole to selfish ends. It strives to subvert the nation, to serve its end in the perpetuance of slavery, or the pride of birth, or hatred of race."—MULFORD.

"If it be right that the conduct of the nineteenth century should be determined not by its own judgment, but by that of the eighteenth, it will be equally right that the conduct of the twentieth century should be determined not by its own judgment, but by that of the nineteenth."— SYDNEY SMITH.

Lactantius, speaking of the universal equality of mankind, says,— "Aequitatem dico—se cum ceteris coaequandi, quam Cicero aequabilitatem vocat; Deus enim, qui homines generat et inspirat, omnes aequos, id est pares esse voluit; eamdem conditionem vivendi omnibus posuit, omnes ad sapientiam genuit; omnibus immortalitatem spopondit. Nemo apud eum servus est, nemo dominus."

"The things which among ourselves are called equal—whether lines, angles, weights, temperatures, sounds, or colors—are things which produce in us sensations that cannot be distinguished from each other."— SPENCER.

"That stupendous invention of 'speech for the purpose of concealing thought.'"—CARLYLE.

" 'Tis you that say it, not I ; you do the deeds,
And your ungodly deeds find me the words."—Sophocles.

" These heroes are dead. They died for liberty : they died for us. They are at rest. They sleep in the land they made free, under the flag they rendered stainless, under the solemn pines, the sad hemlocks, the tearful willows, the embracing vines. They sleep beneath the shadows of the clouds, careless alike of sunshine or storm, each in the windowless palace of rest."—Ingersoll.

" From the successive strata of our historical deposits, they diligently gather all the high-colored fragments, pounce upon everything that is curious and sparkling, and chuckle like children over their glittering acquisitions ; meanwhile the rich veins of wisdom that ramify amidst this worthless *débris* lie utterly neglected. Cumbrous volumes of rubbish are greedily accumulated, whilst those masses of rich ore that should have been dug out, and from which golden truths might have been smelted, are left unthought of and unsought."—Spencer.

" Political freedom, therefore, is, as we say, an external result of an internal sentiment,—is alike in origin, practicability, and permanence, dependent on the moral sense ; and it is only when this is supreme in its influence that so high a form of social organization as a democracy can be maintained."—Id.

" I am consoled if American liberty will remain entire for half a century."—Patrick Henry.

" I come not here armed at all points, with the statute-book doubled down in dog's-ears, to defend the cause of liberty. I can acknowledge no veneration for any procedure, law, or ordinance that is repugnant to reason and the first principles of our Constitution. I rejoice that America has resisted."—Pitt.

" Liberty, that best gift, dealt out by the impartial hand of nature, even to the brute creation."—Tacitus.

" The king ought to use the power of law and right as God's minister and vicegerent ; the power of wrong is the devil's and not God's ; when the king turns aside to do injustice, he is the minister of the devil."—Milton.

" On the other hand, among a people sufficiently endowed with the faculty responding to the law of equal freedom, no such retrograde process is possible. The man of genuinely democratic feeling loves liberty as a miser loves gold, for its own sake and quite irrespective of its advantages."—Spencer.

"I aver that this doctrine, in all its length and breadth, is false and pernicious. It is the foundation on which all slavery rests, and the excuse for all forms of tyranny. It has no support in any sound rule of public law, and has never been acknowledged by wise or virtuous governments in any age since the advent of Christ. You can find no authority for it except in the examples of men whose names are given over to universal execration. Mohammed asserted it when he forced his religion upon the subjugated East, when churches were violently converted into mosques, and the emblem of Christianity was trampled under foot, to be replaced by the badge of the impostor. On the same principle Poland was partitioned, and Ireland plundered a dozen times. The King of Dahomey acted upon it when he sold his captives, and the men of Massachusetts endorsed it when they took them in exchange for captives of their own. You and your *confrères* adopted it as a part of your political creed when, after the Southern people were thoroughly subdued, you denied them all the rights of freemen, tore up their society, abrogated all laws which could protect them in person or property, broke their legal governments in pieces, and put them under the domination of notorious thieves whom you forced them to accept as their absolute masters."—J. BLACK.

THE future solution of all race-problems in America must depend upon the learned and faithful exposition of the historical, political, constitutional, and common-law significance of the pregnant provisions and commandments of these articles. The kind, class, nature, extent, or character of the body of liberties, privileges, and immunities, which are held in common and enjoyed, as freely as the air they breathe, by the white citizens of the States and nation on terms of undisturbed equality, is not involved in this controversy. They have grown to form as much a part of American existence and every-day life as the productions of the country's soil and climate. They are as well recognized by the dwellers in the land as the common highways in their immediate vicinity. They are the elements of civilization which have rocked the cradle of American infancy; they are to the nation a sort of ocean, on whose bosom all its citizens may sail, with calm hearts and tranquil spirits.

The real issue presented in this controversy involves the historical, constitutional, and political construction of the articles of the copartnership contained in these amendments, by virtue of which seven millions of citizens were recently admitted to a full joint and several participation in the beneficent treasures of American civilization. Under the terms of these national compacts, it is admitted that there is an equality of rights by the law of the land between the citizens recently incorporated and those who originally incorporated themselves under the Constitution of the United States. This controversy presents a single, certain, material, and sharply-defined issue, which involves the constitutional, political, and civil equality of the new citizen, in the partition, apportionment, and enforcement of the rights and privileges bestowed by the letter and spirit of the articles aforesaid, in the historical, constitutional, political, and civil signification of the said joint and several national freedoms, liberties, privileges, and immunities.

The primitive, narrow, isolated, pro-slavery paths through which, with such indefatigable zeal, Mr. Justice Clifford has pursued this question, have proved unprofitable diligence, resulting in the formulation of a myth, a mere legal fiction, instead of the establishment, upon an everlasting foundation, of a vitalizing principle,—something solid, evolved from philosophic and judicial acumen, which would grapple and solve the mighty issue. The providence of God, to whom a thousand years are but as one day, after apparently sleeping for centuries, took one mighty leap, and the past centuries vanished, as if time were nothing. Its stupendous handiwork is clearly visible in vast achievements, through mortal instrumentalities, suddenly spreading before its apparently forgotten child in America, with all the signs of lavish power, the treasures of equality before the law, and a civilization whose proud boast it now is, that equality of right is the crown of the national edifice. It is not alone in the artificial technology of the law-term, with which every professional mind is familiar, "due process of law,"—or in those words, "law of the land," as commonly employed by legal writers and by jurists, and which were taken from the celebrated twenty-ninth chapter of King John's charter, where it was provided, as the security of freemen,—that the mysterious key to the true construction of equality before the law is to be discovered. The archives of the past, wherein is recorded the everlasting, irrepressible, irreconcilable conflict between two hostile principles,—

right and wrong, equality and disparity, tyranny and freedom, the lust for dominion and humanity,—can alone afford a philosophic clue to the interpretation of these three amendments, which place equality of civil rights upon a permanent foundation.

Before the empire of Truth can assert the full sovereignty of her reign in America according to the letter and spirit of these amendments; before a sound judicial interpretation of the mighty revolution accomplished through them is attempted; before the historico-constitutional construction of the high privileges, rights, and immunities confirmed to this and all other races through these three articles of amendment to the Constitution can be broadly expounded; before these great postulates of equality, freedom, and liberty can be intelligently approached; it is first necessary that the pretensions of tyranny and power, the spirit of dominion masquerading in America under the guise of a permanently privileged class, should be investigated in the lurid glare of the history of man in the Old World,—his long, perpetual sacrifice and martyrdom through the ages of the past. Read in the broad, clear light of to-day, this series of historical events seems but one continuous working out of the preordained purpose of Providence, to exhibit in America that majestic and ennobling spectacle,—the civic transformation of the state, brought about by a mighty revolution, which should overthrow every remaining vestige of the sovereignty of Tyranny, Power, Force, and Falsehood, and speedily conform the constitutional policy of the state to the eternal decrees of Truth and Justice, Liberty, Right, and Duty, by establishing the inviolable sanctity of the doctrine of the equality of man, upon firm and everlasting foundations.

In his construction of their cardinal provisions, the jurisconsult, whose imperial province is enlarged by the vast domain of the historian, should bring to the aid of a powerful understanding the profound historic and civic significance which attaches to the phraseology employed in these broad guarantees of equality. The bare statement that the legal fiction, " Equality does not mean identity," and its lineal heir, " substantial accommodation," etc., could afford aid in the grave office of expounding these weighty provisions, would appear a bitter satire to the enlightened understanding, which must detect at a glance the broad distinction between the wisdom of the law and the cunning expedients to which its professors and expositors often resort.

To a masculine mind it would seem that the judgment and reason of the framers of these great articles had been employed in vain to extirpate the institutions of slavery, if the Supreme Court was at liberty a quarter of a century afterwards (in the Civil-Rights Cases), to consider whether or not the refusal of the common privileges of an inn was a badge of servitude. The point would appear too narrow for difference of opinion. Obviously such a refusal could be solely on account of color; and, if not alike applicable to all other citizens, under like circumstances and conditions, should subject the public servant to the common-law action of " trespass on the case." It would seem to be too apparent for argument, that, if neither slavery nor involuntary servitude may hereafter exist in America, and if the rights of these citizens include that of assisting in the regulation of their several States and the nation by their ballot; if they are now full partners with the individuals who formerly composed the nation, in the national glory and treasures of Civil Liberty in America, the perpetuation of any insignia, ceremonialism, emblem, device, token, custom, ordinance, rule, or regulation, symbolic of the previous condition of slavery, and enforced as such, is a gross invasion of the equality of this race, and an act of infamous violence, second only to the tyrannical force, falsehood, and fraud by which these present members of the state had been formerly held as slaves.

The forefathers, who in an American wilderness laid the foundations of an empire of civilization, understood the historical and political purport of the great guarantee of equality which was proclaimed in the Declaration of Independence; and as they understood and intended it, that doctrine was as far removed from the day-dreams of the heated visionaries of their generation as it is from the ill-omened legal fictions of to-day which, like phantoms of darkness, are struggling for supremacy over it. Their humanity sought and their intelligence discerned a system for the civic gradation and final levelling of those innumerable prejudices which agitate the human breast, by subjecting them to the dominion of the law of the land.

Yet the patriots of '76, like the patriots of '61, clearly foresaw that the solemnization and coronation in America of the doctrine of the equality of man would not be as the dawn of a morning without clouds. In the dire necessity for the inauguration of this *ultima ratio*, this urgent essentiality of freedom, by a decisive, severe, overpowering, irrepressible conflict with hereditary tyranny, the judgment of the early founders and of the recent upholders of the American State wholly coincided. The Declaration of Independence by the former, and the adoption by the latter of these three amendments, are harmonious expressions of the unity of the same great primal truth, the principle of the equality of man before the law.

The great patriots of '61 saw that the institution of slavery, upon the annihilation of which the life of the nation depended, had opened a wide gap, through which manifold miseries had already entered, and which, if ignored, would grow ever more dangerous. It threatened no less than the final overthrow of the organic principle of the Republic, which slavery already held in abeyance. The Abolition, Free-Soil, and Republican parties, the doctrine of State rights, and all the political events which preceded the Rebellion, were different political phases of the irrepressible conflict between the doctrine of equality of rights and the force, falsehood, and fraud which held dominion over it. This political conflict had furnished matter for the debate of a century and had resulted in all the horrors of a civil war. At its termination the saviors of the nation, who had fought for the maintenance of the holy doctrine with calm, unswerving determination, engrafted upon the Constitution those three special and definite structures constituting the very principia of equality, in order that the political symmetry of the state in this regard might never again be interrupted.

It is this stupendous and beautiful growth of the Constitution which is now brought again into jeopardy, by the legal fictions which have endeavored to subvert it and make it amenable to the base uses of race-prejudice. Those common enemies of Christian charity and mankind, the race-maniacs, now struggle to compass the disruption and dismemberment of these huge branches of the tree of the state, seemingly for no graver reason than that the new-born sons and daughters of freedom have sought their umbrageous shelter.

These beings of transcendent excellency, who are now hazarding the life of this organic principle, by monstrous precedents their legal fictions have established, apparently have forgotten that the Supreme Court has judicially ascertained and recorded (in the Slaughter-House Cases), that, when the black storm of civil strife arose, and its sulphureous bolts awoke the grim, saturnine echoes of war, the dark-skinned fathers of these very sons and daughters of freedom stood between the State and its enemies, sternly resolved—

" To shield it, to save it, or perish there too ;"

and, with the cry of freedom on their lips, bared their breasts to the pitiless fury of the war which rained deadly hail upon their serried columns. To all others save the blind devotees of race-prejudice, the daring of these heroic dead would speak trumpet-tongued ; this glorious devotion to duty would sweeten and blossom in their dust.

But it is most extraordinary, as will hereafter appear, that the constitutional expounders of American equality who suffer from strange optical delusions and mental aberrations can see only grains of sand in a Sahara of gold. Their intellectual lens is not strong enough to enable them to see clearly or straight. Their prodigious activity seems employed in the multiplication of reasons, facts, and fictions to offset and overturn the historical, political, and constitutional authorities which are acknowledged by civilized man throughout the world. These unprogressive, intellectual imperialists are bent upon such a construction of equality as will prevent the abolition of race-vestments in America. The dangerous effects in the future of the American State of an all-powerful precedent, which defeats the letter and spirit of the principle of equality, do not seem to have disturbed the serene intelligence of these legal-fiction sophists, who are both courageous and ingenious in substituting the dogmatism of their legal fictions and juristical empiricism for the wisdom which is crowded into realms and ages spanned by the arches of Time.

While the progress of political enlightenment necessitates the perpetual banishment of all caste-insignia, social predilections incline the disciples of race-prejudice to uphold, by hook or by crook, the primitive pro-slavery traditions of the dark ages in America. Its luminaries decline to cross even the threshold of the great edifice of universal history, for fear they may behold the whole human race passing through their periods of barbarous inequality. They refuse to glance at the endless list of remorseless butchers stained with blood and sacrificing each other to gratify their insatiate lust for dominion over the natural and revealed law of the equality of right.

To history heaped upon history, to centuries upon centuries, the records of which contain the struggles of man against man for equality, a vast pile of ruin upon ruin (the dust and blood of antique time), their ears are closed. From this mighty drama, upon the "background of eternity," the legal-fiction doctrinaires turn aside. Their powers of generalization are apparently not sufficiently broad to perceive that the miscellaneous crimes, assassinations, insurrections, banishments, bastiles, reigns of terror, sovereign conquerors, new parties, invasions, executions, revolts, intrigues, councils, treaties, annexations, leagues, reformations, conspirators, policies, cabals, impeachments, all summed up, involve the recognition, denial, and reassertion before God and man, under the ever-varying phases of the political condition of mankind in the present and by-gone ages, of the sacred principle of the equality of man's rights in the State; and that they all seem to be directed towards this end; the fundamental doctrine of Christianity arising from its assertion of the common brotherhood of man by the

> " Divinity that shapes our ends,
> Rough-hew them how we will."

By a gross delusion, a vacant unconcern for this momentous question, and a dogged resistance to the law of reason, jurisprudence has now established, in America, the mischievous precedent, which determines that the balance and splendor of the

American State can endure although it refuses this "natural" and constitutional justice to seven millions of citizens. All these lessons of history American jurisprudence seems either to have read in vain, or it is heedless of the great principles involved. Its unclarified eye has not penetrated beyond the surface of these great events, which teach that universal equality is the foundation of the stability of the State. It is blind to the stern events and terrible truths which glare out from the past. It seems unaware, that the story of man in the Old World is written in the history of princes, kings, and tyrants, who also, and in like manner, trampled this sacred principle beneath their unhallowed feet. These precedents for the disdain of the equality of man are contained in the field-books of ancient conquerors, those butchers of mankind who deluged the earth with blood rather than submit to this "law of right reason" and the whispering of the divinity within them. Jurisprudence in fact does not seem to appreciate the great truth that whatever is most afflicting and degrading in the annals of the human race is the inevitable sequence and the natural accompaniment of the overthrow of the eternal verity of this sacred principle.

If, before setting this terrible precedent, it had paused to inquire, it could have found authority for its ruling only in the prolonged story of the reduction of ancient Asia and Africa; in the history of the Alexanders and Cæsars, of the barbarous North whose savages upturned Europe, or of Europe whose sacred ruffians overturned Asia; in the history of Charles the Fifth, who kept Europe in war for half a century, and of Catherine de' Medici, who deluged it in blood for the other half; in the history of the haughty bigot, Philip, depopulating the Netherlands; in Austria's waste of Germany and the adjoining powers by a thirty-years' war; in England under the Stuarts, and their reign of blood. These are only a few of the witnesses which attest the eternal struggle between the warring elements, tyranny against equality, seeking the overthrow of the divine principle which has entered into the economy of Providence ever since the foundation of governments.

Upon France, following fast upon Louis the Fourteenth and

the iron scourges of their kind, who rebelled against this decree of the great Author of governments on earth, came a terrific avenger, the French Revolution, making war upon the permanently privileged orders of the old states and overthrowing the fiendish tyrants who denied this God-given prerogative of man. It could find no sanctuary on earth; and inscrutable Providence, which does not always stay the impending avalanche, but, suddenly unbending the ordinances and letting loose the powers of nature, sometimes burns and wastes a vast country by the fiery current of a volcanic irruption, called up that gorgeous blood-stained spectre, the terrific apparition of the French Revolution, which, like the bruised adder, turned and struck "its mortal fangs inflamed with rage and hate" into those monsters who claimed the right divine to oppress, brutalize, and torture their brother man.

Jurisprudence should perceive that the perpetual struggle for the establishment of the universal equality of mankind is in accordance with the decree of the Almighty. It should understand, or be made to understand, that the French Revolution, rolled as it was in garments of blood, simply emphasized and accentuated the tremendous nature of the struggle for the equality of all mankind; that the legal fiction of a right divine, or the inequality fiction, by which those august beasts and mischievous apes trampled humanity under their feet, has no foundation in primitive nature or the revealed laws of God, and it, like a "devilish engine, back recoiled;" that Providence cannot be cheated by the substitution of mere words for its divine decrees; that the equality of humanity means far more than idle law-terms; that it cannot be crushed at the pleasure nor spared at the suggestion of the ministers of justice of the state, without sooner or later imposing the penalties of a violated decree as immutable in its workings as that law which binds the ocean to its bed.

The majesty of the principle of equality in the state is indeed inviolable. In the French Revolution, though long delayed, this law, which had been previously grossly violated, struck back "most serpent-like;" and the awful tragedy in which that lesson was veiled spared not any order in its progress. Justice, treading ruthlessly in its slippery, bloody shambles, cried aloud, saying, Why callest thou me murderer, and not rather the wrath of God, burning after the steps of the oppressor, and cleansing the earth, when it is wet with blood ?   And strange, indeed, it must seem, if the working of Providence is not kept steadfastly in view, that, while the sun of liberty was thus eclipsed; while the presiding demons of that storm of havoc from day to day " nursed the dreadful appetite for death;" while the swinish commune sat at their banquet of blood; the multitude, with a fixed and determined will, and in a strange but steadfast handwriting, traced upon the walls of Paris the true watchwords of human progress, *Liberté, Fraternité, Égalité.* It is the misunderstanding or misapplication of these terms which has constituted, through the courses of time, the original sin of all governments.

Is it a task too Herculean for the intellectual backwardness of the enlightened aristocracy of American jurisprudence to apprehend the truth, that upon the divine side of this principle stand the Christian martyrs, the articles of Magna Charta, the Declaration of Independence, Washington, Sumner, Seward, Lincoln, those advance couriers of Equality, those agitators of the slavery-question, the authors of civil rights, and an innumerable array of bright and shining lights?   That by its human side stand Herod of Jewry, the middle ages of serfdom, feudalism, slavery, the original compromise between the North and South embodied in the Constitution which acknowledged slavery, the Fugitive-Slave Law, and the slavery events which preceded secession and armed rebellion in America, the dark shadows of the spirit of the piratical Malay, the assassinating Thug, Booth, Czardom, Nihilism, the socialism of Chicago, and Hall *v.* DeCuir ?

A glimmering perception of this " right reason" is observable in Bentham's idea of the " greatest happiness," but he did not in the early dawn of his glory see clearly how, in the providence of God, it was the destiny of America to demonstrate that the "greatest happiness to the greatest number" can be secured only by the equality of the rights of all the members of the State.   Undoubtedly Wycliffe, Luther, and Knox, in their contests with Popery, were under the unconscious influence of this principle, which afterwards swept away Catholic with Jewish disabilities, and built monuments to the martyrs of the Church and State. From prehistoric ages downward this divine principle has erected temples to the unknown Providence which worked by universal, inevitable law which altereth not; the law of a wise Providence, the unvaryingness of whose rules of action is the same in the workings of nature as in the administration of governments,—a law, the moral and political equilibrium of which can no more be disturbed with political impunity than a cyclone resulting from a disturbance of the atmospheric equilibrium can be controlled by the hand of man.

It was this great law working in their hearts which piloted the Pilgrim Fathers to America. For the preservation of its primitive sacredness, the organic union of the American State was first formed. To the holy covenant for this "rule of right," the hand of Washington afterwards set the crimson seal at Yorktown; for its overthrow, Sumter's bombardment challenged the nation to civil war. After a career of matchless greatness, Grant, the intrepid hero, enthroned at Appomattox the natural justice of this immortal principle. The highest insignia of General Grant's glory as a Christian, warrior, statesman, and citizen, are in the grandeur of the precedent, that illustration of the American principle of equality, which this great conqueror of the New World afforded those of the Old,—an example second to that of Washington alone, who, having also surrendered his sword to the State whose life it had saved, sat down at the foot of Peace, and extended everywhere her olive branches.

Look at the picture of seven millions of citizens degraded by the judicial precedent of Hall *v.* DeCuir, which authorizes the enforced observance against them of many of the customs of slavery, and then on that of Grant, at Appomattox, and to Jurisprudence the hero appears indeed as Hyperion to a satyr. Clad in tatters and rags, there, too, stood the grim remnants of the scarred veterans of Secession, with their arms reversed, their flags furled, and their drums mute, breadless and shoeless; the mere shadow of the grand army of the " Lost

Cause" had surrendered. Its fallen chieftain, the greatest soldier of his age, had striven, with the courage of a hero and the patience of a martyr, to achieve the independence of the Southern Confederacy, which, legitimately interpreted, meant the perpetuation of the reign of the old hag Slavery, and the eternal crucifixion, upon her cross, of that luminous figure, Equality before the Law. In the land of darkness, where the shadow of death so long had hovered, stood the mighty chieftain of Rebellion. In the bloody eclipse of despotic power General Lee saw only the blow of a fate to which the Confederacy was the sacrificial impassive victim. Sustained by the God-given greatness of his own soul; believing that his failure in the right alone constituted the wrong; with an unfaltering trust in the Providence on whose strong arm he leaned, and an unquestioning faith in its inevitable results to nations as to men; this model soldier, the very flower of chivalry,—who had taken the single, awful step between triumph and ruin,—advancing with modest submission, in accordance with the ceremonialism of war, tendered his sword to his conqueror. But Grant, his country's—the world's—hero, " with all his blushing honors thick upon him," breathing the true inspiration of Americanism, and filled with honest indignation at the bare thought of triumphing in the presence of a spirit so great even in its fall, refused to accept the blood-stained sword of his misguided, prostrate foe. By no action of his, this conqueror declared, would he " acknowledge the inequality of any American citizen who had taken sanctuary beneath the glorious drapery of the Republic."

CHAPTER XLII.

" Time, that withers the strength of man and ' strews around him like autumnal leaves the ruins of his proudest monuments,' produces great vicissitudes in modes of thinking and feeling. It brings along with it, in its progress, new circumstances—new combinations and modifications of the old—generating new views and motives, new everything. We ourselves are always changing; and what to-day we have but a small desire to attempt, to-morrow becomes the object of our passionate aspirations."
—PINCKNEY.

" This aid must come before any other aid—is, in fact, that which renders any other aid practicable; for no faculty to which liberty of action is denied can be assisted in the performance of its function until liberty of action has been restored."—SPENCER.

" How truly, indeed, human progress is towards greater mutual dependence, as well as towards greater individuation, how truly the welfare of each is daily more involved in the welfare of all, and how truly, therefore, it is the interest of each to respect the interest of all, may, with advantage, be illustrated at length; for it is a fact of which many seem wofully ignorant."—ID.

" Instead of a capricious and giddy exaltation of spirit, as at new-gained liberty, a sober and solemn sense of the larger trust and duty took possession of their souls ; as if the Great Master had found them faithful over a few things, and had now made them rulers over many."—EVARTS.

" ' God,' says St. Eucher, ' has made three tabernacles,—the Synagogue, which had the shadows only, without the truth ; the Church, which has the truth and shadow together; and Heaven, where there is no shadow, but the truth alone.' "—PASCAL.

" Mr. Grote, the most learned and thoughtful of modern historians, has shown by divers examples that fidelity to the fundamental law—which he terms constitutional morality—is the one indispensable condition upon which the safety and success of every free government must depend. The high career of Athens, from the expulsion of the Peisistratids to a period after the death of Pericles—the marvel and the admiration of all time— was plainly due to the faithful practice of this supreme virtue. It was this that made the steady Roman strong enough to shake the world. England observes not only the theories but the minutest forms of her constitution, when legislating for her own people, and that has given her domestic tranquillity and solid power at home ; her shame and her misfortunes are all traceable to the disregard of it in dealing with colonies and outside dependencies. Constitutional morality was cherished and inculcated by our fathers, in the early ages of the Republic, as the great principle which should be the sheet-anchor of our peace at home and our safety abroad, and, to the end that it might never be forgotten, they imposed a solemn oath upon every legislator and every officer to keep it and observe it with religious care at all times and under all circumstances. In contrast with the self-imposed restraints of the American democracy, Grote mentions the French, a nation high in the scale of intelligence, but utterly destitute of attachment to any constitution or any form of government, except as a matter of present convenience. You know what came of it,— eleven revolutions in less than eighty years, a history filled with wrong and outrage, a people forever alternating between abject slavery and the license of ferocious crime."—BLACK.

" They are certainly hard of belief whom so lucid an argument, coming down from heaven, cannot convince."—MILTON.

THE search after the primal truth of Providence embodied in these amendments is long, obscure, continuous, laborious, and unremitting. It requires the widest sweep of ancient and modern political horizons. In the wailing cry of myriad victims, comprehending nations, peoples, and states, the lesson of its inviolable sanctity is taught. It is not in the vain, farcical garb of " legal fiction," or in temporary expediencies, that jurisprudence can discover its true exposition. It is in tracing the ever-varying lights and shadows of the march of events in states and commonwealths, kingdoms and governments, that the judgment and reason of great jurisconsults can be best employed, in the interpretation, vindication, and maintenance of this vast underlying structure, which supports the national edifice of freedom.

Jurisprudence, as an institution of the state, must adapt its artificial principles to the new conditions which environ it. In the law which extirpated slavery, created a new citizenship, and armed it with the dynamic political force of the ballot, we discern what Guizot calls the " progress," and in Hall v. DeCuir the " resistance," of society. The former expresses the " rightness," the " straightness" of the state's new lines ; the latter, the " wrongness," the " crookedness" of its ancient domain, in the light of the new survey. The amendments introduced a new standard of measurement better adapted to the right lines of equality in the state; and, unless the antique foot-rule of Dred-Scott jurisprudence can by some new graduation adjust itself to the modern system, it is high time that it should be altogether discarded in favor of one more in keeping with the sociological and industrial progress which have naturally followed this new standard of political truth.

The principle of equality, as a generalization, holds multiplied relations to civic life; it underlies all its manifestations. It was founded upon abundant observation, and adopted after half a century's sad experience. The suffering attendant upon the adaptation of the old humanity to the humanity of the new environments of freedom, liberty, and equality is but temporary. The disastrous workings of the principle of inequality under the old institution of slavery entailed far greater miseries upon countless myriads; as already noted, this latter included all those manifold persecutions, class-operations, robberies, and murders which have horrified the country for two centuries; and yet so much social reverence has the institution of slavery in America, that, a quarter of a century after its extirpation, jurisprudence has already, by its loftiest decree, sacrificed the civil rights of seven millions of citizens to this Juggernaut. This is, indeed, counteracting " the propagandism of liberty by the propagandism of superstition." The decree of Hall *v.* DeCuir has none of the large, far-seeing benevolence of the principle of equality before the law. But, with all the force that decree may exert, it cannot uproot this vigorous shoot of civil liberty. Although slow, the growth of the plant is unceasing and powerful.

The struggle in America is between the beneficence of the principle of equality, and what may be termed the narrow social expediency which refuses to allow that principle to run in its constitutional channel. Those whose limited and special constitutional function in the state it is to maintain and enforce the civil rights of all citizens have indirectly usurped the office of constitution-menders. These self-appointed, self-anointed, juristical legislators have inaugurated a policy and set a precedent

of destructiveness at war with the Constitution as amended by
these benign and progressive Articles. The red-tapists of the
by-gone age of slavery shrink with horror at the prospect of
American jurisprudence undergoing the process of adaptation to
the principle of the equality of the civil rights of " free negroes."
In spite of the thickly-strewn proofs that progress does not work
backward in America, the old *régime* doggedly insists that the
American political and social diathesis warrants an aggressive
warfare against the doctrine of equality. The juristical sleight
of hand which assists in the non-distribution of equality by the
ingenious artifices of legal fictions, is powerless, unfortunately,
to avert by any jugglery the dire consequences sooner or later
sure to follow, in a disguised or open shape, their repudiation
of the ethics of the government, the divine Author of which
will not be cheated, even by the judicial authorities whom He
has delegated as His vicegerents in America.

Since it would seem to be the will of the Supreme Being, and
His purpose throughout the ages, that all human liberties be
recognized, the arguments by which it is attempted to prove
that the constitutional claim of seven millions of citizens cannot
be enforced, manifest merely the insurrectionary rage of perverse malcontents. If Providence, throughout an eternity of
past ages, has so sternly negatived these brain-sick theories of
despotism ; if the hand divine is constantly moving through
this principle towards the complete development of a more universal good ; why should American jurisprudence pose in a
glaring attitude of self-stultification in the face of America's manifest destiny ? In the view of the past history of inequality, in
the presence of the mighty progressive movement of to-day, its
agitation, its demonstration, its enlightenment of the masses
lying in outer darkness, why should these representatives of the
state doggedly insist upon fitting the more expansive and constantly increasing growth of the principle of civic equality, to
the antique, primitive, fixed framework of the jurisprudence of
inequality which is a mere relic of barbarism ?

The slowly-evolved result of thousands of ages, of divine right
against human and diabolic wrong, all that gives its charm to
modern civilized life, the liberties of the State, its ponderous but

smoothly-working machinery, the rights of human nature, the happiness of posterity,—Jurisprudence attempts to overthrow in an hour. They cannot be disposed of quite so summarily. The might of Jehovah reigneth ; and against His handiwork—the principle of equality—the highest achievement of political progress—the breath of man shall be as naught, and his feeble hand be raised in vain.

CHAPTER XLIII.

"Well may you say, 'We have made a covenant with death, and with hell are we at agreement; when the overflowing scourge shall pass through, it shall not come unto us; for we have made lies our refuge, under falsehood have we hid ourselves.' But, nevertheless, wait a little while. The waters of truth will rise gradually, and slowly but surely, and then look out for the overflowing scourge. 'The refuge of lies shall be swept away, and the hiding-place of falsehood shall be uncovered.' This mighty and puissant nation will yet rouse herself up like a strong man after sleep, and shake her invincible locks in a fashion you little think of now. Wait: retribution will come in due time. Justice travels with a leaden heel, but strikes with an iron hand. God's mill grinds slowly, but dreadfully fine. Wait till the flood-gate is lifted, and a full head of water comes rushing on. Wait, and you will see fine grinding then."—BLACK.

"The august judge, pronouncer of God's oracles to men."—CARLYLE.

"But as the investigation of the forms and tendencies of hereditary fanaticism and their elaborate absurdities are tiresome, let us postpone a fuller examination until these subjects are resumed."—JOHNSON.

"I know it is the cant of those in power, however they have acquired it, to call themselves the nation. We have recently witnessed an example of it abroad. How rapidly did the nation change in France! At one time Brissot called himself the nation; then Robespierre, afterwards Tallien and Barras, and finally Bonaparte. But their dreams were soon dissipated, and they awoke in succession upon the scaffold or in banishment. Let not these gentlemen flatter themselves that Heaven has reserved to them a peculiar destiny. What has happened to others in this country, they must be liable to. Let them not exult too highly in the enjoyment of a little brief and fleeting authority. It was ours yesterday, it is theirs to-day, but to-morrow it may belong to others."—BAYARD.

"Owls and godless men, who hate the lightning and the light and love mephitic dusk and darkness, are no judges of the actions of heroes."—CARLYLE.

"I stand in the presence of Almighty God and of the world; and I declare to you, that if you lose this charter, never! no, never will you get another! We are now, perhaps, arrived at the parting point. Here, even here, we stand on the brink of fate. Pause, pause, for heaven's sake, pause!"—GOUVERNEUR MORRIS.

454

" The ground is still quaking beneath our feet, under the throes and convulsions of that great social and political change which was first definitely foreshadowed to the world by the Emancipation Proclamation of Abraham Lincoln."—Welling.

" The work of readjustment is the history of civilization. When it is retarded, when the written law has become petrified, or when the natural forces which should transform it are artificially paralyzed, then there is decay and disease showing itself in a deep hatred of law as such, and culminating sooner or later in passionate outbursts of despair, of crime, or of revolution. Wherever there is a nation where law is unpopular, there is a nation whose political constitution is rotten to the core. For law should be the highest expression of the national will, the most sacred embodiment of the conviction of the people. When it is not that, but is merely a foreign, arbitrary, and unnatural legalization of injustice, then against that so-called ' law' we are bound to rebel to the uttermost by our fealty to the higher law. What is the American Republic itself? It is the result of a revolt against law, due in reality to the extent to which the principles of English law had saturated the mind of our American colonists. Speaking of one of the battle-fields on which the Americans won their independence, Lowell sang quite truly :

' Here English law and English thought,
Against the might of England fought.' "—Pall-Mall Gazette.

" By the frame of the government under which we live, the same people have wisely given their public servants but little power for mischief, and have, with equal wisdom, provided for the return of that little to their own hands at very short intervals. While the people retain their virtue and vigilance, no administration, by any extreme of wickedness or folly, can very seriously injure the government in the short space of four years."— Lincoln.

" There is much cause, therefore, to fear lest a thoughtless and lavish dissipation of the noblest mental endowments should become prevalent, or a false and baseless credit-system in thought spring up amidst an absolute deficiency of a solid and permanent capital safely invested in fundamental ideas and lasting truths."—Schlegel.

" For it is the opinion of choice virtuosi that the brain is only a crowd of little animals, but with teeth and claws extremely sharp, and therefore cling together in the contexture we behold, like the picture of Hobbes's Leviathan, or like bees in perpendicular swarm upon a tree, or like a carrion corrupting into vermin, still preserving the shape and figure of the mother animal ; that all invention is formed by the morsure of two or more of these animals upon certain capillary nerves which proceed from thence, whereof three branches spread into the tongue and two into the right hand."—Swift.

"At last, the vapor or spirit which animated the hero's brain, being in perpetual circulation, seized upon that region of the human body so renowned for furnishing the *zibeta occidentalis*, and, gathering there into a tumor, left the rest of the world for that time in peace."—ID.

"Further, nothing less than a violent heat can disentangle these creatures from their hamated station of life, or give them vigor and humor to imprint the marks of their little teeth. If the morsure be hexagonal, it produces poetry; the circular gives eloquence; if the bite hath been conical, the person whose nerve is so affected shall be disposed to write upon politics; and so of the rest."—ID.

"Now, I would gladly be informed how it is possible to account for such imaginations as these in particular men, without recourse to my phenomenon of vapors ascending from the lower faculties to overshadow the brain, and there distilling into conceptions, for which the narrowness of our mother-tongue has not yet assigned any other name beside that of madness or frenzy."—ID.

"The bacilli deoxidize the blood and so kill by what may be called air starvation."—BALLINGER.

"Dr. Saymonne claims to have isolated a bacillus, called by him 'bacillus crinivorax,' which is the cause of alopecia. It is, he says, found only on the scalp of man, other hirsute parts of the body and also the fur of animals being free from it. . . . The theory now especially in vogue is not that they produce a poison directly, but by splitting up complex compounds in the body. Hence of late we have been hearing so much about ptomaines, or the poisons produced in the putrefaction of organic matter, and leucomaines, or those basic substances formed in animal tissue during normal life, either as products of fermentative change or of retrograde metamorphose. With all these doctrines among those who accept the micro-organisms as causes, and then with the doctrines of those who recognize their action and presence but attach more importance to the causes of morbidity pre-existent before their arrival and on which their coming or their production depends, it is easy to see that we are in a great globe of inquiry, and that there is probably much truth yet to break forth."—NEW YORK INDEPENDENT.

"Are we to form an exception to the general principles of human nature, and to all the examples of history? And are the maxims of experience to become false when applied to our fate?"—GOUVERNEUR MORRIS.

"I understood, too, that in ordinary civil administration this oath even forbade me to practically indulge my primary abstract judgment on the moral question of slavery. I had publicly declared this many times, and in many ways. And I aver that, to this day, I have done no official act in mere deference to my abstract judgment and feeling on slavery."—LIN-COLN.

"Who, like the Peak of Teneriffe, has hailed the intellectual sun, before its beams have reached the horizon of common minds; who, standing like Socrates on the apex of wisdom, has removed from his eyes all film of earthly dross, and has foreseen a purer law, a nobler system, a brighter order of things."—COLTON.

"A pure and spiritual religion, the deep fountain of generous enthusiasm, the mighty spring of bold and lofty designs, the great sanctuary of moral power."—EVERETT.

"No ostrich, intent on gross terrene provender and sticking its head into *fallacies*, but will be awakened one day,—in a terrible, *à posteriori* manner, if not otherwise. Awake before it come to that; gods and men bid us awake! The voices of our fathers, with thousand-fold stern monition to one and all, bid us awake."—CARLYLE.

"Custom is a violent and treacherous school-mistress. She, by little and little, slyly and unperceived, slips in the foot of her authority; but having, by this gentle and humble beginning, with the benefits of time fixed and established it, she then unmasks a furious and tyrannic countenance, against which we have no more the courage or the power so much as to lift up our eyes."—MONTAIGNE.

"Sophocles in his Œdipus shows that, anciently in Thebes, the kings were not absolute neither: hence says Tiresias to Œdipus, 'I am not your slave.' And Creon to the same king, 'I have some right in this city,' says he, 'as well as you.'"—MILTON.

"Our constitutions being purely democratic, the people are sovereign and absolute. The faults of absolute governments are to be charged to the sovereign: in ours, they must be traced back to the people."—LIVING-STON.

"These three propositions being true, I think they ought to be followed out, without excess or diminution, by action, not by the declaration of a principle nor the establishment of a law for the future guidance of others. It is a war measure by the President,—a matter of fact,—not a law by the legislature. And as to what is proposed to be done in the future the least said the better. Better leave yourself free to act in the emergencies as they arise, with as few embarrassing committals as possible."—LINCOLN.

"'Would you believe that there was a republic formed in a corner of Italy, which lasted more than five hundred years, and which possessed this Asia Minor, Asia, Africa, Greece, the Gauls, Spain, and the whole of Italy ?' 'It was therefore soon turned into a monarchy ?' said the Brahmin. 'You have guessed it,' said the other; 'but this monarchy has fallen, and every day we make fine dissertations to discover the causes of its decay and fall.' 'You take much useless pains,' said the Indian: 'this empire has fallen because it existed. All must fall. I hope that the same will happen to the empire of the Great Mogul.'"—VOLTAIRE.

JURISPRUDENCE might well pause before it made the fateful cast on which were staked the civil rights of seven millions of citizens; for, in reality, "the hazard of the die" involved the awful forfeit or gain of the sacred principle of the equality of the rights of the whole family of mankind in America. The spectacle of Jurisprudence rattling the iron dice of destiny, with only the stake of the civil rights of a disfavored class at hazard, might prove an agreeable pastime to pro-slaveryites, ecclesiast or secularist. But to the American people, to the friends of civil liberty all over the world, beholding the wrestling of a juristic giant to pull down the noblest pillar under the stupendous fabric of liberty, in order to dislodge a citizen of the African race, who, according to the law of the land, claimed sanctuary in one of its departments, the Supreme Court, it would seem that the mischiefs of despotism were no more preventable in America than elsewhere. If those majestic lords, the public servants of America, by crafty rules and regulations formulated upon judicial fictions, are authorized to gratify the hereditarily consecrated prejudices and revenges of the stronger against the weaker class of citizens, by imposing upon the latter gross and debasing symbols of involuntary servitude (often devoid of the humanities of the institution of slavery), it would seem that by the law of the land jurisprudence had by so doing disfranchised seven millions of citizens, and had jeopardized the constitutional freedom of all others.

Despotic power would clap her hands for joy at the eclipse of the star of liberty, and would view with delight the spectacle of the moping owls, whom its brightness had blinded, leaving their squalid nests, to reign again amidst the darkness. The gradual unfolding of a panorama in America, which represented the civil rights of seven millions of American citizens in the tentative grasp of Jurisprudence, debilitated by superstition and under its strange delusions, would prove diverting to the fiends of despotism. They could not sufficiently admire the constructive skill which had broadened and deepened down from precedent to precedent the false and shallow doctrine of the inequality of mankind in America. To Satan himself, whose clumsy tools of handicraft are tyranny, force, falsehood, and fraud, the subtle device of statutory construction which set the precedent of dwindling down the principle of equality of right to nothing, would prove alike instructive and entertaining. His sable majesty would follow with fiendish glee the tragic drama in its development through nine acts,—Slavery ; Rebellion ; Civil War ; the three Articles of Amendment ; the Enforcement Acts ; the Civil-Rights Bills ; Hall *v.* DeCuir ; the Civil-Rights Cases ; and the tragic *dénouement* of the civil rights of seven millions of citizens obscured in a cloud of words,—and would recall the slow torments of the ancient martyrs, who were first rubbed with honey and then left to be stung to death by wasps and wild bees.

Some Paracelsus of heathendom, " covered with the awful hoar of innumerable ages," and older far than jurisprudence, who had witnessed the mighty formations of the ages, and had come, in these latter days, to testify to the process of blood, through which the crude, coarse principle of inequality had been finally transmuted into that of pure equality in America, just as the mighty Meynour, conjured up by Bulwer, in that marvel of creative genius, Zanoni, had watched the gradual change of gross metals into the gold, the pearl, the diamond, and the ruby, by the fire of the lamp of Rosicrucius ; some political seer, some Solon, familiar with all the precedents, principles, and charlatanry of despotism, would smile an icy smile, when told by explanatory, excusatory, but self-accusatory Jurisprudence, I have relaxed a little from a vigorous construction, a rigid enforcement of the constitutional, organic law, in order to accommodate its strict equality of right to the normal pro-slavery weakness of our humanity, brought about by the prevalence of the social malaria which infects even the vigorous constitutions of our law-

makers and law-interpreters. Such a master in political science,
such an impassive sage, whose calm eye surveyed from afar the
treacherous inroads of despotism upon freedom, would reply,—

" The sacred majesty which renders the court venerable, alone
prevents me from saying, that this course of jurisprudence will,
in the end, lead your country—whither it has conducted all
others which have seen fit to tread the temporary path of unconstitutional expediency—to despotism. This first fatal misstep
you should make sudden haste to retrace, before it is too late;
since, when you have once begun to let down your dikes and remove the barriers, the torrent of arbitrary power easily rushes
in and overwhelms you. Your client, America, represents the
freshness of the world's unfaded youth. She must not be exposed
to peril, nor be led into the way of temptation by the consideration of power, of opportunity, of expediency, of the necessity of the State, or of reasons of state; which always seem
to involve some mysterious iniquity. Political craft quickly
adulterates jurisprudence so that its tendency forces truth to
give way to dissimulation, and honesty to convenience. Political
jurisprudents are oftentimes the ablest architects of ruin in a
free state. In the end they become thorough-paced politicians;
and utterly forgetful to imitate God, as whose vicegerents on
earth they sit. These representatives in miniature of the eternal justice which presides in the dispensations of the Almighty
no sooner grow political than the mist thickens, Egyptian
darkness involves the seat of judgment, and they lose sight of
the standards of right and wrong, of the true and the false.
Their sharp and vigorous intellects, instead of vindicating fundamental maxims, learn to personate a political part and luxuriate
in the palliations of falsehood. By practising the paltry quirks
of semi-political, semi-juristic sophistry, they become the fruitful
parents of tyranny. Blindness, obstinacy, and unsteadiness are
everywhere manifest in their judgments, and even the inheritance
of freedom becomes a prize of disputation. Laws which were
designed for the protection of the poor and weak against the
oppression of the great and powerful are frittered away by false
refinements, glittering *équivoques*, and the order, peace, and beauty
of society are subverted under a non-constitutional administra-

tion. These jurisprudents mistake the shout of the mob for the trumpet of fame. Let the nation beware that their fatal precedents, adulterated by human frailty, are not followed in America.

" The pro-slavery social and political spirit, incarnated into the system of the jurisprudence of your country, has controlled the unconstitutional decision of Hall *v.* DeCuir. But jurisprudence, it must be acknowledged, has no natural tendency, in itself, to any form of social or political anthropomorphism. If there had been an alliance between the politician, the pro-slavery individual, and jurisprudence, scientists who believe in the *bacillus* could probe for the rottenness. If it were true that jurisprudence thus impregnated becomes a martyr to this Heliogabalus of disease, experiments might be made upon the mental body—the brains—of its professors, similar to those which scientists make upon live rabbits. And, wherever such an unnatural alliance exists, it would seem to be the duty of the scientific critic to institute a series of experiments similar to those (*mutatis mutandis*) which have proved so successful in detecting the *bacillus*, and to ascertain whether or not the ghosts of some of these deadly microbes may not have found their way into the mental structures of the jurists and judges who countenance the unholy connection. Your disclosure of the spiritual hollowness of jurisprudence in America is startling. Is its lofty wisdom to be obscured by dust created from movements so far below its sphere? Shall the buzzing of the noisy insects in the vales below be permitted to disturb its noble faculties? Has jurisprudence forgotten that it must either march onward, or be doing nothing more progressive than marking time?

" The professors of jurisprudence should have a wealth of spiritual ideas ; not mere mechanical concepts of artificial, arbitrary rules. The administrators of justice should adopt new methods of thought, and new principles of law, more in accord with the spirit and inspiration of the constitutional amendments which they are to construe. They must invent and furnish broader conceptions of the law of equality of right, and afford less enervated and more progressive reliable rules for the regulation of the conduct of the citizens of the commonwealth under the new charter. A clarified system of strength, majesty, and grandeur, with distinctiveness in its rules and positiveness in its principles, must be promulgated, to take the place of that succession of negations which hitherto has constituted the only construction which the amendments have received. Their very essence and kernel consist in their freedom from, and disregard of, the limitations of those negations. The intellectual circle of jurisprudence must become enlarged and extended, if it would measure up to, and keep pace with, the seeming designs of Providence in the breaking of the magnificent dawn of the Thirteenth, Fourteenth, and Fifteenth Amendments.

"In consequence of the presence of the *bacillus malariæ* of slavery in the mental structures of its professors, it seems that the doctrine of equality of rights by due process of law has been brought into such grave disrepute, when applied to the civil rights of seven millions of your disfavored citizens, that it jeopardizes those of the remaining fifty millions. It must be remembered that the temptation to destroy the natural and acquired rights of men is always present in some shape under every form of government, and jurisprudence must understand, that the race-prejudices of its professors are the oldest and strongest incentive to judicial despotism. It must also know that this malarial fever in its American professors and judges is sometimes accompanied with juristic phantasms. In Hall *v.* De-Cuir it led the court into the extraordinary mistake of deciding that the fifth proposition of the first book of Euclid fails when the figures are drawn with *charcoal.* upon a white board, but applies when they are traced in *chalk* upon a black board. At some stages of this disease that which exists only in the mind of the patient seems to his diseased fancy a real object. The abnormal heat of prejudice in the interior of the patient's body disturbs the action of his nervous system. The controlling cause of the disease must be the insidious influence of the former condition of slavery. But, when it is reflected, that the accumulated filth of slavery has long since been removed from the country, and that the low, humid borders, stagnant lakes, and marshy shores of the slavery commonwealth, with all their poisonous *débris*, are now in the process of purification ; that the geological, thermal, hygrometrical, and barometrical conditions under which this social contagion once polluted the moral atmosphere of the country no longer exist; the reappearance, in spite of all the sanitary regulations of your new institutions, of the old typhus type, is indeed phenomenal, unless your juristic professors are hereditarily diseased, in which event the herb never grew that will cure them.

" But neither jurisprudence nor America should be held responsible for the gangrenous precedent set by diseased ministers of the state. The nation has confided the principle of equality of right by due process of law to the care of her jurisprudents, and, although its fate in America may be to crumble into the dust of Hall *v.* DeCuir, nevertheless, its central position in the universe is impregnable; for it has a sure and steadfast place in the hand of God, whose providence has implanted it deep in the breast of His creatures. The magnitude of that which this great principle has already accomplished in America is only the pledge of a nobler, worthier, fuller development.

" I have witnessed," the seer would exclaim, " from the top of the centuries, the growth and decay of all the germs of imperialism which resisted its progress, and thus am enabled to testify that there is an irreconcilable hostility between the doctrine of equality and the chicanery of inequality. They cannot, as the American professors of jurisprudence suppose, be compromised. I have watched and am watching, and the countless hosts of heaven have watched and are watching, the divine ordering of America among the nations. Your government is to-day the nearest approach to the Christian realization of a perfect state existing in the world. Shall she, then, permit the limitations upon equality established by Hall *v.* DeCuir and the Civil-Rights Cases, to overthrow the eternal principles upon which her natural edifice is builded, and upon which alone the glorious superstructure of equality of rights can be firmly established?

" The deceptive formalism of juristical doctrinaires cannot be substituted for the essence of the truths of equality. That superstructure which has a lie for its foundation is in reality baseless. The old red dragon, Tyranny, has the advantage of many centuries of experience over America. In her grand struggles for life, it is true, America twice overcame him; but wherefore? It was because in those struggles, the people stood by the divine, not the human, side of equality of rights by due process of law. The doctrine of inequality was originally transported to, and planted upon her virgin soil in the form of slavery. It grew apace. Its roots were legal fiction, social expedience, political necessity, the exigency of the nation, the pleasures of power, political supremacy, the greed of gain. These roots took deep hold in the soil of the Southern States; and there sprang up a gigantic, deadly, overshadowing growth which threatened to destroy the vigorous plant 'equality of right by due process of law.'

"The redevelopment and establishment of equality of rights in America by the recent articles, which are made integral parts of the Constitution, were at once soul-stirring, majestic, and brilliant. The angels of deliverance who inspired these amendments had a right to expect in Jurisprudence a handmaiden. To her keeping this one great essential principle was confided as a national compass, that America might not creep forever timidly along the shore, as did the ancient mariners who had no such instrument for directing the course of their ships.

"Take a single retrospective glance. Does not Jurisprudence perceive that what the battle of Sadowa was to Protestantism, to the Germany of Luther and Hegel, Gettysburg was to equality of rights in America, against the despotism of slavery which refused to acknowledge this divine right; that the civic Protestantism, as it may be called, against the institutions of slavery in America, was guided by the invisible arm which marshalled religious Protestantism against the corruptions of Romanism; that both these forms of Protestantism were confident declarations to all mankind of the fundamental law of their inalienable rights to religious and civil equality? Both of these achievements appear to stand as witnesses of God for the redemption of the spiritual and natural powers of man, from all that hold undue dominion over them. Jurisprudence must learn that in government, as in the solar system and the entire universe, permanence and stability depend upon one principle or force: in the material world, the universal law of gravitation; in the political world, the all-embracing principle of equality of right by due process of law. That the course of inequality in the state, as in the heavens, is as that of an uncontrolled projectile force without continuous convergence or obedience to any central, universal law, the result of which is an ascent, a maximum height, and then a sure and hasty descent into chaos. To jurisprudence in America is committed the mighty trust of maintaining the equipoise of the state through the principle of equality of rights by due process of law. The limit of its decisions must reach to this sublime altitude, or jurisprudence cannot fulfil its high destiny.

" After the uncrowning of the monarch of slavery, and the lifting from this race of the maddening sense of its accumulated shame and wrongs, a system of government was adopted which inaugurated a mode of thought and action independent of inherited tradition. What was institutional before, became thenceforward uninstitutional; and the fetters of constitutional construction, so strongly and subtly forged in Hall *v.* DeCuir as to threaten the overthrow of this principle of equality by due process of law, must now be loosened and forever thrown aside. The same subterfuges, shifts, and pretexts which appear in that decision seem to have been resorted to ever since the primitive history of man's dominion over his kind. It is a struggle to assert a legal right over this race, and under color of lawful right to subject it to tyrannies not dissimilar in principle to those which have been exercised throughout the ages, without color of lawful authority, by the stronger over the weaker element of the society of the state. The forces of inequality of right which reappear in that case have been mustered on every battle-field of freedom, under every species of false disguisement. These devices are always allied with the sinister schemes of despotism, and their course is just as tortuous. The world, everywhere and at all times, has been full of the accumulated proof of the evils resulting from such precedents of arbitrary despotism in free states. They are the implacable foe of nations and of individual man. How can America hope to win by the introduction into her state, of any of the practices of a despotic power which would thus attempt the usurpation of the civil rights of seven millions of her citizens ?"

CHAPTER XLIV.

" The articles of Magna Charta embody its protests against oppression and its demands for a better administration of justice. It piloted the Pilgrim Fathers to the New World. It supported the followers of George Fox under fines and imprisonment, and it whispered resistance to the Presbyterian clergy of 1662. In latter days it emitted that tide of feeling which undermined and swept away Catholic disabilities. Through the mouths of anti-slavery orators, it poured out its fire, to the scorching of the selfish, to the melting of the good, to our national purification."—SPENCER.

" The convulsions of a great empire are not fit matter of discussion under a commission of Oyer and Terminer."—BURKE.

" Everywhere else the principles of convenience, or of symmetry, or of simplification,—new principles at any rate,—have usurped the authority of the jejune considerations which satisfied the conscience of ancient times, and everywhere a new morality has displaced the canons of conduct and the reasons of acquiescence which were in unison with ancient usages because in fact they were born of them."—MAINE.

" It is ordained by Divine Providence that the life of nations, like the life of individuals, shall undergo such trials; yet, drawing our predictions from the past, we have no reason to despair of the issue. The thousand years of English history which lie behind us justify our confidence that this nation will rise triumphant out of the struggles before it, and, like the German nation, will find in its own past the best materials for the regeneration of its political system."—GNEIST.

" The nation is organic, and has therefore the unity of an organism, and in its continuity persists in and through the generations of men; it is a moral organism, it is formed of persons in the relations in which there is the realization of personality, it is not limited to the necessary sequence of a physical development, but transcends a merely physical condition, and in it there is the realization of freedom and the manifestation of rights; it consists in the moral order of the world, and its vocation is in the fulfilment of the divine purpose of humanity in history."—MULFORD.

" The nation as it exists in its necessary conception is the Christian nation."—ID.

" The book which illustrates from the beginning of history the divine purpose, and the divine order in the world, has been and is the book of the life of nations."—ID.

" Then all institutions that have not the exact proportions of the momentary schedule are to be levelled to the ground, and all that has been achieved in the work and sacrifice of generations must make room for a structure designed in the individual conceit. It is this spirit, which is the evil of fanaticism, that appears as a vain and destructive force."—ID.

" Beautiful, great soul, to whom the temporal is all irradiated with the eternal, and God is everywhere divinely visible in the affairs of men, and man himself has, as it were, become divine."—CARLYLE.

" The time will come when the dreadful calamity which has so long afflicted our country, and filled so many with despair, will be gradually removed, and by means consistent with justice, peace, and the general satisfaction; thus giving to our country the full enjoyment of the blessings of liberty, and to the world the full benefit of its great example."—MADISON.

" We live in a time of necessary and searching reform. We cannot avoid its duty. Things have already changed. They must be readjusted. The harmony of the great polity has been rudely disturbed. It must be restored in some way. The civil war imperilling the existence of our country has laid bare the roots of evils in our polity, and shown what some elementary errors must lead to when legitimately carried out. We have discovered that a part of our foundation has given way and that repairs are needed. Let every one contribute his share to the reconstruction, be it much or little, so that he helps on the great work of repairing the mansion of Freedom. I offer this contribution to my country's cause. If what I give does not prove acceptable in the form in which it is offered, these pages will, nevertheless, lead to reflections which will not fail to be useful and may prove fruitful."—LIEBER.

> " Strong mother of a lion, live ;
>   Be proud of these strong sons of thine,
>   Who wrenched their rights from thee."—TENNYSON.

" But what's the reason, think you, that men slip in this age wherein we live ? As I told you before, they understand not the works of God. They consider not the operation of his laws."—CROMWELL.

> "What constitutes a state ?
> Not high-raised battlement and labored mound,
>   Thick wall or moated gate ;
> Not cities proud, with spires and turrets crowned ;

> Not bays and broad-armed ports,
> Where, laughing at the storm, proud navies ride ;
> Not starred and spangled courts,
> Where low-browed baseness wafts perfumes to pride.
> No ! Men, high-minded men,
> Men who their duties know,
> But know their rights,—and, knowing, dare maintain,—
> Prevent the long-aimed blow,
> And crush the tyrant, while they rend the chain ;
> These constitute a state,
> And sovereign law, that state's collected will,
> O'er thrones and globes elate,
> Sits empress, crowning good, repressing ill."—Jones.

"Those first bold adventurers on the wide ocean of thought."—Schlegel.

"The world is built upon the mere dust of heroes : once earnest-wrestling, death-defying, prodigal of their blood : who now sleep well, forgotten by all their heirs."—Carlyle.

"And freedom being thus the grand prerequisite to the fulfilment of the moral law, it follows that, if a man is to be helped in the fulfilling of the moral law, the first thing to be done is to secure to him this all-essential freedom."—Spencer.

Whoever is conversant with the history of the make-shifts of despotism knows the legal-fiction-quirk-and-quibble-trick to be an old and stale one. These gross approaches to inequality are the short cuts, the by-roads, over which the loathsome phantom, Despotism, always makes stealthy advances upon the territory of freedom. Other incumbents of the seats of justice, the servile ministers, with a sidelong glance at place and power, in search of authority for unjust judgments, can hereafter, upon discovering the precedent of Hall *v.* DeCuir and the Civil-Rights Cases, extend their scope until the spirit of despotic power is fully intrenched within the citadel of liberty, and, standing upon the prostrate majesty of man, with "jealous leer malign," can laugh aloud at the bare mention of "equality of rights by due process of law."

There is observable in the ear-marks of American civil-rights jurisprudence an astounding similarity to those of the old-fashioned juristic auxiliaries of despotism; and yet, rightly understood and lawfully interpreted, the intent of this Article of amendment to the Constitution clearly was to demolish all the dexterous expedients of such servile jurists who have acted as the priests of despotic power, in all its protean shapes, at every period of governmental history. Jurisprudence, in the legitimate exercise of her authority, should undoubtedly be able to afford the correct constitutional interpretation of those fundamental negations laid down in the amendments, " Neither slavery nor involuntary servitude shall exist within the United States." " No State shall deprive any person of life, liberty, or property, without due process of law. No State shall deny the equal protection of the laws."

What is the constitutional significance of that progressive national legislation which apportions the representation of the national government and that of the States according to the whole number of the persons in each State, so long as the right of no male citizen to vote is abridged except for crime? What is the political import of the constitutional prohibition of any question as to the validity of the public debt incurred in the struggles of 1861 for the re-establishment of the principle of equality by due process of law? Why can no constitutional right under these amendments be asserted, or any claim made for loss by reason of the emancipation from the principle of inequality of those millions of former slaves now citizens? The constitutional, legal import of these cardinal doctrines depends upon the historical, philosophical, and political significance of the terms employed in all the vast negations of the amendments. What is the sound constitutional generalization to be gathered from the great body of truth contained in all the branches of these three Articles? They must be construed *in pari materia.* How otherwise than by a philosophical, political, and historical generalization can the combined realistic force of these amendments be directed towards the accomplishment of the grand civic purposes of their creation, when invoked and applied in the concrete to sixty millions of people of all races, for whose welfare as citizens they were enacted?

The obvious principle to be generalized from the provisions of these Articles of amendment to the Constitution, when their combined aid is invoked in support of the civil rights of a single individual of the state, is, that by the abolition of slavery or involuntary servitude can only be intended the substitution of the equality before the law of each individual in any of the States; equality throughout the United States in its broad, Christian, historical, and political signification. For the freedom of his ballot has created him one of the governing agencies of the State and nation: an American sovereign, and the peer of any other citizen in any of the States, irrespective of color, race, or previous condition. The prohibition by the amendments of any State action in abridgment of life or property without due process of law, or without the equal protection of the law, means the right of each citizen to the beneficent action of that aggregate of the fundamental laws, institutions, and usages of the American state which constitutes its civil rights.

Due process of law cannot be construed as a mere right to a subpoena or writ of summons. The due process of Christian, philosophic, historical, political, constitutional law means an equal protection of the new civic life and of the new civic properties of each sovereign unit in the state, which are created and confirmed by virtue of these three Articles. Even before their adoption, although there were in the Constitution no provisions against adverse action by the States, or guaranteeing equality of right and due process of law, no citizen of the United States could be deprived by the State governments of his life or property without summons, trial, witnesses, counsel, and jury. Before their express addition to the Constitution, technical " due process of law," or equal protection of the law, was commonly and universally satisfied by the exercise of its functions in their limited technical acceptation; and it is remarkable that the active intellects of distinguished jurists have overlooked the all-important consideration of the broad distinction between the technical, professional sense, ordinarily imputed to the terms " due process of law," and " equal protection of the law," and the grave constitutional significance of these terms when introduced into the Constitution as amendments thereto. They became thenceforth fundamental constitutional principles. The terms " due process of law," "equal protection of the law," in rights, properties, and freedoms, constituting an integral part of the Constitution, must be interpreted with reference to the immunities and privileges with which the principle of the equality of all men before the law had now constitutionally clothed all American citizens.

A sound interpretation of equality of right, or equal protection by due process of law, can only be afforded by the jurisconsult who comprehends the mighty changes of the civic convulsion,—the great sweep of events which preceded and succeeded the Rebellion. It was through their combined instrumentality that this Magna Charta was achieved, and finally embodied by these three articles into our Constitution. How otherwise can the enforcement of this great gift of freedom be accomplished than by a broad system of laws, the *rationale* of which is co-extensive with, and analogous to, the new sphere of their action? The department of justice must be enlarged, and refitted with machinery more adaptable to the new school of equality by due process of law, which has been substituted for the one-time fashionable, but now effete, system which the nation has abolished.

How otherwise can the true interpretation of these three articles be discovered than by a profoundly philosophic inquiry concerning the origin, divergent character, counterscope, and irrepressible antagonism of the principle of Equality, and its implacable foe Inequality, which contrarieties brought forth rebellion and civil war? Only by considering them in their Christian, historical, and political significance can we recognize the God-given boundaries, the broad constitutional expanse of the limitations employed in these three Articles, for the grant of equality of right by due process of law. Their political and constitutional significance cannot be overestimated, when it is reflected that to the provisions for the civil equality of rights is added the political right of representation by ballot. By these three amendments to the Constitution (construed *in pari materia*), the strongholds of equality before the law were everywhere widened, deepened, and strengthened, and the borders of the constitutional frontier of equality in America visibly enlarged. The addition to the territory of equality of rights by due process of law was immense. Prior to these three huge strides towards constitutional freedom, the citizens of the United States, under Article IV. Section 2 of the Constitution, were entitled only to the " privileges and immunities of citizens in the several States." The various Constitutions and Bills of Rights of the States of the Union were alone declaratory of the immunities, rights, and privileges of the citizens of each State. The banishment of slavery and involuntary servitude; the inhibition of all State action which refused equal protection of the laws to any citizen in his life, liberty, or pursuit of happiness; the inhibition of the denial to any person of the equal protection of the law; the investiture of all citizens, irrespective of race, color, or previous condition, with the political right of a representation in the State and national government,—wrought changes commensurate with the vast problems solved by the mighty revolution, whose instrument —war—according to Heraclitus, is the "king and father of all things." The destiny of that revolution was to inaugurate the reign of equality before the law.

Whatever natural or positive rights, immunities, or privileges, therefore, are embraced in the broad Christian, historical, and political expanse of the principle of the equality of all men in the state, must reflect in a great measure the sound constitutional import of the terms employed in these constitutional amendments to secure this great freedom. The amendments were adopted after grave debate, and almost in sight of the late civil slaughter and the blood of the nation. By their all-embracing terms the American state was placed upon the most enduring, solid basis for the future superstructure and the fullest attainment of the principle of American equality. American equality thus constituted is the ripest birth of time. For the doctrine of the equality of rights by due process of law is in conformity to, and accordance with, the sacred historical, political, and constitutional truths of the loftiest civilization known to the great family of nations.

After this great result had been accomplished by the constitutional artificers who are now resting from their labors, the duty and obligation of those intrusted with the administration of jurisprudence began. But Jurisprudence, which lives only in intellect, sat long condoling by the death-bed of the old pro-slavery Constitution. She had beheld the awful rising and the dark setting of that blood-red orb of Despotism which lately challenged America to the arbitrament of civil war for the maintenance of the principle of equality by due process of law. And these amendments ought, therefore, to be viewed by her priests as covenants of God with man and as the dawn of a new civilization, and their interpretation should be broad and liberal, cloudless and clear.

A mere symbolical interpretation of the Fourteenth Amendment through the poor and empty form of legal fiction, with such unintelligible ciphers for terms as " Equality does not mean identity," is not, in the lurid glare of the Civil War, a significant interpretation of the words " equality of right by due process of law," which were intended to indicate that realistic force in the jurisprudence of the new state which accomplishes wholesome national, political, and civil reformations commensurate with the purpose of the war. Equality of rights by due process of law means the successful resistance against any individual or governmental agency which touches that integral part of the state individuation—the man—and assails the conditions of his civic life by denying his equality of rights. Equality of rights by due process of law defeats that barren conception of equality which affirms that there is a secondary significance, legal, moral, physical, or spiritual, in the civic relation of any one member of the state to another. That ruling illustrates the meaning of equality of right by due process of law which declares that all the power of the state is pledged to maintain the doctrine that the individual civic type of an American citizen, in the view of the state, is one and the same, irrespective of the character of the type. It requires rules of interpretation more comprehensive than the old rules under a pro-slavery Constitution, and more adaptable to the necessities and requirements of the new and enlarged constitutional field, which these three Articles have opened, for the more perfect development, not alone of this race, but of the universal family who shall hereafter constitute the American nation. The enlarged system of these three Articles makes individual elevation the special end and specific aim of government. Constitutional due process of law created a new organic system. It conferred the fullest authority and power upon the guardian of jurisprudence, for the enforcement of the principles of the new system. The basis of this enlarged field for the exercise of jurisprudential authority, its governing and guiding principles, are traceable to the political necessities and great principles which brought about civil war, for the restoration and establishment upon a more permanent foundation of the equality of the rights of man. Equality of rights by due process of law was intended to remedy defects—*casus omissi*—in the system of equality which existed under the Constitution before the adoption of these amendments. The amended Constitution is antagonistic to and corrective of the pro-slavery principle of the old. Although it had cost centuries of battles in the Old World and the Revolution of '76 in the New, due process of law was not fitly established in America until after another terrible conflict by the adoption of the amendments to the Constitution.

Equality of rights by due process of law is the divine mission of the amended Constitution. It belongs to no particular man or class of men. It is the crowning of that civilization which centuries failed to secure in the Old World. Its meaning is that every individual of the nation is alike sacred, and that his civil rights cannot be judged indifferently, nor weighed lightly, but must be enforced and protected by all the power of the state, executive, legislative, and judicial. Equality of rights by due process of law no more requires that "individuals who are repulsive to each other" should—in the language of Hall *v.* DeCuir—be, by the law of the United States, "locked up in the same apartment" than the general laws of the United States require that persons of different sexes, who are not repulsive to each other, should be locked up in the same apartment. But it does mean the utter abolition of that popular or individual absolutism which under any disguisement whatsoever asserts its authority over the civil rights of any American citizen. It abolishes all those forms of despotism which degrade the individual by destroying the dignity of his personality. The crises through which the family of mankind have passed, and their divine deliverance in America, are thenceforth and forever the competent witnesses, and afford the true key, by which to construe the historical significance of these jewel-words, " due process of law."

Equality of rights by due process of law, as a grand generalization, works the transformation of a *vulgus* into a *populus*. Under its reign the civil adversities and vicissitudes which successive generations of a much-suffering race encountered, are forever wiped out; and their descendants in America are entitled to the rights, immunities, and privileges of American citizenship, not as if these were stars, to be gazed at from afar, but as they are, and were intended to be, as much their properties and possessions, under the economy of the state, as light, air, and water. Equality of right by due process of law flows for all from the new fountain of the state. Its noble, fructifying course cannot be diverted by myths and legal fictions to any special end. There is, under its sanction, no exclusive possessory right or title to the vast national highway of civilization. If equality of rights by due process of law is enforced, the destination of the American people is unified. The imperfections of the individual's external surroundings (save such as are criminal in the eye of the state) cannot exclude him from civic equality, nor can the supposed grandeur of any member of the state exalt the individual, who claims it, above the principle of civic equality. Under the reign of equality of rights by due process of law the rights of the integral units which compose the state, to these very immunities and freedoms which have been claimed and struggled for all through the human cycles, are as sacredly preserved from assaults of factions within, as from infringements without the geographical limits of the republic.

These three Articles construed *in pari materia* give that definition to these sacred words which is most in accord with the political and historical formulæ of the nation which adopted them. And in the same sense that America as a country belongs to the integral individual units who have peopled it, and formed its governments, is equality of right by due process of law through these Articles pledged to these joint and several integral units. The legitimate and necessary sequence of this principle of equality is the affirmation, to every American citizen, of the realities of freedom. It is the sole instrument by which the permanent pacification of great secular contentions in the state can hereafter be secured. By affording to every citizen the same civil and political endowment, the state has so partitioned and enforced the privileges and immunities of freedom that they fall in equal portions to the lot of her children.

The principle of equality by due process of law affords the poverty-stricken, crude, unassimilated offspring of the American people, native-born or naturalized, the same means of holding a respectable position in the great family. Equality by due process of law means such assimilation of Civil Freedom, with its twin-sister Civilization, as will, throughout the future, prevent those convulsions which have overtaken other states because of the absence of that equality which operates in America as a universal civil enfranchisement of every individual in the nation. Equality by due process of law restores the missing link which binds together mankind in the nation. In their constitutional sense, these terms undoubtedly intend that the dissimilarity of social tissue, produced by race and previous condition, should no longer be regarded as the criterion of the rights, obligations, and duties of the newly-adopted American citizen. That interpretation which falls short of effecting such a civil amalgamation as will bring the newly-admitted race into political, civic, intellectual, and moral assimilation with all others as citizens of one country, cannot be called due process of law, nor satisfy the constitutional requirements of these amendments.

The enlightened authors who incorporated this principle into the Constitution hoped and believed that all traces of race-subordination would soon be forever lost in America, and that the great civic transformation which would follow this national unification of American citizens would bind together by cords of sympathy every child of the Republic. It is not for words, artificial rules, and arbitrary legal dogmas to assert the grim tyranny of their distinctions, in the interpretation and construction of the grave principle involved in " equality of right by due process of law," and thereby to overturn and defeat the declared policy of the nation.

If united to stricken jurisprudential sterility, how can due process of law hope for the fair offspring of equality? Equality by due process of law opens in America, as Shalmaneser did in Assyria, a way both for the Samaritans and Israelites of the day. It places the doctrine of equality upon a plane so infinitely high that no power but a despotic one can touch it. Equality of law means that if Rome could assimilate paganism and Christianity, Christianity and these three Articles can assimilate the paganism of the color-line to the Christian civilization of the state; that as mediæval ecclesiasticism conquered its antagonists, the nineteenth century can encounter and overcome the fungus brood of pro-slavery race-antagonism in America.

"Equality by due process of law" intends to silence, not to feed, the wild, terroristic, clamorous brood of race-harpies in America. It creates deep-seated structural changes in the organic jurisprudence of the nation, and is not to be satisfied by merely colorable construction. It clothes each citizen with the real habiliments of American citizenship; it pushes every individual into the competition of the society of the state unhandicapped. The supreme object of the national policy was, by due process of law, to remove forever the dark idolatries of slavery from the sight of the wretched worshippers of caste.

This powerful political factor, compacted with the Constitution, now works hand in hand with ecclesiastical civilization. Equality by due process of law was specially provided by these amendments because the principle of the equality of civil rights had been in the old condition of affairs practically rejected. The absence of rational morality in America rendered the resort to the power of this broad instrument of juristic force, essential to the administration of justice upon the lofty scale of equality before the law.

The authors of this new instrument anticipated that the status of civilization in America would require its coercive force until a nation of slavery-worshippers was elevated to the acknowledgment "that Equality before the law was a more worthy object of its adoration." Its authors foresaw that a foe might arise which mere emancipation could not strike down; that, like the Hydra of old, Slavery might put forth new heads; though crushed, it might receive new life,—that "Achilles absent was Achilles still,"—that, having always the iniquitous will, it could be prevented from fresh injury only by taking from it all its power.

A thorough interpretation of equality of right by due process of law contemplates also the restoration to true ideas of liberty and civil rights of that remnant of the lost tribe of civilization who shun the light of the modern intellectual day ; who, in spite of the world's advancement, adhere to the formularies of their old creed ; whose enforced ascent to the higher level of those who gladly welcome approaching science, virtue, freedom, righteousness, and that equality which comes from Heaven, is difficult and distasteful. It was provided for the enlightenment of the immobile, materialistic worshippers of caste, whose rites in America are below the level of paganism in Japan. The framers of these three Articles foresaw that, unless they annexed to equality of right enforcement by due process of law, the results for which the Civil War in America had been waged were no more secure than those which Christianity had attained by similar shedding of blood in the Byzantine Empire. They recognized the great truth that, when the state was relieved from the sociological asphyxia of slavery, its victims, being restored to their proper senses, would become factors in the noble civilization ; which end, they foresaw, could only be accomplished by this divine instrumentality. Instead of the glittering generality that " all men are born free and equal," they created and substituted a constitutional power, by which jurisprudence could enforce the principle of equality and, by due process of law, maintain throughout the Republic those newly-created spiritual and material immunities, privileges, and rights which centre around life, liberty, property, and the pursuit of happiness in America.

The framers of these amendments agreed in opinion with the jurisconsults of Antonine, " *Omnes homines natura aequales sunt,*" and carried their thought into action. They reflected, that a warranty of the constitutional protection by due process of law could be attained only through the comprehensive practical sagacity of Jurisprudence, armed with authority to formulate rules, systems, and precedents, adapted to the ends of equality.

The words " equality of right by due process of law," they said, " have hands and feet, and their line of march is not in regions of remote abstraction." In the sight of the legions of rebellion, with their garments rolled in blood, they conceived the constitutional polity of equality of right armed with due process of law. They felt the deep significance of past events which might again repeat themselves in America, and they resolved upon this radical constitutional remedy.

All the crises of the world were before the authors of these amendments. The confused noise of battle, its agony and sufferings, its sacrifices, were fully in view when they said, " Let us adopt a policy that no device or jugglery of state-craft can destroy, annul, or evade. We will give a fresh charter to life, liberty, and property in America. We will elevate the principle of equality by due process of law upon a high pedestal. The privileges, rights, and immunities of the citizen shall not be tortured, corkscrewed, and serpentined by juristic proceedings. They shall not be diverted to the vile uses of despotism by any of its swindles, old or new. As Americans we must stand together ; and our onward march shall be marked by the inspiring music of ' Equality of Rights by Due Process of Law.' When equality is embodied, as a cardinal principle, in the Constitution, and is enforced by due process of law, no field will be left for the legal battles of red-tape formulists upon the bench. Those who come after us shall, out of the stones of this temple of liberty, build no sepulchre for equality before the law."

They conceived that the absolute sway of an imperialism which claims for its authority divine right, affords no graver illustration of inequality than the decree of a court (or *sans-culotte*) which through race-prejudice violates the infinite sacredness of a civic personality. Individual rights, they said, were not a matter of mere constitutional parchment, the violation of which was only a technical breach of a technical law. They contended that that decree does not conform its mandate to equality of rights by due process of law, which fails to recognize the inner spirit of man, his individual character, or the awakening of his dormant energies ; but subjects him to the infernal edict of a public servant often no higher than a mere spiteful clown.

Equality by due process of law introduced into the Constitution a new, stupendous, organic provision, conservative of the unity, growth, identity, structure, and development of the new germs of freedom unfolded by the altered conditions which now environ all Americanized races. The terms of this constitutional compact are not susceptible of any other analysis. Whatever judicial interpretation of equality by due process of law falls short of this copious construction grasps but feebly the significance of this potent instrumentality. Equality by due process of law was no longer the theoretical, but the actual, development of the constitutional policy of the equality of mankind in America. It is the most perfect realization, by the state, of the divine relations of mankind, under the best form of government which has ever existed on earth.

"Equality of rights by due process of law" is not a merely local, technical law-term. Its high place is to be found in the archives of the family of nations. In one form or another, its sacred claims have been written and rewritten in the blood of all peoples, of all ages and all climes; but again and again the upper and the nether millstones of despotism have ground its blood-stained charters into dust. Its chief postulate, marked in the records of the ages, is the same to-day as it was in the pre-Socratic age: "That the state was made for man, not man for the state;" that personal rights are as inalienable as personality; that God can, and will, allow no one to rule absolutely but Himself. If the development of this sacred principle is in its essence identical with that of Christianity, its grand growth in America needs not the support of the lame legs of juristical fiction.

CHAPTER XLV.

"Label men how you please with titles of 'upper' and 'middle' and 'lower,' you cannot prevent them being units of the same society, acted upon by the same spirit of the age, moulded after the same type of character. The mechanical law, that action and reaction are equal, has its moral analogue. The deed of one man to another tends ultimately to produce a like effect upon both, be the deed good or bad."—SPENCER.

"You cannot repeal human nature."—LINCOLN.

"Cicero doubts whether it were possible for a community to exist that had not a prevailing mixture of piety in its constitution."—ADDISON.

"We speak of our civilization, our arts, our freedom, our laws, and forget entirely how large a share is due to Christianity. Blot Christianity out of the pages of man's history, and what would his laws have been?—what his civilization? Christianity is mixed up with our very being and our daily life: there is not a familiar object around us which does not wear a different aspect because the light of Christian love is on it; not a law which does not owe its truth and gentleness to Christianity; not a custom which cannot be traced in all its holy, healthful parts to the gospel."—JUDGE SIR J. A. PARK.

"Fellow-citizens, we cannot escape history. We, of this Congress and this Administration, will be remembered in spite of ourselves. No personal significance, or insignificance, can spare one or another of us. The fiery trial through which we pass will light us down, in honor or dishonor, to the latest generation. We say we are for the Union. The world will not forget that we say this. We know how to save the Union. The world knows we do know how to save it. We—even we here—hold the power, and bear the responsibility."—LINCOLN.

"Whoever does not assume unconditionally the might of goodness in the world, and its ultimate victory; whoever starts from moral unbelief, not only cannot lead in human affairs, but must follow with reluctant steps. We live indeed in the kingdoms of the redemption, and no more in the kingdoms of this world."—ROTHE.

"In giving freedom to the slave, we assure freedom to the free,—honorable alike in what we give and what we preserve. We shall nobly save, or meanly lose, the last, best hope of earth. Other means may succeed; this

481

could not fail. The way is plain, peaceful, generous, just,—a way which, if followed, the world will forever applaud, and God must forever bless."—LINCOLN.

"Drive back to the support of the rebellion the physical force which the colored people now give and promise us, and neither the present nor any coming Administration can save the Union. Take from us and give to the enemy the hundred and thirty, forty, or fifty thousand colored persons now serving as soldiers, seamen, and laborers, and we cannot longer maintain the contest."—ID.

"To contend with slavery is the work which, through Providence in history, has been given to the nation. This is only the statement of an historical fact; the work has been given to no individual, and to no special or ecclesiastical association of men, but to the nation. The nation, in the realization of its own being,—in the maintenance of its own unity and its own life,—is borne on to an inevitable conflict with slavery."—MULFORD.

"You can have no conflict without being yourselves the aggressors. You have no oath registered in heaven to destroy the government; while I shall have the most solemn one to 'preserve, protect, and defend' it."—LINCOLN.

"What an astonishing illustration of the defeat of dishonesty by the eternal laws of things we have in the history of the East-India Company! Selfish, unscrupulous, wordly-wise in policy, and with unlimited force to back it, this oligarchy, year by year, perseveringly carried out its schemes of aggrandizement. It subjugated province upon province; it laid one prince after another under tribute; it made exorbitant demands upon adjacent rulers, and construed refusal into a pretext for aggression; it became sole proprietor of the land, claiming nearly one-half the produce as rent; and it entirely monopolized commerce; thus uniting in itself the character of conqueror, ruler, land-owner, and merchant. With all these resources, what could it be but prosperous? From these spoils of victorious war, the rent of millions of acres, the tribute of dependent monarchs, the profits of an exclusive trade, what untold wealth must have poured in upon it! what revenues! what a bursting exchequer! Alas! the company is some fifty million pounds in debt."—SPENCER.

"It is subversive of human energy; it is destructive of institutions of order and law; it is regardless of truth and sobriety; it is alien to human freedom; it guards its domain as its own possession against the advance of thought; it is in alliance with ignorance against the beneficent influences of science; it is in conflict with elements of progress, and confronts them with its own inquisition."—MULFORD.

"First, the gospel has done it, and then justice has done it; and he who thinks it his duty to labor that this happy condition of existence may remain, must guard the piety of these times, and he must watch over the spirit of justice which exists in these times."—Sydney Smith.

"But negroes, like other people, act upon motives. Why should they do anything for us if we will do nothing for them? If they stake their lives for us, they must be prompted by the strongest motive, even the promise of freedom. And the promise, being made, must be kept."— Lincoln.

"I cannot stay to call to your attention these characters, or these incidents, or to renew the gratitude and applause with which we never cease to contemplate them. In this view, these progressive processes were but the articulation of the members of the State, and the adjustment of its circulation to the new centre of its vital power. These processes were all implied and included in this political creation, and were as necessary and as certain, if it were not to languish and to die, as in any natural creature." —Evarts.

"From it, as from a root, spring our aspirations after social rectitude. It blossoms in such expressions as, 'Do as you would be done by,' 'Honesty is the best policy,' 'Justice before generosity,' and its fruits are equity, freedom, safety."—Spencer.

"I felt that measures otherwise unconstitutional might become lawful by becoming indispensable to the preservation of the Constitution through the preservation of the nation. Right or wrong, I assumed this ground, and now avow it."—Lincoln.

Wherever there is equality by due process of law, the tyranny of opinion cannot be stronger than the express commands of the law; and under the reign of this wise principle America is pledged to do away with the decadent formulas of slavery-jurisprudence, and resolutely to maintain for each citizen an opportunity for that development which will bring out the type of his individuality to its fullest expression. The Articles of Amendment established a new condition in the moral life of every American citizen. By the inward working of their deep, eternal truth, it was intended to recast the external national mould of American character. Equality of right by due process of law intended to place in eternal bondage the unconstitutional element of race-antagonism in the society of America.

The doctrine of equality of rights by due process of law broke and shivered to atoms—it ground to powder—the external gyves, grades, and distinctions which cramped and weighed down the spirit of American equality. In its political sense, equality by due process of law is the recognition (independently of any strait-jacket of narrow rules) of those individual rights and liberties which place all citizens upon one and the same true foundation of civic equality, and by its aid conventional fetters which bound the freedom of its spirit were broken and cast away. One of its main postulates is, that the elevation of the lower stratum of society, in the opinion of the nation, does not degrade the higher. Any rule, or any other law, political or moral, which denies this doctrine, operates, if enforced by its courts, as a voluntary outlawry of equality by the state itself; for it loses sight of the relation of the citizen to the nation, and of the nation to the citizen.

The right construction of these Articles, in their political and historical features, depends not upon the rules of the rude justice and the barbaric condition of the social state of slavery. The tortuous and ungodly jungle of that jural system is unfitted for the political, economic, historical, constitutional advancement of the state under its new institutions of equality. The new political and constitutional condition of America is as great an advance upon the old Dred-Scott status of inequality, as the principles of Magna Charta, and the liberal growth which followed them, were superior to the primitive conceptions of law which the precedents of the Chief Justiciar introduced with William the Conqueror from Normandy into England.

Those gifted men who squint with only one eye at these Articles of Amendment through the Dred-Scott precedent, cannot, through that " muddy vesture" of decayed slavery, perceive that the Thirteenth, Fourteenth, and Fifteenth Amendments introduced into the Constitution a new, fundamental civil system, of the noblest nature, and of the deepest constitutional significance to civil liberty. In the formula of the old writs, these Articles practically say to Jurisprudence, In the peace of God and of the American State, I demand your obedience and the conformity of your rules to the great commandment of this law of equality. They do *not* say to the public, We also constitute you co-workers with jurisprudence,—its *posse comitatus*, as it were,—to arrest Civil Rights upon the illimitable avenues now opened for the individual advancement of this race. The most polished and artful human ingenuity cannot evade, or avoid, the far-reaching, all-seeing, all-pervading principle they embody, without repealing the Constitution as thus amended.

The structure of these amendments, framed in simple words of grand significance, grasps the magnitudes of time and space. They are in part the noble inspiration of America's great and best-beloved statesman, Lincoln. The Magna Charta for equality of rights by due process of law proclaims that Lincoln did not enter the temple of Poseidon to hail the death-stroke in vain. It speaks in the name and by the authority of the American State. It does away with words,—" the daughters of men :" it substitutes deeds,—" the sons of God."

These Articles are constitutionally definitive of the relation of every individual unit in the nation to the nation, and that of the nation to every unit composing it. Through them the State says, with Hegel, " Be a person, and respect others as persons."

Properly regarded, equality of rights by due process of law sanctions the natural by means of the positive ; and it creates the positive right out of the natural right—that is, civil rights—by constitutional provision. The one is immanent in the nature of man ; the other positive, and immanent in the Constitution of the nation.

Equality by due process of law, in its constitutional sense, therefore, is the recognition, and leads to the enforcement, of the natural, positive, inalienable rights of the aggregated units which constitute the nation, and must necessarily have precedence over all other considerations of which jurisprudence takes cognizance ; and must extend its prerogatives by a vivifying, invigorating system of laws, rigidly and impartially enforced upon those bases of equality which are adapted to the accomplishment of the great end for which it was granted. Due process of law means the vigorous enforcement by the law of the land of the civil rights of all citizens. By the equal protection of the law, therefore, is meant the permanent maintenance of the primal prerogatives of humanity, admeasured by the actual standard of the positive provisions of these great institutes, which constitute another Magna Charta; the enforcement of the noblest sentiments of the truest humanity, as contradistinguished from the former degraded civil and political condition of a slave-holding nation.

It is to this great height that jurisprudence must be elevated, or these beneficent provisions of positive law will remain forever under the pro-slavery obscuration of its interpreters. In the mean time, sacred, historical, political, and constitutional progress must halt, until the almost Oriental immobility of American jurisprudence shall have appreciated and felt the meaning of these noble guide-posts planted in the Constitution to direct the future march of America in the economy of Providence towards the fulfilment of its destiny. The formation of enlarged precedents and principles, adapted to the internal and external organization of the state in its new conditions; the development of the deeper unity of the nation through the inauguration of its declared polity, under the new constitution of the state, is the cyclopean task of jurisprudence, and not, as it has been suggested, of the legislative department of the state.

The national polity rests upon the ground-floor plan of the three instruments of amendment, the interpretation of which should be plain, and should admit of no hypercritical, scornful, unsympathizing, distant, class, or caste criticism which would tend to the obscuration of its grand civic purposes. Abstract speculations of judicial opinions respecting the national polity, the conflicting judgments of jurisconsults, or the automatic opinions of pro-slaveryites are all only convenient modes of evading the main question, degrading alike to the good faith of the nation and to jurisprudence itself. The plant of equality must take firm root in good soil, or perish. Its full growth can be attained only under the fostering care of jurisprudence, which should develop its germs, by assiduous training suited to its nature and commensurate with the end for which it was planted by the nation.

A proper recognition of the individuality of man, a due working field for his progressive development, can be afforded only by some great progressive force in jurisprudence, which shall work from above downward, from within and from without, from beneath upward, from centre to circumference. This would lead to the establishment of a civilization, of that kind which Mr. Bancroft describes as a "something between men, no less than something within them." It is to this intellectual size, to this enlarged proportion, that jurisprudence must attain before it can establish equality of rights by due process of law in America in place of the trite, ephemeral, empty notions of Hall *v.* DeCuir. Those new patches upon the old garment of Dred Scott— Hall *v.* DeCuir and the Civil-Rights Cases—have made the judicial rent worse. Jurisprudence has refused to impart its quickening touch. Instead of permitting the noble plant of equality to take root deep in the body politic and push upward its fruit-bearing branches, she has placed unkindly soil around its roots. The transmission to seven millions of disfavored citizens of equality of right by due process of law seems too sublime an undertaking for her decadent power. The magnificence of the opportunity offers no temptation to her ambition. In her view, the political alchemy by which Republican politicians sought to transmute the ha'penny of Dred Scott's humanity into the guinea of human equality has created a mixed metal, having a resemblance which is not borne out by the reality ; and the Fourteenth Amendment a political fraud, and an unconstitutional falsification which has necessarily resulted in a sociological failure.

Why is that interpretation of these provisions, which says that American civic society shall be equipped with the same arms and uniformed in the same colors, if it includes the militia of a disfavored race, so exceedingly offensive to the imperial majesty of Jurisprudence? Why is equality of right by due process of law mere, sheer, empty nothingness if the citizens of the United States of African descent can come under its sheltering provisions? The only answer that can be given to these questions is, that the old, withered, pro-slavery ritual of despotic power apparently has still a potent charm for Jurisprudence in America. But the unity and just order of the nation ; the organic life of its humanity ; the characteristic political events which marked the great crises in the American state, closing one age and opening another, and the work of conforming her old system to the new conditions and institutions of the state, are seemingly not weighty considerations with Jurisprudence. The Magna Charta of these great liberties,—for the perpetuation of which America's half million, like Sparta's three hundred, laid down their lives,—as interpreted by Jurisprudence, is to be regarded as the mere, empty symbolism of immunities, rights, and privileges.

A careful study of the history of governments, past and present, will demonstrate the accuracy of the conclusion, that the embodiment of the political wisdom of all ages is massed in the last three Articles of amendment to the Constitution. Yet their brilliant judicial interpreters have declared to the world that these Articles, embodying the collective wisdom of ages of statesmanship, represent only the ideal abstractions of political enthusiasts ; that they are mere political empiricisms ; that the grand portraitures of the gradual ascent of man in the scale of being, of his advance through conflict upon conflict to the realization of full freedom, are only political pageantries, the mere shifting changes of a spectacular political scenery ; that this American Magna Charta conferred only the blessing of an imaginary liberty ; that in reality it added no new foundations to the equality of the rights of mankind in the state, nor any additional due process of law, by which it could be enforced, which might not be readily disposed of by the legal fictions of race-antagonism.

As Laplace swept the whole heaven with his glass and found no God, so Jurisprudence, peering through the blurred spectacles of caste-prejudice, can see no divinity in the golden firmament of the great American charter. That auspicious event in the historical life of the world which meant, as Aristotle said, that "The end of the state is not simply to live, but to live nobly," has no attractiveness for jurisprudence, if the African race is to be embraced within the ample folds of equality of right by due process of law.

The framers of the great Charter, according to Hall *v.* DeCuir and the Civil-Rights Cases, were mere blinkards, simpletons ; there was no keen forecast of political genius about them. Their philosophical perspicacity, as it now stands diagnosticated in the Civil-Rights Cases, was a lamentable hallucination, a mooncalf monstrosity. Those of that illustrious body who dimly anticipated for America in the near future a race of jurisprudential giants whose mighty intellectual stature was suited to the proportions of these Articles, saw through a glass darkly. It now seems that they labored wholly to no purpose, to keep jurisprudence itself unspotted from the leprosy of slavery.

The dead-looking, pallid construction of Hall *v.* DeCuir is all that is left of the simple, natural, grand, colossal figure of equality. Foolish cackle, ephemeral trivialities, inane, sham fictions, enigmatic, false stuffings, equivocal sibylline phrases, all as hollow as the rattle of dried peas in a bladder, are what remain of the equality of right by due process of law, regarding the civil rights, immunities, and privileges of the African race. For the shining sun of equality by due process of law, the dark lantern of Dred Scott has been substituted. The once luminous vital figure of civic equality has now become a dead, dry block for logic-chopping lawyers. The modern construers of this American Magna Charta of equality of right evidently are regardless of its gravity, for in Hall *v.* DeCuir their judicial treatment seems to imitate the example and rehearse the wisdom of the ancient statesmen who, the great humorist says—

> " By geometric scale
> Did take the size of pots of ale."

In so far as the principle of equality of right by due process of law is concerned, Jurisprudence in America has gone backward to the " immeasurable circumambient realm of nothingness and night." And yet the blindest jurisconsult must see that the very form and body of jurisprudence, and all her great achievements and splendor, are owing to the struggles of mankind, century after century, to maintain that equipoise of right in the state which is called equality before the law. It was the spirit of equality by due process of law which first rocked the cradle of Jurisprudence, and it is the same spirit which now stands sorrowfully by the side of its sturdy child in America,—Civil Rights.

CHAPTER XLVI.

"These principles form the bright constellation which has gone before us, and guided our steps through an age of revolution and reformation. The wisdom of our sages and the blood of our heroes have been devoted to their attainment; they should be the creed of our political faith, the text of civil instruction, the touchstone by which to try the services of those we trust; and, should we wander from them in moments of error or alarm, let us hasten to retrace our steps, and to regain the road which alone leads to peace, liberty, and safety."—JEFFERSON.

"But, in truth, the matter in hand bears a far closer resemblance and affinity to natural objects which live and grow than to any lifeless edifice of stone; to a great tree, for instance, nobly and beautifully spreading out on all sides its many arms and branches."—SCHLEGEL.

"It may not yet be felt in high places of office and power, but all who can put their ears humbly to the ground will hear and comprehend its incessant and advancing tread."—SUMNER.

"Why should there not be a patient confidence in the ultimate justice of the people? Is there any better or equal hope in the world? In our present differences, is either party without faith in being in the right? If the Almighty Ruler of nations, with His eternal truth and justice, be on your side, of the North, or on yours, of the South, that truth and that justice will surely prevail, by the judgment of this great tribunal of the American people."—LINCOLN.

"Our sun of political happiness is already risen, and hath lifted its head over the mountains, illuminating our hemisphere with liberty, light, and polished life. We are laying the foundation of happiness for countless millions. Generations yet unborn will bless us for the blood-bought inheritance we are about to bequeath to them. Oh, happy times! Oh, glorious days! Oh, kind, indulgent, bountiful Providence, that we live in this highly favored period, and have the honor of helping forward these great events, and of suffering in a cause of such infinite importance!"—RAMSAY.

"I do order and declare that all persons held as slaves within said designated States and parts of States shall be free; and that the executive government of the United States, including the military and naval authorities, will recognize and maintain the freedom of said persons.
490

And, in order that they may render all the aid they are willing to give to this object and to the support of the government, authority will be given to receive them into the service whenever they can be usefully employed, and they may be armed to garrison forts, to defend positions and stations, and to man vessels. And I appeal to them to show themselves worthy of freedom by fidelity and diligence in the employments which may be given to them, by the observance of order, and by abstaining from all violence not required by duty or for self-defence. It is due to them to say that the conduct of large numbers of these people since the war began justifies confidence in their fidelity and humanity generally."—LINCOLN.

" The progress of evolution, of development, is never in one straight line. It is revolutionary : it is cyclical : it returns upon itself, yet never back to its starting-point, but always like a spiral coiling higher and higher, and every completed turn of the coils is marked by changes that seem to be catastrophes if viewed alone, but appear harmonious and necessary when seen in the light of all that has gone before."—COUES.

" This is no fight for party ; it is a holy crusade for humanity and for liberty, and we expect, as we have a right to expect, the help of every good man who has a heart to feel for his kind or an ambition to leave to his children the inheritance of free institutions, with equal opportunities to all, which he received from his fathers."—C. BLACK.

" We speak of the 'dark ages,' of the ' age of superstition,' etc., of the centuries past, and forget all about the ignorance, darkness, and superstition of the nineteenth century. Galileo stood foremost among the unpopular great men of the sixteenth and seventeenth centuries. There are three in the nineteenth century who were laughed at for advocating 'impossible' schemes,—Mr. Morse, because he said a message could be sent by wire ; Cyrus W. Field, because he said a cable could be laid across the Atlantic ; Edison, because he stated he could light houses and streets by electricity."—RODERICK, IN GROWING YOUTH.

" But what is of most importance is the high sanction given to a latitude in expounding the Constitution, which seems to break down the landmarks intended by a specification of the powers of Congress, and to substitute, for a definite connection between means and ends, a legislative discretion as to the former, to which no practical limit can be assigned."— MADISON.

" We have, in the annals of Roman law, a nearly complete history of the crumbling away of an archaic system, and of the formation of new institutions from the recombined materials."—MAINE.

" The guardianship of the laws and traditions was vested in the chiefs of the colleges, known as ' Scribes,' ' Men of Great Synod,' ' Princes and

Fathers of the House of Judgment.' They instructed the people, preached in the synagogues, and taught in the schools. Nothing was allowed seriously to interrupt their duties. Palestine was ruled by various dynasties; the masters were martyred; the academies were destroyed; to study the law was made a crime against the state; yet the chain of living tradition remained intact. The dying masters appointed their successors, and for one academy destroyed, three new ones sprang up in another quarter."—THE TALMUD.

"We can succeed only by concert. It is not, 'Can any of us imagine better?' but, 'Can we all do better?' Object whatsoever is possible, still the question recurs, 'Can we do better?' The dogmas of the quiet past are inadequate to the stormy present. The occasion is piled high with difficulty, and we must rise with the occasion. As our case is new, so we must think anew, and act anew. We must disenthrall ourselves, and then we shall save our country."—LINCOLN.

"Slavery brought in its train the multiplied curses of a diseased social state; a reign of mutual hatred and terror, of universal demoralization, of sin-begotten recklessness, of extravagant expenditure, of bad cultivation, exhausted soils, mortgaged estates, bankruptcy, beggary. After all, the moral law would have been the safest guide."—SPENCER.

"This church is that great and divine corporation which embraces all other social relations, protects them under its vaults, crowns them with dignity, and lovingly imparts to them the power of a peculiar consecration. The church is not a mere substitute formed to supply or repair the deficiencies of the other social institutes and corporations; but is itself a free, peculiar, independent corporation, pervading all states, and in its object exalted far above them, a union and society with God, from whom it immediately derives its sustaining power."—SCHLEGEL.

"The three main characteristics of political government which mark the modern epoch are the national polity, the general endeavor to define more clearly, and to extend more widely human rights and civil liberty."—LIEBER.

"The war is not waged in any spirit of oppression, or for any purpose of conquest or subjugation, or the overthrowing or interfering with the rights or established institutions of those States, but to defend and maintain the supremacy of the Constitution, and to preserve the Union with all the dignity, equality, and rights of the several States unimpaired."—CRITTENDEN.

"If you order us to examine the works of Grotius, or Puffendorf, of Burlamaqui, or Hutchinson, for what you understand by the law of nature, we apprehend that you are in a great error in taking your notions of natural law, as discoverable by natural reason, from the elegant systems of it which have been drawn up by Christian philosophers; since they have all laid their foundations, either tacitly or expressly, upon a principle derived from revelation, a thorough knowledge of the being and attributes of God: and even those among ourselves who, rejecting Christianity, still continue Theists, are indebted to revelation (whether you are either aware of or disposed to acknowledge the debt or not) for those sublime speculations concerning the Deity, which you have fondly attributed to the excellency of your own unassisted reason."—GIBBON.

" Yet this commentary on the moral code—this history, as we call it—men forever read in vain ! Poring with microscopic eye over the symbols in which it is written, they are heedless of the great facts expressed by them. Instead of collecting evidence bearing upon the all-important question, what are the laws that determine national success or failure, stability or revolution?—they gossip about state intrigues, sieges, and battles, court scandal, the crimes of nobles, the quarrels of parties, the births, deaths, and marriages of kings, and other like trifles. Minutiæ, pettifogging details, the vanity and frippery of by-gone times, the mere decorations of the web of existence, they examine, analyze, and learnedly descant upon ; yet are blind to those stern realities which each age shrouds in its superficial tissue of events,—those terrible truths which glare out upon us from the gloom of the past."—SPENCER.

" Such a magnificent idea is too big for their narrow conceptions, which can neither observe the beauty of the work nor comprehend the grandeur of its authors."—HUME.

" It is enough for me to prove the vastness of the power as an inducement to make us pause upon it, and to inquire with attention whether there is any apartment in the Constitution large enough to give it entertainment."—PINCKNEY.

" And by the war of the Constitution—a war within the nation—the bonds of our unity were tried and tested, as in a fiery furnace, and proved to be dependent upon no shifting vicissitudes of acquiescence, no partial dissents or discontents, but, so far as is predicable of human fortunes, irrevocable, indestructible, perpetual. *Casibus haec nullis, nullo delebilis aevo.*"—EVARTS.

" Where once rolled a fathomless ocean, now tower the snow-covered peaks of a wide-spread, richly-clothed country, teeming with existence; and where a vast continent once stretched, there remain but a few lonely coral islets to mark the graves of its submerged mountains."—SPENCER.

" It has been the misfortune, if not the reproach, of other nations, that their governments have not been freely and deliberately established by themselves. It is the boast of ours that such has been its source, and that it can be altered by the same authority only which established it. It is a further boast, that a regular mode of making proper alterations has been providently inserted in the Constitution itself. It is anxiously to be wished, therefore, that no innovations may take place in other modes, one of which would be a *constructive assumption of powers never meant to be granted.* If the powers be deficient, the legitimate *source of additional ones is always open, and ought to be resorted to.*"—MADISON.

" Their knowledge of mankind showed them that ' this corruptible would put on incorruption,' only when this mortal should put on immortality. Nevertheless, they believed in man, and trusted in God, and on these imperishable supports they thought they might rest civil government, for a people who had these living conceptions wrought into their own characters and lives."—EVARTS.

" In the great system of political economy, having for its general object the national welfare, everything is related immediately or remotely to every other thing ; and, consequently, a power over any one thing, if not limited to some obvious and precise affinity, may amount to a power over every other. Ends and means may shift their character at the will and according to the ingenuity of the legislative body. What is an end in one case may be a means in another ; nay, in the same case may be either an end or a means, at the legislative option. The British Parliament, in collecting a revenue from the commerce of America, found no difficulty in calling it either a tax for the regulation of trade, or a regulation of trade with a view to the tax, as it suited the argument or the policy of the moment."—MADISON.

"Our comfortable expectation and most thirsty desire whereof, what man soever among you shall any way help to satisfy (as we truly hope there is no one among you but some way or other will), the blessings of the God of peace, both in this world and in the world to come, be upon him more than the stars of the firmament in number."—HOOKER.

" You give me a credit to which I have no claim, in calling me ' the writer of the Constitution of the United States.' This was not, like the fabled Goddess of Wisdom, the offspring of a single brain. It ought to be regarded as the work of many heads and many hands."—MADISON.

" But our trust in the Almighty is, that with us contentions are now at the highest float, and that the day will come (for what cause of despair is there ?) when, the passions of former enmity being allayed, we shall with ten times redoubled tokens of our unfeignedly-reconciled love, show ourselves each towards other, the same as Joseph and the brethren of Joseph were at the time of their interview in Egypt."—HOOKER.

"O man of the people, ragpicker of every prejudice, worker of social KARMA! Simple-minded as you are, honestly and hopelessly stupid, you are at any rate the typical man; and those who go about so stiffly in evening dress, ready to cringe before self-constituted authority and kneel to all the golden-calf gods in the fashionable pantheon, are mere monkeys beside you. . . . We will teach you that that instinct of freedom, liberty, equality, and fraternity, which has so often made you heroic, is no myth, but a reality—albeit but the first foam of a wave of human progress which shall in the end carry you higher than the gods you shall have outgrown and cast aside!"—COUES.

"The soul is deemed an aërial ingenious particle, which when separated from the body is reunited to the substance of the heavens."—NAVARRETE.

"I will continue to cherish the belief that, although, like all other human institutions, it may for a season be disturbed, or suffer momentary eclipse by the transit across its disk of some malignant planet, it possesses a recuperative force, a redeeming energy in the hearts of the people, that will soon restore it to its wonted calm, and give it back its accustomed splendor."—PINCKNEY.

"My son, my heart thrills with joy when I contemplate how in this century a beauty, a freedom, and a brotherly love unfold themselves which existed to us only in the germ. As one example, my son, see how the State now educates its children, and does it in a way that no Solon, no Socrates, ever could imagine. . . . Thou shalt live in a time when it will hardly be conceived that there were slaves, serfs, bondmen, monopolies, and the whole trumpery of a false world."—AUERBACH.

"I am loath to close. We are not enemies, but friends. We must not be enemies. Though passion may have strained, it must not break our bonds of affection."—LINCOLN.

"I should indeed rejoice as having, in a great measure, attained my object, if only I shall succeed in directing your attention to some star in the higher region of intellect, which hitherto was either totally unknown or at least never before fully observed."—SCHLEGEL.

"I commit to you, therefore, without further discussion, the cause of my clients, identified with the rights of the American people, and with those wholesome rules which give to public law simplicity and system, and tend to the quiet of the world."—PINCKNEY.

"I pray Him, from whom every good gift cometh down, to grant that this humble attempt may not be without benefit to some of its readers."— D'AUBIGNÉ.

THE genius of American liberty asserted itself in these three amendments, and threw down the gauntlet to that wretched progeny of Despotism, Inequality. But when the infernal peers of the malignant fiend, Race-Prejudice, thrust into the face of American Jurisprudence the Civil Rights of seven millions of citizens of the United States of African descent, she shrank from the ordeal of shaking hands with this form of humanity. That was too great a trial. Such a test, such a proof, taxed too heavily the candor of the court: Christian Jurisprudence, even with the New Testament by its side, where it had read of the Divine Being who washed the feet of his disciples, and said, " My peace I give unto you, not as the world giveth," could not elevate its standard to the sublime, moral height of the Great Master's teachings. The deep, rich meaning of that sacred example touched not the conscience of the court, and whenever this redeemed, disenthralled, emancipated race asked for the enforcement of its constitutional equality of rights by due process of law, Jurisprudence surrendered both the letter and the spirit of the great principle, rather than be put to the rack and subjected to the extreme torture of acknowledging the equality of the civil rights of the African race.

Whenever the ignorant, sycophantic hypocrisy of Caste (which is the chief barrier to American aspiration for further and higher development of individual liberty) nerves its palsied form, and steps in front of humanity's equality of rights, Jurisprudence, only the shadow of its great true self, with crossed legs and frightened mien, crouches upon the woolsacks in deference to the awful presence of this pigmy prince—Race-Antagonism. The smallest dwarf, plated with pro-slavery social assumption, has, it seems, bolder attributes than Jurisprudence itself, enthroned upon the lofty pinnacle of the Supreme Court. For it cannot escape observation that, although the whole question of civil rights was discussed *ad nauseam* in the separate opinion in Hall *v.* DeCuir, yet there was no reference throughout the discussion to the Fourteenth Amendment. The same shaft which struck Mrs. DeCuir smote, with unmerciful severity, upon the nerves of seven millions of citizens. Does it not look, in the light of

Hall *v.* DeCuir, as if the Fourteenth Amendment should be placed on trial for absurdity?

But America cannot afford to laugh at this folly: it must sooner or later deplore the blindness of guides whose judgment says, "Anything for the times, nothing for the truth." The sacred question in America is, whether in administering "due process of law" this measure of God's justice shall be enforced, or be evaded by legal fictions, quirks, and quibbles, so paltry as these: "Equality does not mean identity," "Substantial accommodation," etc. These amendments are either worthless shadows or substantial powers. "It is enough to make mad the thinking, and appall the free," to be told in Hall *v.* DeCuir, that Jurisprudence, armed with its great authority, "can be vehement in words but not in things," that it cannot lift from these American citizens the accumulated shame and wrongs of slavery,—the great motive and object, the grand inducement which led to the grant of this new American Magna Charta.

The future question is, whether the matchless faith and fortitude of the great constitutional artificers, in their efforts to solve that great problem,—the establishment of a government for a nation composed of mixed as well as kindred races,—are to be overturned by the timorous or sagacious misgivings of Jurisprudence; whether the principles of the equality of rights by due process of law, which lie deep and solid as the Rock of Ages, are to be thrown down to gratify the insane lust of Race-Antagonism for despotic power over something or somebody; whether the Cyclopean work of patriots shall be overthrown to defeat the civil rights of seven millions of adopted citizens; whether this tree of freedom, "gray with the moss and beaten with the storms of centuries," shall be torn up by the roots to glut the savage instinct and foolish sentimentality of the worshippers of caste; whether the great safeguards, the landmarks of a nation's freedom, can be obliterated by technical refinements, and namby-pamby distinctions respecting the meaning of words, which bear the same relation to the gigantic growth of equality of rights by due process of law, as a blade of grass to a forest of oaks; whether the principle of equality by due process of law, which extended the domain of civilization further in America than it had reached for the past ten centuries in Europe, shall now be brought into jeopardy by judicial precedents which imperil the status of the freedom of the entire household of liberty in America, in order unconstitutionally to deprive seven millions of disfavored citizens of their equality of rights; whether the equality of rights by due process of law of any race is safe in America, after the discrimination and distinction in favor of privileged orders in the society of the state shall have been established by the law of the land; whether artificial dissolving views of equality of right or forms and symbols of due process of law shall be substituted for their substance and soul.

The mighty voice of nations, the glorious deeds of unnumbered martyrs, attest the divinity of the truth underlying the political principle, equality of right by due process of law. It comes daily into clearer elucidation in the higher development of the civilization of the African race in America; and this inquiry concerning the Thirteenth, Fourteenth, and Fifteenth Amendments is to ascertain whether it is the duty of large-minded, masculine jurisconsults to interpret the law in such a way only as to please the delicate tastes of the powerful members of the States; whether the civil war in America was waged for the destruction of property, or for the unity of the nation, and its continuity, under the principle of equality of right enforced by due process of law; whether the power of the nation, North, East, and West, in its might and totality, was arrayed against the South for the massacre of brethren, and not for the great end, that equality of rights and due process of law, representing the majesty of the state, should be thrown around those civil immunities and privileges which were to be the portion of every branch of the family of mankind in America; whether jurisprudence shall recognize the oldest form of truth, which these amendments acknowledge, in affording the justice of a legal religion to beings having a moral nature; whether there is a divine sanction in this great truth which is impregnable, and can never be put to confusion; whether God's justice can be denied any race which bears His image; whether the grim distinctions of Hall *v.* DeCuir, which in effect treat this race only as an order of inferior animals,—subkingdom Vertebrata, class Mammalia, order Bimana,—can be maintained ; whether the doctrine which refuses to humanize a race of men which Jurisprudence in Dred Scott deserted and left in the enswathement of the Centaur-Nessus robe of slavery is the American doctrine ; whether mankind are separated from one another by any broader line of classification than the environments of each have established ; whether or not it shall be proclaimed in America that man is in his nature neither savage nor hermit nor slave, but a member of a well-ordered family, a good neighbor, a free citizen, acting with others like himself, in obedience to and under the protection of law.

To the sagacious observer of the history of nations, who, through the accumulated wisdom of centuries, reviews the mighty resurrection of liberty from the dead past, it is apparent that jurisprudents need also to wander backward, over the long line of events which have filled the world with the desolating forces of the despotisms which denied the divine principle of equality of right. In America, no matter how saintly its show, Jurisprudence must remove from her face the veil of sanctimonious profession in regard to equality before the boundless extent of this great truth can be fully realized. When her jurisconsults refuse to adopt a system by which this principle will have its full course, and permeate all the arteries, pulses, and veins of the entire commonwealth, they should be led back to the vast storehouse of remote ages, and there behold the ruins upon ruins which the doctrine of inequality has worked.

The history of equality of right by due process of law is the history of progressive liberty. Its great lesson is one which philosophical jurisprudence, from its lofty watch-tower, cannot too closely contemplate. Its overflowing records, bristling with points, invite the fullest exercise of judicial perspicacity. The three amendments which underlie this cardinal principle emanated from those great historical movements, those wonderful political reformations, by which a perfect form of government has been constituted in America. If the grave sociological, political principle of this great charter is to receive no broader constitutional interpretation than Hall *v.* DeCuir affords, its pages are the noblest yet the darkest in American history. It

would almost seem that its full, genuine, massive ring, replete
with the cultus and consistency of historical constitutional equality, has found no worshipper in American jurisprudence, and
the pantheon of a Julian would appear to be almost as fit a place
for a true and spiritual religion as American jurisprudence for
the indwelling of the spirit of Equality of Right by due process
of law.

The manifest intention of the framers of these amendments
was favorably to introduce every member of the family of man
to American civilization. Accustomed to deep reflection on
human affairs, they saw the necessity of a permanent constitutional addition to the political rights of all American citizens.
By these amendments they designed to impart a continuous
power, a living energy to sociological development in America.
They saw that the chain of equality, upon the strength of which
the political rights of all depend, was no stronger than its weakest link,—race-prejudice. They realized that the American
germ " equality," young and yet full of years, was as subject to
multiform and grotesque perversion in the new world as Christianity itself had always been in the old. With the keen inspiration of the spirit of liberty, they arrived at the conclusion
that the doctrine of the brotherhood of man, and the duty of
universal benevolence and charity in the state, constitute the
true foundation of the principle of equality of man before the
law.

Upon this grand, broad, colossal, humane, and Christian
foundation rest the commandments of these three Articles.
They are the embodiment of the experience and wisdom of the
long line of the generations of the sons of men, who sought,
through all forms of government, from the primitive ages of
savagedom downward, for equality of right by due process of
law. The philosophic statesmen who laid these foundations had
long known, that ever since the origin of the American government the divine and human side of equality of rights, like
separate streams, had held divergent courses. They saw that
aggregations of separate races of men, with local antagonistic interests, and lacking that reciprocity and community of interests
which are the true amalgamators of nations, could not without a

war of races or sections long adhere together under any form of government; that the society of the American state must be one in adversity or in prosperity, in sunshine or in storm, in sympathy, in purpose, in sacrifice. In this unity, they reflected, consisted the difference between the Russian and the American systems. To these statesmen it was apparent after the Dred-Scott decision that the principle of equality in its relation to all races had become deciduous, and had established a doctrine of absolutism in America not superior in its primal tenets to those of the Suttee and the Thuggee, and they saw that the principles of the great central truth of the equality of all citizens before the law had a powerful tendency to direct each individual in the nation towards civic homogeneity.

The authors of these three amendments realized, that the expensive, bloody, roundabout process of a war of races, with the result in the hand of the God of battles, might not in its issue be favorable to the arrogant American hypocrisy which boasted on parchment of the supremacy of His laws but openly violated them in fact. They foresaw that this scourge inevitably awaited America unless a constitutional foundation for the perpetuity of the equality of rights of all races by due process of law could be securely laid. It was evident to these profoundly sagacious intellects, that the law towards which all governments tend— the law of equal freedom—must properly be considered the law of nature, and the governing and guiding principle which best preserves the equilibrium of the state; that the principle of the constitutional system which works the necessary cohesion of the individuals of the state by the universal equality of liberty, political, intellectual, sociological, and moral, was the very corner-stone of popular liberty. They reflected that the strength of the nation consists in the just appreciation of the civic grandeur of the station of individual members. Their political reason sought some deep foundation for the firm establishment of kind feelings, and the promotion of good will, between the members of the great political family of America, and they provided the three amendments, each intended to be as substantial as the great pyramids of Egypt.

They embodied in these Articles, as they thought, a practical, complete, cordial recognition of all American citizens. They reflected that in consequence of the pro-slavery principle of inequality the wonderful fabric of the old Constitution had been shaken to its centre. The artificers of these amendments had actually seen it tremble from turret to foundation-stone. They foresaw, that the political tempests and civic whirlwinds which had swept away the short-lived freedom of other governments, and acted so disastrously in the case of their own, could be prevented from recurring only by the inviolable maintenance of the principle of the equality of the rights of each individual member of the state by due process of law; that the despotic denial of this sacred principle, throughout the ages, had constantly created a disturbance in the political atmosphere, producing revolutionary convulsions which had wrecked popular liberty in the enforced struggles of mankind for freedom. These philosophic statesmen cast forth this precious seed of liberty, and watered it with the blood of their brave hearts, that their children might gather the fruit of the full-grown tree when those who planted it were mouldering in peace beneath its shade. Their doctrines declared, with the Great Master upon whose doctrines all really higher civilization is founded, "I am the way, the truth, and the life;" "All ye are brethren;" "Thou shalt love thy neighbor as thyself." Successive generations of heroes, large-souled men, in the long succession of the ages, have fought and struggled, with sore travail and sufferings untold, with the courage of Titans and a fortitude never yielding to despair; but they never could—for it was not so decreed—with all their grand efforts, found any system so happily fitted to guide the family of the state in the way of advancing civilization, and ensure the happiness of the whole people, as that now (it is to be trusted) firmly welded to the Constitution of the United States.

Those colossal builders, buttressed in consciousness of right and invincible in will, did not stop to consider the dot over the *i* nor the cross over the *t*. They knew all about the "excellent foppery" of Jurisprudence: that as the world wagged so would it wag; that its precedents and principles were spiced too frequently with the errors of the Machiavellian policy. But

they maintained, with Cicero,[1] that the state should be formed
for eternity,—" *Debet enim constituta sic esse civitas, ut aeterna
sit,*"—and accordingly they placed the new Magna Charta, for
the security of American liberties, properties, freedoms, and pursuit of happiness, under the constitutional protection of the
American principle, Equality, and armed it with due process
of law. Their constitutional reformations were not empty formulas; they were not mere inactive, shadowy similitudes of
equality. In their reconstruction, their re-establishment of the
American state, these statesmen laid deep and broad the political
foundation of equality. The destruction of the thing itself they
rendered impossible, by the constitutional installation of the
sovereign authority of Due Process of Law. According to their
amended system in its artificial working, the political property
of the principle of equality by due process of law as established
by these amendments is not dissimilar to that of the natural law
of gravitation. It maintains the civic equipoise of the atomic
units which form the state, and preserves the permanence and
perpetuity of their balance. The existent order of the state has
its foundation in the adjustment and balancing of the civic right
of every member of the state through the principle of equality
of right by due process of law. By these three Articles America
testified to her unflinching confidence in the celestial origin, and
the final triumph upon earth, of Heaven-born Justice; and she
commanded her supreme justiciars to follow the lead of this
great evangelical, historical, and political truth, by conforming
the order of the state to the principle of the amended constitutional system, which provides for the enforcement of the equality
of every individual's civic right by due process of law.

Beguiled by Satan, who entered her garden in the glistening
sinuous folds of Race-Prejudice, Jurisprudence has placed such
a construction upon these amendments as entirely to divest seven
millions of American citizens of the harmonious beneficence of
this constitutional system. But Jurisprudence has not ventured
to suggest how a republic whose sovereignty is derived from the
people can be bottomed upon any other system with constitutional

---

[1] The Republic, Book iii. chap. iii.

safety. The principle of equality by due process of law is founded upon the doctrine that "Man is by nature a political being." The principles of equality before the law, by due process of law, occupy great historical places in the arena of the world's history. They cannot be interpreted by mere legal fiction, generated by partisan passion. Their sap is not derived from the scholastic tree of technical jurisprudence. In their political and constitutional interpretation, these venerable provisions touch the life of humanity. Their historical, Christian significance means "the unity of the human in the divine Fatherhood." The noble lineage of these great legal phrases is to be traced through all those proverbs and axioms of freedom and liberty, which represent the coined wisdom and humanity of past ages. In whatever language they are written, by whatever tongue they are spoken, their true interpretation and mission is: "Justice against violence;" "Law against anarchy;" "Freedom against oppression."

DIGEST

OF

LEGISLATIVE AND JUDICIAL PROCEEDINGS,

NATIONAL AND STATE,

EMBRACING THE ORGANIC LAWS OF THE UNITED
STATES OF AMERICA SINCE MARCH 6, 1862,

IN RELATION TO THE

CIVIL RIGHTS OF ALL CITIZENS OF THE
UNITED STATES.

PREFATORY NOTE.

To avoid making the Digest of Cases large and expensive, the plan has been adopted of preparing an accurate, solid, and compact embodiment of the pith and marrow of each decision. This compilation presents to the inquirer, within a narrow compass, without tedious research and laborious erudition, all that is material of law or fact to denote the special application of principles in each case. The citations are invariably in the language of the court, and do not consist of partial and disconnected extracts from opinions. The syllabus of the cases has never been used unless it was *ipsissimis verbis* of the judge's opinion.

In the tabulation of cases the plan of the best reports, in the United States and Massachusetts digests, has been adopted. Ordinal numbers have been discarded, and titles of office ignored. The distinctive word in the name of appellant and appellee has been sometimes made the index-word.

CONTENTS OF THE DIGEST.

TABLE OF CASES.

511

DIGEST

OF

ORGANIC LAW AND CASES

TOUCHING CIVIL RIGHTS.

PROCLAMATIONS.

On March 6, 1862, the President, in a special message, recommended the passage of a joint resolution, "that the United States ought to co-operate with any State which may adopt a general abolishment of slavery, giving to such State pecuniary aid, to be used by such State in its discretion to compensate for the inconvenience, public and private, produced by such change of system."[1] This was passed about a month later,—April 10, 1862.[2]

On May 9, 1862, President Lincoln annulled a reputed "general order" of Major-General David Hunter, setting forth that as martial law had been declared in the States of Georgia, Florida, and South Carolina, and slavery and martial law in a free country were incompatible, slaves in those States were free. The President said, "Whether it be competent for me as Commander-in-chief of the army and navy to declare the slaves of any State or States free, and whether at any time in any case it shall have become a necessity indispensable to the maintenance of the government, are questions which, under my responsibility, I reserve to myself."[3]

On September 22, 1862, President Lincoln proclaimed that "hereafter, as heretofore, the war will be prosecuted for the

---

[1] Stat. at L., xii. 1265. [2] Ib. 617.
[3] Ib. 1265.

object of practically restoring the constitutional relation between the United States and each of the States and the people thereof, in which State that relation is or may be suspended or disturbed;" that he would at the next meeting of Congress "again recommend" the tender of pecuniary aid to the people of such "slave States," not then in rebellion, as might voluntarily adopt immediate or gradual abolition of slavery; that on January 1, 1863, the slaves in States then in rebellion should be free, and that their right to freedom would be recognized by the executive, including the army and navy of the United States; that he would on January 1, 1863, designate the States then in rebellion, and representation in Congress by members chosen by a majority of the voters should, in absence of strong countervailing evidence, be deemed conclusive proof that a State was not in rebellion; called attention to the provisions by Congress just cited, and commanded the military and naval officers to enforce them; and promised that he would in due time recommend that all citizens who had remained loyal to the United States throughout the rebellion should, on restoration of constitutional relations between the United States and their respective States, "be compensated for all losses by acts of the United States, including the loss of slaves."[1]

On January 1, 1863, he designated the States or parts of States " in rebellion;" declared all persons held as slaves therein free; enjoined on them to abstain from violence, except in necessary self-defence; recommended them, when allowed, to labor for reasonable wages; declared that they would be received into the armed service of the United States, and that this was "sincerely believed to be an act of justice, warranted by the Constitution, upon military necessity."[2]

On December 8, 1863, President Lincoln issued a proclamation of pardon to rebels, with certain exceptions, who should take an oath that they would support the acts of Congress and proclamations of the President with reference to slaves, so far as not repealed or held void by the Supreme Court, etc.[3] This

---

[1] Stat. at L., xii. 1267.   [2] Ib. 1268.
[3] Stat. at L., xiii. 737, 738.

qualification was left out of the oath required to be taken by the subsequent proclamation as to pardons by President Johnson on May 29, 1865.[1]

EFFECT.

UNITED STATES COURTS, ETC.

The effect of the Emancipation Proclamation has been several times considered. It has been said that "it could operate no further than as a military order."[2] And "the chief magistrate, in his proclamation of September 22, 1862, is designated not only as 'President of the United States,' but as Commander-in-chief of the army and navy thereof," thereby, it would seem, implying that in assuming to emancipate all the slaves in the seceded States the executive rested his authority not on the acts of Congress,—which, though they may be practically applicable to all the slaves in those States, do not profess in terms to declare universal manumission,—but on that undefined war power the existence of which in the President alone was denied by Senator Sumner and others.[3]

In 1861 the United States issued bonds to Texas, in the arrangement of certain boundary claims; some of these, which were in the State treasury at the secession, were sold by the new government of Texas. The question of title in the purchaser of these bonds being before the Supreme Court in 1868, it was said, "Slaves in the insurgent States, with certain local exceptions, had been declared free by the Proclamation of Emancipation; and, whatever question might be made as to the effect of that act under the Constitution, it was clear from the beginning that its practical operation, in connection with legislative acts of like tendency, must be complete enfranchisement; wherever the national forces obtained control the slaves became freemen; support to the acts of Congress and the proclamation of the President concerning slaves was made a condition of amnesty by President Lincoln in December, 1863, and President Johnson

---

[1] Stat. at L., xiii. 758.
[2] Dana's case, Wheat. Int. L., p. 441, n.
[3] Wheat. Int. L., p. 603, n.

in May, 1865. The emancipation was confirmed rather than ordained in the insurgent States by the amendment to the Constitution prohibiting slavery throughout the Union, which was proposed by Congress in February, 1865, and ratified before the close of the following autumn by the requisite three-fourths of the States."[1]

In 1872 the Supreme Court said, "In that struggle slavery, as a legalized social relation, perished. It perished as a necessity of the bitterness and force of the conflict. When the armies of freedom found themselves upon the soil of slavery, they could do nothing less than free the poor victims whose enforced servitude was the foundation of the quarrel. And, when hard pressed in the conflict, these men (*for they proved themselves men in that terrible crisis*) offered their services, and were accepted by the thousands, to aid in suppressing the unlawful rebellion; slavery was at an end wherever the Federal government succeeded in that purpose. The proclamation of President Lincoln expressed an accomplished fact, as to a large portion of the insurrectionary districts, when he declared slavery abolished in them all. But, the war being over, those who had succeeded in re-establishing the authority of the Federal government were not content to permit this great act of emancipation to rest on the actual results of the contest or the proclamation of the executive, both of which might be questioned in after-times, and they determined to place this main and most valuable result in the Constitution of the restored Union, as one of its fundamental articles; hence the Thirteenth Article of Amendment of that instrument."[2]

STATE COURTS.

On August 29, 1863, A sold B a negro, both parties residing beyond the lines of the Federal army. *Held,* that the owner's rights were in nowise affected by the proclamation;[3] that this was a war measure, intended to act on the fears of slave-holders,

---

[1] Texas *v.* White, 7 Wall. 700, 728.

[2] Slaughter-House cases, 17 Wall. 36, 68.

[3] Dorris *v.* Grace, 24 Ark. 326, 329 (1866).

dependent on the military for enforcement,[1] and could not divest rights of property.[2]

The Alabama court afterwards spoke of slavery as having been abolished by ordinance of the Convention which made the State Constitution after the war. But whether it was sooner destroyed, they did not intend to express an opinion;[3] again, it said, "If, as one of the results of the war, slavery had not ceased to exist before the adoption of this ordinance, it certainly has had no existence since;"[4] again, it speaks of abolition as the "result of civil convulsion and war;"[5] and again, "The legality or illegality of the destruction of slavery by the act of war is a question it would be utterly vain and useless to discuss. It is an historical fact that the consummation was effected by the act of war, anterior to the action of the State Convention; and whether justly or unjustly, legally or illegally, are not practical questions. This was the view, in fact, taken by the State Convention. That body was not guilty of the absurdity of abolishing slavery which did not then exist. But it gave a high and solemn sanction to the truth of a fact before well known, that the institution of slavery had 'been destroyed in the State of Alabama,' by expressly so declaring, and prohibiting its existence in the future except as a punishment for crime."[6]

Afterwards it was held that "slavery in Alabama was abolished in May, 1865." And "whether the State was in or out of the Union at the issuance of the proclamation of President Lincoln in January, 1863, makes no distinction or difference. If in the Union, he had no constitutional authority, nor had Congress any to confer on him, to issue and enforce it at that time; and if out of the Union, it could have no force or validity until the Federal government was enabled by conquest or the power of arms to enforce it."[7]

In a suit in 1866 on a replevin bond executed in 1859 for the

---

[1] 24 Ark. 330. [2] Ib. 331.

[3] Burt *v.* State, 39 Ala. 617, 626 (1866).

[4] George *v.* State, 39 Ala. 675, 676 (1866).

[5] Eliza *v.* State, 39 Ala. 693, 695 (1866).

[6] Ferd. *v.* State, 39 Ala. 706, 708 (1866).

[7] Leslie *v.* Langham, 40 Ala. 524, 529 (1867).

delivery of slaves, the court said, "We judicially know that before the trial slavery ceased to exist in the State of Alabama."[1]

In 1868, in Florida, it was said, "In time of peace the President, with or without the sanction or authority of Congress, had no power to issue a proclamation freeing the slaves; but as Commander-in-chief of the army he had the power during the war to issue any military order authorized by the usages of modern warfare which the circumstances required; but no military orders or proclamation issued by him could have effect over persons or property not within the lines of military occupation, but within the lines of the enemy and over which they had exclusive control. The proclamation was, as it purports to be, a war measure, issued by the President as Commander-in-chief in time of war, and to affect the war; under it slaves coming within the lines of Federal military occupation could not be reclaimed by their former owners. They were thus practically free by means of actual force, by the power of arms. And an owner was allowed to recover for the services of a hired negro from 1863 to 1865."[2]

In 1869, where it was sought to charge an administrator with certain slaves, the court said slavery was a national interest protected by national law, and it could only expire by national act, in case the owners of slaves were unwilling to give them up.[3] "The great national decree, which laid slavery prostrate in the dust forever upon this continent, was the proclamation of President Lincoln, issued on the first day of January, 1863. After that act slavery was maintained only by force. It was thenceforth virtually abolished, and actually so wherever the army of the United States had possession of the territories to which the proclamation extended,—as much as it was at any time in the year 1865. The nation fixed the day for its termination, and after that day it was simply a struggle of the former masters of the slaves to prevent the decree of the nation from being carried into effect. The Alabama Convention of 1865 and its

---

[1] Glover v. Taylor, 41 Ala. 124, 128.

[2] Slaback v. Cushman, 12 Fla. 472, 475.

[3] Morgan v. Nelson, 43 Ala. 586, 591.

ordinance had as little to do with emancipation as they will have with the coming of the day of final wrath when the grave will give up its dead. It would have been all the same had that Convention never met. If the Convention merely ratified the act of emancipation, its ratification had relation to the beginning of the act." [1]

In 1870 it was said "the proclamation was manifestly naught but a war measure, and of no apparent effect till carried into execution by force of arms." [2]

A series of cases involving the amenability of freedmen to the criminal laws were decided at the January term, 1866, of the Supreme Court of Alabama. The first case was an indictment of a party as a slave in 1863 for murder of a white person. All slave murderers were punished with death; for others murder was divided into degrees; the statute making this division, it was expressly said, should not apply to slaves. The court held, that the offences prescribed in the two statutes were not the same; that a prisoner indicted under the first could not be punished under the second; and that, as the judgment under the common law could not be sustained, there was none under which he could be punished. [3]

The second case was an indictment for larceny, found in 1865. It was held, an averment that the defendants were "freedmen" was descriptive of their status and did not vitiate the indictment. [4]

The third was an indictment for murder of a slave by a party "now a freedman, but formerly a slave." The court reiterated its views, as given in Burt v. State, and declared that the party could not be punished. [5]

The next case was one of larceny; for slaves committing this crime there was a different punishment from that provided for freemen; and the court held, that a party could not be punished who had committed the crime while a slave under either statute

---

[1] 43 Ala. 592.

[2] Weaver v. Lapsley, 42 Ala. 601, 614.

[3] Burt v. State, 39 Ala. 617.

[4] Jeffries v. State, ib. 665; affirming Peters v. State, ib. 681.

[5] Nelson v. State, 39 Ala. 667.

or at the common law.[1] But an act approved in 1884, and ratified by the State Convention of 1885, punishing larceny, was held to apply to freedmen as well as others.[2]

In the last case a party was indicted for felony as a "freedwoman of color," and a "free person of color" under a section of the Alabama code which had been promulgated as not applicable to slaves. The court sustained the indictment. It said of the negroes, "Emancipation changed their servile status, but on becoming freedmen they remained as persons, and as persons they are amenable to the existing laws;"[3] and "the fact that they had become free" not by their own seeking, but by a political convulsion in which they took no part, "could not affect their amenability to the laws."[4]

LEGISLATION, ETC.

1. March 13, 1862, Congress adopted an "additional article of war," prohibiting officers of the army or navy from using their forces to "restore fugitives from service or labor, who may have escaped from any persons to whom such service or labor is claimed to be due."[5]

2. On April 16, 1862, Congress passed an act, abolishing slavery in the District of Columbia, appropriating a sum not exceeding one million dollars for the compensation of loyal owners, and a hundred thousand for the deportation to Hayti or Liberia of such liberated slaves as might desire to emigrate.[6] This was extended to slaves from other States, resident in the District since April 16, 1862, by an act passed July 12, same year.[7]

3. On July 17, 1862, a long act "to suppress insurrection, to punish treason and rebellion, to seize and confiscate the property

---

[1] George *v.* State, 39 Ala. 675.   [2] Aaron *v.* State, 39 Ala. 684.
[3] Elijah *v.* State, 39 Ala. 693, 695 (1866).
[4] Ib. 696.   [5] Stat. at L., xii. 354.
[6] Stat. at L., xii. 376.   [7] Ib. 538.

of rebels, and for other purposes" was passed. Its ninth section provided that all slaves of persons engaged in or giving comfort, etc., to rebellion, taking refuge within the lines of the army, or captured from or deserted by such persons and coming under the control of the United States, or found in places occupied by rebel forces and afterwards occupied by those of the United States, should be deemed captives of war, and free. Its tenth section provided that no slave escaping into any State or Territory, or the District of Columbia, from any other State, shall be delivered up, etc., except for crime, etc., unless the person claiming him shall make oath that the person to whom his service is alleged to be due is his lawful owner, and has not borne arms against the United States in the present rebellion nor given aid and comfort thereto; and that no military or naval officer should decide the validity of such claims, or surrender such fugitive to the claimant, on pain of dismissal from the service.[1] Its eleventh section authorized the President to employ persons of African descent in the army and navy "for the suppression of the rebellion."[2]

4. Act approved March 3, 1863, granted permission to the Alexandria and Washington Railroad Company to extend their road into the District of Columbia, provided no person should be excluded from the cars on account of color.[3]

5. An act approved April 9, 1866, entitled "An act to protect all persons in the United States in their civil rights, and furnish the means of their vindication," declared all persons born in the United States and not subject to any foreign power, excluding Indians not taxed, to be citizens of the United States; that they should have the same right to sue, hold property, etc., and the same benefit of laws for the security of personal property, as white citizens, and be subject to like penalties only; that any person subjecting an inhabitant to a different punishment, on account of his previous condition of servitude or his race, should be deemed guilty of a misdemeanor; gave the United States courts exclusive jurisdiction of offences under it,

---

[1] Stat. at L , xii. 589, 591.　　　[2] Ib. 592.
[3] Ib. 805.

and of all causes, civil or criminal, affecting persons who were denied or could not enforce in State tribunals the rights secured by its first section. It gave the right of removal from a State to a United States court of any action against a person for acts done under color of this statute, or under the act establishing the Freedman's Bureau,[1] or for refusal to do any act because inconsistent with this one; charged the district attorneys, etc., to institute proceedings against violators of the act; provided a penalty for those who should hinder officers in the discharge of their duties under it; and that the President might direct judges to attend for speedy trials the places where he might have reason to believe offences against the act had been or were about to be committed, and employ the land and naval forces to enforce its provisions.[2]

6. The "enforcement act," approved May 31, 1870, entitled "An act to enforce the rights of citizens of the United States to vote in the several States of this Union, and for other purposes," provided that all citizens, otherwise entitled to vote, should be so entitled without distinction of race, color, or previous condition of servitude; fixed a penalty for any officer, charged with furnishing to citizens opportunity to perform prerequisites to voting, who should fail to give all citizens the same and equal opportunities to do so; declared that an offer to perform them, failing to be carried into effect through such officer's act of omission, should be deemed a performance, and that the judge, etc., who refused to receive the vote of a citizen making affidavit to such offer should be punished; that any person who by threats, bribery, etc., should obstruct or conspire to obstruct a citizen from qualifying to vote, or from voting, or should attempt to hinder a person, to whom the right of suffrage was extended by the Fifteenth Amendment, from or in exercising that right by threats of depriving him of employment or of ejecting him from a rented house, etc., and any persons who should conspire together or go in disguise on the highway or on the premises of another with intent to violate its provisions or in-

---

[1] Stat. at L., xiii. 507, approved March 3, 1865.
[2] Stat. at L., xiv. 26.

timidate a citizen or hinder his free enjoyment of privileges secured by the Constitution and laws of the United States, should be deemed guilty of a felony ; contained the same provisions as the last preceding act as to jurisdiction of the United States courts and duties of attorneys and marshals and the President's employment of the army and navy ; required the district attorneys to bring *quo warranto* against those holding office in violation of the third section of the Fourteenth Amendment, and made such holding a misdemeanor ; repeated the provisions of the previous act, giving the same rights to all persons " within the jurisdiction of the United States," in regard to contracts, suing, etc., as the whites ; forbade the State to impose greater taxation on emigrants from one country than on those from another ; prescribed a penalty on any person subjecting another to a different punishment, on account of his being an alien, of his race, etc., from those provided for citizens ; re-enacted the previous act ; provided penalties for illegal voting, etc., at congressional elections ; and that the defeat of a candidate for any office, except that of presidential elector or member of Congress, by reason of a denial of citizens of their right to vote on account of race, color, etc., should not defeat the candidate's right to the office ; and gave the United States courts jurisdiction wherever the sole question of the title thereto grew out of the denial of such right on the ground mentioned.[1]

7. Act approved February 28, 1871 (" Ku-Klux Act"), entitled " An act to amend the previous act," provided a penalty for unlawful acts in the matter of registration, though under State laws, and for State or municipal elections ; that in towns of over twenty thousand inhabitants, on petition of two citizens, a United States judge should appoint supervisors of elections of members of Congress, or registration for such election ; which supervisors should inspect and sign the lists, etc., attend at the election, challenge voters, count ballots, make returns, etc. ; and should report, if molested, to the chief supervisor, who should take evidence and report the acts to Congress ; provided for the appointment of deputy marshals to serve at congressional elec-

---

[1] Stat. at L., xvi. 140.

tions, and for the mode of procedure in the United States courts, which were given jurisdiction.[1]

8. Act approved April 20, 1871, entitled "An act to enforce the provisions of the Fourteenth Amendment to the Constitution, and for other purposes," makes any one who, under color of a State law, etc., shall deprive any person "within the jurisdiction of the United States" of any rights secured by the Constitution thereof, liable to suit in the United States courts; provides that any who conspire against the government of the United States, or to take its property, or against its officers or witnesses or jurors of its courts, or who go in disguise on the highway to deprive persons of equal privileges under the laws, or hinder the State authorities from securing them, or to obstruct justice or deprive a citizen of equal protection of the law, or injure a person for enforcing that right, or to intimidate, etc., a citizen from giving lawful support in favor of presidential electors or members of Congress, or injure him for so doing, shall be criminally liable in the United States courts, and the injured party shall have therein his action for damages; that where insurrection, domestic violence, or combinations shall so obstruct the execution of the laws as to deprive any class of people of the immunities named in the Constitution and secured by the act, and the State authorities fail to give protection, the President may employ the militia or land and naval forces for the suppression of such insurrection, etc. By a section "not to be in force after the end of the next regular session of Congress," it provided that, when such unlawful combinations should be able to defy the State government, or the latter should connive at their purposes, and the conviction of offenders be impracticable, it should be deemed a rebellion, and the limits of the district involved should be prescribed by proclamation, in which the President might at his discretion suspend the *habeas corpus*, after commanding the insurgents to disperse; that no person should be a juror in a United States court who was, in the court's judgment, in complicity with such combinations, and that an oath should be taken by jurors suspected of so being; and that per-

---

[1] Stat. at L., xvi. 433.

sons knowing that the wrongs mentioned in the first section were about to be committed, and having power to prevent them, and not doing so, should be liable in damages to the party injured.[1]

9. Act approved March 1, 1875 (" Civil-Rights Bill"), entitled " An act to protect all citizens in their civil and legal rights," recited that, " Whereas it is essential to just government, we recognize the equality of all men before the law, and hold that it is the duty of government in its dealings with the people to mete out equal and exact justice to all, of whatever nativity, race, color, or persuasion; and it being the appropriate object of legislation to enact great fundamental principles into law: therefore all persons within the jurisdiction of the United States should have equal enjoyment of the accommodations of inns, public conveyances, theatres, and other places of public amusement;" allows parties to proceed for violations of the act at common law or under State statutes; requires the district attorneys to institute criminal proceedings in the United States courts against violators, under a penalty; provides that no " citizens" should be excluded from serving as grand or petit jurors in the United States courts on account of race, color, or previous condition, etc., and imposes a penalty on any officer failing to summon a citizen for such cause.[2]

THE AMENDMENTS.

XIII.

Abolished slavery or involuntary servitude except as a punishment for crime. Was proposed February 1, 1865, and declared adopted December 18, 1865.[3]

XIV.

Among other things, declared that persons born or naturalized in the United States and subject to the jurisdiction thereof

---

[1] Stat. at L., xvii. 13.   [2] Stat. at L., xviii. 335.
[3] Rev. Stat., 30.

are citizens thereof and of the State wherein they reside; that no State shall make or enforce any law abridging the privileges or immunities of citizens of the United States, nor deprive any one of life, liberty, or property without due process of law; nor deny to any person within its jurisdiction the equal protection of the laws. Was proposed June 16, 1866, and announced as ratified July 28, 1868.[1]

XV.

Provided that the right of citizens of the United States to vote or hold office should not be denied, etc., by the United States or any State on account of race, color, or previous condition of servitude. It was proposed February 27, 1869, and its adoption announced March 30, 1870.[2]

Each of these amendments contained a provision that Congress should have power to enforce it by appropriate legislation.

CITIZENSHIP.

IN GENERAL.

" I have often been pained by the fruitless search in our law-books and the records of our courts for a clear and satisfactory definition of the phrase ' citizen of the United States.' "[3] The words " people of the United States" and " citizens" are synonymous and mean the same thing.[4]

Citizens are members of the political community to which they belong. They are the people who compose the community and who in their associated capacity have established or submitted themselves to the dominion of the government.[5]

The Constitution uses the words " citizen" and " natural-born citizen," but neither that instrument nor any act of Congress has attempted to define their meaning.[6]

The same person may be at the same time a citizen of the United States and of a State, but his rights of citizenship under one

---

[1] Rev. Stat., 31. [2] Rev. Stat., 32.
[3] Bates op. Att. Gen., x. (1862).
[4] Dred Scott *v.* Sandford, 19 How. 393, 404 (1856).
[5] United States *v.* Cruikshank, 92 U. S. 542, 549.
[6] United States *v.* Rhodes, 1 Abb. (U. S.) 28, 38.

of these governments will be different from those he has under the other,[1] and the distinction between citizenship of a State and citizenship of the United States is clearly recognized.[2] Equality of privilege is the constitutional right of all citizens, but equality of protection is the constitutional right of all persons.[3] What, then, are the essential privileges which belong to the citizens of the United States as such, and which a State cannot by its laws invade? It may be difficult to enumerate or define them. The Supreme Court on one occasion thought it unwise to do so. It is his privilege to have with all other citizens the equal protection of the laws.[4] " It was very ably contended on the part of the defendants that the Fourteenth Amendment was intended only to secure to all citizens equal capacities under the law. That was at first our view of it. But it does not so read. The language is, ' No State shall abridge the privileges or immunities of citizens of the United States.' What are the privileges and immunities of the citizens of the United States? Are they capacities merely? are they not also rights? "[5]

Colored equally with white persons are citizens of the United States.[6] The emancipation of a native-born slave makes him a citizen.[7]

When the Constitution was adopted free men of color were clothed with the franchise of voting in at least five States, and were a part of the people whose sanction breathed into it the breath of life.[8]

In 1838 it was said that upon the Revolution " slaves manumitted here became free men, and therefore if born in North Carolina are citizens of North Carolina."[9] The court said it was difficult to ascertain whether before the Revolution free

---

[1] United States v. Cruikshank, 92 U. S. 542, 549.
[2] Slaughter-House cases, 16 Wall. 36, 73.
[3] Ah Fong's case, 3 Saw. 144, 157.
[4] L. S. Asso. v. C. C. Co., 1 Abb. (U. S.) 388, 398.
[5] Ib. 402.
[6] Matter of Turner, 1 Abb. (U. S.) 84, 88.
[7] United States v. Rhodes, 1 Abb. (U. S.) 28, 42.
[8] Ib. 28, 41.
[9] State v. Manuel, 4 D. & B. (N. C.) 20, 25.

colored persons voted for members of the legislature. But probably few of them did, because a freehold qualification was required. " The Constitution extended the elective franchise to every freeman who had arrived at the age of twenty-one and paid a tax ; and it is a matter of universal notoriety that under it free persons without regard to color claimed and exercised the franchise till it was taken from free men of color a few years since by our amended Constitution."[1] And it was held, that, if a free colored person was a citizen under the State Constitution,[2] the rights of citizenship, irrespective of color, include the right of suffrage, and the African race, although not specially referred to,[3] in the provision that "all persons born in the United States and subject to the jurisdiction thereof," etc., "are citizens," etc., is but declaratory of the common law,[4] and it is not to be presumed that the amendment was meant to change its rule.[5]

In early times free colored persons exercised the suffrage in New Hampshire, Massachusetts, New York, New Jersey, and North Carolina,[6] and this was the case in New Hampshire and Massachusetts in 1856,[7] and colored aliens could be naturalized.[8]

It is not true that the Constitution was made exclusively by and for the white race; it was established by "the people of the United States" for themselves and their posterity; and, as free colored persons were then citizens of at least five States, and so in every sense part of the people of the United States, they were among those for whom and for whose posterity the Constitution was established.[9]

DRED SCOTT DECISION.

In 1824 a United States army surgeon took his slave, Dred Scott, from Missouri to a military post in Illinois, and subsequently removed him to another post, within the Territory of "Upper Louisiana," wherein slavery was forbidden by the Mis-

---

[1] 4 D. & B. (N. C.) 25. [2] Ib. 26.
[3] United States v. Carter, 2 Bond, 389, 391.
[4] McKay v. Campbell, 2 Saw. 118, 129. [5] Ib. 130.
[6] Scott v. Sandford, 19 How. 393, 574 (Curtis's dis. op.).
[7] Ib. [8] Ib. 586. [9] Ib. 474.

souri act of admission. Later he returned with Scott to Missouri, where Scott sued in a State court for his freedom. An action of trespass *vi et armis* was also brought in the Circuit Court of the United States. A judgment for Scott was, on appeal, reversed by the Supreme Court. It was held that the Circuit Court had no jurisdiction, as a negro " whose ancestors were imported into this country and sold as slaves could not become a citizen of the United States,"[1] though a State might confer on him the right of citizenship within her boundaries.[2] But, even if a State made him free, the Constitution of the United States did not then act upon him, and clothe him with the right of a citizen in other States and its own courts.[3]

Chief-Justice Taney, delivering the opinion, says the negroes had, for more than a century before the adoption of the Constitution, " been regarded as beings of an inferior order, and altogether unfit to associate with the white race, either in social or political relations, and so far inferior that they had no rights which the white man was bound to respect; and that the negro might justly and lawfully be reduced to slavery for his benefit. He was bought and sold, and treated as an ordinary article of merchandise and traffic whenever a profit could be made by it."[4] He showed, from the slave trade, the early legislation of the colonies, etc., how general this idea was among English-speaking people;[5] said not citizenship, but freedom, was the question involved in Legrand *v.* Darnell, 2 Peters, 664,[6] and that it was not prepared to say " that there were not cases wherein United States courts might exercise jurisdiction, though a member of the African race was a party, but this was a question of his claim to special privileges, by reason of citizenship;[7] that a change of public feeling in relation to the race could not induce the court to give the words of the Constitution a more liberal construction in their favor than they were intended to bear when it was adopted."[8]

Thus, the first point was settled,—namely, that a negro was not a citizen. The question of citizenship was raised below by

---

[1] 19 How. 393, 403.

[2] Ib. 405.   [3] Ib. 406.   [4] Ib. 407.   [5] Ib. seq.

[6] Ib. 423.   [7] Ib. 425.   [8] Ib. 426.

a plea in abatement, which was overruled; the defendant having
then pleaded a bar, and final judgment being in his favor, some
of the court doubted if the plea in abatement was before them,
on a writ of error. It was held that it was;[1] but, even if it
were not, that the objection to the plaintiff's citizenship was apparent on the record, the plaintiff, in his bill of exception, stat-
ing that he was born a slave, but was made free by his removals.[2]
The court then said it could examine the exception after deciding against the jurisdiction below on the plea in abatement,[3]
and proceeded to inquire whether the facts entitled the plaintiff to
freedom;[4] for, " whatever opinions might be entertained in favor
of the citizenship of a free person of the African race, no one
supposed a slave was a citizen of the State or of the United
States."[5]

The court then held that the power given Congress by the
Constitution, "to dispose of and make all needful rules and
regulations respecting the territory or other property belonging
to the United States," was confined to territory then claimed by
the United States and within the boundaries settled by the treaty
with Great Britain,[6] that is, to the unoccupied land ceded
by several States to the original Confederation,[7] — wherein
slavery was prohibited by the Congress of the Confederation in.
passing the "ordinance of 1787,"[8] which was revised by the
United States Congress, after becoming a nullity, on the adoption of the Constitution.[9] Still, the court concurred in the
opinion that the right of Congress to govern new territory was
involved in the right to acquire it,[10] though the Federal government cannot establish or maintain colonies;[11] and the power of
Congress over territories is limited in the Constitution,[12] by the
Fourteenth Amendment, which provides that no person shall
" be deprived of life, liberty, or property, without due process
of law;" and the court says, " An act of Congress which deprives
a citizen of the United States of his liberty or property merely
because he came himself or brought his property into a particu-

---

[1] 19 How. 427.   [2] Ib. 427.   [3] Ib.   [4] Ib. 430.
[5] Ib.   [6] Ib. 434.   [7] Ib.   [8] Ib. 435.
[9] Ib 438.   [10] Ib. 443.   [11] Ib. 446.   [12] Ib. 449.

lar Territory of the United States, and who had committed no offence against the laws, could hardly be justified with the name of due process of law ;"[1] and that, so far as the Constitution is concerned, there is no difference between a slave and any other property.[2]

And thus, the second point was determined,—namely, that Congress could not prohibit a citizen of a State taking his slave into a Territory and then holding him as property.

Scott, however, maintained that he was free, because of his removal to Illinois, independently of his having been taken to United States territory, and was not again reduced to slavery by being brought back to Missouri. That his status depended on the laws of Missouri and not on those of Illinois was affirmed on the authority of Stradler *v.* Graham, 10 How. 82 ;[3] and the court held that the Circuit Court of the United States had no jurisdiction where by the laws of the State the plaintiff was a slave :[4] which settled the third point in the case.

GENERAL REMARKS ON THE AMENDMENTS, ETC.

They came before the Supreme Court for the first time in 1872, in the Slaughter-House cases, wherein the constitutionality of a Louisiana statute, requiring butchers to do their work in the buildings of a corporation created by it, was involved.[5] The court said, that servitude was used as of larger meaning than slavery, and to prevent evasions, such as practised in the West Indies, after the English government had abolished slavery, by means of long terms of apprenticeship, or reducing slaves to the condition of servants attached to the plantations ;[6] that the purpose of the Thirteenth Amendment was to forbid all forms of African slavery, and, because of legislation unfavorable to the blacks in certain Southern States, the Fourteenth was adopted,[7] and, as their position appeared still insecure, the Fifteenth was passed. The three have one purpose,[8] but they apply to others than those of African descent.[9] One great purpose of these

---

[1] 19 How. 450.   [2] Ib. 451.   [3] Ib. 452.   [4] Ib. 453.
[5] Slaughter-House cases, 16 Wall. 36, 37.
[6] Ib. 69.   [7] Ib. 70.   [8] Ib. 71.   [9] Ib. 72.

amendments was to raise the colored race, from that condition of inferiority and servitude in which most of them had previously stood, into perfect equality of civil rights with all other persons within the jurisdiction of the States. They were intended to take away all possibility of oppression by law because of race or color. They were intended to be, what they really are, limitations of the power of the States and enlargements of the power of Congress. They are to some extent declaratory of rights, and, though in form prohibitions, they imply immunities such as may be protected by congressional legislation.[1]

The object of the civil-rights statutes, as of the Constitution which authorized them, was to place the colored race, in respect of civil rights, upon a level with the white. They made the rights and responsibilities, civil and criminal, of the two races exactly the same.[2] A careful perusal of the amendments and of the civil-rights bill makes it obvious that the design of both was not only to guarantee in the largest sense to every citizen in the United States a sacred right of equality under the law throughout the whole land, but also to protect from invasion all the essential rights that belong to the citizen, and flow from the Constitution.[3] Under them a State (1) cannot establish servitude, or (2) deprive a negro of his privileges as a citizen of the United States, and (3) must recognize as its citizen any negro citizen of the United States who becomes a resident therein, and (4) give him the same privileges as her other citizens; but there is no limitation on her power to protect the rights of her citizens, so as to secure her own internal peace and prosperity.[4]

Prior to December, 1865, when it was announced that the Thirteenth Amendment had become part of the Constitution, the negro population in Kentucky was generally in a state of slavery. The free negroes were not citizens of a State; they were mere residents, without political rights.[5] They were not citizens of the United States, and were not capable of becoming citizens

[1] *Ex Parte* Virginia, 100 U. S. 339, 344, 345.
[2] Virginia *v.* Rives, 100 U. S. 313, 318.
[3] Hobbs *v.* Johnson, 1 Wood, 537, 541.
[4] Cory *v.* Carter, 48 Ind. 327, 358.
[5] Marshall *v.* Donovan, 10 Bush (Ky.) 681, 686.

thereof. The primary object of the Fourteenth Amendment was to relieve this race from the disabilities declared, in the Dred Scott case, to be inherent and inseparable from the African blood. The Thirteenth Amendment abolished slavery and prohibited involuntary servitude except as a punishment for crime, but left the negro under all his former political disabilities and with no political rights except such as the various States might see proper to permit him to enjoy.[1] The main purpose of the first clause of the Fourteenth Amendment was to establish the citizenship of the race of people who had not heretofore been citizens of the State or of the United States; not to abridge the rights of those already citizens, but to elevate the negro to a political status he had not theretofore occupied.[2]

The amendments are the logical results of the late civil war. Practically slavery had been abolished before the adoption of the Thirteenth Amendment.[3] The fundamental idea and principle pervading these amendments is an impartial equality of rights and privileges, civil and political, to all citizens of the United States.[4] Equality of rights, privileges, and capacities is a condition of all citizens established by these organic laws.[5]

For a general review of the effect of the amendments, see Le Grand v. United States, 12 Fed. Rep. 577, Desty's note, p. 583.

THE THIRTEENTH AMENDMENT.

" It trenches directly on the power of the States, and of the people of the States. It is the first and only instance of a change of this character in the organic law.[6] It destroyed the most important relation between capital and labor in all the States where slavery existed. It struck out of existence millions of property. The measure was the result of the strife of opinions and the conflict of interests, real or imaginary, as old as the institution itself; those who insisted upon the adoption of it were animated by no spirit of vengeance. They sought

---

[1] 10 Bush (Ky.) 687.   [2] Ib. 688.
[3] Donald v. State, 48 Miss. 661, 675.   [4] Ib. 677.
[5] Ib. 678.   [6] United States v. Rhodes, 1 Abb. (U. S.) 28, 37.

security against the recurrence of a sectional conflict. They felt that much was due to the African race for the part it had borne during the war. They were also impelled by a sense of right and by a strong sense of justice to an unoffending and long-suffering people. These considerations must not be lost sight of when we come to examine the amendment in order to ascertain its proper construction.[1]

"The present effect of the amendment was to abolish slavery wherever it existed within the jurisdiction of the United States. In the future it throws its protection over every one of every race, color, or condition within their jurisdiction, and guards them against the recurrence of the evil."[2] Present possessions and future acquisitions are alike within the sphere of its operations.[3] It reversed and annulled the original policy of the Constitution, which left it to each State to decide exclusively for itself whether slavery should or should not exist as a legal institution, and what disabilities should attach to those of the servile race within its limits. The emancipation it wrought was an act of great national grace, and was doubtless intended to reach further in its effects as to everything within its scope than the consequences of manumission by a private individual.[4]

In 1867 it was said that a State law relating to negro apprentices, under which the indentures manifestly vary from those of white apprentices, in not requiring education, authorizing the apprentice's assignment and transfer, speaking of the master's authority as "property and interest," etc., is in violation of this amendment,[5] as creating an "involuntary servitude."[6]

In 1874 it was said, "this is not merely a prohibition against the passage or enforcement of any law inflicting or establishing slavery or involuntary servitude, but it is a positive declaration that slavery shall not exist. It enfranchised four millions of slaves, if indeed they had not previously been enfranchised by the operation of the civil war."[7]

In 1870 it was said that "Congress, in the exercise of the

---

[1] 1 Abb. (U. S.) 38.   [2] Ib. 52.   [3] Ib. 53.   [4] Ib. 56.
[5] Matter of Turner, 1 Abb. (U. S.) 84, 87.   [6] Ib. 88.
[7] United States v. Cruikshank, 1 Wood, 308, 318.

power thus given, have the right to authorize the Federal courts
to take jurisdiction of cases of this sort and to enjoin proceedings
in the State courts. But Congress has not yet assumed that
jurisdiction" (case of a monopoly).[1] Without any other provision than the first section of the amendment Congress would
have had authority to give full effect to the abolition of slavery
thereby decreed.[2] Congress may make it a penal offence to deprive a person of the rights secured by this amendment, but
cannot pass laws for the punishment of ordinary crime.[3] But
the acts forbidden must be designed to injure a person, etc., by
reason of race, color, or previous condition of servitude.[4]

The disability of free negroes to testify is removed by it;[5]
and a negress who continued in the service of her former master
after its passage was allowed to recover for her labors, though
there was no proof of any understanding or express promise
that they were to be paid for.[6]

THE FOURTEENTH AMENDMENT.

MARRIAGE.

About 1867, Judge Duval, of the Fifth Circuit, discharged a
white woman who had been convicted of marrying a negro,
under a State statute which inflicted a penalty on the white person alone; but in a later case (1879) he took a different view,[7]
holding that it violated the spirit of the Constitution and the
civil-rights bill,[8] but not its letter.[9] In 1871 it was held that the
Fourteenth Amendment had not abrogated a State statute forbidding marriages between whites and blacks,[10] nor was such a law in
conflict with the civil-rights bill of April 9, 1866, " waiving the
power of Congress to pass a law authorizing any class of persons
to make or enforce contracts in the State." [11] For the power to
make contracts was " to be enjoyed as by white persons;" [12] but

---

[1] L. S. Asso. *v.* C. C. Co., 1 Abb. (U. S.) 388, 404.
[2] United States *v.* Rhodes, 1 Abb. (U. S.) 28, 53 (1866).
[3] United States *v.* Cruikshank, 1 Wood, 308, 319.   [4] Ib. 320.
[5] Handy *v.* Clark, 4 Houst. 16, 17 (1869).   [6] Ib. 19.
[7] *Ex Parte* François, 3 Wood, 367, 368.   [8] Ib. 369.   [9] Ib. 370.
[10] State *v.* Gibson, 36 Ind. 389, 392.   [11] Ib. 394.   [12] Ib. 395.

the court " deny the power of Congress to determine who shall make contracts, or the manner of enforcing them, in the several States,[1] or determine who may marry in a State,"[2] and say that " to assert separateness of the races is not to declare inferiority in either." [3]

In 1871 a law of Georgia declaring a marriage between a white and a colored person void, but prescribing no penalty, though if the parties cohabited declaring them guilty of fornication, was held not to violate this amendment;[4] and so held in 1879 as to a State law forbidding such a marriage and inflicting an equal penalty on both parties[5] (in this case the parties had left the State of Virginia, for the purpose of being married in the District of Columbia).   In 1882, where one section of a State code prescribed a punishment for fornication generally, another a different punishment where committed by persons of different race, but the punishment in the latter case was the same for both parties, *held*, no conflict with this amendment.[6]

A regulation of a pursuit or profession or the use of property is not within it.[7]

THE CHINESE.

An ordinance prescribing the cutting of a prisoner's hair was held to be in conflict with it, as " acting with special severity upon Chinese prisoners, inflicting upon them suffering altogether disproportionate to what would be endured by other prisoners if enforced against them.   Upon the Chinese it operates as a cruel and unusual punishment." [8]   And so with a statutory provision prohibiting " aliens incapable of becoming electors" from fishing in the waters of the State.[9]   And so with a special tax on Chinese emigrants.[10]   And so with a State law prohibiting corporations from employing Chinese, for " it seems quite impossible that any definition of these terms ' privileges and im-

[1] 36 Ind. 402.   [2] Ib. 403.   [3] Ib. 405.
[4] Hobbs *v.* Johnson, 1 Wood, 537.   [5] *Ex Parte* Kinney, 3 Hughes, 9.
[6] Pace *v.* Alabama, 100 U. S. 502.   [7] Munn *v.* People, 69 Ill. 80, 85.
[8] Ah Kow *v.* Nunan, 5 Saw. 552, 561 (1879).
[9] Ah Chong's cases, 6 Saw. 451, 456 (1880).
[10] Ah Fong's case, 3 Saw. 144, 157 (1874).

munities' could be adopted, or even seriously proposed, so narrow as to exclude the right to labor for subsistence." [1] It also violates the statute passed to give the Fourteenth Amendment effect.[2] So with a city ordinance prohibiting laundries " within the habitable portion of the city." [3]

This amendment places the right of every person within the jurisdiction of the State upon the same secure footing and under the same protection as are the rights of citizens themselves under other provisions of the Constitution ; and contracts to labor are contracts which any person has a right to enforce,[4] and the legislature has not unlimited power over corporations, though a State Constitution authorizes it " to repeal or alter" laws concerning them.[5]

MISCELLANEOUS.

United States Courts.

In 1868, in a case involving a tax on non-resident insurance companies, the court said, " the privileges and immunities" secured to citizens of each State in the several States are those which are common to the citizens in the latter States, under their Constitutions and laws, by virtue of their being citizens.[6] In 1870, in a case involving a State tax on non-resident traders, it was said, the attempt will not be made to define the words "privileges and immunities," or to specify the rights which they are intended to secure and protect, beyond what may be necessary to the decision of the case before the court ; beyond doubt these words are words of very comprehensive meaning.[7]

Where the question was as to a female's being licensed to practise law, the court said, " There are certain privileges and immunities which belong to a citizen of the United States as such ; otherwise it would be nonsense for the Fourteenth Amendment to prohibit a State from abridging them." [8] " There are privileges and immunities belonging to citizens of the United

---

[1] Parrott's case, 6 Saw. 349, 374 (1880).   [2] Ib. 376.
[3] Stockton Laundry case, 26 Fed. Rep. 611 (1886).
[4] Ib. 377.   [5] Ib. 381.   [6] Paul *v.* Virginia, 8 Wall. 168, 180.
[7] Ward *v.* Maryland, 12 Wall. 418, 430.
[8] Bradwell *v.* State, 16 Wall. 130, 138.

States in that relation and character, and it is these and these alone which a State is forbidden to abridge."[1] In 1872 it was said that the Fourteenth Amendment protects the privileges and immunities of citizens of the United States and not of the States.[2]

In 1873, where the question was as to a prohibition of the sale of liquor, it was said, "The most liberal advocates of the rights conferred by this amendment have contended for nothing more than that the rights of the citizen previously existent, and dependent wholly on State laws for their recognition, are now placed under the protection of the Federal government and are secured by the Federal Constitution."[3]

In 1874, where the question was as to female suffrage, it was said, "The Constitution does not define privileges and immunities of citizens."[4] "The amendment did not add to the privileges and immunities of a citizen. It simply furnished an additional guarantee for the protection of such as he already had."[5] In 1875 it was said that the right of trial by jury is not a privilege or immunity under this amendment.[6] In the same year, in a case where "banding together" to intimidate colored voters was charged, the court said, "The amendment adds nothing to the rights of one citizen as against another; it simply furnishes an additional guarantee against any encroachment by the States upon the fundamental rights which belong to every citizen as a member of society."[7]

An arrangement by which the St. Louis Court of Appeals has exclusive jurisdiction in certain cases of appeals from the Circuit Court of that city, and the Supreme Court has similar jurisdiction as to other counties, does not violate this amendment.[8]

"Equal protection of the laws means equal security under them to everything on similar terms in one's life, liberty, and

---

[1] Bradwell *v.* State, 16 Wall. 139.　　[2] Slaughter-House Cases, ib. 36, 74.
[3] Bartemeyer *v.* Iowa, 18 Wall. 129, 133.
[4] Minor *v.* Happersett, 21 Wall. 162, 170.　　[5] Ib. 171.
[6] Walker *v.* Sauvinet, 91 U. S. 90, 92.
[7] United States *v.* Cruikshank, 92 U. S. 542, 554.
[8] Missouri *v.* Lewis, 101 U. S. 22 (1879).

property, and in the pursuit of happiness, and this forbids unequal taxation." [1]

The purpose of the Fourteenth Amendment was to restrain the action of States; [2] and when a State has not violated its provisions, but recognizes it, the amendment imposes no duty or power on Congress.[3] And a provision under which private persons are liable to punishment for "conspiring," no matter how well a State may have done its duty, was *held* unconstitutional,[4] as directed exclusively against the actions of private persons,[5] and to be broader than the Thirteenth Amendment would justify.[6] Congress under this amendment cannot legislate unless the "privileges or immunities" are violated by a State or the United States government.[7]

In 1866 a white man was indicted for burglary in entering a colored man's premises. The owner could not testify against the prisoner under the State law. *Held*, that the right to testify was secured to him by the act of April 9, 1866,[8] and that the cause was one " affecting" the owner within the meaning of that act,[9] and the criminal jurisdiction of the statute was not limited to colored persons.[10] The court added that Congress had abolished the distinction between white and colored witnesses, and given the United States courts jurisdiction of causes which concerned the colored man wherever his right to testify was denied or could not be enforced; [11] that the argument that there was no such thing as a right to testify had no force, as the statute was to be construed reasonably, and this right, like that of suing and contracting, was to be exercised only on proper occasions and within proper limits; [12] and, though the fact that white citizens enjoyed the right denied to colored men in this case was vital to the jurisdiction of the United States court, this need not be averred, as the court would take judicial notice of the provision of the State statute herein.[13]

In 1870, in a case involving the creation of a monopoly, the

[1] Railroad-Tax Cases, 8 Saw. 238, 251.
[2] United States *v.* Harris, 106 U. S. 629, 638.   [3] Ib. 639.   [4] Ib.
[5] Ib. 640.   [6] Ib. 641.   [7] United States *v.* Cruikshank, 1 Wood, 308, 326.
[8] United States *v.* Rhodes, 1 Abb. (U. S.) 28, 30.   [9] Ib. 32
[10] Ib. 35.   [11] Ib. 35.   [12] Ib. 36.   [13] Ib. 30.

Circuit Court said, "The new prohibition is not identical with the clause in the Constitution which declares that the citizens of each State shall be entitled to all privileges and immunities of citizens in the several States. It embraces much more. Is it possible that those who framed the article were not themselves aware of the far-reaching character of its terms? They may have had in mind but one particular phase of social and political wrong which they desired to redress. Yet if the amendment as framed and expressed does in fact bear a broader meaning, and does extend its protecting shield over those who were never thought of when it was conceived and put in form, and does reach social evils which were never before prohibited by constitutional enactment, it is to be presumed that the American people, in giving it their *imprimatur,* understood what they were doing and meant to decree what has in fact been decreed. The privileges and immunities secured by the original Constitution were only such as each State gave to its own citizens. Each was prohibited from discriminating in favor of its own citizens and against the citizens of other States. But the Fourteenth Amendment prohibits any State from abridging the privileges of the citizens of the United States, whether its own citizens or any others. It not merely requires equality of privileges, but it demands that the privileges and immunities of all citizens shall be absolutely unabridged, unimpaired."[1]

State Courts.

The term "privileges" is comprehensive, and includes all rights appertaining to the person as a citizen of the United States.[2] "The object of the amendments and of the statutes is to relieve citizens of the black race from the effects of prejudice, to protect them in person and property from its spirit. We are disposed to construe these laws according to their very spirit and intent, so that equal rights and equal protection shall be secured to all, regardless of color or nationality."[3]

"Its object was to prevent any question in the future as to the effect of the war and the President's proclamation of emancipa-

---

[1] Live-Stock Asso. *v.* C. C. Co., 1 Abb. (U. S.) 388.
[2] Coger *v.* N. W. Co., 37 Iowa, 145, 155.   [3] Ib. 158.

tion upon slavery. It had no other office, and its real effect was more for the future than for the present. As to the matter of social and political rights the African was left just where the State Constitution left him, and subject to all the inconveniences and burdens incident to his color and race, except his former one of servitude. He was a person whose place and office in the body politic was yet to be designated and established. He possessed no political rights in the usual and proper sense of that term through this enactment."[1]

" The provision that no State shall abridge the immunities of citizens of the United States does not refer to citizens of the States.[2] It embraces only citizens of the United States. It leaves out the words ' citizens of the State' which are so carefully used, and used in contradistinction to ' citizens of the United States,' in the preceding sentence. It places the privileges and immunities of citizens of the United States under the protection of the Federal Constitution, and leaves the privileges and immunities of a citizen of a State under the protection of the State Constitution."[3]

" There is some reason to believe that the privileges and immunities referred to are those only which arise under the Constitution of the United States, and not those which arise under State laws."[4] " It does not refer to persons of the white race. We know from the history of the times that the main purpose of this amendment was to confer the rights of citizenship upon persons of African descent who had previously not been citizens."[5] " It contains no new grant of power to the Federal government. It did not enlarge the powers of the Federal government, but only diminished those of the States. The inhibitions against the States doing certain things have no force or effect. They do not prohibit the States from doing anything that they could have done without them. The only effect was to extend the protection and blessings of the Constitution to the new class of persons."[6] " Citizenship entitled them to the protection of life, liberty, and property, and the full and equal protection of the laws; but the

---

[1] Cory *v.* Carter, 48 Ind. 327, 347.   [2] Ib. 349.   [3] Ib. 350.
[4] People *v.* Easton, 13 Abb. Pr. N. S. (N. Y.) 159, 164.
[5] State *v.* Gibson, 3 Ind. 389, 392.   [6] Ib. 393.

ratification of this amendment has not in any manner or to any
extent impaired, weakened, or taken away any of the reserved
rights of the States." [1]

THE FIFTEENTH AMENDMENT.

The Fifteenth Amendment had the effect of removing from the
State Constitution or rendering inoperative that provision which
restricts the right of suffrage to the white race, and it is presumed the State recognizes it as binding,[2] especially where there
are no statutory enactments or adjudications indicating the contrary;[3] but it does not confer the right of suffrage, but prevents
the States or the United States from giving preference in this
particular to one citizen of the United States over another on
account of race, etc.,[4] and invests citizens of the United States
with a new constitutional right.[5] That Congress may regulate
the elections of Representatives, etc., was held by the Supreme
Court.[6]

In 1875 two inspectors at a municipal election in Kentucky
were indicted for refusing to receive and count the vote of a
colored citizen under the act of May 31, 1870. The court said,
" This is a penal statute and to be construed strictly; not so
strictly indeed as to defeat the clear intention of Congress, but
the words employed must be understood in the sense in which
they were obviously used;" [7] and it was held that the sections of
this act providing for the punishment of inspectors were not " appropriate legislation," [8] as the right conferred by the Fifteenth
Amendment was exemption from discrimination in the exercise
of the elective franchise on account of race, color, or previous
condition of servitude, but the offence for which the punishment
of inspectors was provided was not limited in terms to such
discrimination.[9] In 1875, where certain parties were indicted

---

[1] State *v.* Gibson, 3 Ind. 394.

[2] Neal *v.* Delaware, 103 U. S. 370, 389.   [3] Ib. 390.

[4] United States *v.* Reese, 92 U. S. 214, 217; United States *v.* Harris, 106
U. S. 629, 637.

[5] United States *v.* Reese, 92 U. S. 214, 218; United States *v.* Cruikshank,
ib. 542, 555.

[6] *Ex parte* Liebold, 100 U. S. 371, 382; see *Ex parte* Clark, ib. 399.

[7] United States *v.* Reese, 92 U. S. 214, 219.   [8] Ib. 221.   [9] Ib. 218.

under section 6 of the act of May 31, 1870, for conspiring for intimidating a citizen, etc., the court said, it must appear from the indictment that the intent of the defendant was to prevent the parties from exercising their right to vote on account of their race, etc.[1] Cases below, involving the constitutionality of the "Enforcement Acts," the form of indictments, etc., are as follows : United States *v.* Sanders, 2 Abb. (U. S.) 456, 466 ; Le-Grand *v.* United States, 3 Cr. L. M. 713 ; United States *v.* Clayton, 10 Am. L. Reg. 737, 741 ; *In re* Quinn, 12 Rev. Rec. 151, 153 ; United States *v.* Crosby, 1 Hughes, 448 ; Harrison *v.* Hadley, 2 Dill, 229, 238 ; United States *v.* Goldman, 2 Woods, 187 ; United States *v.* Jackson, 3 Saw. 59, 60 ; United States *v.* Newcomer, 11 Phil. 519 ; United States *v.* Cahill, 3 McCrary, 200 ; Seeley *v.* Knox, 2 Woods, 368, 371 ; United States *v.* Given, 17 Int. Rev. Rec. 189, 190 ; United States *v.* Amaden, 10 Biss. 283.

A Governor of a State is not an officer of election within the meaning of the act of May 31, 1870.[2] The right to be secure in one's house existed before the Constitution.[3]

REMOVALS—JURIES, ETC.

In 1871, where colored witnesses were excluded by a State law from testifying in a case of murder of a colored person by whites, it was said that a criminal prosecution did not affect a witness in the case,[4] or a person not in existence.[5] In 1877, where a colored man sought to remove his suit for the recovery of a State office from a State court, and failed to declare in his affidavit that his inability to enforce his rights was in consequence of a law, etc., the case was remanded to the State court, on the ground that the act of April 9, 1866, was intended to protect only from legal disabilities, and discrimination from other sources was not ground for removal.[6]

In 1879 a negro arraigned for murder demanded a removal

---

[1] United States *v.* Cruikshank, 92 U. S. 542, 556.
[2] United States *v.* Clayton, 10 Am. L. Reg. 737, 741.
[3] United States *v.* Crosby, 1 Hughes, 448; ib. 457.
[4] Blyew *v.* United States, 13 Wall. 581, 591.   [5] Ib. 594.
[6] State *v.* Dubuclet, 5 Rep. 201, 202.

to the new United States court. A State law provided that "male white citizens," etc., should be eligible for jury duty. It was said of the Fourteenth Amendment, "This is one of a series of constitutional provisions having a common purpose ; namely, securing to the race recently emancipated all the civil rights that the superior race enjoy. It was designed to secure to the colored race the enjoyment of all the civil rights that under the law are enjoyed by white persons, and to give that race the protection of the general government in that enjoyment wherever it should be denied by the States. It not only gave citizenship and the privileges of citizenship to persons of color, but it denied to any State the power of withholding from them the equal protection of the laws." [1]

"It is to be construed liberally to carry out the purpose of its framers. It has evidently reference to the newly-made citizens who, being citizens of the United States, are declared to be also citizens of the States in which they reside. What is this but declaring that the law in the States shall be the same for the black as for the white, that all persons, whether colored or white, shall stand equal before the laws of the State, and, with regard to the colored race for whose protection the amendment was primarily designed, no discrimination should be made against them by law because of their color? The words are prohibitory, but they contain a necessary implication of a positive immunity or right most valuable to the colored race." [2]

"Its aim is against discrimination because of race or color." [3] "A right or immunity, whether created by the Constitution or only guaranteed by it, even without any express delegation of power, may be protected by Congress," [4] "and an appropriate mode of so doing is by a law providing for the removal of a case from a State to a Federal court." [5] "A colored man has a right to a trial on an indictment by a jury selected and impanelled without discrimination against his race or color because of race or color." [6] And it was added that the law would protect whites as well as blacks, and that the denial of a right to

---

[1] Strauder *v.* West Virginia, 100 U. S. 303, 306.   [2] Ib. 307.
[3] Ib. 310.   [4] Ib.   [5] Ib. 311.   [6] Ib. 305.

serve as jurors because of color was "practically a brand" and "a stimulant to that race-prejudice which is now an impediment to securing to individuals of the race that equal justice which the law aims to secure to all others."

In the same year, where a State law made "all male citizens" liable to serve as jurors but confided the selection of names to the county judge, and the fact was that the jury to try a negro was composed entirely of white men, it was held not a ground for the removal of the case.[1] The court added that the Fourteenth Amendment was broader than the section of the statute providing for removals,—the latter authorizing a removal only before trial, not after the trial has commenced, and not embracing a case in which a right may be denied by judicial action during the trial or by discrimination against a prisoner in the sentence or in the mode of executing the sentence; but a violation of the constitutional provisions when made by the judicial tribunal of a State may be, and generally will be, after a trial has commenced.[2] And the court said, "If an officer refuses to select persons of color solely on the ground of their color, he would violate the spirit of the State laws as well as the act of Congress ; but, though his act was in one sense the act of the State and prohibited, inasmuch as it was a criminal misuse of the State law, it cannot be said to have been such a denial or disability to enforce in the judicial tribunals of the State the rights of colored citizens as is contemplated by the removal act ;" and it was held that the denial must appear before the trial ;[3] and if the subordinate officer who selects the jurors, or the sheriff who summons them, or the clerk who takes their names from the books, excludes colored men because of their color, it cannot be said that a right is denied by the State or cannot be enforced in her tribunals ; and it was said that denials of equal rights in the action of the judicial tribunals of a State are left to the revisory powers of the Supreme Court ;[4] and the assertions that the juries which indicted and tried an accused colored person were composed wholly of whites, and that no colored persons have ever been

---

[1] Virginia v. Rives, 100 U. S. 314, 320. [2] Ib. 319.
[3] Ib. 321. [4] Ib. 322.

allowed in the county of trial where a colored man was interested, were not sufficient to show discrimination because of color
or race;[1] and the refusal of the court and of the counsel for the
prosecution to allow a modification of the venire, by which a
portion of the jury should be composed of persons of the peti-
tioner's own race, does not amount to a denial of a right secured
to them by any law providing for the equal civil rights of citizens of the United States.[2] And a mixed jury is not guaranteed
by the Fourteenth Amendment.[3]

In the same year it was said that the right to a jury chosen
without discrimination on account of color is guaranteed by the
Fourteenth Amendment.[4] "Its purpose was to secure equal
rights to all persons."[5] The amendments derive much of their
force from the provision for appropriate legislation, which
enlarges the power of Congress, not of the judiciary. Some
legislation is contemplated to make the amendments fully effective. Whatever legislation is appropriate that is adapted to carrying out the objects the amendments have in view, whatever
tends to enforce submission to the prohibition they contain and
to secure to all persons the enjoyment of perfect equality of civil
rights and the equal protection of the laws against State denial
or invasion, if not prohibited, is brought within the domain
of congressional power.[6] The prohibitions are directed to the
State, and they are to a degree restrictions of the State power;
it is these which Congress is empowered to enforce, and to
enforce against State action, however put forth, whether that
action be executive, legislative, or judicial. Such enforcement
is no invasion of State sovereignty.[7] A State acts by its legislative,
its executive, or its judicial authorities; it can act in no other
way. The constitutional provisions, therefore, must mean that
no agency of a State, officers or agents by whom its powers are
exerted, shall deny to any person within its jurisdiction the
equal protection of the laws. And it was said, " Whoever by
virtue of a public position under a State government deprives
another of property, life, or liberty without due process of law,

---

[1] Virginia *v.* Rives, 100 U. S. 322.　　　　[2] Ib.　　　[3] Ib. 323.
[4] *Ex parte* Virginia, 100 U. S. 339, 345.　　　　　[5] Ib. 347.
[6] Ib. 339, 345.　　　　[7] Ib. 346.

or denies or takes away the equal protection of the laws, violates the constitutional inhibition ; and, as he acts in the name of and for the State and is clothed with the State's power, his act is that of the State; the legislation must act upon persons,—not upon an abstract thing denominated a State, but upon persons who are the agents of a State in the denial of the rights which were intended to be secured. Such is the act of March 1, 1875, and we think it was fully warranted by the Constitution."[1] And " we do not perceive how holding an office under the State and claiming to act for a State can relieve the holder from obligation to obey the Constitution of the United States or take away the power of Congress to punish the disobedient;" and the court added that the judge in making his selection of jurors was not performing a judicial act, and, if he was, he was violating the spirit of the State statute, which gave him no authority to exclude colored men because they were colored.[2] And, where a judge was indicted in a United States court for failing to select certain citizens (unnamed) of the African race on account of their race, etc., and was in custody, having refused to give bail on his petition for a habeas corpus, the court said, " That act of Congress from which the indictment was found (March, 1875), is constitutional, and the prisoner was correctly held to answer under it."[3]

In 1880 it was repeated that the provisions for removals did not embrace a case where a right was denied during trial or in regard to the sentence, etc.[4] The Constitution of Delaware restricted the suffrage to whites; the qualification for jurors was that they should be voters, etc. : *held*, that the Fifteenth Amendment had abrogated the limitation on the suffrage, and a petition for removal was rightly refused ;[5] that it should be presumed that the State recognized the amendment,[6] which presumption was strengthened by the decision of her Supreme Court that the word " white" had been erased thereby.[7]

" The fact that no colored citizen had ever been summoned as a juror in a State court, although the colored population exceeded

---

[1] *Ex parte* Virginia, 100 U. S. 347.   [2] Ib. 348.   [3] Ib. 349.
[4] Neal *v.* Delaware, 103 U. S. 370, 386.   [5] Ib. 393.   [6] Ib. 389.
[7] Ib. 390.

twenty thousand in 1870, and twenty-six thousand in 1880, in a total population of less than one hundred and fifty thousand, presented a *prima facie* case of denial, by the officers charged with the selection of grand and petit jurors, of that equality of protection which has been secured by the Constitution and laws of the United States. It was, we think, under all the circumstances, a violent presumption which the State court indulged, that such uniform exclusion of that race from juries during a period of many years was solely because, in the judgment of those officers, fairly exercised, the black race in Delaware were utterly disqualified by want of intelligence, experience, or moral integrity to sit on juries. The action of those officers in these premises is to be deemed the act of the State; and the refusal of the State court to right the wrong by them committed was a denial of the right secured to the prisoner by the Constitution and laws of the United States." [1]

In 1882 it was said that the removal of a prosecution to the United States court and its quashing of an indictment does not divest the State court of jurisdiction to try the prisoner;[2] and that, where the Supreme Court of a State has declared that its statute excluding citizens of African descent from juries because of their race or color is unconstitutional, and therefore every officer charged with the duty of selecting and summoning jurors must do so without regard thereto, it could not be said in advance of a trial that the accused was denied and could not enforce his equal civil rights, etc.[3]

It must be alleged in the motion to set aside a panel of petit jurors, that the officers who selected and summoned them excluded qualified citizens of African descent because of their race or color. It may have been true that only white citizens were selected and summoned, yet it would not necessarily follow that the officer had violated the law and the special instruction given by the court " to proceed in his selection without regard to race, color," etc. "There was no legal right in the accused to a jury composed in part of his own race. All that he could demand

---

[1] Neal *v.* Delaware, 103 U. S. 397.
[2] Bush *v.* Kentucky, 107 U. S. 110, 114.   [3] Ib. 116.

was a jury from which his race was not excluded because of their color." The allegation that colored citizens were excluded and that only white citizens were selected was too vague and indefinite to constitute the basis of an inquiry by the court whether the sheriff had not disobeyed its order by selecting and summoning petit jurors with the intent to discriminate against the race of the accused.[1]

"The presumption that the State recognized the Fourteenth Amendment, from the date of its adoption, to be binding on all its citizens and every department of its government is overthrown by the fact that twice after the ratification of that amendment the State enacted laws which in terms excluded citizens of African descent because of their race from service on grand and petit juries."[2] And where a grand jury was selected, but the highest State court had declared that the local statutes in so far as they excluded colored citizens were in conflict with the national Constitution,[3] it was ordered, that the judgment of the State Court of Appeal affirming the refusal of the lower court to set aside an indictment for murder on that ground, be reversed, and the cause be remanded to that court, to be thence remanded to the United States court with direction to set aside the indictment.[4]

In 1874, where a negro indicted for bigamy sought to have his case removed to a United States court, it was held that local prejudice by reason of race or color, alleged to be so great that he could not have a fair trial in a State court, was not sufficient ground for removal,[5] and that to entitle to this the cause must show a deprivation of a right guaranteed by the first section of the act of March 1, 1875, and that the act was intended to protect against legal disabilities, not private infringements of rights by prejudice or otherwise where the laws were impartial and sufficient.[6]

SCHOOLS.

United States Courts.

In 1873 it was said that an act which directs that the portion of school tax which is collected from white persons shall be

---

[1] Bush *v.* Kentucky, 107 U. S. 117.   [2] Ib. 121.   [3] Ib. 122.
[4] Ib. 123.   [5] Texas *v.* Gaines, 2 Wood, 342, 344.   [6] Ib. 345.

applied to schools for white children and the portion collected
from colored persons to the schools for colored children violates
the Fourteenth Amendment,[1] and a United States court may
enjoin State officers from obeying it.[2]

In 1878 it was held that, where schools were provided for
colored children in no respect inferior to those provided for
white, but colored children were not allowed to attend the latter,
the Fourteenth Amendment was not violated. The colored
child's parent in this case alleged that the school to which
admission was refused was the nearest to his house.[3] But if
a school is so remote that a child could not attend it without
going to an unreasonable and oppressive distance, and does not
offer substantially the same facilities and educational advantages
with those for the white children, his exclusion from the latter
is a deprivation of his constitutional right.[4]

State Courts.

In 1842 in Ohio it was held that to teach colored children
released a party from his subscription to the common school, the
statute providing that "all white children" should be entitled to
"public school privileges."[5]

In 1850 a case was decided involving the constitutionality
of an act establishing separate schools for white and colored,
wherein the principal point made against it seems to have been
that under it colored men might be elected school directors, and
that the directors might be elected by colored voters, which
would violate the State Constitution; both these grounds were
held untenable.[6]

In 1859 in Ohio it was held that a child of five-eighths
white blood was "colored," within the meaning of the Ohio act
providing separate schools for white and colored children, and
"not as of right entitled to admission into the schools set apart

---

[1] Claybrook v. Owensboro, 16 Fed. Rep. 297.   [2] Ib. 304.

[3] Bertonneau v. Schools, 3 Wood, 177.

[4] United States v. Bunting, 10 Fed. Rep. 730, 735 (1882).

[5] Chalmers v. Stewart, 11 Ohio, 386.

[6] State v. Cincinnati, 19 Ohio, 178, 196, 197.

for the instruction of white youth."[1] And the court said, "That the legislature has the power thus to classify the scholars, even when all are undeniably white, no one will question."[2] The Ohio law gave the colored children a share of the school fund proportioned to their numbers;[3] and, though, "where the number of colored youth was too small to justify the organization of a school for them, such school must be temporarily delayed or suspended, this was no more than might occur with the other class under similar circumstances."[4] And as to the fact that no separate school for colored children had been established in the district where the action was brought,[5] and that the number of colored children there had not at any time exceeded ten, the court said, "It might perhaps have been better if some further and more definite provision had been made for the education of colored youth in districts in which the number is so very limited, but that is a matter for the legislature."[6]

The question of the conformity of the act under which the State officials excluded a colored child from a school for whites first came up in Ohio in 1871. The court remarked, "The application in Van Camp *v.* Logan of the principle settled by it, we are not required to approve or disapprove, for in that case there had not been as in this a separate school established for colored children."[7] And as to the section of the statute making provision for separate schools it would "express no opinion further than is necessary to the determination of this case, in which it clearly appears that the clauses applicable to it do not operate to exclude the colored children of that locality from a common-school education equal to that of the other youth. Were this not the fact more doubt would arise.[8] It seems, however, that the act under which Van Camp *v.* Logan was decided contained a provision that, where the colored children in a school-district did not reach a certain number, or owing to their distance from each other a separate school was impracticable, their share of the public money should be set apart for their education under the direction of the board; and

---

[1] Van Camp *v.* Logan, 9 Ohio St. 406, 415.

[2] Ib. 414. [3] Ib. 409. [4] Ib. 410. [5] Ib. 408. [6] Ib. 414.

[7] State *v.* McCann, 21 Ohio St. 198, 208. [8] Ib. 207.

that it was so set apart was averred in that case (see page 407 ; compare State *v.* McCann, page 206) ;" and the court observed, that the Fourteenth Amendment "includes only such privileges or immunities as are derived from or recognized by the Constitution of the United States, and has no application to this case, for all the privileges of the school system of this State are derived solely from the Constitution and laws of the State ;[1] and it only affords to colored citizens an additional guarantee of equality of rights to that already secured by the Constitution of the United States,[2] inasmuch as the citizenship of colored persons and their right to equal protection of the laws were not denied them in Ohio before the adoption of the amendment ;[3] and that a classification of the youth which does not exclude either class from mutual advantages, is not unconstitutional ; nor can a colored parent dictate where his children shall be instructed, or what teacher shall perform that office, without obtaining privileges not enjoyed by white citizens."[4] In this case the one school provided for colored children in two districts was as convenient of access to the plaintiff's children as that in one of the districts to some of the white children.[5]

In 1849 it was held, that under the Constitution of Massachusetts, under which "all persons without distinction of age or sex, birth or color, origin or condition, are equal before the law," a committee in charge of the Boston public schools might prohibit the attendance of colored children at other schools than those provided for them.[6] The court called attention to the fact that the latter were as well conducted, etc., as the former, and included this under the committee's "power of general superintendent,"[7] and held that the increased distance—one-fifth of a mile—which a colored child was thus obliged to go was not "such as to render the regulation unreasonable, still less illegal."[8] But it says that where inhabitants are widely scattered an arrangement requiring schools for pupils of different ages, etc., might require pupils to go such long distances that it would be quite unreasonable.[9]

---

[1] State *v.* McCann, 21 Ohio St. 210.   [2] Ib. 211.   [3] Ib. 209.
[4] Ib. 211.   [5] Ib. 203.   [6] Roberts *v.* Boston, 5 Cush. 198, 205.
[7] Ib.   [8] Ib. 210.   [9] Ib. 209.

In 1850 the court in Indiana said, " It has been said that the blacks are entitled by the terms of the grant to share the benefit of the school lands donated by Congress. We need not look to this question ; for, even if so, it does not follow that they should enjoy that benefit in schools with the whites. Separate schools may be organized." [1]

But, where the provision of the State statute was that the public schools should be free to white children, the court said colored children had not the right to attend, even if paying for their tuition ; and that the reason for their exclusion was " not because they did not need education, nor because their wealth was such as to render aid undesirable, but because black children were deemed unfit associates of white as school companions," [2] which reason " operates with equal force against all such children attending at their own as at the public expense ;" [3] and this was affirmed in 1874.[4]

In this case the court's attention was called to two sections of the State Constitution, the first providing that " the General Assembly shall not grant to any citizen or class of citizens privileges or immunities which upon the same terms shall not equally belong to all citizens ;" and the second, that, as knowledge was essential to a free government, the General Assembly should " provide by law for a general and uniform system of common schools, wherein tuition shall be without charge and equally open to all." [5] The Constitution in question in this case took effect in 1851,[6] and the court said, the first section was not violated by a statute providing for separate schools, for the trustee's consolidating several districts into one where necessary, or otherwise using the colored children's proportion of the school revenue to their advantage ; as " the privileges and immunities secured were not intended for persons of the African race ; for the section expressly limits the enjoyment of such privileges and immunities to citizens, and at that time negroes were neither citizens of the United States nor of this State ;" and that the provisions of the second clause were not intended for children

---

[1] Lewis *v.* Henley, 2 Ind. 332, 335.   [2] Ib. 334.   [3] Ib. 335.
[4] Cory *v.* Carter, 48 Ind. 327.   [5] Ib. 327, 334.   [6] Ib. 340.

of the African race, because "it is unreasonable to suppose that the framers of the Constitution, who had denied to that race the right of citizenship, of suffrage, of holding office, of serving on juries, and of testifying in any case where a white person was a party, and had prohibited under heavy pains and penalties the further immigration of that race into the State, intended to provide for the education of children of that race in our common schools with the white children of the State; the public sentiment of the State at that time was unfriendly to the African race and their participation in government affairs, and demanded their exclusion from the State;"[1] and they said they must give effect to the intent of the Constitution and construe it as a whole,[2] and that the meaning of a Constitution is fixed when it is adopted and not different at any subsequent time.[3]

The court then said, that under the State Constitution the school system must embrace every portion of the State,[4] and that it must be uniform as to government, discipline, etc.; that the "all" to whom the schools were to be equally open did not embrace the whole people, as "the infant, the middle-aged, the septuagenarian, and the married," nor were they to be equally open to every child; that Congress had no supervision over the States in the matter of education;[5] that the system of common schools was purely a domestic one under State authority; that the Constitution had made it the legislature's duty to provide the system, and imposed no limitation on its power except that tuition should be free and the schools equally open to all,— "that is, to such classes of persons as the legislature may in its wisdom determine;" and that this included the power of classification by age, sex, etc.,[6] and also with reference to race or color if in the legislature's judgment such classification was conducive to good order and the public interest; but since the Fourteenth Amendment no system would be general, uniform, and equally open to all which did not provide for the education of the colored race,[7] and that the classification on the basis of race or color did not amount to an exclusion of either class; that if there

---

[1] Cory *v.* Carter, 48 Ind. 341.   [2] Ib. 342.   [3] Ib. 343.
[4] Ib. 358.   [5] Ib. 359.   [6] Ib. 360.   [7] Ib. 361.

were causes of complaint it was rather with the whites, for the colored class received their full share of the revenue though none of it might have been contributed by them, and where districts could not be consolidated it was to be expended to their best advantage according to number, "a privilège not granted to the white class;"[1] said that there might just as well be cause of complaint that one scholar could not occupy another's seat, or all be put in the same classes, etc., as that whites were taught separately from blacks; that the only allegation was that the plaintiffs were excluded from the school where the white children were taught, not that other means were not provided by the trustees, etc.;[2] that, even if the "other means" not specified by the legislature were not provided, this would not entitle the colored child to admission into the schools for whites, "because the legislature has not provided for the admission of colored children into the same schools with the white children in any contingency;" if they were so entitled under the Fourteenth Amendment "the courts cannot in the absence of legislative authority confer that right upon them;" and it referred to the legislation for separate schools in the District of Columbia,[3] as a legislative construction of the Fourteenth Amendment.[4] In 1869 in New York it was held, that the right to be educated in the public schools was derived entirely from State legislation,[5] and that a statutory provision for separate schools was not in violation of the civil-rights bill, of which the principal object was to confer all the substantial rights of a citizen on colored people, which rights "so far as they are affected by the act are enumerated in the first section," among which a right to attend a school for white children is not included, and nothing is contained in succeeding sections from which such a right can be derived.[6]

In 1869 it was held, that, where a State statute provided that "all residents of any district shall have an equal right to attend any school therein," but that this should not prevent "grading of pupils," etc., a school board could not exclude any resident

---

[1] Cory *v.* Carter, 48 Ind. 362, 363.   [2] Ib. 393.   [3] Ib. 364.
[4] Ib. 366.   [5] Dallas *v.* Fosdick, 40 How. Pr. 249, 251.   [6] Ib. 256.

from any school because of "race or color or religious belief or personal peculiarities." [1] And this statute was not overridden in this respect by a later act allowing boards to fix districts and require pupils resident in each district to attend the schools therein. [2]

In 1871 in Arkansas it was held, that a law requiring separate schools for whites and blacks required these where there were both in the same district. [3]

In 1872, where a State statute prescribed that "negroes, Mongolians, and Indians shall not be admitted into the public schools," but the trustees might establish separate schools for their education and use the public school funds for the same, the court said, "While it may be and probably is opposed to the spirit of the Constitution and laws of the United States, it is not obnoxious to their letter;" [4] and, considering a requirement of the State Constitution "that the legislature should provide for a uniform system of public schools," and a provision that it may "pass such laws as will tend to secure a general attendance of the children in each district," etc., the court said, "The legislature has not acted according to the Constitution when it prohibits the attendance of any children within the State upon the common schools, [5] nor the trustees in denying to any resident person of proper age an equal participation in the benefits of the common schools;" yet it was "perfectly within their power to send all blacks to one school and all whites to another, and make such classification, whether based on age, sex, race, or any other existent condition, as may seem to them best." [6] In this case it was held that the colored boy should have been admitted: *query*, Because there was no other school in his district?

In 1872, where a colored school was "farther from the parents' residence than the white, but there was no evidence that it was not within convenient distance," [7] the court said, "The ground taken is that the relator has an absolute right to send his children to that one of the public schools which is near to

---

[1] People v. Detroit, 18 Mich. 400, 409, 410.   [2] Ib. 413.
[3] Union Co. v. Robinson, 27 Ark. 116, 120.
[4] State v. Duffy, 7 Nev. 342, 346.   [5] Ib. 346, 347.   [6] Ib. 348.
[7] People v. Easton, 13 Abb. Pr. (N. S.) 159, 160.

his residence. Of course, if he has this right every other citizen has the same.[1] In the city in question there were no school-districts, but the schools were those of the whole city." "The school nearest his residence is no more his than that which is most distant."[2] It would not follow that if the exclusion was unlawful the remedy was by mandamus, as the party might sue for damages,[3] but none of his privileges were abridged unless every citizen had the privilege of choosing to which school he would send his child.[4] He had equal advantages with other citizens, as he did not pretend that the school open to him was not as good as the one closed, though if the former were " materially objectionable, or an improper school to attend," a very different question might arise.[5] The court complimented the board whose course was in dispute, and said it had no doubt, if the colored citizens as a body wished the colored schools closed and the admission of their children to the others, their views would have great weight with that body.[6]

In 1874 a negro's cow was seized for taxes under an act " for the benefit of the common schools in B. county." The question was whether the legislature under the Thirteenth and Fourteenth Amendments could pass this act, providing, as it did, that money should be raised by the taxation of the property of white inhabitants and expended exclusively for their benefit.[7] The court said, " Whatever interest the negro may claim in the school fund he must have as a citizen of this commonwealth, and not as a citizen of the United States;"[8] that it is not one of the " fundamental rights under the care of the Federal government, whatever these might be,"[9] but the power of establishing and maintaining a system of public schools was among those rights " reserved to the States or to the people."[10] As to whether the negro, possessing all the constitutional privileges of any other citizen, has a right to demand an equal participation in the profits of the common-school fund and the educational advantages afforded by the common-school system, the court declined to

---

[1] People v. Easton, 13 Abb. Pr. (N. S.) 161.   [2] Ib. 162.
[3] Ib. 163.   [4] Ib. 164.   [5] Ib. 165.   [6] Ib. 166.
[7] Marshall v. Donovan, 10 Burt (Ken.), 681, 687.   [8] Ib. 688.
[9] Ib. 689.   [10] Ib. 690.

determine, as in this case the negro was asserting no such claim.[1] The State statute was held constitutional, "for, as the benefits were special, the contributions might be specially laid,[2] though it would be otherwise with a law by which the negroes were taxed and the money expended, exclusively for the benefit of the whites;"[3] and the court said, "It is for the legislature and not for the courts to determine the time and manner in which the imperfections in our school system growing out of the change in the civil and political condition of the negro are to be remedied."[4] The law in question denied the negro's right to vote on the question whether a tax for schools in the district should be levied or not; the voting on this question was held not to be an "election."[5]

In 1874, putting aside the notion that a State provision for separate education could be in conflict with the Thirteenth Amendment, the court of California added, "The privilege of attending the public schools is not a privilege or immunity appertaining to a citizen of the United States as such. No person can rightly demand admission because of the status of citizenship."[6] As to the clause forbidding any State to "deny to any person within its jurisdiction the equal protection of the laws," the court said, it "did not create any new or substantive legal right or add to or enlarge the general classification of rights of persons or things existing in any State under the laws thereof.[7] But education is the protection of youth; and it would not be competent for the legislature, while providing a system of education, to exclude persons of African descent from its benefits, merely because of their descent."[8] The court said the separation of the races for educational purposes is a mere question of policy, cited a Massachusetts case,[9] and added that the exclusion of colored children from schools where the white attend could not be supported except where separate schools are actually maintained for colored children.[10] In this case the constitutionality of a State statute was involved.

In 1868, where a board of school-directors had provided a separate school for colored children and required them to attend

[1] Marshall *v.* Donovan, 10 Burt (Ken.), 691.   [2] Ib. 692.
[3] Ib. 693.   [4] Ib. 694.   [5] Ib.   [6] Ward *v.* Flood, 48 Cal. 36, 48.
[7] Ib. 50.   [8] Ib. 51.   [9] lb. 52.   [10] Ib. 56, 57.

it, considering a State law providing " for the instruction of youth," the court said, this was " without regard to color or nationality," [1] and, though the board of directors was authorized to have as many schools in their district as they might deem proper,[2] and they might exercise discretion equally operative on all as to residence, qualification in study, freedom from contagious disease, or the like, they could not in their discretion deny the youth admission to any particular school because of nationality, religion, color, or the like.[3] Though they might fix the boundaries within which children must reside, the grade of each school, etc., their discretion was limited to equality of right in all the youth ; that if they could exclude African children they might also German, Irish, etc. ; [4] that the State statute did not " in letter or spirit justify such limitations of privilege on account of nationality ;" that to sanction it would be a " violation of the spirit of the laws" and " tend to perpetuate national difficulties ;" and that it was no justification of the directors that " public sentiment in their district was opposed to the intermingling of white and colored children in the same schools." [5]

This case was twice affirmed in 1875.[6] The question of distance, etc., was not touched upon in the court's opinion in these cases, though alluded to by counsel in the second one.[7]

In 1881, in Kansas, the Fourteenth Amendment and a State act providing that the public schools should be free to all children came up for consideration. The court said, " The question whether the legislatures of States have power to pass laws making distinctions between white and colored citizens, and the extent of such power, if it exists, is a question which can be finally determined only by the Supreme Court of the United States ; and hence we pass this question and proceed to the next, over which we have more complete jurisdiction, which was, whether the legislature had given boards of education the power to establish separate schools for white and colored children.

" *Prima facie* this question should be answered in the nega-

---

[1] Clark *v.* Directors, 24 Iowa, 266, 274. [2] Ib. 269. [3] Ib. 277.
[4] Ib. 275. [5] Ib. 276.
[6] Smith *v.* Keokuk, 40 Iowa, 518; Ward *v.* Ward, 41 ib. 686, 693.
[7] See p. 690.

tive. The tendency of the times is and has been for several
years to abolish all distinctions on account of race or color or
previous condition of servitude, and to make all persons absolutely equal before the law. Therefore, unless it appears clearly
beyond all question that the legislature intended to authorize
such distinction to be made, we should not hold that any such
authority has been given, and we certainly should not expect to
find that the legislature had given any such authority during the
Centennial year of 1876, when the minds of all men were inclined to adopt the most cosmopolitan views of human rights
and not to adopt any narrow or contracted views founded merely
upon race or color or clan or kinship." [1]

" The tendency of the present age is not to make any distinction with regard to school-children except to classify them with
reference to their studies. And is it not better that this should
be so, is it not better for the grand aggregate of human society
as well as for individuals, that all children should mingle together and learn to know each other? As a rule, people cannot
afford to be ignorant of the society which surrounds them; and,
as all kinds of people must live together in the same society, it
would seem to be better that all should be taught in the same
schools." [2] As the legislature had not expressly conferred the
power of discrimination on the boards, it was held not to exist,[3]
and not to be included in a power to divide a city into districts,[4]
or proved from a power, " if it were admitted," to establish separate schools for males and females, for " to so hold would imply
a power to establish separate schools for Irish and Germans, red-
headed children and blondes." [5] The court added, " It must be
remembered, that, unless some statute shall be found authorizing
the establishment of separate schools for colored children, no
such authority exists." [6]

TRAVEL, THEATRES, ETC.
United States Courts, Etc.

Speaking of the act of 1875, c. 114, Cooley says, " In the
absence of any such regulation, it is not very clear that inn-

---

[1] Board *v.* Tinnon, 26 Kan. 18.　　　[2] Ib. 91.　　　[3] Ib. 92.
[4] Ib. 21.　　　[5] Ib. 22.　　　[6] Ib. 23.

keepers and carriers of persons would be warranted in discriminating on the ground solely of a difference in color or because of any previous condition. The common law required impartiality in their accommodations, and personal discrimination must be unlawful, unless the person excluded would be dangerous to others or justly offensive to their sense of decency or propriety, or for other reason would interfere with a proper enjoyment by others of the accommodations which the innkeeper or common carrier affords." [1]

The first case where this matter came before the Supreme Court of the United States was one involving the railroad charter of 1866 [2] in 1873. It was held, that the assigning to colored persons of separate cars " equally comfortable" with those for whites, and the same which were at other times used for the latter, was " an ingenious attempt to evade the obvious meaning of the requirement that no person should be excluded from the cars on account of color." [3]

In 1877 a' Louisiana statute against discrimination by carriers between passengers on account of race or color was held unconstitutional as a regulation of interstate commerce.[4] In this case it appeared that the steamer had two cabins, the fare for the lower one being two dollars less than that for the upper, which was reserved for whites. The plaintiff had refused to occupy the lower cabin, and sat all night in the recess back of the upper one.[5] In this case the court said, that " a steamer carrying passengers might have separate cabins and dining-saloons for white and colored persons, for the plain reason that the laws of Congress contained nothing to prohibit such an arrangement ; and applicants to whom there is no valid objection have a right to a passage, but it is not an unlimited right ; on the contrary, it is subject to such reasonable regulations as the proprietors may prescribe." [6]

The question of the privileges of an inn, a theatre, and a railroad car were before the Supreme Court in 1883, under the first and second sections of the Civil-Rights Act of March 1,

---

[1] Cooley on Torts, 284.   [2] Ib. 15.
[3] Railroad Co. v. Brown, 17 Wall. 445, 452.
[4] Hall v. DeCuir, 95 U. S. 485, 490.   [5] Ib. 492.   [6] Ib. 501.

1875.[1]   The first section of the Fourteenth Amendment was
relied on;[2] but the court said, that only State action was prohibited thereby; that it did not invest Congress with power to
legislate on subjects within the domain of State legislation, or
create a code of municipal law; it secures positive rights but by
way of prohibition against State laws;[3] that Congress could not
act till a State law was passed or some State action taken adverse
to the rights of citizens sought to be protected; and, though it
might legislate in advance, it could only be against the State or
State action; that the legislation of Congress could only be corrective in general;[4] that the law made no reference to any supposed or pretended violation of the Fourteenth Amendment on
the part of the States, but "steps into the domain of local
jurisprudence;"[5] that the provisions of the section already held
constitutional in *Ex parte* Virginia (100 U. S. 339) were corrective in character,[6] as was the previous Civil-Rights Bill of
April 9, 1866, re-enacted with some modifications May 31,
1870;[7] that civil rights, such as are guaranteed by the Constitution against State aggression, cannot be impaired by the
wrongful acts of individuals unsupported by State authority,[8]
though its remarks did not apply to "cases where Congress is
clothed with direct and plenary powers of legislation over the
whole subject, with the express denial of power to the States,"[9]
and such power was not conferred over this subject by the
Fourteenth Amendment; and that it was unnecessary to examine whether the right to equal accommodations in inns, public
conveyances, and places of amusement was one of the essential
rights of the citizen which no State can abridge or interfere
with; and whether the law would be applicable to the territories
or the District of Columbia, or whether Congress might pass a
law regulating rights in public conveyances passing from one
State to another, was not before the court;[10] nor is the denial of
such accommodations a species of "servitude" under the Thirteenth Amendment,[11] and it has nothing to do with the question
of slavery;[12] and whether the civil-rights legislation in 1860

---

[1] Civil-Rights Cases, 109 U. S. 3.   [2] Ib. 10.   [3] Ib. 11.
[4] Ib. 13.   [5] Ib. 14.   [6] Ib. 15.   [7] Ib. 16.   [8] Ib. 17.
[9] Ib. 18.   [10] Ib. 19.   [11] Ib. 20.   [12] Ib. 21.

was authorized under the Thirteenth Amendment without the
support it afterwards received from the Fourteenth, it showed
that at the time Congress did not assume under the Thirteenth
to adjust the "social rights of men and races;"[1] that under the
Thirteenth Amendment legislation might be direct and primary
to eradicate all forms and incidents of slavery, but under the Fourteenth it could only be corrective to afford relief against State
regulations or proceedings.[2]

An indictment, under the act of March 1, 1875, must allege
the citizenship of the person injured.[3] But it may charge that
the accommodations were refused at a certain "inn, to wit, a
restaurant."[4]

It is a violation of the third section of the act to regulate
commerce to subject a passenger to inferior accommodations to
those enjoyed by another passenger, who pays the same rate of
fare on a railroad ; but the company is under no obligation to
put colored passengers into the same car with white, under this
section, if it furnishes cars equally good for both at the same
price.[5] The same principle applies here as applies to the transportation of property.

Following the decision of the Supreme Court of the United
States in the "Slaughter-House Cases," "whatever his own
opinions may have been," Judge Giles, in the Circuit Court for
Maryland, said, in 1876, " The act of Congress of March 1,
1875, under which this action was brought, so far as it seeks to
inflict penalties for the violation of any or all rights which
belong to citizens of a State, and not to citizens of the United
States as such, was the exercise of a power not authorized by the
Constitution of the United States, and the privilege of using
for local travel any public conveyance is not a right arising under
the Constitution of the United States."[6]

In 1879 a colored woman took position as a passenger on a

---

[1] Civil-Rights Cases, 109 U. S. 22.　　　　[2] Ib. 23.

[3] United States *v.* Taylor, 9 Bis. 472 ; Lewis *v.* Hitchcock, 10 F. R. 4, 5.

[4] Ib. 4, 6.

[5] Heard *v.* Georgia R.R. Co., decided February 15, 1888, before Interstate-
Commerce Commission.

[6] Cully *v.* B. & O., 1 Hughes, 536, 540.

steamboat on the upper deck aft, which was assigned to the exclusive use of white passengers; when directed to a place on the lower deck with substantially the same accommodation, she refused to go to it, and tendered the customary fare, which was declined. She was told she would be put off at the next landing-place if she remained where she was, but voluntarily left the boat at that place. The court said, as Congress had not declared that steamboats plying between the several States should be compelled to carry white and colored passengers in the same cabin, etc., it would have to decide the case by the common law [1] (which was affirmed in " The Sue," 22 F. R. 843, 844). That the passenger's right on a steamboat was not unlimited, but the owners or master might make suitable regulations to promote the owners' interests and preserve order and decorum, and could not be required to put passengers in the same cabin or state-rooms who would be disagreeable to each other; [2] but that colored passengers were entitled to accommodations as suitable as those designated for the exclusive use of white passengers, and the court was of opinion that these were afforded in the case before it. [3]

In 1882 there were two cars to a train, one a smoking car and the other a " ladies' car;" a colored woman refused to enter the former and was forbidden to enter the latter; the court said, the company had a right to make reasonable regulations, as to provide one car for ladies and one for gentlemen, but if a gentleman bought a first-class ticket he must have such accommodations as were ordinarily provided for ladies; and if they had a right to require white people to ride in one car and colored people in another they must provide for the colored women such accommodations as were provided for the white women; [4] and the jury was directed to assess " such damages as would make the plaintiff whole, considering the loss of time and inconvenience." [5]

In 1882, where a colored woman was refused admission into a " ladies' car," the court said, she could recover, if given inferior accommodations to white persons because of her race and color,

---

[1] Green *v.* Bridgeton, 9 Cent. L. J. 206, 207.   [2] Ib.   [3] Ib. 208.
[4] Gray *v.* Cin. R.R., 11 F. R. 683, 686.   [5] Ib. 687.

at common law, and it knew of nothing in the laws of Kentucky to prevent this; it would not determine whether the right to travel on railroads without discrimination on account of color was a privilege of national citizenship,[1] but the only protection which Congress could give was from the action of the States,[2] and it was held necessary to allege that the State had denied the equal protection of its laws or abridged the immunities of the party as a citizen of the United States.[3]

In 1885, where a colored woman was excluded from the cabin provided for white women who paid the same fare on the steamer, the court said, " One of the restrictions which the common law imposes is, that a carrier's regulations must be reasonable and tend to the comfort and safety of the passengers generally, and that accommodations equal in comfort and safety must be afforded to all alike who pay the same price;[4] whether a separation on a steamer solely on the ground of race or color is reasonable is a mixed question of law and fact, and whenever it appears that facts do not exist which give reason for the separation the reasonableness of it cannot be sustained ; but the great weight of authority, it seems to me, supports the doctrine that to some extent and under some circumstances such a separation is allowable at common law.[5] A regulation which a carrier may lawfully make, if reasonable, has strong argument in favor of its reasonableness if it is demanded by the great majority of the travelling public who use his conveyance.[6]

" The amendments obliterating color as a distinction with regard to political rights do not make a colored discrimination unlawful in carriers as against the declared policy of the nation ; it is a question with which citizenship has little to do, but the regulation must not only be reasonable in that it conduces to the comfort of passengers, but it must not deny equal conveniences and comforts to all who pay the same fare,[7] and the fact that a smaller number of passengers use the colored cabin than the white does not justify a difference in their accommodation ;"[8] and the court said, " the separation goes to the verge of the

---

[1] Smoot *v.* Ken. R.R., 13 F. R. 337, 342.   [2] Ib. 343.   [3] Ib. 344.
[4] The Sue, 22 F. R. 843, 844.   [5] Ib.   [6] Ib.   [7] Ib. 846.
[8] Ib. 847.

carrier's legal right, and cannot be upheld unless *bona fide* and diligently the officers of the ship see to it that the separation is free from actual discrimination in comfort, attendance, or appearance of inferiority."[1]

This was affirmed the same year, and it was said that colored people and whites might be separated by a common carrier where the accommodations for both are substantially the same ; but where a colored woman was told by the conductor she must ride in the front car and would not be permitted to go in the ladies' car, the court said she could recover damages unless the jury believed the former was equal to the latter in accommodations.[2] The rule as to separation with equality of accommodations was followed in another case in the year 1885 ;[3] but the court said, that the smoking and non-smoking car did not furnish equal accommodations, and that if colored people were excluded from one end of a car whites must be excluded from the other. In this case the colored passenger was ejected from his seat in the " ladies' car" by third persons ; but the court said, that, if the company's employees were aware of the deed, it was their duty to interfere to prevent it,[4] and, though not personally liable for their failure to interfere, the company was liable for it,[5] and that the plaintiff could recover for his mental suffering, etc.[6]

State Courts.

In 1858, where a colored woman was refused " cabin-passage" on a steamer, the court said, the right to be carried was absolute and could not be affected by the company's rules,[7] but these, if reasonable, might determine what part of the boat the passenger would have a right to use,[8] and " reasonable rules" are those which have for their object the accommodation of passengers.[9] Reasonableness is a mixed question of law and fact for the jury under instructions, and must be shown positively,[10] and " does not depend on the party's color or the class to which he belongs or the effect of carrying him on the defendant's business, but on

---

[1] The Sue, 22 F. R. 848. [2] Logwood *v.* Memphis Co., 23 F. R. 318.
[3] Murphy *v.* West. R.R., 23 F. R. 637, 639. [4] Ib. [5] Ib. 641. [6] Ib.
[7] Day *v.* Owen, 5 Mich. 520, 525. [8] Ib. 526. [9] Ib. [10] Ib. 527.

the accommodation of the mass of persons who have the right to and are in the habit of travelling in his boat;"[1] and the rule excluding colored persons from the cabin was held reasonable.[2]

In 1861, where a negro had been excluded from a street-car under the company's regulation, the court said, " A corporation created for the carrying of passengers cannot arbitrarily refuse to carry any class of men. It may, however, lay down rules for the comfort and convenience of those whom it is bound to carry, although to the exclusion of particular individuals or of every individual who falls within the rule. What rules are proper must be left to the discretion of the corporation in the first instance."[3] " The regulation gives rise to a presumption, and maintains an argument in its own favor;"[4] and it held that the company's interest was *prima facie* in favor of admitting negroes, and the decision that they should be excluded is "almost convincing proof that the question would be, and indeed has been, decided in the same way by the community at large;"[5] that it believed that the regulation was a wise one,[6] or, if not, would " work its own cure best when least molested."[7]

In 1867, where a rule of a railroad company required colored persons to sit at one end of a car, a colored woman refusing to take a seat there was ejected. The court said, " No one can be excluded from carriage by a public carrier on account of color, religious belief, political relations, or prejudice;"[8] " if there be no clear and reasonable difference to base it upon, separation cannot be justified by mere prejudice, nor is merit a test;"[9] " it is not an unreasonable regulation to seat passengers so as to preserve order and decorum, and prevent contacts and collisions arising from natural or well-known customary repugnances which are likely to breed disturbances by a promiscuous sitting. The right of the passenger is only that of being carried safely and with a due regard to his personal comfort and convenience, which are promoted by a sound and well-regulated separation of passengers."

---

[1] Day *v.* Owen, 5 Mich. 527.　　　　[2] Ib. 528.
[3] Goines *v.* McCanless, 4 Phila. 255.　　[4] Ib. 256.　　　[5] Ib.
[6] Ib. 257.　　　　[7] Ib. 258.
[8] W. C. Co. *v.* Miles, 55 Pa. 209, 211.　　[9] Ib.

The court said, a guest could not select his room at an inn, though the keeper is bound to entertain proper guests, and that a steamboat passenger must obey the reasonable orders of the captain. But it would not be a reasonable regulation to compel colored and white passengers to bed and room together, and added, " A railroad company has the right and is bound to make reasonable regulations to preserve order in their cars. In order to preserve the conductor's authority as the servant of the company, it must have the power to establish proper regulations for the carriage of passengers. It is much easier to prevent difficulties among passengers, by regulations for their proper separation, than it is to quell them. The danger to the peace engendered by the feeling of aversion between individuals of the different races cannot be denied. It is a fact with which the company must deal.[1]

" The right to separate being clear in proper cases, the question remaining to be considered is, whether there is such a difference between the white and black races within this State resulting from nature, law, and custom, as makes it a reasonable ground of separation. The question is one of difference, not of inferiority or superiority." [2] The court then called attention to the legislation of Pennsylvania, the practical separation of the races in the army, etc., and said, " Law and custom having sanctioned a separation of races, it is not the province of the judiciary to legislate it away." [3] And it held the rule a reasonable one.

This case was decided before the passage of the State act of March 22, 1867, declaring it an offence for railroad companies to make any distinction between passengers on account of race or color.[4]

In 1870, where a colored woman was refused by a brakeman admission into the "ladies' car," the court said, "A railroad company cannot capriciously discriminate between passengers on account of their nativity, color, race, social position, or their political or religious beliefs. Whatever discriminations are made must be on some principle or for some reason that the law

---

[1] W. C. Co. *v.* Miles, 55 Pa. 212. [2] Ib. 213 [3] Ib. 264. [4] Ib. 215.

recognizes as just and equitable and founded in good public policy; what are reasonable rules is a question of law;" and it added, that a rule excluding colored persons could not be justified on the ground of mere prejudice; but "must have for its foundation a better and a sounder reason and one more in consonance with the enlightened judgment of reasonable men ;" [1] and it held that a woman was not obliged to go forward to the car set apart for and occupied mostly by men ; [2] and "public carriers, till they do furnish separate seats equal in comfort and safety to those furnished for other travellers, have no right to discriminate between passengers on account of race or nativity alone ;" [3] and it was said that a party could recover not only for actual damage but for the " vexation and disgrace." [4]

In 1873 a colored woman purchased a steamboat-ticket entitling her to transportation, but " to meals at an assigned table only," etc. A ticket for dinner being offered her having the words " colored girl" written on it, she refused to purchase it ; afterwards a man bought her an ordinary dinner-ticket ; she took her seat at the dinner-table in the " ladies' cabin," and was ejected by the officers of the boat. The court said the instructions below were correct, [5] which were, " All persons unobjectionable in character and deportment, who observe all reasonable rules and regulations of the common carrier, who pay or offer to pay first-class fare are entitled, irrespective of race or color, to receive upon the boats of the common carrier first-class accommodations ; if the plaintiff's right to first-class accommodations was denied her simply because she has African or negro blood in her veins, and if for this reason only she was removed from the table after paying or offering the price, she is entitled to recover. [6] If she voluntarily purchased a ticket limiting her rights as a passenger, she was bound by the special contract ; but if this ticket did not include meals, she was entitled to the privilege of other passengers as to these, except as limited by said ticket." [7] And it held that the rule requiring persons of African

---

[1] C. & N. W. Co. *v.* Williams, 55 Ill. 185, 186.   [2] Ib.
[3] Ib.   [4] Ib. 190.
[5] Coger *v.* N. W. Co., 37 Iowa, 145, 160.   [6] Ib. 150.   [7] Ib. 151.

descent to take their meals in the pantry or on the guards of the boat was an unreasonable one and not to be regarded by the jury ; and the words " at an assigned table" did not give the officers of the boat the right to set a table for the plaintiff in the pantry or on the guards of the boat, but if she paid or offered the usual first-class fare for a meal she was entitled to eat it in the cabin, upon an equality with other first-class passengers.[1]

The appellate court added, that the question was, had the company the right to enforce rules whereby colored persons were required to submit to treatment and accept accommodations different from those of white ?[2] and said, " In our opinion the plaintiff was entitled to the same rights and privileges while upon defendant's boat which were possessed and exercised by white passengers. These rights and privileges rest upon the equality of all under the law, the very foundation-principle of our government. If a negro must submit to different treatment and accommodations inferior to those given a white man when transported by public carriers, he is deprived of a benefit of this very principle of equality."[3] And said, that he might just as well be required to accept an inferior article of merchandise at the same price paid for the superior article by the white man ; that, as to his not being charged so great a price, he might just as well be confined to an inferior article of merchandise. " The doctrines of natural law and Christianity forbid that rights be denied on the ground of race or color; and this principle has become incorporated into the paramount law of the Union."[4]

The court rests its conclusion on the language of the State Constitution, that " all men are by nature free and equal," but also cites the Fourteenth Amendment[5] and the Civil-Rights Bill of April 9, 1866, and proceeds: " Under this statute equality of rights is secured to the negro ; the language is comprehensive, and includes the right to property and all rights growing out of contracts. It includes within its broad terms every right arising within the affairs of life; the right of a passenger under a contract of transportation with a carrier is

[1] Coger v. N. W. Co., 37 Iowa, 151.   [2] Ib. 152.   [3] Ib. 153.
[4] Ib. 154.   [5] Ib. 155.

included therein; the colored man is guaranteed equality and
the equal protection of the laws with his white brother,—equality in all the affairs of life over which there may be legislation
or of which the courts may take cognizance.[1]

"Without doubting that social rights and privileges are not
within the protection of the laws and constitutional provisions
in question, we are satisfied that the rights and privileges which
were denied the plaintiff are not within that class; her rights
of property were invaded, and her right to demand services to
which she was lawfully entitled was denied."[2] "She claimed no
social privilege, but substantial privileges appertaining to her
property and the protection of her person; no regulation could
deprive her of a right to accommodations to which she would be
entitled but for her color."

And as to a violation of the contract on the ticket, to take
"an assigned table," the court said, it would not stop to inquire
whether a common carrier's contract to enforce customs derogatory to the equality of a class of citizens could be enforced,[3]
being "well satisfied that a common carrier could not require
contracts of the character indicated to be accepted by those demanding transportation; and that the conditions of the ticket
for transportation had no relation to the plaintiff's right to a seat
at the table, and her dinner-ticket gave her the right to dine in
the cabin on an equality with other passengers."[4]

Whether plaintiff's treatment resulted from the enforcement
of rules requiring proper deportment, or of others aimed at her
exclusion on account of color, was held to be for the jury; and
as for "deception" in obtaining her dinner-ticket, the court said,
"Having obtained it in a manner not forbidden by the regulations of the boat or by law, she was entitled to all the rights it
would have conferred upon a white person."[5]

Theatres.

In 1873 a negro applied for admission into a theatre; this
was granted. He then asked for a seat in a particular part of

---

[1] Coger *v.* N. W. Co., 37 Iowa, 156.   [2] Ib. 157.   [3] Ib. 158.
[4] Ib. 159.   [5] Ib. 160.

the hall; this was refused, but a seat was offered him in another portion equally good; the refusal was on account of his color, and because the door-keeper believed that to give him a seat where he desired it would interfere with the pecuniary value of unsold seats. The door-keeper's counsel contended, that the State statute providing that "all citizens without distinction of race and color should be entitled to any accommodation of any theatre," etc., was in violation of the State Constitution, which declared that private property should not be taken for public use except upon compensation, etc.; but the court held otherwise.[1]

In 1876 it was held, that to refuse to admit a colored man to a theatre after he had purchased a ticket was a violation of a requirement of the State Constitution, that "all places of business or public resort for which a license is required, etc., should be open for the accommodation and patronage of all persons without distinction or discrimination on account of race or color." The court said, "This does not enunciate a mere abstraction, but it guarantees substantial rights;" and it was held that three hundred dollars was sufficient damages.[2] It appears to have been considered immaterial by the court that the ticket purchased had on it, what was headed " a contract," that the management shall have the right to refuse admission to the holder upon returning the regular price of the ticket.[3]

STATE PROVISIONS WITH REFERENCE TO CIVIL RIGHTS.

NATURAL RIGHTS.

Freedom.—The Constitutions of eighteen States have a provision that men are free:

(A) Thus, in two States the Constitution declares that all men are born free and independent: Mass. C. i. 1. (B) In seven, that they are by nature free and independent: N. J. C. i. 1; O.

---

[1] Donnell *v.* State, 48 Miss. 661, 662, 681, 682.
[2] Joseph *v.* Bidwell, 28 La. Ann. 382, 383.   [3] Ib. 384.

C. i. 1; Ill. C. ii. 1; Io. C. i. 1; Cal. C. i. 1; Nev. C. ı. 1; Fla. C. Decln. Rts. 1. (C) In one, that they are equally free and independent: Ala. C. i. 1. (D) In seven, that they are born equally free and independent: N. H. C. i. 1; Me. C. i. 1; Vt. C. i. 1; Pa. C. i. 1; Wis. C. i. 1; Neb. C. i. 1; Ark. C. ii. 2. (E) In two, that they are by nature equally free and independent: Va. C. i. 1; W. Va. C. iii. 1.

Equality.—The Constitutions of twenty-six States declare: (A) In eight, that men are born equal: N. H. C. i. 1; Mass. C. i. 1; Me. C. i. 1; Vt. C. i. 1; Ind. C. i. 1; Neb. C. i. 1; N. C. C. i. 1; S. C. C. i. 1. This seems to be implied in three other States: Pa. C. i. 1; Ark. C. ii. 2; Wis. C. i. 1. (B) In three, that they are by nature equal: Io. C. i. 1; Nev. C. i. 1; Fla. C. Decln. Rts. 1. And so, in one, that they are equal before the law: Ark. C. ii. 3. And this seems implied in the Constitutions of six other States: O. C. i. 2; Kan. C. B. of Rts. 1; Va. C. i. 1; W. Va. C. iii. 1; Ga. C. i. 1, 2; Ala. C. i. 1. (C) In four, that all men have equal rights when they form a social compact: Ct. C. i. 1; Ky. C. xiii. 1; Tex. C. i. 3; Ore. C. i. 1; N. M. 1851, July 12. (D) In Rhode Island, that all laws should be made for the good of the whole, and the burdens of the State ought to be fairly distributed among its citizens: R. I. C. i. 2.

Life and Liberty. — The Constitutions of twenty-six States declare that all men have a natural, inherent, and inalienable right to enjoy and defend life and liberty: N. H. C. i. 2; Mass. C. i. 1; Me. C. i. 1; Vt. C. i. 1; N. J. C. i. 1; Pa. C. i. 1; O. C. i. 1; Ind. C. i. 1; Ill. C. ii. 1; Wis. C. i. 1; Io. C. i. 1; Kan. C. Bill of Rts. 1; Neb. C. i. 1; Del. C. Preamble; Va. C. i. 1; W. Va. C. iii. 1; N. C. C. i. 1; Ky. C. Preamble; Mo. C. ii. 4; Ark. C. ii. 2; Cal. C. i. 1; Nev. C. i. 1; Col. C. ii. 3; S. C. C. i. 1; Ala. C. i. 1; Fla. C. Decln. Rts. 1; La. C. 1; Ariz. Preamble B. Rts.

Happiness.—In all the above States except Missouri, the Constitution declares that they have such natural right to pursue happiness.

Safety.—In fourteen of the above States, that they have such natural right to obtain safety: Mass., Me., Vt., N. J., O., Io., Va., W. Va., Ky., Cal., Nev., Col., S. C., Fla.

Property.—In twenty-seven States the Constitution declares: (A) In eighteen, that all men have a natural right to acquire, possess, and protect property: N. H. C. i. 2; Mass. C. i. 1; Me. C. i. 1; Vt. C. i. 1; N. J. C. i. 1; Pa. C. i. 1; O. C. i. 1; Io. C. i. 1; Del. C. Preamble; Va. C. i. 1; W. Va. C. iii. 1; Ky. C. Preamble; Ark. C. ii. 2; Cal. C. i. 1; Nev. C. i. 1; Col. C. ii. 3; S. C. C. i. 1; Fla. Decln. of Rts. 1; Ariz. Preamble B. Rts. (B) It seems the right of property is also recognized in other States by the provisions of § 184: Ill. C. ii. 1; Mo. C. ii. 4; Ga. C. i. 1, 2; Ala. C. i. 37, Preamble; La. C. 1; and in Dak. and Wy. by U. S. R. S. 1925. (C) So, in two, that all men have such right to the enjoyment of the fruits of their own labor: N. C. C. i. 1; Mo. C. (D) So the Constitutions of two States declare that the right of property is before and higher than any constitutional sanction: Ky. C. xiii. 3; Ark. C. ii. 22.

CIVIL RIGHTS.

General Provisions.—The Constitution of Georgia provides that the social status of the citizens shall never be the subject of legislation: Ga. C. i. 1, 18. So, in South Carolina, that no person shall be disqualified as a witness, nor be prevented from acquiring, holding, and transmitting property, nor be hindered in acquiring education, nor be liable to any other punishment for any offence nor be subject in law to any other restraints or disqualifications in regard to any personal rights than such as are laid upon others under like circumstances: S. C. C. i. 12. In three States, that all citizens of the State possess equal civil and political rights and public privileges: Va. C. i. 20; S. C. C. i. 31; Ala. C. i. 2. So, in West Virginia, that every citizen is entitled to equal representation in the government: W. Va. C. ii. 4. In Arizona, " that the civil rights of the people shall not be abridged:" Ariz. Bill Rts. 6.

Color Distinction.—By the Constitution of Arkansas no citizen shall ever be deprived of any right, privilege, or immunity, nor exempted from any burden or duty, on account of race, color, or previous condition: Ark. C. ii. 3. So, in Maryland, as to the right of being a witness in a court of law: Md. C. iii. 53. So, in four States, as to the right of suffrage and holding office: Neb. C. xviii. 1; Ala. C. i. 38; Fla. C. xiv. 1; La. C. 188; Terr. U. S. 1860.

And in three, distinction on account of race or color in any case whatever is prohibited, and all classes of citizens shall enjoy equally all common, public, legal, and political privileges: Va. C. xii. 2; S. C. C. i. 39; Fla. C. xvi. 28. So, in two, it is specially provided that all the public schools shall be free and open, without regard to race or color: Col. C. ix. 8; S. C. C. x. 10.

In Pennsylvania, it is forbidden to refuse admission or accommodation in restaurant or hotel, on railroad or street-railway or omnibus, or at theatre, concert-hall, or place of entertainment or amusement " on account of race or color:" Pa. 1887, 71. Penalty $50 to $100.

In Mississippi the Constitution provides that the right of all citizens to travel upon all public conveyances shall not be infringed: Miss. C. i. 24.

Exceptions.—By the Constitutions of seven States the right of voting is confined to whites: O. C. v. 1; Kan. C. v. 1; Md. C. i. 1; Del. C. iv. 1; Ky. C. ii. 8; Ore. C. ii. 2.

By the Constitutions of seven States white and colored children shall not be taught in the same (public) schools: W. Va. C. xii. 8; N. C. C. ix. 2; Tenn. C. xi. 12; Mo. C. xi. 3; Tex. C. vii. 7; Ga. C. viii. 1; Ala. C. xiii. 1.

By that of Oregon no Chinaman can hold real estate, or hold or work a mining claim: Ore. C. xv. 8. And by that of two States no native of China can vote: Col. C. ii. 1; Ore. C. ii. 6.

In South Carolina no person shall be disfranchised for felony or other crimes committed while a slave: S. C. C. viii. 12.

The Constitutions of two States provide that the legislature shall pass laws prohibiting free negroes from coming to or living in the State, and making such action felony: Ky. C. x. 2; Ore. C. i. 35.

By the Constitution of California the legislature is to prescribe all necessary regulations for the protection of the State and the counties, cities, and towns thereof from the burdens and evils arising from the presence of aliens who are or may become vagrants, paupers, mendicants, criminals, or invalids afflicted with contagious or infectious diseases, and from aliens otherwise dangerous or detrimental to the well-being or peace of the State, and to impose conditions upon which such persons may reside in the State, and to provide the means and mode of their removal from the State upon failure or refusal to comply with such conditions; and no corporation shall employ, directly or indirectly, in any capacity, any Chinese or Mongolians, and the legislature shall pass laws to enforce this provision; and no Chinese shall be employed in any State, municipal, or other public work except as punishment for crime: Cal. C. xix. 1–3. And, further, the presence of foreigners ineligible to become citizens of the United States is declared to be dangerous to the well-being of the State ; and the legislature is to discourage their immigration by all means within its power. And Asiatic coolyism is declared a form of human slavery, and prohibited, and all contracts for cooly labor are void ; and the legislature may prescribe penalties for companies or corporations formed in any country for the importation of such cooly labor ; and the legislature is to delegate all necessary powers to cities and towns for the removal of Chinese, or their location in prescribed portions of such towns, and also to provide legislation to prohibit the introduction of Chinese into the State : Cal. C. xix. 4.

Indians aged twenty-one, if civilized, and not members of any tribe, can vote in Wisconsin. So, in Michigan, if born in the United States. So, in Wisconsin, persons of Indian blood who have once been declared by Congress citizens of the United States, any subsequent act of Congress to the contrary notwithstanding. So, in Minnesota and Washington, persons of mixed white and Indian blood who have adopted the customs and habits of civilization; and Indians also, after an examination by the courts, in Minnesota. But in two, no Indian not taxed can vote : Me. C. ii. 1 ; Miss. C. vii. 2. And in one, no Indian can: R. I. C. ii. 4.

MARRIAGE.

Constitutional Provisions.—The Constitution of Mississippi legitimates all children, born before or after its adoption (1868), of persons not married, but cohabiting as husband and wife on December 1, 1869 ; and such persons are to be taken as married :

Miss. C. xii. 22. So, in Virginia, the children of parents, one or both of whom were slaves at or during the period of cohabitation, and who were recognized by the father as his children, and whose mother was recognized by such father as his wife, and was cohabited with as such, shall be capable of inheriting from such father as if born in lawful wedlock: Va. C. xi. 9. By the Constitutions of two States the intermarriage of white persons with negroes or mulattoes, or their cohabitation as husband and wife, is forbidden: N. C. C. xiv. 8; Tenn. C. xi. 14.

Statutory Provisions.—Marriage of colored persons prior to 1867, if by authorized party, valid: Md. 1888, 13. So with their *de facto* marriages prior to 1865 or 1866: Va. 103, 4; 104, 13; W. Va. 121, 8; 1882, 58; Tenn. 3285; 3303; Mo. 2173; Ark. 4609; Tex. 2846 (1870); S. C. 2030–1 (1872); Ga. 1667; Fla. 149, 7 (1866); D. C. 724, 5 (1866).

Provisions for verification of marriage, etc., before justice of the peace: Md.; Mo. 3275–7; see, also, N. C. 1842. Persons prohibited by laws of bondage from marrying, but living together till death of either, or August 15, 1870, considered married, without ceremony: Tex. 2846. Indians contracting according to custom, and cohabiting, married: Dak. Civ. C. 42. Children born in slavery take by descent as brothers and sisters: Mo. 2173. Colored children born before March 9, 1866, legitimate as to mother, and as to father if parents living as husband and wife: Ga. 1669.

Marriages are void: between a white and (1) "a negro or mulatto:" Del. 74, 1; Va. 105, 1; N. C. 1084, 1284; Tenn. 3291; Ark. 4593; Cal. 5060; Col. 2248 (but inhabitants of former Mexican territory may marry according to custom); S. C. 2032; Fla. 149, 8–9; Ariz. 1893; Ind.; Ky. (2) "A negro:" Mo. 3265. (3) "An African, or descendant of Africans:" Tex. 2843; Ariz. 2091; Ga. 1708. (4) "A person having one-fourth of negro blood:" Neb.; Ore. 34, 2; Miss. 1147 (though solemnized out of State); Fla. (5) Or "one-eighth:" Ind. 2136, 5325; Mo. 1540; Fla. 59, 13. (6) "To the third generation, inclusive:" Md. 1884, 264; N. C.; Tenn.; Ala. 4189. (7) "An Indian:" N. C., Nev., S. C. (Query, in Ariz.?) (8) "A Chinese or Mongolian:" Nev., Ariz. (9) "A person having one-fourth Chinese or Kanaka blood :" Ore. Crim. Co. 689. (10) " Or one-half Indian blood :" Ore.

But in Michigan marriages between whites and persons of African descent are valid : 1883, 23, 1. In North Carolina marriage between Indian and negro is void. No license for marriage between white and Mongolian : Cal. 5069. One hundred dollars fine for joining negro and white in marriage : Md. 1888, 27, 194. Misdemeanor (State prison one to two years) for white to marry "a black person, mulatto, Indian, or Chinese :" Nev. 1873, 2472. Not less than one nor more than three years' imprisonment for party marrying such ; from one to five hundred dollars' fine, and six months' imprisonment for white who cohabits with black, etc. : Ibid. 2473–4–5.

The foregoing comprises all the ascertained provisions on the subject down to the following dates :

Alabama	Code, 1886	Missouri	Acts, 1887
Arizona	Acts, 1889	Montana	Acts, 1887
Arkansas	Acts, 1889	Nebraska	Acts, 1887
California	Acts, 1889	Nevada	Acts, 1889
Colorado	Acts, 1887	New Hampshire	Acts, 1887
Connecticut	Acts, 1887	New Jersey	Acts, 1888
Dakota	Acts, 1887	New Mexico	Acts, 1888
Delaware	Acts, 1879	New York	Acts, 1888
Florida	Acts, 1885	North Carolina	Acts, 1885
Georgia	Acts, 1888	Ohio	Acts, 1888
Idaho	Acts, 1889	Oregon	Acts, 1889
Illinois	Acts, 1887	Pennsylvania	Acts, 1885
Indiana	Acts, 1887	Rhode Island	Acts, 1886
Iowa	Acts, 1888	South Carolina	Acts, 1872
Kansas	Acts, 1889	Tennessee	Acts, 1887
Kentucky	Code, 1888	Texas	Acts, 1887
Louisiana	Acts, 1888	Utah	Acts, 1888
Maine	Acts, 1885	Vermont	Acts, 1886
Maryland	Code, 1888	Virginia	Acts, 1888
Massachusetts	Acts, 1889	Washington	Acts, 1887
Michigan	Acts, 1887	West Virginia	Code, 1887
Minnesota	Code, 1888	Wisconsin	Acts, 1889
Mississippi	Acts, 1888	Wyoming	Acts, 1886

ADDENDUM.—A bastardy law which, by its terms, applies only to " white women," is constitutional.[1]

---

[1] Plunkard *v.* State, 67 Mo. 364 (1887).

THE END.